Providence After Dark
and Other Writings

ALSO BY T.E.D. KLEIN

The Ceremonies (1984)
Dark Gods (1985)
Raising Goosebumps for Fun and Profit (1988)
Reassuring Tales (2006)

Providence After Dark
and Other Writings

T.E.D. KLEIN

Hippocampus Press
New York

Copyright © 2019 by Hippocampus Press
Works by T.E.D. Klein © 2019 by T.E.D. Klein

Published by Hippocampus Press
P.O. Box 641, New York, NY 10156.
www.hippocampuspress.com
All rights reserved.
No part of this work may be reproduced in any form or by any means without the written permission of the publisher.

The interview on page 245 is reprinted by permission of Rick Kleffel of NarrativeSpecies.com and The Agony Column Podcast. The interview on page 411 is from *T.E.D. Klein and the Rupture of Civilization: A Study in Critical Horror* © 2017 Thomas Phillips. Reprinted by permission of McFarland & Company, Inc., Box 611, Jefferson NC 28640. www.mcfarlandbooks.com

Cover photograph: "Fairy Tale Way" © 2013 by Donna St. Pierre, facebook.com/DonnaMarieStPierre.
Hippocampus Press logo designed by Anastasia Damianakos.
Cover design by Daniel V. Sauer, dansauerdesign.com

First Edition
1 3 5 7 9 8 6 4 2

ISBN 978-1-61498-268-5 trade paperback
ISBN 978-1-61498-269-2 ebook

Contents

I. On Lovecraft 13
- Providence After Dark 15
- *The United Amateur* 20
- A Dreamer's Tales 31
- The Festival 73
- The Old Gent 111
- T.E.D. Klein: Master of Ceremonies 113

II. On Other Authors 127
- Arthur Machen 129
- Ramsey Campbell: An Appreciation 138
- *Slow* 156
- An Afternoon with Aickman 159
- A Haunted House 166
- Frank Belknap Long 170
- Dr. Van Helsing's Handy Guide to Ghost Stories 172
- Introduction to *Dark Love* 212
- Introduction to David Schow's *Seeing Red* 218
- Whiskey, Popcorn, and Gold 225
- *Gaspard de la Nuit* 231
- *A Connecticut Yankee* 235
- *The Ceremonies*, 2016 edition: A Note from the Author 243
- A Conversation with T.E.D. Klein 245

III. The Twilight Zone 261
- *Stories from the Twilight Zone* 263
- *Twilight Zone* Magazine 270

The 13 Most Terrifying Horror Stories 283
The Book of Hieronymus Bosch 286
Twilight Zone: The Movie 288
Horrors! An Introduction to Writing Horror Fiction 292
Standing Behind the Curtains: A Conversation with T.E.D. Klein 310

IV. On Film 317

They Kill Animals and They Call It Art 319
Animals in Movies—The Abuse Gets Worse 326
On Cutting Up Movie Classics 330
How I Flopped as a Paramount Script Reader 332
Annie Hall 337
Star Wares 339
Master of a Lost Art 343
And Many Happy Returns 347
T.E.D. Klein Interview 349

V. On Other Topics 357

Where Do We Go from Here? 359
Charles Manson, B.M.O.C. 363
The Joy of Losing 366
Working for the *Brown Daily Herald* 369
CrimeBeat 373
Crime and Punishment 397
A Higher Standard 398
Antarctica in the *Times* 400
Quotation & Misquotation 402
Silenced Voices 405
Three Letters to Brown 406
Spalding Gone Gray 409
Lament of an Aging English Instructor 410
Reassuring Words: An Interview with T.E.D. Klein 411

VI. Reviews **423**

Legion by William Peter Blatty 425
The Face That Must Die and *Incarnate* by Ramsey Campbell 430
The Suburbs of Hell by Randolph Stow..433
More Books 436
The Glamour by Christopher Priest 440
Collected Stories by Ruth Rendell..444
The Terrors of Ice and Darkness by Christoph Ransmayr..................447
Bring Me Children by David Martin 450
A Curate's Egg 453
Sci-Fi Entertainment 461
A Swedish Podcast 585

Thanks to S. T. Joshi for originally proposing this collection, for assembling most of its contents, and for arranging them in a reasonable order; to David E. Schultz for putting it all together; and to Derrick Hussey for his patience.

Author's Note

A few years ago, my friend Margie returned from two weeks' travel in Vietnam, where she'd been visiting her niece, who was spending a college semester in, of all places, Hanoi.

By the time I saw her, Margie had been back for a while, and I assumed she was already sick of telling everyone about her trip; nor, to be honest, was I all that interested in hearing about it. So I said simply, "Give me two adjectives to describe the place."

To her great credit, she hesitated barely a nanosecond before delivering her judicious, carefully considered response: "Hot . . . dirty."

I bring up this anecdote not to disparage faraway nations, but because it seems peculiarly relevant to the contents of this volume, which I've just spent the past few days rereading. I felt, as I read, some trepidation and also, I'm happy to say, some genuine relief, but my overriding judgment can best be summed up by two adjectives: long-winded . . . repetitious.

You have been warned.

I. On Lovecraft

Providence After Dark

A very smart friend of mine, impressively well-read, swears that in his early teenage years his favorite books—in fact, the only books he ever read for pleasure—were paperback novelizations of sci-fi and horror films he'd seen. Not, mind you, the original works on which the films were based, but novelizations, that most scorned of genres.

I mention this to illustrate how lowly, plebeian, in fact downright philistine one's entrance may be to the halls of literature. I'm sure there are professional writers, no doubt a few Ph.D.s as well, who'd prefer to forget that they once cut their teeth on Reader's Digest Condensed Books or Classics Illustrated comics. (It's remarkable how often the latter, in my own case, have served as a lifelong substitute for the real thing.)

My earliest encounters with H. P. Lovecraft were just as humble. I wish I could say that I first read him in the celebrated black-bound Arkham House editions that, for those of us of a certain age, are forever identified with his writings, but I didn't discover that series till years later. I was probably in sixth or seventh grade when

---

Written for the college textbook *H. P. Lovecraft: Selected Works, Critical Perspectives and Interviews on His Influence* (Jefferson, NC: McFarland, 2018), edited by University of North Georgia professor Leverett Butts, who "asked current science fiction, fantasy, horror, and weird fiction authors to contribute essays . . . discussing their first encounters with Lovecraft's fiction, the nature of their appreciation for his work, and his influence on their own work."

I first stumbled across a Lovecraft story—two, actually, "The Dunwich Horror" and "The Rats in the Walls"—in the local library's copy of *Great Tales of Terror and the Supernatural,* a mammoth, much-reprinted anthology that has introduced him to generations of new readers; in those days, with mortality unimaginably distant, the fatter a book was, the stronger its appeal.

But what really confirmed Lovecraft's status in my juvenile literary pantheon was a paperback called *The Survivor and Others,* whose cover (from which gazed a scary, scaly monster with, oddly, three nostrils) bore the byline, in large letters, "H. P. Lovecraft" and in smaller, fainter ones, "and August Derleth." In truth the book's contents were almost entirely by Derleth, HPL's most prolific and energetic disciple. After Lovecraft's death in 1937, Derleth had co-founded Arkham House to rescue Lovecraft's work from the pulp magazines where it had originally been published; additionally, he'd taken plot ideas out of the master's commonplace book—sometimes just a single line—and had spun them into stories that I now see were exceedingly mechanical and formulaic. (He also specialized in Sherlock Holmes pastiches.) At the time, though, as a fourteen-year-old, I paid no attention to the warning at the beginning of *Survivor* that these tales were based upon mere "scattered notes" from HPL and that the results were to be regarded as "a final collaboration, post-mortem." All I knew was that I found the stories thrilling.

So what made me a Lovecraft fan was not even Lovecraft. And aside from those two initial tales in the library anthology, I'm not sure I'd actually read much authentic, unadulterated fiction of his (nor was it yet so widely available) when, in the fall of 1964, I found myself in Providence on the morning before my one and only college interview—for Brown, as it happens: the university, aside from Miskatonic, most closely associated with Lovecraft. (I should add that this connection had very little to do with my choice of schools.) Vaguely aware that he had lived somewhere in the area, I stopped in the college bookstore and asked if it stocked any books by him. It did not; but one of the salespeople, providentially knowledgeable, informed me that that I might find what I wanted downtown, at Dana's Old Corner Book Shop on Weybosset Street. In fact, I was told, Lovecraft himself had actually frequented the shop.

Wasting no time, I dashed down College Hill and visited the place, a little low-ceilinged establishment below sidewalk level that smelled of books new and used; on the wall that lined the steps leading down was a mural of Alice tumbling down the rabbit hole. The proprietor, old white-haired Mr. Dana, confirmed that Lovecraft had indeed been among his customers but admitted he had no particular memories of the man. Still, the store displayed a partial shelf of Arkham House titles, my first encounter with that exotic imprint, and I bought two or three—hardcover volumes that in those days sold for three dollars, five dollars, and six fifty (which struck me as a bit steep). This excursion downtown—followed by a hurried visit to the Lovecraft collection at the John Hay Library up the hill—gave me something to chat about at my interview later that day; the interviewer, I recall, had never heard of Lovecraft, but I expect he was impressed by my enthusiastic geekdom.

In fact, comparatively few people had heard of him then. Providence, like the world at large, is far more conscious of him today, seventy-seven years after his death; Lovecraft is practically a minor industry there now. When I began college there, Lovecraft had been dead for some twenty-eight years. That, too, seems a rather long time, and yet, looking back, it sometimes felt as if I had just missed him. The city has changed considerably since I lived there—it's awfully yuppified these days—and it's lost much of what I once treasured about it, the sense of its being a slightly seedy, slightly sleepy old backwater, albeit one with more than its share of well-preserved Colonial architecture. For Lovecraft, it was always a romantic and magical place; for me as well—partly because this corner of New England seemed so full of history (in contrast to the bland, charmless Long Island suburb where I'd grown up), and partly because Lovecraft's presence seemed to haunt every street.

College Hill, in particular, was filled with Lovecraft connections; he had walked the neighborhood's streets throughout his life, and loved them all, and immortalized them in his stories and letters. Exploring them—occasionally prowling the lanes and alleyways after dark as Lovecraft did, seeking glimpses of what he had called Old Providence—became something of a preoccupation during my four years there. I remember one night, with a friend, suddenly coming upon a little cemetery, its centuries-old tombstones standing out against the lights of the city spread out below; only afterward did I learn that this was St. John's churchyard, where Lovecraft, in a modified sonnet, hints that visitors might spy "amidst these tombs the shade of Poe." (One of HPL's early literary influences, Poe had descended on the neighborhood in 1848 in search of a wife. His name is spelled out in the first letters of each line of Lovecraft's poem.) In my freshman year, I spent an evening in a distant part of the city with Cliff and Muriel Eddy, an elderly couple, sadly impoverished, who, as onetime fellow writers, had been friends of Lovecraft's; in fact, HPL is credited with having "revised," or even rewritten, Eddy's story "The Loved Dead," whose necrophiliac theme had supposedly caused a minor scandal when it appeared in *Weird Tales.* The eighteenth-century house where I lived my senior year—the third floor, which another student and I occupied, contained four fireplaces, including one in the kitchen—stood between the old Providence Art Club on one side and the landmark Fleur-de-Lys house on the other; both are mentioned in "The Call of Cthulhu," in which the latter is home to one of the main characters. The so-called Shunned House—today just another piece of desirable East Side real estate—was a couple of blocks away.

Supernatural horror tales, at their best, transform the ordinary world into something scarier, more exciting, more fun; I know that sounds ridiculously simplistic, but I think in essence it's all they should hope to do—to add a little wonder to the world. Lovecraft's tales made living in Providence more fun; and later, during the '80s, when I was spending many a weekend in southern Vermont, that region was likewise enhanced, if a good deal less dramatically, by the fact that he'd used it as the setting for one of his admittedly less successful tales, "The Whisperer in Darkness." I would find myself driving from Brattleboro to Newfane and Townshend on the very same road along the West River that the tale's narrator traveled, and that ordinary scenic journey, and those ordinary, charming, slightly touristy Vermont towns, would seem a shade more magical.

The same is true, to some degree, for all New England—for me, it's all Lovecraft Country. It's not exactly the New England of the guidebooks, the history books, or even the historical novels (endearing though that New England is); rather, it's a more mysterious, more richly atmospheric region that, in Lovecraft's hands, manages to combine the quaint and the cosmic, the specific—specifically named streets, specific actual houses—and the utterly strange. It's a place, as well, where tiny actions can have near-universal significance, where a grubby backwoods hermit can mutter words out of a dusty, worm-eaten old book with earth-shattering consequences, opening the gates to another dimension.

Please understand that, alone, each of those particular elements doesn't seem quite so remarkable; what appeals to me about Lovecraft isn't so much the now-familiar collection of forbidden old books (almost a contradiction in terms, when you think of it) or the menagerie of extradimensional monsters led by that now-practically-iconic winged being with tentacles coming out of its face. What appeals, rather, is the conjunction of such fantastic stuff with staid old New England.

I wish I could say the same for New York, where I live now. Lovecraft spent a couple of years here, during his brief, uncomfortable marriage; he set a few stories here as well. Indeed, every few weeks, when I'm in Brooklyn, I invariably walk past his last local address. Yet somehow the city seems to resist Lovecraftian transformation. Maybe I'm just too old, or perhaps this place is just too busy, too modern, too mired in reality. I can understand why HPL fled back to Providence.

The United Amateur

Lovecraft himself would probably have deplored the fact, but perhaps he should have been flattered: that along with Hemingway, Wilde, Virginia Woolf, Dr. Johnson, and many other colorful figures, Lovecraft's life has become, for many readers, more interesting than the literature he produced. I know a number of Lovecraftians who are well into Volume Five of the letters without ever having made it past the Walls of Eryx; although originally attracted by the horror tales, they're now even more intrigued by the real-life mysteries of Lovecraft's marriage, the saga of his travels round New England, and the tragedy of his final illness.

One aspect of his life, however, has been left relatively unexplored: Lovecraft's involvement in amateur journalism. More than just a hobby, it was for many years the closest thing he had to a career, and remained a central concern from 1915 until his death. He was a regular contributor to amateur periodicals and, at one time or another, served as president, vice president, board chairman, journal editor, and financial "custodian" of the United Amateur Press Association—one of the three most active organizations in the field—and in later life became president of the rival National Amateur Press Association. (The third organization was a competing faction of the UAPA to which Lovecraft and his cohorts gave short shrift.)

Foreword to *Writings in 'The United Amateur': 1915–1925* by H. P. Lovecraft, edited by Marc A. Michaud (West Warwick, RI: Necronomicon Press, 1976).

But though amateur journalism was one of Lovecraft's absorbing interests, it has received comparatively little attention. The fact is, the mentality that supported such publications now appears alien and even somewhat contemptible: One thinks of small-town spinsters contributing florid odes to Spring, and of myopic Midwestern high-schoolers laboring over essays on The Meaning of Idealism. It was a world of civic orations and Sunday sermons.

Still, it was a world to which Lovecraft himself seems to have been devoted. Obviously it fulfilled a number of needs. It provided him with the sort of epistolary social life he preferred; it provided him with a small but congenial readership; and—in the UAPA's "Department of Public Criticism"—it provided him with a chance to pontificate on the literary work of others and, through this, on a variety of other subjects.

Lovecraft's tenure as official UAPA critic forms the largest part of the present collection, although Marc Michaud has included a host of his other contributions to the *United Amateur,* from horror tales to treasurer's reports, thereby throwing light on a neglected aspect of Lovecraft's life and affording us an unusual glimpse of home-front America during the First World War.

While this compilation from the *United*'s pages is by no means complete, it presents a fine sampling of Lovecraft's work under his own name, as well as under such illustrious *noms de plume* as Humphry [sic] Littlewit, Ward Phillips, and Henry Paget-Lowe. Despite the coincidence in initials, however, some may question the editor's inclusion of poems by Perrin Holmes Lowrey, who emerges in these pages as a somewhat better poet than Lovecraft himself. It seems unlikely that the organization's annual Poet Laureate award would have gone to Lowrey if the man were merely one of Lovecraft's alter-egos—especially when Lovecraft himself received Honorable Mention in the same category.

Moreover, in his columns of criticism Lovecraft is always outrageously hard on himself. "Our own poetical attempt," he writes of a typical contribution, "spoils three and a half otherwise excellent pages." Elsewhere he describes one of his poems as "an abominably dull elegiac piece of heavy verse," accuses another of "purposeless obscurity," and dismisses a third as lacking "any remarkable poetic power or elevation of thought." He carries this pretend-modesty even further—and no doubt enjoys a private joke—when he belittles a poem he wrote under the name "Lewis Theobald, Jun.," noting that the "insipidity of the sentiment leaves much to be desired. The whole poem savours too much of the current magazine style." It's doubtful, then, that a man for whom self-disparagement was an article of gentlemanly faith would allow himself the sort of praise he lavishes on Lowrey, whom he hails as a "delectable lyricist. . . . The style of Mr. Lowrey possesses an attractive individuality and delicacy which is already bringing him celebrity in the larger literary sphere." Lovecraft even quotes an entire stanza he's found "thoroughly enchanting"—words he would never use for his own work.

But while Lovecraft has nothing good to say for himself, he's the soul of kindness when it came to others. As a matter of fact, perhaps his greatest talent as a critic is that he finds something nice to say about almost everything. No matter how ludicrous the work in question may sound, he makes sure to send it on its way with an encouraging pat on the head—and sometimes the results are unintentionally comic: "'Did You Ever Go A-Fishin'?,' by Olive G. Owen, is a vivid poetical portrayal of that peculiar attraction which the angler's art exerts on its devotees. . . . 'Little Jack in Fairyland,' by Ruth Ryan, is a well written account of a dream, with the usual awakening just as events are coming to a climax. The style is very attractive and the images ingenious." He can be just as grandiloquent—and as kindly—toward children: "'Spring,' by Randolph Trafford (aetat 10), is full of the exuberant vigour of youth, and speaks well for the future of this bright young bard."

Speaking well for the future was virtually a rule of Lovecraft's. When an author or work merited commendation, no one could match the fervor of his praise. ("*Invictus* for January . . . is one of those rare journals concerning which it is almost impossible to speak without enthusiasm." Of another magazine: "There is scarce a line unworthy of commendation." Of a favorite poetess, later to become a client for his revision work: "Winifred V. Jordan, whose work is never too brief to be pleasing, or too long to be absorbing . . ." Of another: "We feel certain that Miss Lalls has already become a fixed star in the empyrean of the United.") And for those that did not merit praise, it was still possible to say something nice; the trick was to speak of their promise. ("*Toledo Amateur* for December is a wholesome juvenile product . . . and we may reasonably expect to see it improve from month to month, into one of the leading amateur papers. . . . *Stray Leaves* has great possibilities, and will doubtless prove one of the leading papers in amateur journalism in times to come.") Indeed, the first of Lovecraft's "Annual Reports" is little more than a list of names followed by encomiums—a sort of literary pep talk.

Of course, without immediate access to the works in question, there's no way of telling whether or not Lovecraft's judgments were correct. It's hard not to wonder, for example, about "The Redemption," a tale he accuses of presenting "a very repulsive picture of bestial atavism." One's curiosity is aroused: What was it about the tale that provoked, from the mild Lovecraft, this uncharacteristic denunciation?—"We doubt seriously if stories or essays of this type should appear in the press, and especially in the amateur press." Eyebrows may rise, too, when—in a review of the *Cleveland Sun*—Lovecraft writes, "The 'sporting' features should be eliminated at once, as not only being in bad taste, but exerting a noxious influence over the literary development of the younger members." Sporting features? What could he have meant? Surely nothing to do with sporting houses and bordellos. Cockfighting, perhaps? Fortunately, a few pages later we learn that he was merely speaking of that publication's sports column, given over to "the lyrical liltings of the pool-room Muse," to "prize-fight philosophy and race-track rhetoric. . . . We cannot but censure Mr. Dowdell's introduction of the ringside or ball-field spirit into an Association purporting to promote culture and lettered skill."

There are other references that stir the imagination. One would like to see the "attempted reconstruction of a scene supposedly excised from *King Lear*," by Lovecraft's good friend Sam Loveman, and a poem called "Chores" by the ubiquitous Mrs. Jordan—a "sombre, repellent, rustic tragedy," filled with "homely horror." One would also give much to read "An Hour with a Lunatic," which Lovecraft describes as "a very short and very thrilling tale of the 'dime novel' variety," and "Dead Men Tell No Tales," which he calls "a ghastly and gruesome anecdote of the untenanted clay." It certainly sounds more compelling than "Little Jack in Fairyland."

But if some of the references sound provocative and mysterious, especially when read out of context, many of the others—let's be honest—can prove stupefyingly dull; reading them through at one sitting (as I've done) is a little like studying the box scores of long-forgotten cricket matches. What's more, Lovecraft's poetical criticism seldom goes beyond the mechanical questions of rhythm and rhyme. All too often this is the sort of thing we find: "These decasyllabic quatrains are a decided departure from Mrs. Renshaw's usual style, which explains the slight lack of fluency. The last line of the third stanza contains a redundant syllable, a defect which might be corrected by the removal of the article before the word 'louder,' or by the poetical contraction of 'sympathy' into 'symp'thy.'" Even before he turned professional, Lovecraft was always the reviser.

Occasional attempts at humor do little to alleviate the tone: "In the second paragraph we read of a channel 'damned' up by a projecting root of a tree; which somewhat surprises us, since we did not know that tree-roots are accustomed to use profane language. Perhaps the author intended to write 'dammed.'" Concerns of this sort turn the Department of Public Criticism into a litany of misprints and typos, especially after Lovecraft invites authors to send him lists of printers' errors so that he can publish the corrected versions—a lovely idea, from the authors' standpoint, but it makes for rather tedious reading.

End-words, too, were always a major concern. Sometimes the matter could be rather petty, as when Lovecraft rails against "those careless bards who pronounce 'real' as 'reel,' and 'ideal' as 'ideel,'" or when he points out "the noticeably imperfect rhyming of 'garret' and 'carrot.' . . . It is barely possible," he admits, "that according to the prevailing New York pronunciation this rhyme is not so forced as it appears, but we are of New England, and accustomed to hearing the sounds more classically differentiated." (Astonishingly, he later allows that "the native pronunciation of New-England makes of 'scarf' and 'laugh' an absolutely perfect rhyme.")

More often the advice seems well-needed; time and again he's forced to remind his flock that "hope" does not rhyme with "note," that "hours" does not rhyme with "bars" and "stars," and that rhyming "bear" and "appear" is only "correct according to the old-time standards." Still, he never lets these elementary mistakes dull his enthusiasm for a fellow amateur's work; he is nothing if not generous. Sometimes his delicacy toward others' feelings can be rather amusing, as when he writes of one poem: "The thoughts and images are without exception lofty and well selected, and the only possible defect is the attempt to rhyme 'come' with 'run' in the last stanza."

But if the bulk of Lovecraft's poetic criticism is exclusively mechanical, perhaps that's all the work deserved; and perhaps it's just as well to let the original tales and poems remain mysterious and unseen. For the truth is that most of Lovecraft's wonderful praise and encouragement seems sadly misplaced: Judging from the few examples he actually quotes—lines he's liked, ideas he's appreciated, an occasional stanza he's revised—most of this amateur material must have been, by today's standards, utterly, abysmally, atrociously unreadable.

It testifies to Lovecraft's incredible patience that he was able to wade through this stuff each month, treating every sonnet, every imperfect couplet, with close and respectful attention; for if his critical commentaries are scarcely exciting, the works themselves must have been far worse. Yet writing about them must have been, for Lovecraft, a very real pleasure, since it allowed him to play the role he liked best: that of teacher. He had a natural bent for the job. It shows in his letters to friends, filled with lengthy discourses on every area of human knowledge; it shows in his *United Amateur* revisions, often line by line, of each month's crop of poetry; it shows in his erudite references, always apt and never forced, to Pope, to Elizabethan drama, to the correct pronunciation of Indian names, to the Puritan custom of naming children after biblical injunctions ("Praise-God Barebones, a leading and fanatical member of Cromwell's rebel parliament, went a step further than his father, naming his own son 'If-Jesus-Christ-had-not-died-for-thee-thou-hadst-been-Damned'! All this was actually the first name of young Barebones, but after he grew up and took a Doctor's degree, he was called by his associates, *'Damned Dr. Barebones'!*"), and to Samuel Johnson

("As the late Dr. Johnson said of the Ordinary of Newgate's calendar, 'it contains strong facts'").

Indeed, one of the principal goals of amateur pressdom was exactly that: to teach. It was, as Lovecraft said, a kind of "university"—albeit one in which he was more professor than student. Asked "For What Does the United Stand?," he replied: "Naturally, we do not expect to make a Shelley or Swinburne of every rhymer who joins us, or a Poe or Dunsany of every teller of tales; but if we enable these persons to appreciate Shelley and Swinburne and Poe and Dunsany, and teach them how to shed their dominant faults and use words correctly and expressively, we cannot call ourselves unsuccessful. . . . The United, then, stands for education." In another essay included here, "Literary Composition," he relishes the opportunity of advising prospective writers: "A page of Addison or of Irving will teach more of style than a whole manual of rules, whilst a story of Poe's will impress upon the mind a more vivid notion of powerful and correct description and narration than will ten dry chapters of a bulky text-book." (It's gratifying to note that his own advice on the proper methods of description, while worthy of many a good text-book, is a marvel of conciseness.)

Obviously there's a great deal of learning to be found in these pages, as well as (surprise!) much "innocent merriment." There's a catch, though: You must seek it out for yourself. But if that's one of the problems here—to find bits of color amid the grey spaces—it is also this collection's strength: It makes available, in a low-priced format, a great mass of raw material, undigested and untampered with. No apologists have sifted it in the hope of whitewashing Lovecraft's reputation; nor have these pages been cannibalized by ghouls hoping to pull out and print just the damning quotes. They are all here, the eulogies and the tirades, the honey and the venom, Lovecraft the rational and the irrational; the reader must make his own judgments.

He will have a lot to choose from. Buried within the critical notes, the President's Messages, and editorials are dozens of insightful digressions, philosophical asides, and passages of personal revelation—what writer Tom Collins, our leading authority on these amateur materials, has called "mini-essays." Here readers will find the youthful Lovecraft expressing himself on a wide variety of subjects, not a few of which arouse his ire.

On coeducation: "While the advantage of coeducation to young ladies is made quite obvious, it remains far from clear that young men receive equal benefit. A desirable decline of cliques and hazing might, it is true, result from the admission of women to men's universities, but the young men would undoubtedly lose much in earnest, concentrated energy and dignified virility through the presence of the fair." (This from a twenty-four-year-old who'd never gone to college and who'd never had a date—or, as he puts it, "a frigid old critic without experience in romance.")

On pacifism: "The sole ultimate factor in human decisions is physical force.... The present fad of peace-preaching should not be allowed to influence a writer of sense into glorifying a socialistic, unpatriotic fanatic who refuses to uphold the institutions that his fathers before him created with their toil, blood, and sacrifice. It is not the right of the individual to judge of the necessity of a war; no layman can form an intelligent idea of the dangers that may beset his fatherland. The man is but a part of the state, and must uphold it at any cost." (This—and the poems reprinted here, the flag-waving "Ode for July Fourth, 1917" and the bloody-minded "Teuton's Battle-Song," with its "Slay, brothers, Slay! And bathe in crimson gore; / Let Thor, triumphant, view the sport once more!"—from a young man who had to sit out the Great War for reasons explained in an editorial note: "That President Lovecraft and Professor McDonald are not gallantly fighting at the front today is due to no lack of patriotism, but solely to the fact that Army Officials decreed that their bodily physique was not on a par with their valorous spirit.")

The trend toward "simplified spelling" was another of his *bêtes noires*. For a man who still wrote of "labour" and "civilisation," the use of modernisms such as "thru" and "thot" was an outrage. Over and over he takes up the cudgel against "these radical distortions," this "empty innovation," "the destructive bacillus of deformed spelling.... We are inclined to wonder at the possible meaning of the strange word 'alright,' which appears more than once in Miss Ziegfeld's tale. It is certainly no part of our language, and if it be a corruption of 'all right,' we must say that we fail to perceive why the correct expression could not have been used."

There were plenty of other *bêtes;* Lovecraft had more than his share.

On alcohol: "The distiller and vendor of rum is elementally the supreme foe of the human race, and the most powerful, dangerous, and treacherous factor in the defiance of progress and the betrayer of mankind."

On comic strips: "These . . . present the pathetic spectacle of utter inanity and repulsive grotesqueness without the faintest redeeming touch of genuine comedy, legitimate satire, or refined humour."

On free verse: "'Free Verse' has neither the flow of real verse nor the dignity of real prose. It tends to develop obnoxious eccentricities of expression, and is closely associated with bizarre and radical vagaries of thought. It is in nine cases out of ten a mere refuge of the obtuse, hurried, indolent, ignorant, or negligent bard who cannot or will not take the time and pains to compose genuine poetry or even passable verse. It has absolutely no justification for existence, and should be shunned by every real aspirant to literary excellence, no matter how many glittering inducements it seems to hold out." He dismisses it as "scribbling several lines of unequal length, each beginning with a capital letter. It is an admirably easy way to acquire a literary reputation without much effort."

In his collaborative story "Poetry and the Gods," also in this collection, Lovecraft calls *vers libre* "that pitiful compromise of the poet who overleaps prose yet falls short of the divine melody of numbers." Here, too, incidentally, one may find faint foreshadowings of Cthulhu in the lines "*The Gods were never dead,* but only sleeping the sleep and dreaming the dreams of Gods in lotos-filled Hesperian gardens beyond the golden sunset"—just as, in one of the mini-essays from the Department of Public Criticism, readers are given an early glimpse of the Dunwich region:

> The poem intensifies that feeling of hidden terror and tragedy which sometimes strikes us on beholding a lonely farmer, enigmatical of face and sparing of words, or on spying, through the twilight, some grey, unpainted, ramshackle cottage, perched upon

a wind-swept hill or propped up against the jutting boulders of some deserted slope, miles from the town and remote from the nearest neighbour.

This collection provides other foreshadowings as well. One reads Lovecraft's comments on romance within the world of amateur journalism—and recalls that Lovecraft met his future wife at an amateurs' convention. One reads Andrew Francis Lockhart's portrait of Lovecraft in "Little Journeys to the Homes of Prominent Amateurs," based upon the subject's own notes—and witnesses the making of a legend. Here, for the first time, we meet the familiar figure so dear to the popular imagination—the scholarly recluse living in some dream of the past, a veritable Gothic hero. "Lovecraft came from pure-blood stock," one learns, "and he is the last male descendant of that family in the United States. With him the name will die in America."

In "Ex Oblivione" one finds an early treatment of a theme found later in *Fungi from Yuggoth* and the Dunsanian tales; and in "The White Ship"—a personal favorite of mine—one finds his first attempt at fiction after having heard the Irish fantasist at a Boston lecture.

One sees the first appearance of a genuine Lovecraft horror tale, "The Alchemist," in its original form, complete with the inevitable typo in the first sentence; and one sees him comment on his own amateur publication, *The Conservative* (whose maiden issue predictably contained a blast at simplified spelling).

Reading his views on "Americanism," one discovers that, for Lovecraft, the term was nearly synonymous with racism; and elsewhere one learns that the race in question, the British, represent "the noblest human type ever moulded by the Creator."

But the picture this collection provides is a good deal more complex than one might expect. One will find, if one looks, the customary condemnations of the Irish and the blacks—but also some surprisingly sympathetic words. One finds the usual doubts about religion and the Bible—but also praise for their influence on morality and literature. One reads Lovecraft's gibes at the motion picture—but also his prediction of a great future for a medium that can "convey the liberal arts to multitudes hitherto denied their enjoyment." One comes across warlike sallies against rival amateur groups—but just as many overtures of peace. If Lovecraft defends "the true amateur spirit" against the inroads of crass commercialism, he elsewhere holds up professional publication as the ideal for amateurs to pursue.

In short, these pages introduce one to an exceedingly interesting man—a man at once generous, tender-hearted, and ferocious; modest and self-deprecating, yet outrageously smug; eloquent, erudite, endlessly patient; aesthetically conservative and politically reactionary; cynical, yet terribly naive; pompous, often pedantic; wry, solemn, and never at a loss for an opinion. A memorable portrait emerges here—and best of all, it's by Lovecraft himself.

A Dreamer's Tales

*S*traighten your tie; put on your best smile. You're about to meet, in the pages that follow, a gorilla-like thing that crouches in the moonlight with the arm of a child in its teeth; a regiment of zombies commanded by a headless corpse; a horde of winged, web-footed creatures "not altogether crows, nor moles, nor buzzards, nor ants, nor vampire bats, nor decomposed human beings," but some monstrous combination thereof; a host of scaly humanoids "crawling and floundering" across the slime-covered floor of the sea; and "a loathsome night-spawned flood of organic corruption more devastatingly hideous than the blackest conjurations of mortal madness and morbidity."

But you'll also meet a wandering balladeer haunted by dreams of a long-lost golden city of crystalline fountains and lotus-scented breezes; voyage to exotic lands on a delicate white ship that waits for you beside a bridge of moonbeams; and visit a strange high house on a misty mountaintop that's frequented by the gods.

Since these latter pleasures may be unexpected ones, not of a sort generally associated with Lovecraft, some explanations are in order.

Our story begins in 1919, when Howard Phillips Lovecraft (1890–1937) of Providence, Rhode Island, was an oldish young man of twenty-nine—fussy, pompous, prim, prodigiously well-read, his large patrician head bursting with facts and opinions on everything from chemistry to the classics. He had written reams of

---

Introduction to *Dagon and Other Macabre Tales* by H. P. Lovecraft (Sauk City, WI: Arkham House, 1986).

eighteenth-century-style verse for amateur literary magazines of the day ("A Rural Summer Eve," "On a New-England Village Seen by Moonlight," "On Receiving a Picture of Swans"), dozens of essays and reviews both erudite and impassioned ("The Dignity of Journalism," "The Case for Classicism," "The Truth about Mars"), and a handful of short stories, some of which are included in this book. He was fond of archaic English spelling—*honour'd, antient, aesthetick*—and of posing as an aged country squire. ("I was born an old man," he once noted, and throughout his thirties would describe himself as "a comfortable, benevolent old gentleman," a "weary old gentleman," and "a simple old man whose only salient qualities are a love of old times, a penchant for ghosts, and a healthy appreciation of his native soil—things to be found in three-quarters of the rural squires of Old England!" By thirty-six he would be talking of "my sunset years.") Yet in truth he was an overprotected only child as sheltered as a schoolboy, appeared barely capable of making a living, had no experience of sex ("I am unfamiliar with amatory phenomena save through cursory reading"), and, until her confinement in an asylum in March of 1919, had never spent a night away from his doting, increasingly dotty widowed mother. The previous August, just after his twenty-eighth birthday, he had written, with admirable self-perception: "Always a recluse, with no varied events of life to mark the transition from boyhood to manhood, I have retained more of the old juvenile point of view than I would care to acknowledge publicly. I have grown up without knowing it."

It was in September of 1919 that Lovecraft discovered Lord Dunsany (1878–1957). The celebrated Anglo-Irish writer was, in many ways, the very man Lovecraft had always longed to be. Lovecraft's life was one of steadily declining fortunes—a small inheritance left by a maternal grandfather was virtually depleted, condemning him to a life of genteel poverty—yet he played at being a British aristocrat. Dunsany was the genuine article, with a title after his name (Edward John Moreton Drax Plunkett, the eighteenth Baron Dunsany) and an ancient family seat, Dunsany Castle northwest of Dublin, dating back to 1190. Older than Lovecraft by twelve years and destined to outlive him by another twenty, Dunsany was already a widely published author with a dozen books to his credit and some fifty more to come; during the course of his active career he was a soldier, big-game hunter, cricketer, chess master, world traveler, lecturer, poet, playwright, and author of humorous sketches, travel pieces, novels, and fantasy tales.

It was the fantasy that interested Lovecraft. "I had never read anything of Dunsany's," he wrote later, "though knowing of him by reputation. The book had been recommended to me by one whose judgment I did not highly esteem, and it was with some dubiousness that I began reading 'Poltarnees, Beholder of Ocean.'"

The book was *A Dreamer's Tales,* published in 1910, and it begins:

> Toldees, Mondath, Arizim, these are the Inner Lands, the lands whose sentinels upon their borders do not behold the sea. Beyond them to the east there lies a desert, for ever untroubled by man: all yellow it is, and spotted with shadows of stones, and Death is in it, like a leopard lying in the sun. To the south they are bounded by magic, to the west by a mountain, and to the north by the voice and anger of the Polar wind. Like a great wall is the mountain to the west. It comes up out of the distance and goes down into the distance again, and it is named Poltarnees, Beholder of Ocean. . . . Very peaceful are the Inner Lands, and very fair are their cities, and there is no war among them, but quiet and ease. And they have no enemy but age, for thirst and fever lie sunning themselves out in the mid-desert, and never prowl into the Inner Lands. And the ghouls and ghosts, whose highway is the night, are kept in the south by the boundary of magic. And very small are all their pleasant cities, and all men are known to one another therein, and bless one another by name as they meet in the streets. And they have a broad, green way in every city that comes in out of some vale or wood or downland, and wanders in and out about the city between the houses and across the streets; and the people walk along it never at all, but every year at her appointed time Spring walks along it from the flowery lands, causing the anemone to bloom on the green way and all the early joys of hidden woods, or deep, secluded vales, or triumphant downlands, whose heads lift up so proudly, far up aloof from cities.

Like an overture, this formidable opening paragraph displays many of the peculiarities that reappear throughout Dunsany's fantasies: the sentence inversion ("all yellow it is"); the quaint, archaic diction ("behold," "therein," "for ever"); the stately repetition of phrases ("It comes up out of the distance and goes down into the distance"); the invention of names, such as Mondath and Arizim, to suggest the ancient or exotic; and the personification of such natural forces as fever, thirst, and spring—all of them elements one finds in traditional verse (Lovecraft called Dunsany's style "pure poetry despite the prose medium") or in passages from the Bible ("And they have . . . And the ghouls . . . And very small . . . And they have . . ."). Here, too, is the Romantic view of time as the dread destroyer ("no enemy but age"), the ornate description of imaginary landscapes, and, even in this introductory paragraph, a breathless fascination with cities: specifically, with magical cities in far-off lands—a central theme of Dunsany's that would become, for Lovecraft, something of an obsession. Even the title of the book, *A Dreamer's Tales,* was prophetic, for Lovecraft, too, was a dreamer, and so are most of his heroes.

"The first paragraph arrested me as with an electric shock," Lovecraft recalled later, "and I had not read two pages before I became a Dunsany devotee for life."

His new-found enthusiasm received a further boost when, in a happy coincidence, Dunsany himself came to Boston the following month as part of his American tour. Lovecraft was able to secure a front-row seat for "the great event" and noted that Dunsany's manner was "boyish and a trifle awkward," that his face, though "fair and pleasing," was "marred by a slight moustache" (Lovecraft, following the eighteenth-century fashion, was a lifelong foe of facial hair), and that "to Boston autograph seekers he proved very accommodating, refusing none despite a severe headache." Though Lovecraft himself was not among the autograph seekers ("I detest fawning upon the great"), one of his companions later obtained Dunsany's signature through the mail, in return for "a genuine autograph letter of Abraham Lincoln" and several other "tokens of esteem." The Irish writer replied with a brief thank-you note— "written personally," Lovecraft was delighted to report, "with his celebrated quill." It was exactly the sort of idiosyncrasy that Lovecraft prized: Dunsany, he explained elsewhere, "almost invariably employs a quill pen, whose broad, brush-like strokes are unforgettable by those who have seen his letters and manuscripts." He quoted the thank-you note in full to one of his many correspondents, declaring it "a treasure of priceless worth."

That Lovecraft could regard the Irish writer's autograph as more desirable than Lincoln's demonstrates, to say the least, a rare degree of admiration. It's not surprising, then, that he speaks of Dunsany with the highest praise in his essay "Supernatural Horror in Literature," that he eulogized him in poetry ("So now o'er realms where dark'ning dulness lies, / In solar state see shining PLUNKETT rise!"), or that in "Suggestions for a Reading Guide" he includes him in his lifetime reading plan, quaintly terming him "the preëminent fantaisiste."

But something more than mere admiration is suggested in a letter of 1920, in which Lovecraft notes, "Dunsany is really handsome, and has one of the most kindly, winning, wholesome expressions I have ever beheld. Whether serious or whimsically humorous, his blue eyes are alight with an indefinable quality which makes one sure that he is a very good and very generous man. Dunsany left in my mind an exceedingly favourable impression—an impression which made me wish that he were a personal friend of mine. He is, I think, a trifle *unworldly*—if such may be said of a man who has travelled all over the globe and served through two wars."

Clearly there's a real attraction here, both physical and spiritual, to the older man, and also the hint of a growing identification with him—for Lovecraft himself was nothing if not unworldly. And indeed, elsewhere in the letter, he speaks of Dunsany's "engaging, boyish sort of awkwardness," his occasional lisp ("Obviously he has been at pains to correct it"), the "fearful headache" that, during a subsequent lecture, forced him to apply ice water to his head, and the man's pleasing absence of stage presence: "He addresses his audience not as a performer declaiming to a crowded pit, but as a gentleman entertaining friends in his own drawing-room."

One is struck by the similarities Lovecraft must have seen between himself and his idol: Lovecraft, too, was tall, thin, proud, and awkward, declining to stoop to amuse people he regarded as inferiors, perpetually concerned with acting the cultivated gentleman, the man of leisure and learning. Yet he, too, had his engagingly youthful side; a friend describes him as having "a boyish charm and enthusiasm" that belied the stiffness of his demeanor. Like Dunsany, he had a certain peculiarity of voice; those who knew him recall it as "high-pitched" and "piping." He may have envied Dunsany his good looks (for Lovecraft always regarded himself as homely), but he clearly identified with him physically, despite a difference in their heights. "Sometimes," he wrote, in a letter to Frank Belknap Long, "I am provoked by my own hugeness—I am five feet and nearly eleven inches, and vary in weight between 150 and 175 according to my immediate state of health." Long—who, contrary to his name, was quite diminutive—must have been tickled by his friend's generous assertion that "some of the greatest men have been the smallest"; Lovecraft listed Newton, Pope, and Poe, and added: "The catalogue is well-nigh endless. . . . I half fancy that I am too large to be classed among the real literati—though Dunsany's six feet four inches heartens me!"

Dunsany's headaches only added to this feeling of identity, for Lovecraft was prone to "infernal" ones: "Now I know *all* about headaches," he confided. "All there is to be known. Some of mine seem impossible to live through. And I know that if Edward J.M.D. Plunkett's are anything like mine, he *must* put water to his head when they are near their climax."

Aside from the physical peculiarities they shared, Lovecraft's sense of identification with his idol seems to have found its deepest expression in the matter of race—a subject always dear to Lovecraft's heart. In the 1922 essay "Lord Dunsany and His Work," Lovecraft was careful to delineate the man's racial background, noting that he "is a representative of the oldest and greatest blood in the British Empire. His race-stock is predominantly Teutonic and Scandinavian—Norman and Danish—a circumstance which gives to him the frosty heritage of Northern lore."

That Lovecraft considered himself a member of that selfsame breed is made clear in a letter he wrote a year later, once more to Frank Belknap Long, in which he praises that ethereal mystick power which lends frantick and cosmical madness to the work of such men of genius as Mr. Poe, Mr. Machen, and my Ld. Dunsany. This force of supernatural wonder—the faint clawing of black unknown universes on the outer rim of space, as I phrase it in my crude unsophisticated way—is a purely *Teutonick* quality. . . . As an aesthetick observer, you ought to find plain evidences of *Nordick* superiority; and derive therefrom a proper appreciation of your natural as distinguisht from your adopted race-stock. As for me, I am proud to be a Teuton, and wou'd not wish to be taken as any other sort of man. . . . Be proud, boy, to be an Englishman; and remember that no finer breed of men now walks the earth. In us are combin'd the mysticism of the great northern forests that spawn'd us, and the Latin refinements of the Normans that mingled with us.

In his final tour de force of Dunsanian identification, a series of letters on genealogy, he managed to prove—half in jest, half in hope—that he and his hero were distantly related. (That is, when he was not filling page after page with witty speculation on the more remote branches of his illustrious family tree: "Did I mention the Egyptian priest Ra-ankh-Khamses, who voyaged to the Cassiterides on a Phoenician ship in the time of Psammeticus and was cast on the green shores of Quernas near the site of the modern Queenstown? . . . Then, of course, there is the Cro-Magnon Glwkhlghx. . . .") Alluding to his great-grandmother's line, he noted: "Oh—another Fulford hookup is MORETON! Shades of Edward John *Moreton* Drax Plunkett! . . . I'm now calling Dunsany 'Cousin Ned'. We MORETONS always did take to phantasy!"

Lovecraft, who'd started by noting a physical resemblance to Dunsany, had managed to insert himself not only into the other writer's ethnic group but even into Dunsany's own family. There is one step in the process yet to come, and you'll find it in a letter written in June 1923, in which Lovecraft, having praised the work of Welsh writer Arthur Machen, adds (with his own italics): "But *Dunsany* is closer to my own personality and understanding. . . . Dunsany *is myself,* plus an art and cultivation infinitely greater. His cosmic realm is the realm in which I live."

"Imitation," as the widely misquoted Charles Caleb Colton put it, "is the sincerest of flattery," and it's arguable that, personal feelings notwithstanding, the greatest compliment Lovecraft paid Lord Dunsany was to imitate his work.

"Truly," he admitted, "Dunsany has influenced me more than anyone else except Poe—his rich language, his cosmic point of view, his remote dream-world, and his exquisite sense of the fantastic, all appeal to me more than anything else in modern literature. My first encounter with him . . . gave an immense impetus to my writing; perhaps the greatest it has ever had." In later years he recalled the Irish writer's effect as one of "cosmic liberation. When I first encountered him (through *A Dreamer's Tales*) in 1919 he seemed like a sort of gate to enchanted worlds of childhood dream, and his temporary influence on my own literary attempts . . . was enormous. Indeed, my own mode of expression almost lost itself for a time amidst a wave of imitated Dunsanianism."

At first glance, the "Dunsanianism" in Lovecraft's tales seems easy enough to identify. It is marked by archaic language ("With strange art were they builded," etc.) and by evocative place-names such as Ib, Cathuria, Kadatheron, Sona-Nyl, Ulthar, Ooth-Nargai, distant Oonai, the Cerenerian Sea, the Karthian and Tanarian Hills, and the tongue-twisters Nath-Horthath and Mnar.

Yet what are we to make of the "land of Lomar" and of another, more ancient land called "Zobna"? They appear in Lovecraft's story "Polaris," along with allusions to "Olathoë, which lies on the plateau of Sarkis, betwixt the peaks Noton and Kadiphonek," and quaintly inverted sentences such as this: "Long did I gaze on the city, but the day came not."

Ironically, "Polaris" was written in 1918, a year before Lovecraft ever so much as peeked into *A Dreamer's Tales*—proof, if you will, that a writer is unlikely to fall under the spell of a new literary style unless there are already germs of it in his own work. Some of the stylistic similarities between "Polaris" and Dunsany's fiction may derive, in part, from their having had a common ancestor in the King James version of the Bible. (Dunsany's first published work, *The Gods of Pegāna* [1905], was in fact a kind of alternate-universe scripture written in biblical prose, celebrating a pantheon of imaginary deities.) If the determinedly atheistic Lovecraft had little use for religion—see, for example, his contemptuous references to it in "The Strange High House in the Mist"—he nonetheless appreciated "the classic and Hellenically influenced book of Job," the "pure poetry" of Solomon and the Psalms, and the "prophetic music" of Isaiah, all of which may have provided rhythmic inspiration for lines such as "When I awaked, I was not as I had been. Upon my memory was graven the vision of the city, and within my soul had arisen," and so on.

Thematically, too, "Polaris" resembles many a Dunsany tale—"The Wonderful Window," for example, in which a modern-day Londoner, staring through a window newly installed in his flat, watches helplessly as a beautiful medieval city falls before hordes of invaders. But here the resemblance is merely accidental; for "Polaris," like other Lovecraft stories, seems to have had its origin in a dream—in this case one of May 1918, in which Lovecraft envisioned an ancient stone city of "palaces and gilded domes, lying in a hollow betwixt ranges of grey, horrible hills," was puzzled by its statues of "strange bearded men in robes," and was haunted by a sense "that I had once known it well, and that if I could remember, I should be carried back to a very remote period—many thousand years, when something vaguely horrible had happened."

Perhaps it's best to view the story the way Lovecraft himself did, as simply an amusing literary coincidence, "interesting as a case of unconscious parallelism of manner." Contrasting "Polaris" to a later tale, he added: "'Celephaïs' dates from after my introduction to Dunsany, and I will leave to the critic the question of just how much of the style is due to Dunsany's influence, and how much to my own independently similar cast of imagination."

In addition to "Celephaïs," Lovecraft listed as "my most Dunsanian things" the stories "The Doom That Came to Sarnath," "The Quest of Iranon," "The Other Gods" ("It represents me in my most Dunsanian mood"), and "The White Ship," a product of his "new Dunsanian studies." All of them are included in this book.

Lovecraft took his "Dunsanian studies" seriously. "I have read everything of Dunsany's except his new novel," he reported in 1923, and, indeed, from the titles scattered through his letters of the period, one could put together a competent Dunsany bibliography. "I certainly was under his influence in the winter of 1919–20," he told a friend; but that influence, though it waned, lasted till the end of Lovecraft's career. It's apparent in *The Dream-Quest of Unknown Kadath,* in "The Strange High House in the Mist," and in the fragment "Azathoth," reprinted in this book. It may also be seen in "The Tree," a tale of "posthumous vengeance" for a crime barely hinted at—the poisoning of an artist by his rival. (Lovecraft merely noted that the tale combined "the Greek idea of divine justice and retribution" with the "Oriental notion of the soul of a man passing into something else," but one gets a whiff of Dunsany in the heavily perfumed style.) There's a Dunsanian connection, too, in the mysterious desert ruins of "The Nameless City," which, according to Lovecraft, "had its basis in a dream, which in turn was probably caused by contemplation of the peculiar suggestiveness of a phrase in Dunsany's *Book of Wonder*—'the unreverberate blackness of the abyss.'" A phrase in *A Dreamer's Tales,* from the story "The Hashish Man," provided Lovecraft with the title for his 1931 novelette *At the Mountains of Madness.* Even the so-called Cthulhu Mythos tales owe something to Dunsany, populated as they are by a host of awesome new deities as inventively varied as the ones in *Pegāna,* albeit considerably more inimical.

But the Dunsany of *Pegāna* was changing—and as he changed, Lovecraft grew less and less enamored of him. "Instead of remaining what the true fantaisiste must be—a child in a child's world of dream—he became anxious to show that he was really an adult good-naturedly pretending to be a child in a child's world," Lovecraft wrote, describing what he saw as a "hardening-up." In a 1922 amateur press essay he complained that "the serious side of Dunsany has been steadily on the wane," and later noted wistfully to a correspondent that "his recent work . . . seems less closely packed with breathless unreality than the early products." By 1923, though he was still protesting that "the charm of Dunsany is endless" and that "he is the most wholesome and delightful person imaginable," Lovecraft was forced to admit: "Dunsany's newer work has less appeal because of the increasing note of visible irony, humour, and sophistication." Lovecraft obviously knew what he wanted from

Dunsany, and he wasn't getting it anymore.

Yet perhaps the other's penchant for ironic humor might have been evident from the start, for in "The Hashish Man," one of the stories Lovecraft read first, the visionary traveler of the title declares: "Once I found out the secret of the universe. I have forgotten what it was, but I know that the Creator does not take Creation seriously, for I remember that He sat in Space with all His work in front of Him and laughed." The same might be said of Dunsany's attitude toward his own work.

Lovecraft's disenchantment with Dunsany is reflected in his reactions to New York, where he lived from March 1924, when he married Sonia H. Greene, until April 1926, when he returned, joyous but defeated, to his native Providence. As James Turner points out in his introduction to the preceding volume of Lovecraft tales, these two years of exile were "probably the most significant learning experience of his entire adult lifetime."

In a way, it was Dunsany's influence—along with that of Mrs. Greene and several literary pals—that brought him to New York in the first place. From the moment of his first visit there in early 1922, Lovecraft managed to convince himself that the city was a paradise straight from some gaudy Dunsanian fantasy. Apparently the train trip down must have put him in a receptive frame of mind—"I spent the five-hour journey reading Dunsany," he reported—for no sooner did he lay eyes on "the Cyclopean outlines of New-York" than he pronounced the place "dreamlike and Dunsanian . . . a mystical sight in the gold sun of late afternoon; a dream-thing . . . cold, proud, and beautiful; an Eastern city of wonder whose brothers the mountains are. It was not like any city of earth, for above purple mists rose towers, spires, and pyramids which one may only dream of in opiate lands beyond the Oxus; towers, spires, and pyramids that no man could fashion, but that bloomed flower-like and delicate; the bridges up which fairies walk to the sky; the visions of giants that play with the clouds. Only Dunsany could fashion its equal, and he in dreams only."

Even after he'd lived there for seven months, a chance view of the Manhattan skyline—such as the one from the roof of the Columbia Heights apartment building where poets Hart Crane and Samuel

Loveman lived—could send him into paroxysms of rapture: "I nearly swooned with aesthetic exaltation when I beheld the panorama. . . . It was something mightier than the dreams of old-world legend—a constellation of infernal majesty—a poem in Babylonian fire! No wonder Dunsany waxed rhapsodic about it when he saw it for the first time . . . it is beyond the description of any but him!" Clearly, when it came to waxing rhapsodic, the Irishman had nothing on Lovecraft.

But Dunsanian panoramas were simply not enough. Though Lovecraft praised the splendor of the skyline, he professed nothing but disdain for the species that had built it, comparing New York's "pinnacles of breathing stone" to the beauties of a coral reef, and mankind to "the coral insect" that created it. And when it came to describing these "insects called men," he was capable of launching into diatribes that, in exuberance and sheer verbal excess, more than matched his "rhapsodic" passages. A trip to the Lower East Side, for example, taken less than a month after his move to New York, became the occasion for an airing of his personal phobias:

> The organic things—Italo-Semitico-Mongoloid—inhabiting that awful cesspool could not by any stretch of the imagination be call'd human. They were monstrous and nebulous adumbrations of the pithecanthropoid and amoebal; vaguely moulded from some stinking viscous slime of earth's corruption, and slithering and oozing in and on the filthy streets or in and out of windows and doorways in a fashion suggestive of nothing but infesting worms or deep-sea unnamabilities. They—or the degenerate gelatinous fermentation of which they were composed—seem'd to ooze, seep, and trickle thro' the gaping cracks in the horrible houses . . . and I thought of some avenue of Cyclopean and unwholesome vats, crammed to the vomiting point with gangrenous vileness, and about to burst and inundate the world in one leprous cataclysm of semi-fluid rottenness.

His only memory of a human face was a composite one, "a yellow leering mask with sour, sticky, acid ichors oozing at eyes, ears, nose, and mouth, and abnormally bubbling from monstrous and unbelievable sores at every point."

How seriously must one take all that? I'm not entirely sure. Lovecraft's racial prejudices were certainly real—deeply held, in fact, and an integral part of his whole philosophical outlook—yet the passage above also demonstrates his schoolboyish delight in stretching language to exaggerated lengths. (It bears an interesting resemblance to descriptions of "The Lurking Fear," written just over a year before.) In face-to-face encounters he was never less than a gentleman, and his own wife was, of all things, Jewish, of a people he claimed to despise.

It's clear, at any rate, that so racially mixed a city was not for him; "New York is no place for a white man to live," he declared. His initial enthusiasm for his new home also soured in the face of his inability to find steady employment; his futile efforts to find a full-time job—the awkward interviews, the ads placed in newspapers, the letters of entreaty to publishers—make painful reading today. His Brooklyn apartment was burglarized, and his marriage soon proved a failure; he preferred spending nights out with his pals and doesn't seem to have been terribly broken up when business considerations forced Sonia to depart for the Midwest on the last day of 1924. "The turmoil and throngs of N.Y. depress her," he claimed, "as they have begun to do me, and eventually we hope to clear out of this Babylonish burg for good. I find it a bore after the novelty of the museums, skyline, and bolder architectural effects has worn off, and hope to get back to New England for the rest of my life." He became, in a sense, his own Iranon, dreaming of the golden city of his youth, where he'd been the son of a king. "Vistas faded and contracted, and the glitter of adventurous expectancy receded farther and farther," he wrote later. "Came to hate New York, whither I had moved, like poison." Soon he was denouncing the place as "a scrofulous bastard-city" and "an accursed metropolitan pest zone."

He put his loathing—and his longing—to good use in "The Horror at Red Hook" and "He," both from 1925 and reprinted here. The first, he said, was inspired by "the gangs of young loafers and herds of evil-looking foreigners that one sees everywhere in New York," the second by his own plight as one "who comes to New-York as to a faery flower of stone and marble, yet finds only a verminous corpse." But his creative energies were at a low point, and for most of that year he felt oppressed by the "accursed and filthy rabbles that infest the N.Y. streets, and whose clothing presents such systematic differences from the normal clothing of real people along Angell St. and in Butler Ave. or Elmgrove Ave. cars that the eye comes to feel a tremendous homesickness."

In the end he yielded to this homesickness, and by the spring of 1926 he had traded the streets of New York for the Angell and Elmgrove of his beloved Providence. "A man belongs where he has roots," he explained, "where the landscape and milieu have some relation to his thoughts and feelings, by virtue of having formed them.... There *is* no other place for me. My world is Providence." Where once, years before, he had identified himself with his idol, Lord Dunsany, now he wrote (in words that provided the inscription on his tombstone), "I am Providence, and Providence is myself—together, indissolubly one." In later years he would add, "Don't say 'I love those hills, steeples, etc.' Say 'I *am* them.'"

Safely ensconced back in Rhode Island, once more on his native soil like an Antaeus in contact with the earth, Lovecraft found his creative powers returning and, over the next six years of the decade that remained to him, produced some of his greatest fiction. Though he traveled extensively—visits to literary colleagues and correspondents up and down the East Coast, antiquarian jaunts as far away as New Orleans, Key West, Quebec, and Portland, Maine—Providence remained his home.

He had little taste for Dunsany's new work, and his taste for the old had waned: "I am too old for such emotional effects now," he concluded. "Thank Pegāna I came across Dunsany when I did!" Always intensely self-critical, he dismissed most of his own earlier stories: "In the attempts at ethereal phantasy there was probably too much of the unconsciously imitative—second-hand Dunsany, as it were. Some of the stuff—especially 'Iranon'—strikes me as damnably mawkish after the lapse of a decade. I couldn't write such stuff now if I wanted to!"

Those words were written in the summer of 1930. A year later he expressed similar doubts about "The Outsider," another tale from his Dunsanian period, but written under a very different influence: "It represents my literal though unconscious imitation of Poe at its very height. In those days I couldn't help aping the mannerisms as well as reflecting the spirit."

Lovecraft, in fact, regarded Poe as his major literary influence, ever since he'd first read him at seven. At age twenty-five, with his Dunsanian years still before him, he told a correspondent, "When I write stories, Edgar Allan Poe is my model," and he felt the same way at forty, noting that "Poe has probably influenced me more than any other one person." Elsewhere he described him as "my God of Fiction," and in still another letter contended: "Of all the really great workers in the field of the weird, I hardly think there is any reason to question the leadership of Mr. Poe."

Poe's appeal differed from Dunsany's; though Lovecraft spoke admiringly of the former's "vast and cosmic vision" (just as he had once praised Dunsany for his "cosmic point of view"), he claimed to find in Poe's work an "essentially *intellectual* wonder . . . totally devoid of the sensual." Sensual or not, there's a great deal of Poe in the pages that follow, especially in those tales of a darker, more Gothic nature, with their hysterical first-person narrators and horrific endings. Of "The Tomb" and "Dagon," written in rapid succession in 1917, Lovecraft said: "May the shade of the late Mr. Poe of Baltimore turn green through jealousy!" Even his nominally Dunsanian tales have traces of the earlier writer in them; while "The White Ship" and *The Dream-Quest of Unknown Kadath* owe their nautical scenes largely to Dunsany's "Idle Days on the Yann" (an enchanting travelogue, always a favorite of Lovecraft's), they also show the influence of two of his favorite Poe stories, "MS. Found in a Bottle" and *The Narrative of Arthur Gordon Pym*, echoes of which are also found in Lovecraft's *At the Mountains of Madness*. Another Poe favorite, "The Masque of the Red Death," chronicles the downfall of a decadent ruler in much the same way as a supposedly Dunsanian story, "The Doom That Came to Sarnath."

Perhaps the only writer that Lovecraft ever compared favorably to Poe is the Welsh fantasist Arthur Machen (1863–1947). "No one can so well as Mr. Machen suggest dim regions of terror whose very existence is an affront to creation," Lovecraft wrote. "There is in Machen an ecstasy of *fear* that all other living men are too obtuse or timid to capture, and that even Poe failed to envisage in all its starkest abnormality. He is greater than our Eddie in ability to suggest the unutterable." Lovecraft considered Machen's "The White People" one of the two greatest supernatural tales ever written (the other was Algernon Blackwood's "The Willows"), and as he'd done with Dunsany, he couldn't resist tracing a Lovecraft family connection to the man, noting with pleasure that "the Phillipses come from the borderland of Wales, that mystic Machenian land."

Among Machen's favorite themes, to which he returned again and again throughout his career, were some that today might strike readers as peculiarly Lovecraftian. He wrote of odd little newspaper items that provide disturbing hints of ancient survivals; terror amid the natural beauty of the hills and woods; elder races that resurface to prey on humanity; inbred country folk who know more than they let on; and sinister cults, hidden from civilization and given to performing ceremonies that predate Christianity. Of the tales in this volume, his influence is particularly evident in "The Horror at Red Hook," with its epigraph from Machen's "The Red Hand," its reference to Turanian magic (Machen's "The Turanians" had been published the previous year), and its mystical talk of "the hidden beauty and ecstasy of things," "the sense of latent mystery in existence," and "the hellish green flame of secret wonder." Phrases such as those were far more in Machen's line than Lovecraft's.

If on occasion Lovecraft spoke of Machen as greater than Poe, and of Poe as greater than Dunsany, he also admitted to a preference for Dunsany over Machen. (That's not as paradoxical as it seems; he admired each for different things.) A 1923 letter finds him praising the Welsh writer as "a Titan—perhaps the greatest living author," but at one point his praise takes a curiously Dunsanian form: "Pegāna, what an imagination!" The exclamation is revealing, for in the same letter he goes on to hail Dunsany as the more talented of the two.

Behind this preference lay the conviction that Dunsany was the more adept at evoking a sense of beauty—"the beauty," as Lovecraft put it, "of moonlight on quaint and ancient roofs." As the essay that concludes this volume observes, "Beauty rather than terror is the keynote of Dunsany's work"—and it was beauty rather than terror that claimed Lovecraft's first allegiance, despite his reputation as a horror writer. "I am vastly more responsive to beauty than to horror," he confided to a friend, and he deplored what he saw as his own inability to capture them both equally in prose: "When I come to record my imaginative experiences, I generally find that only the horror items have any uniqueness or originality. Others have seen the same beautiful things that I have seen, and have sung them more nobly. Dunsany, indeed, has said exquisitely almost everything I could possibly wish to say; so that when I indulge in sheer phantasy I can do no more than imitate him. Thus horror alone is left as my peculiar kingdom."

It was a kingdom in which he never felt entirely at ease. Art, wonder, beauty—"these," he said, "are all there is in life. . . . The one great crusade worthy of an enlightened man is that directed against whatever impoverishes imagination, wonder, sensation, dramatic life, and the appreciation of beauty. Nothing else matters."

Beauty and horror vie with one another throughout this collection, which, encompassing them both, might with some justice be entitled *A Dreamer's Tales,* presenting as it does the fruit of what Lovecraft called his "visions and nightmares," the one embodying his longings and ideals, the other his fears and detestations. From these twin sources—akin to that memorable construction of Walter van Tilburg Clark's, "the ecstasy and the dread"—Lovecraft drew his inspiration. "I never took opium, but . . . space, strange cities, weird landscapes, unknown monsters, hideous ceremonies, Oriental and Egyptian gorgeousness, and indefinable mysteries of life, death, and torment, were daily—or rather nightly commonplaces to me before I was six years old," he wrote. "Today it is the same."

The same wonders, too, dominated his waking thoughts: "Somehow I cannot become truly interested in anything which does not suggest incredible marvels just around the corner—glorious and ethereal cities of golden roofs and marble terraces beyond the sunset, or vague, dim cosmic presences clawing ominously at the thin rim where the known universe meets the outer and fathomless abyss."

Forced to choose between the ethereal cities and the fathomless abyss—between, in effect, the daydream and the nightmare—Lovecraft, as we've seen, chose to stake his reputation on the latter; his primary talent, he believed, was for writing horror. While that judgment may be true of his work as a whole, I'm not sure it's supported by the present collection, in which, to my mind, the dream fantasies remain fresh, charming, and even at times quite touching, while in comparison the horror tales emerge as somewhat dated. Though a reader of 1920 reported, in the pages of *The American Amateur*, that a Lovecraft tale had left her immobilized with fright ("One night I let the moon shine in my eyes because I was afraid to get up and pull down the shade after reading one of his stories—'Dagon,' I think it was"), modern readers in search of a similar scare will probably find scant pickings. Better, perhaps, to take Lovecraft at his own word: His intention in "Dagon," he claimed, was "purely and simply to reproduce a mood."

This book, therefore, is something of a mixed bag. A publisher's catalogue lists its contents as "the lesser tales," Lovecraft scholar Donald R. Burleson describes them as "early and minor works, for the most part," and August Derleth, in the previous edition of *Dagon*, pronounced them "secondary," though he added, loyally, that many are "certainly among the best short stories of the macabre written in the twentieth century." What is certain is that they're shorter than the stories in Arkham House's two companion volumes, *The Dunwich Horror* and *At the Mountains of Madness*.

There's nothing the matter with shorter tales, early tales, even secondary tales; it's just that, like some of those poor paperback editions of minor Lovecraftiana that still appear on newsstands (and that are invariably picked up by friends new to the genre but "interested in seeing what this Lovecraft fellow's all about"), they're simply not representative of the author's best work. Casting an eye on Lovecraft's juvenile fiction, Tom Collins once observed with admiration, "I'm not sure Lovecraft could ever *not* write a clear sentence." True enough; but (as Collins would agree) the very early tales—such as, in this collection, "The Tomb"—do contain sentences that must sound, to today's readers, a little silly: "It was in mid-summer, when the alchemy of Nature transmutes the sylvan landscape to one vivid and almost homogeneous mass of green; when the senses are well-nigh intoxicated with the surging seas of moist verdure," etc. Clearly this book is not the place to meet Lovecraft for the first time.

Many of these tales reveal a Lovecraft who ignored his own literary rules. He maintained, for example, that horror is best conveyed through suggestion and indirection; yet he sometimes seems, in the pages that follow, unnecessarily explicit. Compare, for example, his treatment of the grotesque humanoid sculptures in "Dagon" with the lightness of tone M. R. James brings to the same device in "Count Magnus" (a story praised by Lovecraft), in which an ornamental band on the lid of a sarcophagus depicts "a man running at full speed, with flying hair and outstretched hands. After him followed a strange form; it would be hard to say whether the artist had intended it for a man, and was unable to give the requisite similitude, or whether it was intentionally made as monstrous as it looked. In view of the skill with which the rest of the drawing was done, Mr. Wraxall felt inclined to adopt the latter idea."

Lovecraft also advised writers to ground their supernatural horror amid the everyday, "building it up insidiously and gradually out of apparently realistic material, realistically handled. . . . Spectral fiction should be realistic as well as atmospheric—confining its departure from Nature to the one supernatural channel chosen." Most important of all is the creation of a convincing sense of place—in the longer and later tales, perhaps Lovecraft's greatest strength. But you'd never know it, judging from most of the stories in this collection. True, there's the stylized New York of "He" and "The Horror at Red Hook," and, in "The Festival" and "The Strange High House in the Mist," a quaint New England setting described in convincing detail (perhaps because the "Kingsport" of the stories was based on the real town of Marblehead). And there's certainly a sense of place in the ingenious "Under the Pyramids," ghostwritten for Harry Houdini—perhaps too much of it, in fact, since Lovecraft's reliance on guidebooks gives the tale, at times, the air of a travelogue. Most of the early fiction, however, makes do either with imaginary settings out of Dunsany or with the improbable England of "Arthur Jermyn," "Hypnos," and "The Hound" (also set in Holland), the picture-postcard Ireland of "The Moon-Bog," and the fairy-tale France of "The Alchemist."

Still, this collection demonstrates Lovecraft's considerable stylistic range—for all the narrowness of his themes, he managed to turn out creditable fantasy tales, fables, prose poems, psychological horror, Gothic horror, and various kinds of science fiction—and some of the offerings, among them "Polaris," "The White Ship," and "The Strange High House in the Mist," are genuinely moving; at least I find them so. The episodic "Herbert West—Reanimator," which Lovecraft himself scorned as "unimaginative hack-work," is nonetheless told with ghoulish relish and wit ("Their outlines were human, semi-human, fractionally human, and not human at all"); though slowed by plot recaps at the start of each section (a requirement of the "vulgar magazine" that commissioned it), the story shows how enjoyable Lovecraft can be when he lets his hair down. Closing out this collection, his groundbreaking "Supernatural Horror in Literature" makes the perfect finale.

Even in the lesser tales, there are some distinct pleasures. Mostly it's the pleasure of watching Lovecraft experiment with themes he'll later develop more fully, and which here appear only in miniature or primitive form. "Dagon," for example, is a precursor of his Cthulhu chronicles (and incidentally the first story Lovecraft sold to *Weird Tales,* his most important market). "Beyond the Wall of Sleep" plays with a theme—bodiless voyaging through space and time—that eventually reemerges in his lengthier SF epics. You'll find the first mention of "the mad Arab" Abdul Alhazred in "The Nameless City," a bridge between Lovecraft's Dunsanian tales (with its allusions to Ib, Sarnath, even Dunsany himself) and his Mythos tales (quoting as it does Alhazred's famous couplet). You'll find the first mention of the dread *Necronomicon* in "The Hound" and, in "Herbert West—Reanimator," of demon-plagued Miskatonic University.

One characteristically Lovecraftian element already in full flower in these tales is that of the neurasthenic narrator. He's a most peculiar breed—in many ways, not surprisingly, an idealized version of Lovecraft himself ("From earliest childhood," says one, "I have been a dreamer and a visionary") right down to his personal quirks ("The odour of the fish was maddening")—and you'll find him virtually unchanged in story after story: high-born, hypersensitive, scholarly, reclusive, and easily unbalanced. These are men of eccentric enthusiasms and the leisure to pursue them; they almost never seem to hold jobs, and the ones who do sound nonetheless like aristocrats. The narrator of "The Tomb" informs us that he is "wealthy beyond the necessity of a commercial life," just as Lovecraft wished *he* were. Like his hero Iranon, who says airily, "I am a singer of songs, and have no heart for the cobbler's trade," Lovecraft, in his midthirties, searched vainly for a position with someone who might need "the assistance of a gentleman" and ruled out work that would bring him into contact with the "garment industries which are almost wholly in the hands of the most impossible sort of persons." "What a man *does for pay* is of little significance," he argued. "What he *is,* as a sensitive instrument responsive to the world's beauty, is everything! . . . A poor but cultivated man is, absolutely, the superior of a *rich* boor. . . . I never ask a man what his business is. . . . What I ask him about are his thoughts and dreams."

Cultivated indeed, his narrators bristle with learning and are by no means reluctant to show it. They're familiar, as Lovecraft was, with astronomy, the classics, and the lore of the occult. ("I couldn't live a week without a private library," he informed one correspondent. "Indeed, I'd part with all my furniture and squat and sleep on the floor before I'd let go of the 1500 or so books I possess.") Even the hero of "The Transition of Juan Romero," forced to work as "a common labourer" in a mine, turns out to have a shady but obviously well-traveled and well-educated past, is able to draw upon an "Oxonian Spanish," and quotes lines from Prescott and Poe. In short, these are men of culture and refinement: so refined, in fact, that with senses grown as abnormally acute as Roderick Usher's, they're forever on the brink of becoming—like the narrator of "The Lurking Fear"—"unhinged."

Which isn't to say that they're weak-willed. Lovecraft's heroes may prefer ancient books to broadswords, and, unlike the case with Dunsany, you'll find no knights or warriors in their ranks, but for most of the story they tend to be brave to the point of foolhardiness, heedless of danger, blundering blindly into the most terrifying predicaments. (In "The Lurking Fear," this includes digging up a wizard's coffin in a lonely graveyard on a stormy night—the very time the man's ghost is said to walk abroad!)

In the end, however, their composure deserts them along with their sanity, which invariably proves as fragile as an eggshell, and they take their leave of us in the same manner as they began: on a note of warning, from one who has seen too deeply into truths hidden from the rest of humanity. Incurably deranged, their nerves shot, their most cherished assumptions shattered from their encounter with the uncanny, they babble of their adventures like those half-mad narrators of Poe's, overwrought, wide-eyed, and breathless; we would scarcely be surprised to see foam flecking their lips. (It's significant that, along with points for physical strength and various technical skills, a popular Lovecraftian role-playing game awards the players Sanity Points.) The narrator of "From Beyond" is left complaining of "shaky nerves," while that of "Beyond the Wall of Sleep"—who, unlike other Lovecraft heroes, actually holds down a job (as an intern in a madhouse, no less)—suffers so badly from "nervous strain" and exhaustion that he's forced to take "a nerve-powder" and later, a long vacation. The "Polaris" narrator is "feeble and given to strange faintings"—for purposes of the plot, in this case—yet one feels that the same might be said for most of Lovecraft's heroes, just as it must once have been said of Lovecraft himself. As he confessed in a letter to the pugnacious Robert E. Howard, "While I have always had an active imagination, I have never had any surplus (or even sufficiency till I was over thirty) of physical energy. In youth—between breakdowns—I had just about energy enough to keep on my feet and no more."

One way of exercising that active imagination of his was to tell his tales in the first person, thus lending them an air of immediacy; no doubt, too, this approach allowed Lovecraft to project himself more fully into the fantasy he was spinning and to indulge in some extremely heightened language that, in a third-person narrative, might have seemed inappropriate. Often, as in "From Beyond," "Beyond the Wall of Sleep," "The Moon-Bog," "The Hound," "Hypnos," "Herbert West," and "Juan Romero," the narrator is an observer—an "active and enthralled assistant," as one of them describes himself—who, like Atal in "The Other Gods," watches in horror as an impetuous companion delves too deeply into cosmic mysteries; as the narrator of "Hypnos" puts it, "I had been halted by a barrier which my friend had successfully passed." The companion pays with his life, but the narrator survives to gasp out his tale to the world. (In "The Unnamable" it's the narrator who dabbles in occult matters and the friend who's the horrified skeptic; the penalty, in this case, is not death but merely adjoining hospital beds.) When there's no friend to act as the story's sacrificial victim, it's the narrator himself who peeks behind the barrier. Even if he manages to escape with his life, it may not be for long: Tales such as "Dagon," "The Temple," and "In the Walls of Eryx" come to us in the form of manuscripts discovered after the writers' deaths.

Readers coming to this collection for the first time will soon discover that, except for the narrator and the occasional obsessive friend, there are no real characters in these stories. Here, once again, Lovecraft modeled himself on his idol Poe, who, he felt, was above such sentimental considerations: "If Poe never drew a human character who lives in the memory," he argued, "it is because human beings are too contemptible and trivial to deserve such remembrance. Poe saw beyond the vulgar anthropocentric sphere, and realised that men are only puppets." Typically, though the Poesque tale "The Tomb" alludes at one point to "the dreaded face of a watcher," it never tells us anything else about him. "My friend Alos" in "Polaris" remains little more than a name; and the narrator of "The Lurking Fear" shares his initial adventures with "two faithful and muscular men" who aren't even named till five pages later. When we do get a relatively vivid description, it's often couched in terms of pedigree, such as the central figure in "Beyond the Wall of Sleep," who, we are told, is "one of those strange, repellent scions of a primitive colonial peasant stock."

If the men in these tales are "only puppets," the women are virtually nonexistent. Except for the few who mothered him—Sonia, his mother, his aunts—and for a pretty young thing named Helen Sully, on whom he seems to have had a mild middle-aged crush, Lovecraft had little use for women ("Females," he wrote, "... are by Nature literal, prosaic, and commonplace, given to dull realistic Details and practical Things, and incapable alike of vigorous artistick Creation and genuine, first-hand appreciation") and even less use for sex, the sort of subject to "engross crude minds when more worthy interests are lacking." Romance struck him as "somewhat trite and boresome" ("I fear if I were to try to become a lady's man," he confided, "I should offend all my charmers at the very outset by weaving them into weird and horrible tales! But fortunately horror-writers are not often ladies' men"), and its physical particulars were bestial, "repulsive," and potentially even dangerous to contemplate: He couldn't help noticing "the apparent connexion betwixt ages of erotic interest and national decadence." "Eroticism belongs to a lower order of instincts, and is an animal rather than nobly human quality," he wrote. "The primal savage or ape merely looks about his native forest to find a mate; the exalted Aryan should lift his eyes to the worlds of space and consider his relation to infinity!!" He claimed that, "being of a scientifick and investigative cast," he had satisfied his childish curiosity about sex by reading his uncle's medical books, and boasted: "I knew everything there is to be known about the anatomy and physiology of reproduction in both sexes before I was eight years old. . . . The entire subject had become merely a tedious detail of animal biology, without interest for one whose tastes led him to faery gardens and golden cities glorified by exotick sunsets." (These words were written in 1924, incidentally, less than a month before his marriage.)

With little interest in their fellow men and none at all in women, Lovecraft's narrators are solitary souls, alienated from the communities that surround them. "Temperamentally unfitted for the formal studies and social recreation of my acquaintances, I have dwelt ever in realms apart from the visible world," explains the narrator of "The Tomb," with more than a passing resemblance to Lovecraft himself. One thinks of novelist Steven Millhauser's observation—"Boredom, properly understood, is the essence of the Romantic temperament"—when one reads that the narrator of "The Hound" is "wearied with the commonplaces of a prosaic world" and that the hero of "The Strange High House in the Mist," yearning for those same "realms apart," is wearied with his middle-class baggage of "stout wife and romping children." (We learn no more about this family, nor do we need to.) Disillusioned with modern-day New York and disdainful of his fellow poets—a passel, it seems, of "loud-voiced pretenders"—the narrator of "He" prefers wandering the silent streets by night in lonely antiquarian walks. The dream-haunted Kuranes, in the Dunsanian story "Celephaïs," finds himself "the last of his family, and alone among the indifferent millions of London." The tone of Romantic self-pity recalls that of Machen's *Hill of Dreams* (1907), which Lovecraft had not yet read—"the story of a man," as Machen explained, "who is . . . lonely in the midst of millions, because of his mental isolation, because there is a great gulf fixed spiritually between him and all whom he encounters"—and anticipates that of Machen's *Far Off Things* (1922), a memoir of his early years in London, "all alone in my little room, friendless, desolate; . . . for me no help, no friends, no counsel, no comfort."

Despite his popularity within his own literary circle, Lovecraft, too, knew all about friendlessness. "You will notice that I have made no reference to childish friends and playmates," he told a correspondent. "I had none! The children I knew disliked me, and I disliked them. . . . Their romping and shouting puzzled me." Describing himself as a stranger in the modern world, he spoke often of his "beloved eighteenth century," maintained he had been "born 200 years too late," and concluded: "I am never a part of anything around me—in everything I am an outsider." (His famous story "The Outsider" was to follow five years later.)

Alienation often brings with it a sense of superiority; it's not surprising that the heroes of Lovecraft's fantasies see themselves as special, a breed apart, like the narrator of "Beyond the Wall of Sleep," who is assured by a grateful alien, "You have been my only friend on this planet, the only soul to sense and seek for me." Poets, to judge from this collection, are practically a separate species, excused by divine right from ever having to work or grow up; and just one day after his own marriage, Lovecraft humorously scolded a friend for deciding to "leave the paths of fancy and settle down to be a 'solid citizen' with a thoroughly adult life. If everybody is going to be so damned adult, then who the h. will sing in gardens at evening when the moon is tender and the west wind stirs the lotos-buds?" He admonished another friend: "An artist must be always a child—that's why I tell you never to grow up!—and live in dreams and wonder and moonlight."

Sometimes, in his delight at his own childishness and unworldliness, he comes off sounding like the airily smug Skimpole in Dickens's *Bleak House*. "The imaginative writer," he declared, with himself in mind, "is the painter of moods and mind-pictures—a capturer and amplifier of elusive dreams and fancies—a voyageur into those unheard-of lands which are glimpsed through the veil of actuality but rarely, and only by the most sensitive. . . . He is the poet of twilight visions and childhood memories, but sings only for the sensitive. . . . He is not practical, poor fellow, and sometimes dies in poverty; for his friends all live in the City of Never above the sunset." (The reference is to a story in Dunsany's *Book of Wonder*, "How One Came, as Was Foretold, to the City of Never.") If these sentiments sound a wee bit self-serving, though, it's probably worth noting that they appear in an essay defending his "Dagon" from a mob of literal-minded philistines who objected to the tale's biological inferences, its geologic depiction of the ocean bottom, and other things that struck them as unnatural, unwholesome, or implausible.

Philistines, in Lovecraft's view, were everywhere (as one might suspect from the title of his essay, "The Omnipresent Philistine"). In contrast to his special pleading on behalf of poets, he was inclined to see the rest of humanity as one great "herd." Worse, like Lovecraft himself on the subway, the heroes in his stories are forever coming face to face with characters who seem to represent a lower order of being, such as the "degenerate squatter population" of the Catskills—"simple animals . . . gently descending the evolutionary scale"—among whom the narrator of "The Lurking Fear" must travel. "Mankind is truly amusing," Lovecraft informed a correspondent, "when kept at the proper distance. And common men, if well-behaved, are really quite useful." Occasionally, of course, the crowd pressed too close; but as he reminded another correspondent, "Your soul and personality are still your own, and if the burthen of the herd mind presses too seriously upon you, you can always retire haughtily within their impregnable recesses."

It's clear that, like Eliot and other intellectuals of his time, Lovecraft had little affection for democracy. When it came to a choice between "civilisation" and "the masses," he said, "I care only for the civilisation. . . . I'm for giving the masses as little as can be given without bringing on a danger of collapse. . . . I would frankly prefer a landholding aristocracy with a cultivated leisure class and a return to the historic authority of the British crown, of which I shall always be spiritually a subject." He wrote those words in 1929, and was saying much the same thing in 1932, describing his "ideal of a government" as "a fascistic one" and dismissing democracy as "a mockery and a jest." Two years later, at the age of forty-three, he was still inveighing against "Dagoes," "Jewish radicals," and "damn coons," and longing for a society based on "the maintenance of intellectual and artistic standards, the welfare of superior types, and so on." Later still, he had a change of heart; dismissing most of his earlier work ("The more I look over my old stuff the more disgusted I get with it") and sensing that he'd finally begun to emerge from a decades-long adolescence, he put his youthful affectations behind him, faced the world more humbly and humanely, and even became a convert to the New Deal ("The liberals at whom I used to laugh were the ones who were right"). But these changes came very late indeed—in the final few years left to him, when he had virtually stopped writing fiction. And even as late as 1936, less than a year before his death, one finds him denouncing the barbarism of "proletarian groups and peasantries" and of "the backward races who hate the white man and all his works."

These lifelong attitudes are reflected in his choice of heroes for the stories in this book. While many are sensitive poets alienated from the ugliness of an unappreciative world, they are also likely to be Aryans stranded amid hordes of darker folk—a situation analogous to Lovecraft's experience in New York, which he drew upon directly in "He," with its blue-eyed New England narrator lost amid "throngs of . . . squat, swarthy strangers with hardened faces and narrow eyes, shrewd strangers without dreams." Iranon, "his yellow hair glistening with myrrh," is equally out of place among the "dark and stern" philistines who have no use for his songs. In "The Doom That Came to Sarnath," one of Lovecraft's earliest Dunsanian tales, "adventurous young men of yellow hair and blue eyes" prove to be braver and more virtuous than the dark-skinned races who are the tale's villains and victims; the pre-Dunsanian "Polaris" pits "tall, grey-eyed men" against invading armies of "squat, hellish yellow fiends." Though Lovecraft satirized his own Teutonic elitism in

"The Temple" and, in "In the Walls of Eryx," assailed humanity's arrogance toward alien cultures, many of his horror tales are studies in racial xenophobia, casting fearful sidelong glances at types such as the "swarthy, evil-looking strangers" who skulk through "The Horror at Red Hook." The title character of "Herbert West—Reanimator," described as "a blond, blue-eyed scientific automaton," is virtually a different species from the black boxer known as "the Harlem Smoke"; the latter, depicted as distinctly less than human, possesses "abnormally long arms which I could not help calling fore legs" and fails to respond to a resurrecting drug that West has prepared with whites in mind.

Race also provided an outlet for Lovecraft's historical pessimism; long an admirer of imperial Rome, he saw Aryan civilization in a similarly golden light—as proud but doomed, a dying culture inevitably losing ground before a rising tide of barbarians. Like Lovecraft himself, overwhelmed by the rabble of New York, white civilization goes down to defeat before the waves of squat invaders in "Polaris"; the swarthy immigrants of "Red Hook" go on practicing their savage blasphemies. "America has lost New York to the mongrels," Lovecraft declared, and later wrote: "I think the old culture with its idea of quality versus size is worth fighting for, *but I don't think it's going to win.* . . . A blighting barbarism of machinery and democracy is inevitably coming. . . . I hate it like poison, but I see it ahead." The brooding tone is occasionally replaced by one of cosmic detachment, but only when Lovecraft is considering the fate of mankind as a whole, eventually to be wiped out by some more adaptive creature, just "as the dinosaurs were wiped out—leaving the field free for the rise and dominance of some hardy and persistent insect species." One finds the same theme—that man was preceded by other intelligent races, and that his present position as master of the earth is only temporary—in this collection's title story, "Dagon," which also hints at an ancient kinship between humanity and a race of gilled sea-dwellers.

Small wonder, then, that Lovecraft's darker tales balance a fear of the past with a fear of the future. We've struggled up from the primordial muck; sooner or later, the stories suggest, we'll be dragged back down. In "Herbert West," the heroes discover that "despite the nauseous eyes, the voiceless simianism, and the daemoniac savagery," a corpse is not that of an animal: "It had been a man." Stories such as "Arthur Jermyn" and "The Beast in the Cave" offer similar metamorphoses, similar revelations. While Lovecraft's letters are filled with light-hearted speculations about his distinguished family tree, his tales are haunted by ancestral horrors such as these. He could envy Lord Dunsany his childhood on "the ancestral estate," but his own imagination conjured up Gothic retreats like the ones in "The Festival," "The Shunned House," "The Dunwich Horror," and "The Rats in the Walls," guarding ancient family secrets, hereditary taints, and racial backsliding.

Degeneration in all its forms was, in fact, his chosen theme, and it's one he came to naturally; Lovecraft scholar Barton L. St. Armand has pointed out how Lovecraft's own experiences—his ill health and the deteriorating mental health of his parents, the dwindling of his family fortune, the successive homes, each smaller and shabbier than the last, the decline of once-proud neighborhoods into slums—all predisposed him to a horror of corruption and decay (St. Armand terms it "the Great Dread of the Viscous"), and quotes Lovecraft's assertion that "no line betwixt 'human' and 'non-human' organisms is possible. . . . Certain traits in many lower animals suggest, to the mind whose imagination is not dulled by scientific literalism, the beginnings of activities horrible to contemplate in evolved mankind." It does indeed seem likely that, as an impoverished but genteel New Englander with aristocratic pretensions, "antierotic views" (his own phrase), an abhorrence of alcohol, and a distaste for animal passions, the rigidly well-behaved Lovecraft had a stake in keeping the beast at bay: the beast around him, in the form of darker races whose forms he found physically loathsome, and the one within, whose thwarted desires are definitively catalogued by St. Armand in *The Roots of Horror in the Fiction of H. P. Lovecraft*. Enthusiasts have noted that the most effective horror tales are those that draw upon the writers' own fears—an observation made by such respected figures as Edith Wharton ("The teller of supernatural tales should be well frightened in the telling"), E. F. Benson ("The narrator must succeed in frightening himself before he can hope to frighten his readers"), and H. Russell Wakefield

("Before you can scare others, you must be scared yourself").

Lovecraft apparently agreed: "No first-rate story can ever be written," he said, "without the author's actually experiencing the moods and visions concerned in a sort of oneiroscopic way." His own private dreads and revulsions produced a body of work filled with cannibalism, bestiality, reverse evolution, fish-gods and fish-men, reptile-men, ape-men, creatures both slimy and scaly, monsters behind human masks, savage tribes, degenerate backwoodsmen, fungoid rottenness that spreads like cancer, and decomposing corpses that walk and speak like men.

What these horrors actually amount to, taken together, is essentially change, impermanence, in its most awful and organic form—for lurking behind them all is the Romantics' implacable enemy, time. Confronted by a world in which all things pass away and in which change is the only constant, Lovecraft—whose outlook was best summed up in the title of his amateur magazine, *The Conservative*—must have felt much as the late Loren Eiseley did, in *The Unexpected Universe*, as he sat at his study window: "For years, I had not seen anything from that particular window that did not spell the death of something I loved."

It is here, in this dread of impermanence and in the desperate need to evade it, that the Lovecraft of the eldritch horrors becomes one with the Lovecraft of the ethereal fantasies. In this his literary mentor once again preceded him, for change, and the escape from its dominion, is also a central concern for Dunsany, a fellow celebrant of the old ways and a lifelong foe of, as he put it, "the hostile hand of Time." His *Book of Wonder* is pervaded by a Romantic's anguish at the transformations time brings, as in this description of "the chaunt called Dolorous: It told of desolate, regretted things befallen happy cities long since in the prime of the world. It told . . . of the malignity of time . . . of autumn and of passing away."

For Lovecraft, a less robust soul, lacking the Irish aristocrat's worldliness and wealth, the anguish must have been all the greater—an aching desire to escape from this world of endless change, and one that equaled, in its intensity, that of the troubled youth in Hope Mirrlees's 1926 fantasy novel *Lud-in-the-Mist*:

... Ranulph's sobs redoubled. "I want to get *away!* to get *away!*" he moaned.

"Away? Away from where?" and there was a touch of impatience in Master Nathaniel's voice.

"From . . . from things *happening*," sobbed Ranulph.

Master Nathaniel's heart suddenly contracted; but he tried not to understand. "Things happening?" he said in a voice that he endeavoured to make jocular. "I don't think anything very much happens in Lud, does it?"

"*All* the things," moaned Ranulph, "summer and winter, and days and nights. *All* the things!"

Lovecraft, for his part, sought to "get away" by several different means. He would lose himself in antiquarian pursuits and, until his later years, in daydreams of the secure, timeless world of the eighteenth century, fancying himself an English country gentleman of that sunnier, more serene age. Another way of escaping time's clutches, and with them the corruption of the flesh, was by casting off one's "gross body" altogether, as the narrator contemplates doing in "Beyond the Wall of Sleep" (and as later characters do in tales such as "The Whisperer in Darkness"), trading "the sallow cheeks" and "repulsively rotten fangs" of one's earthly form to become an entity of celestial light and to journey perpetually round the universe—or, as in "Celephaïs," a mere "violet-coloured gas" dwelling far outside the realm of matter and energy.

But every escape, every "getting away," is also a quest. To flee the ravages of time, casting off this world of instability, is also to seek a refuge, a place of permanence. In Lovecraft's case, this meant the quest for a city, a timeless city where change is unknown. Typically, this enchanted place can only be found in a dream, like Sona-Nyl in "The White Ship," where "there is neither time nor space, neither suffering nor death," or like the title city of "Celephaïs," where "there is no time . . . but only perpetual youth," and which is revisited, along with other scenes from these early tales, in *The Dream-Quest of Unknown Kadath* ("Ever new seemed this deathless city of vision, for here time has no power to tarnish or destroy").

Cities—dream cities, ruined cities, cities seen from afar, cities glimpsed at sunset—were, in fact, the central image of Lovecraft's Dunsanian fantasies, just as they were for Dunsany himself, creator of such magical metropolises as Arathrion, Zorra, Bombasharna, Sardathrion with its "mist-draped marble lawns," slumbering Mandaroon "with her white pinnacles peering over her ruddy walls and the green of her copper roofs," the lonely desert city of Bethmoora, the City on Mallington Moor ("a beautiful city all of white marble"), the dream city of Merimna ("a marvel of spires and figures of bronze, and marble fountains, and trophies of fabulous wars, and broad streets given over wholly to the Beautiful"), Sidith "whelmed by the gods" and Nombros warred over by them, doomed Andelsprutz, long-lost Zaccarath, ancient Astahahn, whose citizens "have fettered and manacled Time," and Perdóndaris, whose ivory gate ("carved out of one solid piece") inspired the throne in Lovecraft's Sarnath, "wrought of one piece of ivory," and, in his *Dream-Quest,* the alabaster walls of Thran, "wrought in one solid piece by what means no man knows."

Yet Dunsany, the adventurer, world traveler, and man of action, could also wax poetic about the countryside, the open fields, the woods and jungles where he hunted game, whereas for Lovecraft, in his life as well as in his fiction, the city was supreme—indeed, the highest achievement of the human race. (Though denying he was "actively hostile toward mankind," he argued that "its only use is to build quaint cities for me to enjoy a century or two later!") "I wish I could get the idea on paper," he wrote, "the sense of marvel and liberation . . . reachable at rare instants through vistas of ancient streets, across leagues of strange hill country, or up endless flights of marble steps culminating in tiers of balustraded terraces." He felt it most keenly "in the late afternoon, when the slanting sunlight throws strange mantles of golden enchantment on roofs and spires, groves and gardens, fields and terraces. . . ." Such a scene never failed to provoke "a quick tightening of the throat—a wild certainty that some strangeness lies just beyond the blazing west, or a singing sureness that some marvel lovely and incredible is about to blossom." This feeling reached its height for him on his initial visit to Marblehead ("God! Shall I ever forget my first stupefying glimpse of MARBLEHEAD'S huddled and archaick roofs under the snow in the delirious sunset glory of four p.m., Dec. 17, 1922!!!"), a moment he described as "the most powerful single emotional climax during my nearly forty years of existence." As Peter Cannon observes in his essay "Sunset Terrace Imagery in Lovecraft," "For H. P. Lovecraft, to gaze down from a height, ideally at sunset, upon a gorgeous city or landscape vista, arguably constituted the supreme emotional experience of his life."

Even if he had trouble getting the idea on paper, he certainly tried. His stories and letters are filled with vivid and picturesque description; so, presumably, was his conversation. (A little boy of his acquaintance, on seeing Niagara Falls, was heard to exclaim, "Gee, what would Mr. Lovecraft say!"—"which may be taken as evidence," Lovecraft added wryly, "that the youth is not unimprest with volubility and flow, whether in aqueous torrents or in childish old gentlemen.")

Curiously, however, the cities in his fiction, especially those of his dream fantasies, are almost interchangeable. Though they vary somewhat in flavor, displaying by turns aspects of ancient Greece, quaint harborside New England, or Arabian Nights-cum-Dunsany, they often end up sounding like a single all-encompassing metropolis. Over and over we find the same list of images, from "Polaris" ("Of ghastly marble were its walls and its towers, its columns, domes, and pavements. In the marble streets were marble pillars . . .") and "The Doom That Came to Sarnath" ("Of polished desert-quarried marble were its walls . . .") to "Beyond the Wall of Sleep" ("Walls, columns, and architraves of living fire . . . extending upward to an infinitely high vaulted dome of indescribable splendour"), "The White Ship" ("lordly terraces . . . gleaming white roofs and colonnades of strange temples . . . golden domes"), "Celephaïs" ("bronze gates . . . onyx pavements . . . cerulean splendour"), "The Quest of Iranon" ("palaces of veined and tinted marble, with golden domes and painted walls, and green gardens with cerulean pools and crystal fountains"), culminating in *The Dream-Quest* ("All golden and lovely it blazed in the sunset, with walls, temples, colonnades, and arched bridges of veined marble . . .").

This catalogue of wonders, repeated again and again with small variations, suggests that Lovecraft built his imaginary cities—or his one great city—by accretion, as with a collage. Once the specific objects (or architectural elements) were listed, he could fill in the details, as if gradually focusing a telescope. In "Sarnath," for example, we get the usual onyx-paved streets, bronze gates, houses of chalcedony, walled gardens, crystal lakelets, and shining domes, followed by this note: "And in most of the palaces the floors were mosaics of beryl and lapis-lazuli and sardonyx and carbuncle." Lovecraft's method of construction, detail by lovingly imagined detail, recalls that of his visionary heroes in "Beyond the Wall of Sleep" ("As I gazed, I perceived that my own brain held the key to these enchanting metamorphoses; for each vista which appeared to me was the one my changing mind most wished to behold") and "Celephaïs" ("it was he who had created Ooth-Nargai in his dreams"), as well as the method employed by the hero of Dunsany's "The Coronation of Mr. Thomas Shap," who forsakes London to live in the city of his daydreams ("Slowly he built up Larkar: rampart by rampart, towers for archers, gateway of brass"). In fact, the Irish writer may once again have been Lovecraft's inspiration. In Dunsany's "The Fall of Babbulkund," for example, members of a caravan wending their way to "the City of Marvel" hear fascinating accounts of this "most beautiful city in the world" from fellow travelers, only to arrive too late and find nothing but desert, with the city living only in their imaginations. "Carcassonne" tells, similarly, of the quest for a miraculous city that, though described in ever greater detail, growing more and more real to the imagination, is never actually reached at the story's end. The planned equatorial city of Erlathdronion, "Earth's Wonder," in Dunsany's "A Tale of the Equator," enjoys an even more problematic existence; it's conjured up so vividly by court poets that the Sultan, after listening to them, calls a halt to its construction, "for in hearing thee we have drunk already its pleasures."

The constructive process, in Lovecraft's case, could not have been entirely intellectual. The stately repetition of images, the litany of simple, rhythmic phrasing and exotic words, becomes a kind of chant—"beryl and lapis-lazuli and sardonyx and carbuncle"—and suggests an author capable of losing himself in a vision, and of savoring such passages for their very sound. There's clearly an element of self-hypnosis in the process; reading the familiar lines aloud, or hearing them inside your head, it's hard not to be lulled into something approaching a hypnotic state. Lovecraft must have been aware of this, for he wrote: "As for the *unconscious* element in composition . . . it is really very considerable. . . . Unless there is actual emotion and pseudo-memory behind a tale, something will inevitably be lacking, no matter how deft, expert, and mature this craftsmanship may be. Emotion makes itself felt in the unconscious choice of words, management of rhythms, and disposal of stresses in the flow of narration." It appears, in short, that just as Lovecraft tapped into his own fears and loathings in his horror tales, frightening himself as he wrote, he gave himself over in much the same way to his Dunsanian fantasies, plunging himself into visions of his personal paradise and, with readers in tow, into the breathless rapture of a dream. "I do best," he explained of such writing, "when I . . . can live wholly in the pictures I am imagining."

But living in imaginary pictures, haughtily retiring into those impregnable recesses of his mind, was a practice Lovecraft recommended not just in literary creation but in life. For him, I suspect, the conjuring up of magical cities in rhythmically sonorous prose amounted almost to prayer, a protective spell to ward off unpleasant reality and keep the modern world from pressing too close. Life, he argued, was simply a set of pictures in the brain, infinitely alterable; "it best becomes a man of sense to chuse whatever sort of agreeable fancies best amuse him, and thenceforward to revel innocently in them; sensible that they are not real."

Judging by the tales in this collection, there's good reason for reveling in fancies; reality is a pretty horrifying place. Contrast, for example, the glorious imaginary city in "Beyond the Wall of Sleep" to the nightmarish reality—"a hideous world in which we are practically helpless"—revealed in a similar story, "From Beyond," which introduces you to "the things that float and flop about you and through you every moment of your life." Lovecraft, who once theorized that "the entire play of creation is pure chaos, and wholly devoid of values," has made the "floundering things" in "From Beyond" a kind of living chaos, the embodiment of all the biological repulsiveness, mob violence, and Darwinian strife that he himself loathed: "Foremost among the living objects were great inky, jellyfish monstrosities which flabbily quivered in harmony with the vibrations from the machine. . . . These things were never still, but seemed ever floating about with some malignant purpose. Sometimes they appeared to devour one another, the attacker launching itself at its victim and instantaneously obliterating the latter from sight." And the worst thing about them is, they're *real*.

Reality, in these tales, comes as a shock. In "The White Ship," the Land of Hope turns out to be an illusion, a monstrous cataract that kills men and crushes their dreams. Another glimpse of reality, less dramatic but a hundred times more dreary, appears in "The Quest of Iranon," when the city of Oonai, so alluring by night, turns out to be "not golden in the sun, but grey and dismal." In view of Lovecraft's New York experience, the tale seems amazingly prophetic. "He," the fruit of that experience, contrasts the Dunsanian wonder-city of Lovecraft's fantasies—"I had seen it in the sunset from a bridge, majestic above its waters, its incredible peaks and pyramids rising flower-like and delicate from pools of violet mist to play with the flaming golden clouds and the first stars of evening"—to the "squalor" of the real New York seen by "garish daylight."

Lovecraft's vision in these tales is a bleak and gloomy one, a series of rude awakenings, of *Wizard of Oz* revelations without the charm. Imagination, Lovecraft says, requires an act of will. The everyday is humdrum; the reality is worse. Even his beloved eighteenth century was merely another fancy—or so he admitted late in life, in a letter that recalls the conclusion of *The Dream-Quest:* "Except in certain selected circles, I would undoubtedly find my own 18th century insufferably coarse, orthodox, arrogant, narrow, and artificial. . . . What I look back upon nostalgically is a dream-world which I invented at the age of four from picture books and the Georgian hill streets of Old Providence."

Providence was one of the few unfailing sources of solace in Lovecraft's life, all the more so during his years of misery and exile in New York, when he had little to sustain him but the vision of an eventual return home. Late in 1924, in the moving poem "Providence," he catalogued the city's beauties in the familiar Dunsanian manner—

> A flight of steps with iron rail,
>   A belfry looming tall,
> A slender steeple, carv'd and pale,
>   A moss-grown garden wall

—apostrophized its "sacred ground," and ended with a testament to the strength of his imagination:

> Thy twinkling lights each night I see,
>   Tho' time and space divide;
> For thou art of the soul of me,
>   And always at my side!

Here, plainly, was another timeless city, a bastion of purity, tradition, and culture. Lovecraft clung to this vision in the midst of the teeming, ever-changing modern metropolis. "New York was a nightmare," he wrote, just after fleeing it, "and I have already form'd a most delightful picture of the gang as meeting in various colonial Providence homes!" (He would soon be speaking similarly of being "ingulph'd in the nightmare of Brooklyn's mongrel slums," and of how, safely back in Providence, "that experience has already become the merest vague dream.") The key to the city's appeal was that, like his imaginary Celephaïs, it never changed: "Home," he reported joyfully, "was just as it had always been since I was born there thirty-six years ago."

His enthusiasm, this time, remained strong; the cataloguing of beauties continued—and did so for years after his return. In letters he praised the city's "gabled and steepled vistas," its "roofs, spires, and domes," and wrote: "Let no one tell me that Providence is not the most beautiful city in the world! Line for line, atmospheric touch for atmospheric touch, it positively and absolutely *is!*"

Paradise, once won, still had to be defended; cherishing Providence's antiquity, Lovecraft found himself appalled (as more than one observer has) by the city's often crass attempts at "progress," including the demolition of a row of ancient brick warehouses, which Lovecraft eulogized as "the links that join us to the years before . . . symbols of old New England thoughts and ways" in a poem in the *Providence Journal*. He discovered, to his horror, that Providence, too, had its slums, inhabited by "slug-like beings (half Jew and half Negro, apparently) which crawl about and wheeze in the acrid smoke which pours from passing trains," and told another correspondent how, immediately after leaving New York, "I thought the crowds of Providence looked refreshingly human and Nordic; but now . . . the business section seems discouragingly mongrel and decadent. . . . But the old hill is all right, thank god."

Yet even within the relative gentility of his old College Hill neighborhood, he still yearned for something more, just as his hero Kuranes, back in the land of his boyhood, longs for that dream within a dream, Celephaïs. "As time goes on, my taste for urban panoramic effects increases," Lovecraft wrote in April 1927, only twelve months after his return:

> The vistas I relish most are those in which the sunset plays a transfiguring and glorifying part. Sometimes I stumble accidentally on rare combinations of slope, curved street-line, roofs and gables and chimneys, and accessory details of verdure and background, which in the magic of late afternoon assume a mystic majesty and exotic significance beyond the power of words to describe. Absolutely nothing else in life now has the power to move me so much; for in these momentary vistas there seem to open before me bewildering avenues to all the wonders and lovelinesses I have ever sought, and to all those gardens of eld whose memory trembles just beyond the rim of conscious recollection. . . . All that I live for is to capture some fragment of this hidden and just unreachable beauty. . . . There is somewhere, my fancy fabulises, a marvellous city of ancient streets and hills and gardens and marble terraces, wherein I once lived happy eternities, and to which I must return if ever I am to have content.

Unless, like Wordsworth, you believe that we're born "trailing clouds of glory" and freighted with memories of a better life in heaven, it requires no great discernment to see that Lovecraft's vision—like the "marvellous sunset city" for which Randolph Carter searches in *The Dream-Quest*—is rooted in the blissful, timeless world of infancy, when all needs are met and all the world is touched with wonder. "Adulthood," as he once remarked, "is hell."

Cannon points out that, in *The Case of Charles Dexter Ward,* with its detailed Providence setting and openly autobiographical hero, Lovecraft inserted an account of what must be "literally among his own first impressions": "The nurse used to stop and sit on the benches of Prospect Terrace to chat with policemen; and one of the child's first memories was of the great westward sea of hazy roofs and domes and steeples and far hills which he saw one winter afternoon from that great railed embankment, all violet and mystic against a fevered, apocalyptic sunset of reds and golds and purples and curious greens." Lovecraft himself later spoke of "a strange sense of adventurous expectancy connected with landscape and architecture and sky-effects" that had haunted his dreams "for nearly forty years," and recalled a time at age two and a half when, viewing a New England townscape from a railway bridge, he felt "the imminence of some wonder which I could neither describe nor fully conceive—and there has never been a subsequent hour of my life when kindred sensations have been absent."

It was this same sense of wonder, Lovecraft admitted, that first attracted him to Lord Dunsany: "He seemed like a sort of gate to enchanted worlds of childhood dream." In his own Dunsanian excursions, he had Kuranes attain the timeless city of Celephaïs by dreaming of "his old world of childhood," and Iranon search all his life for "the city of marble and beryl where my father once ruled as king." Was he remembering, as he penned this fantasy, his birth into a family of wealth and influence, and his early years in the huge house of his grandfather? Or perhaps it was something more common, the memory of an infant state when, for a brief time, we all ruled as kings.

Much as we may miss them, there's a curious drawback to these timeless cities of childhood: They're surprisingly hard to live in. They lie beside the river like gems, timeless and beautiful, but we never see one of Lovecraft's protagonists actually settling down in them; they are merely nice places to visit. Only in the pre-Dunsanian "Polaris" does the hero become involved with the fortunes of a city and the affairs of its citizens; but then, he is already a citizen himself. The more common case is that of the "Yann"-

inspired travel pieces, in which cities are either seen from a distance (such as the sunset city in *The Dream-Quest,* recalling vistas of skylines from Marblehead to Manhattan) or remain virtually unexplored, the hero content to glide by them, perhaps lingering in one for a day or two before pressing on. "The White Ship," for example, offers us the land of Zar, with "lordly terraces . . . gleaming white roofs and colonnades of strange temples"—but one dares not enter, for it's impossible to leave. Into "Thalarion, the City of a Thousand Wonders," we learn, "many have passed but none returned." And as for lovely Sona-Nyl, the narrator cannot remain there for more than a few vaguely alluded-to aeons—which, in this tale, equals merely a few minutes. He must soon set sail again for the adventure that lies out upon the water.

The heaven of our dreams, once we arrive there, can be a pretty tedious place. Kuranes, in *The Dream-Quest,* forsakes his long-sought Celephaïs for a reconstructed Cornish fishing village of his boyhood; one, it seems, can grow tired of absolute permanence and perfection. Wallace Stevens was only echoing an earlier American, Mark Twain, when he wrote "Sunday Morning" and charged paradise with being boring and insipid, a place without death where fruit, though ripe, never falls and where, beneath a "perfect sky," rivers "seek for seas / They never find."

Unlike the heavenly city, the river serves as an ideal symbol of change—change in its promise of travel, change in the water itself. However enticing the shore may be, the man of independent mind must go voyaging again, journeying out upon the waves—like Ishmael, who, in *Moby-Dick,* feels the well-known lure of the sea and is compelled to state a "mortally intolerable truth; that all deep, earnest thinking is but the intrepid effort of the soul to keep the open independence of her sea; while the wildest winds of heaven and earth conspire to cast her on the treacherous, slavish shore."

The sea and the river, in sum, are where the traveler experiences life. The harbor city on the shore may offer security, a refuge to which one can always return, but it also means monotony, stagnation. It cannot be lived in because, paradoxically, it is timeless; it permits none of the change one associates with life. A recent *New Yorker* piece quoted Goethe's Faust and his promise to Mephistopheles: "If I ever say to the moment—'Stay, you are so beautiful!' then you may throw me into chains; then will I readily perish; then may the death-bell toll; then you are free from your service. The clock may stand, the hour-hand may fall: Time will be a thing no more for me!" The writer added: "Perhaps you do surrender to the Devil when you wish time would stop; perhaps you're asking for the stasis of death."

The timeless city is ruled by that same stasis. Like the city of Xura in "The White Ship," the Land of Pleasures Unattained, it is enticing but dead, reeking of decay, "the lethal, charnel odour of plague-stricken towns and uncovered cemeteries." You cannot stay; you must move onward.

The life, it's clear, is in the voyage; the road, as Cervantes said, is better than the inn. It's noteworthy that, before departing for New York, Lovecraft described his beloved Providence as intellectually "sterile"; and that no sooner did he return than he was excitedly making travel plans, plans for journeys farther and more frequent than before. So, too, with his heroes: No sooner does Kuranes arrive in the dream-city of Celephaïs than he must go voyaging again. "More than ever," we read, "Kuranes wished to sail in a galley to the far places of which he had heard so many strange tales." Foremost among them is "Serannian, the pink marble city of the clouds." Nor can Randolph Carter find it in his heart to remain in Dylath-Leen, or in Celephaïs, or in any of the other enchanted cities of *The Dream-Quest*. Like Ulysses, and like a child straying from the shelter of his ancestral home, he is compelled to voyage forth again—to seek another city.

And what does one gain from these voyagings? Nothing less than an appreciation of what it means to be alive in this universe. Describing one such voyager who might just as well have been Lovecraft, Arthur Machen observed: "A man may go on a journey, and see cities of climbing spires and golden palaces, he may view rich vineyards purple and gold in the sunshine, laughing harvests, towering mountains. But, if he cares to stray a little from the highroad, there are deep, dark, and secret places. There are haggard rocks that grin and mouth at him, as if the hag and hungry goblin had been changed to stone. There are hollows in a gloom of ash trees, places holy and enchanted, upon which the traveller will gaze in silence, hardly daring to enter. There are paths that lead down lonely hills, and when the twilight falls, it is evident that they must end in fairyland. . . . There are flaming walls that bound the world of our thought; pillars of Hercules beyond which no ship can sail. And yet it is our privilege that now and again there is one who has passed beyond these walls, these bounds, these pillars, who has looked on the other side and has brought back its secrets."

They are precious, those secrets from the other side. And you're sure to find a few of them in this book.

The Festival

The recollections that follow were written in November and December 1975 for Willis Conover's *Science-Fantasy Correspondent*. No attempt has been made to update them; save for a few minor revisions, they appear here in their original form, complete with references—now happily outmoded—to the Biltmore Hotel's bankruptcy and Lovecraft's unmarked grave.

I am grateful to Bill Desmond for making available to me his tapes of the various panels.

—T.E.D.K.
March 1980

When the traveller in north central Rhode Island takes the wrong fork off the Aylesbury Pike just a few miles beyond Dean's Corners, he comes upon a queer conglomeration of buildings rising dark and lonely amid the ancient hills. Here Portuguese and other seafaring races have commingled with the original Yankee and Indian stocks to produce swarthy-faced beings of oddly sinister aspect—beings who eye the stranger mistrustfully, and who converse with one another in a grotesquely degenerate patois.

The traveler may not choose to linger in this benighted metropolis, especially when he discovers that, but for two unsavory-looking diners, the place shuts up tightly at ten. Yielding to panic as

---

From *The First World Fantasy Convention: Three Authors Remember* (West Warwick, RI: Necronomicon Press, 1980), where it appeared along with essays by Robert Bloch and Fritz Leiber.

the hours of darkness grow interminable, he may gather his belongings and speed madly toward the grey New England dawn, convinced he has just escaped from Dunwich—although in fact that demon-haunted community lies a good sixty miles to the north.

Later, the traveler may learn the truth: that he has passed the night in Providence.

Had he arrived in town on a recent All Hallow's Eve, however, the traveler might well have chosen to extend his stay till the following Sunday, for he would have stumbled upon a quaint and curious festival unique in the annals of literature: Some four hundred fantasy fans, critics, booksellers, collectors, artists, writers, and their respective retinues had gathered together at the Holiday Inn to honor the late Howard Phillips Lovecraft and the *Weird Tales* tradition of which he was part.

That so many made the journey to Providence attests to the magic of Lovecraft's name, as well as to the extraordinarily smooth planning of Donald Grant, Bill Desmond, Charles and Lupe Collins, and New York literary agent Kirby McCauley, who had spent more than seven months organizing the event.

I'd been with Kirby that day last spring when, driving through New England, he'd first alluded to a fantasy convention. "It's something friends and I have talked about for years," he said. "We've put if off and put it off, but now the time is right." I'd been with Kirby when, later that day in Providence, he sat in the convention manager's office at the Holiday Inn, calmly booking two hundred rooms for Halloween weekend—at that time the number seemed to me impossibly optimistic—and assuring the young woman that "fantasy fans are nice, quiet people, much less destructive than the science fiction crowd." And I'd been behind the wheel of Kirby's car when, still later that day, giving him a lightning tour of Lovecraft's College Hill, I ran a stop sign and collided with a truck from Dominick's Pizzeria, reducing our vehicle to a pile of wreckage.

From such inauspicious beginnings had the festival grown. The two hundred rooms were duly occupied; the two hundred sixty banquet tickets were sold out. Kirby's optimism had, as usual, proved correct.

In fact, the place was packed—to the point where the combined body heat of the conventioneers must have raised the room temperature a good five or ten degrees. (Of course, this slight excess of heat might be seen as a tribute to the memory of Lovecraft, who, it's said, functioned most comfortably in temperatures of ninety and above.)

As the only major hotel in Providence, the Inn had been something of a Hobson's choice—but as it turned out, a happy one. The ideal hotel might well have been the huge old Biltmore, a shabbily respectable place familiar to thousands of New England jewelry manufacturers and traveling salesmen as well as to Lovecraft himself, who'd mentioned it in his *Charles Dexter Ward*. Unfortunately, the Biltmore had gone bankrupt in 1974.

A greater disappointment, from the standpoint of Providence history, was the loss of Dana's Old Corner Bookshop, a tiny establishment hidden in the cellar of 22½ Weybosset Street. In its time the shop had been a rich source of Arkham House books (new) and occult literature (used); Lovecraft himself had browsed here and had known old Mr. Dana, the proprietor. Tragically, the entire building had burned to a shell—and with it the thousands of books in the upper stories—only a few months before the convention.

But changes were inevitable. As the lifelong home of Lovecraft and the onetime home of Poe, as well as of Lovecraft collaborator Clifford Eddy (of "Loved Dead" fame), Providence was still the perfect site for this celebration.

In truth it is a lovely, unappreciated city, and from their hotel rooms, convention-goers had the good fortune to see some of its most notable features: its dignified, unpretentious skyline, marred only by the hideous new Hospital Trust offices, yet still dominated by the wonderful old Industrial National Bank tower, an Art Deco curiosity that bears an astonishing resemblance to the *Daily Planet* building of Superman fame; the gleaming white dome of the Rhode Island state capitol, which, though it looks like some scaled-down version of the one in Washington, boasts the second-largest unsupported marble dome in the world (the largest is St. Peter's in Rome); the gloomily atmospheric downtown section, where a new civic center and regional theater rub shoulders with seedy pawnshops, shoeshine stands, and abandoned movie palaces; and rising above the bay and river to the east, the steepled slopes of College Hill, a place of vine-covered brick walls, hidden alleyways, and leafy suburban streets, where Colonial houses—magical old buildings with fanlights over the front door and fireplaces in every room—are fighting a losing battle against the glass-and-cinderblock encroachments of Brown University. For all its benign intentions, the university has been spreading like a cancer over as much of the hill as it can buy; but the neighborhood still has one of the largest concentrations of Colonial architecture in the nation. Seen from above or below, from the waterfront docks at India Point or the decaying lanes off Benefit Street or the neon heights of the Holiday Inn, Lovecraft's old hometown remains a haunted place—haunted not least by the ghost of Lovecraft himself.

He haunts the literature, too—which is perhaps one reason why the First World Fantasy Convention remained gratifyingly free of "superstars" and the teenage-idol mentality that's become so prevalent at similar gatherings devoted to science fiction. Fantasy is a curious genre: Little swayed by fashion, dominated by writers long dead, it offers its adherents a chance for literary immortality unknown in other fields. Science fiction tends to date, as do mainstream novels both contemporary and historical; yet write an evocative fantasy, or an effective horror tale, and you may well be read for generations. Certain traditions appear to be timeless; like fairy tales and legends, the literature of dreams and the literature of fear are never out of date.

Because the dead gods are still worshiped—Morris, Eddison, Le Fanu, James, Machen, Blackwood, Dunsany, Lovecraft, Howard, Smith, Tolkien, and the rest—and because the average fantasy reader looks to childhood as the source of inspiration and joy, the fantasy field tends to be oriented toward the past. (Lovecraft himself professed a desire to recapture in his fiction "the familiar Old Providence of my childhood"; and speaking at the panel on Epic Fantasy, writer Lin Carter listed the "Oz" series, first read in childhood, as a major literary influence: "My entire history of reading books," he said, "has been a search for more of that sort of thing.") Often, then, this sort of literature is revered not because it's good but because it was read when one was young, credulous, and uncritical; the past itself is recaptured by collecting and owning the material that shaped it. By shelling out money for old books and magazines, one is in effect buying up one's own youth—a pleasant pastime, if in the end a futile one.

In light of such pursuits, it's not surprising that, at the convention, the acquisitive instinct often reigned supreme, leaving real literary inquiry in short supply. As they milled about the so-called "huckster room," a small room where books and magazines were sold, fans spent little time debating "Who writes well?" and "Is the work successful?" Instead they concerned themselves with the going rate for a March 1936 issue of *Weird Tales* (cover slightly worn) and with good deals on out-of-print fanzines. The boast was not "I've read" but rather "I *own*."

Cast stones, of course, have a way of rebounding. I confess that I, too, have hoarded a library of fantasy and pulp classics for some mythic rainy day and that, along with typewriter and easy chair, I number among my most cherished possessions an H. P. Lovecraft letter bought several years ago from Roy Squires, the California manuscript dealer and publisher. Still, there's something undeniably sad in seeing the pleasures of fantasy reduced to those of ownership—and even worse, to matters of dollars and cents. Lovecraft, after all, spent most of his life in poverty and was paid next to nothing for his work; yet here we were bidding extravagant sums for relics of his life and times.

Modern names, too, were reducible to cash. Some of the more enterprising convention-goers, in fact, sought to have their books autographed by whatever famous authors were in attendance so that, years later, the volumes might fetch a better price. For others, collecting had long ago become an end in itself. Gleefully brandishing an attaché case filled with books, one veteran conventioneer admitted that, in the past, he would hurry through the aisles of a huckster room wheeling a shopping cart. Although he'd just been nominated for a fantasy award, he had more important things on his mind: "Even if I don't win," he confided, "I've picked up so many collectibles this weekend that it was worth it anyway."

Collectibles! Unfortunate term, that—reminding one of the film in which, rather than ask for food, a fastidious Peter Sellers character declares himself content with "a plate of edibles."

A critical spirit did emerge, however briefly, during the panel discussion on "Investigating Lovecraft," held at ten Saturday morning and attended—surprisingly, in view of the hour—by some fifty or sixty people. It was chaired by Barton Levi St. Armand, associate professor of English at Brown, an old friend and scholar of truly awesome learning. He's devoted most of his life to studies of Poe, Hawthorne, Emily Dickinson, Jung, Wilde, the Hermetic tradition, and subjects more arcane, but he remains one of the most approachable men I've ever known. I'll recall, evermore, the stuffed and mounted raven in his parlor and the "DAGON" plates on his car. As a graduate student at Brown, St. Armand had turned out a brilliant master's thesis on Lovecraft. (His book-length treatise, *The Roots of Horror in the Fiction of H. P. Lovecraft*, is due to be published shortly.) When, several years later, I'd followed him with a Lovecraft thesis of my own, St. Armand had served as my advisor. He had changed little since that time; as he sat there on the panel, he was still wearing the same spectacles, the same rust-colored moustache, and the same ubiquitous Phi Bete watch-chain, but he had just added to this ensemble a small goatee which, at this early stage in its growth, gave him the appearance of a snake-oil salesman or a slightly disreputable magician.

St. Armand began by evaluating Lovecraft's current standing in academic circles, and—in this day of exploding population and terrorist bombs—he addressed himself to a far more gentle phenomenon, the "Lovecraft explosion."

"I can still remember a time when the Lovecraft fandom was a true *fan*dom," he recalled, "and Lovecraft's name itself was a kind of secret sign or code among a certain group. . . . Now Lovecraft studies have become much more general, and as a Poe scholar I'm amazed at the explosion in the academic treatment of Lovecraft himself. . . . He's someone who has come from fandom to near respectability"—*near,* St. Armand was careful to point out, because as yet no scholarly journal in America has "gone deeply into Lovecraft's symbolism."

Here, it appeared, was one area in which the French were far ahead of us—just as they had been in according Poe his high critical reputation. "French journals," said St. Armand, "very *respectable* French journals, are filled with very serious studies of Lovecraft." (He has, in fact, contributed one notable example himself: a paper, "H. P. Lovecraft, New England Decadent," which appeared in the *Annales* of the University of Toulouse–Le Mirail.)

In this country, for the moment at least, the same job is being done by the fan magazines. Thanks, he said, to such publications as *Nyctalops, Whispers,* and the British *Shadow,* "when Lovecraft finally becomes respectable in the academic community, scholars are going to be amazed at what has already been accomplished by fans.... The recognition of Emily Dickinson, the recognition of Edgar Allan Poe, is sure to be followed at some time by the recognition of H. P. Lovecraft."

Tom Collins, another panelist, agreed. He pointed out that the late Sam Russell, a longtime scholar in the field, had written the definitive work on English ghost-story writer M. R. James—and that it had been circulated only in private and was unknown to professors.

Collins, still in his twenties, has the air of a comfortable old British clubman: portly, walrus-moustached, and blessed with a mind as precise as a pocket watch, he's my personal choice to play Mycroft Holmes. Currently, Collins is editing a collection of Lovecraft's unpublished poetry (St. Armand lauded him for "recovering Lovecraft's verse"), and he explained the motivation for such labors with admirable succinctness:

"As you read the magazines," he said, "they crumble to dust in your hand. And you realize that, by golly, if you don't carefully preserve what's on that page, it will be gone."

Examining Lovecraft's critical reputation, Collins brought up a problem that would resurface again and again in subsequent debates. Lovecraft, it's clear, was a man of varied, shifting, and seemingly contradictory views; he had opinions about almost everything—opinions that changed as he grew older—and he invariably committed them to writing, not so much in his fiction as in his amateur-journalism essays and voluminous correspondence. Some of the opinions he expressed are, by today's standards, downright unpleasant, and one is constantly coming across evidence of racism, snobbery, and literary affectation.

"There are a number of things in Lovecraft's life which, looked at on their own, are not all that attractive," Collins observed. "I think that could be said for most of us. But unfortunately, he was very open. We have an awful lot of his letters left in which he said all those private things that he wouldn't necessarily have said out loud."

Lovecraft's fiction presents a similar problem: Not all of it is of high quality, designed to enhance his reputation—yet all of it has been preserved in print. "There is juvenilia in print," said Collins. "There are fragments. There are things which have no conceivable interest to a general reader whatever, that are in mass-market paperbacks—things he wrote when he was fifteen and didn't know how to plot or how to write a clear sentence."

Here Collins paused and reconsidered. "I'm not sure Lovecraft could *ever* not write a clear sentence," he said at last. "He seemed to be born with that ability. Really bad things should be preserved for the scholar and printed, perhaps, in an Arkham House book—but for Pete's sake, in a Ballantine *paperback*? Where people are going to pick this stuff up and say, 'This is Lovecraft? What's all the fuss about?'"

The paperback houses, Collins argued, were doing Lovecraft's memory a disservice by printing too much. But he had equally harsh words for a man who, he felt, had printed too little: August Derleth, the late Wisconsin writer, publisher, and Lovecraft correspondent who'd cleaned up Lovecraft's image after the man's death by repressing the more unsavory letters, particularly those of a racial nature.

"The people who knew Lovecraft have a certain view of him," Collins declared, "and as a result . . . the best scholarship will be done and we'll really begin to evaluate his personality when all of those people who knew him have gone.

"Which," he hastened to add, "I'm certainly not in any hurry for, on a personal basis. But you notice that the explosion in Lovecraft scholarship did not occur until Derleth was unable to interfere with it anymore, and until Derleth was unable to promulgate his view of the correct and official truth of Lovecraft's life." (Collins told me later that the dedication in his book of Lovecraft's poetry will read: "To August Derleth, without whom this book would have been neither possible nor necessary.")

Panelist Dirk W. Mosig took issue with Collins. A professor of psychology at Georgia Southwestern College with a wide circle of correspondents in the fantasy field, Mosig is one of Lovecraft's staunchest and most learned defenders, and is currently preparing a study of his work for the Twayne United States Authors Series. Mosig does not sound like a good person to fight with: He holds a black belt in karate and, I'm told, keeps pet tarantulas at home. Some may also be intimidated, at first, by his Dr. Strangelove accent.

"To say that we have to wait until Lovecraft's acquaintances are dead before we can do scholarship," he told Collins, "is to say that, well, when they are dead we can get away with it! We can get away with saying all kinds of things, and nobody will challenge us. It's like saying, 'Let's get rid of all the eyewitnesses.' The eyewitness is probably more accurate than either one of us, who go back forty years to reconstruct a man we never met."

"But the eyewitnesses are also looking back forty years ago," said Collins.

"But they have their memories," Mosig noted. "We have imagination."

Collins remained unconvinced. "They also have imagination," he said.

Mosig chose to spend most of his time on "the psychological interpretation of the works" and on "their philosophical implications." This, it appeared, was his specialty: examining HPL in light of Jung's theory of "the shadow," which Mosig defined as "an unconscious opposite of the ego, the conscious self . . . which embodies all the archaic, primitive characteristics which each particular individual is afraid to recognize—the things which he considers as evil, as inadequate, inappropriate, irrational.

"But each one of us has this shadow," he continued. "We can't get rid of it. It follows us everywhere we go. And sometimes it erupts, it appears, and we confront the shadow. And what happens then? The Outsider looks in the mirror and sees the shadow—sees himself."

Over and over in the stories, Mosig declared, Lovecraft's protagonists come upon this truth; and usually it destroys them. "The truth of what man learns about himself," he said, "may be too much to take."

Philosophically the situation is similar. As Mosig reminded the audience, Lovecraft was a complete materialist; man was insignificant in his scheme of things. "For man, it may be the most terrifying thing to recognize how insignificant he really is. Can a man really cope with the realization that he is nothing, a mere accident, a speck of dust in the cosmos, with no purpose, no destiny—can a man cope with that? Or is the truth too much?

"In both cases," he concluded—in Lovecraft's philosophy as well as his psychology—"man is afraid to face reality, to deal with things as they are."

A fourth panelist now proceeded to paint an equally dark picture of the Lovecraftian universe. Speaking hesitantly in a shy Baltimore drawl, George Wetzel—whom Barton St. Armand had praised as "a very famous figure in Lovecraft scholarship who kept Lovecraft's name alive through the publication of his Lovecraft Collectors Library . . . a landmark of scholarship"—termed HPL "an artistic altruist" who felt that "the only real reason for living is to lessen the pain of existence for others by creating something to help ease the pain of life." He spoke, in particular, of the "death wish" he'd found in many of Lovecraft's writings.

"Not so much a death wish as a wish for oblivion," suggested St. Armand. He remarked that the only reference he'd seen to suicide in all Lovecraft's letters (save in the so-called "New York exile" period, when the writer was "very close to the point of a nervous breakdown or worse") appeared in a letter Lovecraft wrote to J. Vernon Shea just after Lovecraft and his mother had lost their home on Angell Street, forcing them to move. "Lovecraft writes in this letter," said St. Armand, "that he used to bicycle down to the Barrington River and look at the marshes and think of how wonderful it would seem to lie face down in the marshes and just breathe in the water."

From the marshes the discussion drifted into the sea theme, the sea-as-death theme, the sea-as-oblivion theme, and points south. I myself was the fifth member of the panel (Barton, true friend, had introduced me as a "fantasy author following in the viscous footsteps of the Master himself"), but in all this seawater I was out of my depth; I had long ago forgotten everything I'd ever written about Lovecraft and most of what I'd read. Awed by the poise and erudition of those around me—and at how gracefully Tom Collins had dropped words like "promulgate" into his talk—I said almost nothing and contented myself with staring at the audience. Toward the end of the discussion, I couldn't help noticing Forrest J. Ackerman, old-time fantasy buff and editor of *Famous Monsters of Filmland,* in one of the middle rows. Ackerman was sitting bolt upright in his chair, hands clasped as if in prayer, smiling slightly. He was fast asleep.

If all the philosophizing had been too heady for FJA, the following panel should not have been: It dealt with dollars and cents, the problems of marketing fantasy and of making a living at it—an unromantic subject for a convention devoted to H. P. Lovecraft, yet a perfectly appropriate one, since, as moderator Gahan Wilson pointed out, "the bleak reality of Lovecraft's life was poverty."

Wilson himself radiated prosperity. Impeccably dressed (as always) in a cream-colored three-piece suit, his blond moustache neatly trimmed, he looked like a Madison Avenue version of Richard Brautigan. He proved, too, an able emcee: dapper, sophisticated, and funny, as befits a staff cartoonist for both *Playboy* and the *National Lampoon.* For the latter, Wilson has created a series of childhood vignettes entitled "Nuts!" which are hilarious and also terrifyingly true; his *Playboy* work is in the Charles Addams tradition, only hipper, gorier, and usually more amusing. Wilson is also the creator of the H. P. Lovecraft statuette given to winners of the Fantasy Award; from the hint of Easter Island in the cheekbones to the haunted look around the eyes (a familiar Wilsonian touch), the figure displays both wit and, I think, considerable feeling. It therefore seemed only appropriate when, early in the panel, Robert Bloch dubbed Wilson "the poor man's Richard Upton Pickman."*

---

*In 2015, yielding to pressure by some in the field who preferred their

There was more where that came from—as Bloch soon demonstrated. "When I got into writing," he began, "was in prehistoric times. We didn't even have typewriters! We'd come out of the cave and get a block of stone, and we would hack something out on the stone. Then an editor would take it away and chisel it into final form. Well, millenniums have passed since then, and most writers are still hacks, and most editors are still chiselers!"

Bloch clearly loved playing to an audience, and he proved the weekend's leading entertainer, a horror-comic's answer to Bob Hope, drawing upon what seemed an endless supply of quips, jokes, and one-liners. Some, it's true, were atrocious ("I was following a girl down the street last night, and suddenly she turned into a drugstore!"), others brought enough groans to fill a haunted house, but all of them were thrown our way with enviable grace and delivery.

On the panel Bloch proved funny, affable, and engagingly self-confident, the sleek look of a Beverly Hills agent belying the bizarre nature of his imagination. Of all the honored guests at the convention, he was one of the few who'd really "made it" in the public eye, thanks in large part to his Hollywood screenplays. Granted, *Asylum* and *The House That Dripped Blood* are hardly cinematic milestones, and one may suspect that Mammon enjoys a higher place in his pantheon than even Yog-Sothoth or Cthulhu; still, Bloch has more than paid his dues, having written for *Weird Tales* as far back as 1934, as well as having turned out an impressive line of novels, tales, teleplays, and radio scripts along the way. His greatest fame, of course—as Gahan Wilson was later to remind us—lies in having written the novel on which *Psycho* was based; but Wilson himself preferred an earlier Bloch, the Bloch of the *Weird Tales* days and of classic stories like "Beetles." "Robert Bloch is not the Shower Scene," he maintained. "Robert Bloch means beetles crawling out of a dead man's mouth!"

---

horror icons to be politically correct (a demand that also eliminates Poe) and who declared an award honoring Lovecraft to be insufficiently "inclusive," Gahan's statuette, with its forty years of tradition, was officially discontinued.

Nonetheless, it is *Psycho's* infamous shower scene that's ensured the man's reputation. "I have been told on numerous occasions by various people," Bloch said, "that since they saw this particular film, they've been afraid to take a shower. I've always been grateful that I didn't decide to kill my victim on a toilet seat!"

His own success notwithstanding, Bloch was well able to appreciate the peculiar plight of the fantasy writer in the 1970s. "When *Weird Tales* was in existence," he recalled, "we knew where to send stories." Now, however, the markets have dried up: Thanks to television's new Family Viewing Time policy, "nobody dies before nine o'clock." For that matter, films want only "the more lurid horror material—shock rather than horror, in many instances."

In addition, Bloch pointed out, fantasy and horror writers are paid far too little: Paperbacks have climbed in price from twenty-five cents to $1.25 and $1.95, but word rates have hardly kept pace.

Yes, pay might well be higher. . . . But the lack of markets—that was the essential, the great sore point on which all panelists that day seemed to agree. Indeed, as Gahan Wilson admitted, and as organizer Kirby McCauley had acknowledged from the start, this was the very problem the convention was supposed to remedy. The World Fantasy Awards presented on Sunday afternoon would, they hoped, lend a measure of prestige to the entire field, as well as to the individual works that won; as Wilson candidly observed, prizes help sell books. More important, the convention itself, with whatever coverage it garnered in the media, had been designed to make fantasy respectable in the eyes of the public and the publishers. No longer science fiction's bastard brother, it would emerge as a genre in its own right.

That, at any rate, was the dream; whether or not it comes true may take years to discover. One thing was certain: Most of those who attended the convention did so in the belief that they'd be present at a rather special event—not the birth of fantasy, of course, but perhaps its coming of age. And they left convinced that whatever had started in Providence would survive and grow.

In a group so disparate, however, there can be no unanimity of opinion; surely not everyone came away a believer. And in fact, despite the general pessimism over "fantasy markets" and proper payment, one notable member of the field made it clear he disagreed. Bearded, contentious little Lester del Rey, Ballantine's current fantasy editor (and himself a veteran science-fiction writer, known to *Astounding Stories* readers in the '30s as Ramon F. Alvarez-del Rey),* stoutly defended the status quo.

"Fantasy sales?" he said, speaking from the back of the room in answer to a question from the audience. "If they're a good read, not too quaint and ancient and so on, they sell damned well. The salesmen are asking for more and more and more of them. There's a strong market for fantasy. Usually you want a good-sized book. Fantasy readers seem to like a little more than the thin 60,000-word book, and for a darned good reason: You can't develop a really good fantasy in that kind of length."

He quickly became involved in a dispute over "gross sales figures" with a young man from Brown University.

"You're not gonna get 'em," del Rey snapped, "'cause that's none of your business. That's *company* business."

His questioner declared himself confused; after all, wasn't this supposed to be a conference devoted to the open exchange of information within the field? *"Why?"* he asked. "Why is it secret?"

Del Rey had little patience for such foolishness. "Why should we give that out?" he demanded. "Give me your gross income for last year."

The young man shrugged. "I've been unemployed," he said—and sat down amid laughter and applause.

Most of the panelists that day spoke of a "blurring of the borders" between fantasy, science fiction, and mainstream literature. Popular titles such as *Rosemary's Baby, The Other,* and *The Exorcist* were cited as examples of fantasy masquerading as mainstream fiction; perhaps, as some suggested, that was how they had become best-sellers. Bloch added even *Ragtime* to the list, terming it a fantasy of history. He mourned the fate on the paperback racks of his own mystery novel *American Gothic* ("It's either in the Gothic section or under American History") and added:

---

*But born, it seems, Leonard Knapp.

"I've been agitating for years to get the labels on my books changed to 'Pornography' so there'd be a steady sale!"

Once more Lester del Rey disagreed. "You can ruin a book by not putting it in Fantasy," he said, citing Peter Beagle's *A Fine and Private Place* as a paperback that sold better when presented as "fantasy" than as a straight novel. "The average science-fiction writer who doesn't mention science fiction on the cover is a fool. The average fantasy writer who doesn't mention *fantasy* on the cover is a fool. He's cutting three-quarters of his market out; he's throwing it away. This fear of being categorized is nonsense. We categorize a book just exactly as we put a tomato on a can of tomatoes—so that people will see what it is."

Avoiding what seemed an inevitable debate—i.e., was del Rey being realistically hardheaded, was he a philistine, or did he simply like playing devil's advocate?—I opted for some fresh air and ducked out of the next panel, "New Voices in Fantasy." I had in fact been scheduled to take part in it; but remembering the first panel of the morning and the strain of trying to look intelligent, I had no heart for more.

Instead, I accompanied a group of similarly restless spirits up College Hill. New York editor Kathleen Murray came along, as did Patrick Otte and Diane Burke, both veteran explorers of the Miskatonic Valley; two shaggy South Carolinians, Jim Kent and George Chastain, the latter one of fantasy's most accomplished artists; and the actor Jay Gregory, who, the previous evening, had given a superlative reading of Ray Bradbury's "The October Game."

The autumn day was glorious, and the Hill had never looked more beautiful. We stopped first at Brown University's John Hay Library, its front steps worn by generations of scholars, Lovecraft among them (though poor health had prevented his attending the college). Curator John Stanley had raided the library's special collections and had put together, in honor of the festival, an extensive display of Lovecraftiana: personal correspondence, such as Lovecraft's detailed directions for pronouncing "Cthulhu" (a name, it seems, unsuited for human speech organs); some early magazine appearances (it was surprising to discover that the first issues of *Weird Tales* were huge tabloid-size affairs known as "bedsheets," and even more surprising to see just how lurid their covers were); and assorted juvenilia, perhaps the most fascinating of all. The early sonnets, the schoolboyish horror tales, the intricate little handwritten astronomy magazines complete with title pages, illustrations, and diagrams, all proved that Tom Collins's contention earlier that morning had been correct: Lovecraft was incapable of writing a poor English sentence, even at the age of eight.

Of special note was the small postage-stamp-size drawing at the corner of one of Lovecraft's childhood "newspapers." Emblazoned with ornamental scrollwork, it bore only this enigmatic advice:

SAVE
THIS
COUPON

Stanley's exhibit was worth a standing ovation—and several hours' close study; would that we had had them! But time was scarce, the New England sun was slipping quickly toward Connecticut, and there were other places to see: the one-time Lovecraft homes on Barnes and Prospect Streets, the latter moved from its original site at 66 College Street, hard by the John Hay; the "Shunned House" on Benefit Street, in reality a comfortable-looking old dwelling abutting the sidewalk; the extraordinary Fleur de Lys House at 7 Thomas Street, home of the dream-haunted Henry Wilcox in "The Call of Cthulhu," its façade stuccoed and half-timbered like some cottage from the Brothers Grimm; the Deacon Edward Taylor House next door, built in 1786 and oldest on the block (I'd lived here in my final year at Brown); the venerable slate tombstones of St. John's Churchyard off Benefit Street, where Lovecraft had discerned "the shade of Poe" strolling past the graves with his love, Sarah Helen Whitman (her own house, a few yards away at 88 Benefit Street, remains well preserved); and the park on Prospect Terrace, midway up the hill, where a stern-looking statue of Roger Williams stands blessing the city.

Gentle as the slopes of College Hill may have looked from the windows of the Holiday Inn, they proved more than steep enough for us pedestrians; I refrained from telling the others how much worse the climb could be in a snowstorm. We ended our journey by car, with a brief pilgrimage to Lovecraft's family tomb in Swan Point Cemetery, a beautifully landscaped piece of greenery, more park than graveyard, situated on a bend in the Seekonk. (And let it be set down here, for all time, that this is where I wish to be buried.)

The Phillips family plot is hard to find. After dozens of visits, I still don't know exactly how I got there. Best, perhaps, to trust in chance or the unconscious: One drives aimlessly back and forth through the central part of the cemetery—and suddenly one comes upon the familiar large grey obelisk, not far from the roadway, standing in front of a magnificent beech tree that seems centuries old.

Lovecraft's burial site is unmarked; he is mentioned only on the reverse of the obelisk, the side facing away from the road and the huge carved "PHILLIPS." First his parents' names appear, and then, below them, "Their Son, Howard P. Lovecraft, 1890–1937."

Lovecraft was gone. But while we stood before his grave, half hoping for a sign of some lingering spirit, others were carrying on his tradition. Down the hill and across the city, four younger writers—the "New Voices in Fantasy"—were explaining their own interest in the field.

"I guess my first influence," said Charles L. Grant, "was my grandmother, who was fresh off the boat from Inverness. Her idea of babysitting was to sit me and my brother down and scare the hell out of us by telling us Scottish horror stories, from which we would invariably wake up screaming in the middle of the night. . . . I'd wait for the Silkie to come and get me."

Grant, who's been working on and off as a teacher (writing, he says, whenever he's laid off), has handled both horror and science fiction with unusual grace, bringing to each a vivid sense of atmosphere and elegance of style. No less versatile is David Drake, a cultivated, rather self-effacing young Iowan who's recently emigrated to North Carolina, where he practices law. Drake, like Grant, was one of the few writers that day to mention fairy tales as an influence upon him, though presumably every writer there had grown up on such tales. Had the others remained unaffected by them—or had they just forgotten? Drake, whose own work shares the fairy tale's fascination with violence and doom, clearly had not.

Violence and doom—as well as ghoulish humor—also characterize the world of comic books, which Karl Edward Wagner cited as an early influence on his fiction: specifically, EC horror comics from those wild and woolly days before the Comics Code. (He expressed no love for Dr. Fredric Wertham, whose famous muckraking book, *Seduction of the Innocent,* led to the prohibition of excessive violence in comics and replaced the Old Crypt-Keeper with Mickey Mouse.) Wide of shoulder and of girth, with long red hair and a red beard, Wagner was originally trained as a psychiatrist—working in asylums, he admits, provided him with lots of good horror and fantasy material—but he's now given up his practice to write full-time. Dominating the microphone with his awshucks, down-home North Carolina delivery, he spoke of his boyhood obsession with *The Vault of Horror* and similar comics, the reading of which, his parents warned, would warp his mind. "And it *did* warp my mind!" he reported happily.

For Ramsey Campbell, the gifted young Englishman who acted as panel chairman, the environment in which he grew up was as important an influence as his childhood reading. An awesomely prolific writer, Campbell turns up constantly in anthologies as well as in his own Arkham House collections, *Demons by Daylight* and *The Height of the Scream;* a novel, *The Doll Who Ate His Mother,* is forthcoming. Most of Campbell's tales have modern urban settings and youthful protagonists. His writing is sophisticated, occasionally difficult, and invariably terrifying—qualities which make him, for my money, the finest living writer of horror fiction.

With his moustache, glasses, and shoulder-length hair, Campbell might have been mistaken for still another hirsute member of the Carolina contingent—until he opened his mouth and one heard the warm, plummy accents of a Ringo Starr. He comes, indeed, from Liverpool, and he's used that dispiriting grey city as the setting for many of his stories.

But character, he said, is even more important to him than sense of place, and in creating his fiction he often starts with a particular person in mind: "I'm inclined to say that a story's more frightening if it is happening to people you can readily recognize as being something like people you would meet here . . . or you'd meet anywhere."

He's attracted to the horror genre, he explained, because he enjoys the feeling of working within "a clearly defined tradition." Yet certain things have changed since Lovecraft's time: "I'm happily aware that there really aren't any taboos now in horror fiction."

At this, David Drake pointed out that de facto taboos do exist: With markets as scarce as they are today, editors have the power to enforce their own taboos, leaving the writer nowhere else to turn.

Still, the range of material has recently expanded; no element appears too modern or too discordant to serve as a background for horror fiction. Drake, for example, has set some of his most effective supernatural tales against the fighting in Southeast Asia. So has Charles Grant, who spoke of collecting Montagnard tribal superstitions while stationed in Vietnam and of using them as the bases of stories.

It's important, Grant feels, to bring the old *Weird Tales* tradition up to date by presenting the fundamental horror themes—which themselves never change—amid contemporary trappings. "I wanted to write a werewolf story and a vampire story," he said; "but I didn't want to use a real werewolf, because that's been done to death by Lon Chaney, and I didn't want to use a real vampire. So I combined the two together and wrote 'White Wolf Calling' . . . and instead of a vampire in the form of a wolf feeding on blood, he fed on failure."

Failure and rejection were common themes that day. Grant told of his first professional sale, then added: "It was three years before I sold my second story." David Drake spoke of receiving a letter from his agent, who wrote matter-of-factly: "By the way, you had five stories rejected this week." He spoke, too, of having had to wait eight or nine months for *Galaxy* magazine to pay him for a story, and concluded:

"This is not a business that you want to get into as a professional unless you are very dogged, you don't eat very much, or, of course, if you have a working wife or husband." He intends to stick to his law practice.

Wagner, too, recalled his failures with some of the smaller and more transient fantasy publications. "A lot of those magazines only lasted two issues," he said, "but I've got rejection slips from them." Offering to "compare collections" of such slips with anybody in the room, Wagner described the current publishing scene as a kind of Catch-22:

"In order to be published," he said, "you've got to be a big name. And in order to be a big name, you've got to be published a lot. . . . If you have a good agent, you can get published. However, agents only take writers who've been published a lot!"

Still, he ended on a positive note. "You can't take no for an answer," he said. "Somewhere out there, there has to be an editor who's crazy enough or brave enough to print your stuff."

Ramsey Campbell is one young writer who seems to have led a charmed life in this regard, having been published at the age of sixteen. Yet his tales have not found total acceptance, either. He told of the troubles he'd had with his first book, an Arkham House collection called *The Inhabitant of the Lake*. He had sent several of his stories to the late August Derleth, the firm's cofounder and editor. "After a while," Campbell recalled, "he sent back a letter saying, 'I think you have a potential Arkham House book here.'

"'My God!' I said, and I picked myself up off the floor and then read the rest of what he said, which was considerably more honest, actually. Like the first draft of 'The Church in High Street' he described as 'tending to excite the reader not to horror but to jeering laughter!'"

Drake, too, had been an early protégé of Derleth's. As a longtime fan of Arkham's publications, he had one day left Iowa for a trip to Sauk City, Wisconsin, "to meet Mr. Derleth. And in the course of so doing," he recalled, "while looking through his book room, I turned over a copy of *The Inhabitant of the Lake* to the back cover, and there was this childish little elfin face smiling out! Ramsey—*J*. Ramsey Campbell, at the time—who had sold his first story to Arkham House at age sixteen, and here was his first book. And by God, he was a year younger than I was!"

Drake went home and wrote a story of his own, which he duly submitted to Derleth. Derleth sent the story back, asking for extensive revisions. He returned the second draft as well, advising Drake to "cut out the purple prose"—which had a certain irony, Drake felt, since those were the very passages he'd cribbed straight from Derleth himself.

"Well, instead of getting the third draft back," Drake said, "I got a letter with a check for thirty-five dollars, saying that now I *still* didn't have it, but he would take it for editing, and that I should compare it with my carbon when it appeared in final form, to learn how not to write a short story. Even more embarrassing than that, I didn't *have* a carbon. Jesus, I didn't know you were supposed to keep a carbon!"

To see another's work in print and to feel certain that they could do as well—or, as in Campbell's case, the desire to try his own hand at a Lovecraftian Mythos tale—seems to have convinced all these young writers to take the plunge. Sometimes the motivation was decidedly negative. Grant, for example, told of having read his first Tarzan novel by Edgar Rice Burroughs: "I decided, my God, if *this* can sell, I ought to be able to do something!"*

Karl Wagner also saw what he considered a bad novel: *The Sword Man of Ishtar,* by Charles Nuetzel, put out by an obscure California publishing firm. "It was absolute rock-bottom," Wagner recalls—and he immediately said to himself, "These people will buy anything!"

He mailed them a manuscript he had lying around. "Eventually I got a little letter back saying, 'It's not as good as Charles Nuetzel, but we'll take it.'"

The book was *Darkness Weaves*—the first words of Wagner's original title, which had been much longer. Upon its publication, Wagner discovered that his text, too, had been severely cut, and that at various places in the novel the description of the main character had been altered to fit the cover illustration. What's worse, these alterations weren't even consistent. The book's publisher

---

*Funnily enough, even Burroughs himself seems to have been emboldened to become a writer by what he saw being published: "I had gone thoroughly through some of the all-fiction magazines," he claimed, "and I made up my mind that if people were paid for writing rot such as I read, I could write stories just as rotten."

eventually went bankrupt, still owing Wagner eighty dollars; of that amount, he managed to collect eighty cents.

Obviously it's a hell of a way to make a living; as S. J. Perelman says, the muse is a tough buck. But though poorly paid and for years unrecognized, the young authors remain committed to their work. Asked his goal, Grant replied: "I want to write the consummate horror story—which ought to keep me writing a long time."

The field has many would-be practitioners as well. When, at the end of the discussion, Ramsey Campbell asked the "potential authors" in the audience to raise their hands, a considerable number responded. Impressed, he invited questions from them.

"Wanna buy a story?" asked one.

Until this moment, when panelists had spoken of "Howard" they were usually referring to Howard Phillips Lovecraft. Now they meant someone else: fantasist Robert Ervin Howard, creator of Conan the Cimmerian and other brawny swordsmen—for the topic at hand was "Epic Fantasy," and on the panel were some of that school's best-known exponents.

Epic fantasy? Lin Carter questioned the very term. Former editor of the prestigious Ballantine Adult Fantasy series, Carter—slim, goateed, and denim-suited—has himself created many a muscular barbarian, although his scholarship ranges from the *Aeneid* to the *Necronomicon*. (Years ago he compiled indispensable glossaries of the Lovecraft gods and books; recently he brought forth *Dreams from R'lyeh,* an extraordinary sonnet cycle in the manner of Lovecraft's *Fungi from Yuggoth.*)

"We write *heroic* fantasy," Carter maintained. Technically, he said, the true literary epic is based upon "the national mythology" and deals with "the impulse of the race. . . . When Hollywood says 'screen epic,' they're talking about scope. It hasn't just got a cast of twelve—it's got a cast of forty!"

Therefore he defined epic fantasy as "an action story which has more scope than the ordinary sword-and-sorcery fantasy novel." He cited Wright's *Islandia,* Lewis's Narnia books, Peake's *Gormenghast* trilogy, and Tolkien's *Lord of the Rings* as notable works in this tradition.

Lester del Rey, who has now taken over from Carter as Ballantine's fantasy editor, raised a common criticism: that heroic fantasy runs too much to formula, depending as it does upon the tried-and-true conflict between decadent "civilized" men and the sword-wielding barbarian. "Howard's been imitated until the imitators are imitating the guys who imitated the imitators!" he said. "If you can't put some of yourself in it, why the hell write?"

Carter, who has lucratively reworked many of the Howard themes, disagreed. "If imitation is the sincerest form of flattery," he said, "I think it's also the best way of learning how to write." He declared himself glad to learn from anyone he considers a good writer, and he defended the barbarian-versus-civilization theme as a complex one. "Howard only scratched the surface," he said.

Carter may well be right; the relationship of any man to any society must, of necessity, be complex. Yet there's no denying that, in story after story, the players themselves remain monotonously the same: sinewy heroes, lissome captive princesses, evil wizards, and the like.

Maybe my powers of identification are as slight as my build; I only know that I'm incapable of imagining myself a Viking warrior or Hyborian brawler or Celtic strongman and that I find it impossible to care what happens to such unlikely creations. Although these "heroes" are customarily pitted against whole legions of enemies armed with better weapons and stronger magic, reading this sort of literature is like rooting for the overdog.

Why waste time worrying about a character who's simpler, cruder, and obviously less intelligent than oneself? What sort of man is it who can read such stuff, much less write it? I've known some of the former, and by and large they strike me as pathetic social misfits with sadistic schoolboy minds. Yet the latter group, the writers—at least the ones I saw on the various panels that day—seemed as engaging and agreeable a bunch as one could hope to meet.

Whatever their personal qualities, most practitioners of the genre seem content to offer us, again and again, the same predictable outcome: In the end the virtuous (if violence-prone) strongman always wins.

This is a situation that Fritz Leiber has devoted himself to remedying. In the course of his career he's won five Hugo awards—science fiction's highest honor—and has written everything from horror to straight science; but in fantasy circles he is probably best known for his tales of two likable rogues, Fafhrd and the Gray Mouser, the one a brawny giant from the Cold Waste, the other a diminutive would-be wizard from the south, both of them professional thieves and adventurers operating out of the squalid city of Lankhmar, City of Sevenscore Thousand Smokes.

"The first Fafhrd and Mouser stories were conceived with a certain amount of humorous reaction to heroes who were always winning," said Leiber. "A superman hero tends to become uninteresting."

Leiber himself, built to Fafhrdian proportions, is a tall, distinguished-looking grey-haired man with the slow, sonorous voice of an actor or a minister—both of which he's been.

"You know," he said, "I've always been hooked with these two characters of Fafhrd and the Mouser. I think that's because someone else invented them in the first place." (He meant his old friend Harry Otto Fischer, who in 1936 began a story called "The Lords of Quarmall" but never completed it; Leiber undertook the job, thus giving the world the first story in this continuing saga.)

"And so I felt a kind of loyalty to them," Leiber continued. "I can't kill them off. They aren't quite my own invention, and perhaps for me that makes them more real." He noted that although it has been "around forty years since the characters were invented," he was at the moment in the midst of still another tale.

Lin Carter credits Leiber with having coined the phrase "sword and sorcery," now the generally accepted term for literature of this type. Leiber himself, keenly aware of the field's strengths and weaknesses, described the typical sword-and-sorcery hero as "adolescent," with all the adolescent's impetuousness, rebelliousness, and innocence of the world's true nature.

Some background on this figure was provided by L. Sprague de Camp, who launched into a fifteen-minute prepared disquisition on the barbarian in history. Although not quite the sort of thing for a panel discussion—better suited to a book or lecture, perhaps—de Camp's little talk displayed the wide reading and erudition one has come to expect from him. In the course of a lifetime he has written some sixty books, fiction and nonfiction, on subjects ranging from the Great Pyramid to the Monkey Trial, including a recent controversial biography of H. P. Lovecraft. With Lin Carter, de Camp has also added new adventures to the Robert E. Howard oeuvre and has written a monograph on this author, *The Miscast Barbarian*.

The swaggering hero he has celebrated notwithstanding, de Camp himself is precise and rather machinelike, delivering himself of long strings of facts in the fruity, pedagogical voice of a schoolmaster. He seems above all a self-confident man, little affected by criticism, who takes an apparent delight in being onstage and, like del Rey, playing devil's advocate.

Asked if, as the chronicler of swordsmen, he himself owns any swords, de Camp rattled off an impressive list, including "my grandfather's Civil War sabre, a seventeenth-century Damascene scimitar that I bought in Beirut, one that I got in Spain, an imitation of a Crusader's cross-belted sword, two or three other things that the family's picked up, including one Japanese short sword which is quite good. That is the one that I chased a burglar with."

When the laughter had died down, he continued: "He got away, unfortunately. His head would have looked so pretty over the fireplace!"

Among his own possessions, Lin Carter listed, deadpan, "a seventeenth-century Japanese samurai sword and an enchanted broadsword with runes etched in acid on the blade."

Del Rey admitted he owned none. "A sword is a damned awkward thing to carry around," he explained.

The final word was left to Andrew J. Offut, the veteran science-fiction writer from Kentucky who's now turned his attention to writing heroic fantasy. "Yes, I have a sword," said Offut. "A hara-kiri knife I'm saving just in case."

Offutt also came up with the one really brilliant observation of the panel. Looking from speaker to speaker—most of them skinny or short or out of shape, yet all of them acknowledged masters of Swords and Sorcery—he mused, "Isn't it strange that all of us up here are built like *sorcerers?*"

Lin Carter pointed out that some of the old swordsmen "were about five feet tall—thin people—and you'd swear they couldn't swing one of those damned things."

De Camp spoke of one famous swordsman of a bygone day who was attacked by a "band of miscreants. He killed seven and put the rest to flight. . . . He was a thin little sallow man who died of syphilis at thirty-five."

"Now that sounds like a writer!" said Carter.

If the "New Voices" panel had presented fantasy's Young Turks, the last panel of the day was given over to the Establishment—men who had forged careers in the genre. The topic at hand was "Writing Supernatural Tales: The Whys Explored," and that question—why?—formed the opening theme.

Joseph Payne Brennan, the small, melancholy poet and short-story writer from New Haven, was first to speak. He gave the impression of a sad man sitting wistfully over a bar, like a character in one of his recent tales, "The Business About Fred." Brennan had read some of his poetry the previous evening, and it's one of my regrets that I arrived too late to hear it; he is a fine poet with a good speaking voice, and his sardonic New England accent adds interest to whatever he says.

Why, then, is the man so exasperatingly self-effacing? Why has he so little confidence in himself and his work? Brennan has written his share of classics in the field—"The Hunt," "Levitation," "Canavan's Back Yard," and "Slime" (which many believe to be the unacknowledged source for the film *The Blob*)—yet he speaks so slightingly of his own work, and with such obvious hesitation, that one supposes he must be unhappy with his accomplishments. He shouldn't be; they are considerable.

Attempting to explain his long interest in fantasy, Brennan wondered aloud if his Depression childhood might not have caused him to depend more heavily than other children upon his own imagination, and to spend his time in libraries and at other solitary pursuits. (Today he is a librarian at Yale.) He also cited his Irish heritage. "The Irish," he noted, "are supposed to have an affinity for the supernatural.

"As a child," Brennan recalled, "I was fascinated by ghost stories. Now, *why* I was I'm not sure myself. Whether it was because I was a neglected, lonely child, or whether it was a matter of inheriting some inclination, I can't say."

Interestingly enough, his first published tales had been Westerns. But when the Western pulps disappeared, he said, "I was literally forced into another field—which turned out to be fantasy and supernatural horror. I had a small measure of success in this, and so I stayed with it."

Had he ever tried his hand at science fiction? "I'd *like* to write science fiction," he said wistfully, "but I lack the scientific background which is required."

Robert Bloch was much less hesitant; he spoke quickly, confidently, with well-practiced poise. He told the audience that he'd always preferred writing fantasy to science fiction for a very simple reason: "Because I could be sloppier."

He described the field as "one of the few areas left in which good can still triumph over evil. And that's one of the reasons, I'm afraid, why it's called fantasy.

"When I was a boy back in Arkham," he added, immediately drawing a laugh, "I, too, lived through the Great Depression. As far as I was concerned, it wasn't all that great! When I got out of high school—by expulsion [*more laughter*]—I was faced with the terrible choice everybody had in the Depression. It was a dilemma: to either work or starve. I decided to combine the two by becoming a writer."

Of Lovecraft's influence on him—for the two had corresponded while Bloch was still in high school—he said: "Lovecraft turned me on and turned me loose. . . . I had a natural affinity for this sort of thing [horror stories], because as a kid I had the usual childhood fears of (1) death, (2) life. I was afraid of my fellow children. I was afraid of adults. I was a little bit suspicious of what would happen to you if you did too much breathing. And I knew, of course, that they were all against me. So I merely encapsulated this information and began to distribute it to other people in the form of fiction. . . . I found that I could exorcise these fears while giving vent to them in literary form, and I found that, apparently, some *readers* got a degree of exorcism."

He confessed to an increasing suspicion, as he's grown older, that science doesn't have all the answers. "I'm not saying I believe in ghosts or goblins or vampires or Forrest J. Ackerman," he added. "But I have a rather open mind—which is not altogether accounted for by my prefrontal lobotomy."

Gahan Wilson, acting once more as moderator, provided a glimpse of his own boyhood—but first issued an important apology: "I have trouble saying 'horror,' because I come from the Midwest. So if it comes out 'whore,' excuse me!"

To be the sort of child who grows up writing horror stories, said Wilson, "you've gotta be one of those creepy kids who lurks in alleys and, when they choose up a baseball team, is the last one chosen."

Coincidentally, Wilson had been just such a kid. In baseball games, he said, he'd be stuck out in right field, "the extreme one that nobody ever hit to. So I'd be put there, and they'd say, 'Go further out, Wilson! Go further out!' So I would stand there waiting for the streetlights to go on, which meant that the game was stopped and I could go home and listen to the radio and relax and be done with this horrible business."

Like both Brennan and Bloch, he confessed to having been stumped by science and math. "I was always doodling and failing and so on," he said. Typically, upon his induction into the Air Force, he was made a jet mechanic.

In his comic strip "Nuts!," he said, he hoped to remind us all of the mysterious, confusing, terrifying, incomprehensible world we all faced as children; and, of the strip's hero, he revealed: "This little kid is much better adjusted than *I* was!"

In the face of the world's assorted terrors, it is comforting to make up new terrors out of one's own head. "It's a very satisfactory thing," said Wilson, "when you make your first ghost and then destroy it."

Now well into his seventies, Frank Belknap Long has made and destroyed scores of ghosts in his time, yet still confessed to being haunted by the same feelings that haunt us all—"feelings of *encroachment*," he called them, "of the mysterious and terrifying." Long—who, despite his name is a small, white-bearded man with a wry face half hidden behind thick glasses—had probably known H. P. Lovecraft better than anyone at the convention; they had been longtime friends and correspondents. Long's own work has ranged from science fiction to gothics, and he is particularly well-known for such contributions to the Cthulhu Mythos as "The Hounds of Tindalos" and "The Space-Eaters," as well as for the creation of the fearsome elephantine god Chaugnar Faugn. More recently he has written, for Arkham House, a memoir of his friendship with HPL, entitled *Howard Phillips Lovecraft: Dreamer on the Nightside,* and one of the biggest disappointments of the weekend—especially, no doubt, for Long himself—was that copies of the book were not yet ready in time for the convention.

Long spoke in a frail, whispery voice and often had occasion to use two microphones. As Lin Carter had done in the preceding panel, he mentioned the "Oz" books as an early influence on his work—along with Grimm's fairy tales and the fiction of his friend HPL.

"I'd like to write a great deal more fantasy," he told the audience, "but there's not the market for it there is for science fiction." He seemed unconcerned about whether or not he had the scientific background for such writing; he saw today's science fiction as verging on fantasy anyway, and suggested that making the science sound plausible was sufficient. "As a matter of fact," he laughed, "I'd be ashamed to tell you how little research I have done on several of my science fiction stories that are considered to be based on sound science!"

At last it was Manly Wade Wellman's turn. Wellman, who looks rather like a prosperous old banker and who sounded to these New York ears like Senator Claghorn, is the creator of weird, stirringly beautiful tales drawn from the supernatural traditions of the Ozarks. With his rich Southern gift for storytelling (he now makes his home in Chapel Hill), Wellman was one of the day's most colorful speakers.

"Even when I was a kid," he recalled, "making these things up and telling them and seeing my friends' eyes stick out of their heads . . . I liked that! I *still* like it! I think that's why I write it—to make your eyes stick out.

"I remember back when we had to write stories in school—this was way early in the twentieth century—and they would ask us to write stories, and people would write stories about good little boys, how they did better than the bad little boys. And I would write—" He paused, searching for the right word. "—*peculiar* stories, about winged men fighting dragons up there in the sky, and caves into which you would go, and what you would find there. And the teacher—a very nice teacher, and *boy,* how she could whup ya!—she had me in at recess to talk about a story of mine. 'Where did you get this?' And I said, 'Well, I just thought of it.' 'You thought of this?' 'Yes, ma'am, I did.' And she said, 'If you don't stop thinking about that, you'll go crazy!'

"Well," he continued, after the laughter and applause had died down, "I never stopped thinking about it. . . . I'm sure that my mental processes—well, if a psychiatrist ever got hold of me, he'd be like a kid in a candy store!"

Wellman spoke of fantasy as "a literature of escape—escape from the mundane world," and in differentiating it from science fiction, he repeated an observation that Ramsey Campbell had recently made to him: that science fiction is designed to make the reader feel that it could or will happen, supernatural fantasy that it *is* happening.

Of these two modes, Wellman was solidly committed to the second; the world of the imagination was his greatest love. "Maybe that's why, all my life, I've liked to hang out with the unsophisticated, the simple, the folk people," he said. "Before I could read, I loved to hear such stories. I heard splendid ones in West Africa, I heard them in the hills of Arkansas, I heard them in big towns. . . . I hark back to the word *wonder*—something that makes us wonder."

As the discussion drew to an end, Willis Conover asked a question from the floor, suggesting that the speakers change the "why" of the panel's title to *"how."* What were some of the techniques, the tricks these men used in writing horror stories? he asked—"if you have no objection to giving away your secrets."

Thinking of some of his tales of John, the itinerant Ozark guitarist, Wellman said that he usually began with a main character the readers could identify with.

Frank Belknap Long said that he tried never to plot a story in advance, or else "all the wonder and mysteriousness goes out of it." He often began, he said, with a mood.

Cartoons, too, it seemed, could demand the same process of creation. "What you're doing," explained Gahan Wilson, "is you're fishing in your subconscious."

Joseph Payne Brennan largely agreed with Long. Occasionally, he said, he began a story with a specific plot idea in mind, but most often "something suddenly triggers a plot: an incident, a landscape, someone's appearance, a mood.

"These are the more successful ones," he said. "The ones that are built like carpentry may succeed, but to a lesser extent." He spoke of one story, "Canavan's Back Yard," which had been triggered by the sight of an overgrown New Haven yard he'd passed several times.

"I feel the story grew within me," he explained. "I didn't fabricate it."

Robert Bloch took an opposite track. "How do I get my stories?" he asked. "I have this book called the *Necronomicon*...."

Then he grew more serious. "Unlike Mr. Brennan," he said, "I generally construct stories very carefully. With the kind of mind that I have, though, I start at the end and work backwards—very much the way a writer for a comedian does a monologue for him in which there's going to be some kind of twist, or switch, or topper, or payoff."

By way of example, he detailed the writing of a story called "Catnip," based on "a rather nasty idea." The story ended with the stomach-turning punch line, *"Cat got your tongue?"*

Afterward, he spoke of a unique honor that H. P. Lovecraft had bestowed upon him. As a young writer, Bloch had "killed off" Lovecraft in his horror tale "The Shambler from the Stars":

"What prompted me to write it," he said, "was a genuine desire to express my admiration for this man—and, it being unmanly to profess love for another male, I had to kill him off! But I certainly didn't expect that he would come back with a sequel to it which he would dedicate to me. . . .

"In the course of a long and misspent life, probably the thing that I will always be proudest of is the fact that Lovecraft dedicated that story to me. That meant so much, and I think someday I might be a footnote in literary history because he did that. That was a magnificent thing for him to do."

The story, of course, was Lovecraft's "Haunter of the Dark," about a young writer called Robert Blake and his unholy, eventually fatal attraction toward a demon dwelling within a church on Providence's Federal Hill. Convention-goers were privileged to experience the story in a uniquely appropriate setting that very night at Pembroke's Alumnae Hall, on the Brown University campus, when Fritz Leiber read the tale to a hushed and darkened auditorium. It was a flawless, spellbinding performance, proof that, had he grown bored with his writing career, Leiber could always have returned to professional acting.

The night also brought forth Donald Sidney-Fryer, the slim and greying California troubadour, who recited a long passage from Spenser's *Faerie Queene*. At a similar recitation the previous night he had leapt into the air at the dramatic passages; this time he stood upon a chair and, impersonating a "fair lady," draped his face with a handkerchief. Fryer is himself a superb poet; his *Songs and Sonnets Atlantean* is one of the quaintest, most charming books in the entire Arkham House line.

The evening at Alumnae Hall ended on an appropriately ghoulish note with the rendition of a one-act play called *Rape,* from the repertoire of Paris's famous Grand-Guignol, the "theater of blood and cruelty." Unfortunately, the audience had to content itself with a reading of the play by several Brown students and a faculty member, under the direction of alumnus Barry Alan Richmond, the self-styled "President of the Republic of Montmartre."

Except for the acting of Brown professor Don Wilmeth in two roles, the production was uninspired. The plot, however, commanded attention. The main character is a child-murderer who pretends to be an insane deaf-mute in order to escape the guillotine. Incarcerated in an institution for the criminally insane, he's forced to share a cell with a deranged blind man who, for years, has been promised that someone will bring him "eyes."

The outcome is predictably gruesome: The blind man soon sets upon our hero and begins yanking out his eyeballs—whereupon the unfortunate victim cannot cry out for help lest he give away his deception.

The performance ended with a student stumbling toward us across the stage, eye sockets streaming "blood"—a concoction that actually congeals, or so the director assured me. Its formula, he said, is one of the best-kept secrets of the Grand-Guignol.

Later that night, back at the Holiday Inn, the play was called to mind by a change in clientele. Throughout the early part of the weekend, the fantasy buffs had been sharing the Inn's convention facilities with a gaggle of legal secretaries. Most of these were pleasant-looking ladies with grey hair dyed blonde, and there was thus no danger of confusing them with the fantasy buffs—most of whom were short, hairy, heavily bearded, and male.

However, by Saturday night the ladies had given way to a small convention of deaf-mutes, who could be recognized only because they were the sole guests not talking (save for an occasional unsettling chuckle) and because, when you came up behind them and said excuse me, they didn't move.

Sunday morning brought the last of the panels, "Lovecraft the Man," moderated by the aristocratic-looking Henry L. P. Beckwith, Jr., who had shouted himself nearly hoarse the previous day conducting bus tours up College Hill, on the history of which he is something of an expert. Beckwith's special interest is genealogy; he is part of an old Providence family. Eyes shaded behind dark glasses, he gazed at the audience with what appeared to be cool disdain.

"I'm moderating this thing simply by virtue of being a relative of the deceased," he explained softly. He told me afterward that he's related to HPL on his mother's side—a complicated relationship best described as "fifth cousin once removed."

Willis Conover started the debate—for debate it was—by renewing an argument he'd had with L. Sprague de Camp several months before, at a science-fiction convention in New York. Conover is author of the book *Lovecraft at Last,* a portrait of the master in his final year of life, compiled chiefly from the correspondence he'd exchanged with the then fifteen-year-old Conover. The picture of HPL it presents is a positive one; the man emerges from his letters as sensitive, open-minded, and above all kindhearted.

Immediately assuring the audience that de Camp was "a friend" and that de Camp's recent biography of Lovecraft was "an essential reference," Conover noted: "I've seen reviews in which Sprague's book is described as the objective biography and mine the warm if oversubjective memoir. I disagree completely." How could his book be "oversubjective," he argued, when it was based almost entirely on the subject's own words as they appear in the letters?

Warming to his subject, Conover said that he regarded the de Camp biography as a deliberate attack on Lovecraft; de Camp, he charged, had had a huge mass of correspondence to choose from and had selected the most damaging material in presenting Lovecraft to the world.

By way of support, he read at length from a memoir by Lovecraft's Jewish friend Kenneth Sterling which addresses itself, in part, to the charge that Lovecraft was anti-Semitic. Not so, writes Sterling, and proceeds to give an eloquent defense of Lovecraft—"a man in whose honor," Conover concluded, "four hundred people are meeting here in Providence for the first time. . . . That's who H. P. Lovecraft was. And I ask you, who is the racist oddball about whom Sprague wrote his biography?"

Following the applause, de Camp spoke. Reading from a prepared statement, he immediately discounted the Sterling piece. Lovecraft, he said, "let down his hair in the letters" but kept his real feelings a secret from friends such as Sterling whom he saw every day.

"The biographer's problem," he said, "is that in Lovecraft we have one of the most complex and contradictory characters imaginable—who could on the one hand propose the extermination of the Jews and on the other marry Sonia Greene and make Sam Loveman one of his closest and best-loved friends."

Many of these apparent contradictions, he added, could be explained by the maturing process: "When you make any general statement about Lovecraft, you have to specify whether you're talking about Lovecraft as he was in 1920 or in 1930 or in 1935 or what, because the man changed to an amazing degree.

"Some say they like the Lovecraft of Willis's beautiful *Lovecraft at Last*—which is one of the most splendid examples of book-making I've ever seen—better than they like mine. But that's only natural, because he knew Lovecraft in his closing years, when he was, as it were, at his best."

By way of contrast, de Camp now proceeded to give some examples of Lovecraft at his worst. He spoke of "his lifelong childish dependence on his older female relatives, first his mother and then his aunt. There is his bigoted ethnocentrism. . . . This is not just a passing fancy. . . . It was a major obsession for over twenty years—that he got over," de Camp admitted, "in the course of a few years.

"He long preached a bloodthirsty nationalistic militarism, while too squeamish to take a dead mouse from a trap. He swore he would never abandon Sonia after all she had done for him, and then supinely let his aunt tell her she was not wanted in Providence. While unable to earn a decent living himself, he long expressed scorn and contempt for tradesmanlike persons who did.

"There again," de Camp added, "he got over it later on.

"Was Lovecraft's a good life?" he demanded. "One who, again and again in his later years, writes bemoaning his inability to earn a decent living, laments his non-achievement of longtime ambitions like a trip to Europe, calls himself a has-been and a failure, and predicts his own eventual suicide when his money runs out, as he did several times, can hardly be said to have had a good life."

Lovecraft's non-professionalism seemed a particular sore point with de Camp. "I find it hard not to be exasperated by Lovecraft's incredible waste of his time, talents, and opportunities," he said. "From a professional point of view, he did just about everything wrong. All that a writer could do to ruin his own prospects, Lovecraft did."

De Camp conceded that Lovecraft had always espoused ideals not of the professional writer but of the "gentleman," the "amateur" in the old sense of the word. Why, then, was he being so hard on the man? Perhaps de Camp himself had the answer: "I saw in him," he said, "some of my own shortcomings, though in what I hope was an exaggerated form."

"Lovecraft's tragedy," he concluded, "and it was a tragedy to any but the most insensitive, was that he was unwilling—or to put it more charitably, he was unable—to face the facts of life until it was too late to do any good."

However, HPL's work ethic found a defender in Fritz Leiber. "Lovecraft, in the last years of his life, was trying to become a professional writer," Leiber noted. "I do recall that he wrote very happily to my wife about his income. He was very pleased by the sale of 'At the Mountains of Madness' and 'The Shadow out of Time' to *Astounding Stories,* which had brought him something like five or six hundred dollars, and he said that was really enough to make the difference as far as support went for a whole year."

"I disagree with all these interpretations," declared Frank Belknap Long. The only man on the panel who'd known Lovecraft as a friend, he extolled "the complexity and splendor of his personality." Observing that the other panelists had given Lovecraft "much praise, much blame," he suggested that "there are few writers that could have inspired such controversy."

Harry Beckwith, on the other hand, accepted these disparate views. "I think," he said, "that Lovecraft was all the things that all the people have said he was." He reminded the audience that Lovecraft was the product of another era, as well as of "an old and provincial city." These facts helped explain the prejudices Lovecraft sometimes displayed—prejudices he lost as he matured and made friends with people of different backgrounds.

A question from the floor raised the subject of Lovecraft's politics: Toward the end of his life, the conservative HPL appears to have held strong socialist views. But they were not Marxist or Stalinist, Conover pointed out—just as, he said, "Lovecraft had comparable views on ethics and morality versus organized religion."

Professor Dirk Mosig asked Long if he thought de Camp's image of HPL "the snob" was correct.

Absolutely not, replied Long, and he closed with a comment on Lovecraft's professionalism: "He was never interested in commercial success to any extent. The main chance, the thing that inspires so many Americans to fierce competition—he simply was above that sort of thing." His friend, he said, had never pursued "success in the marketplace."

"One can live for art," observed Leiber, "but it's very lonely." He sounded as if he was talking from experience.

Whatever his virtues or failings, Lovecraft certainly deserves better from his native city and his native state. Although to many of us he is the single most interesting figure in Rhode Island's history, and though his memory colors our perceptions of every street and cobblestone in Providence, he isn't mentioned in the local guidebooks (which nonetheless find room for George M. Cohan and Nelson Eddy), and he fails to appear beside such notables as Ruth Hussey, Ivan Fuqua, Chris Schenkel, Fred Friendly, Napoleon Lajoie, E. M. "Tarzan" Brown, and seventy other illustrious members, living and dead, of the Rhode Island Heritage Hall of Fame. He is honored by no civic holiday; no street or square or building bears his name.

For a little while, though, amid the glow of the convention, it appeared that this oversight would at last be corrected and that Providence's most celebrated writer might someday be immortalized in marble—if Mayor Vincent Cianci was to be believed. The mayor, known as "Buddy" to his friends, made a surprise appearance at the banquet held Sunday afternoon as the culmination of the festival. Citing requests he'd had for a statue of HPL to be erected in one of the city parks, he promised he'd be "very willing to sit down and talk to a committee" about it, as soon as such a group could be formed.

Cianci is a short, brisk, portly fellow built along the lines of Fiorello La Guardia. "I've got a bit of a horror story going myself in the city of Providence," he confided to banqueters. "I'm a Republican, the first Republican to get elected in thirty-eight years." On the current city council, he said, he was faced with twenty-four Democrats and only two Republicans.

Affable and disarmingly candid, the mayor made no attempt to hide the fact that, before this weekend, he'd had little idea who Lovecraft was. "I must confess," he said, "that when I began to work so ardently for Providence as a convention and conference site, I never dreamed that I would be hosting groups other than plumbers, teachers, policemen, and fraternal and veterans' organizations. But as representatives of those who love the occult and mysterious, the supernatural and fantastic, you are most welcome in our city."

After a brief allusion to the local haunts of Edgar Allan Poe, he quoted from a stirring line in one of Lovecraft's letters—"I am Providence"—and concluded with a brief valediction: "We hope that you leave with fond memories and no bad dreams or nightmares about your experiences here." With that, he trotted briskly out the door.

A day or two after the convention, I told a friend on the *Providence Journal* of Cianci's visit. "Imagine," I said, "the mayor himself coming to our banquet!"

"You know what they say about him here?" my friend replied. "He'd show up at the opening of an envelope."

The following weeks brought dispiriting (if predictable) news: The city's administration was doubtful it could afford the estimated $40,000 a statue would cost, and for the time being, at least, in what seems a bizarre consolation prize, it was giving serious consideration to hanging an oil portrait of Lovecraft in—least appropriate of places!—the Providence airport.

The rest of the convention—the jokes at the banquet, the various awards, and Robert Bloch's moving speech on what it meant for a fledgling writer to have Lovecraft as a friend and mentor—is described by Fritz Leiber in the pages that follow.

Suffice it to add that, in concluding his talk, Bloch gave new meaning to those familiar lines from the Cthulhu Mythos by applying them to HPL himself:

> *That is not dead which can eternal lie,*
> *And with strange aeons even death may die.*

Lovecraft's spirit may well have been present that day. I hope it was pleased.

The Old Gent

It couldn't have come at a better time. New York's 1976 World Fantasy Convention had proved a letdown after the memorable gathering in Providence a year before. Now at last it was winding to a close in a noisy round of post-convention cocktail parties. Kathleen Murray and I were wedged into a corner in one of the reception suites, listening to the same jokes and gossip we'd heard all weekend and wondering if it weren't time to fight our way to our coats and leave.

I felt a tap on my shoulder. Willis Conover was standing beside us.

"Before you go," he said, "take a look at this. It might interest you." He reached into the inside pocket of his jacket and brought out a small envelope, from which he withdrew two folded sheets of yellow paper. "I'm not going to tell you anything about this," he said. "Just read it." He returned to another conversation a few feet away.

I read the faint typescript; so did Kathy. At first we were puzzled, even a little suspicious. As we continued reading, however, we

---

Foreword to *The Old Gent* by Willis Conover (Arlington, VA: Carrollton-Clark, 1977). The text of this slim pamphlet purported to be a typewritten letter of greeting from an elderly (but coyly unnamed) H. P. Lovecraft. It seemed to me a sweet and charming little *jeu d'esprit*—who among us didn't wish, after all, that HPL had somehow survived into his eighties and might still be out there, alive and well?—though I recall that Arkham House's Jim Turner, always unpredictable, was outraged at the stunt.

found ourselves exceptionally moved. The party roared on, but we no longer heard it.

Afterward, Willis seemed disinclined to say where the letter had come from. Odd though it may sound, I felt no need to question its authenticity. There is truth in feelings, whatever the facts may be.

I didn't see Willis for the rest of that year; he was overseas much of the time, or doing his work in Washington, and I was busy too. But at Christmastime I sent him a card, to which I added this note:

"I sincerely hope you're going to do something with that rather special letter you showed me; Kathy and I still talk about it. If worst comes to worst you could always Xerox it and send it to a few friends as a memorable Christmas present next winter. But I'd rather see you publish it. More people might appreciate it than you imagine. It may be too late for March 15th, 1977, sad to say. But don't sit on it! There's a *need* for it."

Somehow, I'm pleased to think, my note may have helped persuade Willis to publish the letter here—together with some amplifying words and an introductory letter of his own.

It couldn't have come at a better time.

* * *

Before reading what follows, it might be appropriate to recall these words written by H. P. Lovecraft on June 28th, 1934:

"The difference between a friend who *has lived* and one who *still lives* is not as vast as one might imagine. Both exist as images in the mind, and may be regarded with equal affection."

T.E.D. Klein: Master of Ceremonies

CF: To begin with, I'd like to ask what attracted you to the horror genre in the first place, and which aspects of terror formed your earliest influences.

TK: Peculiar as I know this may sound, my attraction to horror seems somehow connected with, of all things, mother love—or so I've come to suspect, after seven fairly expensive years on an analyst's couch. You Brits, I know, take a rather dim view of Freud, so I guess I'd better explain.

    I grew up with the same insatiable appetite for horror movies, monster magazines, EC Comics, scary masks, and so on that most boys do; the grislier the better, in fact. (I remember being particularly excited about a book called—wonderful title—*Ghosts! Ghosts! Ghosts!*) Most of these things hold a lot less appeal for me now—comics, for one, bore me to tears—but as a child I would absolutely devour them. I'd do so, at any rate, by the light of day. But at night I'd invariably regret it; I'd lie in bed staring at the darkness, too frightened to fall asleep. And there was nothing delicious about that fright, no element of fun in it; it was horrible. I was like an addict who binges by day and, each night, repents. Why, then, did I keep doing it? At the time, I hadn't a clue; but now I can see that working myself into a panic that way, looking back and forth between the door, the window, the closet, and the shadow in the corner (and

---

Epistolary interview by Carl T. Ford in the double-issue festschrift *Dagon* 18/19 (July–October 1987).

worrying all the while about what might be emerging from some secret panel in the wall behind my head) had become something of a nighttime ritual for me—one that ended, more often than not, with my calling out to my mother until she came in and comforted me. She would sit on my bed and try to persuade me that the things I was afraid of didn't exist. And while she was there, they didn't.

What I'm suggesting, you see, is that the horror I fed on so hungrily by day gave me an excuse, at night, to demand love and reassurance from my mother.

My father, on the other hand, was given to telling me scary stories at bedtime, stories with cliffhanger endings that would leave me wanting more. One of them, I recall, was about jellyfishlike things from a flying saucer; they sucked out people's brains, leaving their skulls empty. Often, when he'd come into my room to say goodnight, he'd pretend to be a Frankensteinish monster; he'd turn to face the wall and then walk backward toward my bed, his hands reaching out for me, opening and closing.

Today, decades later, when I read horror fiction or see a scary movie, I think I'm still flirting with these same childhood fears, testing myself to see if I've really outgrown them.

CF: You seem to have done quite a lot of study concerning the work and life of H. P. Lovecraft; in the '70s your work appeared in numerous amateur press journals. Do you ever feel tempted to write more of the same nowadays?

TK: I'm not certain whether you mean scholarly work or Lovecraft-related fiction. I'm not much of a scholar—I can never keep my dates straight, and unless I scribble things down while I'm reading, I forget whatever stray insights may have come to me—so I don't feel equipped to write the sort of informed Lovecraft criticism you get today from people like S. T. Joshi, Don Burleson, Peter Cannon, Steve Mariconda, Robert Price, Will Murray, Darrell Schweitzer, Dick Tierney, and Barton St. Armand. During my senior year at Brown, I did manage to write a superficial but fairly lengthy honors thesis on how HPL was influenced by Lord Dunsany; yet several years later, on a panel at the first World Fantasy Convention in Providence, when I was asked to say a few words about Dunsany's influence, I could remember nothing.

These days Lovecraft the man, and especially Lovecraft the letter-writer, interests me a great deal more than the fiction. The last piece I've written on him—and probably the last I'm going to write—is the introduction to Arkham House's corrected edition of *Dagon and Other Macabre Tales*. It's quite long but, like the thesis, spends a lot of time simply quoting HPL (always a pleasure). It did give me a chance, at least, to say a few words in defense of Lovecraft's more "ethereal" stories, the pseudo-Dunsanian pieces that fans don't seem to care for. I, for one, prefer them to many of his horror tales.

In my own fiction, there are certain identifiably Lovecraftian elements in *The Ceremonies* and in the first three stories in *Dark Gods;* but I don't believe you'll find them in more recent work.

CF: Lovecraft and Machen have obviously strongly influenced your fiction. Are there any other writers who you would say have helped develop the style of the Ted Klein horror tale?

TK: I'm very strongly influenced by everyone I read, from S. J. Perelman to Virginia Woolf. Four horror writers I've learned from (or at least tried to)—in addition to the ones you mentioned—are L. P. Hartley, M. R. James, Walter de la Mare, and Ramsey Campbell.

CF: You edited *Twilight Zone* magazine for a number of years with notable success. What were your fondest memories of working on that 'zine? And why did you finally hand over the editorial reins?

TK: For someone who'd grown up reading *Amazing, Fantastic, Galaxy, If, F&SF,* and other magazines, working on *Twilight Zone* was, no exaggeration, the proverbial dream come true; in many ways it was the greatest fun I've ever had, especially in the second and third years of my editorship—after I had learned the ropes, but before the job became too routine. Though there was constant interference from the publishers in choosing art and copy for the covers, I had virtually a free hand with whatever went on inside the magazine (I suspect because no one else in the office actually read it). I was able to set what passed for "editorial policy"; I chose the stories, edited them, at times even rewrote parts (with the authors' permission or help); I chose the illustrator for each story (and learned, as I'd long suspected, that artists are far more agreeable to work with than writers); I hired (and fired) the columnists; I had the privilege of reprinting tales I'd always loved, of talking to authors I'd always admired, and of sounding off, in editorials, about the things that bugged me. The pay was surprisingly decent, and there were perks such as movie screenings, parties, review copies of the latest books, even a couple of press junkets to Mexico. But the biggest kick of all, each year around Thanksgiving, was telephoning the winners of our annual *Twilight Zone* short story contest and informing them that they'd won. These were people who'd never been published professionally before, and as I heard their gasps and squeals of joy, I felt like a game-show host who's just handed someone a fortune.

Somehow, though, in the end the fun wore off. The office politics began to get me down—take my word for it, *TZ* was published by some pretty unpleasant people—and as I said, after four and a half years the job became routine. I had a vision of the future in which, month after month, I'd be slogging through the same endless piles of manuscripts, choosing ones I liked, making out contracts, fussing over details in the stories, answering the mail, arguing over the covers, explaining to the owners why we couldn't work Stephen King into the magazine *every* month, worrying about how we were going to fill the next issue, and the next, and the next. . . . Besides, I was under contract by this time to write another book. So in the spring of '85, I resigned, and haven't been back since.

CF: Most of your tales contain references to that "cosmic terror" that Lovecraft often wrote about so skillfully. To what degree would you say that the Cthulhu Mythos is represented in your work?

TK: I've always relished Lovecraft's juxtaposition of vast cosmic evil and specific down-to-earth locales—the way an unwashed old man in some seedy New England hamlet, or a half-breed skulking around some waterfront slum, can open an old book, mutter a few spells, and call down forces from beyond the stars. I love HPL's use of specific street names and houses, the sort I walked past every day during my college years in Providence. I love the atmospheric touches, the sense of local history in his stories, the constant suggestion of secrets hidden away in attics, dusty bookshops, backwoods cabins, boarded-up churches, and tunnels beneath city streets. There's horror in these tales, but there's beauty as well. And I admire the way, in his Mythos tales, Lovecraft links events in New England to goings-on in Asia, the Poles, and the South Seas. It's the sort of global imagination that few writers possess.

But the Mythos itself holds little interest for me today; it's been exploited by too many other writers, and overexplained in the pages of too many journals. I have a reference to Lovecraft's Tcho-Tcho people in my "Black Man with a Horn," but I wouldn't want the Mythos connections to go any further than that. I'd rather make up a few myths of my own, as I tried to do in *The Ceremonies*.

I also confess to being a little uncomfortable with the way the Mythos has been turned into a role-playing game, complete with manuals, rulebooks, and dice. I know that your readers enjoy such things, Carl; and as you've pointed out, there are those who might never have read Lovecraft's fiction were it not for their interest in games. Still, the notion of games based on literary works makes me uneasy; the games-playing impulse and the reading impulse just seem too far apart—the one active and social, the other essentially passive and solitary. My suspicion (and it's no more than that) is that the games player, if he reads at all, reads for plot, for facts, for usable data—so that in many a story, he's celebrating what's hokiest about it. Remember, a work of fiction is more than just a series of events set in such-and-such a time and place; it's also about language. When you turn an author's vision into a system of rules and roles and diagrams, so that formerly ambiguous gods and demons are now described with numerical precision, like items in a weapons catalogue—strengths, weaknesses, so many points for *this,* so many points for *that*—it seems to me that you've reduced that vision to something utterly formulaic, the way Derleth did in his pastiches.

I hope I'm mistaken, though; and I'd be eager, the next time I'm in England, to sit in on a game or two with you. Needless to say, I also look forward (with some trepidation) to seeing what sort of a game has been made of my own work.*

CF: Settings play an important part in your fiction; buildings and locale are very detailed, ranging from the American Museum of Natural History in "Black Man with a Horn" to the Poroths' farm in *The Ceremonies*. Sometimes these places seem more important than the people they house. Do you feel this is true? And do you undertake much research into areas that might form the basis for locale in your stories?

TK: Yes, the setting of a horror tale interests me a great deal more than the characters. Judging by the tales I most admire, by writers such as Lovecraft and Machen and M. R. James, the characters are pretty forgettable; what one remembers is the look and feel of their world. But I have to confess that in writing stories of my own, I spend very little time on research, in part because I'm too lazy to leave my apartment, in part because I think one can build a convincing locale out of one's imagination, with just a few well-placed groundings in fact. Too much factual material, I think, tends to clot the story; one senses the author dutifully copying from his notebooks.

CF: Your work seems to incorporate a wide range of fictional props: the Dynnod cards in *The Ceremonies*, the Tarot in "Petey." Do you think such imagery helps bring a sense of realism to the tales?

---

*If such a game was ever created, I'm unaware of it. But there is actually a "scenario" of the game *Call of Cthulhu* "based in part on the fiction of T.E.D. Klein." As presented in the guidebook *At Your Door* (Chaosium, 1990), the plot is extensively detailed, complete with map and illustrations. Writes author Mark Morrison, "The scenario doesn't lift events straight out of Klein's fiction, but rather uses parallel themes and images. It also tries to emulate his style in storytelling, rather than everything being up-front and easily explained. Some things which the investigators come across are never developed, but remain half-glimpsed and lurking."

TK: That's certainly been my intention. I'll stoop to anything—phony references, fabricated quotations, mixtures of false information and fact—to make a story seem more real.

CF: In addition to fictional props, your tales abound in thematic clues. Metaphoric imagery is used to describe everyday objects as things that are both sinister and grotesque. Usually these dark images, as Steve Mariconda has pointed out, take the form of reality as the stories reach their climax. Do you deliberately attempt to lure the detective skills out from the reader? And would you say that such writers' devices are important in a horror tale?

TK: Horror stories—at least the sort I've written, which tend to be fairly subdued and, some might say, oblique—have to drop clues along the way in much the same manner as a detective tale. Both depend on indirection and surprise. One is forever *hinting,* suggesting, nudging the reader . . . but not, one hopes, too clumsily. I'm not a mystery fan—in fact, I find crime novels quite tedious, along with crossword puzzles, quiz shows, and income tax forms—but I do think we can learn a lot from the mystery writer's bag of tricks.

CF: Moving to your novel *The Ceremonies,* "the Old One" is depicted as an evil spirit who has taken over the body of a human so that it can prepare the way for its true incarnation. Is this "Old One" one of the same entities Lovecraft wrote of?

TK: No, I simply liked the portentousness of the phrase. It does have a certain gravity to it, don't you think?

CF: The character of Jeremy Freirs, in the novel, seems to share quite a few characteristics with yourself. You once mentioned in a *Twilight Zone* editorial that you, like Freirs, suffer from an allergy to cats. And you both share the same birthday—July 15. To what extent do you think Freirs carries the Klein personality? Was Jeremy's attitude reminiscent of the way T.E.D. Klein would have reacted in circumstances as outlandish as those depicted in the book?

TK: Yes, Jeremy is very close to me—uncomfortably close, in fact, since a lot of readers seem to find him a bit of an asshole! I, too, spent most of one summer living in an outbuilding on a New Jersey farm (although the area itself was somewhat suburban, the farm had not been worked for years, and the couple who lived there were my good friends from the city who knew scarcely more about country living than I did). I reacted pretty much the way Jeremy does to the bugs—i.e., phobically—and read many of the same books. We differ, however, in that Jeremy appears to have a peculiar lack of friends (they would have complicated an already overlong novel), along with a weight problem that I, thank God, have never had . . . at least not yet.*

CF: The ceremonies which Rosebottom has Carol Conklin unwittingly perform seem to resemble, in part, several of those once performed by Aleister Crowley's occult groups. Are those in the novel based on any true occult rituals?

TK: Nope. Perfectly imaginary, so far as I know. Though I do have a Crowley reference in the novel and find him—as I gather his contemporaries did—an extremely colorful figure. (Machen, on the other hand, was genuinely terrified of him and regarded him as one of the most dangerous men he'd ever met.)

CF: How much research do you undertake concerning the *real* occult lore and legend when preparing your fiction?

TK: Very little—just enough to give me the feel of its ground rules, and of the spooky, earnest quality of its prose. I find the "real" occult fascinating, infuriating, seductive, and above all, preposterous.

CF: Some of your characters hold very pessimistic attitudes towards such matters—these are usually the ones who come to a sticky end. Are you also a materialist, or do you believe that the supernatural holds any elements of truth?

---

*Reading this sentence more than three decades later, I can only shake my head and sigh.

TK: I'm with Lovecraft; religions, all of them, the occult included, strike me as nonsense—pernicious nonsense, as often as not. I'd describe myself as a pretty thoroughgoing materialist, insofar as modern science allows the term "material" at all (i.e., I know the world's more complicated than atom striking atom like so many billiard balls). So it was a pleasure, in "Nadelman's God," to make fun of the occult crowd, most of whom are out-and-out creeps. Yet I suppose the realm of the mystical still has a certain emotional appeal for me, since I continue to love the work of Arthur Machen; and in my fiction, if not in life, I enjoy seeing rational characters like Nadelman forced to admit the possibility that there's something out there which reason can't explain.

I've never had an occult or psychic experience of any sort, and I've even been somewhat systematic in searching for one. I've met half a dozen professional psychics; none has ever demonstrated any psychic ability. On several occasions I've dreamed about various people dying, or have had waking premonitions of their deaths, and in every case (thank God) my "vision" was totally wrong and the people remained very much alive.

However, I know that for true believers, these examples are invariably dismissed; instead they cling to the one time in twenty, the one time in a *thousand,* that some premonition proved correct, or even partially correct. It's an example of what has been called "the ratchet effect": Like a ratchet mechanism designed to turn in only one direction, people who are disposed to believe in astrology, saucers, telepathy, etc., tend to reinforce their belief by considering only the "positive" evidence—the coincidences, the lucky guesses—and disregarding the negative.

I'll give you another example from my own life. Years ago, shortly after getting out of college, I fell in love with a girl named Leslie and for a while came very close to marrying her. Three things occurred, during this time, which now seem merely coincidental; but feeling as I did then, I seized upon them all as proof that we were "destined" for each other. One was admittedly pretty trivial: I met her for a weekend in Chicago, and she showed up at the airport carrying the very book that I had under my arm—Stendhal's *The Red and the Black,* in the very same paperback edition. (It was a book we'd never previously discussed.) Later, I entered a *New York Magazine* competition—like the humorous weekly competitions you see at the back of the *Spectator*—and, a day or so later, had another idea for it. Since contest rules forbade multiple submissions, I mailed the second one in under Leslie's name. Well, not only were both submissions published, but the one with Leslie's name was printed just below my own. Needless to say, I took it as a sign from God! Finally, there came a time when, in an expansive mood, I found myself telling Leslie about a vision I'd had back in college (no doubt while my lungs were full of pot smoke; it had been in the late '60s), a vision of what I was seeking in life. It was vague and difficult to describe, I admitted; all I could remember was the image of a small, serene green meadow. She looked amazed and said, "Why, Ted, that's just what my name means—'little meadow.'"

Now, if life were a movie, we'd have married at that point and lived happily ever after. But first of all, I've never once seen anything anywhere to indicate that "Leslie" actually means "little meadow." (Do we have any etymologists out there?) And further, she and I eventually parted: she picked up and moved to London, got married, had kids, and is living, I hope, happily ever after, but with someone other than me. And I'm with someone else as well. Leslie's remained a close friend and, in fact, happens to be my British agent . . . but so mundane and businesslike and merely affectionate a relationship is hardly consistent with those wonderfully cosmic omens, those messages from Fate.

CF: Turning back to your short fiction again, "Black Man with a Horn" is another one of those tales which borrows from Lovecraft's Mythos but which doesn't seem to milk the references dry. Can you explain how the development of that tale came about? And was the narrator based on a real member of HPL's circle?

TK: I recall that Ramsey Campbell had invited me to try my hand at some sort of modern-day Lovecraft story for his Arkham House anthology, *New Tales of the Cthulhu Mythos,* and that I kept mulling it over while visiting an assortment of elderly relatives who, in time-honored New York Jewish fashion, had retired to Miami Beach.

There's something sad and slightly ominous beneath the blue skies and sunshine down there, and I recall wanting to capture it in a story—and to exploit, as well, the horrific possibilities of the canal that ran past the garden apartment where several of my relatives lived. I was struck the same way—always have been, in fact—by the suggestively gothic atmosphere of the Natural History Museum here in New York. Finally, I wondered what it might be like to be a survivor of the so-called "Lovecraft Circle" and, like Frank Long, to have young fans constantly asking you not about your own lifetime of work but about your memories, even the most trivial ones, of the great H. P. Lovecraft, "the Master." I thought it must be extremely humbling, and also amusing, and also very sad.

CF: I think some of your work would be ideally suited for film adaptation. Have you ever thought of perhaps writing a screenplay, or possibly directing one of your tales? If so, which one do you think would translate to the screen most successfully?

TK: I acquired a master's degree in film history back in 1972 and worked for three or four years as an assistant story editor at Paramount Pictures (the East Coast office here in New York); so, yes, I do have a strong interest in film and, like almost every other writer, a lust to see my name up there in the credits, whether as screenwriter or "based on a story by ———." Long ago I tried to write a few screenplays and extended treatments, always with a collaborator, and I must admit that the process itself was rather fun. One of them involved a snowmobile expedition that turns into a sort of icebound *Deliverance;* another pitted an elderly witch against a South Bronx street gang; another tried to update *Cat People,* before Paul Schrader came along with a version of his own; and still another was entitled *Come Back, Quasimodo!* I even tried, once, to write a screen treatment of Lovecraft's *Dream-Quest.* Aside from the fact that these scripts were all pretty derivative, they faced another difficulty: As New Yorkers, my friends and I never knew just what to do with our scripts once we'd written them. We'd mail them to a few people, then give up and file them in a bottom drawer. It really does help to live in Hollywood and to have a few contacts out there, just as, despite what some may claim, it helps to live in New York if you want to be published.

As for what piece of mine might work best on film, I really can't say. Whatever the case, I suspect I'd have trouble recognizing my original story.

CF: Have you ever thought of writing something outside the horror genre?

TK: All the time; in fact, I'm impatient to do so. I'd really prefer not to write horror for the rest of my life. I've never been very comfortable trying to scare readers, and I don't think I'm especially good at it anyway. If I had my druthers, I suppose I'd be writing light, humorous fiction with perhaps a touch of weirdness here and there—or else some sort of informal weekly newspaper column in which I could vent my spleen in whatever direction I pleased.

CF: Do you have much time to read nowadays? What books and tales form part of your literature diet, and which are your favorites?

TK: I read far, far too much, and write far too little and too slowly. I'm a magazine junkie, for one, and can happily spend hours on end reading through a pile of magazines at the kitchen table, stopping only to snip out some article worth saving or sending to a friend. You'd be appalled at my mail each week: literary magazines, financial magazines, regional magazines, political magazines of every stripe, travel, humor, science, film, even magazines on postcard collecting and flying (both of which I do only in my imagination).

As for books, I tend to juggle several at a time—one for the bedside, one for the bathroom, one for the subway, etc. At the moment, I'm finishing up the recent Orwell biography by Bernard Crick while reading, in dribs and drabs, the following: *The Road to Xanadu* by John Livingston Lowes, about how Coleridge came to write his "Kubla Khan" and "Ancient Mariner"; an ecological history called *Man and the Natural World* by Keith Thomas, filled with all sorts of fascinating trivia; *West with the Night,* a travel book by Beryl Markham (who seems to have been a combination of Isak Dinesen and Amelia Earhart); and a very funny sequel by Keith Waterhouse to the Grossmith brothers' *Diary of a Nobody*.

I seldom read horror fiction these days; perhaps I just got horrored out at *Twilight Zone*. (And while I'm at it, let me air a longstanding prejudice of mine: that by and large, horror fans appear to read almost nothing outside the genre. To call them culturally deprived is putting it mildly; they are virtual ignoramuses whose only points of reference are the paperback racks and a bunch of B-movies.)

CF: Finally, can I ask you what the future holds from your pen? Can you give readers a sneak preview of any plots you've got lined up?

TK: I'm already a year overdue on a sort of paranoid New York City horror novel for Viking, about a man whose life is threatened by what he first assumes is a lone psycho, then thinks is a gang, and eventually comes to realize is a kind of tribe. I'm a little uncomfortable talking about the plot; let me just say that I hope it'll meander less than *The Ceremonies,* with perhaps a bit more action and a livelier pace.

After that, I think I'd like to retire to the country and raise daffodils.

II. On Other Authors

Arthur Machen

In 1937, London's *Left Review* published a pamphlet called *Authors Take Sides on the Spanish War*, in which 148 mostly British writers, in response to a questionnaire, set forth their views on the civil war then raging in Spain. Notable leftists such as W. H. Auden, C. Day Lewis, Arthur Koestler, and Stephen Spender, but also less political figures such as Thomas Burke, A. E. Coppard, Aldous Huxley, Olaf Stapledon, and even the black magician Alastair Crowley—127 writers in all—sided with the Spanish government, i.e., against fascism. Another sixteen—including T. S. Eliot and Ezra Pound on the right and H. G. Wells on the left—were, for better or worse, classified as neutral.

And at the end of the pamphlet, bringing up the rear, a mere five writers—including Evelyn Waugh—declared themselves foes of the regime. Among them was a certain seventy-four-year-old Welshman whose response was among the shortest and bluntest in the entire pamphlet: "Mr. Arthur Machen presents his compliments and begs to inform that he is, and always has been, entirely for General Franco."

Without in the least endorsing Machen's own endorsement of the general, I have to laugh. Machen (rhymes with "blacken") was

---

Introduction to *Masters of the Weird Tale: Arthur Machen* (Lakewood, CO: Centipede Press, 2013). A shorter version, with some bibliographic notes, had previously appeared in *Horror: 100 Best Books,* edited by Stephen Jones and Kim Newman (London: Xanadu; New York: Carroll & Graf, 1988).

always a square peg—delighting, like H. P. Lovecraft, in his own eccentricities, proud of being a man out of his time—and it's pleasing to see him thumbing his nose at the prevailing view, even when that view happened to be right. "He was as strongly opinionated as a country clergyman," wrote Philip Van Doren Stern, introducing a collection of Machen's tales, "and, in his own way, was almost as conservative. He was convinced that the modern world had little to offer in exchange for the ancient customs and beliefs that perished under the onslaughts of an industrial civilization, and he seldom missed a chance of saying so."

Machen was, in fact, a country clergyman's son. He was born in southern Wales on March 3, 1863, in a town on the River Usk called Caerleon, best known today as the site of an ancient Roman fortress. "I shall always esteem it as the greatest piece of fortune that has fallen to me, that I was born in that noble, fallen Caerleon-on-Usk, in the heart of Gwent," he told his readers. "My greatest fortune, I mean, from that point of view which I now more especially have in mind, the career of letters. For the older I grow the more firmly am I convinced that anything which I may have accomplished in literature is due to the fact that when my eyes were first opened in earliest childhood, they had before them the vision of an enchanted land."

As a young man, he left the countryside behind and moved to London—for Machen, an equally enchanted place—in the hope of becoming a writer, nearly starving in the attempt. (Mark Valentine, in his biography of Machen, alludes to "his years of privation and struggle in the city, living in a narrow garret room in Clarendon Road and sustained mostly by dry bread, green tea and quantities of shag tobacco.") Later, following the death of his first wife, he toured with a company of Shakespearean actors, but from 1908 onward he supported himself—and his second wife, Purefoy—as a journalist and essayist. He spent his final years in Amersham, outside London, dying on December 15, 1947. I was privileged to share the earth with him for precisely five months.

"It is wonderful," Purefoy wrote in her old age, "how little money has to do with happiness." It's well she felt that way, because finances were often precarious. "The Machens lived with great sumptuousness on almost no money," an American friend, the poet Robert Hillyer, recalled. "He never escaped from the poverty that had dogged him since his birth."

Machen did enjoy moments of relative security. For several years, like Lovecraft, he lived off a small inheritance; at seventy he was awarded a modest government pension, and on turning eighty he was presented with a fund of over £2,000 raised by friends and admirers. He also enjoyed brief periods of renown, particularly during World War I after publication of "The Bowmen," a patriotic fantasy in which ghostly medieval archers come to the aid of retreating British troops; it was widely misconstrued, by a public hungry for miracles, as a factual account.

Nonetheless, as his friend Father Brocard Sewell wrote in 1959, "Arthur Machen was never a best-seller. He was content to live quietly, and he did not seek the help of publicity to advance his fame or the sale of his works. His death in 1947, at the age of eighty-four, caused little stir or comment. . . . Most of Machen's books are out of print, and most of those who know his name think of him only as the author of a few tales which continue to be reprinted in anthologies. Yet those who were reading him thirty, forty, or fifty years ago are reading him still, and his works are keenly sought for, both by new readers and by collectors."

One collector—an autograph hunter from Chicago—wrote him in the fall of 1921. He asked Machen for his signature and told him that he would place it alongside some of the greatest names in literature (whom he then proceeded to list). Machen wrote back:

> *My dear sir,*
>
> *Thank you very much for your kindly expressions. I subjoin my signature with pleasure, but you will do wrong to place it among the names you mention. These are the names of men who have succeeded; mine is the name of a man who has worked hard for forty years & has received as his reward insult, cruelty, beggary.*
>
> *With my best wishes*
> *Believe me yours sincerely,*
> *Arthur Machen*

Machen's letter—more wry than bitter, one suspects—now hangs framed on the wall of my living room (surrounded by names that, as far as I'm concerned, can't hold a candle to him), a small reminder of the perils of the literary life.

As it happens, Machen's best-known memoir was first serialized in newspapers under the title "Confessions of a Literary Man." Later it was expanded into *Far Off Things,* published in 1922. *Things Near and Far* and *The London Adventure* followed in '23 and '24. Together these three volumes constitute a sort of rambling autobiography that is exceedingly vague as to names and dates but so beautifully written and atmospheric that it's hard to resist quoting from it. (Those lines quoted above, about being born "in the heart of Gwent," come from the first book. I agree with Roger Dobson, who considers that and the second "among the greatest autobiographical writings of our time.") Indeed, with the very best writers— and for my taste that's Updike, Orwell, and Machen—you can open them anywhere, turn at random to any page or passage, and find something to savor. Whether it's fiction or nonfiction, whatever the genre or form, you know you're in good hands.

Not everyone agrees, of course. S. T. Joshi, in *The Weird Tale,* contends that "Machen's worst flaw . . . is that he wrote too much" and that "one must be constantly making apologies for Machen: so much of his work consists either of total failures or inessential items. One of the stock defenses is to argue for the 'charm' of much of this inessential writing; but this attempted exoneration becomes, even in the mouths of his loyal defenders, an unintentionally patronizing condemnation."

He may well be right; I've certainly done my share of apologizing for Machen when recommending him to friends, and I do fall back on "charm" occasionally as an explanation for his remarkable appeal. But charm is a fairly precious commodity; it's not something most writers can confidently count on over a long literary career. Machen is one of those who could, but in his case I prefer to give it another name: For me, everything the man wrote has genuine magic, a mysterious combination of style and attitude, of rhythm and metaphor and point of view, that seems uniquely and effortlessly Machen's and that makes reading him like opening a door to the same sort of enchanted land he found all about him in his childhood. That goes not only for his fiction but for his memoirs, his essays, his introductions to other people's work as well as to his own.

Still, as Sewell reminds us, it's the fiction on which today his reputation rests, and the present collection provides an enormous helping of it. Here Machen puts his style in the service of a higher task than Fleet Street afforded: With the eye of visionary and a language that, for all its simplicity, is at times truly incantatory, he reveals the wonder, and sometimes the horror, that lies hidden behind everyday scenes. No other writer's work so perfectly blends the two elements of Walter Van Tilburg Clark's haunting phrase "the ecstasy and the dread." (In fact, Machen's longest foray into literary criticism, *Hieroglyphics,* sees the key attribute of great literature as "the master word—Ecstasy.") Jack Sullivan has noted that in Machen's best tales "beauty and horror ring out at exactly the same moment" and praises Machen for "his ability to make landscapes come alive with singing prose." Philip Van Doren Stern saw Machen's imagery as "rich with the glowing color that is to be found in medieval church glass." No one is better at evoking the loneliness of the Welsh hills or the sinister allure of dark woods; no one makes London a more terrifying or magical place, a latter-day Baghdad filled with exotic dangers and infinite possibilities. Wherever he looked, he saw a world filled with mystery. Every word he wrote, from youth to old age, reflects his lifelong preoccupation with "the secret and hidden truth, the reality, remote from the outward shows and appearances."

It's remarkable how faithful Machen remained to his chosen themes. What he writes of the hero of his final novel, *The Green Round*—"If he had ever thought of the mysteries as things hidden away and apart, remote from the general stream of life, he saw now that he was mistaken. The mysteries were part of the very tissue and being of man; they were not to be avoided"—might just as well have been said of characters he'd written about four decades earlier.

He sounds the note again in the introduction to W. Townsend Collins's *The Romance of the Echoing Wood*—"It is the office of romance to deal with reality; to unveil, as far as may be, the essential, the real, and eternal truth of things"—and again in an introduction to his own youthful translation of Casanova: "The solid earth beneath our feet, the stars in the heavens, the air we breathe; these are but congealed energies and power; and so the physical science of to-day repeats in its own terms the doctrine of Böhme, the seventeenth-century mystic. . . . The more it is explored, the more evident it becomes that the nature of things is a great mystery, that the world is compact of secrets. . . . The smallest grain of sand is an insoluble secret." His essay "With the Gods in Spring" opens: "We shall go on seeking it to the end, so long as there are men on the earth. We shall seek it in all manner of strange ways; some of them wise, and some of them unutterably foolish. But the search will never end." And what is this "it" to which he refers? "The secret of things; the real truth that is everywhere hidden under outward appearances."

But perhaps this "secret of things" is too shocking for the human mind to accept. That, at least, is the premise of one of Machen's earliest and best-known stories, "The Great God Pan," in which a ruthless scientist seeks to rend the "veil" of everyday reality. ("I tell you that all these things—yes, from that star that has just shone out in the sky to the solid ground beneath our feet—I say that all these are but dreams and shadows: the shadows that hide the real world from our eyes.") In a laboratory set amid "the lonely hills," he performs a delicate operation on the brain of a young girl, reawakening atavistic powers and enabling her to glimpse that real world—a process he calls "seeing the god Pan."

The result is not enlightenment but horror. And here, in recognition of the pages that follow, I should say no more.

Today, for all its power, the tale's decadent *frissons* may seem rather dated, but at the time, "Pan" outraged the more prudish English critics. Machen, who took a perverse pleasure in his bad reviews (he even collected them all in a book, *Precious Balms*), relished "the remark of a literary agent whom I met one day in Fleet Street. He looked at me impressively, morally, disapprovingly, and said: 'Do you know, I was having tea with some ladies at Hampstead the other day, and their opinion seemed to be that . . . "The Great God Pan" should never have been written.'"

Two other early stories, "Novel of the Black Seal" and "The Red Hand," can still provoke a shudder, even today. (The former is included in *The Three Imposters,* which serves as an unpleasant and improbably contrived framing device for it; but like another section of that book, "Novel of the White Powder," it's often presented as a stand-alone.) They play with the notion—as do later Machen tales—that the so-called Little People of British legend, the fairy folk, were in fact the land's original inhabitants, a dark, squat, malevolent pre-Celtic race now driven underground by encroaching civilization, yet living on in caves beneath the "barren and savage hills" and still practicing their unsavory rites, occasionally sacrificing a young woman or some other luckless wanderer they can catch alone outdoors at night. Writers such as John Buchan have also made use of this theme, but none so chillingly. ("Who can limit the age of survival?" muses a character in "The Red Hand," meditatively puffing on his pipe at the window of his London flat as he gazes out at the evening. "The troglodyte and the lake-dweller, perhaps representatives of yet darker races, may very probably be lurking in our midst, rubbing shoulders with frock-coated and finely-draped humanity, ravening like wolves at heart and boiling with the foul passions of the swamp and the black cave.")

Machen's strangest story is "The White People." (It was the direct inspiration, incidentally, for my own novel *The Ceremonies,* which quotes from it at length.) Most of it purports to be the notebook of a young girl who, introduced by her nurse to odd old folk rhymes and rituals, has a series of nearly indescribable mystical visions involving supernatural presences in the woods near her home. The girl's stream-of-consciousness style, naive yet disquietingly suggestive, lends a spellbinding immediacy to the narrative, and for all its confusion and repetitiveness it remains the purest and most powerful expression of a supernatural tradition that sees, behind everyday reality, a world of forest magic, ancient ceremonies, and sinister pagan deities. Most other tales of this sort, such as Algernon Blackwood's "The Wendigo," E. F. Benson's "The Man Who Went Too Far," and Machen's own "Black Seal" and "Pan," merely *describe* encounters with dark primeval forces inimical to man; "The White People" seems an actual product of such an encounter, an authentic pagan artifact, as different from the rest as the art of Richard Dadd is different from the art of Richard Doyle.

Lovecraft, who regarded Machen as "a Titan—perhaps the greatest living author" of weird fiction, and who in letter after letter rhapsodized over Machen's "magick and witchery," his "ethereal genius" and "daemoniac spell," ranked "The White People" beside Blackwood's "The Willows" as one of the greatest horror tales ever written. Machen—who often denigrated his own efforts, and who once summed up the destiny of all writers as "He dreamed in fire; he has worked in clay"—termed the tale merely "a fragment" of the one he'd intended to write, "a single stone instead of a whole house," but acknowledged that "it contains some of the most curious work that I have ever done, or ever will do. It goes, if I may say so, into very strange psychological regions." E. F. Bleiler's assessment strikes me as equally just: "This document is probably the finest single supernatural story of the century, perhaps in the literature."

Still, Machen isn't for everyone. Even his most devoted readers know this. Roger Dobson hails him for "producing some of the most extraordinary stories in the English language" but finds him enjoying mere "cult status" today. Godfrey Brangham notes that "he had spent a lifetime in literary pursuits and had contributed to most forms. Yet in none did he achieve the reputation he really deserved." Mark Valentine considers Machen "a towering figure" in the field of supernatural horror, but one who "remains outside of the literary mainstream. . . . Machen is a traditionalist when the avant-garde has been in the ascendant; a mystic and ritualist when existentialist humanism is the vogue; a Romantic when kitchen-sink realism is called for; a rhapsodiser of beauty when ugliness is more eagerly worshipped."

In his Twayne guide, Wesley Sweetser saw Machen's readership as falling into diverse groups, none of them sizable: "mystery story addicts," "book collectors," "terror and supernatural readers," "Bohemians" in search of "the pagan element," a "small occult following," "true mystics—never a large number in any age," and "genuine intellectuals, again a fairly small group." R. B. Russell (who, as a publisher, would know) suggests something even gloomier: "Arthur Machen's books are highly collectable, and, sadly, it is probable that collectors of his first editions are more numerous than those who read his books for enjoyment." S. T. Joshi sees Machen appealing chiefly to "a devoted band of cognoscenti" and concludes: "In the short run the care of Machen's reputation will rest in the hands of horror aficionados. Whether he will ever again attract a mainstream audience is difficult to say; I honestly suspect not, and I also suspect that Machen would have wanted it that way. I think he enjoyed his position as a literary curiosity . . . and he would have wished to be read only by a small band of sympathetic followers."

Machen himself, nearing sixty, wrote to an American admirer: "I read little; & usually in the old books. . . . As to modern writers of fiction, I know very little about them. When I do read a modern novel, I often make two reflections. Firstly: 'How very clever'; secondly: 'And yet this can never last.'"

For us, at least—we few, we band of devotees—Machen will last.

Ramsey Campbell: An Appreciation

> That was the first time you were afraid of nothing—that day when you were catching butterflies—when you had reached the patch of sunlight. You were not afraid in the shadow, but you were afraid in the sun.
>
> The sunlight was still, desolate, and arid. And you knew that something huge was just behind you. You ran. You fell and cut your knee. You got up and ran again, panting, your heart thumping, much too frightened to cry.
>
> But when you got home, you cried. You cried for a long time; and you never told anybody why.
>
> —Jean Rhys
> *After Leaving Mr. Mackenzie* (1930)

This is a story of how a young man crawled out from under H. P. Lovecraft's shadow, saw the sun, and wrote *Demons by Daylight*. . . .

Back in 1969, after Arkham House had exhausted its supply of Lovecraft fiction and had run through three volumes of miscellaneous "Lovecraftiana," it dipped still further into the barrel and came

---

Written in 1974, this piece was published in *Nyctalops* 13 (May 1977), edited by Harry O. Morris, Jr., reprinted in *Fantasy Reader's Guide to Ramsey Campbell*, edited by Mike Ashley (Chatham, UK: Cosmos, 1980), and again in *Discovering Modern Horror Fiction II*, edited by Darrell Schweitzer (Mercer Island, WA: Starmont House, 1988). I believe it was the first critical article written about Ramsey and his work.

out with *Tales of the Cthulhu Mythos,* a collection of pastiches in the Lovecraft tradition.

Most of them were simply embarrassing; as Mike Heron might have put it, they knew all the words and they sang all the notes, but they never quite got the song. Yet I recall that even the Lovecraftiest of the tales, those closest to the originals, were somehow unsatisfying; forcing my way through them, trying hard to become excited, I realized that what I missed most was not the Lovecraft style (which, let's face it, is eminently imitable; indeed, several of the writers had mimicked it to perfection) but rather his *name.* Similarity wasn't enough; I wanted something that, by definition, no pastiche can provide: authenticity. For me, as I suspect for many of his readers, Lovecraft's life has become as fascinating as his tales; and knowing as we do of the man's solitary existence, his eccentricity, his erudition, his opinions and beliefs, the very name "Lovecraft" above a story seems to stamp the work with a kind of sincerity, the sense of its affording a glimpse into a unique, deeply fascinating soul, that sets it above that of his disciples.

What this means is that the most stylistically accomplished of the pastiches felt also the most artificial. One might almost apply to them the adage about translations being like women: the more beautiful, the less faithful; the more faithful, the less beautiful.

It isn't as surprising as it might seem, then, that of all the *Tales of the Cthulhu Mythos,* the most effective were those that departed most radically from the original canon. The best of the lot—and certainly the most haunting—was a short piece called "Cold Print." The title itself, in its very understatement, stood out in contrast to all the Dwellers in Darkness, Shadows from the Steeple, and Shamblers from the Stars that proliferated throughout the book; and the story stood out even more.

It began, it's true, with one of those portentous epigraphs from a Forbidden Work—in this case something called the *Revelations of Glaaki,* Volume 12 (certainly the most unsavory title since *De Vermis Mysteriis*)—and in fact the quotation itself was even more portentous than most, claiming as it did that "even the minions of Cthulhu dare not speak of Y'golonac"—a rather arrogant assertion for a relative newcomer to make, akin to the sort of movie poster that once proclaimed the She Beast to be "Deadlier than Dracula! Wilder than the Werewolf! More frightening than Frankenstein!"

Happily, though, this unholier-than-thou air was dispelled by the story's opening sentence, in which a young schoolmaster with the disreputable name Sam Strutt "licked his fingers and wiped them on his handkerchief." The tale went on to include such untraditional elements as sexual frustration, loneliness, and outright horniness; the commercialization of Christmas, and the despair that only a holiday can breed; pornography of the kind known euphemistically as "discipline"; hints of homosexuality and pedophilia; allusions to Burroughs, Robbe-Grillet, Hubert Selby, Jr., and B-movies ("The neon sign outside the window of his flat, a cliché but relentless as a toothache . . . garishly defined against the night every five seconds"); throwaway images both comical and grotesque ("Once he met the gaze of an old woman staring down at a point below her window which was perhaps the extent of her outside world. Momentarily chilled, he hurried on, pursued by a woman who, on the evidence within her pram, had given birth to a litter of newspapers . . ."); not to mention such un-Lovecraftian details as bus fumes, slush, snot, and dogshit; all capped by one of the most breathtakingly gruesome endings I had ever read.

Save for that memorable finale, and the fact that the story was miserably proofread, this was hardly the kind of thing one expected to find in a volume of Lovecraftiana. It was much too good. It seemed a product of that bleak land somewhere between *New Grub Street* and the "New Town" of *Jubb* (two of my favorite British novels); it was a tale Lovecraft might have written if he'd had the benefit of an excellent editor, if he'd survived into the '50s, and if he'd been unsettlingly honest.

The tale's author, one J. Ramsey Campbell, was listed in the back of the book. It was noted, with old-maidish redundancy, that he had "the same background as the popular Beatles—Liverpool, England," and that he had been born in 1946—a fact inspiring much consternation, at least in this writer, born but one year later. One prefers one's heroes older.

The biographical note went on to mention two books of Campbell's; one, *The Inhabitant of the Lake and Less Welcome Ten-*

ants, was, it declared, "published by Arkham House when he was but 18"—further consternation and a gnashing of teeth—and the other, *Demons by Daylight*, was forthcoming.

There was obviously nothing else to do but send for that first volume and wait for the second.

The former proved something of a letdown. Like Frank Utpatel's rather cartoony cover and end-paper maps, the tales seemed too eager to spell everything out. They told too much. So did the introduction, in which the young author announced, with bold naïveté, his intention to create a new setting for the Cthulhu Mythos, the Arkham area having been "saturated." (God knows he was right about that.) He went on to describe each imaginary city in considerable detail, as well as the "esoteric volume" from which he intended to quote—thereby saving readers much work but also much pleasure, a mistake he was never to repeat. The effect was as if the bravado of the epigraph of "Cold Print" had found its way into the text. That story had been uncomfortably candid about the secret urges of its protagonist; here, unfortunately, the Campbell of an earlier day was proving all too candid about his own authorial ambitions.

Throughout the book, one was conscious of a deliberate striving after a Lovecraft corpus, a deliberate dropping of names, a deliberate setting up of the horrors. Except for one understated little piece called "The Will of Stanley Brooke," done largely in dialogue, the stories seemed filled with artifice; Campbell hadn't yet learned to cover his tracks.

That it was an extraordinary work for an eighteen-year-old boy to have produced was, of course, obvious in every line; but obviously, too, this was the work of a writer still laboring in Lovecraft's shadow.

As I recall, probably the most interesting thing about the book was the author's photo on the end-flap. Describing him as "one of the youngest and most promising recruits to the domain of the macabre"—as if the entire field were some colossal boys' club (and perhaps it is) or the refuge of some crackpot pressure group (and perhaps it is)—the picture showed a gloomy-looking youth with plastic glasses and short hair, very British-public-school-looking in a sweater, jacket, and tie. His expression was both sullen and amused, with a slight touch of sneer, as if he'd really wanted to smile but was afraid it wouldn't do for a horror writer to look too jolly (a quite reasonable consideration). He looked like a boy who could be guilty of anything: the face of a mathematics prodigy, a child molester, or simply a repressed Catholic schoolboy gone wrong. It was obvious from his serene expression and level gaze that he had impure thoughts, and often. He looked, in a word, creepy. Which is to say, he was one of us.

In succeeding years other Arkham House editions were sent for, as finances permitted. One by one the Derleth anthologies arrived, each with its spurious "unpublished Lovecraft" tale written by Derleth himself, testifying less to his modesty than to his marketing sense; and each time, the first thing I looked for was the Campbell offering. He made, I believe, every volume.

They were a mixed bag. If no story ever excited me quite as much as "Cold Print," largely because of that one's unusually evocative atmosphere, they were nevertheless far superior to those tales in the *Inhabitant* volume. "The Church in High Street" was, to be sure, an example of Early Campbell, bearing that period's distinguishing feature, the overexplicit first-person narrator; it seemed, in fact, to belong more to *Inhabitant* than "The Will of Stanley Brooke" had, and perhaps preceded that tale. "The Stone on the Island" seemed heavy-handed too, but the story did offer pleasant hints of things to come: a protagonist desperately alone, his alienation seeming to distort the workaday world around him, rendering it surreal, dismal, absurd; the halfhearted passes at girls in the office; the office itself, convincingly dull, filled with obtuse people doing trivial things; and the conclusion, whose grisliness made up for whatever lapses the plot may have had.

"The Cellars," "Napier Court," "The Scar"—the tales grew better and better with each new volume, subtler and more difficult. "Cold Print," I began to realize, had been a kind of Campbell primer, containing nearly all the elements that distinguished these later stories. The Early Campbell was gone, and so was the corpus he'd initially tried to create; at last we were witnessing the formation of a genuine body of work, unified not by mere intention but by vision.

That observation, of course, is one calculated to embarrass any writer, and to Campbell himself I apologize for it; it sounds entirely too grandiose, too pretentious. Yet a vision there was, a sustaining one; and with the publication of *Demons by Daylight* it was clear that this vision of the universe—paranoiac, often confounding, always haunting, dreadful, unique—had been sustained throughout an entire book.

It was, to say the least, quite an event.

Judging from the several reviews I saw at the time, a lot was made of the book's cover by, we are told, "the eminent British artist and illustrator, Eddie Jones." It is, in fact, a very good one, and particularly appropriate: An attractive young girl, head up, hair frazzled and free, mouth agape, stands before us in a state of either awe, terror, submission, or sexual excitation, wearing only a thin dress (through which, should you chance to hold the book up to a strong light and squint ever so slightly, you can see her nipples) and a large ornamental cross—useless, we may be sure, against the insectoid demon skull that's superimposed over her.

The back cover, too, is of interest. Campbell himself adorns it, looking very cocky and self-assured. In the earlier pose, he'd looked like a fan; the photo was the sort one sees reproduced in the letter columns of monster magazines, complete with boasts about the subject's age. Now he looks more like a writer. Somewhere along the way between the two collections, the "J." has been dropped from his name—shed, perhaps, like a caterpillar skin when he crawled out from beneath Lovecraft's shadow and took flight on his own—but the lack is more than made up for by a cascade of hair as long as the girl's on the front of the book. He has acquired, too, a new pair of glasses (still plastic, but better-looking), a black turtleneck sweater (the kind Colin Wilson wears in most of his pictures), and a wife—the former Jenny Chandler. (One might expect that after marriage his stories would have changed, his lonely heroes growing less haunted, less horny, to be ultimately replaced by cool, pipe-puffing Carnacki types.... Happily, this does not seem to have occurred.) Campbell's sneer has grown; so, too, has his smile, though it's still knowing rather than welcoming. Standing with arms folded in the Liverpool Public Library (where he has worked), he holds—as if in a gratuitous plug—a book whose title is maddeningly hard to read;

it seems to be *The House on the*—what? *Brink*? I can't help thinking that this book, which I don't recognize, must be of vital importance; perhaps readers will enlighten me. (Still, I'm a little disappointed that it isn't a copy of *We Pass from View,* an imaginary book supposedly written by an obscure dabbler in the occult named Roland Franklyn, first encountered in "Cold Print." Its appearance in the photograph would have been, for me, an amusing reminder of a Lovecraft exhibit at the Brown University library arranged by Professor Barton Levi St. Armand, in which one of the airtight glass display cases contained, or so the card declared, "the legendary *Necronomicon*"—a fat, sinister-looking volume, unfortunately lying shut, the leather of the spine having long since rotted away.)

Among the first things that strike one about Campbell's stories in this new collection is that—following the trend of his earlier pieces—they are extremely difficult. In fact, let's not mince words: I found them hard as hell. More often than not I came to the end without realizing it, turning the page only to find myself faced with a new story, like one of those cartoons in which a man walking the plank strides several feet in the air before realizing he's gone past the end of the board. Frequently I had to retrace my steps, rereading the last few pages to see what I'd missed; on two occasions I remained still baffled and my girlfriend had to explain the endings to me—demonstrating her own patience and, I suppose, the fact that I'm as obtuse as any of Campbell's Brichester revenue clerks.

Still, being difficult is not necessarily a fault; and for horror, in fact, it is almost always a virtue. Several years ago, when I was teaching school, a fellow teacher was criticized for being "too difficult" for students; the material he presented was allegedly "over their heads." I recall his reply: "I think it's important to give them a little more than they can handle," he said. "I like to remain a little beyond them."

For an English instructor, this may or may not be a good idea; but for a horror writer, it should probably be the rule. Writing horror stories is rather like playing the Pied Piper; if the tune one pipes is too fast, too difficult, or too subtle, the reader grows bored and drops out of the dance. If, on the other hand, the tune is too plodding and predictable, the reaction is the same: boredom, loss of attention. The trick, presumably, is to dance just a little ahead of the reader, teasing him, leading him on.

The risk, of course, is considerable: If one balks at making the slightest concession to the reader, one may end up with something akin to abstract art or the most demanding poetry. In that case, as Kirby McCauley has pointed out, one runs the risk of writing stories for oneself alone; even if a few readers have the means to decipher them, no one will care to try.

Yet the other extreme presents an even graver danger: Write a tale too easy to grasp and the reader begins to realize he is more intelligent than the writer—which is the case with so many dismayingly predictable Lovecraft pastiches, from August Derleth's onward.

Campbell, fortunately, seems to have mastered that trick of dancing just beyond our reach. Most of his stories have a hazy, dreamlike quality in which events are comprehensible as discrete units, but they are piled upon one another so frantically that one gets lost in the swirl. Take, for example, the mad rush of images that we find at the beginning of "The Lost":

> It was in Rudesheim that I had my first important insight into Bill's character. The previous night, outside Koblenz, we had caught a bus in an unsuccessful attempt to find the town centre and when our three marks fare ran out had been abandoned in the country, by a filling station railed off by leaping brilliant rain. I'd been sure there had been hefty figures following us as we walked into the stinging darkness—but Bill had seen a bus heading back to our hotel; he hadn't wanted a fight. So we'd joined the rest of our coach party that morning. Chairlifts were strung down a hillside of vineyards to Rudesheim; I stood up until Bill protested, although I had already seen that there could be no danger at all unless you fell on one of the vinepoles. Our courier led us down into Rudesheim, through the contorted cobbled streets of aproned women selling souvenirs, between tables full of tankards and huge packed laughing Germans, and into an inn. Here Bill revealed himself.

Quite an opening paragraph—by no means Campbell's best writing, but typical of the way he buffets the reader with a succession of unrelated images, so that one finds oneself growing winded, a little punchy—and at the same time more susceptible to Campbell's attack. Or (to mix metaphors) one cries "Slow down!" but the tour has moved on, back to Rudesheim.

The fact that all these incidents are crowded into a single paragraph (the journalist in me would run them down the page) makes the writing seem even more compressed and difficult than it really is. Often entire conversations receive the same treatment, with considerable atmospheric effect; at any rate, though it may be typographically problematic, it all saves space and, one assumes, publishing costs. As it happens, this effect is further compounded by the very size of the typeface used—abnormally tiny for an Arkham House edition. In a way, this minuscule type is as symbolic of this collection as Utpatel's thick heavily drawn lines were of the previous one.

Add to this the fact that, whether or not Campbell intended it, the tales are almost totally lacking in line breaks, and you have something very confusing indeed. One example from among dozens; in "At First Sight" we follow the heroine onto a bus: "As she passed the seat where she'd seemed to see the face she stretched out her hand and touched the leather. It was cold as the stones of a well." The new paragraph begins immediately: "A glass was held toward her, half-full of some dark liquid." Huh? Where, on the bus? Coca-Cola vendor, perhaps? But no: "Her eyes refused to look beyond the hand which held the glass. Then she saw that it was not a glass; it was a girl, struggling among her fingers, one bare arm thrust out beneath the thumb. Nor was it a hand that held her." And then a third paragraph: "Val sat up in bed." Etc. Somehow we've jumped from the bus seat into a bed, after having plunged through a most confusing dream. My own guess is that Campbell made some allowance for a break after that first paragraph but that Arkham House ignored it; and it's probably significant that in the first issue of *Whispers*, Stuart Schiff alluded to some "errors on the part of the printer" (perhaps he means the typeface) that marred production of the book. This may be one of the few times that sloppy printing has actually accentuated the atmosphere of a story collection.

The hand holding the glass that turns into a hand holding a girl

("Nor was it a hand that held her") typifies another characteristic of Campbell's fiction: distorted images seen always through the eyes of the protagonist, images that tend to shift and disappear as we try to understand them. "Their heads—no, they couldn't be heads," realizes one character. "On their shoulders were set huge paper masks like balloons, nodding horribly, their grinning mouths stretched wide as if bloated from within. . . . Heads inflated by mud." That comes from a nightmare in "The Old Horns," but the images need not be confined to dreams. For example, in a city at night: "I saw a totem-pole striding toward me down a side-street. It was a child stacked on his father's shoulders." In "Concussion," a sentimental science fiction story reminiscent of Robert F. Young, based on a kind of nostalgia for the present, we find: "A colossal green leper stood on the horizon; the Liver Clock, flaking off each second from the future." Or, from a pub scene in "Made in Goatswood": "His face swam forward through the yellow light like a shark closing for the kill." And a few lines down: "Footsteps plodded up the stairs toward them. It was her father. Kim watched, unwillingly fascinated. The father took shape from the shadows, looming above them. The footsteps continued." It is as if we've been forced to look at the world through a fish-eye lens or the spectacles of some astigmatic stranger. People dream, even in daylight; they are prone to visions any place they go—city streets, even—and thus any place can be frightening. It's a world in which a totem pole can come striding down the sidewalk toward you, and even after it's been "explained away" the surreal quality lingers. In short, it's a world in which anything can happen. Expect anything. Expect the worst.

What this leads to is a kind of dreamlike paranoia that affects his characters' perceptions—not a new thing for horror stories, it's true, except that Campbell does it so much better, and he does it in crowds more often than not. In the paragraph I quoted from "The Lost," one of the first things the narrator mentions is the "hefty figures following us as we walked into the stinging darkness"; and later in that same tale, the narrator finds himself in a German tavern, staring at a girl at the bar: "I was fascinated," he reports. "She seemed to be with three overflowing men. She must have known when eyes were watching her whenever they were, just as I do, for she turned and stared at me. . . . She said something to the man on her right, and he swung round trailing smoke, his cigar like a blackened gun-barrel, to train his gaze on me. I knew he was hostile; I always do."

Granted, the tale presents us with—as we discover—a patently insane narrator whose vision of the world is deliberately distorted; but such distortion is the norm throughout this book. (And for all the narrator's paranoiac delusions, events bear out his philosophy: A mere flood of German curses provokes the longed-for murder of his companion.)

One effect of this distorted vision is that the reader becomes even more paranoiac than the protagonist. After reading several Campbell stories, one's ear grows extraordinarily sensitive to conversations overhead at the next table (something about that girl they found dead in the park), and one learns to pay scrupulous attention to stray scraps of wind-tossed newspaper bearing ominous references to *"mutilations"* and *"police baffled* . . .*"* The ladies on the bus, one seat behind us, are talking about a series of murders, and we find ourselves nodding cynically—"Uh-huh, somebody's going to *get* it!"—aware as we are that Campbell is above all an economical writer and that half-heard conversations and muttered warnings are seldom inserted simply as window dressing; they are clues, and like as not the protagonist—who ignores them—is going to wind up just as mutilated as the corpse the news vendor hinted of.

But stray snatches of barroom conversations are by no means required to raise the hackles of a veteran Campbell reader; simple code words are often enough. Shadows, gloom, an alley, a deserted park on an evening in February, a row of abandoned warehouses—we don't ask for much. A cave, perhaps, as in the brilliant "End of a Summer's Day," but that's hardly necessary—a mere hint of underground passages, a dark doorway that might perhaps lead to catacombs, a trapdoor in the floor of a basement . . . No need for elaboration, no need for mapping out the subterranean network of tunnels (a Campbell staple). Just give us the doorway or the trapdoor and we'll fill in the rest. After all, we've been here before.

Such is the cumulative power of the best horror fiction—Lovecraft's, Machen's, and certainly Campbell's. Each new tale gains drama and atmosphere from those that have gone before—which, like it or not, gives writers such as Campbell an immediate edge over newcomers to the field. Take a story by an unknown writer and, if it opens with a picnic on the beach, we'll be yawning by page two. After all, an ordinary summer's outing . . . what's scary about that? Who cares if the title is "The Slime Monster" or something equally lurid? Yet Campbell can rivet our attention with just such a scene, and we'll react with a shudder to every mention of dunes and mud puddles—despite a title as innocuous as "The Old Horns."

That may be one reason why the genre tends to spawn such apparent "addicts"—and conversely why the uninitiated reader who comes upon some classic horror tale for the first time may well react with little more than boredom: Up to a certain point (after which, we may suppose, the returns begin to diminish), the effect of horror is cumulative. Which isn't to say that one should read through *Demons by Daylight* at one sitting—that would be an unfortunate mistake, akin to gorging oneself on a pound of macadamia nuts. The individual stories are too rich, and need a day or two for the psyche to digest.

Once initiated, however, Campbell's readers become acutely sensitive to phrases that evoke atmosphere, as well as to carefully placed hints of imminent doom. As with most horror stories, the reader customarily finds himself one step ahead of the protagonist, leading to a kind of reluctant fascination, the old "Don't go in there, you fool" syndrome—for, of course, the protagonist does go in there, and ultimately pays for it.

The fact that so many of his main characters end up dead suggests that Campbell's universe is not a particularly moral one; innocent people are just as prone to die as the guilty, and that Campbell primer, "Cold Print," ends on just such a note: "Strutt's last thought was an unbelieving conviction that this was happening because he had read the *Revelations;* somewhere, someone had *wanted* this to happen to him. It wasn't playing fair, he hadn't done anything to deserve this—but before he could scream out his protest his breath was cut off . . ."

No, it isn't particularly fair; Campbell's obsessive young men and neurotically passive young women don't deserve to die. And yet, in a sense, all of them are guilty of *something*—an overweening curiosity, perhaps, or, as in Strutt's case, simply evil thoughts. I can't help but wonder (as one is supposed to wonder in essays like this) if such retribution isn't some sort of holdover from Campbell's Catholic upbringing; Catholicism is, after all, a religion that punishes one for sinful thoughts as well as actions. We are, in that case, all of us guilty.

Not that the Church represents any "force of goodness" in these stories. It seems, in fact, rather impotent, indeed quite fatuous: a collection of lithograph Jesuses and a herd of sheep trotting into a cathedral. (This image, from Bunuel's *The Exterminating Angel*, represents one of Campbell's many film references. For that matter, his narrative makes frequent use of cinematic devices: A hideous face at the window, out of focus, is revealed as a friend; flash cuts to the details of a city street yield a kind of cinematic fragmentation, etc. Campbell has, in fact, written film criticism for the BBC.)

When it comes to Catholicism I'm out of my depth, so I'd prefer to leave heavy analyses of Good vs. Evil in the Campbell Oeuvre to future generations of grad students; but it is worth pointing out that such a conflict doesn't even exist in these tales. There *is* no force of goodness to pit against evil; we are given no heroic Dr. Armitages or Professor Rices to battle against Campbell's Yog-Sothoths. In fact, Campbell eschews heroes of any kind; many of his creations are criminal, and the rest enjoy a stature no better than our own: They are weak, timid, and if in love, selfishly so. Were they suddenly to receive magical powers, they'd certainly abuse them. They are, in short, refreshingly easy to identify with, after years of cool-eyed psychic investigators and aristocratic aesthetes.

Ironically, the only force arrayed against the sundry evils of the universe is the force of human stupidity. By that I mean the very blindness, insensitivity, slavishness to habit and dogma, that keep Campbell's minor characters busy with their daily rounds in the office while the protagonist is quietly going mad from fear. The effect is, once again, dreamlike, for if the reader customarily knows more than the main character, *he* in turn knows a great deal more than the minor ones and therefore finds himself in that horrifyingly familiar world in which no one else quite understands what's going on. Such paranoia reaches its height in "The End of a Summer's Day," one of those perfect stories that, like Lovecraft's "Hypnos" and "Polaris," allows for two satisfactory sets of explanations: one quite natural, one less so. On the one hand it's the apotheosis of that infantile nightmare, "I'm screaming and no one's listening," and in fact it appears in the section Campbell labels "Nightmares." (Perhaps we should take him at his word.) On the other hand, one can't help theorizing the existence of strange subterranean cults who, for reasons of their own, inhabit certain English caves where, every ten years or so, they trap a luckless tourist, substituting for him their previous captive—who, by this time, is as blind as a mole.

Exasperating as they are, these herds of common humanity with their heads stuck in their newspapers—muttering about "all this godlessness going around" and "Don't get involved" and other banalities—do constitute a kind of strength, maintaining their sane little world in the midst of a mad universe. "What do you believe in?" asks a Campbell hero, and his girlfriend's father answers, quite seriously, "What's around me. Not politics disguised as panaceas, not poets trying to be philosophers. This house. My job. Reality." One senses real wisdom here, in this middle-class sage; it's obvious that he speaks from long experience. Believe deeply enough in the ordinary and nothing can harm you. (One senses, too, Campbell's ambiguity toward the character; he's given him some good lines.) At any rate, it isn't the people like him who get hurt; it's the meddlesome few who learn, as in Lovecraft, More Than Mortals Were Meant to Know. They pay for it, these characters, in suffering and death; and those who aren't killed find their perceptions of the world forever altered.

If darkness is to be defeated, then, it won't be by any mystical powers or Catholic saints; it will be by unimaginative men keeping their minds on their work. One would almost be tempted to advise, "In banality there is strength"—but ultimately that doesn't offer much protection. The title *Demons by Daylight* notwithstanding, there isn't any light in Campbell's world to hold back the darkness; and this does tend to make the tales inexorably grim and pessimistic. Lovecraft, at least, offered a wide variety of panaceas: Science, the Great Race, Childhood, Dreams, the very notion that "It's All in Your Mind" (à la *Kadath*) and hence not to be feared. In the world of M. R. James there's a kind of Victorian social stability to rescue us from ancestral ghosts; one flees the cemetery or the swamp and returns to a comfortable seat by the fire. And Arthur Machen balances his pagan atrocities with hymns to pagan joy; to use Walter Van Tilburg Clark's phrase, Machen gives us both "the ecstasy and the dread." But in Ramsey Campbell's world, there is only the dread.

It's absurd, of course, to take a horror writer to task for writing horror, especially when he does it with such originality and grace; indeed, I think Campbell reigns supreme in the field today. Yet horror *per se* can be, in the end, somewhat limiting; and now that he has mastered it, one might hope for an occasional ray of light to alleviate the gloom. Black magic, by its existence, implies white magic; and while I'm not looking for a collection of fairy tales, it strikes me that an occasional vision of something beyond a glass of stout and a secretary's knickers might add a needed dimension to the world Campbell has created.

Yet as far removed as Campbell's world may be from that of M. R. James, he does seem to embody one of that scholarly writer's most memorable virtues: He can create a monster in a single felicitous phrase. We've all read of the famous "face of crumpled linen," but James has come up with other descriptions just as clever, such as this passage from "The Treasure of Abbot Thomas," in which the speaker is describing his attempt to pull a bag of gold from a hole in the side of a pit:

> Well, I felt to the right, and my fingers touched something curved that felt—yes—more or less like leather: dampish it was, and evidently part of a heavy, full thing. . . . I pulled it to me, and it came. It was heavy, but moved more easily than I had expected. . . . My left elbow knocked over and extinguished the candle. I got the thing fairly in front of the mouth and began drawing it out. . . . I . . . went on pulling out the great bag, in complete darkness. It hung for an instant on the edge of the hole, then slipped forward on to my chest, and *put its arms round my neck.*

In "Napier Court" Campbell paints a similar image:

> Resting against the beacon was a white bag, half as high as Alma. She'd seen such bags before, full of laundry. Yet she could not force herself to pull back the gates and pass . . . the shapeless mass, for deep within herself she suppressed a horror that the bag might move toward her, flapping.

"Flapping"—a perfect word, reminding one of the "horrible hopping creature in white" from James's "Casting the Runes," a creature "which you saw first dodging about among the trees, and gradually it appeared more and more plainly."

Words ending in "-ing" are clearly an effective device; "The Old Horns" offers "a prancing figure," and in "The Sentinels" Campbell uses one such word to bring the tale to a climax:

> "The face," Maureen sobbed, clutching Douglas. . . .
> "Oh, God," Douglas shouted, "Barbara!" The car whipped about . . . and skidded into the road.
> A tunnel of trees sprang forth, into which it plunged. The figure ran alongside, skipping high.

As if this weren't enough, we get one more brilliant phrase—constituting our final sight of the thing:

> Ahead the tunnel of light dwindled: Barbara was gone. Only the last light of the car and, as it turned the corner, the shape which leapt easily onto the roof.

Hopping, skipping, prancing . . . All are deliberately innocuous words; so is "the shape which leapt easily onto the roof" (note the wonderful adverb), and the crack in the ceiling which "suddenly, with a horrid lethargy, detached itself from the plaster and fell on Peter's upturned face." The last is ostensibly an excerpt, the only one Campbell provides, from an apocryphal story by his creation, Errol Undercliffe. My only question is why, of all the possible lines to attribute to Undercliffe, he attributes one so characteristic of his own work ("with a horrid lethargy"—how perfect), and why, of all the stories in the book to bear Undercliffe's name, he has chosen "The Interloper"—a terrifying piece that, from catacombs to classrooms, bears the Campbell stamp in every line. It even reintroduces us to poor Sam Strutt.

Whatever Campbell's reasons for adopting this alter ego (it obviously isn't to write a kind of work alien to his own), both the story and the line are magnificent creations. I find the latter particularly memorable because it's precisely the sort of image that would "make" many a successful horror story—sometimes a good line is all that's really needed—and yet Campbell seems able to toss off such lines without half trying. (See, too, the marvelous twist in "The Second Staircase" as to the protagonist's sex, and how casually Campbell brings it off.) This easy facility, this feeling of "talent to spare," reminds me of the baseball star Stan Musial, who, when asked what he would do if he suddenly found himself in a batting slump, replied (after a long pause and much head-scratching), "Well, I can always hit to third." He meant that, even on the worst of days, he could always get on base. For any player of even normal ability, that would have been an impossible boast; for Musial it was a simple statement of fact. Campbell's ability seems just as extraordinary; judging from his recent work, he can always write scary. How many other young writers can say the same?

However, if we're going to honor Campbell—and that's what this essay is all about—it should be not so much for his style as his content. As his own short career demonstrates, he has changed the shape of the modern horror story; he has done for our own field what other young British writers are doing for science fiction. And for a onetime Lovecraft disciple to have done so is all the more impressive; it's as if E. E. Smith had suddenly begun producing self-referential literary experiments in the style of J. G. Ballard.

Best of all, he has made the horror story relevant (a word that, quite rightly, makes one wince). At last, in *Demons by Daylight*, we have a volume in which the hero is convincingly human, not a neurasthenic antiquarian or a gentleman of leisure or a mad scientist or an eccentric sculptor. We have, instead, a fellow who works in a boring office or library and who wishes he had time to read *The Golden Bough* but hasn't gotten around to it yet. He wishes, too, that he were more clever, so that he could impress the girls at the office; he'd willingly (and on occasion literally) stab his best friend in the back for a chance to snake his girlfriend. He desperately needs women, and longs for them; he also loathes, fears, and despises them. (From "The Second Staircase": "Women—he hated them, their soft helpless bodies, passively resisting, unattainable.") Like her male counterpart, the Campbell heroine spends a great deal of her time feeling lonely, wishing she looked as sexy as her flatmate, wondering how far she should let that new boy go with her, wondering if that fellow she met in the pub will call her like he said.

If such characters seem real and ordinary and (at times) embarrassingly easy to identify with, it's because in every story Campbell appears to have risen to a challenge; he's taken a dare, broken a rule, violated a taboo. When it comes to characters, this challenge may be unstated but implicit in the long horror tradition that one's protagonists must be exotic creatures without genitals or neuroses. When it comes to setting atmosphere, the challenge may be spelled out:

> No author . . . can conceive of the difficulty of writing a romance about a country where there is no shadow, no antiquity, no mystery, no picturesque and gloomy wrong, nor anything but a commonplace prosperity, in broad and simple daylight. . . . Romance and poetry, ivy, lichens, and wallflowers need ruin to make them grow.

So declares Hawthorne in *The Marble Faun,* and so declares Isaac Bashevis Singer in our own day:

> Even if demons do exist, they are not in New York. What would a demon do in New York? He could get run over by a car or tangle himself in a subway and never find his way out.
> —"Lost," *The New Yorker,* 23 June 1973

One might almost suspect Campbell has read such assertions—no daylight! no demons in the city!—and has dedicated his career to disproving them. *Demons by Daylight* is the triumphant result.

Slow

Ramsey Campbell isn't one to wait for the opening bell. Other writers hook you with their first lines, but Ramsey is more ruthless: He hooks you with the title.

"The Cellars" . . . "The Sentinels" . . . "The Scar" . . .

The names have, in their very terseness, an undertone of dread, the article serving—as it does in English pub signs (The Black Friar, The Green Man, The Chimes) and in the Tarot deck (The Hanged Man, The Tower, The Moon)—to impart a kind of sinister gravity, the suspicion that we're face to face with something ancient, archetypal, and inimical.

"The Puppets" . . . "The Dark Show" . . . "The Depths" . . .

The more familiar we become with Campbell's vision, the more this suspicion grows. He teaches us that malevolence lurks in the simplest words.

"The Chimney" . . . "The Old Horns" . . . "The Lost" . . .

Even before we've read a single line, we're sure "The Urge" will prove to be a dark one; we sense, from the title alone, that we'd be foolish to befriend "The Companion." And are we offered a tale called "The Change"? Not likely a change for the better!

Beyond these ominously suggestive creations—and such quintessential Ramsicampbellianisms as "The Whining," "The Tugging," and "The Sneering"—come the everyday expressions used, à la EC comics, for their ghoulish irony: "Call First" . . . "Reply

---

Introduction to *Slow* by Ramsey Campbell (Round Top, NY: Footsteps Press, 1986).

Guaranteed" . . . "Wrapped Up" . . . "In the Bag" (which graphically depicts what your mother always warned you would happen if you played with plastic bags) . . . "Heading Home" (in which a severed head does just that).

But perhaps the creepiest of all, reverberating like a cackle in the dark, are those rare titles that reduce a whole lifetime of menace into a single leering word: "Baby" . . . "Bait" . . . "Pet" . . . and now—*Slow*.

Wary readers would do well to remember that this word is not only an adjective; it is also a verb, at times a transitive one. Such a warning may seem needlessly cryptic, but I assure you, it's highly relevant to the story.

It is, as stories go, rather special, as befits its publication in this unusual form. (Allen Koszowski's illustrations seem particularly well-chosen, their clarity an excellent match for the precision of Campbell's prose.) *Slow* represents one of Campbell's few forays into science fiction, where the bleak, garbage-strewn landscape of some contemporary urban hell-hole is replaced by a cozy—yet equally bleak, and equally hellish—cottage-cum-cage on a far-off planet, ruled by aliens so mysterious that they're rarely seen outside parentheses (an ingenious touch), and about whose intentions, like God's, you must draw your own conclusions.

But the story has another distinction; it contains an element seldom found in Campbell's work.

Back in 1974, in an admiring essay called "Ramsey Campbell: An Appreciation," I argued that "Campbell reigns supreme in the field today," but added: "Yet horror per se can be, in the end, somewhat limiting; and now that he has mastered it, one might hope for an occasional ray of light to alleviate the gloom. . . . An occasional vision of something behind a glass of stout and a secretary's knickers might add a needed dimension to the world Campbell has created."

Six years later, taking up where I'd left off, Jack Sullivan noted that "the light" was still missing from Ramsey's work. "If anything," he said, "Campbell's recent fiction is darker than ever, an uninterrupted nightmare in which the setting, a grey and grubby modern world, is as frightening as the demonic force that assaults it." He concluded that, for those of us "who have been waiting half a decade for that elusive ray of light, Campbell seems perfectly willing to leave them grumbling and groping in the dark."

Well, dear friends, grumble no more! The story that follows, written in 1975 but unpublished till now, does indeed contain a ray of light, a dash of hope amid the gloom. It is, to be sure, a pretty fragile thing—the most fleeting of hopes, the feeblest of lights—but it is there, flickering dimly, locked within the hero's mind.

Its presence is, I think, a welcome one, for it demonstrates a relatively little-known facet of Ramsey Campbell's talent—a talent as tenacious and unpredictable as the monster you're about to meet.

An Afternoon with Aickman

Robert Aickman's voice spoke softly from my tape recorder, reading his supernatural tale "Larger Than Oneself." Chris Barker—the man behind this magazine—had sent me the tape in an effort to revive my memory of an afternoon I'd spent with Aickman more than a quarter century ago, accompanied by my friend Kathleen Murray.

I wish I could say that hearing the tape's refined, cultured tones brought back a flood of recollection, but in truth I didn't recognize the voice. Whether in imagination or memory, the Aickman I'd been recalling for twenty-seven years had sounded graver and more somber. But perhaps I'd just been matching a voice to the personality I remembered: sensitive and rather sad; lonely; an air of having known suffering. When, a few years after meeting him, I learned that he had cancer (stomach cancer, I believe), it seemed almost fitting, in an awful unsurprising way; he seemed, somehow, a doomed soul.

That, at least, was the quality he projected, but it was by no means an unattractive one. There was something very touching about Aickman, something that made one worry about him, and in fact he's among the few instances I can recall of an author whose work I liked and appreciated more after having met him; usually it's

---

Originally published in the British magazine *Weirdly Supernatural* (Besthorpe, UK: Haunted River, Winter 2001–02); reprinted in *Masters of the Weird Tale: Robert Aickman* (Lakewood, CO: Centipede Press, 2018).

quite the reverse. He seemed someone who cared earnestly, deeply, even painfully about everything he wrote, and it's impossible now to read him without that sense of the man behind the words.

It was Kirby McCauley, my friend and agent, who first told me about Aickman, and who later, from afar, introduced us. Along with Ramsey Campbell and Frank Belknap Long, Aickman was one of his most celebrated clients, and Kirby revered him greatly. I still have Kirby's letter of July 17, 1973, from Minneapolis, where he was then living, in which he enclosed a copy of a note to him from Aickman containing some words of praise for my first published story.

"Dear Ted," Kirby wrote, "A very quick one, chiefly to pass along this pleasant opinion by Robert Aickman. As I believe I've remarked before, Aickman seems to me the finest living author of strange stories, and one in the front rank for any period and all periods. Do you know his work? If not, I'll be happy to send you a couple of books as well as his fine articles on the supernatural. His outlook and view of potential for the weird tale is extremely discriminating, and you must consider it high praise indeed to gain his notice. . . .

"I say that because not only is he a very perceptive critic but chiefly because he is strongly into the very direction in supernatural fiction you are. He believes that the supernatural is a quality *in* real life and not outside it. His view of the genre, which he prefers to call ghost stories because the other names displease him, is partly as follows: 'The essential quality of the ghost story is that it gives satisfying form to the unanswerable; to thoughts and feelings, even experiences, which are common to all imaginative people, but which cannot be rendered down scientifically into "nothing but" something else. . . . Ghost stories should be stories concerned not with appearance and consistency, but with the spirit behind appearance, the void behind the face of order. Ghost stories inquire and hint, waver and dissemble, startle and astonish. They are a last refuge from the universal, affirmative shout.'"

To this moving and elegantly phrased credo, which I believe appeared in the introduction to one of the Fontana anthologies Aickman edited, let me add the final paragraph from the note of his that Kirby enclosed. It, too, seems pure Aickman:

"I continue to be haunted by noise. I have now been haunted

for about a year and a half—as well as by divers other problems, but noise is by far the worst. Currently, it is the noise made by a telephone exchange, which simply was not working when I viewed the premises in January, but which now works by day and by night, and which is going to drive me out, despite many great advantages of the place, so that the situation is conflictual. I simply do not produce enough at the best to base my life *entirely* on the quest for relative silence; and I suspect that where the relative silence might be found, inspiration—for me—would be lacking."

The figure those words conjured up—a tortured individual, or certainly, at least, an unhappy one, as acutely sensitive to noise as Roderick Usher—fascinated and somewhat intimidated me; and I gathered from subsequent conversations with Kirby that this obsession of Aickman's was all too real. His exquisitely written short stories, which I dutifully proceeded to read, in part because I was flattered by his attention, were also a little daunting; in self-protection one might call them "challenging," but in fact most were so subtle they left me baffled.

Kirby was eager for me to meet Aickman, and in September of the following year, when I set off on a six-week trip to England, he gave me Aickman's number in London and urged me to contact him; he wrote Aickman as well and told him I'd be coming. On the assumption, which proved correct, that a youthful American visitor might be decidedly more welcome if accompanied by an attractive young woman, I waited for Kathy to join me—she arrived in London around ten days after I did—before phoning Aickman and nervously introducing myself. "Oh, yes," he said. "You'd like to see me." He would be gone, he told me, until October 4. "Hold on a moment, I'll get my diary."

The quiet, matter-of-fact way he declared that I wanted to see him must have amused me, because I find it recorded in my notebook along with the date, 9/25/74. And that is the only blessed thing I have recorded from that time; I must have thought everything else would be so indelible that I'd never forget it.

I do remember that, on whatever October afternoon it was that we arranged to meet, Kathy and I waited near the tube stop and Aickman came to get us, convinced that that would be easier than our trying to find his flat. An older man with dark wavy hair, glasses, and a trench coat strode up and looked us over. "You're Klein?" he asked simply. I said I was, and after a few awkward greetings we proceeded to follow him to his home.

One final, slightly jarring image remains in memory: When Aickman smiled, he revealed a nearly black front tooth. Kathy, who'd gone to school in London, would later remind me that the English were famous for their terrible teeth. (I've heard people blame it on all those Cadbury's chocolate bars.) In America, no upper-middle-class person, as Aickman was, would dream of walking around that way.

Aickman's home was also a surprise. He lived in the Barbican, a gloomy grey cement complex in the City that reminded me of the blocky modular housing I'd seen at the Montreal world's fair. I'd expected that a man like him would want elegant old-fashioned surroundings with a bit of atmosphere, not the cold, somewhat institutional modernity of the flat in which we found ourselves.

And cold it certainly was—another reminder that I was among the English, noted throughout the world for their love of freezing houses. (Later, when Kathy and I were the guests of Ramsey Campbell in Liverpool, he proved to be precisely the opposite of Aickman; notwithstanding a repressive childhood and the grisliness of his fiction, he was funny, life-embracing, almost Rabelaisian—except in one memorable respect: His house was so chilly that Kathy and I slept in our overcoats.) For some reason I had worn, on the day I visited Aickman, a cheap imitation-leather jacket, which may have looked as déclassé to him as his dentition did to me; nonetheless, I kept it on, and Kathy kept her coat on.

We sat and talked for around three hours in his cold, rather bare living room. Of our conversation I remember, sadly, very little, except that both Kathy and I found him extraordinarily charming, interesting, and wise. I recall that he spoke of a longtime fascination with haunted houses, and of a British researcher who'd written extensively on the subject. He told us that he himself had had a ghostly experience in this very flat: One day he'd been sitting alone and had distinctly heard a voice—a woman's, I think—speak his first name. No, he assured us, there was no chance that it had come from another flat; the walls were too thick. Indeed, it was these thick concrete walls, and the silence they afforded, that had drawn him to the place. (I assume, but am not certain, that this was not the house he'd complained about a year earlier to Kirby. My guess is that he'd moved out of that, as he'd vowed.)

Undoubtedly we talked about writers and the state of the weird tale, but the only particular I recall is his enthusiasm for a short story called "Levitation," by Joseph Payne Brennan, which he'd included in one of his Fontana anthologies. He was disappointed that neither Kathy nor I was familiar with it at the time, and he proceeded to recount it with great delight. It's about a traveling carnival whose mesmerist, at an outdoor show one evening, invites an unruly volunteer from the audience to lie down on the stage, whereupon he puts the subject in a trance and causes him to rise slowly into the air. Suddenly the mesmerist drops dead of a heart attack, and as the horrified crowd watches, the sleeping man continues floating upward till he's out of sight. Aickman's admiration for this story was another surprise; it's a memorably clever little yarn, but—aside from the absence of violence—it's hard to imagine anything more unlike the sort of story Aickman himself produced.

A few years later, incidentally, when accompanying Kirby on a trip to New Haven, Connecticut, I had the chance to meet Brennan. He turned out to be a small, diffident man with a rueful, self-deprecating quality all his own, but he did wear, in common with Aickman, a certain air of melancholy.

One source of Aickman's melancholy was clearly the modern world. (He'd closed a letter to Kirby with the postscript, "I think that television and the automobile and the flying machine are all worse dangers to man than the atomic bomb!") That afternoon with Kathy and me, he seemed especially pained about England; it was now an impoverished nation whose great days were behind it. Once, he told us, foreigners had treated English travelers with respect. Today things were different. "They laugh at us!" he said, bitter and amazed.

I recall that he talked a good deal, with both fondness and sadness, of Elizabeth Jane Howard, whom he'd tutored in writing ghost stories and with whom, in the end, he'd produced the now-legendary collection *We Are for the Dark,* in which their individual contributions are not identified as to author. (Kathy and I both admired her highly atmospheric story "Three Miles Up," based on a voyage she had taken with Aickman when he was active in the Inland Waterways Association, a society he'd helped found to preserve Britain's canals.) She was now the wife of Kingsley Amis. From everything Aickman said, it was apparent that he'd been in love with her and still missed her.

Kirby, I believe, had mentioned something about a long-ago divorce in Aickman's background. At any rate, when I saw him, he seemed, as I've said, a lonely man. I could tell he was quite charmed by Kathy, a slim, pretty blonde who was formidably well-read, especially in English history and literature. Later he would fall in love with, or certainly develop a crush on, Leslie Gardner, another attractive young American woman, who moved to London and in the end became his literary agent and close friend. He may well have felt similarly toward Kirby's sister, Kay. For his part, I think Aickman inspired, in women, real devotion and affection; he seems to have been someone they were touched by, felt sorry for, and perhaps even wanted to mother. Yet for some reason, at least from what I know of him, there does not seem to have been a satisfying relationship in the latter years of his life.

As evening approached, Aickman more than once suggested going out for dinner. I'm not sure why we didn't take him up on it; it seems unlikely there'd have been anywhere else we had to be. Did I worry he was merely being polite and that we'd imposed on him long enough? Perhaps I thought our encounter had gone so agreeably that it would be foolish to press our luck. (Now I know it's foolish to have said goodbye so soon.)

Aickman had never been to America, and I remember that, during our conversation, Kathy and I were intent on luring him here. Though he seemed somewhat skeptical—partly, I think, because of the expense—we urged him to come to New York; and after leaving his flat, when we were alone but still under his spell, she and I talked excitedly about what we could do to convince him. I believe Aickman had mentioned something about having lectured, at one time or another, on his Inland Waterways project and also, perhaps, on ghosts and the supernatural; at any rate, recalling celebrity lecturers who'd spoken at my college, I was sure that someone as erudite as he was could make money in the U.S. lecturing on ghosts. I actually contacted one or two lecture bureaus on his behalf when I got home, and was disappointed to find no interest. I corresponded sporadically with him for a few years, then kept in indirect contact with him through Kirby and Leslie. He died in early 1981, aged sixty-six. Whenever I think of him, it's with regret at never having seen him again, but with gratitude at having shared, at least, those few hours.

A Haunted House

I met Donald Wandrei only once, on a chilly January afternoon in 1979. He was, even then, something of a legendary figure, reclusive, eccentric, and notoriously difficult; but while I remember how privileged I felt at having spent several hours in his company, my memories of our meeting are as sketchy as the notes I made the next day in my diary.

My visit, I recall, was made under false pretenses. I'd been traveling through the Midwest with my friend and agent, Kirby McCauley, and before returning home we had stopped for a few days in Kirby's native Minneapolis. He and Wandrei had been close once, back in the days when Kirby was a struggling young agent still dreaming of coming to New York—I gather, in fact, that Wandrei had been almost, at times, a second father to him—but relations had soured as Kirby had grown more successful and as Wandrei's longstanding feud with Arkham House, the company he'd helped found, consumed more and more of his time, money, and energies. Though I'm not clear about the legal issues involved, I'm under the impression that Wandrei's dispute went far beyond the publishing house's balance sheet; it was as if, like some betrayed lover, he was doing battle with August Derleth's ghost. Anyone with any connection to the company was suspect, and he'd long since added Kirby, who'd begun to act as Arkham House's agent, to his increasingly crowded enemies list. He was particularly in-

---

From *Studies in Weird Fiction 3* (Fall 1988); reprinted in *Conversations with the Weird Tales Circle* (Lakewood, CO: Centipede Press, 2009).

censed by the annual World Fantasy Convention, largely a brainchild of Kirby's, and each year's festivities were the occasion for a long, loony diatribe filled with puns, innuendos, and personal abuse, copies of which were mailed to (I assume) dozens of figures in the fantasy field. As the years passed, I received more than my share of these bizarre manifestos; I'm rather glad I was never mentioned in any of them.

Wandrei knew I was a client of Kirby's—it's clear he knew a great deal about what went on in the outside world, though perhaps not as much as he imagined—but he didn't know I'd come to Minneapolis with Kirby, or else I doubt he'd have admitted me to his home. I told him, when I telephoned, that I'd come to town on business with my father, and that, having just finished his novel *The Web of Easter Island*, I was eager to meet him. (This much, at least, was true, although in fact I'd found the book a disappointment.) Sounding, on the phone, surprisingly cordial, he invited me to visit him at two the following afternoon.

His house was in St. Paul, on a wide, fairly prosperous-looking street. I recall the street, the grey sky, and my concern about the January weather: I'd been told that here in Minnesota, people had been known to freeze to death while waiting for a bus, and I had visions of the same happening to me when, as planned, I would leave Wandrei's house and telephone Kirby from some street-corner booth to come and pick me up.

Wandrei met me at the back door. He looked, I thought, a bit like Raymond Massey—a tall, gaunt, angular old man whose grey hair needed combing. I recall that the house seemed large and, from inside, large and gloomy, an authentic haunted house, perpetually in shadow, with overflowing ashtrays, furniture hidden by drop cloths and dust, and shades that looked as if they hadn't been drawn for the last thirty years. I recall an overflowing basket of wrinkled peaches in the kitchen, and teetering piles of papers and books throughout the living room and hall (to confuse potential burglars, he explained). But as for our conversation itself, despite the three hours or so we spent together, I remember very little.

Perhaps that's because it was so trivial. Several weeks earlier, the Lovecraft world—a grandiose term for what must have amounted to thirty or forty people, at the most—had been rocked by a minor scandal: A flyer had been mailed out from Warwick, Rhode Island, purporting to come from Marc Michaud's Necronomicon Press and advertising, if memory serves, a collected edition of Donald Wandrei's correspondence with Lovecraft. I'd sent for a copy myself. The offer turned out to be a hoax, perpetrated by parties unknown for reasons unknown—whether to embarrass Michaud or Wandrei more, it's hard to say. No such book existed; none had ever been contemplated. But the prank appeared to weigh heavily on Wandrei's mind, feeding an already active paranoia, and judging from our conversation, he must have spent days, or even weeks, wrestling with the problem of who the culprit was.

Here, let me fall back on my few disordered notes. I described Wandrei as

> periodically throwing back his head and screeching, crowing, with triumphant laughter, talking about things "falling into place," how he was "indebted" to me for giving him info on things I don't even suspect. . . . God! What a waste of a good mind! He believes Kirby was "a jewelry salesman" when he first came to NYC, that Kirby's business associate John Troll is a myth ("No one could have a name like *that!*"), and that Tom Collins was behind the fake Necronomicon Press flyer; it's clear, he says, that Collins hates Marc, proven by Tom's lawsuit against him. (Yet he ruled out Randy Everts for the same reason. Though he regards Everts as "vile" and "unscrupulous," Everts has lawsuits pending and "too much to lose.") Likewise, he thinks it had to be someone as close to Rhode Island as Collins, who could take a bus up on the weekend, whereas it's too costly for Everts to fly. Why, I asked, didn't the perpetrator simply have a *friend* mail the stuff? "It's too risky," said Wandrei; don't spread guilt. . . . Yet to explain why one of the "Warwick, R.I." return addresses appeared as "N.J.," Wandrei figured someone who lives in Jersey must have typed it. I said, "But Tom's a New Yorker." "Yes," he said, "but he wouldn't have wanted to use his own typewriter. He'd have the typing done by an accomplice!"

Regret that, on departing, I left a pack of Winchesters and a Harvey's Chelsea Restaurant matchbook; with that address, he'll probably conclude I'm in league with Tom.

Before leaving, I asked him to autograph *The Web of Easter Island,* which I'd brought with me. He did so graciously ("For Ted Klein—with pleasure and the hope of a happy return"). "There," he said with evident satisfaction as he handed it back. "This is going to be an extremely valuable item to collectors in the future."

I hope he's right; but perhaps a more fitting epitaph came from Carl Jacobi, another Minneapolis friend and client of Kirby's, whom we visited the next day. He was old and ailing, horribly debilitated by a stroke and nearly voiceless, living in a small apartment with *Weird Tales* illustrations on the wall and a photo of himself as a dashing young author in a trench coat and hat. As he spoke with us, he held a handkerchief in one hand and kept dabbing at his lips. Relations between him and Wandrei, he said, had ended years ago; he, too, was on the man's enemies list. I told him about my visit of the previous afternoon. He nodded and observed, in a voice just above a whisper, "That's what comes of living alone."

Frank Belknap Long

Here's a good deed I'm rather proud of, a letter of October 10, 1993, on behalf of Peter Cannon and myself, addressed to Eric Pace, a *New York Times* reporter connected to the paper's obituary department. I had gotten to know him slightly while working part-time at a private club where he was a member.

* * *

Dear Eric,

You may recall, some years back, when you were a much-valued member of the Century's Committee on Memorials, that I served as its staff secretary. . . .

But this isn't a Century matter. I'm writing to you because, as a longtime reader of supernatural horror, it recently occurred to me (and to several friends in the field) that one of its most venerable authors, Frank Belknap Long, is probably close to death—he'll be 91 next spring—and that his passing is unlikely to be noted in the *Times*.

Though his writing career spans literally 60 years and dozens of books (some under pseudonyms), Long remains largely unknown outside the world of genre fiction. And even within it, his own work isn't the main thing that distinguishes him; it's that he is the last surviving friend of the legendary H. P. Lovecraft, and thus the final member of the "Lovecraft Circle" that flourished in New York in the '20s and, via the mail, into the '30s.

Frank Long is, today, a tiny, white-haired man with thick glasses and a wispy little goatee. Few in the field have had much contact with him lately—I haven't seen him myself in several years—in part because his mind is beginning to go, in part because his wheelchair-bound wife, Lyda, can be extremely "difficult," and in part because the Longs no longer have a telephone. (Lyda has a tendency to run up enormous phone bills, and their phone was disconnected several times in the past.) According to Kirby McCauley, Long's literary agent, Frank has been in and out of St. Vincent's Hospital in recent years; but he and Lyda can still be found at their old 421 West 21st Street address.

I don't know whether you have anything on Long in your files; for all I know, you may not particularly *want* anything. But I'm sending you the enclosed biographical material—certainly more than you'll ever need—in the hope that, when he dies, you'll consider giving his passing some mention.

Thanks.

* * *

When Frank died, less than three months later, the *Times* gave him a gratifyingly lengthy obituary at the top of the page, complete with photo.

Dr. Van Helsing's Handy Guide to Ghost Stories

> Of all the common and familiar subjects of conversation . . . there is none so ready to hand, nor so unusual, as that of visions of Spirits, and whether what is said of them is true. It is the topic that people most readily discuss and on which they linger the longest because of the abundance of examples, the subject being fine and pleasing and the discussion the least tedious that can be found.
>
> —Pierre le Loyer, *Livres des Spectres*

M. le Loyer may have been a trifle too enthusiastic—he was writing in 1586—but there's truth in what he said. Ghosts are indeed a fine and pleasing subject, in fiction as well as in life, and in the pages that follow I'll do my best to introduce you to a few, as well as to the men and women who've written about them.

For writers, as you'll discover, the ghost story has always had a singular appeal. It offers them a chance to sport with major issues, from morality to mortality, while raising a shudder or two. It also offers them, in a field whose critical standards are by no means daunting, a shot at literary distinction of the more enduring sort.

This series of articles appeared in the August, September, October, and November 1981 issues of *Twilight Zone* magazine under the byline "Kurt Van Helsing." It should be noted that their primary purpose was a pretty humble one, to add some nonfiction material to the magazine.

As for its appeal to readers, we shall talk of that later. For now, lest critics quibble, we'll begin this overview in time-honored academic fashion by defining our terms—which isn't quite as simple as it sounds.

What, exactly, is a ghost story? In the narrowest sense, it's a tale in which a disembodied spirit returns from the dead, usually to perform some familiar task:

- haunting a particular spot (such as the site of its unconsecrated burial or the house in which it met a violent death) or a particular person (one who has violated its grave, perhaps, or defied an ancient curse);
- visiting retribution upon its murderer, or upon the murderer's family or descendants;
- guarding a tomb or treasure (or, conversely, leading others to it);
- warning the living of impending good fortune or catastrophe;
- doing penance for crimes committed in life.

Such activities are traditionally confined to the nighttime, during which the ghost may make its presence known in any of a variety of ways:

- by becoming visible (in its former earthly shape, or as a corpse, a sheeted figure, even a severed limb);
- by characteristic sounds or speech (anything from echoing footfalls and spectral howls to whole pages of dialogue);
- by animating physical objects such as doors, tables, daggers, and the like;
- by altering the atmosphere around it, whether literally (chilling a room, for example) or spiritually (chilling the blood).

That, anyway, is a strict definition of the form. In truth, however, the "ghost story" as we know it need not—and usually does not—contain anything resembling a ghost. In common usage, the term has come to stand for any tale in which some supernatural force impinges on the world of mortal men.

Origins of the Ghost Story

All the elements of the classic ghost story can be found as far back as the first century, when Pliny the Younger describes a haunted house in Athens occupied by the specter of an emaciated old man, complete with long beard, bristling hair, and clanking chains. After most of its residents have succumbed to disease brought on by sleeplessness and terror, the house is left deserted until an intrepid philosopher named Athenodorus agrees to spend the night there. Some time after darkness the specter appears; beckoning the man to follow, it leads him to a spot in the courtyard outside. "Human bones were found buried there," writes Pliny, "and bound in chains. Time and the earth had moldered away the flesh, and only the skeleton remained. It was publicly buried; and after the rites of sepulcher, the house was no longer haunted."

Yet the ghost story is in fact far older than this. Ghosts appear in the literature of ancient Greece (as in Homer's *Odyssey*), Egypt (in *The Book of the Dead*), China (in the *Analects* of Confucius), Babylon (in the Gilgamesh epic), and Assyria (in which elaborate rituals guarded the home from roving ghosts who peered through windows), as well as in the Old Testament and the Apocrypha. (1 Samuel 28 describes how the Witch of Endor conjures up the apparition of a dead prophet; Ecclesiasticus 39 warns the faithful, "There are spirits that are created for vengeance, and in their fury they lay on grievous torments.")

In fact, spirits of the dead are central to the folk myths of virtually all primitive cultures, and there is good reason to believe that the ghost story is as old as mankind itself. "Who told the first ghost story?" asked Montague Summers, the noted Catholic authority on the supernatural. "Some son of Adam, I suppose, far back in dimmest antiquity, housed in a cave, as he looked up at the vast endless spaces of heaven powdered with nightly stars, as he wondered at the mysterious darkness, the depths of shadow, the remoteness of shapes familiar by day but which took on strange forms at the approach of evening: marveled and told his children how he seemed to see the shadow of their grandsire who had gone from them so short a while, who had lain stark and motionless and cold. The old hunter had returned, yet he brought terror in his train, for now he had something of the night and the wind, of the great untrammeled forces of Nature with which man contended daily for his right to live. And his brood listened with awe; they trembled, they scarce knew why, and were afraid."

Fear—the very word *ghost* is rooted in it. "The derivatives," says the *Oxford English Dictionary,* "seem to point to a primary sense *to wound, tear, pull to pieces.*" Consider, too, some of its original pre-Teutonic associations: the Sanskrit word for *fury,* the Old Norse for *to rage,* the Persian for *ugly,* the Gothic for *to terrify.* Ghosts, in short, were humanity's fear made manifest—for "fear," as the late Harold C. Goddard noted, "is faith: it ultimately creates what at first it only imagined."

The fear took many forms. It was, from the start, a fear of nature, of all the dark, mysterious, and overwhelming forces with which early man was surrounded. Spirits, or *anima,* inhabited the trees, the rivers, the mountains, the thunder; jealous spirits, prone to anger and revenge. Animism is a fundamental assumption of all primitive cultures—nor is modern man a stranger to it, when the normal restrictions on his imagination are relaxed: "A house is never still in darkness to those who listen intently," the British playwright James M. Barrie once wrote. "There is a whispering in distant chambers, an unearthly hand presses the window, the latch rises. Ghosts were created when the first man woke in the night."

But he is also heir to a more specific fear: a fear of the human dead—which, in *The Golden Bough,* James Frazer termed "probably the most powerful force in the making of primitive religion." Often attached to slain enemies and departed ancestors, this fear is founded, in part, upon a sense of guilt—in the latter case, upon the survivor's traditional guilt at remaining alive (thus the phrase "the envious dead"), the ingrate's guilt at having failed to pay proper homage to the deceased, even the murderer's guilt at having "willed" another's death through half-buried feelings of rage or resentment. (Children, those primitive beings of our own world, often believe they have caused a sibling's death in this manner.) Significantly, ancient funeral rites were largely concerned with placating the dead (thus the admonition to "Rest in Peace"), and tombstones may have originally been a way of ensuring that they would not rise again.

But ghosts need not always punish: They may also trace their origins to humanity's more positive attitudes toward the dead. Like parental figures, the spirits can bestow rewards for good behavior; more important, they are expressions of our hope for personal immortality, and of our longing for departed loved ones. "Without death," Schopenhauer maintained, "there would be no philosophy, no poetry." Nor, indeed, would there be ghost stories.

According to Freud, the primitive *id* is unable to distinguish between fantasy and reality; its daytime cravings can thus be fulfilled each night in sleep. As we all learn in times of bereavement, the dead haunt our dreams—and the more recent our loss, the more powerful their hold. Hence Alexander Laing's assertion that "a ghost's visitations usually are confined to a brief period after the death of the body," and the claim, so common in ancient literature, that "the ghost came to me last night as I slept."

Yet not all apparitions need be born in dreams; current research hints that some people may also conjure them up during hypnosis. According to one recent report, even the most experienced hypnotists are unable to tell if a subject is in a genuine trance or if he's simply pretending—except for one curious difference: "When hypnotized subjects are told that a nonexistent friend is sitting in a nearby chair, most of them will enter into a convincing conversation with the empty air. So will the simulators, who almost invariably guess that this is what a real hypnotic subject would do. But about a third of the real hypnotic subjects will also report that their friend is looking slightly transparent—they can see the back of the chair right through his body. So far . . . no simulator has ever invented this detail on his own."

Lost in dreams, some men greet departed relatives; others, under the spell of hypnotic suggestion, chat with absent friends transparent as ghosts. But at the dawn of civilization mere *thinking* may have been enough to summon spirits—or so Princeton psychologist Julian Jaynes suggests. In his controversial study, *The Origin of Consciousness in the Breakdown of the Bicameral Mind* (1977), Jaynes theorizes that the various unspoken commands issuing from the right hemisphere of the human brain were, in ancient times, interpreted by the left half not as thoughts but as "voices" from outside—originally as the voices of dead ancestors, later as the voices of gods. Not until the first millennium B.C. did man learn to identify these commands as coming from within. Thus, if Jaynes's research is to be believed, a regard for ancestral ghosts may have been the genesis not only of religion but of consciousness itself.

History of the Ghost Story

Since ghosts are, as one observer has noted, "the true immortals," they easily survived the transformation of man's consciousness. Classic literature abounded in them; during the Middle Ages they received earnest scrutiny in many a monastic treatise, along with a host of goblins, gnomes, demons, familiars, incubi, and succubi. Their less solemn exploits were largely confined to unrecorded folk tales, but by the fourteenth century writers such as Boccaccio and Chaucer were chronicling them in poem and prose. Though dozens of learned discourses continued to appear, the ghost had at last entered the province of pure fiction.

With the publication of Horace Walpole's *Castle of Otranto* in 1764, the supernatural found its own literary form: the gothic novel, characterized by somber atmosphere, melodramatic plot, and the medieval architecture of its setting. Of course, Walpole's imagination may have been nurtured by many earlier works: The *Arabian Nights,* for example, were rich in magic and colorful incident. (Compiled by fifteenth-century Moslem scholars but based upon Near Eastern, Indian, and Oriental folk tales dating back literally thousands of years, they had been translated into French as early as 1704 and—in the words of mythologist Joseph Campbell—"struck Europe with an impact that initiated a new era of Occidental romance.") There were, as well, early Continental sources equally exotic; in fact, *Otranto* itself was originally purported to have been translated from the Italian of a twelfth-century Neapolitan scribe, one "Onuphrio Muralto"—a play on the author's own name.

But if Walpole had set out to re-create a dark medieval romance, the result surpassed mere pastiche; though now quite dated, his book proved the inspiration for an entire school of fiction, and

E. F. Bleiler suggests that it may well be "one of the half-dozen historically most important novels in English." In his remarkable essay "Supernatural Horror in Literature" (1927), the late Howard Phillips Lovecraft, himself perhaps America's greatest exponent of the terror tale, enumerated *Otranto*'s most characteristic elements:

> First of all . . . the Gothic castle, with its awesome antiquity, vast distances and ramblings, deserted or ruined wings, damp corridors, unwholesome hidden catacombs, and galaxy of ghosts and appalling legends. . . . The tyrannical and malevolent nobleman as villain; the saintly, long-persecuted, and generally insipid heroine who undergoes the major terrors and serves as a point of view and focus for the reader's sympathies; the valorous and immaculate hero, always of high birth but often in humble disguise; the convention of high-sounding foreign names, mostly Italian, for the characters; and the infinite array of stage properties which includes strange lights, damp trap-doors, extinguished lamps, mouldy hidden manuscripts, creaking hinges, shaking arras, and the like. All this paraphernalia reappears with amusing sameness, yet sometimes with tremendous effect, throughout the history of the Gothic novel; and is by no means extinct even today, though subtler technique now forces it to assume a less naive and obvious form. An harmonious milieu for a new school had been found, and the writing world was not slow to grasp the opportunity.

Aside from Clara Reeve, whose *Old English Baron* (1777) used many of the same plot devices—a disinherited nobleman and his father's helpful ghost, archetypes that predated *Hamlet*—Walpole's first major disciple was Ann Radcliffe, best known for *The Mysteries of Udolpho* (1794), a romantic thriller about kidnapping and banditry in an Apennine castle. Oddly enough, though an accomplished stylist, Radcliffe chose to violate one of the primary canons of supernatural fantasy. "However improbable the happenings in a detective story," wrote British novelist L. P. Hartley, "they can and must be explained in terms that satisfy the reason. But in a ghost story, where natural laws are dispensed with, the whole point is that the happenings cannot be so explained. A ghost story that is capable of a rational explanation is as much an anomaly as a detective story that isn't." Or as Arthur Reeve put it in a 1919 essay, "The detective's case is solved at the end. But even at the end of a ghost story, the underlying mystery remains." This is a key to the literature's eternal appeal—that ghosts embody, in Reeve's words, "the very quintessence of mystery"—and even critics of the day objected when Radcliffe's apparitions, save in the posthumously published *Gaston de Blondeville* (1826), invariably turned out to be masqueraders, errant nuns, or magic lantern slides.

Readers who craved "rational explanations" of this sort could always turn to an anonymous book called *Ghost Stories; Collected with a Particular View to Counteract the Vulgar Belief in Ghosts and Apparitions* (1846—Summers traces this to 1823), in which every one of the twenty phantoms described turns out to be a fraud. "What is a ghost?" asks the introduction.

> If visible, it must be matter . . . substantial flesh and blood and bones. . . . If it is not matter, it can only exist in the imagination of the holder, and must therefore be classed with the multifarious phantoms that haunt the sick man's couch in delirium. . . . Is it nude? Oh no! Oh shocking! This is contrary to all the rules. It always appears dressed. If the man has been murdered, it appears in the very clothes he was murdered in, all bloody, with a pale, murdered-looking face, and a ghastly wound in the breast, head, stomach, back or abdominal region, as the case may be; but always in decent clothes. If the person died quietly a natural death, in bed, then the ghost is generally clad in long white robes, or a shroud; but still properly dressed. So then, we have the ghost of the clothes also—the ghost of the coat and unmentionables—the ghost of the cocked hat and wig. How is this?

As if in anticipation of this hard-headed school, gothic novelist T. J. Horsley Curties, in the preface to his *Ethelwina, or The House of Fitz-Auburne* (1799), pointed out: "The Author of this Work . . . in one circumstance . . . has stepped beyond the modern writers of Romance, by introducing a *Real Ghost*."

Real ghosts also make their appearance in two other famous gothics: Matthew Gregory Lewis's *The Monk* (1796), in which the lustful Brother Ambrosio enjoys some pleasantly prurient delights before he's finally dispatched by a demon; and the Reverend Charles Robert Maturin's *Melmoth the Wanderer* (1820), a long, highly digressive work about a pact with the devil, filled with excruciating scenes of torture, madness, and cannibalism amid the dungeons of the Spanish Inquisition, and complicated by narratives within narratives within narratives within narratives.

Many sources list Mary Shelley's *Frankenstein* (1818) as another of the major gothics. But for all its heavy German trappings (and heavy allegorical content), it might more reasonably be seen as an early form of science fiction, in that its controlling force is Science. In true fantasy, the controlling force is Magic—thus distinguishing Mrs. Shelley's work from two well-known vampire novels, Dr. John W. Polidori's *The Vampyre* (1819) and Bram Stoker's *Dracula* (1897), both of them fantasies—not SF—in that they deal with supernatural, rather than natural, beings. (The former, coincidentally, was started the same night as *Frankenstein,* in what proved a remarkably fruitful horror-writing competition.)

Perhaps because of its thinly disguised sexual content, vampire literature found a ready audience in nineteenth-century England, but the Victorians were also enthusiastic devotees of the traditional ghost tale, and these were a staple of popular journals such as *Blackwood's* and Charles Dickens's *All the Year Round.* Robert Louis Stevenson referred to them as "crawlers," presumably because they were designed to make one's skin crawl. "In the magazine ghost stories," the Society for Psychical Research noted in its 1884 *Report of the Committee on Haunted Houses,* "the ghost is a fearsome being, dressed in a sweeping sheet and shroud, carrying a lighted candle, and speaking in dreadful words from fleshless lips. It enters at the stroke of midnight, through the sliding panel, just by the bloodstain on the floor. . . . Or it may be only a clanking of chains, a tread as of armed men heard whilst the candles burn blue and the dogs howl."

Today, with all their lurid melodrama, many of these tales seem hopelessly crude; Edward Bulwer-Lytton's celebrated "Haunted and the Haunters," for example, long a favorite of the anthologists, is practically unreadable. Others, often written by and for women, now seem as insipidly sentimental as the romantic novelist described in a 1931 sketch by Walter de la Mare. ("Mrs. Florence Barclay, the author of

The Rosary, is said to have returned thanks to Heaven that she had never admitted to the hospitality of her fiction any character whom she would not have welcomed to the Vicarage and to afternoon tea.") The title of one collection, *Ghost Stories and Presentiments* (1888)—to which A. Conan Doyle contributed several unsigned tales—suggests one of the problems: Thanks, perhaps, to the family audiences for which they were intended, as well as to the prevailing worship of technology, many Victorian ghost stories display an excessive concern with pseudoscientific psychic paraphernalia, while the ghosts themselves are all too occupied with missions of mercy.

Such benevolence is—at least from the literary point of view—a mistake; "in fiction," says Summers, "the good and kindly ghost has little or no place." Just as A. A. Milne maintained that the proper detective novel required not merely a jewel theft or forgery but outright murder, Henry James observed that "good ghosts . . . make poor subjects," and the English supernatural writer M. R. James (no relation) warned that "amiable and helpful apparitions" were better left to fairy tales; he preferred his ghosts to be "malevolent or odious." But for all their bloody trappings, many Victorian ghosts bore an unsettling resemblance to godmothers, or else emerged as harmless spirits more tormented than tormenting.

Some exceptions to this rule can be found in the work of Irish writer Joseph Sheridan Le Fanu, author of some thirty gruesomely memorable ghost stories, as well as the classic mystery novel *Uncle Silas* (1864). Conventional morality appears to play little part in his shorter fiction: In tales such as "Green Tea," "The Familiar," and "Schalken the Painter," innocent parties tend to suffer quite ghastly fates—and so much the worse for readers who've identified with them.

Unpleasant but undeniably effective, Le Fanu was esteemed as "the Master" by a later writer whose work is at once more comforting and more chilling: the aforementioned Montague Rhodes James, provost of King's College, Cambridge, and later of Eton, who, solely for the fireside amusement of his friends and students, produced some of the finest ghost stories in the English language. The earliest were published in 1904 as *Ghost Stories of an Antiquary;* three slim volumes followed. Typically, many of the most successful stories concern not "ghosts" per se but reanimated corpses ("The

Mezzotint," "The Haunted Dolls' House," "Martin's Close"), demons of various persuasions ("Count Magnus," "Casting the Runes," "The Treasure of Abbot Thomas"), monstrous spiders ("The Ash-Tree"), vampires ("An Episode of Cathedral History"), and even a malevolent hotel room ("No. 13").

Himself an authority on church history and medieval manuscripts, James drew upon this knowledge in his fiction. "The ghost story," he wrote, "is a slightly old-fashioned form; it needs some deliberateness in the telling; we listen to it the more readily if the narrator poses as elderly, or throws back his experiences to 'some thirty years ago.'"

The tales themselves often concern malign beings from even further in the past, stirred back to life by the researches of some bumbling antiquarian. Their atmosphere is scholarly, stuffy, and distinctly High Church, their time gentle and urbane; for all the terrors they may provoke in passing, in the end they impart a feeling of cozy security. In his study *Elegant Nightmares: The English Ghost Story from Le Fanu to Blackwood* (1978), Jack Sullivan traces this "antiquarian" tradition through the work of later English writers (often, like James, associated with Cambridge), including R. H. Malden, T. G. Jackson, E. G. Swain, A.N.L. Munby, L.T.C. Rolt, W. F. Harvey, and, to a lesser extent, H. Russell Wakefield and L. P. Hartley.

In contrast to this initialed and often obscure crew, Sullivan points to a second great supernatural tradition shaped by "transcendental" writers such as Arthur Machen, Algernon Blackwood, Walter de la Mare, E. F. Benson, and, to a degree, Oliver Onions, A. E. Coppard, and Lord Dunsany. Though their work is disparate in tone and technique—de la Mare ("A:B:O," "Seaton's Aunt," "The Riddle," "The Tree") is the subtlest, Dunsany ("The Wonderful Window," "The Death of Pan," "A Shop in Go-by Street") the most whimsical, Onions ("The Rope in the Rafters," "The Beckoning Fair One") the most psychologically insightful, Coppard ("The Bogey Man," "Ahoy, Sailor Boy," "Arabesque the Mouse") the most cynical, Blackwood ("The Willows," "The Wendigo," "The Camp of the Dog") the best at evoking the forces of nature, and Machen ("Change," "Out of the Picture," "Novel of the Black Seal," "The Great God Pan") at once the most lyrical and the most consistently terrifying—all these writers share a certain mystical outlook, a conviction that the supernatural world exists around us and within us, at this very moment, and that to experience it, one need only "rend the veil," whether through madness, drugs, trauma, magical or poetic incantation, genetic predisposition, or the influence of some special person or place. At its best (as in Machen's "The White People" and its earlier incarnation, "The Ceremony"), the transcendental ghost story is pagan, persuasively ecstatic, and as immediate as a dream; at its worst (as in some of some of Benson's cruder efforts, or in Blackwood's novels about "Crackland," a fairyland hidden in "the crack between Yesterday and Tomorrow"), it smacks of, as Sullivan puts it, "a sentimental pantheism gone sour."

Most writers, of course, cannot properly be grouped within any "school"; as with Edgar Allan Poe, their work may reveal wide and complex influences. In any overview of supernatural fiction, however, mention must be made of British writers as Richard Harris Barham (whose *Ingoldsby Legends* recount ghost stories in light verse), "Captain" Frederick Marryat (*The Phantom Ship*, "The Werewolf"), Amelia B. Edwards (author of "Monsieur Maurice" and other Victorian classics, some with an Egyptological slant), E. F. Benson's religiously inclined brothers, A. C. and R. H. Benson (*Paul the Minstrel; The Light Invisible* and *A Mirror of Shalott*), M. P. Shiel (a hypnotic prose stylist, most successful in the post-apocalyptic *The Purple Cloud*), Edward Lucas White ("Lukundoo," *The Song of the Sirens*), and William Hope Hodgson (who specialized in maritime horror, and whose *House on the Borderland* is one of most powerful works of cosmic fantasy ever written); the Americans Fitz-James O'Brien ("What Was It?") and F. Marion Crawford ("The Upper Berth," "The Screaming Skull"), the one born in Ireland, the other in Italy; literary collaborators Emile Erckmann and Alexandre Chatrian of France; the Germans E. T. A. Hoffmann ("The Nutcracker," "The Sandman," and other allegorical nightmares) and Gustav Meyrink, author of *The Golem;* Poe's Japanese disciple, Hirai Taro, who, in homage, called himself "Edogawa Rampo" and wrote a strange erotic story about a man who lived inside a chair; and the American expatriate Lafcadio Hearn, who retold the ghostly legends of Japan and China in exquisitely lyrical prose poems.

In fact, few authors have pursued literary careers without at least some excursions into supernatural fantasy, and so in ghost-story collections it has never been uncommon to find such celebrated names as Defoe, Goethe, Scott, Irving, Balzac, Hawthorne, Thackeray, Dickens, Hardy, Bierce, Twain, Stevenson, de Maupassant, Kipling, Wells, Chesterton, Forster, and Dinesen. Henry James, an illuminating critic of the genre, is often accorded pride of place here for tales such as "The Turn of the Screw"; its hyper-analytic style has made it a particular favorite among the academics (who see, in its narrator's ambiguous motives, room for still another dissertation) and among those who prefer psychological abstractions to atmosphere.

Unlike the Victorian, the modern age has not been kind to ghosts or ghost stories. "To most modern men having ceased to recognize their own souls, the spectral tale is out of fashion, especially in America," declares Russell Kirk, the conservative political theorist. Author of *The Surly Sullen Bell* (1962), an atmospheric, if didactic, collection of traditional ghost stories, he's convinced that the genre demands "a skill innately conservative."

The celebrated novelist Edith Wharton, author of such hauntingly beautiful tales as "Afterward" and "The Eyes," was equally pessimistic. "Since I first dabbled in the creating of ghost stories," she said in a memoir, "I have made the depressing discovery that the faculty required for their enjoyment has become almost atrophied in modern man." She blamed the form's decline on "those two world-wide enemies of the imagination, the wireless and the cinema."

One would assume, then, that she'd agree with the poet Osbert Sitwell, who, in an essay in *Penny Foolish* (1935), remarked that ghosts had gone out with the advent of electricity. "Only by night do I believe in ghosts," he wrote, "and then more especially in a house that lies buried in the depth of the country and in which there is no electric light." Yet in "All Souls'," Wharton's feminine narrator dismisses Sitwell with a scornful "What nonsense! As between turreted castles patrolled by headless victims with clanking chains, and the comfortable suburban house with a refrigerator and central heating where you feel, as soon as you're in it, *that there's something wrong,* give me the latter for sending a chill down the spine!"

The late H. R. Wakefield was similarly glum, and, in the end, similarly undecided. "Many—perhaps most—people simply *can't read* ghost stories," he complained in 1961. "They'd as soon read binomial theorem stories. . . . I've found that the cult of such tales is confined mainly to a small subset of highest brows." He concluded with an oft-heard warning: "I assure would-be aspirants that no one in his senses ever tried to write ghost stories for a living." Yet this is the same author who'd written over a hundred such tales and who, in one of them, "The Red Hand," had spoofed his own bad faith; the story's hero, an aging horror writer with, like Wakefield, a hundred titles to his credit, has a change of heart, vows he'll have nothing more to do with this "chain-clanking tripe"—and is found strangled by one of his own ghostly creations. Though in the essay "Farewell to All Those!" Wakefield at last turned his back on the genre, he ended with the reflection, "Don't be too sure that none of the old magic endures!"

Is there an enduring human fascination with ghosts? For all her pessimism, Edith Wharton thought so: "Deep within us," she observed, "the ghost instinct lurks." Arthur Koestler thinks so, too—"We can no more escape the pull of magic inside us than the pull of gravity," he writes—and so did Violet Paget, author (under the pen name Vernon Lee) of such classic Victorian ghost tales as "Oke of Okehurst," whose narrator confesses:

> We have all heard of ghosts, had uncles, cousins, grandmothers, nurses, who have seen them; we are all a bit afraid of them at the bottom of our soul. . . . I am too skeptical to believe in the impossibility of anything.

Indeed, skepticism can have this curiously reverse effect; a total disbelief seems as foolish as belief. Anyone who doubts this might try asking several friends to "sell their souls" to him, in writing, à la *Doctor Faustus;* though offered several dollars, most people—even professed "skeptics"—are likely to refuse. As Arthur Reeve has noted, "In our inmost souls, secretly perhaps, we are as full of superstition as an obeah man."

Perhaps, then, it is not ghost tales that are out of place in the modern age, but simply the more dated types of ghosts themselves—"the violent old ghosts," as Virginia Woolf wrote in 1921: "the blood-stained sea captains, the white horses, the headless ladies of dark lanes and windy commons." Perhaps we need bid good-bye to only a few of the more worn-out props.

As to this, novelist Elizabeth Bowen was optimistic: "On the whole, it would seem, ghosts adapt themselves well, perhaps better than we do, to changing world conditions. . . . Hitherto confined to antique manors, castles, graveyards, crossroads, yew walks, cloisters, cliff-edges, moors, or city backwaters, they may now roam at will. They do well in flats, and are villa-dwellers. They know how to curdle electric light, chill off heating, or de-condition air. Long ago they captured railway trains and installed themselves in liners' luxury cabins; now telephones, motors, planes, and radio wavelengths offer them self-expression."

"In the past," noted L. P. Hartley (whose best-known horror tales include "W. S.," "The Killing Bottle," and "The Travelling Grave"), "ghosts had certain traditional activities; they could squeak and gibber, for instance, they could clank chains. They were generally local, confined to one spot. Now their liberties have been greatly extended; they can go anywhere, they can manifest themselves in scores of ways. Like women and other depressed classes, they have emancipated themselves from their disabilities."

If ghosts are now emancipated, it is largely due to the inventiveness of writers such as Fritz Leiber, Robert Bloch, Ray Bradbury, Henry Kuttner, Clark Ashton Smith, Henry S. Whitehead, Seabury Quinn, August Derleth, Frank Belknap Long, Manly Wade Wellman, Joseph Payne Brennan, Richard Matheson, Charles Beaumont, Jack Finney, Dennis Etchison, Ray Russell, Henry Slesar, Kingsley Amis, John Metcalfe, John Collier, Charles Birkin, John Keir Cross, William Peter Blatty, Ira Levin, Thomas Tryon, Robert Marasco, Stephen King, and Ramsey Campbell. These modern practitioners of the supernatural tale have written for the major publishing houses and specialty firms such as Arkham House, for pulp magazines such as *Weird Tales* and contemporary slicks such as *Playboy;* they have even written for television and for Mrs. Wharton's two great villains, radio and film. H. R. Wakefield notwithstanding, some of them have even managed to make a decent living at it. More than a few have prospered.

But before we proclaim The Triumph of the Spirit, we'd better listen to the argument that's raging between Montague Summers and H. P. Lovecraft—an argument that calls into question the very foundations of the ghost story. The discussion resumes in next month's *TZ;* for now, class is dismissed.

Part II

"In the end it is the mystery that lasts and not the explanation."
—Sacherell Sitwell, "For Want of the Golden City"

Despite the popular successes of some of today's paperback horror writers, and despite the verdict of the box office (where SF and horror films now count for forty percent of ticket sales), the modern world has shown a diminished regard for shorter fiction and has proved inhospitable to the more traditional sorts of ghosts. They've been faced with the choice of adapting or dying out. Explaining why he'd included no "conventional ghost stories" in a wartime anthology, writer Julius Fast argued that the "last original ghost plot was hashed to death along with the vampires and werewolves" (a somewhat debatable point, I should think); and in a recent anthology, *Unlikely Ghosts* (1969), James Turner asserts: "The ghost has become as absurd today as he was serious yesterday. There is little of the world left for him or her to haunt. . . . Satire has almost destroyed him."

Many writers blame this situation on a general "loss of faith" and, specifically, on the loss of belief in individual spirits. For Russell Kirk, the culprit is a decline of religion and, in its place, the modern worship of "St. Science," while British writer Hugh Walpole—distantly descended from both the gothic novelist and, on his mother's side, *Ingoldsby Legends* author Richard Harris Barham—deplored the prevailing skepticism of our times: "The human flesh creeps in every kind of way," he wrote. "What makes one man creep merely makes another yawn. In these scientific days, in fact, creep-making is not so easy. Everyone is wise, incredulous, and scornful."

But is skepticism really so modern an attitude? Is it a loss of belief that's made ghost fiction unfashionable? History suggests otherwise. Though in ages past the belief in ghosts was more widespread, there were always those who doubted. Confucius was unable to make up his mind about ghosts; some ancient Greeks claimed to see them, but others questioned their existence. Cicero was a believer; he concluded that ghosts were the damned, condemned to linger near the scene of their crimes, and noted that a fellow Roman "has seen such spirits a thousand times and, from long habit, has lost all fear of them." (In this the man may have been characteristic of his age: "In the first and second centuries," writes historian Samuel Dill, in *Roman Society from Nero to Marcus Aurelius,* "apparitions became the commonest facts of life, and only the hardest minds remained incredulous.") Yet Pliny, a contemporary, remained skeptical, asking one correspondent, "I would . . . willingly know if you are of the opinion that phantoms are real figures, and carry in them some kind of divinity; or are empty vain shadows, raised in our imaginations by the effect of fear." On this question St. Augustine, too, admitted ignorance: "I confess I am not able to understand it," he wrote. "The finite cannot deal with the infinite."

If there were any skeptics during the Middle Ages, they knew enough to hold their peace; like angels, demons, and the Little People, ghosts were regarded as simply a different order of being in the divine scheme. Paracelsus listed spots in Germany where woodland elves patrolled the land in "little coats some two feet long," and Michael Constantine Psellus, an eleventh-century Byzantine philosopher in the Greek emperor's court, held that demons were quite corporeal, having "aerial bodies, that they are mortal, live and die, that they are nourished and have excrements, that they feel pain if they be hurt or stroken." If their bodies were cut in two, they would immediately come together again.

Yet by the Renaissance the doubters were everywhere, openly questioning established belief. There were always many, of course, to take the side of the faithful. Ludwig Lavater, a much-cited sixteenth-century spiritualist, maintained that ghosts were "frequently seen in monasteries and about churchyards, marshes, great buildings, solitary places, or places notorious because of some murder, &c." (all the settings later used by Victorian writers), and ghosts were equally visible on the Elizabethan stage: "When Kemble at Drury Lane in 1794 let Macbeth gaze upon an empty seat in the scene of royal revelry and apostrophise the vacant air," says Montague Summers, "all this was absolutely alien to Shakespeare's intention and practice."

Most Elizabethans, though, were decidedly skeptical about spirits: Reginald Scot's *Discovery of Witchcraft,* for example, attributed such visions to sheer hysteria, and Shakespeare himself has a character in *King John* deride those who can see

> No natural exhalation in the sky,
> No scope of nature, no distempered day,
> No common wind, no customed event,
> But they will pluck away his natural cause
> And call them meteors, prodigies, and signs,
> Abortives, presages, and tongues of Heaven.

The same doubts prevailed throughout the following century. Though in his *Anatomy of Melancholy* (1621) Robert Burton noted that "Devils many times appear to men, and affright them out of their wits, sometimes walking at noonday, sometimes at nights, counterfeiting dead men's ghosts," and that the ghosts themselves "often foretell men's deaths by several signs, as knocking, groanings, &c.," elsewhere he admitted that "the question is very obscure, according to Postellus [sixteenth-century French scholar Gulielmus Postellus] 'full of controversy and ambiguity,' beyond the reach of human capacity."

The issue was still controversial in Victorian days. In 1831, with tongue in cheek, Walter Scott wrote an erudite essay on the question of "ghosts before the law" (they are, it seems, difficult to swear in as witnesses—a fact which Isaac Asimov and Fred Pohl exploit in their comic ghost story "Legal Rites"), and as late as the 1880s a few eccentric Irish litigants were still trying to break the leases on their homes by claiming that the premises were "haunted." When, in 1882, the newly formed Society for Psychical Research asked seventeen thousand Britons whether they'd ever experienced "a vivid impression of seeing or being touched by a living being or animate object, or of hearing a voice; which impression so far as you could discover, was not due to any external physical cause," some 1,684 people—nearly ten percent—said that they had.

No doubt there would still be a sizable percentage were the question posed today; the credulous are always with us. But is it this same ten percent that forms the audience for supernatural fiction? Montague Summers, himself a professed believer, felt that such was indeed the case, and went even further: The ideal supernatural *writer,* he argued, must believe in ghosts. "The ghost stories told by one who believes in and is assured of the reality of apparitions and haunting," he said,

> will be found to have a sap and savour that the narrative of the writer who is using the supernatural as a mere circumstance to garnish his fiction must inevitably lack and cannot attain. . . . Very fine tales have, no doubt, been written by authors who regarded the supernatural as just a fantasy and a flam. They topple, however, whether on the one side into nightmare indigestion or on the other into vague aridities that are in fine meaningless. . . . He may succeed in duping his readers, but not for long. Presently his wand will snap short, his charms will lose their potency and mystic worth; he will soon have turned the last page of his grimoire; he steps all involuntarily out of the circle, the glamour dissipates, and the spell is broken!

Unfortunately, Summers weakened his case by singling out the work of Bulwer-Lytton, "a serious and discriminating student of the occult." Summers found his tales "convincing"; others prefer to see them as, in Alexander Laing's words, "all chair-snatching tarradiddle."*

Edith Wharton makes perhaps a more convincing case; her fiction is beautifully controlled, and she herself appears to have been something of a believer. "Till I was twenty-seven or eight," she wrote, "I could not sleep in the room with a book containing a ghost-story, and I have frequently had to burn books of this kind, because it frightened me to know that they were downstairs in the library!"

---

*Today, in fact, Bulwer-Lytton may be best known for the annual bad-writing competition, established in 1982, that bears his name.

Writing a decade later, H. R. Wakefield expressed a somewhat more cautious faith: "I am a sceptic of sceptics, but not, I hope, a wooden one. That there are many things in Heaven and on Earth for which we have no explanation, and for which, in all probability, we shall *never* have an explanation, is certainly part of my philosophy, and I have never written a tale in which are recorded happenings that I do not believe could occur.... For us there are only those faintest of glimpses and softest of whispers. Sometimes I fancy I see something flicker and hear something stir. And that is why I sometimes write a story. There is, I believe, something there, but I shall never know what; and, rest assured, neither will you."

Yet writers equally as powerful expressed no doubts at all. A. E. Coppard boasted that he didn't believe in ghosts. Arthur Machen confessed, a trifle wistfully, that he'd never seen any of the spirits he wrote about. Throughout his life H. P. Lovecraft, describing himself as "a clear-cut atheist and materialist," saw the cosmos as "a mindless vortex, a seething ocean of blind forces," and scorned "the immortality myth" as one of "the sugary delusions of religion." ("A life snuffed out," he wrote, "survives no more than an electric light smashed to pieces.") Thomas Hardy was another unbeliever, though obviously unhappy in the role; he once declared he'd give ten years of his life to see a ghost—which more than rivaled Houdini's famous offer of five thousand dollars to any "spiritualist" whose feats the great magician couldn't duplicate.

Both men would probably have liked to make good on their offers; after all, what is ten years, or five thousand dollars, against the chance of immortality? Even if one hasn't seen a ghost, one may still want to *be* one.

The skeptics' case is persuasive on this point. Prefacing *The Haunted Omnibus* (1937) with a warning that "the editor does not admit to a belief in ghosts," Laing argues that "a non-believer has as much right to enjoy a ghost story as anyone else. Dante's *Inferno* is not dependent for its effect upon a literal belief that the narrator's guide was in truth the shade of Virgil." Another anthologist, Bohun Lynch, goes even further: "People who 'believe in ghosts,'" he argues, "are seldom able to write good ghost stories, or to enjoy reading them." He finds such people to be more interested in logical exposition than in good atmospheric writing

Bulwer-Lytton's graceless prose lends support to this argument; yet how to explain the fact that a cultured, highly sophisticated modern British ghost-story writer such as Robert Aickman was also a believer? Is this sort of belief a help or a hindrance? The answer, of course, is that, as literary historian Edward Wagenknecht says, "The word *belief* may be spoken with many different accents. The actor believes in the character he is creating, though he does not believe as the theologian believes, nor yet as the devotee."

One of America's foremost critics, I. A. Richards, illuminated these differences in his 1929 essay on "Doctrine in Poetry." There are, he theorized, two forms of belief—"intellectual belief" and "emotional belief." The former has little bearing on a writer's art, but the latter, founded on a strong emotional commitment to the theme of the work, is absolutely vital. "In primitive man, as innumerable observers have remarked, any idea which opens a ready outlet to emotion is quickly believed. We remain much more primitive in this phase of our behaviour than in intellectual matters. . . . There are obviously countless ideas in poetry which, if put into this logical context, must be disbelieved at once. But this intellectual disbelief does not imply that emotional belief in the same idea is either impossible or even difficult—much less that it is undesirable."

One of the "illogical" ideas he cites appears in a key passage in *The Rime of the Ancient Mariner*—"The horned Moon, with one bright star / Within the nether tip"—which, while logically inconceivable (though optical illusions of this kind have occasionally been recorded), is yet one of the most haunting images in the entire poem. Coleridge himself might have attributed the image's power to, in his famous phrase, "the willing suspension of disbelief," and Richards does not disagree—although he has some reservations about the wording: "We are neither aware of a disbelief nor voluntarily suspending it in these cases. It is better to say that the question of belief or disbelief, in the intellectual sense, never arises when we are reading well."

Apropos of Wakefield's complaint in "Farewell to All Those!" about modern readers' inability to read ghost stories ("They'd as soon read binomial theorem stories"), Richards ends with a timely warning: "The absence of intellectual belief need not cripple emotional belief, though evidently enough in some persons it may. But the habit of attaching emotional belief only to intellectually certified ideas is strong in some people; it is encouraged by some forms of education; it is perhaps becoming, through the increased prestige of science, common. For those whom it conquers, it means 'Good-bye to poetry.'"

Richards's conclusions must not be construed as an invitation to doublethink; the levels on which we may enjoy an idea are quite distinct from those on which we analyze it, for as Wagenknecht says, the reader or writer of supernatural fiction "may disbelieve with his mind . . . yet believe with his blood." Therefore the oft-quoted comment of Madame du Deffand, who, when asked if she believed in ghosts, replied "No, but I'm afraid of them," is, in Edith Wharton's estimation, "much more than the cheap paradox it seems to many"; it is simply a description of the truth—and one to which all the authorities subscribe. Forced to acknowledge M. R. James's cool skepticism—"Do I believe in ghosts? . . . I am prepared to consider evidence and accept it if it satisfies me"—Wakefield concluded that "unless the writer can, at least temporarily, alarm himself, he will never alarm anyone else." Alluding to a classic James tale whose intruding spirit displays "a horrible, an intensely horrible, face *of crumpled linen*," he suggested: "While James was writing 'Oh, Whistle, and I'll Come to You, My Lad,' I'm certain he was also casting a furtive inner eye at spectral heaped bed-clothes forming into fearful shapes. No doubt he soon laughed the image away, but he must have known it for a time."

"The teller of supernatural tales should be well frightened in the telling," advised Wharton, and Wakefield agreed: "Before you can scare others, you must be scared yourself. Ghostly fear is transmitted, not concocted." Indeed, Russell Kirk says that "for the sake of his art, the author of ghostly narrations ought never to enjoy freedom from fear." He cites as an example the case of the Anglo-Irish ghostly writer J. Sheridan Le Fanu, whose death, it's believed, came during one of his recurring nightmares and who, therefore, may be said to have died "literally of fright."

Part III

> Long before there was a Stephen King or a William Blatty or a string of movies shot in the dark and celebrating knives, there was an Anglo-Irish writer named Sheridan Le Fanu. Le Fanu lived in Dublin in the mid-nineteenth century.... His nights were haunted by nightmares about a house on the verge of collapse, and when he died unexpectedly a friend said, "The house has fallen at last."
>
> —*New York Times* editorial, June 7, 1981

Though Le Fanu was rumored to have scared himself to death, few writers have followed his example. They're much more interested in scaring the reader: to which end the supernatural tale is singularly well suited.

The trick is to make the reader believe in things he knows are not—and could not be—true. Some writers have professed to find this little trouble. A. E. Coppard felt that the supernatural mode "makes work easy, for with its enchanting aid a writer can ignore problems of time and tide, probability, price, perspicuity, and sheer damn sense, and abandon himself to singular freedoms on the aery winds of Never-was." Robert Bloch is somewhat more blunt; he chose to write fantasy rather than science fiction, he says, "because I could be sloppier."

But Edith Wharton begged to differ ("It is, in fact, not easy to write a ghost story"), H. Russell Wakefield agreed with her ("Ghost stories are very difficult to write"), and Walter de la Mare thought that the form demanded absolute perfection—as we shall see below. "It is certainly the most exacting form of literary art," said L. P. Hartley, "and perhaps the only one in which there is no intermediate step between success and failure. Either it comes off or it is a flop."

One way to diminish the chances of a flop, crass as it may sound, is to employ the salesman's ancient device of allowing the customer to "sell himself"—which in this case means allowing the reader to *scare* himself. (The concept predates salesmen. In "The Scholar of Changchow," a folk tale from twelfth-century China, the hero confirms that "nothing in the world should be feared, but there are men who scare themselves.")

Like the customer, the reader must be made to feel he has reached his own conclusions—even when, in fact, he has been led to them. There is nothing immoral in this; all art involves manipulation, and what distinguishes good art from bad is that, in the former, one either doesn't notice or simply doesn't care.

Supernatural fiction manipulates best when certain details are left up to the reader's imagination; "reading," Edith Wharton said, "should be a creative act as well as writing," and she spoke gratefully of her audience's "meeting me halfway among the primeval shadows, and filling in the gaps in my narrative with sensations and divinations akin to my own." It's not surprising that many of the most successful ghost tales are told in fragmentary form, or in a style that savors of a certain disquieting vagueness, or as M. R. James suggested, with "a slight haze of distance."

Of course, *too* much haze—too much obscurity and ambiguity—produces more frustration than fright, as de la Mare's work all too frequently proves. But when a ghost story fails to move the reader (and, sadly, the majority do fail), the fault is generally in its excessive need to "spell things out," for clarity is an enemy of spectral fear. "Isn't it more devastating to one's sanity to see the shadow of a revenge ghost cast on the wall—to know that a vindictive spirit is beside one but invisible—than to see the specter himself?" asked Columbia professor Dorothy Scarborough, writing of Mary E. Wilkins Freeman's classic New England horror tale "The Shadows on the Wall." "Under such circumstances, the sight of a skeleton or a sheeted phantom would be downright comforting."

If clarity is to be avoided, so, too, should excessive length; the mood of fear is difficult enough to arouse, much less to sustain for page after page. "It is, I think, well-nigh essential for success that the ghost story should be short," wrote historian Montague Summers. "Only the adroitest skill and talent of no ordinary kind can avail to keep the reader in that state of expectancy bordering on the unpleasant, yet never quite overstepping the line which is the true triumph of this *genre*. All too frequently a tale spun in many chapters is apt either, on the one hand, to fall slovenly flat, to become banal and to bore; or else on the other to swell into crude physical disgust and end as a mere mixen of horror." In truth, as anthologist

Alexander Laing observed, "the effort to be unremittingly horrendous defeats itself. . . . Even fright, alas!, can die of monotony."

Today, of course, Summers's and Laing's warnings have been all but forgotten, and we are now witnessing the triumph of the supernatural novel—a triumph more commercial than literary. The vast majority of them *do*, in fact, resemble a "mixen," i.e., a midden or dung heap; British writer James Herbert's books are cases in point, relying upon periodic dollops of gore in place of mood and feeling. Even the better novels in the genre, such as William Peter Blatty's *The Exorcist* and Thomas Tryon's *The Other*, while skillful and deservedly popular, tend to lapse into a predictable succession of chapter-by-chapter shocks—an approach which, in less skilled hands, becomes (as Laing warned) increasingly monotonous.

In truth, supernatural horror is a form that lends itself best to the short story or novelette; it is not well suited to the full-length novel, and certainly not to the five- and six-hundred-page blockbusters so prevalent today. Some classic examples of supernatural fantasy—William Hope Hodgson's *The House on the Borderland* and H. P. Lovecraft's *The Case of Charles Dexter Ward* and *The Dream-Quest of Unknown Kadath*—are fifty thousand words or less in length: very thin novels indeed.

Although one looks in vain through Henry James's prose for a short sentence or a thought simply expressed, he, too, apparently favored brevity in the horror tale, though unable to achieve it himself: "Prolongation and extension constitute a strain," he wrote, "which the mere apparitional . . . doesn't do enough to mitigate." The late Dashiell Hammett—whose style tended to the other extreme—felt much the same: "Few weird stories have run successfully to any great length," he said, noting that even the most powerful tales depend upon one or two fortuitous phrases (Lovecraft called them "high spots")—a chilling line, perhaps, or some image in which the developing mood seems to crystallize in a shudder of terror. "This shudder," said Hammett, "is almost always momentary, almost never duplicated."

Characteristically, this shudder does not come until the climax of the tale; in fact, some of the shortest ghost stories on record are little more than climaxes. A couple called the Gibsons won a *New*

Statesman competition in Britain with a 200-worder about a man who grows increasingly nervous while walking down a winding moonlit road:

> Yet what had he to fear if this place were evil—was he not an upright and godly man who held no traffic with evil? If wicked spirits had power over such men as he, there would be no justice in it.
> "That's true," said a voice behind him, "there isn't."

Such succinctness is surely laudable, but it is hardly new; as far back as the fifth century A.D. a Chinese prince named Liu Yi-ching, in his *Records of Light and Dark,* was recounting snippets as short as this: "Once in the privy Juan Teh-Ju saw a ghost. More than ten feet tall, black with bulging eyes, it was dressed in a dark coat and cap. And this apparition was less than a foot from his side. Quite calm and composed, Juan told it with a smile: 'People say that ghosts are hideous; they certainly are!' Then, red with shame, the ghost made off."

There is also the diminutive tale of the two figures walking one night across the moors. "Do you believe in ghosts?" asks one.

"No."

"I do," says the first—and vanishes.

And there is, too, that famous short-short attributed to Thomas Bailey Aldrich—"The last man on earth heard a knocking at his door" (to which, in our own century, Fredric Brown added a happy ending, the visitor turning out to be the last woman)—as well as what pulp writer E. Hoffmann Price has dubbed "the shortest weird story ever written: *He crept into a crypt and crapt.*" We have even seen the ghost tale reduced to a single word—"Boo!"

Brevity such as this is best left to prize contests and license plates, for it comes at the expense of a quality even more necessary to weird fiction: atmosphere. Walter de la Mare called it "all important." "The fine ghost story," he said, "must be far more than decently, it should be excellently written—every word, every cadence, every metaphor apt to the matter in hand. Here the finer shades make a supreme difference; not merely the dot over the *i* but where it's put. How else is all that atmosphere to be conveyed?"

In fact, atmosphere is the life-blood of the ghost story. In most short fiction, character and plot are of supreme importance, and in mystery, plot predominates; but in supernatural fiction they are secondary, for too complicated a plot detracts from the emotional belief on which ghost tales depend, and the vicissitudes of individual characters pale beside the extraordinary circumstances into which they've been thrust. In science fiction the major element is usually the *idea,* but most weird fiction plays variations upon a single basic idea: an individual's growing awareness that "natural explanations" are useless and that the world has been invaded by some supernatural force—one which, in the end, he may yield to or attempt to combat.

Because they dispense with the "natural explanations," no forms of literature make so many demands upon our emotional belief as ghost tales and fairy tales. The latter, however, *presuppose* a world in which magic works, while the former must persuade us that magic works in our own.

This, then, is the function of atmosphere: to take the reader, by easy stages, from the natural to the supernatural. We must first be grounded in a world that is convincingly normal; "a good ghost-story," wrote Henry James, "to be half as terrible as a good murder-story, must be connected at a hundred points with the common objects of life.... The extraordinary is most extraordinary in that it happens to you and me."

Only after a successful grounding in reality can the story produce in the reader, as de la Mare hoped, "the gradual conviction that this workaday actuality of ours—with its bricks, its streets, its woods, its hills, its waters—may have queer and, possibly, terrifying holes in it." The ultimate goal, as M. R. James saw it, was to put the reader "into the position of saying to himself, 'If I'm not very careful, something of this kind may happen to me.'"

To produce this sort of conviction in the modern reader is no easy task. In ages past, writing for audiences who already believed in ghosts, writers had little need of a fine style and provided few touches of spectral atmosphere; they were preaching to the converted, and emotional belief easily came when intellectual belief could simply be assumed.

It's extremely significant, therefore, that supernatural fiction as a literary form—and the first efforts at a really persuasive style—appeared when belief was on the wane. Maurice Richardson speaks of "the outcrop of Gothic romances in the eighteenth century and ghost stories in the nineteenth: They could only be engendered in an allegedly rational age when superstition had been supposedly surmounted." As Pamela Search observes in *The Supernatural in the English Short Story*, "Ghosts, in a word, suddenly became much worse."

Just how much worse can be seen in the public's reaction to *The Castle of Otranto;* though it seems crude today, Walpole's use of atmosphere overcame the age's newfound skepticism and successfully fostered an emotional belief. "It makes some of us cry a little," wrote the poet Thomas Gray, "and all in general afraid to go to bed o' nights."

Creating that sort of fear today requires a far more subtle hand. Since the slow, careful buildup of atmosphere is absolutely essential, the ghost story depends, as no other genre does, on plain old-fashioned *good writing*—another respect in which it differs from science fiction. Wrote the late August Derleth:

> The incontrovertible fact—however distasteful it may be to . . . others who go in for s-f heavily and uncritically—is that there are very few science-fiction stories which have literary value; for every one that does, there are a hundred supernatural stories which do. No impartial critic could fail to agree. . . . I personally enjoy science-fiction and get all the s-f magazines. But my personal enjoyment cannot blunt my critical faculty.

Derleth was no doubt overstating the case a bit—he himself wrote horror stories, not science fiction, and was hardly the "impartial critic" he pretended to be—but his point is well taken: The successful ghost story must possess real literary merit.

Because writers in this genre are forced to pay so much attention to style, and because the necessary atmosphere must be built up with some degree of subtlety, the ghost story is among the most fragile of literary forms. Like humor, sex, or high romance—forms equally vulnerable to shifts of mood—the ghost story is forever at the mercy of boredom, distraction, or ridicule. A single laugh can shatter it. The hero of Dunsany's "The Ghosts" disperses "a herd of black creatures" that haunt a Scottish manor house by concentrating hard on some algebraic equations; in another Dunsany tale, "How the Enemy Came to Thlunrana," a daring young adventurer breaches the walls of a fearsome enchanted castle, tremblingly makes his way past glowering magicians to the legendary sanctum sanctorum, spies the unnamed thing that waits behind an ominous silk curtain—and laughs. The magicians flee; the castle falls; the spell is broken.

Because fear is dispelled by laughter—and is perhaps one of the main reasons we laugh at all—the humorous ghost story is therefore something of a contradiction. Summers disapproved of them, Richardson warns that "humor is fatal to the ghost story," and none other than Sigmund Freud has written: "Even a real ghost, as in Oscar Wilde's 'Canterville Ghost,' loses all power as soon as the author begins to amuse himself at its expense."

Indeed, there are probably more uneasy chuckles to be found in stories that set out to terrify, such as Marjorie Bowen's chilling account of "The Crown Derby Plate," than in all the deliberately "comic" efforts of Wilde, Don Wenceslao Fernandez Florez *(Laugh and the Ghosts Laugh with You),* John Kendrick Bangs, and Richard Middleton. (Bangs's *Houseboat on the Styx,* inhabited by the shades of Shakespeare and other historical figures, offers little more than a few smug caricatures, and his famous "Water Ghost of Harroway Hall" is a callously unfunny piece of sadism. Middleton, a suicide at twenty-nine, wrote a few gentle but haunting supernatural sketches and one coy attempt at whimsy, "The Ghost Ship"—which, mysteriously, has become his best-known work.) Ignoring the ancient Chinese, whose legends were spiced with low comedy, and also ignoring the Victorian English humorist Jerome Klapka Jerome, whose collection *Told After Supper* is perhaps the only consistently amusing writing in the entire field, Dorothy Scarborough asserted that "the humorous ghost is not only modern, but he is distinctively American." A sampling of her anthology *Humorous Ghost Stories* serves only to prove that, for the most part, this form is neither funny nor scary.

Aside from laughter, there is another sure way to kill a ghost:

by imprisoning him within some narrow political or theological framework. Ghost stories have been written to damn or defend the Pope, to promote temperance, and to attack abortion. (One such tale conjures up the spirits of dozens of "murdered" fetuses.) Some authors have given their fiction a tilt toward the right (Russell Kirk's villains tend to be "oily" and "vulturine" immigrants with unsavory manners and liberal ideas), while the Red Chinese have put their specters to work in the service of International Communism. "Belief in ghosts is a backward idea, a superstition and a sign of cowardice," says the preface to *Stories about Not Being Afraid of Ghosts* (Peking, 1961), compiled by the Institute of Literature of the Chinese Academy of Sciences and addressed to an audience of "thoroughgoing dialectical materialists and genuine proletarian revolutionaries."

> A man who is cowardly at heart and has not emancipated his mind will be afraid of non-existent ghosts and gods. But if he raises his level of political understanding, does away with superstition and emancipates his mind, he will find not only that ghosts and gods are nothing to be afraid of but that imperialism, reaction, revisionism and all natural or man-made calamities that actually exist are also nothing for Marxist-Leninists to be afraid of. . . . There are no ghosts . . . but there are actually many things in this world which are like ghosts. Some are big, such as international imperialism and its henchmen in various countries, modern revisionism represented by the Tito clique of Yugoslavia, serious natural calamities and certain not-yet-reformed members of the landlord and bourgeois classes who have usurped leadership in some organizations at the primary level and staged a comeback there. Some are small, such as difficulties and setbacks in ordinary work, etc. All these can be said to be ghost-like things.

Imposing political doctrines on the supernatural tale can be as unfortunate a mistake as poking fun at it; in either case this fragile form tends to wither. Nor can it survive for long under adverse conditions; its success depends upon a certain patience and good will on the part of the reader. Like most short fiction, for example, but perhaps to a greater degree, ghost stories tend to diminish in power if a number of them are read at one sitting; just as in a tale that goes on too long, the horror is seldom cumulative, and the tales' essential similarities become all too apparent.

For that matter, because atmosphere must be built up one dab at a time, ghost stories must not be read too quickly; nor do they lend themselves to easy summarization. A critic once praised the horror tales of H. P. Lovecraft for being so powerful that "they can raise a chill even on the subway," but few tales in the genre can truthfully make such a claim; "ghosts," said Edith Wharton, "to make themselves manifest, require two conditions abhorrent to the modern mind: silence and continuity." Requirements like these are rarely met today; noise distracts our concentration, and we devote less of our leisure to reading. Surely it is these circumstances, and not the prevailing climate of scientific skepticism, which account for the ghost story's decrease in popularity.

L. P. Hartley once complained that he found it difficult to so much as *think* about ghosts "in the bright sunshine of an Italian morning." Aware of the genre's unique vulnerability to surrounding mood, many ghost-story writers and anthologists have prefaced their works by admonishing readers to sample the stories only under the most ideal conditions. "If you can induce your friends to read what follows after nightfall, and when the fireside talk has run on for a while on thrilling tales of shapeless terror," wrote J. Sheridan Le Fanu, the genre's first great practitioner, "I will go to my work, and say my say, with better heart."

Darkness appears to be a prerequisite—ideally, as Boris Karloff suggested in a 1946 preface, "the hour between dog and wolf when the mind is disposed to marvels," or to what Henry James aptly called "apparitions and night-fears"—for night is the time when even the most sophisticated are forced to entertain the possibility of evil spirits, and most supernatural collections make some mention of it in their titles. (Summers alludes to a number of nonfictional works that repeat this same motif, from Lavater's *Of Ghostes and Spirites Walking by Nyght and of strange Noyses, Crackes, and Sundry Forewarnynges* [English translation 1572], Peter Thyraeus's 1594 *De Apparitionibus . . . et terrificationibus nocturnis* [*Of Ghosts and of Midnight Terrors*], and Thomas Nashe's *The Terrors of the Night, or A*

Discourse of Apparitions, also 1594, to Catherine Crowe's *The Night Side of Nature,* 1848.)

The ideal night for ghostly reading was described by E. F. Benson in his introduction to *The Room in the Tower,* whose stories, he said, were "written in the hope of giving some pleasant qualms.... So that, if by chance, anyone may be occupying in their perusal a leisure half-hour before he goes to bed, when the night and the house are still, he may perhaps cast an occasional glance into the corners and dark places of the room where he sits, to make sure that nothing unusual lurks in the shadow."

Yet why would anyone in his right mind *want* to experience these so-called "pleasant qualms"? Who but a fool or a masochist actually wants to be *scared*?

The fact is, there's a basic fallacy in the question so posed, and I'll examine it next month in my concluding visit to these pages. My topic, optimistically titled, will be "Pleasures of the Ghost Story." Until then, class dismissed.

Part IV

Why should anyone in his right mind want to scare himself before going to bed? What in the world are the "pleasant qualms" that E. F. Benson spoke of? Or the "fearful joy" that Russell Kirk claims he strives for in his supernatural tales? Or the *Fearful Pleasures* after which A. E. Coppard named a 1946 collection? Or the "pleasure in being frightened" that, in a 1947 essay, Maurice Richardson saw as "the secret of the ghost story"?

Is there a pleasure in being frightened? Or are ghost-story enthusiasts slightly mad, as Hartley suggests? ("Even the most impassioned devotee of the ghost story would admit that the taste for it is slightly abnormal, a survival, perhaps, from adolescence, a disease of deficiency suffered by those whose lives and imaginations do not react satisfactorily to normal experience and require an extra thrill.")

Many commentators assume that we *do* want to be, quite simply, frightened. Master fantasist M. R. James suggested that the successful ghost story should evoke "the touch on the shoulder that comes when you are walking quickly homewards in the dark hours, full of anticipation of the warm room and bright fire," and anthologist Bohun Lynch agreed: "We ask of a ghost story that it should thrill us," he wrote in a 1925 collection, "that it should make our rising from the fireside, our crossing of the hall, our approach to the staircase adventures of real uneasiness. We should be brought to that plight when the cold wet nose of an Irish terrier unexpectedly thrust at our hands, or the subtle touch of a cat rubbing against us in a dark passage, will produce sudden sweat upon our brow."

If that sounds like an invitation to masochism, he is not alone in extending it; though Alexander Laing, another editor, deprecates the notion of the supernatural tale as "a mere shudder-producer," elsewhere he asserts that "a ghost story as such is meant to play hob with the standard habits of nature—and good ones should give proof of their power to reverse the ordinary state of affairs by quickly turning the reader's spine into a chord of quivering rubber, his blood into thin red sprigs of ice."

This "ice" metaphor is a popular one. According to Edith Wharton, always worth consulting on this subject, the successful ghost story "must depend for its effect solely on what one might call its thermometrical quality; if it sends a cold shiver down one's spine, it has done its job and done it well." H. Russell Wakefield, likewise, dared his readers to "glance inside this book at your leisure, and then defy my hardest efforts to bring upon you the odd, insinuating little sensation that a number of small creatures are simultaneously camping on your scalp and sprinkling icewater down your back-bone." Even the mild Henry James seemed to delight in inflicting this unpleasantness upon his readers; moved by "The Turn of the Screw," an impressionable fan named William Lyon Phelps wrote (in a 1916 *Yale Review*): "This story made my blood chill, my spine curl, and every individual hair to stand on end. When I told the author exactly how I felt while reading it . . . he said that he was made happy by my testimony. 'For,' said he, 'I meant to scare the whole world with that story, and you had precisely the emotion that I hoped to arouse in everybody.'"

Do any of us really want our blood to chill and our spines to curl? Elizabeth Bowen is another who thought so—but she, at least, made one important distinction: We enjoy ghost stories, she said, because "it is nice to *choose* to be frightened, when one need not be. Or it may be that, deadened by information, we are glad of these awful, intent, and nameless beings as to whom no information is to be had. Our irrational, darker selves demand familiars."

Here, at last, we are approaching a phenomenon that Arthur Koestler has analyzed in his study *The Act of Creation* (1946): the phenomenon he terms "bisociation," an ability to appreciate two contradictory sets of information at the same time. "The spectator knows, in one compartment of his mind, that the people on the stage are actors, whose names are familiar to him; and he knows that they are 'acting' for the express purpose of creating an illusion in him, the spectator. Yet in another compartment of his mind he experiences fear, hope, pity, accompanied by palpitations, arrested breathing, or tears—all induced by events which he knows to be make-believe. . . . Of course, these people know that they are watching actors. Do they nevertheless believe that the characters are real? The answer is neither yes nor no, but yes and no. The so-called law of contradiction in logic—that a thing is either A or not-A, but cannot be both—is a late acquisition in the growth of individuals and cultures. The unconscious mind, the mind of the child and the primitive, are indifferent to it. So are the Eastern philosophies which teach the unity of opposites, as well as Western theologians and quantum physicists."

As Koestler sees it, one does *not* read ghost stories to be scared; one reads to be "scared." Like the emotional belief with which critic I. A. Richards balanced intellectual belief, Koestler's concept of "vicarious emotion" allows for a reader's pleasurable identification with the protagonist, the villain, even the victim of a horror story, "for whose sake he temporarily renounces his preoccupations with his own worries and desires. Thus the act of participating in an illusion has an inhibiting effect on the self-asserting tendencies, and facilitates the unfolding of the self-transcending tendencies. In other words, illusion has a cathartic effect—as all ancient and modern civilizations recognized."

Because this "vicarious emotion" is so different from genuine emotion, writers like Kirk can legitimately speak of "a fearful joy" and "delightful frights" to be found in horror fiction. "Most of us enjoy being scared," he says, "so long as we are reasonably confident that nothing dreadful really will overtake us. Thus the fun of the Gothick tale is the fun of the roller coaster or the crazy-house at the county fair." The quote-unquote "terror" of a roller coaster is acceptable, then, even sought after—but not the *real* terror of a speeding, out-of-control automobile. Few of us would want to be frightened for our lives.

Appropriately, there are two kinds of people who avoid ghost stories and horror films: those who get no thrill at all from them, and those for whom such subjects are genuinely—as opposed to vicariously—terrifying. Contrary to what some writers may claim, a true devotee of the supernatural can appreciate a horror tale without losing any sleep over it.

It's fitting, then, that this sort of tale is enjoyed most during times of security and peace—typically, by a warm fireside. (The fireside theme appears frequently and no doubt hearkens back to cave days.) "It is worth remarking," Kirk goes on, "that the grand milieu of the ghost story was in nineteenth-century Europe, and especially England. Despite its revolutionary changes, the last century now seems to us an age of security and normality; and England particularly was safe and cozy."

He calls particular attention to "the Christmas ghost story, told by the blazing fire, with all the strong defenses of a rich and triumphant civilization to reassure the timorous." Christmas is, in fact, the archetypal occasion for recounting such tales, not despite but *because* of its inherent cheerfulness and serenity. Walpole's *The Castle of Otranto,* father of the gothics, was published on Christmas Eve of 1764; tradition demanded the Christmas numbers of Victorian magazines contain at least one ghost story, and Dickens's famous *A Christmas Carol* appeared originally in this form. Marjorie Bowen's classic tale "The Crown Derby Plate" opens by informing us that Christmas is "the correct time to see a ghost," and Victorian humorist Jerome K. Jerome opens *Told After Supper* on this note:

> It was Christmas Eve ... It always is Christmas Eve, in a ghost story. Christmas Eve is the ghosts' great gala night. . . . Ghosts with no position to maintain—mere middle-class ghosts—

occasionally, I believe, do a little haunting on off-nights: on All-hallows Eve, and at Midsummer; and some will even run up for a mere local event—to celebrate, for instance, the anniversary of the hanging of somebody's grandfather, or to prophesy a misfortune. . . . But these are the exceptions. As I have said, the average orthodox ghost does his one turn a year on Christmas Eve, and is satisfied. . . . And not only do the ghosts themselves always walk on Christmas Eve, but live people always sit and talk about them on Christmas Eve. Whenever five or six English-speaking people meet round a fire on Christmas Eve, they start telling each other ghost stories. Nothing satisfies us on Christmas Eve but to hear each other tell authentic anecdotes about specters. It is a genial, festive season, and we love to muse upon graves, and dead bodies, and murders, and blood.

Small wonder that M. R. James offered the public a collection of his tales in the hope that "someone's Christmas may be the cheerfuller for a story-book," and that Henry James described the average ghost story as "the time-honoured Christmas-tide toy." In "Lucky's Grove," H. R. Wakefield even turns the Christmas tree itself into a murderous monster.

The association between ghost stories and the holiday season proves that the genre's goal is to provide not fear but "fearful pleasures." In fact, as Laing points out, "many of the best ghost stories are not terrifying at all."

What pleasures do *these* provide? For one, predicated as most ghost tales are upon a belief in personal immortality, they foster a kind of optimism: There is a chance, at least, that our personalities will survive after death. Stephen King noted in these pages several months ago, "it doesn't matter whether the supernatural forces are good or evil; all that matters is they exist. It means that after this life, there's more." Elizabeth Bowen points out, more specifically, that the typical ghost story plot involves a case of "obsession, or will, so strong that the moment of death goes by unperceived, innocuous—the intended action pursues its course or vision continues, without a jar."

Usually this "intended action" is an act of revenge, the fulfillment of some furious dying curse. In delineating its consequences, the ghost story provides another pleasure—the pleasure of returning to a moral order. (That's one reason why so many observers, like critic Arthur Reeve, have described it as performing the function of "a new religion.") Although many successful modern terror tales ascribe to no morality in particular, with innocents victimized as often as the guilty, most traditional tales (Le Fanu notwithstanding) are grounded in a strict old-fashioned code. Milton's *Comus* alludes to the ancient belief that "no evil thing that walks by night . . . blue meagre hag, or stubborn unlaid ghost / That breaks his magic chains at curfew times . . . hath hurtful power o'er true virginity," and Kirk, a moralist of the old school, observed two decades ago: "A return to the ghostly and the Gothick might be one rewarding means of escape from the exhausted lassitude and inhumanity of the typical novel or story of the sixties. . . . The fictional ghostly tale can possess plot, theme, and purpose. It can touch keenly upon the old reality of evil—and upon injustice and retribution."

That ghost stories might spring from a longing for a simpler, sterner morality seems no less than fitting, for they are an essentially nostalgic form. (This explains why the good ones age so well, and why a prolific "mainstream" author such as Robert Hichens is today remembered only for ghost stories such as "How Love Came to Professor Guildea," the humorist W. W. Jacobs for the chilling "Monkey's Paw," and Robert Chambers for his *King in Yellow* tales; while most forms date all too rapidly, the supernatural genre gives a writer his best shot at immortality.) Unlike mainstream fiction, with its concern for the present, or science fiction, which looks ahead, ghost fiction looks to the past. Freud, surveying "The Uncanny" in volume four of his *Collected Papers,* describes it as "that class of the terrifying which leads back to something long known to us, once very familiar," and Kirk quotes the philosopher George Santayana in *Reason in Religion* (1930): "Faint vestiges may be found in matter of forms which it once wore, or which, like a perfume, impregnated and got lodgment within it. Slight echoes suddenly reconstitute themselves in the mind's silence; and a half-stunned consciousness may catch brief glimpses of long-lost and irrelevant things. Real ghosts are such reverberations of the past." At times this haunted feeling of "recognition," this odd, inexplicable nostalgia, may lie beyond all telling, as Irish novelist Flann O'Brien hinted at in *The Third Policeman:* "It was so faultless and delightful that it reminded me forcibly, strange and foolish as it may seem, of something I did not understand and had never even heard of."

But for most readers of supernatural literature, the past is not so ineffably mystical; it is the past of one's own childhood, when one could savor fearful pleasures from the safety of one's own bed. "Have you ever looked back with wistful regret to your childhood," asks T. Everett Harré in a 1929 collection, "when impressions were so keen, and you thrilled with rapture or affright at your first apprehensions of demons and dragons, fairies, ogres, hobgoblins, and ghosts? And when you were safely tucked within your covers, when . . . rattling shutters conjured witches on broomsticks, and a creaking of doors made the dark alive with phantoms and perils. And when your little world—teeming with miracles and marvels and monsters, with adventures around any corner and back of every bush—was truly an enchanted place!"

Within this nostalgic evocation there lies an important point of logic—and one that accounts for still another pleasure bestowed by ghosts and other horrifying creatures: Their very existence makes possible a host of more pleasant things. Just as Hell presupposes a Heaven and punishment reward, the assembled forces of Evil presuppose the existence of Good; and though supernatural fantasy is primarily concerned with black magic, there is, by implication, a white. Therefore, if ghosts, goblins, vampires, and witches inhabit our world, they bring into being such benign wonders as unicorns, enchanted castles, and all the elements of the fairy tale. (Indeed, Henry James saw the ghost story as a type of fairy tale.) "Alas," Harré continues, "that the witchery should vanish so soon and the glow-of-gold on life's window-panes fade to an outlook of such unromantic reality! Most of us lead humdrum lives. In our day-by-day routine, the glamour of the mysterious and marvellous—which alone gives luster to life—is dulled by a constant brushing of shoulders with the practical and commonplace." Weird literature, he argues, provides a kind of "magic carpet . . . an 'open sesame' to chambers as fearful and fascinating as those of Bluebeard, Ali-Baba, and Aladdin."

To be both fearful and fascinating, to encompass, in Walter Van Tilburg Clark's phrase, both "the ecstasy and the dread"—that is the highest goal of all. Some supernatural tales, notably those of a "transcendental" nature, are concerned solely with the ecstasy; most others, especially those in the "antiquarian" tradition, treat only of the dread. Either sort may make your hair stand on end or, as the Fat Boy said in *Pickwick Papers,* "make your flesh creep," but in the most successful tales these responses need not arise from fear alone. Beauty, too, can make the flesh creep; beauty can make the hair stand on end. Consider the British poet A. E. Housman in *The Name and Nature of Poetry* (1933):

> I could no more define poetry than a terrier can define a rat, but we both recognize the object by the symptoms which it provokes in us. One of these symptoms was described in connection with another object by Eliphaz the Temanite: "A spirit passed before my face: the hair of my flesh stood up." Experience has taught me, when I am shaving of a morning, to keep watch over my thoughts, because, if a line of poetry strays into my memory, my skin bristles so that the razor ceases to act. This particular symptom is accompanied by a shiver down the spine....

It is precisely this merging of fear and beauty—as Montague Summers observed, "a beauty not without awe"—that marks the greatest supernatural tales. "Fear has its own aesthetic," said Elizabeth Bowen, "and also its own propriety.... That austere other world, the world of the ghost, should inspire, when it impacts on our own, not so much revulsion or shock as a sort of awe." To the ghost-story writer J. D. Beresford, introducing his *Nineteen Impressions,* that awe derived from the "impression of something bright beyond, something that shines." To Ann Radcliffe of *Udolpho* fame, it was born of terror rather than horror—a sort of sublime, cosmic terror that "expands the soul, and awakens the faculties to a high degree of life."

To be moved so profoundly, one need not believe in ghosts. "There *is* a magic door, is there not?" asks Lynch, "through which we sometimes catch a glimpse; there *are* moments of ecstatic enlightenment which have nothing at all to do with *planchette* boards, or tumblers, or crystals, or *séances,* or societies. Somewhere—out, beyond, or far within us—there is a region of terror and of unimaginable beauty, too."

In short, the pleasures of the ghost story are manifold and deep. They appeal, in Henry James's words, "to wonder and terror and curiosity and pity and to the delight of fine recognition, as well as to the joys, perhaps stronger still, of the mystified state." Like all great art, they gratify "that faculty of wonder"—for, as Lafcadio Hearn reflected, "There is something ghostly in all great art. . . . It touches something within us that relates to infinity."

Introduction to *Dark Love*

There's a question—just one—that I'd like to ask the writers in this book:
Do you really let your parents read this stuff?
I ask because, while the writers themselves are nice enough—most of them, anyway, if you catch them on a good day—the stuff they've got in store for you is not. Some of it's bloody, some of it's sick, and none of it provides a shred of comfort.

In fact, the stories in this book plunge boldly into what another disturbing writer, back in the '20s, called some "very strange psychological regions." The writer was that old master, Arthur Machen, and he was talking about an early story of his own, "The White People," probably the most daring thing he'd ever written and still one of the best horror tales in the language. "It contains," he said, with wry understatement, "some of the most curious work that I have ever done, or ever will do. It goes, if I may say so, into very strange psychological regions." And he would speak of it no further, as if the tale unnerved even him.

These twenty-two chronicles of Dark Love venture into similarly strange regions, only more explicitly and a great deal less politely; and though, to my knowledge, no one has ever handed out medals for Conspicuous Courage to mere writers, the twenty-two assembled here deserve some sort of credit for the sheer unflinching audacity with which they've followed their personal visions into

---

Dark Love, edited by Nancy A. Collins, Edward E. Kramer, and Martin H. Greenberg (New York: ROC/Penguin, 1995).

manifestly dangerous territory. The tales in this volume respect neither taboos nor good taste; many of them set out to shock, and quite a few succeed. Whatever the world's reaction to them, one thing's for sure: They're not going to end up as episodes of *Tales from the Crypt* or some other TV show.

Yet love, good old human love, is undeniably their focus. They're even, in an odd way, romantic—assuming, of course, that there's something romantic about (to take just three examples) necrophilia, pyromania, and an unrequited passion for an eight-foot-long insect.

And why not? Even in real life, love can take some pretty odd forms.

Just a few minutes after I'd finished reading these stories, for example, a report came over the radio of an Ohio man who, back in 1964, was given a lift to Toledo by an eighteen-year-old girl. Apparently, over the course of the drive, he fell in love with her.

Romantic? You bet.

The man never saw the girl again—not for thirty-one years. But just last week, while reading the newspaper, he came across her name in an obituary of her mother, and managed to track her down. She's now, of course, a woman of forty-nine. According to the news report, he sent her four dozen roses and a stack of letters—thirty-one years' worth of letters, in fact. And when police searched his home, they found thirty-one years' worth of Christmas and birthday presents that, with admirable devotion, he'd been buying her year after year.

Yes, the police. It seems the woman has taken out an order of protection against this fellow, and he's currently under arrest for "misdemeanor stalking."

Still, as I said, it's a romantic story. Thoroughly human. We can all identify with it—some of us with the woman; some of us, admittedly, with the stalker.

Or take, if you prefer, a more sublime example: Take the author of *The Divine Comedy*. Dante was barely nine years old when he first glimpsed Beatrice in the street—"At that instant," he wrote later, "I may truly say that the spirit of life, which dwelleth in the most secret chamber of the heart, began to tremble with such violence that it appeared fearfully in the least pulses," etc., etc.—and nine more years passed before he so much as exchanged a word with her. Yet these few chance encounters were all he needed; he spent the rest of his life celebrating his love for this "most beautiful of the angels in heaven" whom he'd barely spoken to.

One more romantic, just to keep you in the mood: the artist Rockwell Kent. In 1929 he was strolling through a barren little fishing village in Newfoundland when, he says, "I saw a girl's face at a window—just for a moment. I was ashamed to stare. And oh, I thought, how beautiful it would be to live here, and never go away—forever!" When, the next day, he set sail, "I thought how never again I should see the girl in the square house at the turn of the path."

And, by George, he never did. But years later, he was still dreaming about her.

Now, the only difference between those stories and the romantic little stories in this book is that, in the latter, the girl at the window would have a ravaged face and a knife clenched in her teeth, Dante would have orgasms over whipping Beatrice bloody, and the forty-nine-year-old focus of the Ohio man's affections would be dead by now. Dead? Her body parts would probably be scattered from Toledo to Tacoma.

Nothing the matter with that, of course. Each to his own, and all perfectly human. There's no love without obsession, this book seems to say, and obsession is the underlying theme of every story. If love is here, the stories ask, can lunacy be far behind? Make that homicidal lunacy; indeed, if there's one thing these stories make painfully clear, it's that down deep, down real deep, love and violence are as inextricably linked as Mom and apple pie. (And I speak as one whose mother has never made a decent apple pie in her life.)

The source of the fear in these stories is, in essence, the source of the fear in *all* horror stories: fear of the Other. Only in this case, in the twenty-two stories that follow, the Other looks remarkably like ourselves. He or she may be a hitchhiker, a pickup in a bar, or a bow-tied stranger in a crowded café; he or she may also be our coworker, perhaps one we've secretly lusted after, or our neighbor, whether just across the alley or separated from us by the thinnest of walls. He or she may even be our lover or our spouse.

It's an unsettling thought, albeit on the printed page a pleasantly intriguing one. Once, around twenty years ago, while I was engaged in putting together a gothic romance magazine for women (it was called *Rosebud*, for the record, and died before its launch), I came across a scholarly article analyzing that particular genre's popularity. It had, I remember, a wonderful title, one that summed up the basic appeal not just of gothic romance but of a large segment of commercial suspense fiction: "Somebody's Trying to Kill Me, and I Think It's My Husband."

And who knows, maybe he is. Husbands murder wives (and ex-wives) all the time; wives return the favor. Even a handsome ex-football star turned actor—I'm speaking hypothetically, of course—may turn out to be a raving psychopath in the grip of a jealous obsession. The stories in this book remind us of a terrifying fundamental truth: that our understanding of our fellow beings is decidedly limited. We can never really know what's inside another person's skull; we can never know what demons are crouching just behind their eyes. Given the right pressures, the right family history, the right combination of heartbreak and hope—or given, perhaps, the right set of provocations supplied so abundantly by modern urban life—any one of us might be pushed beyond reason, over the edge, into the pit of psychosis.

I've been there myself. I remember walking the streets once, just after dawn, having lain awake all night in pain over a failing love affair, when I noticed that a woman I'd passed was eyeing me strangely. I realized, suddenly, that I'd been talking to myself—*but I didn't care*. I felt not a trace of embarrassment; the problems that preoccupied me seemed of far greater importance than what some stranger thought.

Looking back, it's clear to me that, at that moment, I was crazy. Nuts. Certifiable.

Could it happen again? Of course.

And it could happen—only with far more alarming consequences—to the harmless-looking fellow citizens we bump into every day on the street. They may well have a screw loose already; they may well be, as Machen once luridly suggested, "lurking in our midst, rubbing shoulders with frock-coated and finely draped humanity, ravening like wolves at heart and boiling with the foul passions of the swamp and the black cave."

More lethal still—potentially, at least—are those we believe we know most intimately; for intimacy makes us vulnerable. The therapists assure us that that's a blessing; a lot of us aren't so certain. Vulnerability is scary. Writing about the movie *Psycho,* a critic once noted that the reason the shower scene is so effective is that it exploits "one of the archetypal moments of human vulnerability." But surely there are many more such moments. Riding in an elevator with a stranger, for example. Using a public restroom. Picking up a hitchhiker. And most of all, climbing naked into bed with another human being, even one you think you know well.

It's this treacherous quality of sexual encounters—the supreme vulnerability they impose—that fuels the horror in this book. I was going to say, glibly, that horror makes strange bedfellows; but the lesson of these stories is that, ultimately, *all* bedfellows are strange bedfellows.

The bedroom, of course, holds other dangers as well. As visions of contemporary life, most of these stories allude in one way or another to the ever-present threat of AIDS. But viruses are really beside the point here. The stories demonstrate, among much else, that condoms or no condoms, sex isn't safe. And it never was.

It isn't pretty, either. I want to warn you right now that with very few exceptions, the descriptions of the sex act in the stories that follow, and of the people themselves—their fears and desires, their fantasies and needs, their all-too-mortal flesh and pitilessly observed reproductive organs—are so disquieting, so devastatingly unflattering, from writers male and female alike, that they're enough to send anyone packing off to a monastery. No need for saltpeter or cold showers; the tales in this volume are a more persuasive argument for sexual abstinence than anything you'll ever hear from your doctor, your teacher, or your priest.

In fact, between the lethal danger and the sheer disgust, this book might actually have a salutary effect on the population problem. You'll find stories here calculated to raise eyebrows, goose bumps, and even a few laughs—but nary an erection. (Yes, there's humor here, all right, though it's of the blackest sort; and the main laughter one hears is the sinister cackling of the writers.) Just as second marriage has been called, waggishly, "the triumph of hope over experience," a similar challenge is presented here: If, immediately after finishing these tales, you still feel like getting down and dirty with another human being, it's clearly the triumph of biology over imagination.

However, if you're still determined to carry on the race (and I certainly hope you are), please heed one last warning born of having immersed myself quite deeply in the contents of this book. Obey if you must those famous final words of *The Thing*—"Keep watching the skies!"—and feel free each night, if you're so inclined, to look beneath the bed. Meanwhile, though, for safety's sake, keep an eye on something even closer, something midway between the heavens and the floor: that endlessly mysterious thing in bed beside you.

Introduction to David Schow's
Seeing Red

Exactly thirteen months ago, seeking a weekend retreat from the city, I bought myself a cozy little house in the Catskills. Immediately after I moved in, two things occurred: Real estate prices began to drop, diminishing the house's market value, and Lyme disease suddenly became the scourge of the East Coast, making me afraid to set foot outside.

And now, having read the last story in this collection, "Not From Around Here," I'm going to be equally afraid to stay *inside* the house. It won't be so bad when someone's with me, but whenever I'm alone I'll be listening for a furtive scratching at the window and the patter of feet on the floorboards. It'll probably be hard to get to sleep, and taking a shower without someone standing guard by the door is going to be out of the question. I mean, the house is pretty much ruined for me.

Nice going, Dave. Thanks a lot.

Actually, "Not from Around Here" is extreme even by the standards of this book. It's an authentically nightmarish story that, as they say, pushes the envelope a bit, and it's (as they used to say) Not For The Squeamish. I gather that it's already offended a few people. I doubt I'd have bought it for *Twilight Zone*.

I did, however, buy a number of the stories you'll find here, and

---

Seeing Red by David J. Schow (New York: Tor, 1989).

Twilight Zone, I'm proud to say, is where they originally appeared. The first of them, an earlier version of "Pulpmeister," appeared in our December '82 issue, along with an explanation by the author. "I spent a goodly chunk of 1981 writing six violence novels under a pseudonym, more or less exactly as described," he wrote. "Both the series and the publisher shall remain nameless." The photographs he'd sent us showed a strange-looking guy with a moustache, soulful-looking eyes, and an indecently long ponytail; he looked as if one of the Kean children had mated with a tomcat. In one photo, for reasons unknown, he was about to smash a bottle on his desk with a hammer and was smiling bemusedly. After comparing him to L. P. Hartley, S. J. Perelman, and George Gissing (*Twilight Zone* was nothing if not high-toned), I informed readers that Schow would soon be reappearing in our pages with a four-part nonfiction series chronicling *The Outer Limits.*

By the time it was over, the series had grown to twice that length, Schow had become a familiar name to *TZ*'s readers, and chattily introducing him had become something of a habit. His face, too, had become a familiar one in the magazine, though now, thanks to a new photograph, it looked simply Mephistophelian. So prolific was Schow—and so much more talented than the competition—that during the course of the series we also ran two more of his short stories, "Coming Soon to a Theater Near You" and "Lonesome Coyote Blues," and I later bought another, "The Woman's Version." In doing so, I violated four of my own most sacred unwritten rules:

1.—No stories about Viet vets.
2.—No stories about rock musicians.
3.—No writers appearing twice in the same issue.
4.—No violence so excessive as to turn readers' stomachs.

I've got nothing against veterans, but stories hearkening back to the bloody days of Vietnam have a way of bringing out the worst in many writers; "all too often," I once wrote, "they're just excuses for macho chest-thumping and a curious kind of in-the-know elitism" that I've always thought of as "Nam-dropping." Still, "Coming

Soon" was just too good to pass up; as I said in *TZ*, it was "both horrifying and humane enough to overcome my prejudices."

The same goes for "Lonesome Coyote Blues," one of the most haunting stories in this book. Rock-and-roll fiction usually leaves me cold (maybe it's all that smug music-industry jargon), but "Blues" is an absolute stunner, at once hip, spooky, and tender. Each time I read it, I'm moved.

Both "Blues" and "Coming Soon" also violated Rule #3. It doesn't look good for a magazine to depend too openly upon a small coterie of writers (though I think *The New Yorker* once featured an Updike story *and* a book review in the same issue), and I was reluctant to publish these tales while the *Outer Limits* series was still running. True to his pulp-writing roots, Schow was willing to appear pseudonymously as "Oliver Lowenbruck"—the hero, incidentally, of "Pulpmeister."

As for Rule #4, "The Woman's Version" comes awfully close. There are some descriptions in it, like that of the "dry cinnamon odor of flesh to which rot was but an ancient memory," that make your nose wrinkle, and a few that may make you want to wash your hands, such as this one of a landlord who hails from "some unfathomably strange Middle Eastern country":

> Gnomelike and dull-eyed, he exuded the smell of stale dates and sour sweat. There were brown gaps between each of his teeth, and the tips of his slicked-back hair were perpetually gravid with droplets of an opaque liquid.

Phew! Not someone you'd want to spend the night with—which is precisely the point, since Schow is writing from the perspective of a nasty-minded man-hating spinster whom sex both repels and obsesses. The world is filtered through her sensibility, and it comes out ugly. While for the euphoric young family man of "Not from Around Here" the moon is "a hard silver coin, its white brilliance . . . shimmering on the sea-ripple," for this woman it hangs in the sky "like a slice from a spoiled orange."

The fact is, Schow is something of a chameleon at this game; in story after story he adopts widely varying points of view, and does so convincingly. One story, striking an attitude so determinedly punk that it makes the thugs of *A Clockwork Orange* sound like preppies, gives the middle class a thorough thrashing ("Fat-assed visitors with their squawking brats and cellulite and cameras clogged the walking space. . . . None of the men looked stiff; none of the women, fuckworthy. They were the missionary position missionaries of America. They were doughy and dissipate"). Another celebrates those same bourgeois values—the nuclear family, the joys of home owning, the gorgeous wife and adorable kid and harmless little "marital spats"—with the fervor of a genuine family man (albeit one whose family winds up dead).

Yet there's one quality that nearly all the stories share, for in each case Schow writes with the confidence of a somewhat jaded insider who's seen it all, knows the score, and knows the way things really work. He comes off, in short, as almost preternaturally *knowing*. In "Red Light," which leads off this collection, his narrator, a photographer, sounds like a genuine pro; so does the narrator of "Lonesome Coyote Blues," who can speak familiarly of the rock hits of the past, as well as of some "cheezoid garage band called Abduction." You can hear the experience in his voice, the affection and the contempt.

In "Pulpmeister," of course, Schow's hero is an authentic insider, our tour guide to a modern-day Grub Street where hacks churn out "prestige soft porn" and "books with numbers instead of titles." Yet in "Night Bloomer" he's an insider too, perfectly at home in the soulless world of the corporation, where the goal of sex is "a good technical orgasm" and adultery's just "a squirt of randiness," and where thinking you're happy is as close to true happiness as you're ever going to get.

The ultimate insider's picture is probably the one offered by "Incident on a Rainy Night in Beverly Hills": the vision of a nationwide conspiracy so loonily ingenious that you almost believe it might be true. (The story also offers, among other pleasures, a novel explanation for why Hollywood makes so many bombs, why *Star Wars* was so popular, and why it's so hard these days to get real butter with your popcorn.) The analyst in the story sounds genuinely analytical; his screenwriter friend sounds capable of actually turning out a clever script. Indeed, the one thing Schow's heroes have in common is sheer intelligence; no matter what their station in life, their talk is invariably hip, self-aware, cleverly metaphoric, and just plain knowledgeable.

Most of all, it's a knowledge about film. In fact, after savoring tales such as "One for the Horrors," "Coming Soon," and—wait for it—"Blood Rape of the Lust Ghouls," you're half convinced that Schow himself must have spent at least twelve hours a day since infancy in the fleapit cinemas described so lovingly in his fiction, taking in movie after movie, and the rest of his waking hours thumbing through movie magazines or watching TV. Even if you've never read *The Outer Limits: The Official Companion*, Schow's astonishingly detailed, painstakingly well-researched book-length retrospective of the classic TV series, these stories alone would suggest a writer unusually savvy about film.

And why not? Schow is a longtime denizen of Hollywood, and peered at from the safety of the opposite coast, the world of his stories seems very much a Hollywood one, where "the past" means old movies and a plot to control the United States is enacted through the movie screen. That staple of traditional fantasy, the quaint little shop full of books left unwritten or uncompleted, has here become a theater showing legendary "lost" films, or a mysterious radio station. It's a world where pop culture reigns and where that East Coast icon, Lovecraft, must get by with only two passing references (one of them to a man wearing "a hangdog H. P. Lovecraft face"). When a chapter in "Visitation" mentions Poe and observes, "All this place needs is a tarn," he seems to have stepped out of an entirely different universe, for out here the cultural coordinates are right off the screen: A woman doesn't kill herself, or get murdered by her boyfriend, or go mad; she "pulls a Marilyn Monroe," has "a Dorothy Stratten pulled *on* her," or goes the way of Frances Farmer. While there are nods to TV's *Twilight Zone* and *Leave It to Beaver*, almost everything else reminds Schow's characters of a movie they've already seen. The sinister hotel in "Visitation" is "Gothically overstated" and (for reasons made clear in the story) resembles "a Hollywood set for a horror film." A man's heroic death in a fire reminds him, as he dies, of the climax of an old movie. A sidewalk encounter with his neighbors reminds someone of *The Good, the Bad, and the Ugly*, and, in a further Eastwood reference, a ticket-taker's voice, "strep-throat dry," reminds another character of "a bad parody of the Man With No Name."

The "strep-throat dry" points up another of Schow's strengths, an irrepressible sense of the comic. He's too bright, and probably too impatient, to turn out the sort of straight, plodding journeyman's prose that suffices for so many writers in the genre. His wit is arch and knowing. Why say "smart enough" when you can say "possessing enough intellectual candlepower"? Why opt for a "sickly smile" or some other cliché when you can offer "the smile of a terminal cancer patient laughing at a tumor joke"? Writing "unless you've been out of touch" would be too dull; Schow prefers "unless you've spent the last decade eating wallaby-burgers in the Australian outback." Down a Hollywood street comes not merely "a car" but "a rented LeBaron full of townies from some Texas hog wallow." A character inhabits "the West LA smogscape" and another, with mottled complexion, is "a victim of a spill in the birthmark department." A professional skeptic describes his ambition as "to put a bogey in the paranormal plumbing." The main characters in a sleazy horror film are deftly summed up as "the teen hero and his plucky bimbo squeeze"; and as for the film itself, consider the reaction of a critic aptly named Hackamore: "He'd hated it going in. Coming out, he wanted to fuck it till it bled." Whatever you want to say about David Schow's prose, it ain't colorless.

And he can't resist a throwaway gag; he's overflowing with them. He likes to make up mock newspaper headlines, lurid book titles, and parodic names for bands; when you're cursed with an overfertile imagination, it's hard to hide it under a bushel. In "Bunny Didn't Tell Us," the literary equivalent of a Jack Davis EC comic, full of ragged texture, raffish detail, and wild caricature, someone isn't merely the wife of a millionaire, she's "married to a toilet-paper tycoon"; a would-be grave-robber enjoys a quiet moment to pick his nose, and a series of gruesome grave-site killings becomes an exercise in slapstick horror. In another, grimmer story, a coughing smoker, "with the attitude of a true nicotine addict, puffed his cigarette for relief." Even in a tale as unrelievedly bleak as "Not from Around Here," with its images of bloody bedsheets and broken glass, Schow can't resist a fiendish pun involving a severed limb, as well as this comment on a retarded neighbor: "I've seen more raw intelligence in the eyes of goldfish."

I know that it amuses Schow to think of himself as something of a punk horror writer, a founding member of the "Splatterpunk" school (a name he invented) whose mission in life, like that of a punk rocker, is *épater le bourgeois*. But judging by the intelligence of his writing, I suspect that he's wrong about his own work. In truth, I think, he's a practitioner of something far more interesting than Splatterpunk and considerably rarer; call it Smart Horror. He's certainly too smart for some of the schlocky paperback originals he used to produce under house names, and for the gory scripts he's turning out today. Personally, I think he's too smart for the genre altogether.

Horror, let's face it, is basically pretty dumb. You're writing about events that are preposterous, and the trick is to dress them up in language so compelling that the reader doesn't care. But when you're really good at it, and as smart as David Schow, your language does more than merely carry the reader along; it becomes a joy in its own right.

Nice going, Dave. Thanks a lot.

Whiskey, Popcorn, and Gold

"A Jorkens Omnibus would fill a great need, if some present-day publisher were inclined to publish one." Darrell Schweitzer wrote that in *Pathways to Elfland*, a study of Lord Dunsany's writings, back in 1989. And here it is fifteen years later, and Darrell is getting his wish. From what I know of the publishing world, I'd say that's reasonably fast service.

Aside from this Night Shade edition and its two companion volumes, Jorkens doesn't come cheap; you'll not have a story from him today for the price of a whiskey and soda. I've just checked the net, and *The Travel Tales of Mr. Joseph Jorkens*, the first book in the series, will set you back at least forty dollars—seventy in a tattered dust jacket, like the copy that's peeking from my bookshelf—and you can't find a jacketed *Jorkens Remembers Africa* for less than two hundred fifty. A decent copy of *Jorkens Borrows Another Whiskey*, almost as rare, costs a hundred seventy-five; a battered copy, one-fifty. The Arkham House edition of *The Fourth Book of Jorkens*—through which many of us first made the acquaintance of the Billiards Club raconteur, and whose contents form half the book you're now reading—can be had for as little as twenty dollars without a jacket, twice that amount with one. But the other half of the present volume, *Jorkens Has a Large Whiskey*—a book I thought I'd never live to see—is so rare as to be virtually unobtainable; all my searches turned up empty.

Foreword to *The Collected Jorkens, Volume Two,* by Lord Dunsany (San Francisco & Portland: Night Shade Books, 2004).

So whatever you've paid for *The Collected Jorkens, Volume Two*, you definitely got a bargain.

Presumably you've already met Jorkens in Volume One, where the very first story spoke of him as "old Jorkens" who "had seen a lot of the world." Well, he's even older now, though you'd never know it, except for the fact that he's "been sleeping a good deal more after lunch"; at any rate, he still "knows many a thing which the hurried world forgets." In that previous collection, he looked back on the First World War; in the present volume, he anticipates the Second (in "Jorkens Looks Forward"), and in a later tale ("The Welcome") he hints that, despite his age, he was something of a hero in that war. He's described in this book as "the old traveller," but in fact he's been old since the moment of his conception: "I declined [a publisher's] suggestions to write of my own travels," recalls Dunsany in *Patches of Sunlight* (1938), "but put many lands and adventures that I had seen into the mouth of a drink-cadging old man called Jorkens, with a reputation at his club of being by far its greatest liar." (Dunsany mentions, incidentally, that "the tale that I believe is the best that I ever put into the whiskey-moistened mouth of Joseph Jorkens" is "The Electric King" in *The Travel Tales*. Remember, though, that when he wrote those words, only the first two Jorkens books and a handful of tales from the third had been published.)

Patches is the first of Dunsany's autobiographies, followed by *While the Sirens Slept* (1944) and *The Sirens Wake* (1945). It presents an author who, like his creation, is not only a world traveler but a dedicated hunter—for me the least attractive aspect of his, and Jorkens's, character. He beguiles us at first with some of his earliest childhood memories, "marigolds in the gardens of Regent's Park" and the moon at a family house in Kent:

> I remember it now, over the top of a lime-tree, and it certainly did not seem as though it could be the same as the ones in London. . . . I remember the leaves of the lilac pushing out through railings and shining, when London sighed for spring. . . . I remember . . . spiders' webs in the morning, with dew gleaming all over them, spread about the grass in a field at the top of the hill on the other

side of the woods; and I remember sheep-bells heard on our side of the hill from a valley away at the back of it, carried upon a wind, and carried now on the years.

He remembers English sunsets made all the more glorious because of the dust carried halfway round the world from the explosion of Krakatoa. And he remembers the moment when, as a child, "I first saw a hare one summer's evening: my father . . . clapped his hands for me to see it run."

Yet before the book is over, we find him recounting how, "Returning to Dunsany, I shot a rabbit one day with a .470 rifle, which blew the rabbit to pieces." (The gun, you see, was for bigger game; he was merely testing it.) Along the way, he boasts of having shot, with a more sporting .250, thirty-five rabbits in a single day. Except for the books and plays he turns out with astonishing regularity, his life seems to be a succession of foxhunts, "shooting parties," and "shooting visits" to the homes of fellow gentry, interspersed with African safaris; he bags grouse, snipes, ducks, deer, gazelles, a rhino, and a warthog. The latter has "two neat seven-inch razors like a boar and two eleven-inch tusks in his upper jaw"; the one Jorkens shoots in "The Ivory Poacher" has just ten-inch tusks and "two little razors"—a rare case of Jorkensian modesty.

And yet, dammit, "The Ivory Poacher" is one of the very best tales in the book. Its description of a voyage up the Nile, "that dream of a river," brimming with wonder, color, and exotic beauty, reminds one of the Dunsany of "Idle Days on the Yann," the most beautiful by far of *A Dreamer's Tales*. Again and again in the Jorkens series, a story that, like "Poacher," might easily be summed up in a single sentence, and whose ending we may well anticipate pages ahead of the narrator, is saved by passages of vivid, lyrical prose or startling imagery or even a memorable detail.

"I'm not especially observant," declares Jorkens in "A Life's Work"—another case of modesty, here amounting to an outright joke, for Jorkens's powers of observation are acute and his recollections masterfully expressed. The haunting evocation of the night-shrouded forest in "Jorkens in Witch Wood" and some of the scenic touches in an otherwise negligible tale, "The Ingratiating Smile," both set in a realistically rendered Irish countryside, remind one of Dunsany's atmospheric novel *The Curse of the Wise Woman*. The descriptions of a pair of fanciful cities—Loom-bah in "The Sacred City of Krakovlitz" and Ullumslagi in "Jorkens' Ride"—remind one of his special gift, in his tales of fantasy, for conjuring up magical urban vistas. "Jorkens Handles a Big Property" and "A Deal with the Devil" may go on too long, and the latter's ending may be feeble, but in the one, the scenes of the swamp with its grey-bearded trees, and in the other, the little encounter with the stranger who asks for a light, are almost worth the price of admission.

And who can forget the menu of that dinner in "The Neapolitan Ice," so casually thrown in: "We had turtle soup; fresh turtle, you know; red mullet; good enough in its way, only too many bones; and then we had hare; just the common hare, but they could cook it at that restaurant. . . . And really I think that was about all; and then the Neapolitan ice. Quite a small dinner; but good, you know."

If some future generation of scholars should ever set about analyzing the Jorkens canon with the zeal of, say, Sherlockians—and who knows, stranger things have happened—I hope they'll consider tackling what are, for me, five burning issues. First, there's the character of Jorkens himself. Is he the Billiards Club bore, a figure to be shunned, indeed fled from? (After all, as Agatha Christie assures us in the opening line of one of her mysteries, "In every club there is a club bore.") Or is he its star storyteller, someone to be courted and encouraged?

The evidence suggests both are true; Jorkens seems to be by turns dreaded and beloved. At times the members are at pains to steer him away from holding forth; at other times they practically beg for a story, plying him with whiskey to loosen his tongue. (In much the same way, the narrator of *My Talks with Dean Spanley*, Dunsany's most charming novel, plies the old clergyman from the Olympus Club with Imperial Tokay in order to get him to reveal what life was like in his previous incarnation as a family dog.)

Second, there's Terbut, whose role is equally ambiguous, encompassing that of Jorkens's nemesis, rival, straight man, fall guy, butt, inquisitor, scoffer, and general conversational enabler. He's apparently a lawyer and nontraveler, has "dark hair" and a "rather low brow" (this from "Mrs. Jorkens," in the previous volume), and like Jorkens himself, he's put on weight over the years (this from "The English Magnifico"). What we need, obviously, is a full-scale biography.

Third, there's the intriguing question—prompted in part by the two tales I've just mentioned—of exactly how many wives Jorkens has had, if any. In the former tale, he marries a mermaid; in the latter, he's forgotten her and denies he's ever been married. But he, like his listeners, seems to have forgotten someone else: We know from "Jorkens' Ride" that "as a very young man" he had a Zulu wife.

Which brings up a fourth area worthy of scrutiny: sex. There's barely a hint of it in these stories, except for "Magnifico" and a few of the tales involving mythical beings like the mermaid, a siren (in "The Grecian Singer"), and a satyr (in "The Development of the Rillswood Estate," a tale that might make an amusing film). I suspect a cover-up.

Finally, there's the Billiards Club itself. It's clearly the place to go for food, drink, and talk—but what about billiards? If any such scene exists, I've missed it. In the previous volume, in "Our Distant Cousins," we're informed that "they don't play much billiards there." Yet in that volume's "Tale of the Abu Laheeb," we're told flat-out that the club "had no billiard-table." Sounds like a matter for further investigation.

Still, normal readers will forgo such esoteric questions in favor of simple entertainment. And for them, a book of this kind—a collection of short pieces—often comes with a warning not to read too many at one sitting. They're like candy or popcorn, the advice usually goes: delightful to consume in limited quantities, less so if devoured in a single helping. That's true, up to a point; no one's going to want to read all sixty-one of the stories in this book without coming up for air.

But there's another side to that popcorn metaphor: Eating just one piece is not very satisfying. Individually these stories are rather slight: trifles and diversions, for the most part. Thanks to their all-purpose framing device—the club—and their casually conversational tone, they're a highly disparate mixture of Munchausenesque tall tales, jests, parables, puzzles, ghost stories, shaggy-dog stories, and science fiction that depends more on vagueness than on science. (Jorkens makes an art form out of vagueness; a typical remark—"These are details . . . of which I know nothing and would not be allowed to tell you if I did"—admirably sums up his approach.) If I'd first come across one of them in its original magazine appearance—see S. T. Joshi's invaluable list on page xxi—and had never before read a Jorkens tale, I might have been somewhat disappointed; if I were asked to select just one to represent Dunsany in an anthology, or if an uninitiated friend said, in effect, "I have time for only one story, so show me the best," I'd be hard put to find one that could comfortably stand alone.

Instead, the Jorkens stories have a kind of cumulative power, and I think their enjoyment depends on it; your fondness for them grows as your expectations become more realistic (you aren't going to be left with a lump in your throat or a chill down your spine, or particularly wiser) and as certain conventions—the cozy setting, the quirks of the speaker and his listeners, the little verbal games they play as preamble to most of the stories—become more familiar. Like colorful gewgaws in a shop window, they work better in the aggregate; take one home and it loses some of its luster.

That's why it's so welcome to have all these tales together at last in three plump double-decker volumes; there's something about the Jorkens stories that makes you want to own the entire series. I suppose this is a tribute to their very slightness, as well as to, for most of them, their brevity. As with candy or popcorn—or as with, if you prefer, the gold nuggets that, Jorkens swears, litter the island of Umboodwa—you're always tempted to say, "I'll have just one more."

Gaspard de la Nuit

In an ideal world, or so it's been said, a work of art would stand blissfully untouched by biography; it would be approached, judged, and enjoyed entirely on its own, with no thought for the human life behind it.

But you know that's not how things work; we're all gossips at heart, prurient and envious and sentimental, and our response to art is inevitably colored by what we know of its creator. It is impossible to read Dunsany, say, without remembering that he had a long, privileged life and traveled round the world shooting big game; it's impossible to forget that the novels of Trollope were written methodically each morning by a hardworking British postal administrator; or that Rimbaud gave up poetry and became a gunrunner (and possibly a slave trader); or that Chekhov and William Carlos Williams were doctors; or that Pound was a fascist; or that Conrad spoke no English till his twenties; or that Joyce cobbled together the Dublin of *Ulysses* while living in Trieste; or that John Clare spent half his life in a madhouse.

So, too, with *Gaspard de la Nuit*. Once you've absorbed Donald Sidney-Fryer's authoritative and extremely moving introduction to the life of *Gaspard*'s creator, Aloysius Bertrand, it's impossible to read the pieces that follow without being aware that they're the work of a sensitive, sickly, impoverished young man in his early

---

Foreword to *Gaspard de la Nuit* by Aloysius Bertrand, translated from the French by Donald Sidney-Fryer (Tarzana, CA: Black Coat Press, 2004).

twenties (with some material, no doubt, from his teenage years and some additional tweaks from a few years later); a bookish, ambitious, stagestruck youth, in love with words and with the past, doomed to die at thirty-four after a career of hardship, frustration, and failure, his plays unproduced except for a single abortive performance, and without ever seeing his masterpiece in print.

But if you haven't read *Gaspard,* you're in for a surprise.

Yes, its author lived in a time long gone, in the distant age of Poe, his death roughly coinciding with the birth of the Victorian era. He wrote his book 175 years ago, in another language, and filled its pages celebrating centuries earlier still.

Yet in Sidney-Fryer's translation he speaks to us in every line with remarkable intimacy and immediacy. There is nothing stuffy, precious, or effete about his writing—quite the contrary. It's crowded with life: with movement, humor, violence; with conversation and carousing; with bandits and buxom serving wenches and farting mules. For a collection of prose poems composed by a tragic young bohemian who to some degree died for his art, it's—surprisingly—a lot of fun.

I think of the pieces more as vignettes than as poems; many of them read like very brief short stories, others like scenes from longer works. They can be—as in the slapstick pratfalls of "Messire Jean," for example—as robust and rowdy as Rabelais, who, appropriately, is cited in one of *Gaspard*'s many epigraphs. (These epigraphs, incidentally, attached to each piece—from writers as familiar as Byron, Scott, and Cooper to sources as arcane as the *Memoirs of Olivier de la Marche, The Paternosters of Monsieur the Marshall,* and the *Biography of Martin Spickler*—attest to Bertrand's omnivorous reading and are alone worth the price of admission.)

Other pieces are reminiscent of Hugo, dominated as they are by fickle, unruly, potentially dangerous mobs that threaten to rise up at any moment. Some offer operatic or melodramatic endings, such as our final glimpse of Isaac, the Jewish butcher, who, cursing a squad of soldiers about to arrest him, throws himself out the nearest window into the Rhine. (Whether it's to his death or to freedom I cannot tell.)

Later we make the acquaintance of an unhappy "young recluse" in a monastery, the descendant of Gypsies and robbers, who dreams of a life of action and adventure and secretly amuses himself "by tracing diabolical faces on the white pages of [his] prayer book" (a bit of business that I can't help attributing to Bertrand himself). This young monk, too, will make his escape out a window.

And some vignettes seem touched by an almost Chaucerian spirit. See "The Five Digits of the Hand," with each finger representing a very real, very human character, delineated in only a few lines, yet overflowing with life, from the "corpulent Flemish tavern-keeper, bantering and obscene, who smokes at his door," to the man's youngest child, "a whimpering brat who is always toted about at the waist of his mother." They might just as easily be pilgrims on their way to Canterbury.

In a few passages, inspired as they are by paintings, one has the sense—and we've all done this, haven't we?—of our youthful author staring so intently, so longingly, at a picture of the past that he can almost feel himself enter it. Here, as in certain poems of Whitman's, Bertrand essentially presents us with a list, an inventory of things observed; or like Lovecraft in the poem "Providence"—HPL's heartfelt evocation, when in exile in New York, of his beloved hometown—Bertrand conjures up scenes through a systematic piling up of image after image, detail upon architectural detail, as if a frenzied camera were darting about, then zooming in for an unexpected close-up.

In Bertrand's own long and curious introduction, we're offered just such a catalogue, almost to the point of incantation, a building-up sight by sight of the old Dijon that he so loved, "the Dijon of the fourteenth and fifteenth centuries, that Dijon around which ran an ostentatious dance of eighteen towers, of eight gates ... with the houses made of hard-packed loam, with the pointed gables like a jester's cap, with the façades barred with St. Andrew's crosses; with the fortified mansions that have narrow barbicans, double spyholes ... with her churches, her *sainte-chapelle,* her abbeys, her monasteries, that once flaunted their processions of belfries, of steeples, of spires, unfurling as their banners their stained-glass windows of gold and azure." And swarming through this scene, like figures in a Brueghel painting, are "burgers, nobles, country people, soldiers, priests, monks, clerks, merchants, varlets, Jews, Lombards, pilgrims, minstrels, officers of Parliament and the Chamber of Accounts, officers of the salt tax, officers of the coinage, officers of the forest authority, officers of the Duke's household;—who clamor, who whistle, who sing, who complain, who pray, who curse."

What energy! What life! What a wonderful way to create a vanished city! Like a series of miniatures, the book's first vignette offers a similar, if more compressed, vision of old Haarlem: "And the canal where quivers the blue water, and the church where flames the stained-glass windows adorned with gold. . . . And the storks that beat their wings around the city clock. . . . And the carefree burgomaster who caresses with his hand his double chin, and the enamoured floriculturist who wastes away, his eye fixed on one tulip."

A section called "Chronicles" runs red with swordplay, fires, and gibbets, all served up with gusto, and is filled with the dialogue, in the mouths of many characters, of someone who's read, and been roused by, scores of historical romances. Another section, "Night and Her Glamours," offers liveliness of a different kind: lurid gothic horror with a certain cheerfully ghoulish Tim Burton quality, spooking us with the image of a figure "who wanders about, each night, through the deserted city, one eye fixed on the moon and the other—gouged!" The poor narrator himself is informed that, upon his death, "you would be food for the dung beetle that goes hunting, late in the afternoon, after the tiny flies blinded by the setting sun." Later he discovers in his lap—"O horror!—a monstrous and misshapen larva with a human face!"

Throughout these wildly diverse moods, settings, and situations, Bertrand has clearly been well served by Sidney-Fryer, who's brought to the task more than merely a translator's skill. A productive and highly regarded poet himself, he too has conjured up, and memorably, many a fantastic scene of bygone days. He's also brought to it a lifelong devotion to Bertrand's work; making *Gaspard* known and accessible to the English-speaking reader has been, for him, the labor of decades and one, most certainly, of love.

A Connecticut Yankee

Mark Twain was more prophetic than he knew when, in 1879, in a conversation with his friend William Dean Howells, he confessed: "A man can't write successful satire unless he be in a calm judicial good humor. I don't ever seem to be in a good enough humor with ANYthing to *satirize* it; no, I want to stand up before it and curse it, and foam at the mouth—or take a club and pound it to rags and pulp." *A Connecticut Yankee in King Arthur's Court,* completed ten years later, in May of 1899, exhibits much of the good humor Twain prized, but also much cursing and club-wielding. The book proves that he was a good judge of his own character—and that he was right about the prerequisites of successful satire.

Satiric the book is, from beginning to end; but the nature of its satire, its spirit, tone, and intention, changes as rapidly as Twain's mercurial personality. *Yankee* reads, in fact, like a novel written by a committee, a committee split by artistic differences and clashes of temperament, for it offers us by turns slapstick comedy and high tragedy, vaudeville routines and impassioned jeremiads, the cruelest of graveyard humor and the most unabashed sentimentality.

The novel's inconsistency of tone may be, in part, the result of Twain's efforts to ride herd on his own tempestuous nature; at times the narrative seems to follow the veering course of a deeply angry man who writes himself into rages, then lightens the mood

---

Afterword to *A Connecticut Yankee in King Arthur's Court* by Mark Twain (Pleasantville, NY: Reader's Digest, 1984).

with a joke. Twain was, moreover, a deeply divided man (this, indeed, is the theme of the excellent biography, Justin Kaplan's *Mr. Clemens and Mark Twain*) who longed, on the one hand, to be true to his rough-hewn Hannibal background, yet who craved the approval of the genteel world into which his talent and fame had thrust him. By the time he came to write *Yankee,* this former riverboat pilot and frontier journalist was married to a rather straitlaced coal heiress and was living with three demure daughters in one of the most imposing mansions in Hartford. The reception accorded his two previous novels was very much on his mind. He had seen *The Prince and the Pauper* (1881) extravagantly praised, especially within his own family, for its polished prose and wholesome sentiments. He had seen *Huckleberry Finn* (1885), with its broad humor and earthy language, damned by some of the country's more "respectable" critics and even banned from a few libraries—then go on to become a great popular success. Twain himself sought both kinds of acceptance; he was determined to please both the masses and the gentry.

Not surprisingly, it proved a difficult task. Twain suffered what he called "a dry interval of two years" in the middle of the book, put in seven-hour workdays on it, and often had trouble sleeping. At one point he wrote: "The fun, which was abounding in the *Yankee at Arthur's Court* up to three days ago, has slumped into funereal sadness, and this will not do—it will not answer at all. The very title of the book requires fun, and it must be furnished. But it can't be done, I see, while this cloud hangs over the workshop." Later his spirits improved, but *Yankee* remains, for all its comic moments, a bleak and bitter book. Kaplan terms its ending "a gruesome practical joke" and calls the novel "a book which, as far as it preaches anything, preaches irreverence, the guillotine, a reign of terror, and a kind of generalized despair."

The earliest notes for it, however, show Twain at his jocular best, the teller of funny stories, usually at his own good-natured expense. The original idea came to him from reading Sir Thomas Malory's fifteenth-century masterpiece, *Le Morte d'Arthur,* a primary source of Arthurian legend (though it was based on still earlier works) and an inspiration for such disparate chronicles as Spenser's *Faerie Queene,* Tennyson's *Idylls of the King,* T. H. White's *The Once and Future King,* and the historical romances of Mary Stewart. Malory, whom Twain quotes approvingly in *Yankee,* is full of high heroism and lordly language—just the sort of writer to excite not only Twain's admiration but also his sense of the ridiculous. He jotted down his initial thoughts during the early months of 1885:

> Dream of being a knight errant in armor in the middle ages. Have the notions and habits of thought of the present day mixed with the necessities of that. No pockets in the armor. No way to manage certain requirements of nature. Can't scratch. Cold in the head—can't blow—can't get at handkerchief, can't use iron sleeve. Iron gets red hot in the sun—leaks in the rain, gets white with frost and freezes me solid in winter. Suffer from lice and fleas. Make disagreeable clatter when I enter church. Can't dress or undress myself. Always getting struck by lightning. Fall down, can't get up.

These observations were soon to form one of the best-realized sections of the novel, the chapter entitled "Slow Torture." It is well researched and convincing; after reading it, one can never fantasize in quite the same way about deeds of derring-do in full armor.

Yet Twain was more than a storyteller, more than the stand-up comic lecturer so beloved of nineteenth-century audiences around the world. He was also, as Twain scholar Charles Neider says, "a bloodhound sniffing out injustice," "a self-proclaimed correction officer for the species," and in *Yankee* he had a more serious goal than merely poking fun at romantic conventions and the foibles of our ancestors. There is a moral to it. Twain, who grew up in a slaveholding society and who saw impoverished Southern whites throw away their lives in the Civil War to preserve a system that kept them in their place, realized a full century ahead of *1984* how easily victims can be made to internalize the worldview of their masters, until, like many of the downtrodden in *Yankee,* they become enthusiastic collaborators in their own oppression. The book makes clear that freedom must be taught, taught early; and that for all the horror of slavery, far more horrifying—and more common— is a mind in chains.

Twain himself stated the case a good deal more modestly. As he recounted in his *Autobiography* (a loose collection of memoirs, opinions, and occasional fabrications assembled by Twain over the course of many years):

> *A Connecticut Yankee in King Arthur's Court* was an attempt to imagine, and after a fashion set forth, the hard conditions of life for the laboring and defenseless poor in bygone times in England, and incidentally contrast these conditions with those under which the civil and ecclesiastical pets of privilege and high fortune lived in those times. I think I was purposing to contrast that English life, not just the English life of Arthur's day but the English life of the whole of the Middle Ages, with the life of modern Christendom and modern civilization—to the advantage of the latter, of course.

Contemplating these "hard conditions of life," however, whether of the poor serfs and slaves of medieval Britain or the oppressed subjects of colonialism in his own day, aroused the club-wielder in Twain. Thus it's not surprising to learn that, from the start, his plans for *Yankee* included an ending much like the one he eventually chose: a cataclysmic battle between the knights of England and (at least in his original notes) a modernly equipped military force with Gatling guns, heavy artillery, and iron warships armed with torpedoes.

The contrast between the wry humor of "Slow Torture" and the despairing apocalyptic vision of the end, with the Boss's small band of loyalists imprisoned within a ring of 25,000 moldering corpses, makes it clear that the work was a divided one from its earliest conception. The sense of discontinuity appears even in the opening pages, sometimes in the very progression from one paragraph to the next. At one point, for example, Twain the satirist, employing the colloquial language of which he was a master, describes the Knights of the Round Table as a gaggle of "big boobies":

> There did not seem to be brains enough in the entire nursery, so to speak, to bait a fish-hook with; but you didn't seem to mind that, after a little, because you soon saw that brains were not needed in a society like that, and indeed would have marred it, hindered it, spoiled its symmetry—perhaps rendered its existence impossible.

Suddenly, in the very next sentence, the diction makes an abrupt switch into mock-Malory as Twain the sentimentalist takes over:

> There was a fine manliness observable in almost every face; and in some a certain loftiness and sweetness that rebuked your belittling criticisms and stilled them. A most noble benignity and purity reposed in the countenance of him they called Sir Galahad, and likewise in the king's also; and there was majesty and greatness in the giant frame and high bearing of Sir Launcelot of the Lake.

These are the same knights, incidentally, who later come to the hero's rescue pedaling furiously on bicycles!

Much the same discontinuity recurs throughout the novel, the coarsest of belly laughs alternating with scenes of high moral indignation. You can see it, for example, in the novel's almost schizophrenic attitude toward death, often within a single chapter. Take, for example, Morgan le Fay's murder of a handsome young page who has the ill luck to trip and fall lightly against her, and who is stabbed to death for it. "Poor child!" says the narrator, "he slumped to the floor, twisted his silken limbs in one great straining contortion of pain, and was dead. Out of the old king was wrung an involuntary 'O-h!' of compassion"—and out of most readers as well. Yet the very next paragraph, noting how swiftly the queen has the body and blood removed, opens with a gag: "I saw that she was a good housekeeper."

That evening Morgan's banquet is interrupted in a highly melodramatic fashion by an intruder, "an old and bent and white-haired lady, leaning upon a crutch-stick." Raising her stick, she proceeds to curse the queen for the murder of the page, her grandson. Morgan, predictably, is about to have the woman put to death—"To the stake with her!"—until the Boss humanely intervenes. Yet a couple of paragraphs later the spirit of satire resurfaces, and the old woman's erstwhile savior, tongue once again in cheek, reports that he had the queen's entire band hanged for their sorry performance of a song. Thus on one page he's helping an old lady, on the next he's hanging musicians!—just as, later in the book, while traveling with the king, the narrator will glorify humanity on one page ("A man is a man, at bottom. Whole ages of abuse and oppression cannot crush the manhood clear out of him") and damn it on the next ("There are times when one would like to hang the whole human race and finish the farce").

The visit to Morgan's castle draws to an end, but not without still another shift in sensibility. Immediately after the unexpected jest about the hanging, we are taken on a tour of the queen's dungeon and given a series of vignettes—the book abounds with them—illustrating the variety of human ignorance and cruelty. In the first of these, a peasant undergoing torture on the rack has refused to confess to his crime, the poaching of a deer, lest his property be forfeited to the queen and his family starve. "In a corner crouched a poor young creature, her face drawn in anguish, a half-wild and hunted look in her eyes, and in her lap lay a little child asleep." Babies, often clasped to breasts, are an inevitable feature of the novel's sentimental scenes; another is tears. "Why, her eyes were as grateful as an animal's, when you do it a kindness that it understands [the Boss has ordered her husband freed]. The baby was out of her way and she had her cheek against the man's in a minute, and her hands fondling his hair, and her happy tears running down." Before the tour is through, the Boss has another occasion to eulogize, in the flowery Victorian rhetoric he adopts for such occasions, "that poor grandma with the broken heart, and that fair young creature lying butchered, his little silken pomps and vanities laced with his golden blood."

Yet how does this visit conclude? Predictably, with a gag—a bit of black humor. Watching the procession of ravaged, half-starved prisoners he's just had released from the dungeon, the Yankee remarks, "I *wish* I could photograph them!" Moments later the queen, having mistaken his meaning, is "moving on the procession with an ax!" Twain returns to his familiar colloquial tone:

> Well, she certainly was a curious one, was Morgan le Fay. I have seen a good many kinds of women in my time, but she laid over them all for variety. . . . She had no more idea than a horse of how to photograph a procession; but being in doubt, it was just like her to try to do it with an ax.

And so, after pages of sustained horror, the chapter ends with some amused head-shaking.

Twain varies his narrative's pace and perspective as radically as he does its tone, choosing which events he'll describe in detail—and which he'll ignore—in accordance with his own peculiar whims and the dictates of the story. His hero, unlike most of us, wastes no time worrying *how* a blow on the head in a Hartford factory could have transported him to Arthurian England and devotes barely a moment to mourning the loss of friends and loved ones. Yet later, no doubt with an eye to entertaining audiences of the day, Twain spends page after page, during the Boss's travels with Sandy, on a sort of medieval Burns and Allen routine, contrasting the girl's ornate chatter with the Yankee's 1880s slang. Yielding, perhaps, to his personal enthusiasms, Twain provides far more details about the medieval laborer's wages and living costs than most readers probably want to know; yet great historical changes and years of upheaval are hurried over, as in a tall tale, with barely a word of explanation. On one page a naked Hank Morgan is saved from the stake through the extraordinary good luck (also not explained) of having just happened to know the exact time and date of a convenient solar eclipse; just one page later he is already "the second personage in the kingdom," and by the following chapter he's become "the Boss," the most powerful being in the land. (His talent for predicting eclipses remains undiminished; he even appears to know the date of every *lunar* eclipse.) In less than half a dozen years, sixth-century England has been transformed into a fair approximation of nineteenth-century Connecticut, complete with a stock market and telephones; yet by the novel's end this entire civilization has been all but obliterated.

The key to this civilization is technology, for in many ways *Yankee* is an expression of Twain's continuing fascination with, and faith in, the machine. You might wonder how you'd fare if you found yourself thrust back 1,300 years into the past; most of us could barely knock together a bookshelf. The Boss, however, is confidently able to "make anything a body wanted—anything in the world," and he's therefore Twain's ideal mouthpiece (even to the extent of holding forth on *Roderick Random,* Arkansas journalism, French history, and other subjects few Hartford factory superintendents might have felt competent to expound upon). Typically, the first thing the Boss does after gaining power is to open a patent office, even before founding newspapers and schools. (Establishing churches is noticeably absent from the list.)

At the time of *Yankee*'s writing, Twain was involved with a machine of his own: a typesetter invented by James W. Paige of Rochester, New York. Twain had first seen it in 1880 at the Colt arms factory in Hartford, where it was under development, and had promptly invested $2,000—which quickly grew to $5,000, then more—in the "mechanical marvel." In fact, just a week before beginning work on *Yankee,* he'd organized a company to market and manufacture the machine. Twain termed it "very much the best investment I have ever made," anticipated a worldwide sale of 100,000 units, and hoped to finish his novel, symbolically, on the day the typesetter was finally perfected.

Unfortunately for all concerned, Paige's invention proved a technological dead end and was soon outmoded by the more efficient Mergenthaler Linotype machine. Its failure eventually cost Twain some $200,000 and, in 1894, plunged him into bankruptcy, a state from which it took him years to recover. Even before *Yankee*'s completion in 1889, it was clear that the machine had run into problems. In the face of Twain's increasing anxiety, the novel paints a reassuring fantasy world in which all machines work splendidly.

Whether glorifying the wonders of machinery, vilifying the monarchy and the church, or refusing to come to a conclusion about that exasperating species known as man, *A Connecticut Yankee* speaks for Twain himself, one of the species' most remarkable personalities. It bears the stamp of his troubled genius on every page; and that is perhaps the greatest strength of this complex, flawed, fascinating book.

The Ceremonies, 2016 edition: A Note from the Author

It has often been said . . .

But why am I resorting, in the very first line, to a voice so vague and passive? Because the observation that follows seems to have been credited, if the web is any guide, to nearly a dozen distinguished names, from Da Vinci to Auden.

Well, then, to repeat: It has often been said that a work of art is never finished, merely abandoned. And while I'm not sure I'd proclaim this book a work of art, it was most definitely abandoned—in fact, a little sooner than I'd have liked. I was late—characteristically late, some might say—in delivering the manuscript; and weeks or months after that, I missed the publisher's deadline for turning in the proofs. I remember literally scribbling last-minute changes to the final pages as I rode the elevator up to the Viking offices. (Still, when I recall that I was also editing *Twilight Zone* magazine at the time, I'm a bit amazed I ever managed to complete the book at all.)

On top of other problems, likely as a result of the delays I caused, the hardcover edition was never properly proofread. So in sending the book out into the world a second time, after more than thirty years, I've tried to correct what strikes me now as some clumsy writing here and there, as well as a few mistakes and inconsisten-

---

Introduction to the revised edition of *The Ceremonies* (Hornsea, UK: PS Publishing, 2016).

cies. Though I doubt anyone but me would notice the changes, I'm a lot happier with the present version.

One thing I haven't attempted to do, however, is to update it. *The Ceremonies* was first published in 1984, but the story it grew from was written at the start of the '70s. The book is set, therefore, in a pre-cell-phone, pre-Internet world, and the places it describes are considerably different today, if certainly no better. Attitudes have changed about what's dangerous (cigarettes, suntans); so have salaries, food prices, and rent. You might even say that the past is a foreign country . . . although I believe that, too, has been said before.

Imagine, no laptops! No e-books! I invite you to return to that strange, vanished world.

A Conversation with T.E.D. Klein

Just who is T.E.D. Klein? Certainly one of the most noted and notable authors and editors to emerge in the 1970s and 1980s. The span from his first publication, "The Events at Poroth Farm" (1972), to his latest collection, now out from Subterranean Press, *Reassuring Tales* (2006) (which, coincidentally, concludes with that first story), is long enough that his name might have passed from memory. That is clearly not the case. A winner of the British Fantasy Society's Best Novel award for *The Ceremonies* and the World Fantasy Award for his novella "Nadelman's God" (collected in *Dark Gods*), Klein and his work remain important and relevant to horror fiction and American literature because Klein is one of the horror genre's most careful writers. Every word is placed for maximum impact with minimal fuss. He writes in a normal voice, from points of view that anyone can understand, yet he offers us visions of horrors and ages unseen.

My first encounter with Klein was in Kirby McCauley's definitive collection *Dark Forces*. His story, "Children of the Kingdom," haunts me to this day with its fleeting glimpses of the horrors under our feet, under our streets, the horrors that entwine with every day of our lives. It's the everyday quality that makes Klein so unique. He creates characters who seem like our neighbors, who live resolutely in our world. Then he shows us just how little we know of that world. How much there is to fear.

Klein himself has distinguished himself not just with his writing

---

Interview by Rick Kleffel, *Cemetery Dance 58* (2008).

but his editing as well. His time as editor of *Twilight Zone* magazine saw the introduction of authors we still read. He's written poetry and nonfiction as well. Klein is more than anything else a name who remains, a man who is reliably reprinted for and enjoyed by new generations of horror fiction readers. *CD* tracked him down on the event of the release of *Reassuring Tales* to unwrap some—not all—of the mystery behind some of the best-loved horror fiction of the last century.

RK: What writer do you first remember reading, and why?

TK: Booth Tarkington's *Penrod* books—sort of an early-twentieth-century *Tom Sawyer*. My father had a big black omnibus volume when he was a boy, and he passed it on to me, in a fairly battered state, when I was eight or nine. I read it over and over and still remember many lines—like the description of a caterpillar resting on a twig, looking as if it were "lost in reverie." The writing's quite brilliant and very funny.

RK: When and how did horror fiction catch your attention? Did you always like the genre?

TK: I suppose I got into it via science fiction, which holds almost no interest for me now. At a fairly young age, I began reading the old Tom Corbett series, loved all eight books, and actually wrote to Grosset & Dunlap asking if there'd be more; I even suggested that one of the characters be dropped and an old one be brought back. I remember getting a letter from the publishers assuring me that "Mr. Rockwell"—the books were written under the house name Carey Rockwell—"is currently at work on a new manuscript." At the time, of course, I wasn't quite sure what a "manuscript" was, but I kept waiting for further adventures to come out . . . and they never did. Meanwhile, like so many other readers, I was discovering Robert A. Heinlein's juvenile novels in the elementary-school library; it was probably the title *Space Cadet* that first caught my eye.

RK: Could you sketch for us your development as a reader of horror fiction? Once you started, how did you explore the genre? Via anthologies, recommendations, vague guesswork . . . ?

TK: Lovecraft—no surprise—was the first horror writer whose work I actively began seeking out, and I first came across him in Wise & Fraser's *Great Tales of Terror and the Supernatural,* one of two immensely popular and influential Modern Library Giants; the other, which I already owned, was Healy & McComas's *Famous Science Fiction Stories.* I also read just about every other anthology in the local library's SF section. Today, I find big fat books daunting; I'll still consider settling down with an 800-page history, but the idea of reading, say, that new 1,100-page Pynchon seems absolutely ludicrous. In my school years, though, I felt as if I had all the time in the world, and the thicker the anthology, the better. The library had dozens.

RK: What was the feeling towards the horror genre in the culture around you when you grew up? Did it change in any way that changed your feelings towards horror?

TK: Long before I started reading horror fiction, I had an insatiable fascination with horror movies, EC comics, monster magazines—and they were all readily available. I'd devour them by day, yet would fervently regret it at bedtime, when I'd occasionally work myself into a real terror. My suspicion, looking back, is that this was all a way of getting my parents to come marching into my room to comfort me. At the time, though, it felt like—and I know this sounds glib—being addicted to the very thing I was allergic to.

RK: When and why did you decide to start writing horror fiction?

TK: Primarily, I was trying to imitate the sort of writing I most enjoyed.

RK: Your first published story was "The Events at Poroth Farm." How did the novella come to being, and how did you get it published in *Beyond the Dark Gateway #2*?

TK: Well, I recount it—not that there's all that much to it—in the introduction to the Necronomicon edition of "Poroth," and I've more or less cannibalized myself in the intro to *Reassuring Tales*. Suffice it to say that I wrote "Poroth" one summer, in the locale where it's set, with the vague hope of sending it to Arkham House—only to learn, when I'd finished, that August Derleth had died. That it ended up in an illustrated fanzine seemed quite wonderful, since I had no idea what else to do with it.

RK: This story is notable for its use of other fiction that bleeds through the reality of the tale itself, just as your story bleeds through into the reader's reality. Did you think of yourself as a metafictional writer?

TK: Not until this moment! But it's an interesting question. My main object was to acknowledge—gratefully, sometimes guiltily—the genre's long tradition and the many works of fiction that have helped make the world a bit more interesting. And of course there's the sheer pleasure of sounding off about the things one likes or doesn't like.

RK: Come to think of it, it strikes me that the horror fiction genre itself is rather metafictional. Care to comment on how that affects the genre and your work?

TK: Does an acknowledgement of other fictional creations make a work metafictional? Because if so, all those hip new horror movies—I don't see many, but I'm more or less aware of them—would qualify: the kind in which characters say, "Yikes, this is just like a movie." Maybe the horror genre's a self-conscious one. On the other hand, it often relies on a sort of self-imposed amnesia. For example, Robert Bloch once suggested that his sequel to *Psycho* was a science fiction novel, since it was set in an alternate universe in which the book and movie *Psycho* never existed.

RK: Could you talk about the subsequent history of "The Events at Poroth Farm" after its first publication? It underwent several reprints and several revisions.

TK: I tend to tweak it a bit each time I reread it.

RK: What else were you doing during the time you were writing in the 1970s? How did it affect your writing? How has your second life affected your writing?

TK: I was working as the in-house script reader at Paramount Pictures' East Coast story department, on the thirty-ninth floor of a building at Central Park West and Columbus Circle. I was paid to read novels—usually just before they were published—and screenplays, but I spent a lot of my time staring out the window, watching ships sail up and down the Hudson. It's funny; I'd go to a party in those days and someone would ask me what I did, and when I talked about reading for Paramount, their eyes would light up and I'd be peppered with questions as to what things I'd read had become movies, etc. etc. (And by the way, I had a terrible track record; I remember writing dismissive reports about *Death Wish* and *All the President's Men*.) But later, when I was editing *Twilight Zone* and, after that, *CrimeBeat*—in other words, at times when I was convinced I had the coolest, most enviable job in the world—most people I'd run into, unless they happened to be fantasy or crime buffs, would just look sort of blank and uninterested, as if I'd told them I worked for the phone company.

At any rate, the one thing I can say about my work life—as opposed to writing and editing—is that I wish I'd studied something besides English back in college; I wish I had a degree in engineering or biology or history. Not to make more money, which has never been a problem, but just to know more about how the world actually works. As it stands, the only thing I know for sure is how to punctuate a sentence.

RK: And then you connected with Charles L. Grant. Tell us about "Petey," monsters, madmen, and narratives that combine the two.

TK: My friend Kathy Murray once remarked how wouldn't it be neat if, in a story, the pictures in a tarot deck kept changing slightly, like in M. R. James's "Mezzotint." I suppose at that point I was off and running.

RK: You hooked up with Ramsey Campbell and Arkham House for "Black Man with a Horn."

TK: As I recall, the germ of that was my speculation about what it must be like to be a sort of Frank Belknap Long figure, who's been writing for decades, laboring diligently but producing essentially uninspired work, and who was once the friend of someone famous, like Lovecraft, so that he's become little more than a footnote in the other's biography. It's obviously a common predicament.

RK: Tell us about "Children of the Kingdom," *Dark Forces,* and Kirby McCauley.

TK: Kirby's an amazing, colorful, erudite, eccentric, sometimes exasperating character whom I've been friends with ever since the early '70s, when he wrote me from St. Paul, introducing himself as a young agent and offering to take me on as a client; I think he'd read "Poroth" in a *Year's Best* collection. This was pre-King, of course, but I was impressed that he already represented a number of writers familiar to me, including Frank Long and Ramsey Campbell. *Dark Forces* was, for Kirby, a labor of love. What excited me—and what prompted me to write "Children"—is that Isaac Bashevis Singer was going to have a story in the anthology, and I very much wanted to be in the same book.

RK: There's a real sense of place to your stories. One gets the feeling with every story that you, the author, must have lived in these places and even been in the situations—perhaps minus the supernatural elements, perhaps not. How do you create that sense of place? Did you live in these places?

TK: In "Poroth," I think—or maybe in *The Ceremonies,* or maybe both—the protagonist pens a note in his journal about mainstream fiction being built upon character, mystery as built upon plot, and horror as built upon a sense of place. Often, for me, that's what works best in a story I've read—even one that isn't otherwise successful—and what I most remember afterwards: the setting. It's also, I think, what Lovecraft most responded to in his reading. The settings of my own stories are—as with any other writer, I suppose—inspired by places I'm familiar with, sometimes directly, sometimes in a form that's scrambled or piecemeal or exaggerated.

RK: How did you move from writing acclaimed stories into the editor's job at *Twilight Zone* magazine?

TK: That was due to Kirby; he had the idea for the magazine and installed me as editor, for which I'll always be grateful. He and I collaborated on the official proposal for it, and Eric Protter—then the editorial director of *Gallery,* a sort of poor man's *Playboy*—was instrumental in getting *Gallery* to buy it; *Twilight Zone* shared their offices and staff. I wasn't entirely inexperienced—I'd edited the daily newspaper at Brown, I'd put together a prototype for what was to be a gothic-romance tabloid for women (the project died when the money man was exposed in the press as a mobster), and before *TZ* was launched I served an apprenticeship as *Gallery*'s copy editor—but I sure didn't know much.

RK: Your tenure at *Twilight Zone* saw the introduction of many of today's most important science fiction, horror, and fantasy authors. Could you tell us about your favorites, who stood out, who was easy to deal with and perhaps not so easy to deal with?

TK: I loved almost all the stories I published, and it always seemed to me that there were three or four times as many good ones as there was room for. And it was often a real pleasure to sit down to lunch with various writers, though I tried to bear in mind what Bob Sheckley—who at that time was *Omni*'s fiction editor—had warned me: "Everyone's going to want to be your friend."

Yet what struck me most, in dealing with writers and illustrators, was how much more agreeable it was to deal with the latter. The writers were brainy and clever, God knows, but they were also, to some extent, an envious, ambitious, rather neurotic bunch who were, on some level, unhappy because they weren't Stephen King. The illustrators, on the other hand, were sort of easygoing and cool and good-looking, especially the women. They genuinely seemed to enjoy one another's work; when they'd meet in the office, they seemed to get along rather than sizing one another up. They all seemed quite dazzling to me, and still do. So-called fine artists—you know, the sort whose work fetches great sums at galleries—often strike me as poseurs and frauds, and musicians have always seemed at best strange and at worst creepy; their talent is completely alien to me. But I've always admired illustrators and wish I had their gift.

Selecting the stories for *Twilight Zone* was something of a burden—I felt terrible rejecting submissions and did it badly, sometimes giving writers the impression they'd come closer than they really had—but selecting the illustrator for each story was a joy.

Well, I did have one joy regarding the writers: We had a yearly competition for unpublished writers, and, as you can imagine, it was a thrill to phone someone with the news that his or her story had been selected as one of our winners. It's awfully nice to think that you've made someone's week, or month, or year.

RK: How much did you have to do with *Night Cry*? Could you tell readers a bit about this digest-sized companion?

TK: Eric Protter was—happily, still is—a lifelong magazine veteran and was always trying to come up with ways to reprint stories and recycle them for relatively little money. I'm pretty sure that *Night Cry,* in its inexpensive digest size, was his idea.

RK: I believe that *Night Cry* may have been the first place I saw the artwork of J. K. Potter. Did his visual style influence your writings or your editorial choices?

TK: Hmm, was Potter in *Night Cry*? I'd forgotten; maybe it was after I left. All I can tell you is how I feel now, which is that, while I know he's an extremely nice guy and very talented, I don't care for his stuff at all; I think it's cheapened everything he's been allowed to illustrate and that it's had a pernicious effect on the field in general. Too hard-edged and precise, too blatantly freakish—exactly the sort of things one doesn't want in a horror illustration. And by now, way too familiar. Ironically, as it happens, he did an extremely nice cover for *Reassuring Tales*—quite restrained and surprisingly atmospheric—but I'd had in mind something lighter, more humorous, and the publisher was kind enough to indulge me.

RK: Tell us about writing *The Ceremonies* and its relation to "The Events at Poroth Farm."

TK: Once again, it was Kirby's idea. He said, "You know, Ted, if you expanded that story, I'll bet I could sell it as a novel." That seemed an astonishing notion. You mean, all I have to do is expand this story I already wrote and I'll have an actual book? I plunged right in.

RK: This is perhaps a good time to talk about how you create fear in your writing. There is a scene in *The Ceremonies* that I'll never forget where a baby is attacked by bees. How would you slot that scene into your pantheon of frights?

TK: I recall that my aim in that scene was to describe the horror somewhat offhandedly. During film school at Columbia, I saw a really devastating war movie, *The Red and the White,* by the Hungarian director Miklós Jancsó. His camera sort of drifts away from scenes of anguish and violence as if they were of little import and not very interesting, so that sometimes terrible things happen offscreen. I think that makes the horror more powerful.

RK: What are your feelings about the supernatural in life? Have you ever had any experience that will not yield to logical explanation? Do you believe or want to believe?

TK: As children will do, I once asked my mother, "Is there really a Santa Claus?" A few years after I got that piece of disillusioning news, I asked "Is there really a God?" I don't think she ever firmly answered that one, but I've been an atheist ever since, and it's always amazed me that any thinking person could *not* be. In junior high, I did go through a stage when I was fascinated by the occult, yoga, voodoo, self-hypnosis, UFOs, poltergeists, numerology, Druids, yetis, reincarnation, magic spells, jujitsu, ventriloquism, astrology, and other alluring subjects, but I like to think I've put that sort of stuff behind me. I don't believe in God, I don't believe in ghosts or goblins, I don't believe we have immortal souls, and I don't subscribe to the paranoid antigovernment conspiracy theories of the far left and right.

RK: If you look at the online bibliographies, you may see an entry for a novel titled *Nighttown*. Can you tell us about the novel?

TK: I sold the idea to Viking without ever quite figuring out how I was going to accomplish all I'd promised. I got around halfway through the novel and began to think it was getting too damned *big*—I'd set out with the hope of writing something lean and fast-paced, like *The Thirty-Nine Steps*—and increasingly preposterous (a word that, when you come down to it, surely applies to most horror fiction). Still, dumb as it may sound, I may go back to it someday.

RK: Let's talk about *Dark Gods*. It's a collection of three novellas we've talked about already, and a new one, "Nadelman's God." This one brings to mind your sense of humor.

TK: Thanks. When Doug Winter was interviewing me for *Faces of Fear,* he asked what sort of writing I'd like to do if I weren't writing horror, and I immediately said that I've always wished I could write humor. He told me that a number of others he'd asked had said the same thing. Makes you wonder, doesn't it?

RK: We also note that you seem to like this length, the novella, more than most. What is it that appeals to you about this format?

TK: Well, unless it's tale of pure gimmickry, you do want some space to build up atmosphere. And sometimes, even *with* a gimmick, you want to pad it, swaddle it, disguise that gimmick amidst a fog of prose, hoping thereby to make it seem less naked and silly.

RK: You've published poetry as well. Tell us where and when and if you can, why.

TK: It was really just an exercise to see if I could. However, I want to point out that I do actually *read* poetry and have a whole bookcase of it. Call me a poetry consumer; I buy a lot more than I read, and I read a lot more than I understand. Literally last night, prompted by a Mark Strand essay I'd come across on the web, I found myself rereading this famous Archibald MacLeish poem called "You, Andrew Marvell"—about time, mortality, and the wonder of finding oneself on this planet rolling through space—which I strongly recommend to everyone.

RK: Your stories seem very finely written, yet never one bit overwritten. Do you rewrite, let stories simmer, so to speak?

TK: I *hope* my stories aren't overwritten, but it's hard to judge, sometimes, what to tell and what to merely hint at. Recently—just a few weeks ago, in fact—I wrote a story for an anthology aimed at teens. One of the boys in it is haunted by something vaguely like a giant furry caterpillar. (No, it's not homage to E. F. Benson; it's just what seemed to work.) At one point he shocks everyone by attacking a new teacher visiting the school, and no one can figure out why. I thought I would provide a little shudder by mentioning, just in passing, that the teacher was an ordinary fellow with "glasses, dark hair, and a beard." I thought the beard would be as unsubtle as a red flag, but in fact the editor missed it and—noting that teen readers would be sure to do the same—had me change the description to "glasses, dark hair, and a dark, fuzzy beard."

RK: You've spoken about writer's block before. Why did you say what you did when you said it, and do you still feel that way now?

TK: Hmm . . . Maybe you're talking about how once, at a long-ago party in the Village, I was chatting with a psychoanalyst about my difficulty finishing *The Ceremonies*. He nodded sympathetically and said, "And how long have you had this writer's block?"—at which point, as I was assuring him, "Oh, no, it's not that at all," I somehow dumped my entire glass of Scotch all over his corduroy jacket. I remember laughing in embarrassment as I dabbed at his sleeve with a napkin. I'm not sure whether he was laughing too.

RK: Horror was the genre of the 1980s, which saw Stephen King become a household name. As the boom exploded, how did you feel about the quality and the quantity of what was being written?

TK: You know, at that time I was so busy putting *Twilight Zone* together that virtually everything I read—I mean, everything in the genre—was read with the magazine in mind. I do remember that when King was nice enough to give us a story—and believe me, he did it out of niceness—the sales inevitably went up. Which prompted the publishers, every fucking issue, to complain if I didn't have King on the cover.

RK: How did horror films influence your fiction? Start at the beginning, then take us through the heyday of the 1970s and the 1980s.

TK: I'm a very easy mark at horror movies. I remember seeing *Alien* shortly after it opened and wondering, as I left the theater, why my right arm felt sort of stiff. Then I realized that I'd been holding it up for the past two hours—that is, I'd been viewing most of the movie through the fingers of my right hand. It's interesting that what's always scared me most is simply an ugly humanlike face; I mean, with all the horrifying things that can happen in a movie, the scariest for me is simply, tritely, the moment when you first get a look at the face of the monster. And for someone who, in theory, has a fairly sophisticated knowledge of the field, I have the absolutely dumbest, simplest, most basic and primitive nightmares: like being chased by a bear or hiding from a wolf. When I was at film school back in the '70s, I asked a number of my fellow students to tell me the scariest movie they'd ever seen. I got dozens of different answers; not surprisingly, it was always a movie that the person had seen as a young child. One friend of mine said he'd never been scared by anything except his mother's vacuum cleaner.

RK: Horror fiction has been seen as both subversive and conservative; some horror undermines the status quo, other horror subtly or not so subtly supports the powers that be. Where do you think your horror fiction fits into that spectrum, and do you think that horror tends to default to one or the other end of that spectrum?

TK: I used to discuss this with my friend Jack Sullivan, who put together *The Penguin Encyclopedia of Horror and the Supernatural;* we never quite came to an agreement on it. All I can say is that my own tastes—and my politics, and my morality—run to the conservative.

RK: Your wrote the screenplay for the movie *Trauma*, directed by Dario Argento, starring Asia Argento and Piper Laurie. Tell us how that came to pass and what the whole experience was like for you. Did you have input while the movie was being filmed? How did it feel when you first saw your work on the screen? How does it feel now, on DVD?

TK: Argento's original treatment struck me as something of a mess—illogical, rambling, not entirely worked out, pointlessly sadistic—but I was eager for the screenwriting job, and I think my pitch was essentially: Hey, yeah, sure, it's great, I can work with this, no need to make many changes. So much for integrity. I did, in the end, make as many changes as I could.

It was great fun to work with Argento, and God knows he's an amusing, eccentric character—maybe a tad *calculatedly* eccentric; one could never be sure. We spent some time scouting locations in Pittsburgh, and later he got excited at the prospect of maybe filming in New Orleans, but in the end it proved cheapest to film in bland old Minneapolis. Bummer! During the early stages of production I was installed in a hotel out there to write some revised scenes, and that's the last time I ever saw him.

Of course, it was a tremendous kick to be working on a film—all this while putting out *CrimeBeat* and at one point trying not to let my colleagues there know that for a few days, at least, I wasn't actually in New York. Sometimes, though, it was a little frustrating. Typically, I would show Dario a scene I'd written, say three or four pages long, and he would look it over and nod and smile, and then he would say—gesturing at the page, in his imperfect English—"Ah, yes. You cut, you cut, yes?" Meaning, whittle this dialogue down to around twenty seconds. I had a cute, elaborate beginning involving a construction site, scaffolding, and a severed head; it ended up costing too much. Passages of exposition got cut, too, so that the resulting film makes no sense. At least, I suspect it doesn't; I've never actually watched it in its entirety, though I've watched a number of times the scene where Asia takes off the cloth binding her breasts. Interesting family.

Andy Sands, a friend from the production, has said that the trouble with *Trauma* was "too much plot, too little time." He's right. Dario wanted a serial killer with a backstory and a weird murder weapon, he wanted a mystery, he wanted a love story, he wanted a story that took place over a number of years, and he wanted, most peculiarly of all, to make a statement about the horrors of anorexia, a disorder that seemed completely out of left field but that for some reason fascinated him. And each time he'd see another movie or hear an interesting anecdote from someone he happened to run into, he'd want to incorporate elements of that into the movie. I remember that after he saw the Woody Allen film *Shadows and Fog*, he wanted the movie to look like that. And after he saw, on TV, the old Hitchcock film *Shadow of a Doubt*, he wanted that to be our model. He was forever changing his mind and coming up with new ideas—he could be extremely inventive, and he was an excellent mime and a mimicker of voices—all of which is nice, in a way, if you have a plot that makes sense, a basic logical structure to support the material. I always imagined that my role would be to provide some discipline, some structure, some logic. But I sure don't think I succeeded.

I don't own the DVD, but it's nice to know it's out there. Oh, and by the way, let me give credit where it's due: It was Kirby who came up with the title.

RK: How did Bill Schafer coax those *Reassuring Tales* from you?

TK: I spend a couple of pages in the book explaining that. Or maybe just grumbling. I think I say somewhere that, as I look back, I can see that basically it's been hard to get any work out of me without arm-twisting, ego-stroking, or the dangling of money.

RK: Nice title, of course. Care to comment?

TK: I'll quote, if I may, from the book: "Blame that on one of the living writers I admire most, Ramsey Campbell, who, back in 1980, in the introduction to his collection *Dark Companions,* declared: 'I believe that horror fiction cannot be too frightening or too disturbing. Too much of it seeks to reassure.' Seriously as I take whatever Ramsey says—and I'm proud of having written what may have been the first critical appreciation of his work—I don't share this curiously punitive sentiment. Personally, I've never had the ability, the temperament, or the intention of scaring the shit out of anybody, and I don't especially enjoy being scared myself. No, really. I think it's a pretty rough world out there and that we need all the reassurance we can get. And so, for years, I played with the idea of naming a collection—by way of a joking nod to Ramsey—*Reassuring Tales*. As it happens, I never actually sat down and wrote those tales (surprise!), but I thought it would be fun at least to use the title, especially if I could convince Jason Eckhardt to do a suitably mock-pulpish cover.

RK: Horror has seen a resurgence of late. How do you feel today's efforts compare to those of the 1980s?

TK: I have to tell you that I almost never read it, unless it's written by a friend who's counting on a response. In fact, I read very little fiction at all. Life is too short. Like every other upstanding white middle-aged American male, I've become a Civil War buff and a World War II buff, and I'm also trying to remedy my very sketchy education in science—which means dutifully plowing through four or five science magazines each month. I'd like to learn a few things before I die.

RK: How many years until our next new novella?

TK: Well, you never know. Keep watching the skies.

RK: Thank you for speaking with us. We look forward to reading and rereading your work.

III. The Twilight Zone

Stories from the Twilight Zone

If you were born in the twentieth century and, sometime during the past thirty years, happened to pass within viewing distance of a television set, you're probably acquainted with the man who wrote this book. Rod Serling—who died, age fifty, in 1975—is surely one of the most familiar figures in the annals of broadcasting, and was the possessor of one of the screen's most distinctive voices: a sometimes wry, sometimes somber voice that, even today, is instantly recognizable. You can hear it in every line he wrote.

In fact, if you've seen a single episode of TV's original *Twilight Zone*, chances are you'll never get that voice out of your head, with its echoes of daddy, wise uncle, camp counselor, professor, and network anchorman all rolled into one. Thanks to that voice, and to the series' continued popularity in syndicated form, the tales in this book are coming to you with certain uncommon advantages—ready-made faces to go with the characters' names, the presence of an expert storyteller speaking into memory's ear—and a certain disadvantage: You may be less likely to approach them as stories that can stand on their own.

And that would be a shame. Because even if the series had never graced the airwaves and Rod Serling had never stepped onto America's television screens, hands folded gravely before him, the phrase "the Twilight Zone," as this book demonstrates, would still signify

---

Introduction to *Stories from the Twilight Zone* by Rod Serling (New York: Bantam, 1986).

something special: a world of "what if?" where wishes come true (sometimes horribly), where illusion reigns and magic really works (but only so long as you believe), where little guys are blessed with the strength of titans, where miraculous machines spell our salvation—or our doom—and where the most frightening monsters of all turn out to be ourselves.

It's also a world whose coordinates are ever-so-slightly askew: where, on the railroad line between Stamford and Westport, you'll find a town called Willoughby that isn't on the map; where a transatlantic jumbo jet is liable to arrive at the right destination but in the wrong year; and where, according to "The Mighty Casey," the Brooklyn Dodgers played not at Ebbets Field but at Tebbet's. Baseball aficionados may quibble; but then, the Twilight Zone has always enjoyed its own unique geography.

TV aficionados may do likewise, noting that, in the televised version of "Casey," the team was not the Dodgers but a ragtag bunch known as the Hoboken Zephyrs. There are many such changes in each of the stories that follow, from initial script to TV show to printed page, right down to the way you distinctly remember seeing the show when you were twelve. But these and a thousand other tiny alterations and elaborations are merely the stuff of late-night arguments among trivia buffs. While you're sure to discover lines of familiar dialogue in the pages ahead, and even patches of the original narration, they are simply the skeletons on which Serling hung the tales.

What matters is that, lovingly expanded and embellished, the stories have been given a new life here. For every character who wears a perfunctory description pulled straight from the teleplay, like the "attractive widow in her thirties" in "The Big, Tall Wish," we have others who reveal a recognizable humanity, such as the construction foreman in "Escape Clause," warily approaching the scene of a gruesome accident: "He covered his eyes because of a normal reluctance to view mangled bodies. He also peeked between two fingers, because of the equally normal trait of being fascinated by the horrible."

The short-story format has also allowed Serling the room to indulge a gift for language and imagery:

It was night when Martin Sloan returned to Oak Street and stood in front of his house looking at the incredibly warm lights that shone from within. The crickets were a million tambourines that came out of the darkness. There was a scent of hyacinth in the air. There was a quiet rustle of leaf-laden trees that screened out the moon and made odd shadows on cooling sidewalks. There was a feeling of summer, so well remembered.

That's from my favorite story of the lot, "Walking Distance." I get a lump in my throat each time I read it, even when proofreading the script version for the first issue of *Twilight Zone* magazine. (Maybe that's why I missed so many typos.) It also held a special meaning for Serling himself, who was careful to set the short story in upstate New York near Binghamton, his boyhood home—just the sort of personal note that TV leaves out.

And television can't convey the scent of those hyacinths or the cool of those sidewalks.

Or the fact that the doctor's feet hurt in "Escape Clause."

Or, in another tale, the hint of John Dillinger in a small boy's freckled face. (That Serling identifies the outlaw, whose middle name was Herbert, as "John J. Dillinger" may simply be further proof that things are awry in the Twilight Zone.)

Or another tale's conclusion, as dry as if penned by John Collier, in which a minor character, having had his fill of mystery, enjoys "a Brown Betty for dessert" and goes happily to bed.

We'd miss that Brown Betty on TV.

We'd also miss the occasional aside—"His volume of business was roughly that of a valet at a hobos' convention"—and the rhythm of this simile: "Beasley was a little man whose face looked like an X ray of an ulcer."

And we'd miss the description of the bloated, sadistic Oliver Misrell in "A Stop at Willoughby," sitting at the conference table and "blinking like a shaven owl."

Misrell, whose name suggests a wedding of "dismal" and "miserable," exemplifies Serling's relish for colorful Dickensian names—Luther Dingle, Mouth McGarry, the snobbish Bartlett Finchley, the gunslinger Rance McGrew—and, indeed, this book features a gallery of memorably grotesque characters that might almost have stepped from the pages of Dickens: the complete hypochondriac, Walter Bedeker; the thin-lipped, narrow-shouldered, prune-faced Franklin Gibbs, "a sour-faced little man in a 1937 suit"; Harvey Hennicutt, the silver-tongued con man who can even sell a Sherman tank; and Henry Corwin, the drunken department-store Santa. One larger-than-life character, the swinishly avaricious Peter Sykes, even sports a Dickens villain's name.

It's clear, in fact, that Serling was a Dickens fan. His TV play *Carol for Another Christmas* updates Dickens's *A Christmas Carol,* and he consciously echoes the latter's opening lines in his story "The Night of the Meek." There's also a reference to Scrooge in "Where Is Everybody?" and, though not by name, in "The Odyssey of Flight 33," when a distraught airline pilot, face-to-face with the impossible, decides, "It was a bad dream that followed a late lobster snack and an extra quart of beer."

Yet Serling's real inspirations were a lot closer to home. If many elements of his fantasies are, inevitably, universal—superheroes and saviors, pacts with the devil, wishes with unexpected consequences, magic spells and several Deadly Sins, characters who overreach themselves and meet ironic but appropriate dooms, a modern-day jetliner whose mysterious fate recalls the lost ships in sea legends of old, extraterrestrials who drift in and out of the tales at will, meddling in human affairs like the gods of Greek myth—there is also something uniquely American in these tales. Presided over by a pantheon of homegrown heroes—baseball stars, Hollywood stars, astronauts, gunfighters, and ingenious inventors, as well as such lesser figures as snake-oil salesmen, soda jerks, admen, shady small-time politicians, and a handful of endearing losers—they are set amid classic American locales: suburbia, the Wild West, the seductive glitter of Vegas, the Mexican border, the ballpark, the prizefight ring (which provided the background for Serling's celebrated *Requiem for a Heavyweight* and which he knew from the inside, having boxed during his army days), and the corporate boardroom (another territory he'd explored before, in the TV play *Patterns*). While, like fairy tales, his stories are not afraid to teach a moral lesson, many of them focus on such modern American concerns as business ethics, brotherhood, and the ever-present threat of nuclear war.

They are also invincibly democratic, displaying a typical American irreverence for stuffed shirts and snobs. At times they approach the tall tale in their penchant for exaggeration and slapstick. Characters in "Casey" blunder into water buckets and swallow lit cigars, and a nervous young pitcher throws the rosin bag instead of the ball. ("As it turned out, this was his best pitch of the evening.") The inept cowboy hero of "Showdown with Rance McGrew," unable to extricate his gun from its holster, eventually sends it flying over his shoulder to shatter a barroom mirror.

You have a sense of Serling enjoying himself in these scenes, adding a bit of wise-guy humor to the story out of sheer high spirits: "The sigh Bertram Beasley heaved was the only respectable heave going on within a radius of three hundred feet of home plate." And:

> The three pitchers that scout Maxwell Jenkins had sent over turned out to be pitchers in name only. One of them, as a matter of fact, had looked so familiar that McGarry swore he'd seen him pitch in the 1911 World Series. As it turned out, McGarry had been mistaken. It was not he who had pitched in the 1911 World Series but his nephew.

One hears, in the rhythm of that passage, echoes of Runyon and Twain.

There's even a hint of the later, bitter Twain—the Twain of "The Man That Corrupted Hadleyburg"—in "The Rip Van Winkle Caper" and "The Fever," with their bleak view of the human species in extremis. You'll find it, too, in Serling's three cynical end-of-the-world fantasies: "The Shelter" (with its hero "suddenly realizing that underneath . . . we're an ugly race of people"), "The Midnight Sun" (in which man's darker nature emerges only briefly), and "The Monsters Are Due on Maple Street" (with its deliberate parallels to the Communist witch hunt of the fifties).

Serling resembles Twain, as well, in his love-hate relationship with that modern American god, the machine—a god on whom we've come to depend but of whose disposition we're a little uncertain. Serling's fascination, so apparent in the TV series as well as in this book, dates back to the early fifties, to a youthful radio script, *A Machine to Answer the Question,* about a computer that "can break down every human problem into a mathematical equation"—and provide the answer to whatever question it's asked, even as to the prospect of an alien invasion. (Says the script's pre-*Twilight Zone* narrator: "Man's small mind can only project so far. . . . What's needed is a device to explain the mystery, to probe the void—a machine.")

In fact, Serling himself seems to have had, in the words of the title of one of his stories, "A Thing about Machines." That particular tale—the paranoid fantasy of a man whose relation to mechanical objects is one of, at best, uneasy coexistence—ascribes to machines a distinctly human will, and a pitiless one at that. So does "The Fever," in which a fiendishly inimical machine defeats a mere mortal . . . or helps him, rather, to defeat himself. The inhabitants of "Maple Street" prove ripe for conquest because of their reliance on modern conveniences (to conquer them, "just stop a few of their machines and radios and telephones and lawn mowers"); one suspects that the passengers and crew of "Flight 33" are similarly undone by their unquestioning trust in machinery and the known laws of the universe. Robots, a constant presence in Serling's TV series, come to humanity's aid in "The Mighty Casey" and "The Lonely," though the mannequin in "Where Is Everybody?," like the impersonal voice at the end of the phone ("This is a recording"), makes the hero's agony all the greater as he longs for the touch of a fellow human being.

This last aspect of modern American life—its underlying loneliness and sense of dislocation—provides an even more fundamental theme. Like so many of the televised episodes, the tales in this book are pervaded by a fear of being alone; it is presented, in fact, as the most unbearable of punishments. In "Escape Clause," "The Lonely," and "Where Is Everybody?" (in which the ubiquitous presence of brand names and advertising slogans proves to be of little comfort), the anguish of isolation can drive a man to madness or death. Characters in this unsettling world are perpetually in danger of getting lost (sometimes at the most unlikely moments), disconnected from their fellows, disoriented in time as well as space. "Showdown with Rance McGrew" is a comic nightmare about being yanked willy-nilly into the past; "The Odyssey of Flight 33" is the same nightmare on a grander and more horrifying scale (if tempered by a boyish excitement at the idea of seeing real dinosaurs). "The Rip Van Winkle Caper" is a cautionary tale about travel in the opposite direction.

But for an unhappy few, traveling in time seems the only way out—because the sense of dislocation, which in some tales appears as the most hellish of fates, is depicted in others as an inescapable condition of modern American life. Lost in a world of high pressures, power plays, and false values, the alienated heroes of "Walking Distance" and "A Stop at Willoughby" yearn for the simplicity and serenity of the past: in the former tale, for the hometown, Homewood, of the hero's own past; in the latter, for the quintessential small town of America's past. (Though Willoughby itself is an idealized construction found only in Currier-&-Ives-induced dreams, the story, like "Walking Distance," must have had a personal meaning for Serling, who'd spent the early days of his career commuting from Connecticut to New York on the New Haven line.) Of Homewood we read, "Somewhere at the end of a long, six-lane highway . . . Martin Sloan was looking for sanity," while Willoughby, too, is described as "a doorway that leads to sanity." Clearly both towns offer solace in the same achingly desirable form—a return, through time, to the timelessness of childhood—and both, typically, are stumbled upon in the full flush of summertime. Perhaps, as a character observes, "There's only one summer to a customer," but Serling, it seems, got more than his share.

Twilight Zone Magazine

Required Reading...

Though written eighty years ago, M. R. James's "The Ash-Tree" is neither gone nor forgotten. If you search diligently, you'll find it in his *Collected Ghost Stories,* published by Edward Arnold in London and St. Martin's here, and in Dover's reissue of *Ghost Stories of an Antiquary,* with an introduction by the incomparable E. F. Bleiler. For that matter, over the years virtually all of James's stories (he wrote only thirty) have turned up in various anthologies. Technically, then, his work is still in print.

But just because a story is "in print" doesn't mean it's readily available. Until quite recently, if you tried to find Algernon Blackwood's "The Willows" at your local bookstore, you'd be out of luck; nor can you find, even today, Arthur Machen's masterpiece "The White People." Yet both of them are long-acknowledged classics, described by H. P. Lovecraft as, respectively, "the greatest horror tale ever written" and "a close second." Lovecraft's own work has, for some time now, been almost impossible to find outside the standard hardcover editions published by Arkham House in Sauk City, Wisconsin; and though Ballantine plans to reprint six Lovecraft titles early next year, they'll be using texts riddled with errors, and few of the major stories will be represented.

Each issue of *Twilight Zone* opened with an editor's note, chatting, as such notes do, about the contents and the various authors. Herewith, some excerpts.

Moreover, even when stories *are* available, it doesn't mean they're read. A dismaying number of readers today think of themselves as "horror fans" or "fantasy fans" but know absolutely nothing of, say, Walter de la Mare, E. F. Benson, Lord Dunsany, Robert W. Chambers, Mervyn Peake, William Hope Hodgson, Clark Ashton Smith, H. Russell Wakefield, L. P. Hartley, Oliver Onions, M. P. Shiel, and other fantasists. They buy, in the millions, bestselling books by Stephen King and Peter Straub, but they totally neglect the earlier masters who helped shape the very tradition King and Straub are working in—a tradition both men know intimately.

We had a recent illustration of this phenomenon while talking with a young writer from whom we'd just bought a story. "Horror," the young writer informed us, "is my favorite sort of reading."

> TZ: Ah—and whose work do you like?
> YW: Stephen King, mainly. I buy everything he writes.
> TZ: Uh huh. And how about some of the older guys? You know, people like Arthur Machen, M. R. James . . .
> YW: *Who?*

This is the question we hope to answer in "The Essential Writers," a series that begins in this issue with MIKE ASHLEY's profile of M. R. James. Ashley, a literary historian and bibliographer living in Chatham, Kent, is the author of *Who's Who in Horror and Fantasy Fiction,* an indispensable reference work for all aficionados of the genre. In the months to come, he'll be acquainting *TZ* readers with other major figures in the field.

Accompanying these profiles will be a series of representative works which we present, without apology, as "Required Reading"—tales from the recent or distant past that are deservedly regarded as classics. This month's selection, "The Ash-Tree," is a fine example of its type, and shows why, when it comes to good old-fashioned English ghost stories with all the trappings—the fireside, the country home, the stuffy old books—M. R. James is truly "the master."

Throughout the seventy-three years of his life, James wrote dozens of scholarly monographs but only thirty stories. The subject of this month's *TZ* Interview, HARLAN ELLISON, has already written nine hundred stories and sees (by his own reckoning) a good forty more years of writing still ahead of him. Ellison, whom author Frederik Pohl has described as "one of the twentieth century's greatest sources of *tsouris*," is colorful, quotable, and gloriously impolite—which is why we've made this the longest interview we've ever run in a single issue, and why (with a nod to Paul Krassner of *The Realist,* who coined the term) we've labeled it, by way of warning, "An Impolite Interview."

Interviewer TOM STAICAR, however, remains the politest of men. . . .

December 1981

Pleasant Dreams . . .

Last weekend I found myself playing reluctant host to a stray dog that a friend of mine (*Twilight Zone*'s embattled proofreader, as it happens) had rescued from the streets. The animal was at that randy adolescent age when all a dog wants to do is rip apart slippers and masturbate on people's legs, but he was pleasant enough once he fell asleep. He appeared to spend a lot of time dreaming; his limbs would twitch, his body would stir, and I'd hear him growl softly—at what, God only knows. Perhaps he was merely playing back the events of the day, but I couldn't help thinking that, like other sleepers, he was taking part in wholly *imaginary* scenes: tales of make-believe.

When it comes to dreaming, I suspect we're all, dog and man alike, creative geniuses—in effect writing, several times a night, love stories, suspense thrillers, and slapstick comedies. Moreover, we're all *fantasy* writers, since for most of us, dreams provide the only experience we'll ever have of the supernatural, complete with strange landscapes, terrifying monsters, and bizarre metamorphoses.

Some of Lovecraft's best horror stories, for example, like "The Statement of Randolph Carter," are little more than dream transcriptions, and his sleep was haunted by beings he called "night-gaunts"—"black, horned, and slender, with membraneous wings"—which "in dreams . . . were wont to whirl me through space at a sickening rate of speed," taking the by-day-unadventurous Lovecraft on fabulous voyages. (Similarly, my canine guest may have dreamt of chasing pigeons high above Manhattan's rooftops.)

The painter Fuseli reportedly stuffed himself with undercooked meat before going to bed in the hope of producing nightmares to inspire him, while Coleridge claimed his poem "Kubla Khan" came to him word-for-word in a dream, and that he'd have written hundreds of lines more if he hadn't been interrupted in the process by "a person on business from Porlock." (Australian poet A. D. Hope, in his bitter "Persons from Porlock," sees Coleridge's intruder as an agent of the bourgeoisie, sent out deliberately to thwart such divine visions.)

"We are somewhat more than ourselves in sleep," wrote Sir Thomas Browne, seventeenth-century physician, "and the Slumber of the Body seems to be but the waking of the Soul." Even in more modern times, some have clung to this belief; I once came across a remarkable letter of A. Conan Doyle's, written in 1922, in which he wrote of having "several times had prophetic dreams exact in detail. In sleep the soul is freed and has enlarged knowledge. This it endeavors to pass on to the body, but it seldom succeeds. When it does, it is just at the moment between sleeping and waking."

But wait. There's a darker side. "It has been established by our investigations" write psychologists Calvin Hall and Vernon Nordby in *The Individual and His Dreams*, "that dreams of misfortune outnumber dreams of good fortune. Many more bad things than good things happen to the dreamer in his dreams. We have never found an exception to this rule."

And darker still: If the soul really leaves the body during sleep, might it not, in its nocturnal wanderings, fall prey to accident or enemy attack, like the hero of Lovecraft's *Dream-Quest of Unknown Kadath*?

These random reflections are prompted by *Sleep* by STEVE RASNIC TEM, a cautionary tale about the perils of slumber. . . .

March 1982

Market Report . . .

In last month's book column, Thomas Disch gave a pretty thorough going-over to Barry Malzberg's *The Engines of the Night: Science Fiction in the Eighties* (Doubleday, $10.95). While I have no intention of gainsaying Tom's review, I've read the book myself and found much to admire. One of the most interesting sections, for me, is "Memoir from Grub Street," in which Malzberg describes his experience as the editor of *Amazing* and *Fantastic* during six months of 1968. Several years earlier, these venerable magazines (which kept me sane through junior high and high school) had been dropped by Ziff-Davis and had fallen on hard times. Their circulations, Malzberg estimates, were down to 24,000; they were coming out bimonthly, largely with reprint material, and paying most writers, on publication, just a penny a word. Malzberg edited them from his bedroom, at a starting salary of $100 a month.

For writers and would-be writers, these magazines were, as he says, "at the absolute bottom of the list," paying less than *Playboy, Analog, Galaxy, Worlds of If, Fantasy and Science Fiction, Venture,* and *New Worlds,* and publishing only 12,000 words of new fiction each issue. Yet during his tenure as editor, Malzberg says he received an average of a hundred manuscripts a week, many from established names in the field and often, he says, of the highest quality: "It is no exaggeration to recall that I received throughout my editorship sixty stories a month which by any standard I could ascertain were as good or better than anything published in competing magazines."

Today, of course, the market is even more limited. *Omni*'s good for two or three stories a month, and there are odd new magazines like *Pulpsmith* and smaller magazines like *Fantasy Book, Weirdbook, Whispers, Eldritch Tales, Space & Time,* and the like, but they're published infrequently—quarterly, at best—and their presence is more than offset by the loss of *Galaxy, If, Galileo, Quest/Star, Destinies,* and all the other nationally distributed SF and fantasy magazines that have struggled and gone under. (For real blues, compare this to the situation in 1939 as described by Frederik Pohl on page 18 of this issue.)* As Malzberg asks at the conclusion of his memoir,

---

*That page featured a photo of an enormous 1930s newsstand displaying a vast array of magazines. We printed beneath it a passage from Pohl's memoir *The Way the Future Was,* estimating that during that era "there were close to five hundred pulp magazines, with aggregate annual sales of around a hundred million copies."

"How many stories in oblivion, how many careers unable to begin? What can there be for all of these writers?"

One finds an echo here of Tillie Olsen, who, in *Silences* (Dell, $4.95), laments "the silencing—or being driven to the novel form—of story or novella writers because 'there is no market for stories.'... Public libraries, starved for funds, buy less and less books. Published writers of good books, if their books haven't been respectable money-makers, more and more find themselves without a publisher for their latest one. Younger writers (that is, new ones of any age) find that fewer and fewer first books are being published. The magazine market for fiction has shrunk—what? 75 percent?—in the last two decades."

I wish I could pretend that *Twilight Zone* makes a real difference—that our seven or eight or ten stories a month offer even the beginnings of a solution—but of course that would be nonsense. We receive, just as Malzberg did, hundreds of submissions each month and can find room for only a few; we're forced to send back others that are just as publishable. It's as I said back in November: "We could easily fill a magazine twice this size without a notable decline in quality." (Cf. the standard disclaimer of Ivy League admissions departments, who note that half the applicants they reject could have handled the college work perfectly well.)

The best hope, as I see it, is that we'll be successful enough to generate a little competition. My heart sinks every time I read a cover letter that says (as so many do), "Thank God, at last there's a market for the kind of stories I like to write." Would that there were other markets around, other *Twilight Zone*s, be they imitators, rip-offs, or clones. We'd like some company.

Whatever the state of the market, one writer who's always thrived is ROBERT SILVERBERG. Back in the 1950s he'd sometimes be represented by two or three stories in the same magazine (all under different bylines), and after several years' exile from the field he's once again become one of SF's most polished and prolific authors....

July 1982

Winners . . .

You remember the ancient parable about the bird who, every thousand years, comes flying by with a single grain of sand in its beak and drops it in a little pile, and how, when that pile eventually grows into a thousand-mile-high mountain, it's still just the briefest eye-blink in the mighty vastness of eternity? Sure you do. Well, reader Joseph Tarulli of Brooklyn has come up with an equally vivid illustration—not quite as hopeless, thank God—regarding the chances of winning *Twilight Zone*'s story contest:

> Imagine a large three-story women's department store. Amid the tremendous inventory hangs a blue dress, one appropriate for the office, a dinner, or a house party. The style is tasteful, the fit complimentary, and the price reasonable. There is nothing in the world wrong with this dress, and there is no other dress exactly like it.
>
> Now, only one woman passes through this huge store each week—which means that just fifty-two people a year are choosing among literally thousands upon thousands of garments. Moreover, at least half of these people enter the store without any intention of buying, merely to browse or kill time. And of the other half, perhaps only three would actually be in the market for a dress; the rest are more interested in girdles, shoes, slacks, blouses, etc. Furthermore, the odds are great that the three potential dress buyers will reject the blue dress because they don't happen to like the color or the style, or else it simply isn't their size.
>
> Every year, a writer has about as much chance of selling a story as our hypothetical department store has of selling that blue dress.
>
> Sincere congratulations to the winners!

Jesus! I didn't know things were that bad in either *The Twilight Zone* or publishing in general. Still, I suspect Tarulli's a lot closer to the mark than ninety-year-old publishing great Alfred Knopf, who claimed in a recent *Newsweek*, "It must be impossible to write a book so bad that no house will take it." Obviously it's been sixty years since the guy's seen a slush pile.

But even though *TZ*'s contest wasn't a one-in-a-million proposition, we did receive more than four thousand entries this year, despite the fact that we'd limited the contest, for the first time, to just one entry per writer.

Because of the huge number of submissions, and because so many of them were of genuinely high quality, picking a winner proved a lot harder than expected, and in the end, after endless bickering, bloody noses, and page after page of abstruse statistical analysis, we editors simply threw up our hands and decided that, instead of consigning our three favorite stories to first, second, and third place, we'd award "first place" to all three and let the writers split the total prize money—a thousand dollars—among themselves. (The leftover penny, I'm told, has been plowed back into research and development.) . . .

April 1983

Cone Fever . . .

Psycho is, as we all know, the movie that made millions of Americans afraid to take a shower. (Having been forced to hear this over and over for the past twenty years, Robert Bloch was finally driven to remark, "I'm just glad I didn't have my heroine killed while on the toilet.") But the movie had, on me, a different effect: It gave me an almost superstitious awe of psychiatrists.

It wasn't the movie itself that got to me; I was unimpressed by that improbable Hollywood shrink who shows up at the end of the film just in time to tie up the loose plot threads. Rather, what remains in memory is a real-life psychiatrist—a family friend we'll call Joan—who happened to come along when my parents and I first saw *Psycho* back in 1960, a few days after it opened. The shower scene had just ended, I recall; the amateur taxidermist, Norman Bates, was staring horror-struck at the carnage in the bathroom and moaning, "Oh, *Mother!*" And suddenly Joan clapped her hand to her head and exclaimed, in a voice loud enough for people in the next row to hear, "My God! He killed his mother and he thinks he's her!"

We all greeted this crazy, off-the-wall comment with the derision it deserved; so, no doubt, did the people in the next row. And soon afterward, Joan agreed that she must have been mistaken, since the voice of Norman's unseen mother was so clearly different from that of Anthony Perkins. (Recently I've heard that the mother's voice was, in fact, dubbed by someone else—which, if true, is rather a cheat.)

But of course, in the end, Joan turned out to be right. We were all extremely respectful. Later, when I congratulated her on her insight, she denied it was anything special. "Sheer luck," she said.

Readers will soon be able to test their own insight—or luck—by attempting to guess the ending of *Psycho II*. JAMES VERNIERE, who previews it on page 53, was kept unusually busy this time, interviewing Perkins and director Richard Franklin, as well as Michael Mann, who directed *The Keep*, and Australian star Mel Gibson of *Road Warrior* fame. (Don't miss that one.) . . .

June 1983

Paranoia Preferred, But Not Necessary

Even if you lead the most sheltered of lives, there are moments when, like it or not, you find yourself starring in what might turn out to be a horror movie. You've just seen a revival of *Psycho,* and that night, when you're taking a shower, you think, *Hmmm, what if* . . . ? And maybe you rinse the soap out of your eyes a little bit faster than usual. Or you stop to pick up a hitchhiker, and as he opens the door you suddenly remember all the Menacing Hitchhiker stories you've heard (including that *TZ* episode "The Hitch-hiker," featured in our next issue); and maybe, if it's nighttime, you remember the way Dan Aykroyd's face changed in *Twilight Zone—The Movie.*

Then there's the stranger in the elevator who probably *isn't* a psychopath, but who begins to look like one when the other passengers step out and you find yourself alone with him; and the taxi driver who, now that you're inside his cab and have glimpsed his face in the mirror, just might turn out to be a maniac . . .

It's worse if you're a paranoid, of course—or maybe a professional horror writer; then even bright sunshine can be fraught with terror (as Ramsey Campbell had a character realize in his aptly titled

Demons by Daylight). But you don't have to be any of these things, or even particularly xenophobic; all you need, as Rod Serling used to say, is imagination.

The stories in our last issue made something fantastic out of getting a haircut and something horrifying out of hiring a baby-sitter. This issue offers still another example of Horror in Everyday Life: the subway ride. . . .

. . . Though he's better known today for his supernatural fiction (it's appeared in everything from *Weird Tales* to *Esquire*), JOSEPH PAYNE BRENNAN may be remembered in times to come as a poet. The selection printed here—which we've paired with some eerily atmospheric montages by New York photographer ARTHUR PAXTON—comes from Brennan's latest collection, *Creep to Death*, published by Donald M. Grant of West Kingston, Rhode Island. The book takes its title and tone from a passage in *Death's Final Conquest* by James Shirley: "Early or late / They stoop to fate, / And must give up their murmuring breath / When they, pale captives, creep to death."

AN OFFER YOU CAN'T REFUSE

Tom Schiff, our controller, is always pestering me with money-making ideas. "Listen, Ted, you really should fly out to Cleveland and meet the wholesalers." (Right, Tom, next November, without fail.) "Maybe we should sponsor a *Twilight Zone* writing seminar." (Whose desk can I stick *this* one on?) "You know, we'd save a lot of money on stationery if you just wrote your replies on the bottoms of the original letters." Stuff like that.

The other day he came in with a clipping from some trade magazine, all about how John Cole, editor of the *Maine Times,* had increased its subscriptions in a refreshingly direct way: He asked readers to send in the names of friends who might enjoy the paper, then sent those friends free copies. "Our circulation started to climb," Cole modestly reports, "on a gentle inclined plane."

Inclined plane? That was all we had to hear. We immediately decided to try the experiment for ourselves, and Ray, in the mailroom, has already begun stockpiling manila envelopes. So now, filled with enthusiasm, postal meters at the ready, we're making the following offer:

INTRODUCE A FRIEND TO TWILIGHT ZONE

TZ isn't for everyone. It's a magazine for lovers of supernatural fiction, fantasy films, classic horror, and the imaginative genius of Rod Serling. You know the kind of person. Presumably someone like you.

Presumably, too, you have friends who might enjoy *TZ*, friends who might want to join—what's that wonderful cliché?—Our Growing Family of Readers.

Here's a chance to give them a free look at the magazine. Just print your friend's name and address on the coupon below. . . .

June 1984

Bye!

Recently, while leafing through a boys' science fiction adventure published in 1910, entitled *Through Space to Mars* (Chapter 1: Two Chums. Chapter 2: Jack Makes Oxygen), I was struck by something that's probably more typical of SF than of any other genre—the tendency to *quantify*. A spaceship travels to Mars at a hundred miles a second ("That's 8,640,000 miles a day," some know-it-all in the novel explains); a man standing on the planet's surface weighs exactly fifty-seven pounds; a Martian's head looks like a leprechaun's and is "about three times as large as that of an ordinary person."

All this math isn't necessarily a bad thing; it lends some stories an air of credibility, and you can pick up stray bits of potentially valuable information. ("Slowing 150,000 pounds of Orbiter from 200 miles per hour to a dead stop isn't done without a lot of braking effort," a recent tale from *Analog* informs us.)

But the practice seems out of place in works of fantasy—which is one reason I'm dubious about the fantasy games that GAHAN WILSON describes so entertainingly in this issue's cover story. Instead of a true sense of wonder, they offer odds and numbers. Take this passage from one of the instruction manuals for *Call of Cthulhu:* "Fully-grown Cthonian—Tentacles 65%, Crush 80%. Each round, the Cthonian can attack 1D8 times with tentacles.

After hitting, a tentacle will hang on and drain 1 STR point worth of blood from its victim each subsequent round. Subtract one from the number of attacking tentacles for each tentacle draining blood. The crush covers an area 8 feet across. It regenerates from damage at the rate of 5 points per round, until slain."

This sort of thing tends to reduce Lovecraft's unsettling cosmic vision to the level of a military game, a series of blow-by-blow encounters with a bunch of monsters. What makes Lovecraft so enjoyable is the richness of his New England atmosphere—not the stopping power of a Flying Polyp's windblast (pretty lethal, it appears, for the first fifteen yards). There seems too little room in these games for the writerly virtues.

And sometimes too little for the writer himself. Another instruction book, *Curse of the Chthonians* [sic], features a thirty-one-page game scenario called "The Curse of Chaugnar Faugn," and only on the twenty-seventh page is there the teeniest, most grudging reference to Frank Belknap Long, the man who actually *invented* the dread Elephant God back in 1931. (Frank's original story is "recommended to those wishing to act as keepers in this scenario, though it is not absolutely necessary.") Two pages later, we're given a passage from the story—and that's it. If I were Frank, I'd be pretty put out.

At least, though, his creation has attained a fiendish life of Its own—the dream of many a writer. For every writer's *nightmare,* however, see this issue's installment of "My Darkest Fantasy" . . .

Over the years, the stories submitted to TZ have tended to fall into certain familiar types, and one of the most common is the pact-with-the-devil story. It's a species I'm generally not fond of, in part because the endings are always so predictably defeatist (with "The Devil and Daniel Webster" a notable exception); Satan always triumphs in some ironic or "humorous" fashion over a Mere Mortal Who Thought He Could Cheat Fate. But in the hands of someone like BRUCE JAY FRIEDMAN, the theme seems brand new. . . .

. . . Speaking of resettlements, it's time for my VALEDICTORY ADDRESS.

Ladies and gentlemen, friends and alumni, we are gathered here today because . . . um . . . *cough, cough* . . . to honor the, uh . . .

(*Drops speech. Bends down for it, loses glasses.*)

Oh, well, the hell with it. It's time to wave goodbye. Like someone once said (I think it was that guy from Ecclesiastes, but I'm more familiar with the Byrds' version), to everything there is a season, and 'tis now the season for the old buckaroo to pack his gear, steal a few bottles of Liquid Paper from the stockroom, and go riding off into the sunset of New York's teeming Upper West Side, pausing here and there to drop a crumpled candy-bar wrapper into the outstretched hand of a beggar. In other words, I'm hitting the trail. I feel it's high time I stopped monkeying around with other people's deathless prose and attempted to turn out some of my own. I'm going home to sleep late, read the classics (maybe even *Daniel Deronda*, if I get really desperate), eat good healthy tofu-filled lunches, and Write That Novel—you know, the one *you've* always meant to write if only you could take a little time off from work.

The new guy around here is going to be MICHEL BLAINE, an extraordinarily gifted (and award-winning) writer who's worked for a variety of publications, from *Redbook* to the *Village Voice*, and has headed up the journalism program at New York's La Guardia College, but who is best known to *Twilight Zone* readers as the author of "Kush" (Dec. '84) and "The Screening" (June '85). He has, to put it simply, The Right Stuff—though it's nice to know that, in a pinch, he'll be able to depend on the two people who really know how to put this magazine together, Alan Rodgers and Miriam Wolf.

Mike will be taking over as *TZ*'s editor—and dealing, alas, with the reams of inventory I've left him—beginning next issue. Looking at the field today, I'm more firmly convinced than ever that *Twilight Zone* is the last, best hope of good supernatural fantasy and horror fiction. It's a pleasure to have worked on the magazine from its inception back in the fall of 1980, and I only hope that Mike has as much fun with it as I've had.

August 1985

The 13 Most Terrifying Horror Stories

1. "Casting the Runes" by M. R. James
Despite their cozy fireside atmosphere, James's tales of poor doomed antiquarians always raise a chill. This one made a dandy film, *Curse of the Demon*. Other James masterpieces: "Count Magnus," "The Ash-Tree," and "The Treasure of Abbot Thomas."

2. "Novel of the Black Seal" by Arthur Machen
Machen's lyrical, visionary fiction tends to provoke wonder rather than fright, but this tale, about a surviving race of "Little People" in backwoods Wales, has moments of real terror. Also noteworthy: "The White People" and Machen's little-known "Out of the Picture."

3. "The Willows" by Algernon Blackwood
Otherworldly encroachments on a desolate island in the Danube. Lovecraft regarded this as the greatest horror story ever written; certainly it's the greatest horror story about camping out.

4. "The Dunwich Horror" by H. P. Lovecraft
Quintessential HPL, mixing cosmic horror and a brooding New England locale. Another classic: "The Call of Cthulhu," a documentary-style tale that takes the whole world as its province.

Twilight Zone, August 1983. This was part of a series ("The Fantasy Five-Foot Bookshelf") in which various friends of the magazine—Tom Disch, Karl Wagner, R. S. Hadji—listed their 13 favorite fantasy classics, 13 masterpieces of the macabre, etc.

5. "Bird of Prey" by John Collier
Collier is renowned for his sophisticated wit, but in this account of a malevolent thing that hatches from an enormous egg, he's also bloodcurdling—with the real shocker unveiled in the final line.

6. "Who Goes There?" by "Don A. Stuart" (John W. Campbell)
Antarctic horror, the genesis of *The Thing*. You may wonder, after reading it, if your best friend is actually a tentacled alien bent on world domination.

7. "They Bite" by Anthony Boucher
Boucher invents a totally new—and terrifyingly convincing—breed of monster, the desert-dwelling Carkers.

8. "Stay Off the Moon!" by Raymond F. Jones
Published in the December '62 *Amazing* (and now thankfully out of date), the story suggests that something rather nasty lurks beneath the lunar surface. If the Apollo astronauts had read this one, they might have stayed home.

9. "Ottmar Balleau X 2" by George Bamber
First published in *Rogue* and then in Judith Merril's seventh annual *Year's Best S-F* (1963), the tale introduces us to a letter-writing psychopath who seems to have taken his cue from L. P. Hartley's "W. S."

10. "First Anniversary" by Richard Matheson
Just the thing for anyone who's ever suspected that his wife isn't entirely human. Domestic paranoia in full flower. Another fine example: Matheson's "Prey," which became a film to avoid watching alone.

11. "The Autopsy" by Michael Shea
Published in the December '80 *F&SF,* this tale of alien possession in an isolated West Virginia mining community features a monster even more demonic than The Thing.

12. "The Trick" by Ramsey Campbell
Hopeless, inescapable horror from a child's point of view, by the genre's grimmest practitioner. Appears in Karl Wagner's *Year's Best*

Horror #10. Other Campbell contenders: "Cold Print," "The Interloper," and "The End of a Summer's Day."

13. "To Build a Fire" by Jack London
Natural rather than supernatural horror: the harrowing account of a walk in the woods that becomes a race with death. Reminiscent, in its growing sense of dread, of Captain Scott's doomed journey from the Pole.

Honorable mention to two literally monstrous tales from Donald A. Wollheim's 1955 anthology *Terror in the Modern Vein:* "Fritzchen" by Charles Beaumont and "Mimic" by Wollheim himself; to Fritz Leiber's meditation on Evil, "A Bit of the Dark World," written to match its wonderful cover illustration in the February '62 *Fantastic;* and to two short horror novels that, where so many fail, manage to sustain a sense of the uncanny—*Ringstones* by "Sarban" (John W. Wall) and *The House on the Borderland* by William Hope Hodgson.

The Book of Hieronymus Bosch

A Sestina

Although no atlas maps the world of Bosch,
The wanderer knows it: Hidden in the heart
There lurk the crowded images that dance
Across the paintings; and within the pit
Of even sane men's souls there lies the mad
Arena, Bosch's carnival of pain.

Impaled on harp-strings, sinners sing in pain,
As taloned apes (those pets beloved of Bosch)
Take wing and swoop about a sky gone mad —
A throbbing furnace. Trumpets shriek! The heart
Drums faster as the show starts. In the pit
A cortege of the damned joins in the dance.

Nyctalops 8 (April 1973); *Twilight Zone* (February 1988). The sestina is a challenging medieval poetic form made up of half a dozen six-line iambic-pentameter stanzas in a complex pattern: ABCDEF, FAEBDC, CFDABE, ECBFAD, DEACFB, BDFECA. Instead of rhyming, the same recurring six words end all the lines and are repeated throughout the poem. It ends with a seventh stanza three lines long incorporating all six end-words. The result, unfortunately, is sometimes more puzzle than poem.

The Book of Hieronymus Bosch

Around a bagpipe fools and demons dance,
Carousing beasts that celebrate men's pain.
A duck-billed monk emerges from the pit
Of hell to join this dancing throng; and Bosch
Knows every step those dancers take by heart,
Where some go with God's love, and some go mad.

Nearby this red arena lies a mad
Putrescent garden. Thorns on vines that dance
In grotesque tangles pierce a human heart,
Like fruit that's swollen red as if in pain.
But is this tattered plum the heart of Bosch?
Or is it but a plaything of the pit?

The wanderer through this world within the pit
May first dismiss its architect as mad.
In time he comes to understand that Bosch
Has drawn the tune to which all mortals dance;
For each man dreads the demon-prod of pain,
And each must dance to bagpipes in his heart.

So Bosch has ripped these horrors from his heart
To make a Traveler's Guidebook to the Pit:
The thorns a symbol of the spirit's pain,
The monk a faith denied and driven mad.
And that tremendous bagpipe in the dance?
An emblem of the body's lust, said Bosch.

The traveler sees that Bosch has searched his heart
To illustrate our dance around the pit.
And who that's witnessed pain dare call him mad?

Twilight Zone: The Movie

For once the public and the critics seem to agree. *Twilight Zone: The Movie* is a decidedly mixed bag, in which big-name directors Steven Spielberg and John Landis fall flat on their famous faces while two lesser-knowns, Joe Dante and George Miller, walk off with the laurels.

With clinkers and winners evenly matched, the producers have wisely arranged the movie so as to save the goodies for the second half. At one time Spielberg's segment was going to be last, but now the movie ends with Miller's, the acknowledged audience favorite.

Younger filmgoers, especially those fifteen or less, may well leave the theater smiling, but I doubt they'll have much to remember the next day. Even acknowledging that the Miller and Dante episodes are fun, the movie reminds us of why anthology pictures are almost always so unsatisfying: It's hard to create a fully developed character in the space of half an hour, much less provide the little atmospheric details that make an imaginary world seem real.

And while the freedom to rearrange the order of sequences is nice enough in theory, it comes at the expense of continuity. As originally planned, for example, the film was going to use the simple device of having characters from adjoining episodes run into one another. But the finished film lacks even such simple transitions, so that we're left with four totally unrelated stories, each prefaced by a bland little voice-over from series regular Burgess Meredith and concluding with the rather tired device of a pan up to the sky.

Review in *Cinefantastique* (September 1983).

The lack of structure may be due, in part, to the tragic circumstances under which the film was made. Normally an overachiever type like Spielberg might have been expected to involve himself in all stages of production, but some reports suggest that after last July's accident on the Landis set which killed Vic Morrow and two child actors, followed by the lawsuits and publicity, Spielberg virtually washed his hands of the film and went off to pursue other projects. Perhaps as a result, *Twilight Zone* seems to lack a guiding hand.

And it certainly lacks the one thing that no filmmaker could have duplicated, the central presence of a Rod Serling. I'm convinced that the success of the *Twilight Zone* television series lay not so much in its stories—there've been other such anthologies with stories nearly as clever—but in the spooky yet reassuring figure of Serling himself, who, week after week, would step out onto the set to deliver his opening and closing narrations, deliberately breaking into the drama's reality and reminding us that it was only a TV show. The film badly needed a presence like his, and the unseen Meredith doesn't come near to providing one.

Even people who disliked the movie seem to get a kick out of Landis's brief prologue. The skit is really an extended gag reminiscent of the sort one hears around the fire in summer camp, and its strength comes largely from the familiarity of the characters played by Dan Aykroyd and Albert Brooks, who work well together.

But Landis quickly wears out his welcome. His second episode, in which a stereotyped bigot gets his cosmic comeuppance, is undoubtedly the weakest part of the film, and as far as I can determine its weakness has nothing to do with the death of its star during the final night of shooting, since Landis's original conception has remained relatively unaltered. It's hard to understand why Landis chose to tell so crude and sophomoric a story and, more important, why the others involved in the project allowed him to do so. The segment is pointlessly cruel, sending a man off to the death camps for daring to utter a few barroom slurs; it trades, ironically, in the sort of coarse racial clichés that accounted for some of the cheap laughs in Landis's recent *Trading Places,* and it slanders the U.S. Army in Vietnam by equating them with Nazis and the Ku Klux Klan.

Steven Spielberg's contribution, an expanded version of George

Clayton Johnson's "Kick the Can," is a mawkish exercise filled with self-congratulatory kiss-me-I'm-Jewish bits of business. The original TV version, directed by Lamont Johnson, was considerably more affecting, and its old folks had the good sense to stay young. This new version wags its sticky finger at us and reminds us that You Can't Cheat Father Time. We're offered the improbable vision of eighty-eight-year-olds turning down a second chance at life (all but one bright fellow) and preferring their decrepitude.

The only saving elements in this dispiriting tale are the children—they're well matched with their grown-up counterparts—and Scatman Crothers, who turns in a radiant performance, perhaps because, judging from interviews, he resembles the sunny character he played.

Joe Dante's reworking of "It's a Good Life" is a distinct improvement. In fact, while most people single out Miller's episode as the best in the film, Dante's is in many ways the cleverest, and it's the only one that has even a shred of complexity. In a *Twilight Zone* magazine interview, Dante noted that the original TV version, scripted by Serling from Jerome Bixby's short story, was "a rather atypical *Twilight Zone*" in that it was "bleak and hopeless," lacking one element common to the series—a sense of redemption.

This time Dante and scriptwriter Richard Matheson have shifted the point of view to a new character (played with surprising stiffness by Kathleen Quinlan), exploited the situation's inherent comic possibilities, curbed Anthony Freemont's unsettling powers (the boy can no longer read minds), and provided a more satisfyingly upbeat ending.

George Miller's segment is graced by what is probably the film's best performance, that of John Lithgow, and wrings high suspense from the simple shot of an airplane window with its shade pulled down. The more Lithgow contemplates opening it, the more certain we are that a nasty shock is waiting for him just beyond the glass.

However, I wonder if Miller hasn't erred on the side of confusion: He's piled on the storm effects so heavily, concealing his monster behind so much rain and fog, that although I knew in advance what the creature was up to, in the brief glimpse Miller allowed I could make out almost nothing.

In the end, the film leaves one with rather little: three memorably jarring images—Dan Aykroyd in full flower, Anthony Freemont's mouthless sister, and Miller's wing-riding monster shaking its bony finger at Lithgow—and a single question: Why did they bother?

Horrors! An Introduction to Writing Horror Fiction

*E*veryone's got a horror tale inside him—and chances are that when he gets around to writing it, he'll submit it to a magazine like *Twilight Zone*. As *TZ*'s editor for four and a half years, I saw it grow into America's most popular market for horror fiction, with knee-high piles of manuscripts checkerboarding the office floor. Keeping up with them all was a never-ending job. I remember reading through a bundle of stories (and scribbling rejection slips) by flashlight inside a tent in the Pecos Wilderness of New Mexico while a storm raged outside, and, on another vacation, climbing New Hampshire's Mount Washington with 40 or 50 submissions stuffed into my backpack—all, I'm sure, many months overdue.

Recently I read that the same Mount Washington is inhabited by ghosts (not, I hope, the ones I brought with me). According to a major news magazine, the meteorological station high atop the mountain is haunted by a being known only as "the Presence." Does it make life unpleasant for the lone weatherman who lives up there year-round? Not in the least. "I love to be scared," he explained, "because you forget all your worldly troubles."

I can't think of a better explanation for the appeal of the horror tale. The world, with its troubles, is indeed too much with us, and the horrors it lays before us each day are all too real, ranging from

---

From *The Secrets of Writing Popular Fiction* (Writer's Digest, 1986).

the petty to the monstrous to the nearly unthinkable. Horror fiction offers us a means of keeping these realities at bay. As Stephen King observes in *Danse Macabre,* "We make up horrors to help us cope with the real ones."

In the real world, evil tends to be a grey, grubby, half-hearted thing born of complex human interrelationships, a subject fit for social workers and analysts; the most vicious of psychopathic murderers turn out to be tormented beings with chemical imbalances and abused childhoods. The world of the horror tale is a simpler one, and far less ambiguous; like the world of fairy tales or the Bible, it is a vast arena in which the forces of good are locked in a perpetual struggle with a purer, more thoroughgoing evil than one meets in real life. It is, in short, a hundredfold more satisfying. Enemies of the imagination (and they are legion) who sniff disdainfully, "How can you read horror stories when there's so much horror in the daily newspaper?" might just as well ask how readers living in a high-crime area of some modern American city can enjoy Sherlock Holmes.

As the question demonstrates, the word *horror* can mean many different things. Technically, it should be regarded as a particular branch of fantasy (in fact, it's sometimes known, a bit pretentiously, as "dark fantasy"). As for fantasy itself, whatever its hue, its one distinguishing feature is the presence, somewhere, of a supernatural element. Fantasy is thus set in a world where magic works—as opposed to science fiction, in which events have at least some sort of scientific explanation. It's handy to remember, with this distinction in mind, that *Frankenstein* is a work of SF, *Dracula* a work of fantasy.

But most readers would regard them both as simply "horror" novels, for in the popular view the word tends to signify something much broader and by no means confined to the supernatural; it is used to describe any sort of literature that inspires an emotion of horror in the reader, ranging from the schlockiest paperbacks in their glossy black jackets to works of real artistry approaching, at times, the sublime. It includes supernatural tales as subtle and demanding as those of Walter de la Mare and Robert Aickman, but it also encompasses what H. P. Lovecraft called "the literature of mere physical fear" and what the rest of us might call "cheap thrills." It finds room for tales that are essentially science fiction, such as John W. Campbell's "Who Goes There?" (better known on-screen as *The Thing*), works of surrealism such as Jerzy Kosinski's *Steps,* gothic romances such as Ann Radcliffe's *The Mysteries of Udolpho,* religious parables such as R. H. Benson's "The Watcher," man-versus-nature tales such as Jack London's "To Build a Fire," tales of vengeance such as Poe's "Hop-Frog" and "The Cask of the Amontillado," tales of madness such as Wells's "Pollock and the Porroh Man," tales of cruelty such as Villiers de l'Isle-Adam's "The Torture of Hope," and atrocity tales such as Bram Stoker's "The Squaw"—in short, everything from the delicately dreamlike to what one editor has called the "mere shudder-producer."

But why would any reader want to shudder? Where's the fun in that? Who but a masochist would like to stay up all night biting his nails in terror? When you look at the explanations supplied by horror writers themselves, they seem, at first, preposterous exercises in oxymoron: Russell Kirk tells us he strives, in his supernatural tales, to inspire a "fearful joy." A. E. Coppard entitles a 1946 collection *Fearful Pleasures.* Maurice Richardson argues that "the secret of the ghost story" is the "pleasure in being frightened." Victorian writer E. F. Benson claims his stories have been "written in the hope of giving some pleasant qualms." How can joy be fearful and qualms be pleasant?

Benson himself may have stumbled on the answer when, one winter's night, he read his latest horror tale to the aging Lord Halifax, who, according to one account, "sat, hand cupped to ear, in a state of growing agitation. Suddenly he interrupted: 'This is dreadful. I can't bear it—do go on!'"

The old man's reaction provides us with a clue. The tale that so unnerved him wasn't forced upon him; he asked for it, with full knowledge he could stop it whenever he liked. As writer Elizabeth Bowen once noted, "It is nice to choose to be frightened, when one need not be." The key word is *choose*. The emotion ghost and horror tales inspire is not fear after all, then, but a kind of toothless substitute, vicarious fear. It's what Dr. Johnson called "terror without danger . . . a voluntary agitation of the mind, that is permitted no longer than it pleases."

The pleasure here is in the game of "just pretend"—and on some level we never forget that fact. It's the pleasure of lying in a warm bed reading about polar exploration (a favorite pastime of mine), or of riding on a roller coaster that you're perfectly certain is safe. It's the pleasure of the carnival "house of horrors"—more commonly known as the "fun house." And fun is what this genre's all about. One isn't scared by a horror tale; one is "scared."

Consequently, there are two kinds of people who dislike the genre: those who get no thrill at all from horror movies, ghost tales, and the like, remaining utterly unmoved; and those who are genuinely, instead of vicariously, frightened—not "scared" but *scared*. For these impressionable souls, fiction and nonfiction are effectively the same, and the roller coaster is as real as a runaway car.

It's no wonder, then, that the classic English ghost story has traditionally been told before a cozy Victorian fireside (which sometimes serves as a framing device to the tale). The secure domestic setting serves as a dramatic contrast to the terrifying events being narrated—but it also helps distance us from them. For similar reasons, I'm convinced that the key to the success of the original *Twilight Zone* TV series was the comforting presence of Rod Serling himself, who, like some counselor spinning yarns before a campfire, stepped onto the set to remind us that, no matter how grim the situation, it was all only a story.

There's another sort of comfort the horror tale provides. Its vision of a world menaced by dark supernatural forces has, within it, a happier corollary, one that may offer another clue to the genre's appeal. The existence of a supernatural evil presupposes the existence—or at least the possibility—of an equal force for good. Black magic begets white; a killing curse may well be matched by a beneficial spell. If the werewolf, vampire, and demon are real, so are gentler spirits; a world of witches might also have, hidden behind the scenes, a fairy godmother or two. And if Satan exists, surely angels do as well. Populating the universe with such forces is one way of making sense of our condition, which is, without them, uncertain at best and often overwhelmingly bleak. In so coldly rational a modern world, supernatural fantasy represents a harmless dance before the void. It's not surprising that many critics, over the years, have linked its appeal to religion, for which fantasy may serve as an emotional substitute.

But *only* an emotional one. It should be clear by this time that in order to enjoy a tale of horror, one need not believe in the supernatural. In fact, this is one of the things that makes horror so unusual: the tremendous disparity between what the tales imply and what readers actually believe. The philosophical underpinnings of the genre—the very bedrock of virtually every plot—is the reality of the supernatural. Unlike science fiction, which abounds in new ideas, horror tends to content itself with playing elegant variations on only that one. The traditional horror tale involves a skeptical character who, in the course of the story, discovers (sometimes too late) that certain mysterious or bizarre events have a supernatural origin. Yet I've no doubt that nine out of ten readers remain skeptics themselves.

But if the story does its job—if the style is properly persuasive and the characters convincing—the reader's skepticism will be, for the moment, set aside: the "willing suspension of disbelief," in Coleridge's famous phrase. As a later critic noted, "the effective weird tale should give us what the Scots call a 'cauld grue'—a moment in which intellect is in abeyance and emotion rules, the emotion of half-instinctive fear." Read at the proper time, such as the dead of night, it should make even the most confirmed rationalist glance under the bed; for just as there are no atheists in foxholes, there are no skeptics when the wind howls outside and branches tap eerily on the windowpanes. So long as the reader remains immersed in the story, he's a believer. He may disbelieve with his mind, but, as another critic noted, he will still believe with his blood.

And the same goes for the writer: Whatever his personal convictions, while writing the horror tale he must believe in it; it's only fitting, after all, that he work the same magic on himself that he ultimately hopes to perform upon the reader. Though H. P. Lovecraft, for example, one of the great masters of the form, derided "the sugary delusions of religion" and boasted that he'd "never had the slightest shadow of belief in the supernatural," he admitted that "no first-rate story can ever be written without the author's actually experiencing the moods and visions" of his characters. And here, for once, the experts all agree: Edith Wharton ("The teller of supernatural tales should be well frightened in the telling"), E. F. Benson ("The narrator must succeed in frightening himself before he can hope to frighten his readers"), H. Russell Wakefield ("Before you can scare others, you must be scared yourself"). All of them knew whereof they spoke, as their tales attest.

Other genres, of course, demand an emotional commitment, too. Humorists snicker happily over their gags; pornographers are secretly aroused by what they write (if it's any good); Erich Segal reported that he broke down and sobbed as he penned the closing lines of *Love Story*.

But horror is capable of driving its practitioners to even greater heights . . . or depths. "In order to arouse any real emotion in the reader, it is vital for the writer to feel something of that emotion himself," the veteran fantasist Henry Kuttner observed. "The writer must hypnotize himself. More than once, when I'm writing a yarn and have my character in a tough spot, I find myself unconsciously emitting the most extraordinary sounds—gasps—groans—hoarse rasps and the occasional 'Oooooh God!' If anybody is in the room with me at the time, they are startled, to say the least." He noted that in writing a story whose hero is buried alive, he threw himself into the spirit of the thing, "even to the extent of holding my breath."

Still, autohypnosis is hardly enough to guarantee a good horror tale; otherwise every daydreamer would be a successful writer. Horror, in fact, requires the same qualities of prose, the same care and calculation, as any other brand of fiction—and perhaps even more so, for style counts more heavily here than in other genres. Science fiction may often get by on a particularly novel idea, and mystery on a sufficiently intricate plot; a mainstream tale can occasionally be carried on nothing but colorful dialogue. But the writing in a horror tale is crucial; it must be insidiously persuasive, skillfully orchestrating suspense, building up atmosphere by subtle accretion, one dab at a time. You are trying, above all, to create a mood—and, in the process, to convince the reader of something he knows just isn't so. The major obstacle, as Joel Rosenberg lamented in a *Writer's Digest* article on fantasy, is that, "in a fundamental way, this stuff is ridiculous." The trick is to write so well that readers forget this fact.

One sign of a well-written story is visible right away: the use of specific, concrete images that enable readers to see, hear, smell and even taste as if they were there inside the story. Alice Turner, *Playboy*'s fiction editor, has pointed out that this is probably the single most important element that immediately distinguishes strong writing from run-of-the-mill, and I think she's right; it's also the difference between a successful, full-fledged piece of fiction and a mere barroom anecdote. Of course, the commandment "Show, don't tell!" is an ancient one for writers, but it's especially pertinent to horror. A marvelous example is Richard Matheson's "First Anniversary," in which a man, upon kissing his attractive young wife, discovers that she tastes oddly sour; later he smells what he thinks is rotting garbage, then realizes that it's her smell—her *real* smell, before she manages once more to disguise it from him. By the end of the story, rest assured, we're given a shocking glimpse of what the creature he lives with really looks like.

Sharp, vivid sense-images are the lifeblood of all forms of fiction. What's unusual, perhaps unique about horror is that it also depends on the reverse: a deliberate narrative blurring. Because the genre gains its power from playing on the reader's imagination, the horror tale is at its most effective when it suggests instead of spelling out. It's one genre, in short, in which clarity of exposition can be a failing and vagueness a virtue.

There's a danger, obviously, in generalizing about fiction of any sort; the good writers always prove you wrong. They are, after all, the ones who break the rules and get away with it. But anyone familiar with the horror genre has to be struck by the deliberately vague, fragmented quality of many of the best stories, such as those by the modern English horror writer Ramsey Campbell, relying as they often do on snatches of half-heard conversation, ominous phrases on scraps of old newspaper, murky dreams, odd bits of childhood memory, shadowy figures at windows, and faces dimly seen in the fog. ("Vague reflections of the flame hung on the walls . . .; the roof was a hovering blotch.") Some of his tales, in fact, employ a kind of narrative myopia in which a shape perceived as a corpse crumpled in a doorway will turn out to be, on closer inspection, an innocent heap of trash.

Though Campbell almost never hits a false note, some of his imitators carry this penchant for misdirection too far, leaving readers lost and baffled in the fog. Still, it's hard to disagree with this dictum of Lovecraft's (written in his characteristically archaic style): "One shou'd never state an horror when it can be suggested."

The record shows that, for the most part, he practiced what he preached—and so did his peers. Lovecraft's minor tale "The Hound" has characters shudder at the mere "suggestion of baying," and his terrified narrator never seems to see anything clearly: "I saw a black shape obscure one of the reflections of the lamps in the water. . . . I saw on the dim-lighted moor a wide nebulous shadow sweeping from mound to mound. . . . I had hastened to the terrible scene in time to hear a whir of wings and see a vague black cloudy thing silhouetted against the rising moon."

Silhouettes against the moon may be old hat, but they haven't lost their power to stir (as Spielberg has frequently proven), especially in the right hands; witness the shadowy winged thing that escapes into the night at the start of John Collier's "Bird of Prey" ("He thought he saw a bird—a big bird, an enormous bird—flying away. He just caught a glimpse of it as it crossed the brightness of the moon"), leaving behind a raped pet parrot. This unlucky bird, the living evidence of some vague supernatural evil wisely left offstage, meets its match in another classic tale, Robert Hichens's "How Love Came to Professor Guildea," in which the movements of an invisible ghost are grotesquely mimicked by the one creature that can see it—a caged parrot.

Both birds illustrate the masterful use of suggestion; the exact nature of the horror they hint at is left for us to imagine. So do the bizarre cone-shaped holes in the sand made by the unseen beings in Algernon Blackwood's classic novelette "The Willows," and the ominous knocking at the door at the climax of W. W. Jacobs's endlessly reprinted "The Monkey's Paw."

Horrors need not remain completely invisible, as the title creatures are in Ambrose Bierce's "The Damned Thing" and Guy de Maupassant's "The Horla"; but when they are described, the details should be telling and few. One of the most unsettling images in Anthony Boucher's "They Bite" is this tantalizingly incomplete description of a desert-dwelling monster with lethal jaws, a monster you never see except out of the corner of your eye: "It's something very dry and thin and brown, only when you look around it isn't there." We don't get to meet the thing till the end of the story, but we're already nervous. In M. R. James's "Casting the Runes," we never catch a glimpse of the monster described only as "a horrible hopping creature in white . . . dodging about among the trees," but we fill in the details ourselves—as we also do with the "frightful loping nameless thing on Meadow Hill" that stalks through Lovecraft's "The Unnamable." (Even the title is vague!)

Despite his own warnings, Lovecraft was as prone as anyone to overwriting, but he knew how to catch his readers by surprise, as in this description, at once comic and nightmarish, of a horde of "hybrid winged things" in "The Festival": "They were not altogether crows, nor moles, nor buzzards, nor ants, nor vampire bats, nor decomposed human beings; but something I cannot and must not recall." An impossible amalgam, of course, but what's important is the effect: It certainly stimulates the imagination.

Not all horror tales—and not all great horror tales—leave the details to the reader's imagination. Today, for every work that seeks to inspire a sense of unease, there are a dozen more that set out, more or less successfully, to shock or appall. It's instructive, therefore, to contrast Ray Bradbury's 1945 "Skeleton" with a supernatural tale of more recent vintage. The Bradbury concerns a man with an *idée fixe* that his bones are the source of all his troubles. He has them removed—how it's not quite clear—by a sinister little stranger named Munigant, who strolls off playing a flute made out of bone. After a discreet fade-out, the story ends with the man's wife discovering his body: "Many times as a little girl Clarisse had run on the beach sands, stepped on a jellyfish and screamed. It was not so bad, finding an intact, gelatin-skinned jellyfish in one's living room. One could step back from it. It was when the jellyfish *called you by name* . . ."

Mining the same theme but written forty years later, "Jacqueline Ess: Her Will and Testament," one of the stories in Clive Barker's wildly popular *Books of Blood,* typifies the current trend toward explicit violence and gross physical detail. In an early scene the heroine, who possesses psychokinetic powers, loses patience with her husband and—mentally willing him to "Shut up!"—watches as he does literally that, whereupon we're treated to a full page of graphically depicted carnage, complete with teeth that snap shut, grinding, "cracking and splitting," severing the tip of the tongue and leaving "pinkish foam on his chin as his mouth collapsed inwards," eyes that sink back into the skull as "his nose wormed its way into his brain," head flattening, "telescoping flesh and resistant bone into a smaller and yet smaller space," until the man is reduced to a bundle of "neatly packaged entrails" wrapped in stomach tissue. The book, incidentally, won a best-of-the-year award in 1985.

Twilight Zone has traditionally shied away from chronicles of bloodletting, in part because of commercial constraints (Grand Guignol would seem out of place in a magazine bearing Rod Serling's name), but more because of editorial taste; I preferred tales of a milder, more sentimental sort to the mailbags full of *contes cruels* and remain to this day a sucker for happy endings. My successor, Michael Blaine, was somewhat more partial to experimental fiction; and I suspect, though it's too soon to say for sure, that the present editor, Tappan King, may be more open than I was to wizards, spells, and other trappings of traditional "high fantasy." Those with a taste for the gruesome might look into *Night Cry*, *TZ*'s companion magazine, which, under editor Alan Rodgers, is open to horror of the more explicit sort. (Despite the enormous quantity of submissions, both publications remain good first-time markets for newcomers, with tales fresh from the slush pile in almost every issue. *TZ* also runs an annual story contest for hitherto unpublished writers.)

Whether monsters are seen in close-up or kept offstage, and whether violence is lovingly detailed or merely hinted at, there's one element over which authors discreetly draw a veil: the explanation. Horror need not, and dares not, explain too much; we don't have to know how the monkey's paw actually works, or why the Horla has it in for the hero. This fundamental withholding of information is one of the major differences between supernatural horror and most other genres. At the end of a detective tale, the mystery is solved; but—as fantasy writer Fritz Leiber has observed—at the end of a horror tale, the mystery remains.

Science fiction, too, is more forthright; while horror gets by with a coy wink and a shrug, SF must supply at least a shred of explanation, and one that, as *Analog* editor Stanley Schmidt notes in his article on page 16, is "plausible in the light of known science."

But rational explanations are anathema to the tale of supernatural horror, in which "a certain atmosphere of breathless and unexplainable dread of outer, unknown forces must be present." So, at least, wrote H. P. Lovecraft in his groundbreaking essay "Supernatural Horror in Literature," which draws a careful line between the genre and science fiction: While SF may occasionally stretch the physical laws of the universe, horror sets out quite consciously to violate those laws, deriving its power from "a malign and particular suspension or defeat of those fixed laws of Nature which are our only safeguard against the assaults of chaos and the daemons of unplumbed space."

You can hear, in those words, more than a trace of paranoia; but then, that's probably the number one prerequisite for writing horror. While the science fiction writer is the sort of intrepid soul who goes off with joyful heart to explore the cosmos, the horror writer, anxious and mistrustful, realizes that whatever it is that's out there, it undoubtedly wants to hurt him.

Even though he's often wrong, there's something inherently pessimistic about the genre. In story after story, the protagonist ends up defeated, punished, overcome by supernatural forces. That's why, in horror tales, the "hero" is frequently a villain of some sort, like the spy in "They Bite" and the grave-robber in "The Hound"; it makes his inevitable supernatural comeuppance seem that much more appropriate—the horror equivalent of divine retribution.

But just as often, in these tales, even the innocent come to bad ends. (It's one of the ways, unfortunately, that horror resembles real life.) A middle-aged cleric and a retired sea captain are driven to madness and death for no explicable reason—the one by the apparition of a monkey with glowing red eyes, the other by a malevolent caped figure—in "Green Tea" and "The Familiar," two classic works by J. Sheridan Le Fanu, who has been called "the foremost writer of supernatural fiction in English literature." In another, "Schalken the Painter," a sixteen-year-old girl is carried off shrieking in the arms of a corpse to whom her greedy uncle has betrothed her. "Beginning with Le Fanu," says critic Jack Sullivan, "the ghost story often presents terrifying visions of the universe in which good conspicuously does not triumph and is often absent altogether. The more ambitious specialists in the field, such as Machen, M. R. James, William Hope Hodgson, and Walter de la Mare, frequently portray panicked characters who are cruelly destroyed by malignant forces they often never even understand."

He might have been talking about the poor English traveler in M. R. James's "Count Magnus," hounded to a hideous death simply because he chanced to peer into the wrong mausoleum; or the luckless schoolmaster of Ramsey Campbell's "Cold Print," who meets his doom in a shabby back-street porn shop: "It wasn't playing fair, he hadn't done anything to deserve this—but before he could scream out his protest his breath was cut off, as the hands descended on his face and the wet red mouths opened in their palms."

The reader may be just as horrified as these hero-victims—but probably not quite as surprised. Chances are he saw the trouble coming a lot sooner than they did. (In "Count Magnus," for example, we're chilled to learn that a lock on the evil count's sarcophagus has mysteriously fallen open; but the traveler fails to see this as a warning.) This points up another unusual aspect of the genre: The reader often perceives far more than the hapless heroes and heroines. While a recent science fiction novel was praised in *The New York Times Book Review* as "a fast-paced entertainment that keeps the reader a half-step behind the main characters all the way—not a bad place to be in such a narrative," the situation is entirely different when it comes to supernatural horror: The reader is likely to be a half-step ahead of the characters, who wander blithely into danger and death, unaware they're living in a horror tale.

Yet, in turn, you, the writer, should be one step ahead of the reader, who must always be kept guessing about what's going to happen next. The reader may have his suspicions, and usually does; he may see a lot farther ahead than the people in the story. But he shouldn't know precisely what's in store for them all, or else he'll lose interest in the game. Better to risk making a few demands on the reader's intelligence than to make your tale too obvious, lest the reader realize he is smarter than you are—something, inexplicably, that an otherwise decent writer like August Derleth allowed with his tired and dismayingly predictable Lovecraft pastiches.

In a sense, then, writing horror stories is a bit like playing the Pied Piper. If the tune you pipe is too fast, too difficult, or too subtle, the reader grows confused and eventually bored, dropping out of the dance. If, on the other hand, your tune is too plodding and predictable, the reaction is the same: impatience and boredom. The trick, clearly, is to dance just a little ahead of the reader, teasing him, leading him on. In this respect, the horror tale is like a mystery: the goal is to outsmart the reader without losing his interest.

But don't dance *too* far ahead, or you'll end up outsmarting yourself. I know, because I've done it. I remember how, in writing "The Events at Poroth Farm," the short story that later became the novel *The Ceremonies,* I had what I thought was a terrifically bright idea. The story involves, at one point, a household cat that, unbeknownst to my narrator (but plain to readers), has become possessed by a demonic intelligence. I establish early on that the narrator is violently allergic to cat hair. In a later scene, he discovers that someone has broken into his bedroom and that his possessions have been mysteriously rearranged. As he sits up late that night writing in his journal, I have him complain that his nose is "pretty clogged." He blames it on "the dampness" and dismisses the matter from his mind, but my hope was that, if readers had been paying attention, they would realize—with, I liked to think, a little shiver of horror—that the unknown intruder has in fact been the cat.

And did it work? I asked the best readers I knew, including a couple of editors, and so far as I remember, not a single one of them had even noticed. So much for little shivers.

It's clear that the information you provide the reader must be parceled out shrewdly. You must ask yourself, at each new point in the story, *How much does the reader know? How much does he suspect? What will catch him by surprise?* While a subtle hint in just the right place is almost always more effective than a total revelation, you have to strike a balance between dropping too few clues and giving away the game.

There's another balance to be carefully maintained: the balance of the supernatural and the everyday.

It's been said many times before, but it's so seldom practiced among aspiring writers that I'd better repeat it here: You can't introduce the terrifying and the fantastic into your fictional world, or conjure up a proper supernatural horror, until you've first grounded your tale in reality. Horror, after all, generally consists of a supernatural intrusion—one that alters, in some way, the natural world and changes the lives of your characters. And it will have no emotional impact unless you've already established, so thoroughly that we can believe in it, the reality of the world you're going to change. The abnormal is meaningless unless measured against the normal.

Above all, two aspects of the story must be brought convincingly to life. The first is locale. It has been said that SF is a genre of ideas, mainstream fiction one of character, and horror one of place. The setting of a horror tale is likely to be the greatest single conveyor of mood (and the element readers remember longest), whether it's the decaying Massachusetts hamlet of Lovecraft's "The Dunwich Horror," the isolated Maine community of King's *'Salem's Lot,* the haunted Danube island of Blackwood's "The Willows," the malign fairy-haunted Welsh hills of Arthur Machen's "Novel of the Black Seal," the seedy alleys of Ramsey Campbell's Liverpool, or the dark, mysterious ocean that seems a living presence in the maritime horror tales of William Hope Hodgson.

The other element of realism lies in the circumstances of the characters' lives—their family relationships, their backgrounds, their homes, right down to the ways they make their living. During my years at *Twilight Zone,* we saw too many stories about wizards, and criminals, and rock stars, and religious maniacs, and bestselling novelists, and innocent travelers who find themselves in menacing small towns, and fey Lovecraftian students of the occult who never did a day's work in their lives. (For more on these horrors, see the sidebar, "Horrible Clichés.") I had nothing against such stock figures—I'd used a few myself—but there wasn't a breath of real life in them. And I began to wonder: Don't those writers out there know anything but other horror stories?

Many prospective *TZ* contributors are still in college or high school. They haven't seen much of the world, and their fiction shows it; it's not easy, I know, to invent convincing situations outside one's own experience. They've watched too much TV and read too little outside the fantasy field, and they've failed to draw on the one world they do know, the world of childhood, that perennial source of material for good writers.

But most of our submissions came from working adults. Many of them were journalists of one kind or another; usually, not unreasonably, they wrote stories about reporters. Yet other stories came from those in careers outside the writing field, and inevitably they'd prompt the same questions: Why aren't these people turning their real-life jobs into fiction? Are they ashamed of them? Do they think they're too boring? Not glamorous enough? Not horrific?

To my mind, that's a distinct advantage. Horror stories work best when they're grounded in ordinary, unhorrific everyday life. That's why, as an editor, I was always partial to what I came to call "workaday horror" (and I don't mean an overbearing boss). We saw far too little of it. I was pleased to buy stories about such mundane characters as a waitress in a diner, a watchman at a factory, a border patrolman, a social worker, a janitor, a weary commuter, a professional exterminator, and a woman who, with her husband, runs a shabby hotel. To say nothing of a bored suburban housewife or two.

You don't have to travel to Transylvania to find the inspiration for a horror tale. In fact, you'd be better off staying home. Chances are, like it or not, you've got more than enough material already.

Horrible Clichés
The 21 Most Familiar Horror Plots

Judging by the extraordinary volume of submissions that *Twilight Zone* receives, as well as by letters from readers, horror fans seem to have an inordinate interest in becoming horror writers. Perhaps it's just the desire to step behind the scenery and scare the daylights out of someone else for a change.

Most of those who submit stories are convinced, I'm sure, that they're the first to invent the plots they've used. The truth is that, in the realm of horror and supernatural fantasy, there simply aren't very many fresh plots; what's important is the freshness of the writing. The vast majority of the stories I received in my years at *Twilight Zone* fell into a few distinct categories. Here are the most common:

1. I'm really dead!: a.k.a. "Dead but doesn't know it." Victim of car crash or some other accident discovers, at story's end, that he didn't survive after all. Often he can't understand why friends look right through him (or scream when he approaches), or he hitches a ride from a driver who turns out to be Death. Final image: funeral, or corpse in crumpled car. (Cf. *Twilight Zone* episode "The Hitchhiker," Isaac Bashevis Singer's "A Wedding in Brownsville.")

2. I'm really in hell!: The TV's on the fritz again, the wife or job grows more annoying (or just boring), and suddenly the hero realizes he's actually died and gone to hell. (Cf. famous *Twilight Zone* ending: "Send me to the other place." "This *is* the other place!") Gloomy attempt to make sense of life's little miseries.

3. I'll show them! (version 1): Shy, misunderstood youngster is rejected by schoolmates for being "different." Is vindicated when he (though it's usually a she) turns out to be gifted with startling psychic powers. Frequently submitted by sensitive teenage girls, perhaps with *Carrie* in mind.

4. I'll show them! (version 2): Parents don't believe child's tale of invisible playmate (or monster in closet, etc.). It turns out to be real, saving child's life (or killing child or Daddy, etc.). Famous examples: "Thus I Refute Beelzy" by John Collier; "The Thing in the Cellar" by David H. Keller.

5. The magic picture: It draws one in. Hero or heroine disappears from the real world, is later discovered inside an old painting, photo, tapestry, wallpaper design, etc. Usually the unchanging world inside the picture is an improvement on real life.

6. The magic typewriter: Author (or would-be author) acquires supernatural typewriter that either transforms his writing style or churns out bestsellers all by itself. Sometimes it's haunted by the ghost of its previous owner. A perennial writer's fantasy ever since

John Kendrick Bangs wrote *The Enchanted Type-Writer* in 1899, right up to Stephen King's 1982 variation, "The Word Processor."

7. The forgetful vampire: He fails to remember that it's daylight saving time and emerges from his coffin one sunny hour too soon.

8. Not just a game (version 1): Child gets so caught up in fantasy role-playing game that he murders friends or family.

9. Not just a game (version 2): Video or computer game provides training for galactic combat, or the "game" is actually a real war. (Cf. movies such as *WarGames, Tron, The Last Starfighter,* etc.) Plays on hope that our most trivial pastimes have world-shaking consequences, that we're actually being trained for something important, or that at least someone's watching us and is impressed.

10. Ironic retribution: Classic horror plot, beloved of EC Comics. Murderer is haunted by victim and driven to suicide, strangler is strangled, man who blinded someone is blinded himself, cat-killer is killed by a real (or ghost) cat, hunted animals take revenge on cruel hunter, machines get back at cruel owner (as in a famous *Twilight Zone* episode), etc. See Hans Christian Andersen's "Girl Who Trod on a Loaf," who pulled the wings off flies and was punished when they crawled over her frozen face.

11. Meet the myth: Hero or heroine encounters hitchhiker, seductive woman at beach, new neighbor, tramp, etc., who turns out to be centaur, mermaid, Pan, or the Medusa.

12. The living house: Yes, it's really alive, and it eats anyone foolish enough to enter. Or imprisons visitors. Or crashes on the head of an evil real estate developer.

13. The henpecked hubby: Milquetoast plans intricate murder of wife. Often ends with "Come in, dear, I have something to show you!" as husband waits for her in room full of carnivorous plants. Usually submitted by men.

14. You can't cheat fate: Prophecy proves true, usually in irritating ironic way. Someone fated to die of "cancer" is murdered by an astrological Cancer; future "plane crash" victim refuses to fly but is killed when a plane hits his home, etc. A plot as old as Oedipus.

15. You can't cheat the devil: Tedious variation on #14 in which the devil always wins. (Notable exception: Stephen Vincent Benét's "The Devil and Daniel Webster.")

16. Cannibals: Funeral ends with eating of corpse, isolated town barbecues unlucky strangers, mysterious dinner turns out to be old Fred, etc.

17. Gotcha!: Stories that end with "And then the great jaws opened," "And then it sprang," "And then it was upon him," or "He had time for one final scream." (Cf. William Tenn's classic "The Human Angle": "Because her teeth were in his throat.") Often the ending is a moral one: The mass murderer gets his comeuppance when a seemingly helpless victim turns out to be a werewolf, etc.

18. It was only a dream: Believe it or not, this wasn't retired with *Alice in Wonderland*. Variations are still being dreamed up.

19. Trick or treat: Costumed Halloween celebrants turn out to be monsters, aliens, dead kids, etc. Sometimes they take revenge on a child-killer.

20. Ho ho ho!: UFO sighted over the North Pole in late December is taken for a Russian sneak attack, turns out to be guess who. Commonly submitted in winter. Most frequent ending: "Merry Christmas to all and to all a good night!"

21. The jaws of sex: Hero or heroine (sometimes with dishonorable intentions) meets attractive stranger, perhaps in bar, and anticipates night of romance. Shock comes when they climb between the sheets: Stranger turns out to be vampire, werewolf, alien, squid, giant spider, gelatinous mass—all the things we've always feared in a one-night stand. Sexual paranoia at its most basic. Best example: William Sansom's "A Woman Seldom Found," whose arm snakes out across the room and switches off the light.*

---

*Needless to say, a list like this can be extended endlessly, and in fact I couldn't resist doing so in a booklet called *Raising Goosebumps for Fun and Profit*, published in 1988 by Bill Munster's Footsteps Press. Along with an expanded version of the *Writer's Digest* article above, it included "The 25 Most Familiar Horror Plots," each paired with a startling full-page illustration by Peter Kuper. For the record, the added items were "They're All Against Me!" (a paranoid is proven right), "Make a Wish" (it comes true, but horribly), "Yankee, Go Home!" (yet another isolated town, travelers beware), and "The Punch Line" (tales that end with a ghoulish pun).

Standing Behind the Curtains: A Conversation with T.E.D. Klein

In the early 1980s, horror fiction had reached a wider audience than ever before. Authors such as Peter Straub, Clive Barker, Ramsey Campbell, and, of course, Stephen King raised the standards of writing quality, deftly scaling the summits of popularity and bringing the genre to a new level of literary appreciation. Among their ranks was a writer named T.E.D. Klein, who would ultimately become one of the most important voices in modern horror fiction.

Theodore Donald Klein (the "E" stands for "Eibon," a literary reference to Clark Ashton Smith's Hyperborean sorcerer) was born and raised in New York. A graduate of Brown University, Klein would later study at Columbia, which led to a stint in the late 1970s at Paramount as a script reader. In 1981, he became the founding editor of the highly acclaimed *Rod Serling's Twilight Zone Magazine,* publishing works by authors such as Stephen King, Peter Straub, and Harlan Ellison before parting ways in 1985.

In 1984, Klein published his first, and so far only, novel, *The Ceremonies*. An expansion of an earlier novella titled "The Events at Poroth Farm" (itself in turn inspired by "The White People," a classic short story by Welsh dark fantasy author Arthur Machen), *The Ceremonies* was an excursion into cosmic horror set against the back-

---

Email interview conducted by Barry Lee Dejasu, 2014–15, for *Shock Totem* magazine. It was published in *Dead Reckonings* (Fall 2017).

drop of contemporary American culture. *The Ceremonies* enjoyed a brief ride on the *New York Times* bestseller list, and although it's now long out of print, it is considered a classic.

The following year, Klein released a collection of four novellas, known as *Dark Gods*. Although three of its novellas were previously published elsewhere (one in Kirby McCauley's legendary 1980 anthology *Dark Forces*), one of them, "Nadelman's God," was original to the collection and would subsequently go on to win the 1986 World Fantasy Award for Best Novella. And just like *The Ceremonies, Dark Gods* is unfortunately very much out of print.

As the years went by, Klein would go on to publish fewer than a dozen short stories, most of which (along with "The Events at Poroth Farm") were collected in a 2006 limited-edition book from Subterranean Press, *Reassuring Tales*. As with his previous works, this has unfortunately become an out-of-print rarity, and due to its limited print run (only 600 signed and numbered copies exist), it's even harder to find than the others, often being listed for over $100 in online stores.

Klein may have estranged himself from the genre that he helped shape, but even after nearly three decades his influence has never been forgotten. To date, authors such as Thomas Ligotti, John Langan, Laird Barron, Paul Tremblay, and Simon Strantzas look fondly upon his works as a direct influence upon their own.

In a rare and exclusive gesture, Mr. Klein broke his silence to generously discuss his life, writings, and career.

BLD: While you were growing up, what did you like to read? Who were some authors that you just couldn't get enough of, and not necessarily in horror?

TK: I loved a series of maritime adventure books by Howard Pease (or rather, by one of the authors with that name; there appear to have been two), who wrote about tramp steamers plying the South Seas. As a boy, I used to clip out the daily shipping news from the back of the *Times*—those listings still seem pretty romantic to me—and I imagined, crazily enough, that I would someday ship out on a rusted freighter and visit all sorts of exotic ports of call. Actually,

I'm a lousy traveler and have always been afraid of the water.

My favorite childhood book had also been my father's favorite: Booth Tarkington's *Penrod* trilogy, in a thick black omnibus volume with my father's name stamped all over it. It's basically an early-twentieth-century *Tom Sawyer,* albeit a little more domesticated, and the writing's extremely droll. I read the book again and again and still remember many lines from it—like the description of a caterpillar motionless on a twig, looking as if it were "lost in reverie." Two friends from the neighborhood and I were even inspired to form a secret club we called the P.S. of A.P.B. (which stood for "the Penrod and Sam of All Penrod Books").

BLD: Around what age did you become interested in writing? What were some of your earliest writings about?

TK: At a point—probably in junior high—when I had read most of the celebrated Robert A. Heinlein juveniles and was moving on to the stuff for older readers, I remember getting involved in a writing competition with a brainy friend over who could complete a book first. He was going to write a history of the world (I said he was brainy), and I was going to write a science fiction novel.

Neither one of us got very far, but I remember a few things my manuscript contained that, at the time, struck me as extremely neat but may well have been cribbed from things I'd read. I had my hero, a Heinleinesque space cadet, finish his training in a graduation ceremony that ended, symbolically, with each new graduate being shoved off the rostrum into a pit of mud. There was a space-travel scene—also Heinlein-inspired, I'm sure—in which a sleek ship rocket ship brought travelers up to some sort of giant, drab, ungainly interstellar transport chamber, floating somewhere beyond the moon, inside of which they stood around impatiently like a crowd of commuters in the main hall of Grand Central Station, smoking cigarettes and chatting; and when they filed out a few minutes later, they were at the other end of the galaxy. And there was a time traveler who miscalculated and somehow materialized where a brick wall had once been standing (or would someday be standing)—"and before he could be rescued," I wrote, "his heart had turned to cement."

BLD: What about dark fiction appealed to you so much, to read it and to write it?

TK: Well, if you mean what's usually described as "supernatural horror," I think it just makes the world more interesting. A world with room in it for the supernatural would be both darker and potentially lighter than the one I believe we're actually living in; it would be a world richer in meaning, scarier and yet more charming. On the other hand, if there were even an ounce of religion among the things I happen to believe in (and there isn't), supernatural fiction would probably hold little appeal for me. I'd have no emotional need for it.

As for writing it, I suppose initially there's the normal desire to imitate the authors who've given one pleasure, followed later by the desire to modify, critique, and even poke fun at those same formative figures. (I guess you'd file that under "anxiety of influence.") Plus—and I'm sure this has been said a million times—for anyone who's ever been frightened, as I have, by a scary story or a horror film, there's a certain gratification in creating something of the same sort yourself, where it's you that's standing behind the curtains, controlling the action. It's akin to the reassurance a child may feel when he sees a behind-the-scenes photo of the guy in the rubber monster suit, or learns the secret of how special effects are produced, or gets the autograph, at a horror convention, of some actor who once scared him in the movies.

BLD: It's pretty obvious, from the themes and subject matter of your works, that you were a fan of Lovecraft and Machen. When did you get into them?

TK: I first encountered those writers in the most commonplace, boring old way—by coming across their work at my local library (in that celebrated Modern Library Giant, most likely).* Later, at college in Providence, I found myself strolling daily through Love-

---

Great Tales of Terror and the Supernatural (1944), edited by Herbert A. Wise and Phyllis Fraser.

craft's beloved old neighborhood, buying Arkham House books at a shop he himself had frequented, and, during my senior year, living next door to a house that figures in "The Call of Cthulhu."

So for a while, I really became quite consumed with HPL—with his life as well as his fiction. Plus I've always had a tremendous fondness for New England, and Lovecraft is surely a key part of that; he's made it—the entire region, crazy as this may sound—a somewhat magical place.

BLD: If you don't mind my asking, which house had you lived in? (I myself am a Providence resident, and was born only a couple of blocks away from Lovecraft's own birthplace.)

TK: It's great that you were born so near HPL's birthplace. That's certainly one of the charms of Providence—feeling that his presence is so close. The house I lived in was the Deacon Edward Taylor House, 9 Thomas Street. I loved that building and felt grateful to be living in it. I remember the third floor, where I lived, had wide plank floorboards—creaking slightly, I think—and fireplaces in all four rooms.

BLD: Were any of your stories, or even *The Ceremonies,* ever optioned for film?

TK: Some blessed person did option *The Ceremonies* a few years ago, but obviously nothing has come of it. And a filmmaker in England has an option on "Children of the Kingdom." I wish him luck.

BLD: How does it feel, knowing how many established and up-and-coming authors were greatly influenced by your work?

TK: I'm actually astonished to hear that anyone's ever said such a thing; it's news to me. I'm pleased, I guess, but it's awfully hard to imagine anyone being influenced by anything of mine, especially considering how little I've managed to turn out.

BLD: Your work is *very* highly regarded. In fact, you have an entire stretch of a chapter in S. T. Joshi's *The Modern Weird Tale: A Critique* *of Horror Fiction,* right alongside Shirley Jackson, William Peter Blatty, Stephen King, Clive Barker, Ramsey Campbell, and Robert Bloch. A renowned author once told me that your story "Black Man with a Horn" was in particular a big inspiration upon his work.

TK: That sort of thing is always a bit shocking to hear, but very nice, obviously.

BLD: Back in the '80s, you announced work on a new novel. Whatever became of that? Did you just never finish it, or is it pending heavy edits and in some sort of hiatus?

TK: It was going to be called *Nighttown;* it still may be! I got around halfway through, by which time I began to worry that it was getting out of hand—I mean, getting too long and complicated. (I had originally intended it to be a lively, fast-moving read, on the order of *The Thirty-Nine Steps*, but clearly that sort of thing isn't a natural fit.) And then, unfortunately, I got distracted, which is always a problem. I find writing quite difficult, and I'm good at finding ways to avoid it.

BLD: So what did you end up doing instead? What have you been up to since?

TK: Thanks for asking. Life is definitely full of distractions, if you're looking for them. At one point, in the early '90s, when I should have been hard at work on the new book, I happily spent my time editing a true-crime magazine called *CrimeBeat,* which made a bit of a splash on newsstands but alas ran out of money after fourteen issues—though while it lasted it was great fun and something I'd always wanted to do. (I should add that although it was based on my own proposal, the initial capital was raised by my old mentor from *Twilight Zone,* Eric Protter, who died this past year; as did, more recently, my agent, Kirby McCauley; as did, even more recently, Alice Turner of *Playboy*. All three were friends I was very close to, for decades, and to whom I owe a lot.)

During that same period—this time thanks to Kirby—I also had the chance to write a screenplay for the Italian director Dario Argento, adapted from a treatment of his. The movie itself turned out to be unwatchable; I, at least, have never managed to sit through it. (You know how Machen said something like "I dreamed in fire, but I worked in clay"? He might have been talking about that woeful little film.) Still, it was exciting to work on a script, and actually explore locations, with a colorful, amusing, albeit exasperating character like Argento.

Subsequently I did some teaching at John Jay College, part of the city university system. (Enjoyed it. I once spent a year teaching high school English in Dexter, Maine—one of the best years of my life.)

For the past decade, I've been working for *GQ*; my official title is senior copy editor. The senior part is appropriate, as I'm probably the oldest guy on the staff. Basically I spend my day inserting and deleting commas; I really know my commas. When I first got the job, my friend Margie said, "What?!! You're the most un-*GQ* person I've ever known." I still take that as a compliment. The company, Condé Nast, has just vacated its offices in the heart of Times Square and is now ensconced, for better or worse, in the new World Trade Center downtown. I can't say I'm warming to the place, and I expect to retire soon.

BLD: Would you ever consider returning to writing fiction again?

TK: Definitely—although I have to admit I'm somewhat less interested in horror fiction, and fiction in general, than I used to be; it's probably a consequence of age. I find I prefer to read big fat history books these days, and a smattering of popular science—trying to make up for too many years of ignorance.

BLD: Would you like to say anything to all the authors, artists, etc., who have been inspired by you over the years?

TK: Yeah. I'm truly grateful, but now please try some good nonfiction.

IV. On Film

They Kill Animals and They Call It Art

I've just returned from *The Holy Mountain*. It was quite a trip. I saw an old man pluck out his glass eye and hand it to a little girl. I watched three men impale themselves over and over on bayonets. I passed a man whose face was covered with flies, and another whose body was covered with giant spiders. I met an armless psychopath, a quadruple amputee, a religious chimpanzee, and a man whose excrement was turned into gold. I witnessed mother-son incest, transvestism in the church, several dozen executions, and one public castration.

Oddly enough, none of this bothered me. None of this was real. It was just a charade, courtesy of Alexandro Jodorowsky, the Chilean director whose *El Topo*—a blood-drenched fairy tale shot in Mexico—became the first cult film of the seventies. His new film, now playing at midnight on Fridays and Saturdays at the Waverly, is entertaining enough at first, but it soon becomes filled with the sort of thing Stewart Brand has described in his *Whole Earth Catalog* as "dime store mysticism." It squanders a truly incredible amount of props, images, and money—all to little effect, for Jodorowsky tries so hard to be shocking that, in the end, he becomes merely monotonous. He reminds one of a Fellini without the feeling.

What did bother me, though, was Jodorowsky's use—or misuse—of animals. Their corpses fill the screen. A parade goes by carrying dozens of crosses on which the butchered bodies of sheep hang crucified. A tree stands decorated with hundreds of slaughtered

---

Sunday feature, *New York Times* (January 13, 1974).

chickens. During a "spiritual operation," the lump on a sinner's back is sliced open to reveal the inky body of an octopus.

A dead pig is used as a vat for carrying plaster, a man sits within the carcass of a bull as if it were a bathtub, and the director himself, playing The Alchemist, reclines upon a throne made from the bodies of goats. When this same character offers to let his head be cut off by a disciple, the camera cuts away, then returns to find the decapitated body of a lamb, which spurts fountains of blood while Jodorowsky squats nearby, chuckling heartily at his joke.

He further offers us what looks to be a genuine dogfight, and in an early scene he dresses up a wagonload of frogs and horned toads to resemble Aztecs and Spanish conquistadors, then films the parched creatures as they die slowly in the noonday sun. Those left alive he destroys in a dynamite explosion.

This may hardly seem a major issue, of course, for frogs and the like die every day. They die in schoolrooms and they die in laboratories. Fishermen use them for bait, gourmets eat them, and small boys kill them for sport. These frogs, however, died so that Alexandro Jodorowsky could make *The Holy Mountain,* and therein lies the difference. This is a new kind of violence, a kind apparently ignored by all but a few humane groups, bleeding hearts, and, I daresay, children. It points up a curious—and alarming—trend in filmmaking: what can only be called Death for Art's Sake.

As I've tried to suggest, Jodorowsky is one of its leading practitioners in Mexico. But when it comes to ego trips, Mexico has nothing on the U.S.A. Our own directors, too, enjoy playing God with the lives of their fellow creatures. Consider, for example, Dennis Hopper, who chopped off chickens' heads in *Kid Blue* and who went to Peru to film *The Last Movie*—another Personal Statement. In a 1970 article in the *Times,* entitled "A Gigantic Ego Trip for Dennis Hopper?," writer Alix Jeffry vividly described the making of *The Last Movie:*

> For the sacrifice scene, seven sheep are lying on their sides, feet tied, waiting for their throats to be cut. Several hundred Indians have been engaged as extras for the day, for a little less than one American dollar apiece.... The blood-letting takes place matter-

of-factly after a religious ceremony. An animal raises its head, blood streaming from its throat, and looks with glazed eyes at its executioner, and then its head slowly drops. Death is just another phase of life. . . . Violence breathes in and out of this film.

Violence—it's become something of a catchword. These days, of course, all right-thinking people have denounced "violence in the movies"—and, indeed, with good reason. But sometimes they get a little carried away, and act as if the violence on the screen were *real:* as if, in *Dillinger,* Warren Oates' victims bled real blood; as if, in *Charley Varrick,* Walter Matthau's character died a real death.

Whatever the eventual effects of such carnage upon our psyches and our society, it may be worth reminding ourselves that Hollywood's bullets are blank. But for animals, the bullets and the knives and the blood are real; and more and more directors are using the deaths of innocent creatures to provide shocks their films might otherwise fail to deliver.

As one might expect, horror movies are among the worst offenders. There are, for example, several Filipino imports—B-movie fare at its most primitive. One, *Mad Doctor of Blood Island* (seen on New York TV earlier this season, under a new title and, appropriately, butchered), features the usual hacked-off human limbs, glistening viscera and dangling eyeballs. But all this stuff is patently papier-mâché.

It's all good clean fun—until, halfway through, there's a scene in which a native tribe hacks to death a flock of sheep and pigs for some ritual sacrifice; and suddenly it's no longer very funny, for it's clear that real animals are being killed, and far from quickly.

Not that Asian horror films are the only such offenders; one may also point to such recent European imports as *The Devil's Nightmare,* in which the bloody body of a cat is riddled with steel spikes, and the German-language *Jonathan,* in which the still-kicking bodies of slaughtered livestock add "color" (or at least one color) to the panorama of a massacre.

Billed as "the first adult vampire film," *Jonathan* also features close-ups of a mouse being slowly crushed to death beneath the heel of a boot. The intention? Simply to show that the prison guard in question is a cruel man—something we might have gathered already, since he's just finished whipping the hero bloody.

Yet for all his blood and crying, the hero's pain somehow failed to move me half so much as the mouse's. Maybe it's because the mouse's cries were authentic.

Authenticity is nice when you can get it, but when it comes to filmmaking I've always been perfectly content to look upon stuffed animals, or trained animals, or animals drugged or sleeping (e.g., the monkey in *The Andromeda Strain*), and to make believe they were dead. *The Godfather* employed an actual horse's head for that horrifying bedroom scene, but the object came from a nearby slaughterhouse.

Patton, on the other hand, actually killed the two donkeys that George C. Scott "shot" because they were blocking the advance of his troops. ("The two old donkeys were put to death when a doctor gave them painless lethal injections," explained the film's producer.) That may sound relatively humane, but I'd hate to think a filmmaker would actually destroy an animal just to make a scene look "real" or—as in *The Hellstrom Chronicle,* when a mouse dies in convulsions from a bee sting—just to prove a point.

Of course, some people aren't bothered by all this. They merely smile, shrug, and point out that millions upon millions of animals die each year, killed by everything from bombs to mousetraps to speeding cars. Indeed, one can take a kind of gloomy solace in this fact, just as, to put things in perspective, one can profitably turn one's thoughts to the livestock regularly killed in our meatpacking plants—as Georges Franju pictured it years ago in *Le Sang des Bêtes.* After all, amid carnage of this magnitude, what can a few more deaths possibly mean?

Certainly it's of no consequence to the buffalo and elk killed in *Jeremiah Johnson* that they died for Art instead of for Sport; nor would it matter to a deer that it died for the Richard Burton film *Bluebeard.* Jean-Luc Godard had a pig's throat cut for *Weekend,* Fernando Arrabal did the same for a steer in *Viva la Muerte,* and a goose's head was chopped off amid the feasting of *The Grande Bouffe*—but these animals would hardly care that their butchered bodies appeared not on the dinner table but on the screen.

Unfortunately, *I* care.

And so does Harold Melniker, head of the American Humane Association's Hollywood office. "More and more, we hear of mistreatment of animals on overseas sets," Melniker wrote in a recent issue of *Screen Actor* magazine. "It would indeed be a giant step forward if an actor on a set in Spain or Italy, for instance, were to step forward and protest such action." He cites only one actor, Edd Byrnes, who's been willing to speak out.

Acting as a sort of unofficial advisor to the film industry (and, all too often, as its conscience), Melniker bemoans the current trend toward foreign production. Typically, Kirk Douglas had to go to Yugoslavia to shoot his new western, *Scalawag,* which makes use of the notorious trip-wire to yank the legs from under horses; typically, too, the first TV movie to use trip-wires (and so far the only one) was ABC's *Hardcase,* shot in Mexico.

Overseas productions are by no means the only culprits. In its monthly classification list, which rates films "acceptable" or "unacceptable" in their treatment of animals, the American Humane Association has recorded violations by every American studio, from the cockfight in *The Legend of Nigger Charley* to the recent Burt Lancaster western, *Ulzana's Raid,* filmed in Arizona, which—despite previous assurances to the contrary—went ahead and used trip-wires while an A.H.A. representative protested in vain to the local sheriff.

"When you want action," says Melniker bitterly, "tripping horses is a way of getting it. It's easy and it's quick." Though John Wayne has always abided by A.H.A. guidelines, using only trained horses in his films, directors like Sam Peckinpah prefer to take the easy way out. Peckinpah's recent *Pat Garrett and Billy the Kid* got an "unacceptable" rating for both the trip-wiring of horses and the casual use of chickens, buried in the ground up to their necks, for target practice.

What has the Motion Picture Association of America been able to do about the abuse of animals in movies? As far back as 1939, it acted against *Jesse James,* in which a horse was propelled over a cliff by means of a tipping plank, heavily greased. Until that time, the industry's production code had contained only vague references to the treatment of animals; a type of trip-wire called the "running W" was a commonplace in westerns, as were concealed pits, so that spills cost many a horse a broken leg—or even a broken neck.

The death of the horse in *Jesse James*, however, resulted in such a public outcry that, in 1940, new stipulations were written into the code specifically outlawing the running W, and in 1956 it was further decreed that "in the production of motion pictures involving animals the producer shall consult with the authorized representative of the American Humane Association, and invite him to be present during the staging of such animal action."

Thanks to the provisions of the code, animals in American films were afforded decent and humane treatment under A.H.A. supervision—until, in 1966, the entire production code was discarded, and with it all mention of trip-wires and mistreatment during shooting. No longer was it required that an A.H.A. representative witness scenes involving animals; his presence on the set was left to the whim of the producer.

Since 1966, the abuses have grown, and the trip-wire has made a triumphant return. Where once Melniker's office received copies of virtually all American film scripts involving animals, so that the A.H.A. might act as consultant in the filming, Melniker says he now receives "very few," and spends far more time going over the 25 to 30 television scripts sent him each week.

"It seems as though we have, as a nation, entered into an era of permissiveness," he wrote in the *National Humane Review*. "In all phases of life, individuals are making their own rules and anything goes! Regrettably, this attitude is reaching over into the handling of animals."

But perhaps there is still room for hope. Perhaps an Alexandro Jodorowsky, or a Dennis Hopper, or a Sam Peckinpah will one day go too far, and will unwittingly bring about a return to the 1956 provisions.

Or perhaps these artists will experience a change of heart similar to the one apparently experienced by actor-director Cornel Wilde. In the late 1960s, Wilde appeared on an odious ABC-TV show called *American Sportsman*, in which the camera followed various celebrities as they tracked down and disposed of a wide variety of animals. Aided by a guide, a camera crew, and a high-powered rifle with a telescopic sight, Wilde was shown bringing down an Alaskan grizzly with two shots, chortling like a child over his kill. "Boy, oh boy, oh boy," he exulted. "We did it!"

However, by 1970, Wilde seems to have had second thoughts, as evidenced by *No Blade of Grass*, his film depicting the effects of a worldwide agricultural famine. To be sure, Wilde stuffed his film with motorcycle gangs, graphic rape scenes, and lots of mashed-looking animal carcasses. It was, at best, enjoyable trash—hardly the responsible plea for environmental protection it pretended to be.

But catching *No Blade of Grass* recently at a drive-in, I was unexpectedly gratified by the words that appeared on screen after "THE END" had replaced all the carnage. They said: *"No animal was killed or mistreated for the purpose of making this film."*

How good it would be if those words could follow all films.

Animals in Movies—
The Abuse Gets Worse

"Pit 'em!" Earle shouted. . . .

Juju climbed again, cutting and hitting so rapidly that his legs were a golden blur. . . . He broke one of the red's wings, then practically severed a leg.

"Handle them," Earle called.

When the dwarf gathered the red up, its neck had begun to droop and it was a mass of blood and matted feathers. The little man moaned over the bird, then set to work. He spit into its gaping beak and took the comb between his lips and sucked the blood back into it. . . .

"Pit 'em," Earle said.

The lines above, from Nathanael West's *The Day of the Locust*, describe the preliminary rounds of a cockfight. Both birds have been fitted with "gaffs"—three-inch steel spurs, sharp as needles, fastened to their legs. Midway through the fight the "big red" loses the top half of his beak. The struggle ends when Juju, the smaller bird, drives a gaff through the other's eye, into the brain.

Like dogfights, bullfights, and other barbaric spectacles, cockfights have been outlawed throughout the United States since about the turn of the century. Not many New Yorkers would pay to see one. Yet that's exactly what they're doing when they line up for

---

Sunday feature, *New York Times* (June 8, 1975).

Paramount's *The Day of the Locust,* which opened here May 7—right in the middle of Be Kind to Animals Week. For, in a misguided attempt to remain true to the West novel, director John Schlesinger has staged a genuine cockfight, complete with blood, spurs, and a bird that dies twitching at the actors' feet while the camera lovingly records every detail.

Such self-indulgence in the name of "realism" is totally unnecessary. Hollywood has effectively staged cockfights before—most memorably in *The Cincinnati Kid* and *Ace Eli and Rodger of the Skies*—but they've been simulated. "No birds were hurt, injured, or killed," says Harold Melniker of the American Humane Association, whose office worked with the filmmakers. "The only trouble with simulation is that it requires a little extra time and money."

But time and money are luxuries in this industry, especially in the precarious world of the small-time independent producers—two of whom, sensing the exploitation value of chicken blood, are about to cash in on the trend with forthcoming films of their own: Both *Supercock,* shot in Manila, and *Born to Kill,* shot in Georgia, will feature real cockfights.

Inexcusable in any circumstances, such practices are even more so in a $6 million movie from a major studio. Yet Vincent Canby lauded *Locust* for its fidelity to the original novel, and Pauline Kael praised actor Billy Barty for "the tenderness of his handling of the wretched, mutilated bird." All of the critics seemed to overlook the fact that, unlike Donald Sutherland's bloody death at the hands of a mob, the bloody death of the fighting cock was real.

Perhaps they just didn't care. Last summer, in a *Village Voice* column whose flip title—"On Being Beastly to the Beasties"—matched the tone of his prose, critic Andrew Sarris waxed poetic over the deaths of "all those marvelously expressive rabbits in *The Rules of the Game*" and suggested that animals killed in films "should have felt honored to be called upon to contribute their ephemeral lives and bodies to such immortal works of art."

There is, of course, a precedent for this ghoulish aesthetics: Watching a group of Ethiopian horsemen blown up by an Italian bomb, Mussolini's son compared the sight to "a budding rose unfolding." Presumably the horsemen should have felt honored.

Like the critics, directors have long considered animals expendable in the cause of art. In a 1974 article for the Arts and Leisure section, I cited a few such examples from the likes of Sam Peckinpah, Dennis Hopper, Alexandro Jodorowsky, and others: rabbits roasted in the sun, sheep with throats slit, mice crushed beneath boots, horses made to fall by means of "trip-wires," often with enough force to break their legs—or necks.

The piece drew a furious two-page reply from Robert Redford, who justified the killing of an elk and buffalo in *Jeremiah Johnson* on grounds that the animals were "diseased and earmarked for an early death." If that's true, let's hope his friends stay healthy.

The same year the Motion Picture Association of America received an unprecedented 1,400 letters decrying animal abuse. Its president, Jack Valenti, agreed to a much-publicized meeting with the heads of four humane societies, at which he spoke of the M.P.A.A.'s determination "to abolish inhumane treatment of animals" and urged filmmakers to let American Humane Association personnel supervise the filming of animal scenes. Unfortunately, compliance with the resolution was left strictly voluntary.

Recently two state legislators—New York assemblyman Leonard Stavisky and California state senator David Roberti—have introduced bills making it a misdemeanor to show films for which animals were killed or mistreated, and industry spokesmen have reacted with predicable cries of government interference; like Valenti, they prefer appealing to the "conscience" of those involved. But Paramount's *The Day of the Locust,* with its arrogant disregard for law as well as for the M.P.A.A. pledge, illustrates the futility of such appeals. "They never consulted us at all," says the American Humane Association's Harold Melniker.

During filming of Paramount's *Jonathan Livingston Seagull,* dozens of birds were reportedly killed by caustic bleaches and hair sprays, others were crippled by control cords, and some 88 suffered eye injuries; the same studio's *Posse* employs trip-wires, as do two other major films involving horses: Columbia's *Bite the Bullet* and MGM's *The Wind and the Lion.*

It has become increasingly obvious that animal abuse is no longer confined to shoestring American productions and foreign films. Assuming the industry is permitted to maintain its present hypocritical standards of "self-regulation," we can look forward to the next logical step: a major studio's biography of Shakespeare, complete with real bear-baiting.

On Cutting Up Movie Classics

To the Editor:

Question: Name two classic scenes from the Marx Brothers' movie *A Night at the Opera*.

Answer: The backstage scene in which Groucho and Chico go over a legal contract (containing the famous "party of the first part, party of the second part" routine, etc.); and the justly celebrated stateroom scene, in which a crowd of passengers, waiters, and crew members jam themselves into Groucho's tiny cabin.

Now, guess which scenes were cut during the film's recent showing at the Carnegie Hall Cinema.

Answer: Audiences saw only the early stages of the stateroom scene and a few lines from the beginning of the contract sequence. All remaining footage had been snipped out, along with most of the opening credits. (One never even got to see the title.) A Saturday-night full house, with a dozen or more people standing in the rear, had shelled out $3 a head to see this mutilated print, cut-up and jumpy as an old stag movie, with words and lines missing every few seconds, to say nothing of entire shots.

One hesitates, of course, to criticize a revival house such as the Carnegie; there are too few places left in New York that show old films. Unfortunately, though, this is no isolated example.

Letter, *New York Times* (August 4, 1974).

When restaurants become health hazards, the city closes them down as a public service. I humbly suggest that the city take similar action against irresponsible theaters such as this—for they, too, pose a health hazard: high blood pressure and excessive secretion of adrenalin, due to frustrated rage; and sprained jaws, due to a gnashing of teeth.*

---

*A couple of weeks later, the *Times* published a long, detailed apology from the theater's program director, essentially blaming an "indifferent distributor."

P.S. This was not the first time I complained about a cut-up classic movie. I recently discovered, in my files, a May 1971 letter to, of all places, *Screw* (I think because they'd print just about any letter, the more splenetic and obscene the better), denouncing that spring's rerelease of my all-time favorite film:

"Dear Screw—In case any of your readers are contemplating paying $3.50 to see *Lawrence of Arabia* at the Rivoli, let them be warned: The movie has been cut, hacked, abridged, and mangled by a gang of ignorant functionaries at Columbia Pictures. If you admired the original *Lawrence* as much as I did, watching this version with some of the most dramatic scenes omitted (recovering from the torture, the shock-cut from his face to his army of cut-throats, the scene in the Damascus hospital, etc.) can be a pretty painful experience." I ended by suggesting some appropriate punishments for the offending executives, including that they be "raped by a gang of Turks."

The good news is that Columbia eventually restored *Lawrence* to its full length, no doubt in response to my threat.

How I Flopped as a Paramount Script Reader

It isn't every day one gets to identify with Robert Redford, but at last he and I have something in common. In *Three Days of the Condor* he plays a professional "reader"—a man who's paid to sit in his office all day with his nose in a book—and that's a role I, too, have played. Redford reads spy novels for the CIA; my employer was Paramount Pictures, and spy novels were only a small part of the material I covered. I approached each book or screenplay with three questions in mind: Is there a movie in it? A commercial movie? A *Paramount* movie? Unlike Redford, as often as not I guessed wrong.

If there are any special qualifications for such a job, I've never heard of them. Although I was hired right out of film school, I suspect my typing ability had more to do with it than my master's degree. The work kept me occupied two or three days a week at thirty-five dollars a day—it was forty-five by the time I left three years later—but there were fringe benefits as well: I was invited to all the free screenings, and I had access to the studio's Wats line to call my grandmother in Florida. My office was small but offered a fine view of the Hudson thirty-seven floors below, and I'd often spend the greater part of my afternoons watching ocean liners pull majestically into the docks. Sometimes the maneuvers took hours.

During my years there, Paramount employed half a dozen free-

Sunday feature, *New York Times* (October 26, 1975).

lance readers who worked out of their homes. They were usually assigned the more important books by the bigger-name writers. As its "in-house" reader, I found myself faced with the trashiest novels and the most dubious screenplays our office received. As a rule we were only allowed to consider material submitted by literary agents; all other manuscripts were sent back unread.

Still, an agent's name on the covering letter was no guarantee of quality, and I acted, in effect, as Paramount's first line of defense. If a book appeared hopeless by chapter four, I would skim the rest (paying particular attention to the ending), then write a few lines of comment on an index card for our files. In this way I might plow through half a dozen manuscripts in a single morning.

Within my first month on the job, for example, I was assigned a dreary French romance ("Unless a story's really special," I was told, "we don't want it set outside the U.S."); a children's fantasy about worms ("Kiddie pictures don't make money unless the name Disney's on them"); a gothic ("We're not too keen on gothics, but we do want strong parts for women"); a tennis novel ("Sports movies never make it at the box office unless they're biographies"); an epic about Lady Jane Grey ("Costume dramas are too expensive these days"); a mystery in which a mentally retarded girl drowned her mother in a tub full of raw eggs ("Retards are a no-no here"); a sex novel in which a naked young woman was kicked to death with a soccer ball ("Perversions are *out!*"); a comedy about an impotent husband ("You mean you wasted a whole day reading a book about *impotence?* That's absolutely taboo"); a black cowboy saga (the first of dozens); and, to my astonishment, a screenplay by Michelangelo Antonioni. The script's presence on my desk was unnerving: Why did Antonioni have to go through me?

Perhaps the script's battered appearance should have warned me that it was no stranger to rejection. Indeed, it proved to be one of the master's lesser efforts, a mélange of angst, canasta, and championship Ping-Pong. "Except for a few flashes of skin and the car crash at the end," I wrote on the card, "this would make a very tedious film.... An unfunny parody of Antonioni at his pretentious worst." Playing critic gave me a sense of power.

When submitted material was promising, however, I might spend a whole day with it, composing a detailed plot summary followed by a page of evaluation. Those synopses were passed on to my boss, the East Coast story editor, who in turn sent the best each week to the vice-president in charge of production. His office was in Hollywood, where most of the decisions were made.

Usually my synopses were well under ten pages, but important books might warrant twenty pages or more. The longest I ever wrote was a forty-three-page synopsis of *Ragtime*—a freelance piece for United Artists. "It's easily one of the most beautifully written novels I've read in years," I said, "but I'm amazed and appalled that it's being seriously considered as a movie. . . . It deserves to be left as it is." Less than a week later, I learned that Dino De Laurentiis had bought the rights for Robert Altman.

Synopsis-writing is an acquired art; the secret is to fill the pages with dialogue and lots of vivid metaphors. Unfortunately, it took me years to discover this simple rule. During the early part of my tenure at Paramount, my synopses ranged from bland to incomprehensible, and my summary of *The Taking of Pelham 1-2-3* was so confusing that I almost lost my job over it. Perhaps that's one of the reasons why the movie was eventually made by United Artists.

Because synopses were so much harder to write than rejections, there was always a slight predisposition to *dislike* a manuscript. I had other prejudices as well: against spy novels and mysteries (difficult to skim, difficult to summarize); against published books (if material were hot, I'd have seen it in manuscript); and against screenplays (shorter than books, but often a chore, since they're written to be shot rather than read).

Still, I like to think that my strongest prejudice was simply in favor of good writing. God knows, I saw precious little of it. Most of what I read was junk. When Nixon visited Red China, I was forced to read every novel even remotely connected to things Chinese. During the last Mideast crisis, I read Arab-Israeli intrigues—dozens, it seemed—till every Puerto Rican I passed on the street looked like a fedayeen. During my first year at Paramount, when the word came down from the Coast that "Bob Evans is looking for a love story about pretty people," I spent the next few months reading jet-set fantasies and inside looks at the world of high fashion. I began to feel like a peasant.

Then there were the hordes of *Godfather* imitations (New York gangsters, funny gangsters, Jewish gangsters); *Day of the Jackal* imitations (with such targets as Eisenhower, Churchill, Patton, Kissinger); and big-business novels ("He was as ruthless in bed as he was in the boardroom"). I became an expert on that new form of literature, the book written solely in hope of a movie sale.

Amid such company, serious fiction was a rare treat. Yet even when I fell in love with books—and I think of unappreciated novels by J. G. Farrell, Lloyd Kropp, Thomas Allen, William Kotzwinkle, Herbert Kastle, Francis Irby Gwaltney, William Hjortsberg, Sumner Lock Elliott, and Josiah Bunting III—there was no way I could help beyond saying a few kind words about them. It took me a while, but I eventually realized that the "power" I'd so delighted in was entirely negative. If I gave a book a long synopsis and a highly favorable comment, there were still dozens of people above me who had to agree before it could be purchased. If, on the other hand, I dismissed the book with a card, chances were that no one would ever look at it again.

The one exception to this rule was *Death Wish*. In my wisdom I'd rejected it as "too simple-minded for the American public." Fortunately the studio got a second chance at the property when Dino De Laurentiis produced it; Paramount became the film's distributor, and it proved to be one of the biggest moneymakers of 1974.

How about books I *did* recommend? I can't think of a single one that was made into a movie. I read lots of properties that other people filmed—tripe like *Rosebud* and TV fare like *The Six Million Dollar Man*, as well as *The Odessa File* ("the least suspenseful suspense story I've ever read") and Visconti's recent *Conversation Piece* ("very limited appeal")—but in my three years there I never read a book or script that Paramount actually went on to film.

Perhaps the blame is not entirely mine. Having learned that, in recent years, more than fifty per cent of each week's film gross is reaped by a mere half dozen pictures, Hollywood has grown less adventurous. Aside from the prepackaged disaster films and celebrity bios, the only properties it wants are the best-sellers—and you don't need a story department to find them; any newspaper will do.

Needless to say, when the "discovery" has given way to the deal, the reader's job becomes obsolete. Today the East Coast story departments in most of the major studios are struggling to justify their existence. My own small job was terminated in the fall of 1974 when Paramount disbanded its department. I bear them no ill will; the job was fun while it lasted. Though it's a relief not to have to read any more Mafia novels and scripts about oil tycoons, I miss the Wats line and the view of the Hudson. I also miss the free screenings. It was nice to see Robert Redford doing my job in *Three Days of the Condor*, but hardly worth paying for.

Annie Hall

Sir,—I wish I could agree with the recent *Sight and Sound* review of *Annie Hall* and, indeed, with prevailing critical opinion, which seems to consider it Woody Allen's most successful film. I, too, see it as something of a departure for him, but only in a more damaging sense: Where once he was content to poke fun at himself, he's now taken to putting down the rest of us—and patting himself on the back.

For example, *Play It Again, Sam* has Allen getting so nervous at the start of a blind date that his voice turns into a croak and he accidentally flings a record across his living room. Yet in *Annie Hall* it's Diane Keaton who becomes inarticulate and flustered; Allen himself remains cool and a trifle amused. He's a hit on a TV talk show, he scores equally well at a political rally, and college audiences worship him. We get, in effect, an anthology of his best routines, complete with applauding crowds and lines of admirers eager to congratulate him after the show.

Yet how does Allen regard his fans? The same way, apparently, he regards everyone else: with contempt. In *Annie Hall*, these "fans" appear as a pair of grinning Neanderthals who bother him when he'd rather be alone; a family of mid-American Wasps are seen as closet anti-semites, with a hint of lunacy beneath the barren exterior; Hollywood types become a collection of straw dummies who stand around like people in a cartoon, mouthing the latest catch-phrases. He also gets in a few jabs at his repressive old school-

---

Letter in the British film journal *Sight and Sound* (Spring 1978).

teacher, his self-centered Jewish aunt, vapid Beautiful People (who, in Allen's fantasy, openly acknowledge their shallowness), blacks (they steal, we're told, but some Jews still feel sorry for them), and a pathetic nightclub comic who wants Allen to write for him. (Young Woody is, of course, too virtuous to sell out.) In this world of caricatures, Method actors are charlatans hoping to impress women; academics are out of touch with reality (as opposed to our hero, who prefers watching a basketball game on television to the pseudo-intellectual chatter of a cocktail party); and movie buffs are (here the man goes too far!) pompous asses who pontificate on the ticket line.

Not that Allen has anything against pontificating. Time after time, more or less at random, he gives himself the opportunity to deliver pronouncements on things that irk him. We learn that he disapproves of drugs, TV laugh tracks, and arriving late to films; a poetry collection, conveniently among Annie's belongings, provides the prop for a dismissal of Sylvia Plath. The ultimate effect of such preaching is that Allen emerges as a kind of latter-day Voltaire, the only sane man left amid a fatuous world; in short, he applauds his own authenticity. Even his weaknesses are really strengths. His inability to drive well lifts him above the empty freeway culture of Los Angeles; he gets a queasy stomach at the hypocrisies of Hollywood. In fact, the very ending of the film shows him off to moral advantage: it is the beloved Annie, shallow after all, who "goes Hollywood" (literally), while our hero remains true to himself and Manhattan.

Annie Hall is a very funny movie, but I am bothered by its tone of self-aggrandizement—the same self-aggrandizement I've seen in recent interviews, in which we are offered a new, "profound" Woody Allen, brooding about fame and death and the pressures of the fans, dreaming of a day when he'll make serious, Bergmanesque films. I fear he may be halfway there already, for in *Annie Hall* he's given up playing the clown and has taken on the mantle of sage. It is, I think, a most regrettable transformation.

Star Wares

A bearded emperor sits upon a golden throne, his uniform gleaming with medals, epaulettes, and yards of gold braid. He rules a world of dynasties and dukedoms, scheming barons, ancient trade guilds, monks in cowls and sandals, armored guards and knife-wielding assassins. A world of deadly court intrigues, poisonings, stabbings, conspiracies, prophecies, and spells. A world where troops clash in hand-to-hand combat, warring over fortresses with crude stone battlements and palaces with ornately tiled floors.

But this is no historical epic, for all its resemblance to *The Prisoner of Zenda* or even *I, Claudius*. In fact, it's the world of *Dune*, billions of miles from earth, set so far in the future that mankind has conquered the speed of light, colonized the galaxy, and now counts the years in five figures—10,191, to be exact.

Actually, *Dune* involves not one world but four: four planets, each with its own peculiar culture. Based on Frank Herbert's bestselling 1965 novel, the movie—which opens Dec. 14—is a kind of ecological "what if" tale, depicting how humanity might adapt and survive in widely different environments, from the fertile waterworld of Caladan to the arid desert planet of Arrakis.

In creating this vision of the future, the makers of *Dune*—director David Lynch and production designer Tony Masters—have drawn heavily on the past: Moorish architecture, Venetian interiors, Czarist Russian uniforms, Elizabethan dress, ancient Celtic sym-

---

Sunday feature, *New York Daily News* (December 2, 1984).

bols. Masters, the man responsible for giving each of *Dune*'s four civilizations its own distinctive look, even admits that the carved wooden columns on one of the planets was inspired by a Victorian chandelier in his London living room.

Another world, that of the treacherous Harkonnen dynasty, is Victorian in a more horrifying way: It's a world out of the early industrial revolution, a nightmarish extrapolation of William Blake's "dark satanic mills," complete with grey skies, rusty iron bolts, and a ruling class fond of bathing in machine oil. Baron Harkonnen himself is so grossly fat that, rather than walk, he depends on a small antigravity device which keeps him floating in the air like a malign Peter Pan.

By contrast, the makers of *2010* (opening Friday) enjoyed no such freedom. Set a mere quarter of a century from now—a piddling leap forward by *Dune*'s standards, and one that many of us may live to see—this sequel to the Stanley Kubrick–Arthur C. Clarke *2001* takes its cues from technicians. It's a future designed to *look* like the future.

A few aspects of the film, it's true, seem vintage 1984. The U.S. and Russia are seen squabbling over an American naval blockade of Honduras, a crisis with an all-too contemporary ring; and computer buffs may notice that Roy Scheider does his calculations on an Apple IIc, a popular little portable which, though it may turn up under a lot of Christmas trees this year, is unlikely to do so twenty-five years in the future. By and large, however, director Peter Hyams has relied closely on his scientific advisors.

"Everything was checked and counterchecked," he said recently. "We asked things like, 'What do the shoes they wear look like?'" The goal, he explained, was to make the movie's marvels appear "feasible."

A feasible future is, in fact, what the movie provides, even down to the glimpses we're offered of twenty-first-century TV ads (for voyages in space on a Pan Am rocket and vacations at a futuristic Sheraton) and the chance to hear the earthbound twin of the previous film's HAL 9000 computer. (It answers to the name of SAL 9000 and has the voice of a sexy young woman.) HAL makes a return appearance in this sequel, and so does *2001*'s spaceship, the

U.S.S. *Discovery,* which from a distance resembles—perhaps deliberately—a gigantic version of the bone the ape hurled heavenward in the first movie's opening scene.

By contrast, the Soviets' spaceship looks far less elegant—a cross between a knocked-together wooden lobster trap and a mechanism from inside your washing machine. Its interior is a relatively gloomy one, a network of angular passages lit as dimly as a basement, but the ship's main control room, filled with a rainbow of dials, glows as brightly as a midtown video-game arcade.

For all its scientific accuracy, there may be nothing in *2010* to equal the stunning visual impact of the original film's closing scenes, in which the astronaut played by Keir Dullea awakened somewhere near Jupiter to find his space vehicle parked inside an elegant eggshell-blue hotel room, complete with room-service meals and a large comfy-looking bed.

What made that scene so jarring was the juxtaposition of the far out and the familiar—the sort of juxtaposition one finds throughout *Dune,* whose colorfully garbed cast whizzes about the galaxy in faster-than-light starships furnished in antique style. (Not so coincidentally, *Dune*'s Tony Masters also served as art director on *2001.*) It's the same device that made the covers of the science-fiction magazine *Analog* so memorable back in the early '60s, when Frank Herbert's epic first appeared there. One cover, not for *Dune* but by the artist who illustrated it, John Schoenherr, depicts a medieval monk in his study surrounded by alchemical tools, occult books, a skull—and on the wall beside him, a black plastic telephone.

In this quiet, rather simple scene lies the essence of successful fantasy: The situations it presents may be bizarre, even impossible, but they always contain an element of the ordinary. As the society matron in a 1930s *New Yorker* cartoon said, introducing a guest lecturer to her women's club: "Now, ladies, Mr. Hollingsworth will tell us something about the Spanish Civil War—but not *too* much." The same might be said of the fantastic in art: We want it, but only within limits. The notion of a completely untrammeled imagination, free of all earthly restraints, may sound fine in theory, but in practice it becomes alienating, frightening—or merely boring. Even the great American horror writer H. P. Lovecraft once confessed that what he craved most in fantasy literature were "familiar things & scenes . . . I would feel completely lost in infinity without a system of reference points based on known & accustomed objects."

This is especially true in movies, which bring these imaginary worlds to visual life. What moves us is not so much the fantastic, but seeing the familiar transformed—magnified, as in *Mothra, Them, Tarantula,* and all the other Big Bug movies (including *Dune,* with its subway-size sandworms); undermined, as in *Invasion of the Body Snatchers,* where the most ordinary forms of human behavior begin to seem sinister; or updated, as in *Blade Runner,* which combines androids, hover-cars, 1940s fashions, tough-guy detectives, and a noisy, neon-lit city of the future that makes Times Square look sedate.

Peter Hyams' previous film, *Outland,* attempted a similar trick, hitching a classic Western plot—*High Noon,* complete with stolid marshal—to an outer space locale, a rugged mining colony on one of Jupiter's moons. The plot strained credulity, but the sets did not: You could almost smell the overcooked food in the crowded little cafeteria and the sweat socks in the miners' locker room.

Probably no films have exploited familiar elements as successfully as the *Star Wars* saga, in which a robot chats like the time-honored English butler and Ewoks are a living reminder of the teddy bears we all owned as children. Its most popular and talked-about scene remains the one in the barroom, which packs a gallery of grotesque-looking aliens into the traditional Western saloon.

"Familiar things & scenes"—surely Lovecraft was right; all of us need such points of reference. They're like glimpses, in a foreign country, of our neighbors, whom we greet with an enthusiasm we'd never feel at home. In *Dune,* the fun comes from seeing characters from costume dramas strutting their stuff on extraterrestrial soil. In *2010,* it's hearing, at the end of a perilous space voyage, the familiar honeyed tones of the HAL 9000 computer as he renews an old friendship with his human trainer.

It's a voice audiences recognize—and cheer.

Master of a Lost Art

In the early 1970s, when I earned my bread as a script reader for one of the major Hollywood studios, my working guide was a set of rules handed down by the chief story editor. I was to summarily reject all costume dramas ("too expensive"), scripts with foreign settings ("Middle America's not interested"), sports sagas ("box-office poison"), and stories aimed at children. "Kiddie pix never make money," my boss explained, "unless they have the name 'Disney' on them. That's the only name parents feel they can trust."

A lot has changed in the past decade, and the old certainties have crumbled. The once-dependable Disney has had a string of dismal flops, most recently with its soggy dinosaur saga, *Baby* (though the studio may still buck negative reviews of its *Return to Oz* and hopes to bring back the good times with this summer's animated fantasy, *The Black Cauldron*). The wizard's cap Walt Disney once wore has now settled firmly on the brow of Steven Spielberg—who, appropriately, considers the filmmaker his No. 1 influence and dreams of making an animated feature himself someday. As many an observer noted after seeing *E.T.*, it was precisely the sort of movie that, once upon a time, Disney could be counted on to make.

Not that Spielberg's movies are strictly for kids (though it's hard to think of his latest offering, *The Goonies*, as anything but kid stuff); they appeal, rather, to that much courted and much catered-to being, "the child in us all." But it's clear that, like Disney's, his

---

Sunday feature, *New York Daily News* (June 30, 1985).

imprimatur on a film—whether "directed by Steven Spielberg" or, as in this year's quartet of titles, merely "presented by"—has become something of a guarantee, promising fare that's well-crafted, relatively clean, and resolutely upbeat; filmgoers know, in short, they can bring the whole family. (In fact, he may already have become a prisoner of his own decency; witness, for example, the outcry over the violence—quite restrained compared to films today—in *Indiana Jones and the Temple of Doom*.) As one critic has put it, Spielberg's productions invariably demonstrate "quality control."

That counts for a lot. In this era of $6 movie tickets, we want someone who'll give us our money's worth.

But Spielberg gives us more. Indeed, in that "more" may lie his greatest talent: creating scenes that are bigger and more wonderful than we expected. In film after film—most of them, typically, shrouded in secrecy until the day they open—he has never lost his ability to surprise. A few memorable examples:

- In *Jaws,* Spielberg's fist colossal hit, a couple of beer-guzzling middle-aged buddies go shark fishing from a pier, one of them using his wife's roast for bait, attaching it to a chain wrapped around one of the pilings. Wisecracking smugly, the two settle down to wait. The night is quiet—too quiet—and we're already nervous because one of the men is sitting too close to the water's edge. We wait for the inevitable, expecting the unseen shark to bite right through the chain—or if we're true pessimists, that the beast's huge jaws will soon be snapping through the man's leg.

    What happens, of course, is even more jolting. The shark grabs the bait and swims away with it—yanking the entire pier out to sea.

- When we finally catch a glimpse of the shark, it's even bigger than we'd expected. As it glides swiftly toward a helpless boatful of Boy Scouts, we see its familiar fin knifing through the water, and then, far, far behind—farther than we'd ever imagined—we see the dark triangle of its tail. We realize, suddenly, that we're dealing with a monster.

- In *Close Encounters of the Third Kind,* the quarry is not a shark but a saucer—or rather, a whole fleet of them, in different shapes and sizes. Our first encounter with a UFO proves to be one of the best-orchestrated visual surprises on film, when Richard Dreyfuss, at the wheel of his repair truck, sees the headlights behind him rise straight in the air.

- When, at last, the "mother ship" reveals itself, Spielberg once again exceeds our expectations. Nothing has prepared us for the sheer monumental size of the thing that rises magnificently into view, seeming to fill the entire horizon. It's like expecting a look at the Chrysler Building and getting, instead, the entire Manhattan skyline.

    Spielberg once told a BBC interviewer, "When I go to the movies, I want to see something that overwhelms me." But overwhelming audiences takes genius; to see how rare that is, simply compare Spielberg's grand finale with the strictly human-scale ending of *Cocoon* or that of last year's amiable but trite *Star Man,* whose mother ship resembles nothing so much as a huge, boring ball bearing.

- *Raiders of the Lost Ark* ends with a shot whose scale is similarly vast. Spielberg's camera pulls back through the government warehouse in which the mystical Ark has been stored—and as before, we are unprepared for the immensity of what's revealed. Packed high with grim-looking crates, the place appears as large as several aircraft hangars, reducing the human figures to insignificance.

- In Tobe Hooper's *Poltergeist*—which Spielberg produced and had more than a hand in directing—there's another visual surprise, albeit on a more domestic scale, when JoBeth Williams, as a housewife harassed by poltergeists (literally, "mischievous ghosts"), finds her kitchen chairs have mysteriously been pushed away from the table. She slides them back into place and moves to another part of the room, the camera never leaving her. When, moments later, she returns to the dining area, the chairs have moved again—but not in the same manner we've anticipated. Silently, in just seconds, they've been piled on the table!

- Even in *The Goonies,* directed by Richard Donner (but with some sequences reportedly shot by Spielberg, who wrote the original story), there's a hint of wonder in the climactic scene near the end—one that almost makes up for the film's sitcom sensibility. Searching for buried treasure, the movie's band of treasure hunters come upon something even greater: an entire pirate ship, complete with hidden lagoon.

Sights such as these reduce us all to the level of wonder-struck children. We feel an inkling of what the three-year-old child in *Close Encounters* must have felt when the UFO arrived in his yard.

That little boy looms larger than one might suppose in Spielberg's work, for as critics have been fond of pointing out, what links many of these films is a concern with reuniting children with their parents: the Goonies, the little girl in *Poltergeist,* the slave children in the Temple of Doom. Spielberg is a well-known *Dumbo* fan; one of his all-time favorite movies is *The Searchers,* whose theme is much the same. And I have to admit that, until reading William Kotzwinkle's novelization, I assumed that E.T. himself was a precocious alien baby brought along on the scientific expedition by his parents; I didn't realize he was a botanist, and hundreds of years old to boot.

These parent-child concerns will be central, as well, in such future Spielberg projects as *Peter Pan* and *The Talisman.* They'll also surface, in a novel way, this week in Spielberg's *Back to the Future,* directed by Robert Zemeckis (director of *Romancing the Stone* and co-writer of Spielberg's *1941*), in which a high school senior of 1985 journeys thirty years into the past via a homemade nuclear-powered time machine—housed in, of all things, a DeLorean sports car—and meets his own parents as 1950s-style teenagers.

With *Future* scheduled to open Wednesday, *The Goonies* currently on screen, *Close Encounters* televised just last week, *E.T.* due for re-release July 19, and the TV series *Amazing Stories* due to air on NBC next fall, there's going to be a lot of Spielberg on view.

As moviegoers, it's a good time to count our blessings.

And Many Happy Returns

In his celebration of *2001,* Matt Zoller Seitz ("Film," 1/9)—the literate half of your movie-reviewing team—focuses on "Kubrick's metaphors." They turn out to be, for Seitz, "round shapes" like eyes and planets vs. "machine-tooled rectangles and squares" (huh?). Another, more obvious metaphor he discusses, and one that makes more sense to me, is that this story of man's development as a species is told as "a series of voyages."

Let me add to this list what I've always thought of as the film's controlling metaphor: *birthdays*.

There are at least five of them, and clearly they embody the central theme of the movie. The first section ("The Dawn of Man"), and the one I've watched again and again with the most pleasure, depicts the birthday of the human race as the alien black slab plants a new idea—the first tool (which just happens to be a lethal weapon)—into the brain of an ape, thereby turning the creature into Man the Tool-User.

Jump forward a few million years, in one of the medium's most famous cuts, and what was a bone is now a spaceship; however, the movie suggests that it's only a more sophisticated version of the earlier tool. In this section of the story, as Seitz reminds us, the hero, Heywood Floyd, makes a videophone call to his little daughter back on earth "and tells her that Daddy can't come to her party because he's traveling." What Seitz neglects to mention is that it's her birthday party.

Letter, *New York Press* (January 16, 2002).

The next, and longest, section of the movie, the Jupiter mission, carries on the theme when one of the two astronauts, Frank Poole, gets a videophone message from his parents. They're sitting at a table with, of all things, his birthday cake, and they proceed to sing him a rather strained "Happy Birthday."

This section also features the birthday of Hal 9000, the computer. When astronaut David Bowman has finished dismantling his higher brain functions, we hear Hal repeat his first childlike words, from the day he was activated, and sing "Daisy, Daisy."

The film's final section, of course, culminates in still another birthday courtesy another black slab—the birthday, via Bowman's transformation, of a brainier and presumably more peaceable being ("the Starchild") representing the next step in humanity's evolution.

T.E.D. Klein Interview

Serious Questions

WFR: Are you still in New York? What's the best thing about where you live now?

TK: Still here. I was born in this city and tend to agree with something John Updike said—that all true New Yorkers believe "people living anywhere else have got to be, in some sense, kidding." While it isn't quite, as some claim, the city that never sleeps, it's a relatively twenty-four-hour sort of place, and the subways, unlike London's, run all night. Also, there are almost no mosquitoes.

WFR: What's your role in editing and publishing today? What's been your response to the digital revolution? How has the definition of "good writing" changed over the past 10–20 years?

TK: As senior copy editor at *GQ*, I spend a lot of my day putting in commas and taking them out. I really know my commas. As for the net, even after all these years and thousands of hours online, it remains, for me, something of a novelty, and wow, am I grateful for it; I feel as if I've been given a pass to wander around Borges's infinite library, or at least a Barnes & Noble the size of an aircraft carrier.

[I won't attempt to answer that third question.]

Interview by Dave Roberts, *Weird Fiction Review #6* (Lakewood, CO: Centipede Press, 2016).

WFR: How do you feel about e-books? Will we one day see an e-book from you that collects all of your stories and novellas?

TK: Like most readers, I guess, I've got mixed feelings about them. Obviously they're perfect for the subway or if you're backpacking around Europe, and I keep hoping some generous friend will give me a Kindle, just to play with; but I continue to love ordinary books and have thousands of them, in the city and in a house upstate. I don't expect there'll be a Collected Klein anytime soon, though an e-book version of *The Ceremonies* will probably be along in the next year or two.

WFR: Do you have any opinions on the self-publishing movement?

TK: In principle, it's a wonderful idea, but . . . well, let me put it this way. When I was editing *Twilight Zone,* we probably received fifty submissions for each story we bought. Can you imagine if we'd run every one of them? That would have been somewhat analogous, I think, to the self-publishing universe. Or take *GQ,* where review copies of upcoming books from major and minor publishers arrive by the crateload each week. Since the magazine is mainly interested in selling clothes and fawning on celebrities, the books are left out for the staff. Like a proper addict, I'm always going home with one or two; it pains me that if no one takes them, they end up in a Dumpster. All these books were presumably screened and approved by publishing professionals, yet only one in ten or twenty even seems worth looking at. If self-published works were added to the pile, it would probably be twice as large, but I doubt it would contain many additional gems.

WFR: According to IMDb, you worked on the screenplay for *Trauma,* which was released in 1993. What was the process of writing a screenplay for/with Dario Argento like?

TK: Great fun, just as you'd imagine—especially hanging out with a colorful and eccentric character like Argento for a couple of days, scouting possible locations in Pittsburgh. Of course, it says something about the realities of filmmaking that, for reasons of budget, the movie ended up being shot not in Pittsburgh, nor in New Orleans (which was also considered), but in the quaint, picturesque, richly atmospheric city of Minneapolis. (I'm being ironic.) Argento's English was limited, and whenever he'd read over something I'd written—some scene in which I'd attempted to be creative and clever—he'd invariably nod and say hopefully, "Ah, yes. You cut, you cut, yes?" And so I'd cut. I'm just sorry the script turned out so lousy (I've got plenty of explanations and excuses, but it would take hours) and sorry the film turned out so unwatchable.

WFR: There are key region-specific historic moments in some of your stories, such as the New York blackout in "Children of the Kingdom." What are some recent events that you think would tie well into a good story?

TK: Great question, though in general that's not the way I seem to work. Well, I did once write a story based on some brain research coming out of Geneva, in which patients who had a section of their cerebral cortex stimulated—an area called the angular gyrus—were convinced that a shadowy figure was standing behind them. But I don't think that's exactly what you're asking.

WFR: You've written a number of canonical works, stories that are clearly and deservedly lasting the test of time, that show their influence and that continue to influence stories that have come after. What's your perspective on this today?

TK: I'm just very pleased and gratified that you think so. And I do find it curious, regarding your reference to "the test of time," how certain genres—horror, fantasy, the supernatural—seem to date less and enjoy a greater longevity than mainstream fiction. I think, for example, of Robert Hichens, Robert W. Chambers, Marjorie Bowen, and W. W. Jacobs, to name just a few, whose weird stories keep turning up in anthologies but whose more mainstream work is seldom read.

WFR: Who is your favorite character that you created? Why?

TK: I once conceived of a bad self-published poet named Julian Stilton—sweet but self-deluding and pretentious—that I thought might be an amusing figure in a novel of mine that I seem to have set aside for the past twenty or thirty years. If I ever go back to it, he'll probably be fun to write about.

WFR: My copy of "The Events at Poroth Farm" was revised in 2012. What is the importance of revision on previously published works? What spurs your need to revise?

TK: Well, after all, I've been making my living as a copy editor for the past decade, and it's always been difficult for me to read anything of mine without wincing and wishing I could tweak it a bit. I guess my inner critic is fairly severe.

WFR: Do you keep in touch with any of the writers or illustrators that you worked with at *Twilight Zone*? Are there unsung writers/artists from that time that we need to seek out and revisit?

TK: Happily, I've kept in touch with some of them, both writers and illustrators. It gave me tremendous pleasure to work with them—in fact, that was really the best part of putting out *Twilight Zone*—though as I've mentioned in the past, I discovered that I tended to enjoy working with the illustrators more, in general, than with the writers. The writers—I guess understandably—could sometimes be egotistical, thorny, and competitive; they all seemed to want to be Stephen King. The illustrators were a cooler bunch—delighted to run into one another at the *TZ* offices and to show one another their work. They took the whole enterprise less seriously.

I don't keep up enough with the field to recommend any unsung writers or artists—I'm proud of everything we published—but looking back right now, I'd call your attention to Paula Goodman's amazing woodcut illustrations and to Lawrence Connolly's "Echoes," which seems the perfect little *Twilight Zone* story.

WFR: What do you like to read? Who are your favorite writers?

TK: Off the top of my head, Orwell, Updike, Machen, S. J. Perelman, Bruce Jay Friedman, Wilfrid Sheed, Loren Eiseley, Heather Mac Donald, Ann Coulter (yes, you heard me), Charles Krauthammer, Max Hastings. The latter's a historian; these days I mainly read history. No doubt it's a consequence of old age.

WFR: What nonfiction titles do you think everyone should read?

TK: *Dreadnought* by Robert K. Massie. *Battle Cry of Freedom* by James McPherson. *Nineteen Weeks* by Norman Moss, about the summer of 1940. Machen's three autobiographical volumes (curiously boring, yet quite magical). Anything by or about Winston Churchill. And since you're kindly allowing me to pontificate, I would encourage people—particularly your audience—to read more nonfiction in general and less fiction than I suspect they currently do. So many readers of genre fiction seem to read nothing *but* genre fiction.

Fun Questions

WFR: Are you a Beatles fan or a Rolling Stones fan? Or a little of both? Or neither?

TK: Glad you asked. Stones, all the way.

WFR: How do you prefer to communicate: email, texting, phone calls, or handwritten letters?

TK: Email, by far.

WFR: What are your top five songs and/or pieces of music of all time?

TK: I'm not very musical; at home, in my car, walking home (from the new World Trade Center) with an iPod, I tend to listen to talk radio, podcasts, and audiobooks. But I do like big-band music; also

Randy Newman, some Bob Seger, Kristin Hersh, Syd Straw, some long-ago Kate Bush. Yeah, I know: pretty uncool.

WFR: What ghost would you not mind being haunted by?

TK: I've had a number of good friends die in recent years, and my life is certainly the poorer for it. So of course it would be nice to have them back.

WFR: What is the most insignificant thing that you are proud of?

TK: Knowing all the presidents in order. Coming from behind in a high-school relay race to put our team ahead. Building a stone wall behind my house. Refusing, for many years, to kill mice; rescued them instead. (Big mistake.) Collecting all eighty-eight Space Cards back in the '50s (which probably meant chewing a lot of bubble gum).

WFR: What's your "white whale"? Something you've been searching for for years but haven't been able to find?

TK: As someone who follows politics rather than sports, I'd like to find a politician—and in the present season, a presidential candidate—whose positions on a wide range of issues reflect my own, someone whom I could support without having to keep making allowances. And then there's movies: I'm a lifelong moviegoer with an MFA in film, and there are dozens and dozens of movies I'm crazy about—yet I can't think of a single one in the past ten years that's really excited me or inspired that same passionate enthusiasm. (Granted, this probably says more about me than about movies.)

WFR: What is your favorite verb?

TK: To putter. To dither. To woolgather. I'm adept at all three.

WFR: H. P. Lovecraft and Arthur Machen get in a fistfight. Who wins? Why?

TK: Both those guys were gentlemen, God bless 'em, and I'd like to think hell would freeze over before they'd resort to fisticuffs.

WFR: What's something that people worry about that really isn't a big deal? What's a big deal that no one seems concerned about?

TK: I've never understood people's obsession with clothes and cooking (which, considering my current place of work, with *Vogue* a few floors above and *Bon Appétit* a floor below, seems downright perverse). The entire fashion industry sickens me; once my armies take over the country, we'll all be dressing comfortably in jeans and old pajamas.

Conversely, when you ask about an unacknowledged "big deal," I wish I could give you a light-hearted answer, but in truth my thoughts once again immediately turn to politics—to the unquestioning, reflexively left-leaning conformity of the media, Hollywood, and academia, and to the climate of political correctness they've imposed. As a conservative/neocon/just plain hawk who works in publishing and who lives on Manhattan's notoriously liberal Upper West Side—in short, as the proverbial square peg—I'm acutely conscious of how maddeningly pervasive (I would even say, at the risk of sounding like Sax Rohmer, how insidiously pervasive) this mind-set is.

I also happen to be an animal-lover—a condition that, I regret to say, does not usually go hand in hand with conservatism—and so your question inevitably prompts even gloomier thoughts, about the mistreatment and exploitation of animals throughout the world. True, it's an issue that's hardly unnoticed—few things inspire greater public outcry than the plight of an abused animal—yet despite thousands of news stories, thousands of well-meaning organizations, and thousands of years of human progress, the fundamental situation is never going to improve, nor can it, as long as humans and animals share the earth.

V. On Other Topics

INTRODUCTION

Where Do We Go from Here?

>"What was it all for?"
>"You got me."
>—*The Graduate*

Probably the main reason *The Graduate* has become such a popular film with college audiences is that Benjamin Braddock's plight will soon be their own: In less than a month the Class of '68 will graduate—and then what?

Obviously the most immediate question facing this year's senior class is What to Do About the Draft; many students are not going to live long enough to experience Benjamin's curious state of anomie. Polls here at Brown indicate that a substantial majority of students oppose the Johnson administration's Vietnam policy, favoring a more drastic de-escalation in bombing and troop strength than the administration is now prepared to initiate. Furthermore, a recent survey of some thirty "student leaders" has shown only two of them supporting our country's involvement in the war.

But while it may be a campus of doves, Brown is apparently a campus of prudent ones. A poll undertaken by the *Brown Daily Herald* revealed that more than a third of the graduating seniors—the largest plurality—intend to seek berths in officer candidate schools.

From the *New York Daily Column* (May 8, 1968). This short-lived publication was a newsprint tabloid, but it wasn't exactly a newspaper. The notion behind it, I think, was to print reports from correspondents at various colleges around the country on the state of their campuses.

Most of them are in for an unpleasant surprise. The Navy, Coast Guard, and Air Force officer programs are all vastly overbooked, with waiting lists spilling into next fall. Only the Army and Marines promise no delay in officer training; but then, the Marines also promise that 100 percent of their second lieutenants will be sent to Vietnam.

Members of the Resistance—and their number continues to grow as June approaches—have adopted an "I told you so" attitude. Just as they have reason to deplore the foggy morality that lets a student train for officership when he opposes the war, they have reason to pity his naïveté in falling for the recruiting-poster spiel.

Armed forces recruiters, like any salesmen, have been known to lie—although it may be kinder to say that they merely withhold certain portions of the truth. An Army recruiter who came to Brown this spring, for example, gave a big pitch for the Judge Advocate's Corps—which naturally attracted a number of students with visions of desk jobs, clean clothing, Stateside duty, and free law training to boot. What the recruiter didn't tell them was that the Corps already had a waiting list of 37,000 applicants for a mere 200 positions.

Many an ex-peacenik here at Brown has had his application to Naval OCS in Newport rejected—and now sits in his room wondering what he will do when he graduates; he may be making the most important decision of his life. Draft resistance, with all its physical dangers and moral glories, its promise of jail and martyrdom, may look more inviting. As one student admitted, "I haven't made up my mind yet where I'll be next year—Saigon or San Quentin."

* * *

For many students, military service offers a welcome three or four years of delaying the inevitable question, What to Do With My Life. For the more than 200,000 graduating males who will *not* be drafted, however, the question is of immediate importance. And if they're anything like the liberal arts students so common at Brown, they're going to be in the same boat as Benjamin Braddock—and drifting with the current.

Benjamin is "too rich" to be drafted, explained director Mike Nichols in a rather confusing press conference. If few Brown graduates are going to find themselves in so enviable a position, they may at least resemble Ben in having graduated from a distinguished university with outstanding academic careers behind them—and no clear prospects before them.

I came to Brown three years ago with every expectation that, after a couple of years here, I'd know pretty well what my career goals would be. Yet this year's senior class, and the liberal arts majors in particular, are as uncertain as I know I shall be at this time next year.

If one majors in English—here a very popular concentration, but also a garbage heap for students who flunk out of the sciences—one is generally assumed to have two options for the future: writing or teaching. And everybody wants to write these days (plans for wild, semi-autobiographical first novels are particularly common), and everybody knows that writing is too risky.

If one majors in history, it's a similar story: Teach it, or, like the luckier political science majors, try to land a government job. Philosophy? Religion? Art history? Languages? All are lots of fun to take in college.

And all prepare students for very little—except, perhaps, to teach *new* crops of students about English, history, political science, philosophy, religion, art history, or languages.

Brown is very proud of how truly liberal its liberal arts are; it has tried harder than other Ivy League universities to ensure that its liberal arts courses bear no taint of professionalism. "Conceptual approaches" are the order of the day, in keeping with most progressive educational philosophy.

Unfortunately, the desire to mold "well-rounded gentlemen" and "thinking individuals" can place a very real limit on the more practical value of an education, and in the current educational environment "practical" is a word one uses with a slight shudder. Liberally educated Ivy League gentlemen are not expected to know how to *do* anything, and the liberal arts aren't *supposed* to be practical; therefore, when one student found his roommate fixing a broken window with putty and paint, he could only shake his head and marvel, "My God, it's amazing to see a Brown man actually doing something real!"

Whether it is their fault or not, universities today have fostered a new breed of graduate with a peculiar liberal arts mentality; I speak, in part, as a member of this group. As far back as Dreiser's *American Tragedy,* it was apparent that the "standard American youth . . . felt himself above the type of labor which was purely manual," and today the contempt has grown to encompass a number of other fields, notably business. Future businessmen—like future engineers, doctors, or lawyers—are among the few here at college who seem to know exactly where they're going. But since where they're going seems to be after The Dollar, they are held in particular contempt by the more liberal breed. "Going into Daddy's business? Tsk tsk tsk."

The super-literate literature students, on the other hand, are not going anywhere that they can determine, and they are neither prepared for nor interested in careers involving the traditional nine-to-five routine; everyone knows his life *must* be exciting and "meaningful" and (best word of all) "creative," but no one is very sure where the openings are. As one senior Phi Beta Kappa who intends to travel for several years said, "Four years from now, I'll know what the story is—I hope."

Thus we find a colossal senior-year *anomie,* which Paul Williams, speaking at a convocation here, summed up with the conclusion, "Everything's so *vague,* especially in college." The twenty-year-old editor of *Crawdaddy,* the only intellectual magazine of rock music, expressed the modern student's aimlessness: "You say, 'I guess I'll take this course, I don't know. . . . I'd go out into the world, but I'd even be more ridiculous out there. . . . I don't know, let's hang on and see what happens.'"

What happens, interestingly enough, is that more than half the students who graduate college end up in some sort of business, current preferences and ambitions notwithstanding. But let us not be cynical: Perhaps that "creative" job was in Daddy's business after all. Tsk tsk tsk.

Charles Manson, B.M.O.C.

If the entire population of California went mad tomorrow and released Charles Manson from prison, he could make a handsome income for himself on the college lecture circuit. He wouldn't even have to write a book. In the ranks of academia he has a growing body of admirers, and a speaking engagement at Columbia would pack the hall. Most of his audience, of course, would merely be curious, seeking to fathom that charisma so touted by the magazines, but some would arrive with a more consuming interest: They are fans of his.

It's no exaggeration. With the trial over and the verdicts in, with the definitive study already published and the atrocities of the sixties giving way to new ones, the name Charles Manson continues to excite controversy wherever students gather.

That young men who once paid lip service to nonviolence are now quoting with approval the ideas of a convicted mass murderer, a racist, and a sexist seems a bizarre phenomenon. One's initial conclusion is likely to be that they merely enjoy a good argument, that in order to shock their listeners these self-proclaimed Manson freaks will champion any cause, the more disreputable the better, even if it means taking the side of a thrill-killer.

True, the Manson freaks are indeed devil's advocates—but in a more literal sense. It's surprising how seriously they take themselves. Mongering slogans about "the destruction of all property" seems relatively mild, and cheering at the murder of policemen

---

Op-ed piece, *New York Times* (March 28, 1972).

("wasting the pigs") is probably harmless, however sickening. Greater cause for concern is the new fashion of carrying knives wherever they go.

After an evening's conversation with one Manson freak who bore an unsettling resemblance to his hero, I am convinced it is not frustration so much as fear that attracts the weak to Manson's banner.

He identified himself at the outset as being "heavily into Manson," and before very long he was showing off some karate blows and the huge steel hunting knife he carries in his pack. I asked him if that was meant for protection against muggers, and he replied that, yes, its original purpose had been self-defense. "But now I'm getting into armed robbery," he explained in a soft, gentle Manson-voice, and proceeded to argue for the lifestyle of a criminal. He assured me that he would only rob from the rich—"Don't worry, I'll stick to the East Side"—and that such activity offered one's only chance for a non-parasitic existence. He had once had dreams of writing, but now realized that even the life of an artist in the wilderness was devoid of honor.

Only later did it become clear that he had never robbed anyone—"not yet, anyway." In fact, he had seldom removed the knife from its sheath except to show it around or to sharpen the blade. Several embarrassing minutes were spent trying to make the knife stick in my hardwood floor. He'd been, he said, a typical middle-class college student and, typically, had been rather frightened by the threat of street crime. Finally he had discovered the solution, the way to keep panhandlers and potential muggers at bay: "When you walk down the street, you have to show that you're ready to use violence if anyone hassles you." One's clothing, one's expression, one's style of walking—none of that matters. The violent attitude is what makes the difference. No one has hassled him since.

Pretend you're a criminal and you need no longer fear being a victim. Muggers don't get mugged. The logic is simple, and it has a special appeal to children: When they act out scenes from television or comic books, the strongest usually gets to play the villain. On Halloween they dress up as monsters and make believe they're the beings they fear most.

A lot has been written about the attractiveness of evil, and speculation continues on whether a Hitler could ever rise to power in America. I believe now, as I never did before, that this could come to pass—and with no necessity for entire populations to go mad. Given the same frustration and fear that rule the Manson freaks, people will gladly identify with what they know to be evil. Just before he slung his pack over his shoulder and left my apartment, my visitor admitted that he hadn't had a fistfight since junior high. "I still begin to tremble a bit when I'm faced with violence," he said, "and my legs feel weak." But as he walked out the door, I could see him putting on his evil like a shield.

The Joy of Losing

NEW YORK—"I think I should have voted for Bush," said a disappointed friend. "Since everyone I vote for always loses, maybe it would have thrown the election to Dukakis."

It's true that, in my neighborhood, we've backed a lot of losers. Here on Manhattan's Upper West Side, which has one of the most liberal electorates in the nation and a congressman, Ted Weiss, with a record to match, the lines at the polling booths bristled with never-say-die Dukakis-Bentsen buttons and pessimistic frowns. The returns from around the nation came as no surprise, but election night was nonetheless a gloomy one.

There was no surprise, too, in the reactions of my friends. Most of us are in our late thirties or early forties, professionals and academics of one kind or another with rent-stabilized apartments, postgraduate degrees, and some experience, back in the '60s, with the anti-war movement. Predictably, the feelings that I've heard expressed by almost everyone I know are deeply at variance with the rest of America. It's a given, around here, that George Bush is a goofily grinning mediocrity whose election bodes ill for the environment, for women's rights, and for the poor; that his running

---

Op-ed piece, *Los Angeles Times* (November 14, 1988), when I was still a scornful young liberal. The paper headlined it "For Children of '60s and Their Ilk, a Government to Despise—Again." (Actually, there's stuff here to offend both sides, and it's easy to see why the piece provoked a barrage of angry and disgusted letters.)

mate, Dan Quayle, is a national embarrassment (and potentially a national catastrophe), and that in handing the two of them so lopsided a victory, American voters have once again demonstrated their blindness, their anti-intellectualism, and their susceptibility to the crudest sort of flag-waving demagoguery. "Those morons out there have done it again"—that's what people in these parts have been saying ever since the election. I hear it all the time.

But I've also begun to hear something else—something I first became aware of eight years ago with the coming to power of Ronald Reagan. I heard it again after his reelection, but it seems even more apparent today. Beneath the genuine anguish and disappointment, beneath the grumbling and the sighs, as my friends and I contemplate another four or even eight years of Reaganism and enumerate the disasters that await us, I hear a secret satisfaction.

In part, of course, it's just the melancholy satisfaction of the doom-cryer; there's something undeniably enjoyable about playing Cassandra. There's also a hint, in my friends' worried tones, of the excitement one tends to feel in a crisis. Adversity is not without its appeal.

This time, though, the appeal is of a very special kind: that of the outcast, the rebel, who defines himself by his opposition to those in power. Disturbing as it may sound, it is by no means entirely unpleasant to live under a regime one truly loathes—at least here in America. One is free to criticize the government's hypocrisy and stupidity; one can dissociate oneself from its blunders. Most of all, one can feel superior to it. It's small satisfaction, but very real.

It's also an exercise in nostalgia, for not since the Vietnam War era has this outcast's role come quite so easily. It came, in those days of undergraduate proclamations and draft-card burnings, with a peculiar certainty. The war was criminal, and we knew it. The government was wrong, and we knew it. Millions of Americans—a vast majority, at one stage—may have supported the war, but they, too, were wrong. We knew we were morally and intellectually superior to them.

Several years ago a social observer at the *New York Times* noted the rise of a new class of Americans: those who defined themselves not so much as representatives of a particular region, ethnic group, or social background but, foremost, as members of the intelligentsia—smarter, in short, than the average Joe. That's the way we saw ourselves in our college days. We were ashamed, appalled, outraged at the things our country was doing—and the feeling was curiously agreeable.

Jimmy Carter changed all that. For me and for most of my acquaintances, his election remains the only time we actually voted for a winner. Suddenly we felt obliged to take the government's side—a rather uncomfortable position for self-styled dissidents. We found ourselves defending the administration, or trying to, when it waffled on some issue. We winced when the President was criticized, because it was no longer quite so easy to dissociate ourselves from his failures; after all, we'd elected the guy. It was alternately enraging and humiliating to watch the nation blunder, as nations will, into crises at home and abroad. Despising the government turned out to be a lot more pleasant than having to apologize for it.

Now, once again, we've got a government we can despise. Once again we can feel superior to the rest of the citizenry; they've turned their future over to a couple of slickly packaged know-nothings and they deserve everything they're going to get. As for us, we've been given another four years to feel young and defiant. It's just like old times.

Working for the *Brown Daily Herald*

Back in the '60s (and for all I know, maybe today), at the end of the academic year, everyone on the *Brown Daily Herald* managing board received handsome clothbound volumes of the newspaper with their names stamped in gold on the front. I have three such volumes, huge cumbersome things; for the past twenty years I've been storing them beneath my TV. The other day, in an attempt to revive a fading memory, I hauled them out.

But I could barely bring myself to look at them. All those pieces about ROTC (and anti-ROTC demonstrations), and CIA recruitment (and anti-CIA demonstrations), and anti–Dow Chemical demonstrations, and draft-card burning, and sit-ins at Faunce House and peace vigils on the Green, and assorted boycotts and rallies and protest marches, and dramatic appearances by the likes of Jimi Hendrix and Janis Joplin . . . All that moral fervor, all that posturing . . . It was like being plunged head-first into a PBS documentary on Those Crazy Turbulent Sixties; but somehow the clichés of that era ring truer for me today on TV, embodied in footage from Berkeley and Wisconsin and Harvard. Brown circa 1968 seemed then, and seems now in those yellowed pages, a self-important little backwater, imitating the more momentous goings-on at other schools.

Then there are mysterious headlines like "Cam Club & SGA:

This memoir appeared in *100 Years of Daily Publication,* the Alumni Weekend issue of the *Brown Daily Herald* (November 2, 1991).

Possible Merger" and "CAC Policy Statement: Responsive Resistance" and "USCA to Sponsor Student-Faculty Discussion Sessions This Semester"—stories which were no doubt as deadly then as they seem today. (There's also one chillingly prescient headline on a 1967 story by Richard Cohen, soon to be our business manager: "Ronald Reagan Is for Real.")

And then there are the dozens of stories about the Magaziner Report (which poor Elliot Maxwell '68, who also worked on it, kept vainly reminding us was in fact "the Magaziner–Maxwell Report"). This document, the brainchild of Ira Magaziner '69, represented a watershed in the university's history; the transformation it wrought in the curriculum, a profound and enduring one, may well be responsible for Brown's current popularity. Yet somehow, for all its importance, I never actually read the damned thing; I tried—several times, in fact—but never made it past page one.

Two changes I noticed, before I shut the bound volumes and shoved them back beneath my TV for another twenty years: In 1968 "Negro" began giving way to "Black" in the *BDH*'s headlines, and "Daily Since 1891" gave way to "Founded in 1866" beneath the *Brown Daily Herald* logo.

That logo, incidentally—an old-fashioned line engraving of the Van Wickle Gates, with a treetop, probably one of the long-vanished campus elms, obscuring the "o" in *Brown*—gave me tremendous pleasure; it was as if we were carrying on some quaint New England tradition, from a century bathed in golden light. I'm writing this without having seen the *BDH*'s present logo (I seem to recall that the Van Wickle design was dumped ages ago), but I hope the current managing board has at least had the sense to restore, in some form, the reference to 1891.

If all this makes the members of my own board sound like figures from a history book, well, we were, in several ways, fairly historical. We were the first, so far as I know, to divide the job of editor-in-chief between two people, myself and Jeff Blumenfeld (a fact that's never stopped me from describing myself, on résumés and wherever else it will do me some good, as "Editor-in-Chief"), and we were the first board to name, in turn, a female editor, Beverly Hodgson '70.

More important, we were the last *Herald* managing board to operate out of Faunce House—from a suite of offices on the second floor, the central room dominated by a giant U-shaped table—and the last board to print the paper the traditional way, on a clattering, oil-smelling old linotype machine using hot lead, trays of heavy type, and the expertise of a pair of veteran typographers.

For years the university had been trying to pry the *BDH* from Faunce House; it wanted the rooms, I recall, for other student activities. We were offered the building that the paper currently occupies. We turned it down. Though the proposed new quarters offered more space, we wanted to remain at the heart of the campus, a place where people could casually drop in after classes or a snack in the Blue Room.

And we turned down the chance to typeset the paper ourselves. (These were the days before desktop publishing and personal computers, but even then, salesmen were peddling various innovative devices that would have allowed us to create the pages in-house.)

We had no quarrel with modern technology. The new process would probably have made life simpler, saving us countless moonlit drives halfway across Providence to the typographers; and in the long run, it would have saved us money. But we didn't want to give up those gigantic, noisy old linotype machines, three of them crowded into a shabby little cinderblock building near some God-forsaken cemetery; we didn't want to give up reading proof on cheap cream-colored galley sheets at three A.M. and ruining our stomachs on box after box of Dunkin' Donuts (the only late-night food available in that neighborhood); we didn't want to give up the novelty of seeing our words turned into actual hunks of lead, not so different from the process Gutenberg must have used. I found it—I think we all found it—romantic as hell.

What's more, we didn't want to abandon the two men whose livelihoods, we feared, depended on the *Herald:* typesetter Larry McGee, who took so great an interest in what he was setting that he'd discuss the articles with us, and who attributed the survival of his marriage to the fact that, as a night worker, he seldom saw his wife for more than an hour at a time; and compositor Frank Crump, a temperamental Southerner given to exotic redneck imprecations—a man who, true to his profession, read backward faster than forward.

For once, Richard, Jeff, managing editor Mark Hochberg, and I agreed about something: that while it was delightful to make money, there'd be time enough for that when we graduated. The *Herald* represented a tradition, and Larry and Frank were a part of it. We felt a responsibility toward them; we didn't want to see them thrown out of a job.

I'm telling you, it was our finest hour; how often does one get to feel so virtuous, and at so little cost? You can imagine our surprise when the first thing the subsequent board did was to take the university up on its offer, moving the paper off campus, and to arrange for the purchase of in-house typesetting equipment. The rest, as they say, is history.

CrimeBeat

Why crime?

That's what a friend of ours wanted to know. He meant, *Why devote a magazine to crime?*

That's easy. Because crime, while undeniably horrifying, is also fascinating—as fascinating as any great drama.

But ask the millions of Americans who read true-crime books, and the millions more who watch documentary crime shows on TV. Ask the millions, from coast to coast, for whom crime is the single most gripping subject in the daily newspaper; ask anyone who's ever devoured the latest crime news—whether of a mugging on the next block or a murder halfway around the world—and has been left wanting more. More background. More details. More updated information, after the publicity's died down.

That's why we created *CrimeBeat*—because sometimes the newspaper isn't enough. And because there's simply no other mag-

---

Over lunch one day in 1990, my old friend Eric Protter—former editorial director of *Gallery* and *Twilight Zone*—asked me if I had any ideas for magazines, as he thought he might have a source of funding. I told him I'd always wanted to start a true-crime magazine, and duly wrote up a proposal. Somehow, miraculously, thanks to Eric, late 1991 saw, on the nation's newsstands, the premiere issue of *CrimeBeat*, "the newsmagazine of crime." (A cynical friend dubbed it *Popular Crime.*) Alas, by the spring of '93 we'd run out of money and had not been snapped up, as we'd privately hoped, by some major publisher. Still, as these editor's notes suggest, I'd enjoyed the opportunity of sounding off on subjects close to my heart.

azine on the stands today that covers so many aspects of contemporary American crime, from trackdown to trial, from the stories of individual cases to statistics on national trends.

But why, one may ask, is there such a fascination with crime?

That's easy, too. It's a fascination with the mysteries of human behavior—with the extremes of human good and human evil, sometimes within the same soul.

It's also the fascination of conflict, of struggle—the essence of every great plot. And it's a conflict in which we can all too easily imagine ourselves. For while few of us are criminals, most of us are—or will be—crime victims. The same is true of friends and loved ones: We're all potential victims today.

So our fascination with crime is also a matter of self-protection, of sheer survival. In a world where outlaws have the cops outgunned (see page 6) and where serial murderers may look as trustworthy as lawmen (see page 35), the more we know about what's lurking out there, the better we'll be able to avoid it.

Why now?

Because crime—the threat of crime, the human cost, the corrosive fear that crime inspires—looms larger in America today than ever before. Eighty-two percent of Americans believe that crime is on the increase, and they're right. The rates are soaring.

- In 1965, there were 9,850 murders in the U.S. Since then the population has grown 25 percent, while murders have more than doubled.
- The odds that you'll be robbed or raped are three times greater than they were twenty years ago.
- Over the past decade, while their embattled police forces have grown no larger, America's cities have seen a 43 percent rise in violent crime.
- There were more murders last year in New York City (population 7 million) than in Japan and Great Britain combined (population 178 million). In fact, during the six weeks of war this year, more than two and a half times as many Americans were killed in New York City as in the Persian Gulf.

- According to the FBI, an American home is burglarized every 10 minutes and a car stolen every 20 seconds. (See page 32.)
- The justice system is no longer doing its job—assuming its job is to ensure that dangerous criminals don't walk free. See, for example, this issue's "Courthouse Blues" by *Baltimore Sun* reporter David Simon, taken from his new book *Homicide: A Year on the Killing Streets,* probably the best book ever written about day-to-day police work in America.
- The courts are swamped. Last year, out of 80,000 cases filed in Manhattan Criminal Court, only 350 went to trial.
- Four out of five children will be victims of violent crime at least once in their lifetimes.
- Each year one in four American households—30 percent in urban areas—has a member victimized by criminal violence or theft.
- In all, 36 million Americans are the victims of crime each year.

Our goal is to keep you from becoming one of them.

So think of CrimeBeat as a sort of illustrated case-by-case survival guide for the nineties. We wish you didn't need it, but chances are you do.

October 1991

Child's Play

Shortly after taking office, President Bush made a promise to the American people. "By the year 2000," he declared, "the high school graduation rate will increase to at least 90 percent."

He also made another promise: "Every school in America will be free of drugs and violence and will offer a disciplined environment conducive to learning."

There are those—and you'll find them in this issue—who'd argue that these seemingly laudable goals are, in fact, mutually exclusive: that if you insist on keeping teenagers in school who might otherwise drop out (or be thrown out), you're retaining the very element most responsible for the drugs and the violence.

This is Rutgers criminologist Jackson Toby's view, but it's one shared by former principal Joe Clark (who's tossed out more than his share of violent and disruptive students) and junior high school English teacher James Sweeney (who's still forced to endure them).

Clark is a formidable character. He may be a tough man to work for, but he's a colorful speaker who delivers his rhetorical broadsides with the fervor and wit of one who's clearly enjoying himself. (Even his phone-machine greeting is a typical blend of no-nonsense and whimsy: "Succinct data at the beep will result in a response of great promptitude. Thank you.")

While Clark has abandoned the school corridors for the lecture hall, Sweeney has remained in the battle zone. When he sent us a copy of his article, he wrote: "My apologies for the delay. The end of the year is the busiest and roughest time at my school. On the second to last day, one of our assistant principals was robbed at gunpoint by a well-dressed man who walked into her office at 3:05 P.M. and got her engagement ring and all her cash. She was quite shaken by the incident; when he asked her to turn around so he could make a getaway, she thought he was going to shoot her."

More often, in schools today, the gunmen are the kids themselves; and more often than adults, they do shoot. The towheaded tyke on our cover may be only a model, but he illustrates a disturbing trend: the growing murder rate among the young. Children are acquiring guns (which isn't surprising, since there are twice as many handguns in America as there are households), they're bringing guns to school (an estimated 400,000 kids have done so at least once in the past year, and 135,000 of those carry guns daily), they're using guns in the schools and on the streets, and they're dying from them. In May 1990, a survey of FBI crime statistics (released, all too appropriately, by the Centers for Disease Control) revealed that, since 1984, murders from firearms had climbed 46 percent among children under five, 27 percent among children from five to nine, 77 percent among children from ten to fourteen, and 107 percent among youth from fifteen to nineteen. Virtually no adult group had so dramatic a rate of increase.

What this means is that, inside school and out, fights that used to be settled with fists are now settled with bullets; the shoving match has become a shooting match. Any child has the strength to pull a trigger, and the consequences may not seem very real; killings, after all, are as commonplace on TV and in the movies as they are on the streets.

And it doesn't take much to start a fight. Any offense will do—a taunt, a threat, a dirty look. A few years ago, a student at Columbia was robbed at gunpoint by a teenager who, as he was walking away with the victim's cash, chanced to drop a dollar bill. The college student, whether out of reflex courtesy, bitterness, or misguided bravado, called after him, "You dropped one." The youth whirled and shot him dead.

Or it may be no offense at all. A woman friend, a psychologist, was sitting in a parked car waiting for her husband to come out of a supermarket one evening when—like the luckless schoolteacher on page 27—she suddenly saw a gun pointing at her through the window. It was held by a boy in, she guessed, his early teens. He demanded her money. Aware that the gun was only inches away, she carefully opened her pocketbook and removed her wallet. She was unnerved when, after she'd handed it over to him, he continued to point the gun at her. "You don't have to shoot me," she said slowly. As if to contradict her, he fired. The shot hit her in the leg. She still limps—but she's alive. The next victim may not be so lucky.

Executive editor Marc Lichter has also looked down the barrel of a loaded gun; check out his gripping account on page 6. I've never had the experience myself—not yet. But when I do, I hope the gun's not in the hands of a child.

November 1991

83% Safe

... A certain number of parolees—at least 17 percent, if Mike Kass is to be believed—are *expected* to go on committing crimes.

Kass is an outstanding parole officer; it's clear both from reading his column "In Defense of Parole" (page 10) and from talking with him at length that he's an extraordinarily dedicated, thoroughgoing professional and, more important, a shrewd judge of character. We'd be a lot better off with more parole officers like him.

But the system he defends is one that regularly sets thieves and murderers free to prey on the public—in large part because there aren't enough jail cells to hold them, and little inclination on the part of that same public to pay for new ones. Thanks to this overcrowding (and perhaps to misplaced compassion), few convicts serve their full time anymore; the average murderer in this country spends less than a third of his sentence behind bars.

Consider: A New York State civil service employee was arrested this summer for robbing banks on his days off. The press treated it as a bit of joke: "He Called in Sick to Rob Banks" was how *Newsday* headed it; *Time*'s story was entitled "Extracurricular Activities." No one seemed bothered by the fact—buried in the news reports—that, back in the '70s, the man had served three years for murdering a guard during a previous bank robbery.

Three years for a human life? Are the prisons really that crowded?

Kass is the first to admit that the system makes mistakes, and that the mistakes are the stuff of lurid headlines. He notes that newspapers don't seem to spend much time talking about the successes, and points out that the parole system has a success rate of 83 percent.

But is that really good enough? Would you get on an airplane that had an 83 percent chance of reaching its destination safely?

One of the most time-honored precepts of our justice system is that it's better to let ten guilty men go free than to punish one innocent man. In other words, protecting the innocent is the number one priority. Yet by freeing known criminals after an absurdly short time in jail, we're admitting, in effect, that we're prepared to sacrifice a certain number of innocent lives.

Why aren't we more concerned about these future victims? Because at the time of a convict's release, they're mere phantoms. They don't exist yet; they have no names, no voice. They're still just statistical projections, faceless victims of the convicts who'll return to crime—the seventeen failures in every hundred.

CrimeBeat intends to be a voice not just for the victims whose identities we know, but for those potential victims whose existence, while easily overlooked, is just as real.

December 1991

A Sin of Silence

Imagine that you're a female college student on a date with someone you met in class; and imagine that you innocently invite him up to your room for a cup of coffee, whereupon he proceeds to force you, using physical threats and coercion, to have sex with him.

There's no mystery about what's happened. Call it rape or call it date rape, he's committed a crime.

Do you turn the guy in? Of course you do—if you feel any sense of social responsibility.

Not everyone does, of course. It's been estimated that half of all violent crimes, perhaps even two crimes out of three, go unreported; and in the case of rape, the figures may be as high as nine out of ten.

But the *right* thing—the responsible thing—is to blow the whistle. Inform the authorities. Call in the law.

Even if you're a timid soul; even if you know that you yourself will never make the same mistake again; even if you leave the college behind and will never again cross paths with that particular student, you owe it to others to speak out—if only to prevent some other woman, some future victim, from undergoing this experience.

That's what you do with a crime. You report it. To protect the innocent.

You'd do the same in the case of a child molester. Even if you knew that your own child had nothing to fear from him, you'd inform the authorities—in order to prevent him from victimizing others.

But let's change the nature of the offense to something less dramatic. Let's say your boss comes on to you at the office, in a manner that's extremely upsetting. He's crude; he's abusive. And though you tell him how you feel, he won't stop. It's a clear case of sexual harassment. What should you do?

Ideally, you report him.

Maybe, out of fear, you wait until you've found another job. But in the end, you report him—to protect other women like yourself.

Now let's take the case of Professor Anita Hill. Let's pretend, for the sake of argument, that every charge she raised about Judge

Clarence Thomas was true. Let's pretend that he made Anita Hill's life as miserable as she claims.

Did she blow the whistle on him? No. Did she at least warn her successor? No.

Even after she'd left his employ, even after she'd established herself in another career in another part of the country, did she come forward? Did she inform the authorities (with whom, incidentally, she was more than familiar)? Did she have the courage to speak out, if only to shield other women from having to endure what she did?

No. Not for ten long years.

Is Professor Hill a liar? As Leslie Berman says on page 36, we'll never know.

One thing we do know, however. If Clarence Thomas was as abusive as she claims, if he really offended her so deeply, then she had a duty to blow the whistle on him. Not just for herself, but for others.

By remaining silent, Anita Hill failed her fellow women. Whether she's a liar is anybody's guess. But she's certainly no heroine.

January 1992

Mugged by the Law

... One man who did his part to bring a criminal to justice is Chuck Hollom, the San Francisco cab driver whose story is told on page 9. Having pinned a fleeing mugger to the wall of a building with his cab, Hollom has now been ordered to pay the man nearly $25,000 in damages—all this determined by a jury of his peers, men and women you'd normally expect to be grateful to someone who, at considerable risk to himself, had collared the sort of urban predator who might just as easily have preyed on *them*.

The jurors' reprehensible decision leaves the city with a black eye, but perhaps their action reflects upon more than just San Francisco. As a lawyer friend observed when she heard the story, "God, what a sick country this is!"

The $25,000 is supposed to pay for mugger Ocie McClure's medical expenses—specifically, for the broken leg he incurred during the incident. Hollom is at pains to point out that this injury was far more likely inflicted by the man's own deliberate twisting movement after he was pinned than by the pressure of Hollom's cab. He vividly recalls the sight of McClure "up against the wall. And he stood there yanking Japanese yen out of the purse he'd stolen, and staring at it with these bulging eyeballs, and going, 'All right, man, you got me. Let me go. Back off. Go away!' And I just sat there with the car in park—I put the emergency brake on, but did not shut off the engine, because that would have caused the car to sag back—and waited for the police and ambulance to come. And he started lifting the right side of his body, wrenching his leg. . . . He managed to lacerate it all the way around, cracking the bone and tearing his pants leg"—the sort of damage, Hollom maintains, that the bumper itself could not have caused.

McClure's injury, he says, "is only explicable in light of the fact that, at twenty-two years of age, at 210 pounds, with no fat on his body, the weightlifter Ocie McClure was on crack cocaine, which anesthetized his leg. As a three-time loser with convictions in '85 and '86, he knew that he was facing jail. Apparently he preferred the hospital. He had crack in his head and was feeling no pain."

It's sad that Hollom feels the necessity for such explanations, and that the courts compel them. Forcing a decent man to prove he didn't *really* injure a criminal seems a moral travesty. His story is a painful illustration of the old saying, "No good deed goes unpunished."

April 1992

Don't Blame Me!

Leave it to Ernie Anastos. The New York TV newsman has never been known as a sage, but when asked if he didn't get jaded, serving up crimes and disasters day after day, year after year, he put his finger on a fundamental truth. "It's always the same awful stories," he admitted, "but they're happening to *different people.*"

. . . Everybody's got an explanation. Death Row denizen Joseph O'Dell (page 10) blames Virginia police for framing him. Spike Lee, in the magazine *Paper,* blames racist whites for the rape conviction of Mike Tyson (page 24), the so-called black role model.

"How can he get a fair trial in Indiana," Lee demands, "a hotbed of the Ku Klux Klan?"

And street-gang apologist Léon Bing, whose book *Do or Die* (excerpted in November's *CrimeBeat*) offers a sympathetic portrait of the L.A. gang world, ends a March 16 *Time* magazine interview with this chilling example of Gangbanger Chic:

> Q. You still see the gang members socially.
> A. They are among my best friends.
> Q. How can you call them your friends?
> A. I trust them. They are there for me.
> Q. But you are talking about people who freely told you of torturing strangers.
> A. I know. They're killers. But I separate deeds from individuals.
> Q. Isn't that condescending? Don't you hold other people responsible for their actions?
> A. I don't excuse them. I try to understand them.
> Q. One gang member spotted an enemy on the street and machine-gunned him, along with his wife and baby. Yet he is such a good friend that you attributed the killing, in your book, to another gang member in order to protect him.
> A. Because I knew his mother was going to read the book. It would have killed her.

Let's hope his mother doesn't read *Time*.

May 1992

Meeting Mr. Wright

Sometimes the most shocking part of a news story is buried near the bottom. Last summer, when a New York State civil service employee was arrested for robbing banks on his days off, the press treated it as little more than a joke. "He Called in Sick to Rob Banks" was *Newsday*'s headline; *Time* entitled the story "Extracurricular Activities." I've mentioned it before; it was the sort of humorous piece that, here in *CrimeBeat,* usually ends up in the Rap Sheet section.

Only in passing did the press reports mention that this colorful, amusingly eccentric fellow had a *history* of robbing banks—and that, back in the 1970s, he'd in fact spent three years in prison for killing a bank guard during a robbery.

Three years?? This, for me, was the *real* story: that a man could serve a mere three years for armed robbery and murder.

I had the same reaction when, this spring, the *New York Post* ran a front-page story—a pretty typical one, considering the source—entitled "Coed Call Girl," illustrated by the photo of a beautiful young Eurasian NYU student.

The story itself wasn't terribly interesting—the girl had allegedly pumped five shots into the owner of the escort service she worked for in a dispute over money—but in the middle, six paragraphs down, came this remarkable sentence: "For three weeks after the shooting, she eluded the police by staying at her mother's house in Paramus, N.J."

Three weeks?? It took New York's Finest (not, incidentally, the same Finest celebrated on page 48) three full weeks to track a would-be murderess to her *mother's* house? (Paramus, New Jersey, is just across the river—a quick commute.)

What both these figures—the three years in prison, the three weeks on the lam—suggest isn't necessarily that the police are incompetent or that those who run the prisons are fools; it's that our criminal justice apparatus is so ludicrously overburdened that it's barely functioning. The safety net we take for granted is largely imaginary.

"Misplaced Trust" happens to be the title of the article on page 43 about a lawyer who looted his clients' trust funds—the money on which they'd staked their futures. But in some ways it's also the theme of this issue. Certainly it might describe the tragedy of Mr. and Mrs. William Fischer (page 40), who entrusted the life of their baby daughter to a Swiss nanny who's now on trial for murdering the child.

And in "Discount Sentencing" (page 53) you'll learn that citizens who've entrusted their safety to the Florida penal system are in for a nasty surprise; convicted lawbreakers there, and in many other states, are now walking free after serving as little as 10 percent of their time. The following passage—perhaps the most horrifying one in a horrifying article—bears repeating, especially because the case, we're told, is "not unusual":

> Manuel C. Wright was sentenced in August 1986 to two and a half years in prison for robbery, battery on a law-enforcement officer, and criminal mischief. He got out soon enough to be arrested and sent back in February 1988 on a one-year sentence for aggravated battery. He served only two months of that time. In August 1988 he got five years for car theft but was released in September 1989. In January 1990 he got seven years for armed burglary, grand theft of a firearm, resisting an officer with violence, attempting to kill an officer, and car theft. He was released in September 1991. He recently was arrested again and charged with three burglaries after police found $125,000 worth of stolen merchandise hidden at his mother's [clearly a popular hideout] and his girlfriend's homes. He's in jail awaiting—but probably not worrying about—his next trial.

Think about Mr. Wright the next time you're planning your Florida vacation. You may run into him down there—or a lot closer to home.

June 1992

Same Old Song

> I shouted out, "Who killed the Kennedys?"—when, after all, it was you and me.
>
> —"Sympathy for the Devil"

Mick Jagger's sophomoric pieties struck me as a bit trite when I first heard them back in 1968, and they sound even triter today. We're all of us, God knows, guilty of enough wrongdoing, great and small, without having to declare ourselves the moral equivalents of Lee Harvey Oswald and Sirhan Sirhan.

But such pieties have never lost their appeal for America's editorial writers and professional pundits—who, thanks to last month's riots, are purveying them again, accompanied by the usual breast-beating over "police brutality," "white racism," and "black rage." "What, as a nation, did we really expect?" asked the earnestly liberal

New Yorker. "The residents of our inner cities have for many years now been unable to lay claim to our national sense of common humanity and simple decency. On what basis can we expect to suddenly lay claim to theirs?" (Translation: Serves us right.) "It Takes a Nation of Millions to Make L.A. Burn!" cried the *Village Voice.* (Translation: We're all guilty.) An *Observer* cartoon showed two road signs, one pointing to "San Andreas Fault," the other to a charred Los Angeles labeled "Society's Fault."

You'd think, to read the papers, that the riots were society's long-overdue, richly deserved comeuppance. You'd think the devastation and the fifty dead bodies were a perfectly reasonable response to the *real* outrage, the acquittal of the four cops.

Even safe, determinedly middle-of-the-road *USA Today* couldn't resist the chance to sermonize. "The violence in Los Angeles has shown us the racism that still permeates our whole society," it declared, castigating President Bush for talking too much about "the need for order" and not enough about "the perceived injustice that ignited the disorder."

All this preaching about "racism" and "injustice" may sound high-minded, but it has a certain pernicious effect. It dignifies the looting, the lawlessness, the murder. It legitimizes, excuses, indeed *justifies* such behavior. Worse, it encourages it—by ceding the moral high ground to the criminals. It allows them to pretend, if only to themselves, that their actions are merely a response to injustice. "People may feel bad about what they're doing," said a Boston psychologist, speaking of the looters, "but they rationalize it somehow."

Consider the words of a "former gang member" quoted in the *New York Times.* "A lot of people feel it's reparations; it's what already belongs to us." Consider the rioter quoted (with approval, one suspects) by the *Voice:* "If we don't got no rights, and nobody gives a damn about us, hey, why not riot? Ain't nobody watching us. I'm going to do what I want to do. I'm going to loot all these white man's stores. . . . I'm just taking back what's mine, what's ours, for free. . . . Like, yeah, we're doing this to the white folks; yeah, we're doing this to the Koreans. I said, when they come in and see their store burned down or broken in, they'll see how we feel. That's justice."

The most insightful words about the rioting were written back in 1988 by the black essayist Shelby Steele. "I think the real trouble between the races in America," he said, "is that the races are not just races but competing power groups. . . . But the human animal almost never pursues power without first convincing himself that he is *entitled* to it. And this feeling of entitlement has its own precondition: to be entitled, one must first believe in one's innocence. . . . Of course, innocence need not be genuine or real in any objective sense, as the Nazis demonstrated not long ago. Its only test is whether or not we can convince ourselves of it." And he adds, "To be innocent, someone else must be guilty."

Each time a writer or speaker proclaims that "society" or "all of us" bear the guilt for the riots, he fuels this conviction of innocence—and a consequent sense of entitlement—in the hearts of potential rioters. He allows them to convince themselves that they're looting in a just cause, merely "taking back what's ours." In short, he helps promote *next* year's riot.

So when someone tells you he's to blame for the riots . . . he is.

July 1992

Feds on Film

Peggy Coler doesn't understand. Seventeen years ago her husband, FBI agent Jack Coler, was murdered in cold blood along with his partner, Ronald Williams. Assigned to the Pine Ridge Indian Reservation in South Dakota, the two young agents, both in their twenties, were following up a routine robbery case when they unwittingly blundered into an armed encampment of the American Indian Movement. Totally outgunned, with no more than pistols at hand against a barrage of high-powered rifle fire, they were quickly wounded—and, minutes later, executed by AIM leader Leonard Peltier.

Yet today, thanks to a mixture or radical chic and antigovernment paranoia (the sort that blames Earl Warren and the CIA for Kennedy's assassination), the two lawmen are vilified—as one New York tabloid snidely puts it, "the feds bit the big one"—and Peltier hailed as a hero. "Ron and Jack have become victims of media desecration," says Peggy Coler. She has seen her husband and his partner go from being treated as "heroes and martyrs" to being made to seem "guilty as their killer."

That's certainly the impression left by the *60 Minutes* account of their deaths, and by the recent documentary *Incident at Oglala*. The story they've been spreading is ugly and distorted, but it's the one that's sanctioned by the media, and it's probably the one most Americans will hear. On page 14, *CrimeBeat* presents the other side.

We've come a long way from 1959's *The FBI Story,* in which daring G-men defended society from the likes of Ma Barker and Baby Face Nelson. The feds were heroic, it's true, in *Mississippi Burning*—but that was set in the '60s. The more modern conception of lawmen is that of *Tequila Sunrise,* with its grubby and corrupt government drug-enforcement agent outwitted by a hip, handsome, fresh-faced coke dealer (played by Mel Gibson, no less) who dresses more stylishly, lives in a funky house by the Pacific with his button-cute son, and is looking forward to an honorable retirement. In Hollywood, at least, dressing well is more important than decency.

Of all the government agencies reviled by Hollywood, the CIA ranks supreme. Ever since *The Spy Who Came In from the Cold* (1965), which taught us that we were more treacherous than the Russians, and *Three Days of the Condor* (1975), in which an assassination squad shooting CIA operatives turns out to have been hired by the CIA, the Central Intelligence Agency has become Hollywood's villain of choice, right up there with rogue cops, industrial polluters, Arab terrorists, and right-wing hate groups.

Which is one reason the new film *Patriot Games* is so unusual. It's one of the few times we've seen the CIA as the good guys. The bad guys, this time, are the IRA.

However, the film isn't as politically incorrect—or as daring—as one might wish. One set of villains from the Tom Clancy novel, a radical black group, has been prudently left out, and the film is careful to emphasize that the bloodthirsty terrorists bedeviling British royalty aren't *really* the IRA, they're merely a psycho splinter group. In fact, they're at war with the *real* IRA. (Never mind that it's the real IRA who've been known to pack bent nails around their London bombs so as to kill or maim as many people as possible.)

Furthermore, the film's hero happens to be Irish (or at least Irish-American), and several of its terrorists turn out to be renegade Englishmen. Still, all this hasn't stopped the Irish-American press from denouncing it as racist.

The film does have one virtue: It shows that terrorists are difficult to fight because they're so difficult to find. As "Endless Stalemate" (page 32) makes clear, the real-life war the British are waging may not be as exciting as the one on the screen, but it's every bit as nerve-wracking.

August 1992

Quantifying Evil

It should come as no surprise that this issue of *CrimeBeat* presents a pretty bleak picture of humanity. True, we feature a heroic young mother who came to the aid of her victimized daughter (page 25), and an outraged father who came to the aid of his accused son (page 56); but the latter was, unfortunately, a psychopathic murderer.

Murderers abound in these pages, even more than they do in the world at large. But in fact, over the past year, *CrimeBeat* has covered the gamut of human misbehavior, the entire hierarchy of wrongdoing, ranging from the lowliest case of sexual harassment—a type of transgression so common, so subjective, and so difficult to define that it's hard to know where crime begins and mere boorishness leaves off—on up the scale (or perhaps it should be down) to a host of more serious offenses—streets scams, video bootlegging, various forms of counterfeiting—in which the greedy prey on the naive, but at least do so nonviolently. And then there are the robberies, and the drug crimes, and the crimes of violence, ranging all the way from assault to the extremes of human depravity—crimes so monstrous they defy comprehension.

Yet even here, in the realm of the monsters, there are arguably gradations of evil. Judges in the court of law make such distinctions all the time. Which, one might ask, is really more horrible: the still-unsolved murder of three-month-old Kristie Fischer (page 48), or Diane Lumbrera's murder of her four children (page 44)? The killing of all three members of the Brendel family of Barrington, Rhode Island (page 36), or the massacre of 23 innocent strangers in Killeen, Texas, by gunman George Hennard (page 26)?

For anyone tempted to measure evil by sheer numbers, the murder of twenty-three people may seem twenty-three times as heinous as the murder of just one. But in matters of morality, statistics seem beside the point; more than one philosopher has argued that it's a mistake to weigh the enormity of a disaster by the number of lives lost. Here, for example, is Jorge Luis Borges, paraphrasing Shaw:

> The tumultuous general catastrophes—fires, wars, epidemics—are but a single sorrow, illusorily multiplied in many mirrors.... What one person can suffer is the maximum that can be suffered on earth. If one person dies of starvation, he will suffer all the starvation that has been or will be. If 10,000 other persons die with him, he will not be 10,000 times hungrier, nor will he suffer 10,000 times longer. There is no point in being overwhelmed by the appalling total of human suffering; such a total does not exist. Neither poverty nor pain is accumulable.

In the record books, of course, a hundred people dead is a hundred times more horrible than a single death; but in another sense, the figure is meaningless. We each die only once; we're each a universe unto ourselves, whether we die alone or with millions of others. Jewish law declares that he who kills a single man destroys the world.

October 1992

Let him rot!

The above sentiment, a perfectly understandable one, was voiced by Ellen Levin. She's learned that "preppie murderer" Robert Chambers—who strangled Levin's teenage daughter Jennifer in 1986—will shortly be up for parole.

Ellen Levin has launched a petition drive to keep Chambers in prison. She's already amassed more than 5,000 signatures and expects to get thousands more.

They probably won't be necessary. As John Marr notes on page 22, parole boards—more concerned, one suspects, with protecting their careers than with protecting the public—usually pass over the really notorious murderers, the ones who've made the headlines. It'll be a long time before you see Charles Manson, Sirhan Sirhan, or the Son of Sam walking free.

But the more obscure killers, as well as the sex offenders, habitual thieves, and career criminals—in short, the kind of sociopaths for whom "rehabilitation" is a joke—these can be released without fanfare. The public doesn't hear about them . . . until they find new victims.

And inevitably they do. Whether it's as few as 17 percent of them who return to lives of crime (as parole officer Mike Kass estimated in last December's *CrimeBeat*) or as many as 39 percent (the return rate in Georgia, according to Robert Fleming's article in this issue), a sizable number of them will prove to have been bad risks, gambles by the parole board that didn't come off.

But unlike most gamblers, parole boards don't lose when they guess wrong. It's *your* life they're gambling with. It's *you* who lose.

. . . Not all parolees turn to murder, like the ones you'll see chronicled in this issue. But chances are good that they'll leave the world a little worse for their presence.

According to the U.S. Department of Justice, 69 percent of young parolees are rearrested within six years of their release from prison. (The rate is a whopping *93 percent* among parolees with six or more prior arrests—and these repeat offenders are usually rearrested within seven months of their release.) "Over a 20-year period," the Justice Department concludes, "an estimated half of all releasees will return to prison, most in the first three years after release."

How would you feel about a hospital that released a steady stream of patients from quarantine, knowing that half of them were carrying the plague?

November 1992

Words on a Wall

You may have heard it read aloud in school, or seen it embroidered on a sampler framed in a grandparent's parlor. You may even have memorized it for some youthful oration. It's a famous old poem called "Invictus," written more than a century ago by an Englishman named William Ernest Henley, and the sentiments may sound terribly corny today.

Out of the night that covers me, it begins,

> Black as the Pit from pole to pole,
> I thank whatever gods may be
> For my unconquerable soul.

In case the notion of a poet rhapsodizing about his "unconquerable soul" sounds a bit grandiose or immodest, it's worth noting that, when he wrote it, Henley was in his mid-twenties, broken in health, and confined to the tubercular ward of the Edinburgh Infirmary, facing his own expected death.

> In the fell clutch of circumstance
> I have not winced nor cried aloud.
> Under the bludgeonings of chance
> My head is bloody but unbowed.

Even if lines like that have lost their power to stir, you probably recognize some of those phrases; they've become part of the language, and once inspired generations of English-speaking people to fight on through adversity, to refuse to surrender to circumstance. Among them was Franklin Delano Roosevelt, crippled from polio, who once cited "Invictus" as his favorite poem (and promptly received dozens of lovingly hand-printed copies from fans around the nation).

The poem's final stanza is perhaps the most famous of all:

> It matters not how strait the gate,
> How charged with punishments the scroll.
> I am the master of my fate:
> I am the captain of my soul.

Those lines were penned in the early 1870s, when taking responsibility for one's own life was a matter of pride. It's hard not to contrast them with a poem written just a few months ago and reprinted in the *New York Times*. It was spray-painted by two men in their twenties onto the wall of a South Bronx bodega, on a street notorious for drugs, gangs, and violence:

> Never forget!
> What we may do is wrong, but it is a way of life!
> We are forced to survive by any means necessary!
> Why? Because we're just products of our environment.
> Created by the getto [*sic*], born in the getto, also taught in the getto.
> All we really are is victims of the getto!!!

We've come a long way from masters of fate to victims of the ghetto. In the distance between these two poems, we can trace the grim trajectory of crime in America—mirrored by a century-long decline of personal responsibility.

The pattern is visible even in the past few decades. In 1965, there were 9,850 murders in the U.S. (up six and a half percent from the previous year), and the population stood at 195 million. Since that time the population has grown by a quarter—but the total number of murders has more than doubled. Last year we had 25,000 of them.

You can blame the crisis on drugs; you can blame it on TV; you can blame it on the easy availability of guns. But when we offered criminals a convenient scapegoat called "society" and told them that they were its victims, we armed them with something more dangerous than guns: We ceded to them the moral high ground, absolved them of guilt, and gave them an excuse—indeed, a justification—for breaking the law.

Once a young poet gloried in his strength of will. Now young men his age boast of their powerlessness, and criminals are encouraged to perceive themselves as victims.

Maybe it's time to dust off those old samplers.

January 1993

Pollyanna Time

In a recent editorial entitled "The Inmate Riddle, and Its Moral," the *New York Times* warned that "serious violent crimes" remain at an all-time high, with no sign that the crime rate is decreasing.

Old news.

The editorial then revealed that in a 1988 survey of eight states, "only 12 percent of the 144,916 people arrested for violent crimes went to prison. And even the 144,916 probably constitute less than half of all those believed to have committed serious crimes in those states that year. So only about six percent of criminals go to prison."

Now, if there's one thing that's known about controlling crime, it's that the key to deterrence lies in the certainty (as opposed to the severity) of punishment; one deters crime by increasing the probability that an offender will serve time. "As sanctions become more likely, crime becomes less common," says our foremost criminologist, James Q. Wilson, a professor at Harvard and UCLA. For example, he notes, "The higher the probability of being imprisoned, the lower the robbery rate."

When it comes to violent crime, a six percent chance of going to jail clearly isn't much of a deterrent. One might suppose the *Times* would want to increase this dismally low rate.

Quite the contrary. Its editorial deplores what it sees as "America's prison binge," and instead advocates a greater reliance on probation, the use of "electronic monitoring," and such classic liberal nostrums as "education and work programs." (To be fair, it also adds "military-style boot camps" to the list.) Its conclusion? "Progress against crime won't be possible until America gets over its obsessive belief that the remedy is simply to throw people behind bars for ever-longer prison terms."

At a time when the average murderer serves less than seven years, "ever-longer prison terms" sounds pretty good to me.

One offender who should have stayed behind bars is Leslie Allen Williams (see November's *CrimeBeat* and page 27 in this issue), whom the Michigan penal authorities saw fit to parole in 1990 after seven years in prison for kidnapping and rape. Upon release, he proceeded to murder at least four teenage girls, kidnap another young woman, and rape a nine-year-old.

Two of the girls he killed were sisters—Michelle and Melissa Urbin, ages sixteen and fourteen. At a graveside ceremony following their funeral, their mother, Kathryn Urbin, told reporters: "I have no anger toward Williams. It's for the system which released him."

While I have no quarrel with her priorities, I suspect that, for most of us, the anger is deep enough to encompass both the criminally stupid system *and* the monster it released into the world.

An even more remarkable magnanimity has been expressed by Reginald Denny (see page 35), the white truck driver who, during the Los Angeles riots, while the nation watched, was set upon by a black mob, dragged from his truck, and beaten into a coma. (His accused assailants, now described on T-shirts as the "L.A. Five," have attained the status of neighborhood heroes.)

Denny, currently recovering from ninety-six facial fractures and a brain hemorrhage, refuses to condemn his attackers. "I've never walked an inch in their shoes," he told reporters. "Man, who knows what these guys went through? That's not to excuse their behavior. But you know, anyone who gets hammered on long enough is going to retaliate sooner or later."

That's L.A. for you. Beat somebody's brains out and he begins to think he's Jesus.

March 1993

Why Crime Pays

A year and ten months for murder? Sixty days' imprisonment for rape? Sentences that short sound like a joke—or like one of those nightmare visions of the future in which criminals rule the world.

But the joke's on us, because that's what a murderer actually *does* receive in America today—if your calculations are wide-ranging enough to encompass all the murders in a given year and all the jail time likely to be served.

That's the approach taken by Professor Morgan Reynolds. He's an economist at Texas A & M University, and he approached the subject like an economist should, weighing anticipated costs against anticipated benefits, and keeping an eye on the bottom line.

His calculations for 1990 (the year from which his statistics are drawn) are based on total days served for each of the various crime categories, divided by the total number of offenses. They take into account, as Reynolds explains, "the fact that the vast majority of offenses don't result in any punishment. Ninety-eight percent of reported crimes may not result in a prison sentence."

Furthermore, he says, "only 20 percent of the crimes are cleared by arrest." He points out, though, that this figure is dominated by property offenses. "The clearance rate is much higher for violent crimes. Nationally, you might get 69 percent of murders cleared by an arrest, and for robbery on the order of 30 percent, using the standard FBI numbers." Even after being processed by the courts, he adds, "only 45 percent of felony convictions go to prison."

What you're left with, Reynolds says, is "a rational, economist's approach to the expected punishment." And the bottom line, he admits, is "shockingly low": not only two months for rape and less than two years for murder, but just 23 days for robbery, 6.7 days for arson, and 6.4 days for aggravated assault. For stealing a car, the expected sentence is a mere day and a half.

Don't misinterpret these figures. Reynolds isn't saying that if you kill someone and go to jail, you can expect to get out in 22 months; in fact, the median sentence for those who actually serve time is around four and a half years (a term which is *still* shockingly low). Reynolds's figures include those who don't serve any time at all.

Nor is he saying that criminals sit down and perform calculations like these before they turn to crime. His figures reflect a purely intellectual world-view, a hardheaded balancing of risk with reward. There's no reason to assume that criminals are as rational as economists.

Yet surely *some* element of calculation is involved, however crude—or else penalties and the visible presence of police would have no deterrent effect at all.

It's clear they do. It's also clear that experienced criminals have a far more accurate idea of the risks of crime than the rest of us. In a sense, they work with Reynolds's figures every day.

And they behave accordingly. "States in which the probability of going to prison for robbery is low are also states which have high rates of robbery," notes James Q. Wilson in *Thinking about Crime*. "The chances of being imprisoned for murder do seem to affect the murder rate."

For Reynolds as well, the solution to our rising crime rate is "one that appeals to common sense"—which, he adds pointedly, "isn't so common in some circles. We have an unpleasant method that works, and a lot of pleasant social programs that *don't* work . . . or at least have not been proven to work."

His conclusion? "If you're going to reduce crime to pre-1960 levels, you must raise the expected cost to criminals by increasing the probability that they'll serve time and by lengthening the median sentence. The basic message—it's a straightforward, old-fashioned one—is that punishment works."

April 1993

Crime and Punishment

To the editors:
Jean Bethke Elshtain asks rhetorically, "How on earth will executing Timothy McVeigh ... expiate for 168 deaths? Will the moral universe be thereby righted?"

To which I would answer: yes, somewhat. More, at any rate, than if he were merely kept in jail. A *lot* more than if he were set free. Simply because we can't execute a murderer 168 times doesn't mean we shouldn't execute him once.

Letter in the *New Republic* (July 28, 1997). For years, I would write letters at the drop of a hat, mainly to the editors of magazines—letters with suggestions, letters of complaint, praising an article, disagreeing with another, never without an opinion. Looking through my old files, it appears I wrote letters to practically every magazine I opened. And of course, only a small portion were ever printed. I would certainly like all those hours back.

A Higher Standard

I've never known a publication to have as many angry, discontented readers as the *NY Press*—though perhaps that's only appropriate in a city where more than half the inhabitants reportedly claim they can't wait to move somewhere else. "Mugger's an asshole," they cry at the beginning of their letters, just to show where they're coming from. "Mugger sucks." "Get rid of Mugger."

The grousing is awfully predictable, and most of it, beneath the personal invective, comes down to the same tired complaint: "How *dare* someone in a Soho-based newspaper speak well of the Republicans? Don't you know this is New York?"

Recently, while raging at columnist Todd Seavey, one of your readers ("The Mail," 5/31) inadvertently revealed her peculiar world-view—peculiar because it's so far removed from reality, yet common, I suspect, among your audience. "If I wanted to read about how the cuts to social programs for the poor by Newt & Co. were really a good thing for everybody with that supply-side trickle-down theory crap, I could pick up the *New York Post* or *The Wall Street Journal*," she fumed. "I am inundated with this propaganda every day." Describing "the majority of all the media" as anti-choice and Seavey as "a card-carrying right winger," she claimed that his views merely "parrot what the mainstream media has to say."

Letter in the *New York Press* (June 14, 1995). The paper's editor/publisher, who contributed a regular column as "Mugger," was a libertarian.

Reality check. Part of my job involves reading a wide range of newspapers and magazines, and I can assure you that, in a city that went 81 percent for Cuomo last November, Republican and conservative voices are hardly the "majority"—and the same is true of our national press, whose reporters (according to a recent *Time* poll) are overwhelmingly more liberal than the populace in general. Whatever their place in the political spectrum, *The New York Times, Newsday, The New Yorker, New York, The Village Voice, Paper,* the *Amsterdam News,* the *Forward,* and every free newspaper I've seen in this city—except for the *NY Press*—are demonstrably left of center and express implacable hostility toward the GOP. So do *Time* and *Newsweek,* at least since the Bush years (columnist George Will notwithstanding); so, to a lesser degree, do all three network anchors (most notably Peter Jennings, who characterized November's voters as a bunch of spoiled two-year-olds). And so does that bastion of liberal piety, WNYC. So spare us this nonsense about Republicans running the media.

Antarctica in the *Times*

The Love of Penguins

To the Editor:

An abortion foe named Ron Arthur has written a paean to parental love among the penguins, presumably seeing in the child-rearing practices of these birds examples of behavior that our own species would do well to emulate (letter, Aug. 4).

Let me submit, as a corrective, some penguin observations by the early Antarctic explorer Dr. Edward Wilson (described in Elspeth Huxley's *Scott of the Antarctic,* New York, 1978):

"Each chick was carried on the feet of a parent and protected by a loose flap of the adult bird's abdomen. Chicks were constantly falling off, and in the scramble to get hold of them by adults overcharged with mother-love, a great many—Wilson estimated three-quarters—were trampled to death, a drastic but efficient form of population control. 'I think the [chicks] hate their parents,' Wilson commented, adding that this was not surprising."

New York Times (August 12, 1985)

Cold War

To the Editor:

As Caroline Alexander notes in her essay "The Race to the Bottom" (Oct. 31), Roland Huntford's *The Last Place on Earth* paints sharply contrasting portraits of the Antarctic explorers Roald Amundsen and Robert Falcon Scott—even in its index. Amundsen, the Norwegian, is given entries on "leadership, capacity for," "rectitude, sense of," "loyalty," "modesty," "sensitivity," and "stoicism." For Scott, the Englishman, we find phrases such as "inadequate preparation," "ignorance of snowcraft," "command, unsuitability for," "insight, lack of," "leadership, failure in," and "panic, readiness to."

Alexander takes these contemptuous notations as an indictment of Scott; I see them, rather, as an indictment of the ludicrous, monotonous, unceasing tendentiousness of Huntford's book, an example of the debunking impulse run wild. Huntford, whose treatment of Amundsen amounts to unadulterated hagiography, does not allow Scott a single virtue. Both expeditions, for example, sacrificed their animals—the killing of worn-out sled dogs to feed the others was, from the start, a key element of Amundsen's plan—yet Amundsen actually receives an index entry, "animals, love of." (Scott's dismay at animal suffering is dismissed as "mawkishly sentimental.")

In the same spirit, the Book Review chose to trumpet Alexander's essay with a peculiarly snide cover line: "Upper-class twits at the South Pole." Scott, in truth, was hardly upper-class; his father, a small-time brewer, was prosperous for a few years but died leaving the family virtually penniless. Scott himself had already begun training as a naval cadet by age 13.

Furthermore, there's something a little unseemly about a bunch of modern-day editors, snug and smug on West 43rd Street, belittling a man who froze to death after trekking nearly 1,500 miles to the South Pole and back, and who managed, in his final hours of life, to write some of the language's most moving letters of farewell.

New York Times Book Review (December 12, 1999)

Quotation & Misquotation

To the Editor of *Commentary:*

It's clear from Gertrude Himmelfarb's article "The Right to Misquote"—and even more so from the actual opinion handed down by the U.S. Court of Appeals for the Ninth Circuit—that in his suit against Janet Malcolm and *The New Yorker,* Jeffrey Masson had the misfortune of running into a couple of judges with tin ears. Any judge who can write, as Arthur Alarcon did for the majority, that the phrase "intellectual gigolo" is no more

---

Letter in *Commentary* (July 1991). The libel suit in question involved *New Yorker* writer Janet Malcolm's shockingly unflattering portrait of Jeffrey Masson, who'd been fired as projects director of the Freud Archives. Malcolm had put words in Masson's mouth (e.g., that he'd been regarded by colleagues as "an intellectual gigolo") and had edited taped quotes to alter their intended meaning. Nonetheless, California's Ninth Circuit ruled summarily for Malcolm. A unanimous Supreme Court later reversed the decision and allowed the case to go to trial, but Masson eventually lost.

(P.S. The same issue arose in 2012, when George Zimmerman brought suit against NBC for having doctored the tape of his 911 call the night he shot Trayvon Martin. Zimmerman had said, "This guy looks like he's up to no good, or he's on drugs or something. It's raining and he's just walking around, looking about." The operator asked, "Okay, and this guy, is he black, white, or Hispanic?" "He looks black," replied Zimmerman. In NBC's hands, this had been compressed to "This guy looks like he's up to no good. He looks black.")

defamatory than, and means substantively the same as, a "private asset but a public liability" has no feeling for words.

That's the example Professor Himmelfarb cites; the court's opinion lists many more. Readers may be interested in an even more glaring example, to be found in the section entitled "Misleadingly Edited Quotations." Here the issue isn't one of putting words in someone's mouth; rather, it is altering a quotation so that it means very nearly the opposite of what was actually said. The following remarks of Masson's, concerning Freud Archive director Kurt Eissler, come directly from the tape:

> He was constantly putting various kinds of moral pressure on me [to keep silent about what Masson felt he'd discovered in Freud's papers].... "Do you want to poison Anna Freud's last days? Have you no heart?" He called me up. "Have you no heart? Think of what she's done for you, and you are now willing to do this to her." I said, "What am I? What have I done? You're doing it, you're firing me. What am I supposed to do, thank you? Be grateful to you?" He said, "Well, you could never talk about it, you could be silent about it, you could swallow it. I know it's painful for you, but just live with it in silence." "Fuck you," I said, "why should I do that? Why? You know, why should one do that?" "Because it's the honorable thing to do, and you will save face, and, who knows, if you never speak about it and quietly and humbly accept our judgment, who knows, in a few years, if we don't bring you back?" Well, he had the wrong man.

After Janet Malcolm got through with them, Masson's words appeared as follows:

> He was always putting moral pressure on me. "Do you want to poison Anna Freud's last days? Have you no heart? You're going to kill the poor old woman." I said to him, "What have I done? You're doing it. You're firing me. What am I supposed to do, be grateful to you?" "You could be silent about it. You could swallow it. I know it is painful for you. But you could just live with it in silence." "Why should I do that?" "Because it is the honorable thing to do." Well, he had the wrong man.

In the taped transcript, Masson refuses to be bought off by the prospect of a future job. In Malcolm's version, with thirty-three crucial words deleted, he seems to be saying that appeals to his sense of honor are a waste of breath.

Yet the Ninth Circuit refused to see anything malicious in this alteration, ruling that "The statement Malcolm ascribed to Masson was a rational interpretation of his ambiguous remarks."

Judge Alex Kozinski, in his eloquent dissenting opinion, showed himself to be far more sensitive to language—and its corruption—than his colleagues. "Because," he noted,

> quotations possess an immediacy and resulting credibility often lacking in ordinary narrative prose, minor changes in quoted language can have a major effect on how a speaker is perceived. A skilled writer can shade a speaker's words in subtle ways that will color a reader's perception far more effectively and permanently than if the writer paraphrases or otherwise discloses her editorial role.

Now that the case has reached the Supreme Court, I find it disturbing that a number of professional writers' groups, whom one might expect to be equally sensitive to the use and misuse of language, have filed briefs on behalf of the defendant. It strikes me that they have come in on the wrong side.

Silenced Voices

To the Editor:

Gary Orfield contends that "the critics of affirmative action are wrong," and that "hard data" drawn from surveys of law-school students at Harvard and Michigan "demonstrate that affirmative-action policies do indeed confer benefits on all students, members of majority and minority groups alike."

It seems to me, rather, that all these opinion polls demonstrate is the prevailing liberal mind-set on today's American campus. Quizzed about affirmative action and "racial diversity," it's the rare student who won't find something positive to say. I'm not sure that would be the case if he or she were asked about "racial preferences" or, more bluntly, "racial quotas."

More important, I wonder how the results might have differed if the survey had focused not on these elite law-school students but on another population entirely: the white and Asian applicants denied admission because they were passed over in favor of black applicants with significantly lower grades and test scores. These rejected applicants are the injured parties here, and their voices deserve to be heard.

Letter in the *Chronicle of Higher Education* (January 28, 2000), written at a time when I was an adjunct at John Jay College of Criminal Justice. (It's probably just as well that no one there ever read it.)

Three Letters to Brown

"Architectural Monstrosities"

For the past dozen years, I've been getting phone calls from well-meaning fellow alumni, asking me to donate money to Brown, and for the past dozen years I've been giving them pretty much the same answer: that while I have terrifically fond memories of the place, I would never contribute a cent to it, because whenever Brown gets its collective hands on some money, it promptly defaces College Hill by putting up another one of its godawful architectural monstrosities—usually knocking down two or three beautiful old homes in the process.

Judging from the photo of something called the "Geology-Chemistry Research Building" in November's issue, a dreary, factory-like affair hailed in your pages as a "slumbering giant" (zzzzzz) with "ninety-six offices" and "41,350 square feet of laboratories," all I can say is: Gentlemen, I rest my case.

Performance Anxiety

Based strictly on the article "Judging Merit" in your March/April issue, I wonder if Harvard law professor Lani Guinier might not be

---

Letters in the *Brown Alumni Magazine* (February 1983, May/June 2004, and May/June 2018). The first of these prompted, in a subsequent issue, a series of six indignant alumni letters under the rubric "Answering Ted Klein," all castigating me for my stinginess and lack of school spirit.

reasoning fallaciously when she disparages tests such as the SAT and the LSAT. The latter, she claims, "is only 9 percent better than random at predicting first-year law school grades, and yet we call it merit!"

What I suspect she's not taking into account—assuming her figures are correct—is that LSAT scores are customarily used in helping decide who gets into law school in the first place, with the highest scores determining, in part, acceptance at the most selective schools. The range of test scores at each school is therefore a limited one, and consequently the test will have less predictive value, since it has *already* been employed during the admissions stage.

As Steven Goldberg, chairman of the sociology department at City College, CUNY, explains in *When Wish Replaces Thought,* "To the extent that a variable is used by a college in the selection process, the ability of that variable to predict performance at that college is diminished."

He goes on to imagine a college "that accepted only students with 800 SATs. At such a college, the students would exhibit the full range of grades.... Yet because all had the same 800 SAT scores, there would be no correlation between SAT score and college performance."

Similarly, no doubt, among the general population, height would be an excellent predictor of prowess on the basketball court—but would be distinctly less so if the field in question were confined to players over six feet tall.

Who Works Harder?

Justice Sonia Sotomayor, speaking at Brown ("Supreme Perspective," March/April), warned minority students that someone might say, "You're only here because of affirmative action." (Considering her own history, she was probably being a bit defensive.) In truth, such a taunt seems rather unlikely; I suspect, in a place like Brown, it might even be regarded as hate speech and get the speaker branded as a racist. It would also, of course, be plain discourteous.

Her suggested response: "Tell them, 'That may be true, but I've earned it, I've had to work harder than you.'"

That's awfully self-serving. If affirmative action essentially means holding a prospective applicant to lower standards, how does meeting those reduced standards require harder work? Or maybe she means that once the applicant is actually in college, he or she has to work extra hard merely to keep up with fellow students. That, at least, makes sense.

In 2008, as an appeals court judge, Sotomayor notoriously joined in dismissing—initially without even issuing an opinion—the appeal of twenty white New Haven firefighters who'd been denied expected promotions after scoring higher in exams than black test takers. Later, the Supreme Court—just before she herself came on board—overturned this patently unfair decision.

One of the white firemen whose appeal Sotomayor rejected was a dyslexic who gave up a second job to spend more time preparing for the exam, took practice tests, and created tapes and flash cards to help him study. He's someone who really did have to "work harder"—which, when you think about it, is pretty ironic.

Spalding Gone Gray

Douglas Davis's love song to Spalding Gray was touching, despite a rather addled reference to *Swimming to Cambodia* as "a film that exposed the genocide in Cambodia." No film "exposed" the genocide, of course—the news was old hat by the time that film came out. I suspect Davis is confusing *Swimming* with *The Killing Fields*.

I used to be a fan of Gray's myself, though not so worshipful as Davis. What finally turned me off was Gray's surprisingly mean-spirited monologue *It's a Slippery Slope,* in which, in his patented "I'm just a lovable neurotic" manner, he made an amusing, self-celebrating story, with himself as victim, out of how he'd cheated on his longtime girlfriend and abandoned her for a younger woman. I began to think of Gray as a fellow who'd been to the well a few times too often. The monologues, with their manufactured spiritual crises, had begun to sound formulaic, and the comic stories that he told on himself were stale and a little smug.

When I read last summer about his very public flirtation with suicide—he'd stood on a bridge in Sag Harbor and threatened to throw himself off until cops and a crowd had gathered—I was skeptical. Now we hear that he may have jumped off the Staten Island ferry. The only way I'll believe that his latest disappearance isn't merely a stunt designed to furnish him with both publicity and material for some future monologue is if he actually turns up dead.*

New York Press (February 11, 2004)

---

*He turned up dead.

Lament of an Aging English Instructor

What irks:
Soon my students will
speak of me
(if they speak of me
at all)
in the third person
past tense. And I
shall not be around
to correct them.

Reassuring Words:
An Interview with T.E.D. Klein

TP: I'd like to begin by asking a question to which I'll return, in part, later. What does horror (fiction or film) mean to you in 2016?

TK: Thomas, I'm somewhat abashed to admit this, as it suggests a lack of serious commitment, but I have far less interest in horror fiction (and horror films) than I used to. In fact, I read very little fiction of any kind these days; like a lot of men my age, I prefer reading nonfiction—generally twentieth-century history and some easy popular science. I'm sure this has something to do with mortality breathing down my neck.

TP: Your response makes sense on a number of levels, Ted. For one thing, it also suggests that what we *do* commit to carries weight. To what, we might ask, are we committing when absorbing the imagery, be it literary or filmic, of horror? The issue begs the question as to the value of what we allow into our lives, particularly given how brief these lives ultimately are. But on that note, I wonder (and please don't feel pressure to get too personal): Does the proximity of mortality precipitate an interest in the relatively prag-

---

From *T.E.D. Klein and the Rupture of Civilization: A Study in Critical Horror* by Thomas Phillips (Jefferson, NC: McFarland, 2017). Phillips, who's also a composer, teaches literature at North Carolina State. His book is a closely argued academic treatise, in regard to which I'm a bit out of my depth—as this interview may suggest.

matic disciplines of history and science, or does your lack of interest hinge more on a general aversion to horror?

TK: Normally I'd reply that in reading history and science, I'm attempting to make up, late in the game, for my woeful ignorance after a lifetime of avoiding nonfiction. I used to complain—still do, actually—that majoring in English in college was a mistake, since it's left me envying people who actually *know* things.

But that doesn't explain the almost physical satisfaction I get, these days, when settling into some big fat history book—whereas books that set out to make my skin crawl . . . well, that's just not a sensation I particularly crave anymore.

Speaking a bit more broadly, after a lifetime of reading fiction for pleasure, I suspect I'm becoming a bit jaded; I find I'm increasingly critical of, and impatient with, the fiction I've been reading lately. The contrivances, the labored attempts to shoehorn in—or shovel in—exposition, the withholding of vital information, the overelaborate set pieces, all seem too obvious. (Mind you, I'm not pretending I can do any better. I see these failings in my own stuff as well.) I feel the same about the movies. I used to be a passionate filmgoer—I actually have an MFA in film—but in recent years I certainly don't feel the wild enthusiasms I once did. Again, I think it may come down, at least in part, to having seen so damned many movies.

TP: I certainly share your reticence around fiction/film, especially that which has appeared in the twenty-first century. Some of the recent novels to come from the French publisher Les Éditions de Minuit, however, have gone a long way to revive my literary enthusiasm. Somehow I can imagine you enjoying Christian Gailly's *An Evening at the Club* or Jean Echeno's *Piano,* to name two examples. But on the English major topic, please allow me to share a quick anecdote. A student recently made a similar point in class discussion about Philip K. Dick's *Ubik,* claiming that nonfiction offers information and knowledge, while fiction provides us with "lessons." Fair enough, though I suggested that the rather clever manner in which Dick exposes and repudiates racism, and further, ascribes to his protagonist—and possibly the genre of science fiction—the role of "professional agitator," would seem to be a "lesson" we (still) can't do without. That said, I certainly know the experience of being a humanities professional and feeling at odds with a techno-savvy, STEM culture.

On a related note, I recall your having mentioned the correlation between yourself and Jeremy from "The Events"/*The Ceremonies*. This may very well be a stretch, but I wonder if Jeremy's immersion in gothic/horror fiction prepares him in any way for the heroism of the novel's dramatic conclusion?

TK: That's an interesting thought. In fact, his heroism, such as it is, bothered me so much that when I recently reread the novel for the first time in thirty years, with an eye to revising and correcting it, I rewrote most of that final scene. But I'm not sure I managed to make his actions any more convincing.

I guess you're asking, in part, if a steady diet of horror fiction might make the supernatural seem a little more familiar and hence less threatening; and I suppose it could, just as a lifetime of reading military histories and tales of bravery might conceivably make someone behave more courageously in battle. Yet I suspect that immersion in horror fiction—especially the work of someone as gloomy as, say, Le Fanu—might just as easily have the opposite effect, affirming one's sense of helplessness and futility vis-à-vis the supernatural, the way a diet of antiwar fiction might demoralize our hypothetical soldier.

TP: In another interview, with Carl T. Ford in the 1987 special issue of *Dagon,* you claim "there's horror in these [Lovecraft's] tales, but there's beauty as well." Can you elaborate on the beauty of horror in general? Does it have to do with the particular atmospheres horror evokes, or is it more complex in your estimation, a product of the sublime, for example?

TK: That's an interesting question, but I'm not sure what you mean by "the particular atmospheres horror evokes." Maybe you yourself can elaborate a bit?

For whatever it's worth, I've argued in the past that supernatural horror logically has a bright and shiny flip side, so to speak, since a universe with room in it for malevolent forces presumably contains benign ones as well; the existence of demons presupposes that of angels. But now, I have to say, that notion strikes me as a bit glib; I guess I've made my peace with living in a universe where science rules, where magic spells don't actually work, and where no houses are really, truly haunted.

TP: By the atmosphere of horror I mean, with reference to Lovecraft's claim on the subject in *Supernatural Horror in Literature,* that horror has a way of provoking especially striking and visceral "sensations," as opposed to merely entertaining, or even deeply engaging plots. A fantastic example from *The Ceremonies* is that incredible moment when Carol catches Rosie glaring at her malevolently, showing his true face in the flickering light, at an otherwise pleasant dinner table. Astonishing. Or when he emerges as a "bundle," and then "a gaunt and wrinkled old woman" on the verge of killing Carol's roommate. But let's move on to the next question that may take us further into the appeal of the genre.

TK: Thank you (if I may interject). I'm always curious as to what works or doesn't work for a reader.

TP: What might it say about the generalized "us" that a provocative and often quite violent form of beauty is so popular?

TK: Sorry, not sure I follow.

TP: Sure—how about I reframe it in this way. Despite most evidence to the contrary (or simply a lack of compelling evidence), many people *want* houses to be haunted. What might this say about humanity, particularly given that we seek representations of hauntings, among other unsettling events, on such a large scale in fiction and film? Do you think we need horror, at least at certain points in our lives, as a medium for transcending, however briefly, what might be otherwise banal and not necessarily "beautiful" lives?

Or does it come down to Stephen King's notion that we're all a bit mad and need to nourish the unconscious in relatively safe ways?

TK: I agree that there's a desire to transcend the banal. A world in which houses can be haunted is definitely a richer, more exciting place, and in fact a more *meaningful* place—though not necessarily one I'd prefer to live in.

TP: I find that there's a great deal of cultural critique in your work, particularly "The Events at Poroth Farm"/*The Ceremonies,* "Petey," and "Nadelman's God," in terms of religious and class ideologies. How important is such critique in your overall project of writing horror?

TK: Well, I'm a little conflicted about this. On the one hand, it's hard to disagree with the common assumption that art which carries a message is bad art. And this surely goes double for fantasy; as a general rule, I'd say that political messages and, as you put it, cultural critiques have no business in fantasy fiction. Whenever I sense some sort of agenda in a story, I resent it. I accept the notion that insofar as art is political, it isn't art. But that's speaking in the abstract. I also happen to be a fairly opinionated fellow, even about stuff I know nothing about; I like to argue; I spend a lot of time (maybe too much) reading the news; I'm quite politically engaged, not necessarily in ways you'd expect from someone living on the Upper West Side of Manhattan. And it's hard to resist taking advantage, so to speak, of the humble platform that a work of fiction affords me. When I'm writing, I fancy myself as a truth-teller—I mean, don't we all?—and it's a pleasurable indulgence to inject some opinions into my work. As to whether they belong there, I'm not sure I can say.

TP: On a related note, you mention Edmund Wilson's notion of "homeopathic horror" and similar descriptors in *Raising Goosebumps for Fun and Profit.* I understand that this term speaks to the (important) entertainment value of the genre, but is the provocation of critical analysis in some horror the homeopathic poison, so to speak, that provides a possible antidote to cultural ills (including but not limited to the raw egotism of individuals and collectives)? What does "homeopathic horror" signify for you?

TK: Was I really that insufferably pretentious? I've looked through *Goosebumps,* and I see that, yes, I guess I was—although I seem to have quoted Wilson explaining that notion ("injections of imaginary horror, which soothe us with the momentary illusions that the forces of madness and murder may be tamed") without actually using the phrase itself. Looking back at Wilson's essay, I see he agrees that "a political element . . . seems clumsy and out of place in a ghost story." Unfortunately, he also suggests that horror has a special appeal to readers during wartime ("Gestapo . . . tank attacks and airplane bombings, houses rigged with booby-traps"), which seems to me quite doubtful, and he thinks highly of "The Turn of the Screw," which I find the most overrated ghost tale ever written.

I don't believe, on reflection, that a passion for horror fiction and films has much to do with current events, the world situation, etc. Our fascination with the genre starts when we're quite young, don't you think?—long before we have the slightest interest in the day's news. Historians and critics used to maintain that the revived-dinosaur and giant-bug-and-lizard movies of the '50s were, quote unquote, a response to the real-life terrors of the Atomic Age, the uncertainties of the Cold War, blah blah blah—but that strikes me as silly. True, "atomic testing" supplied filmmakers with a handy explanation for how these creatures got so damned big; but I was crazy about those movies when I was growing up during that era, and believe me, their appeal had nothing to do with any concerns about the Bomb, because such concerns never entered my mind, nor the mind of anyone I knew.

TP: Oh, I absolutely agree that such fascination begins when we're young! Those mid-'70s Saturday nights with Chiller Theater were quite formative for me. I do think, however, that the genre often calls its reader out—on the convenient illusions of suburban safety and immortality, for example. But I also find your critiques of the Gilead community in *The Ceremonies*/"Events" or of George's financial and other improprieties in "Petey" to be not only insightful but organic elements in the respective narratives. Perhaps there's an inherent impulse to seek (and possibly destroy) human presumptuousness without necessarily negating the potentiality of what you called "benign" forces in life in the act of creating horror scenarios. Any further thoughts on this quagmire of an issue?

TK: I think you're quite right about "Petey," but in fact, when you mentioned cultural critique, I thought you were alluding to the other three stories in *Dark Gods,* all set in New York City and all, at times, a bit snarky.

TP: I was initially drawn to writing horror for the sake of both fun and what always feels like genuine experimentation relative to other forms of writing, including so-called experimental fiction. There's something tremendously compelling in creating an alliance between such disparate modes of writing as the nouveau roman, for example, and horror. Have you generally felt unimpeded by tradition or stylistic convention when writing horror or are there particular constraints that inform how and what you write?

TK: When I hear the words "experimental fiction," I reach for my gun. I live among thousands of books, but have I ever read any experimental fiction? Beats me. Did I ever publish any in *Twilight Zone*? I doubt it. Have I ever dabbled in it myself? I don't believe so. I'm not even sure what it is.

TP: Your writing style comes across to this reader as effortlessly literary, by which I mean it pushes well beyond attempts to emulate Lovecraft or conventional, post-MFA writing that's peppered with the usual similes and attempts at hyper-realism, surrealism, or some kind of baroque arcana, etc. Rather, it seems to ride a fine line between exceptionally graceful, sophisticated prose and the grittiness that is more or less integral to horror. To quote the Ford interview again, you suggest that "a work of fiction is more than just a series of events set in such-and-such a time and place; it is also about language." What is it about your particular relationship to language that both sets it apart from others and has inclined you to give it voice in the horror genre?

TK: You're very kind, first of all. I only wish my writing were so effortless. It doesn't come easily at all, which is one reason I've done so little of it. You know, I've recently gone over the full text of *The Ceremonies* and two of the tales from *Dark Gods,* making hundreds of tweaks and small revisions, wincing (and occasionally cringing) at what struck me as embarrassingly clumsy writing. I hope I've improved it. I'm not sure exactly what it is that I'm after when it comes to style—certainly it never works out, on the page, the way I imagine it's going to—but I have to tell you, I've always been inspired, to the point of imitation, or at least attempted imitation, by the writers I most admire. And they're not necessarily writers in the genre.

TP: Just a comment here: I believe that reading horror alongside (or even behind) writers outside the genre is tremendously useful. Among the most fascinating parallels I've happened upon in this book is between "Petey" and T.S. Eliot's *The Cocktail Party*. The overlap is mostly to do with content, though the two texts can illuminate each other in very, very interesting ways.

TK: Thank you; I'm honored—though candidly, all I remember of *The Cocktail Party* is that, offstage, some woman ends up getting improbably crucified in Africa. Permit a free association. There's a scene in a Patrick White novel I read many decades ago in which an aging writer is leafing through his youthful notebooks and comes across an Eliot poem that, as a young man, he'd admiringly copied down, albeit without attribution. The old writer doesn't recognize the poem, takes it for one of his own, and thinks something like, "Gee, I really turned out some good stuff in those days."

TP: Well, despite the irony in this delightful and poignant example, and at the risk of overdoing the praise, I for one think that you've undoubtedly "turned out some good stuff." Regarding *The Cocktail Party,* perhaps where horror ends and where Eliot begins (thematically, that is) is where "Petey's" George gets what's coming to him and the crucified woman, and in yet another irony, locates redemption (albeit a painful one, to put it mildly) in the context of what is otherwise a drearily confused existence. Here's where your fiction really shines to me: in its ability to land the reader in some serious murk, cosmic or otherwise, and often on a rather dark note, without necessarily eschewing the value of humanity.

You are obviously a fan of cosmic horror, which often ends badly for protagonists, though you've also stated that you enjoy happy endings. Some critics have reacted negatively to what they perceive as a discrepancy here. What are your thoughts about this reaction, and more broadly, about what appears to be an underlying imperative or ideological position concerning the related notion of cosmic pessimism?

TK: Hmm, "cosmic pessimism" certainly sounds like the sort of philosophy I can subscribe to! (I wish it were otherwise.) But yes, I continue to prefer happy endings—as happy, at least, as the demands of the work will allow. Do you mention, in whatever precedes this interview, anything about my titling that little collection of mine *Reassuring Tales*?

I'm fond of something the late Robert Bloch once observed: that the fantasy genre is "one of the few areas left in which good can still triumph over evil. And that's one of the reasons, I'm afraid, why it's called fantasy."

TP: Oh yes! In fact, I look at "Well-Connected" as an example of your work that provides reassurance not only of being "snatched back from the abyss" but of the possibility of tenderness in the human experience (in this case, between a father and son). That said, it's impossible not to be aware of the title's irony, given certain of the collection's other stories. I suppose the difference between your vision and proponents of "cosmic pessimism" is that they don't seem to "wish it were otherwise." Rather, they come across as strangely and paradoxically religious about their adopted cosmology to the point of criticizing others who dare to allow for any semblance of optimism.

TK: Yes, interesting thought. It reminds me of a collaborative horror novel I read years ago by two young writers I'd published in *Twilight Zone,* John Skipp and Craig Spector. I don't recall the details, and I'm paraphrasing what follows, but something unexpectedly shocking and gruesome happens to one of the minor characters, and after describing the carnage, the authors remark, "God's funny that way."

Meanwhile, in the godless universe we actually inhabit, I'm convinced we have far too many "village atheists," despite the fact that I share their outlook. The late philosopher Sidney Hook used to say that though he himself was an atheist, he was not about to argue with a mother who, grieving for her dead son, found comfort in the thought that she would eventually be reunited with him in heaven.

TP: Laird Barron's controversial story "More Dark," a satire on the antinatalism of Thomas Ligotti and his followers, is quite caustic in its critique. You, too, have made critical remarks in the past regarding the general demographics of horror readers and, through your fiction, occultists. Is there anything that contemporary horror can do to productively counter the "fantasy, play-acting, and delusion" of "creeps," as the protagonist of "Nadelman's God" puts it, while maintaining the genre's intent to unsettle?

TK: Once again—forgive this refrain—I'm not entirely sure what you're asking. If you mean, is there some way of wresting supernatural horror from the goths and the occultists and their ilk, I'm not sure how we'd accomplish that, and I suppose I should hate to lose a portion of our audience. I must say I'm intrigued and amused by that type—by their earnestness—and a teeny bit contemptuous of them (okay, more than a teeny bit), and sometimes alarmed.

Going slightly off-topic for a moment, have you ever noticed that sports fans seem to have barely any interest in fantasy, and vice versa? That's certainly the case among friends of mine. (And sorry, whispering the phrase "fantasy football" is not an argument!)

I often go back, even today, to a remark a therapist once made, and which I quoted approvingly in "Nadelman": I was telling him about how a girl I knew believed she'd been a Pharaoh's mistress in a previous life—not a slave, mind you, but a Pharaoh's mistress, maybe even a Pharaoh—and how she'd walk out onto her apartment building's roof once a month to pay elaborate homage to the moon. And he nodded as if he'd heard it all before and said, "Reality is never enough for some people."

TP: I suppose my question is ultimately more about the genre than its readership. Of course, readers arguably inform a given genre as much as they are formed by it. While few writers or artists wish to alienate their audiences, I wonder if horror (and this takes us back to a number of points made above) is an appropriate or even necessary venue for engaging the "reality" that isn't sufficient for some, a project that has the capacity to disrupt certain identities or identifications, even and perhaps especially those that deem themselves marginal? In other words, perhaps horror, despite its supernatural components, is an especially effective mode of grounding one in "reality" that appears to care very little if at all about our precious egos. Would you agree with that?

TK: If you mean that a work of horror can serve as a reminder of the cruelty or at least indifference of the universe, I'd agree that it can. But then, unfortunately, so can many a history book.

VI. Reviews

Legion
by William Peter Blatty

It sounds promising enough, at first. Exactly twelve years after the events of *The Exorcist,* the Washington area is witness to a series of grisly occult murders, and the killer or killers may well be supernatural. Characters from the earlier novel are back in action, confronting the forces of darkness.

The first victim is a little black boy who delivers the *Washington Post;* he's found crucified to a pair of oars in the Georgetown University boathouse. Then a couple of local priests are polished off in an equally gruesome manner. It sounds as if we're in store for another horror blockbuster.

No such luck—for this time around Blatty has made a peculiar decision: He's chosen to tell his story from the point of view of a garrulous old police detective, Lieutenant William Kinderman, a veteran of forty-three years on the force. Kinderman played a supporting role in *The Exorcist,* but now, in a kind of fictive Peter Principle, he's been elevated to the position of central character.

And a more tedious character could scarcely be imagined. From the start, he displays little interest in the crimes he's supposed to be investigating; he's far more concerned with such theological problems as the existence of God, the problem of evil, and the nature of

---

Washington Post (July 4, 1983). Writers in newspapers generally aren't responsible for the titles of their pieces, and I remember cringing at the title the *Post* gave this one: "More Blather from Blatty."

the human soul. As a result, until the novel's final chapters, the events of the story take a backseat to Kinderman's interminable soliloquies on the Bible, quantum mechanics, electrons, the Neanderthal, elephants, chimpanzees, Shakespeare, Occam, Blake, Leopold and Loeb, genetic theory, quarks, neutrinos, Kafka, Teilhard de Chardin, B. F. Skinner, Darwin, Alfred Binet, and the role of the Prime Mover.

It's typical of the book that one of the first clues in the case—that two strands of hair match—is revealed only after we've been forced to sit through a meandering eight-page discussion on the Gnostics, angels, and the miracle of the autonomic nervous system.

That Blatty would rather write a novel of ideas than a horror novel seems a perfectly laudable ambition; *The Exorcist*, in fact, managed to be both, combining authentic chills, strong narrative drive, and a gripping presentation of such complex intellectual problems as catching the Prince of Lies in a contradiction and determining whether the main character was a victim of possession or merely psychosis. *Legion*'s philosophizing, however, is long-winded, intrusive, and, in light of the book's simple-minded supernatural ending, ultimately pointless. Worse, it's served to us, via Kinderman, in a singularly off-putting style, a mixture of Hollywood Yiddishisms (he describes God as "blithely *shtravansing* through the cosmos like some omnipotent Billie Burke"), literary name-dropping ("Kinderman thought of the passage by Plato . . ."; "He remembered 'Visions,' an essay by Jung . . ."; "He remembered a line from G. K. Chesterton . . ."), and a certain sour preachiness that I've always associated with Lee J. Cobb, the actor who played Kinderman in the 1973 film of *The Exorcist*. In the original novel, the lieutenant admitted of himself, "Schmaltz—that's the Kinderman method: pure schmaltz." He hasn't changed much in the intervening twelve years; if anything, his schmaltz quotient has increased.

The detective is, in short, a classic bore, and viewing the action through his baggy eyes tends to distance us from it. When, as the novel opens, we find him at the scene of the crime, he's busy musing about Beethoven, Gerard Manley Hopkins, and *The Brothers Karamazov*, and throughout the book he constantly interrupts the narrative to deliver monologues on whatever strikes his fancy. At the second murder, in which a priest has been decapitated in the confessional, the chapter opens on a similarly irrelevant note:

> The existence of life on earth was dependent on a certain pressure of the atmosphere. This pressure, in turn, was dependent on the constant operation of physical forces which in turn were dependent upon the earth's position in space which in turn was dependent upon a certain constitution of the universe. And what caused that? wondered Kinderman.

The old policeman's reverie is blessedly interrupted at this point, but a few lines later we're off on another detour: "Kinderman retreated into his thoughts. Was the universe eternal? Could be. Who knows?" He proceeds to spend most of the next three pages mulling over the divine game plan, and before the chapter's over he's unloading himself to Sergeant Atkins, his long-suffering assistant—"One more thing about evolution"—followed by four more pages on the subject ("As regarding this theory about the fish . . ."). Isaac Bashevis Singer routinely gets away with this sort of thing; with Blatty it just seems self-indulgent.

There is a plot, of sorts, hidden somewhere amid all the philosophizing. It's discovered that, though each of the murders is different, certain aspects of the modus operandi, including the severing of the victims' index fingers, ominously parallel that of a San Francisco psychopath called "the Gemini killer," who was believed shot to death back in 1971. And while Kinderman is busy grappling with the big questions, dimly in the background there are bodies piling up.

But you have to keep a sharp eye out for them, for speculations like this keep getting in the way:

> "What we see is only part of the spectrum," brooded Kinderman, "a tiny slot between the gamma rays and radio waves, a little fraction of the light that there is. . . . So when God said, 'Let there be light,'" he pondered, "it could be that He was really saying, 'Let there be reality.'"

In the face of such brooding and pondering, Atkins, we learn, "didn't know what to say."

Poor Atkins, in fact, is not a character at all, he's merely a foil for Kinderman, patiently listening to his monologues ("Consider Bell's law, Atkins: in any two-particle system, say the physicists . . .") and feeding him lines, on occasion, like a brown-nosing student at a college lecture. When Kinderman natters on—"He stared at the Kleenex box on his desk. 'Thalidomide cures leprosy,' he said absently. Abruptly he leaned forward toward Atkins. 'Have you any idea why the speed of light should be the top-limiting speed in the universe?'"—Atkins, the proper straight man, obediently asks, "No. Why?" When Atkins tries to interject a thought of his own, the old windbag interrupts with, "Wait, I'm not finished."

Even in the final scene, with Kinderman sitting in a White Castle still yakking ("You know, we talk about evil in this world and where it comes from. But how do we explain all the good?"), Atkins is made to say: "Would you do me a favor, Lieutenant? Would you please explain your theory?" Kinderman is, of course, only too glad to oblige, and as the novel ends, there's no sign he'll ever shut up: "The physicists now are all certain that all the known processes in nature were once part of a single, unified force . . ." He's a Yiddish Mr. Wizard.

In his own apparent eagerness to instruct us, Blatty has gone so far as to throw in a short allegorical dialogue about Creation, the kind of thing usually confined to obscure occult books. The dialogue comes in the form of that hoariest of devices, a dream, one in which Kinderman sees, so help me God, a big blue light exchanging theological chitchat with a little white light. ("In his mind he heard the light on the left begin to speak. 'I cannot help loving you,' it said. The other light made no answer.")

If Atkins is merely cardboard, Kinderman's relations with his own wife are cloyingly saccharine ("I think not, precious angel. . . . Hugs and kisses, darling dumpling"), and other characters in the novel emerge as little more than "cuts of meat in a supermarket cooler" (to use Thomas Disch's term for horror-tale victims trundled onstage merely to be butchered). A nurse we've barely met gets hers in a typically grisly little throwaway: "Her torso had been slit open, her organs removed, and her body—before being sewn back up—had been stuffed with light switches taken from a storeroom in the hospital basement."

Even one of the supposedly sympathetic characters, a survivor from the previous novel, is introduced mainly to be slaughtered, and though we're offered a few little hints ("Is it true the way he died? . . . And was he mutilated?"), the exact manner of his death is coyly withheld for a full thirty pages before we learn that the man's entire blood supply has been drained, without spilling a drop, into "twenty-two specimen jars arranged neatly in symmetrical rows." Clearly from the way they're presented, these deaths are intended to titillate.

Suddenly, in the book's closing pages, Blatty becomes all business, staging several confrontations between Kinderman and the killer during which, in another artificial device reminiscent of old detective films, the latter simply looks Kinderman in the eye and, in a brief lecture delivered with cool villainly hauteur, Explains All. ("Haven't you guessed it, Lieutenant? Why, of course you have. You've finally put it all together.") There's also a mildly dramatic scene in which Kinderman realizes his own family is in danger and ends up dashing home to save them. It's as if the author's realized, just before the end, that he has a responsibility to tell a story. Kinderman moves quickly for an old man; but for Blatty himself, it's much too late.

The Face That Must Die and *Incarnate* by Ramsey Campbell

Tales of violence and horror, it's said, offer readers a form of catharsis—and they evidently do the same for writers, judging from Ramsey Campbell's highly personal introduction to *The Face That Must Die,* a novel written, in part, from the point of view of a razor-wielding psychopath.

Campbell's introduction recounts with almost painful candor the bloody breakup of his parents' marriage, his father's sudden absence, his mother's descent into madness, and his own reaction to it all: "More than once I grew so frustrated that I ran at a wall of the room head first. I wasn't always sane myself." It's clear that writing a novel as savage as *Face* must have been, among other things, therapeutic—a kind of exorcism.

Not surprisingly, it proved a difficult book to sell. It appeared as a paperback in Britain in 1979, but here in America it was turned down by publisher after publisher; no doubt its protagonist was just too hateful and its violence too explicit. (One key scene graphically depicts a throat-slashing from the point of view of both killer and victim. Another intended victim has his face cut with a straight razor, the killer snarling, "I'll have his eye out in no time.")

Now, however, with the success of Campbell's more recent novels and his growing reputation as a horror writer's horror writer, a small California publishing house with the off-putting name

---

Washington Post Book World (November 20, 1983).

Scream/Press has brought out *Face* in what it calls "The Definitive Edition," complete with Campbell's introductory memoir, a rather innocuous chapter somehow deleted from the British paperback, and eighteen full-page illustrations by the photographer J. K. Potter. These last are, I think, a mistake; ordinarily Potter's work is imaginative and atmospheric, but here his images are lurid and downright crude, like publicity stills from some home-made splatter film.

Indeed, the book's central character—called, wonderfully, Horridge—makes a quintessential splatter-film villain. Crippled in mind and body, he limps through Liverpool like a sex-hating Savonarola with a particular horror of homosexuality, savoring his own cunning and justifying his murderous behavior with the twisted logic of a paranoid who reads dark things in people's faces and finds hidden meanings in every word and name. He's the sort of man who, on visiting a pub, soon convinces himself that government agents are spying on him from the telly by the bar. Listening to him run through the inevitable list of crank grievances—gays, blacks, snooping police, young layabouts, etc.—I couldn't help thinking of the title character of Keith Waterhouse's brilliant novel *Jubb,* which, two decades earlier, examined so many of the same obsessions but turned them into comedy.

Ironically, what's most disturbing about *Face* is not the violence—that, after all, is purveyed by any number of writers these days—but Campbell's unremittingly bleak view of humanity, one that will be familiar to admirers of his short stories. Repulsive and bloody-minded as Horridge is, he's much more fun to read about than any of the "normal" characters Campbell gives us, and he's no more unpleasant than Peter, nominally the book's hero, a selfish, shallow fellow perpetually absorbed in drugs, comic books, and Conan. Nobody ends up looking very attractive here.

Humanity fares little better in Campbell's new novel, *Incarnate.* The world appears to be populated by an army of rude barmaids, sneering bosses, nasty ticket clerks, callous teachers, brutal policemen, sadistic customs inspectors, bad-tempered neighbors, and various menacing strangers. Everyone seems sullen, angry, spoiling for a fight. Children are invariably mistreated or, at best, ignored. Even one's own unconscious can betray one.

It's this last danger that forms the basis of the novel. The extremely tangled plot concerns five disparate Londoners who, eleven years before, had participated in a rather vaguely described Oxford experiment in "prophetic dreaming." Recently, in their own individual ways, they've each begun to grow a little mad, and, unbeknownst to them, the unconscious material of their dreams has begun to take on tangible form: A mother begins lavishing affection on a strange, menacing little girl at the expense of her own daughter; a social worker finds herself playing hostess to a mysterious bedridden old woman; a sexually repressed, violence-prone male not unlike Horridge sees his secret spanking fantasies enacted on the television.

It's an annoying necessity in books of this type (and one Campbell handles with more finesse than anyone else I know) that, until the end, characters must be kept in ignorance of their own condition. For most of the way, therefore, the novel cuts back and forth among the five as their daily lives grow increasingly removed from reality. They never get in touch with one another, never answer letters, never simply sit down, compare notes, and talk about their fears; though two of the women meet by chance and become friends, even working in the same building, they fail to recognize each other. When at last they all do come together, we're treated to glimpses of various dream worlds (including a dream London) and are witness to a clash of wills between characters real and unreal, the latter mutating, merging, and recombining like putty. It's a scene reminiscent of *Altered States* and Machen's "Novel of the White Powder," and it's all pretty confusing.

But maybe that's the nature of the subject. Campbell has always been a skillfully impressionistic writer, locking us within his characters' distorted perceptions: "Headless men were queuing in the market, or dwarfs in coats too big for them, and then he saw they were empty coats, hanging on the wire mesh." In this book, however, the distortions affect entire chapters; a detailed scene in a police station goes on for pages, rich in dialogue and description, but is revealed several chapters later to have been "only a dream." The fact that such revelations inspire pleased surprise rather than irritation demonstrates the power of Campbell's spell.

The Suburbs of Hell
by Randolph Stow

"They could make a spooky film in Old Tornwich when it's foggy," remarks one of the town's inhabitants.

This is clearly a case of British understatement, for fog and spookiness appear to be two of the little East Anglian fishing village's major exports, along with chills (both atmospheric and literary), gloom, loneliness, and murder. Indeed, as depicted in Randolph Stow's novel, the town resembles the setting of some English film noir, complete with echoing cobblestones, dark waterways, and streetlamps casting long forbidding shadows. There's even a menacing intruder who arrives at the beginning of the novel: "Something ugly," says a frightened child who glimpses the figure stalking up a night-shrouded street. "A loony, I reckon. With an anorak with the hood pulled up, and underneath this mask, the worst I ever seen. And hands with hair on, and claws."

The reader rubs his own hands and settles down to what seems, at this point, a good old English thriller. And at first that's exactly what one gets: In short order three innocent people—a solitary young school teacher, a retired military man, and a good-hearted widow who tends Old Tornwich's lighthouse—are murdered, apparently at random, by an unseen gunman.

Fear spreads like a plague through the community, throwing the little town into, as one inhabitant says, "the buggeredest mud-

---

Washington Post Book World (August 19, 1984).

dle." Once-popular pubs suddenly stand empty. ("It's that outside Gents of mine," grumbles one publican. "Nobody dares risk a pee in case he gets shot.")

The villagers feel only slightly safer in their own homes. "When you think of your house, normally, you think of doors and windows that lock and walls that are solid," says one. "But suddenly you find yourself thinking about windowpanes that break and bolts that don't hold and smugglers' tunnels into the cellar."

Throughout this reign of terror, Old Tornwich seems so cut off from the modern world, so much a separate universe, that one is jarred by the occasional references to current television shows, the tabloid *News of the World,* and once, dimly seen, some teenagers playing electronic games.

The authorities, too, remain conveniently out of the picture. Though we hear, in passing, that all the local men have been fingerprinted, the town never swarms with the crowds of police and newsmen that such crimes would attract in real life. Still, it's an omission sanctified by literary convention; similar liberties are routinely taken in almost all novels of this sort, in which small, isolated communities are the scenes of multiple murders.

The ones in Old Tornwich bring out the worst in its populace—and ultimately lead to more violence. Neighbor suspects neighbor, racial prejudices surface (the local taxi driver is a black man), seamy crimes are brought to light, and before the book is through, the surviving characters fall prey to madness, suicide, and new murders, until one by one, as in Agatha Christie's *Ten Little Indians,* they're eliminated. Warily the reader waits for the original killer to show his hand, but as the bodies continue to mount up, the list of suspects dwindles, and the book's relentless grimness—unrelieved by a trace of humor, sex, or joy, and with only an occasional hint of pity for the poor doomed victims—begins to take its toll. So does the Suffolk dialect: "Frank fink he knows somefing," we read. "There int nofing goonna happen to you. . . . Thass all over, monfs agoo." And, "Fanks for everfing, Harry."

Soon one finds oneself waiting impatiently for the next hapless character to bite the dust and looking forward to the novel's conclusion, where in time-honored fashion the author can be counted on to supply the necessary explanations, the revelation of the culprit's name, the ruses, tricks, and modus operandi. When someone in the book declares, "I'm sure there is a motive to be found, however mad it must be. . . . There must be some reason, some connection that makes sense," the reader silently agrees.

But that connection never comes, for writing a standard whodunit isn't Stow's intention; unfortunately for us, he is far more ambitious than that. Like Doris Lessing, who's lately turned to writing political parables disguised as science fiction (to the dismay of SF fans and many of her own); like John Fuller, whose recent *Flying to Nowhere* gave us a *Name of the Rose*–like historical mystery that ultimately petered out into metaphysical mystification; and like his fellow Australian, novelist Joan Lindsay, whose *Picnic at Hanging Rock* chronicled a community's reactions to a mysterious disappearance that remained, at the end, unsolved, Stow has written a novel that masquerades as a murder mystery but which is in fact a parable on (and the capitals seem called for) The Human Condition, The Fallibility of Man, and the Supremacy of Death.

The loftiness of his intentions is made painfully clear in the one-or-two-page interludes that alternate with his main chapters. They are written in the voice of a curiously omniscient narrator who may or may not be the murderer, in a style so oblique as to become, at one point, almost incomprehensible, leaving the reader unsure whether he's just read about a homicide or a daydream. Each of these mini-chapters is preceded by a portentous epigraph from some classic English work from *Beowulf* to *Titus Andronicus*. (The title itself comes from Webster's *Duchess of Malfi:* "Security some men call the suburbs of hell, / Only a dead wall between.")

Woe to anyone who picks up *Suburbs* expecting to find a neat, buttoned-down little crime puzzler. Forget convincing motives; forget, for the most part, sympathetic characters; forget the pleasures of ratiocination. And don't expect a sensible, satisfying ending with the mystery neatly solved. On the final page, when the narrator's identity is revealed, the reader may be moved, or he may feel, as I did, that he has been the victim of an elaborate literary joke.

More Books

Shortly after putting the world on notice, in the July/August *TZ*, that "the two best novels ever written about childhood" were undoubtedly Booth Tarkington's *Penrod* and Steven Millhauser's *Edwin Mullhouse,* I received an odd-looking package from Phil Zuckerman, president of Applewood Books (Box 2870, Cambridge, MA 02139), containing five slim, brightly colored paperbacks, and a brief note—"Please add these books to your list"—and an equally brief postscript: "They're a little like Jerome K. Jerome."

The books were the first five installments of a "serial novel"—a breed you probably thought had died with Dickens—whose full title is *The Personal History, Adventures, Experiences & Observations of Peter Leroy*. The author, Eric Kraft, is a transplanted Long Islander now living in Newburyport, and *Peter Leroy* is his fictionalized autobiography. (His hometown of Babylon appears as "Babbington," Clam Capital of the Western World.) As the full title suggests, Kraft's tale is whimsical, cozy, old-fashioned (despite, as Peter moves through boyhood, the growing presence of sex)—and, yes, it *is* a little like Jerome K. Jerome. It's also like a cross between James Thurber and that fat new book ". . . *And the Ladies of the Club,"* recounting family anecdotes and small-town gossip with humor and affection—though not without a sigh for times gone by.

The *Peter Leroy* series, which comes out four times a year, began in 1982 with *My Mother Takes a Tumble* and is now up to book #8,

---

Twilight Zone (December 1984).

Call Me Larry. Each title, at 96 pages, sells for $4.95, but one can subscribe to four books for $16 or to eight for $30. Neat idea.

Here's another: *The Psychotronic Encyclopedia of Film* (Ballantine, $15.95), a fact-packed 815-page paperback guide to B-movies (and some a good deal farther down the alphabet) by Michael Weldon, assisted by Charles Beesley, Akira Fitton, and *Fangoria*'s own Bob Martin. "Psychotronic," says Weldon, "was originally meant to suggest a combination of weird horror films and electronic gadget-filled science fiction movies. I thought I'd made it up, but later it turned out I'd stolen it from *The Psychotronic Man,* a Chicago-made film about a maniac barber who kills people with psychic energy."

Weldon's book surveys, in capsule form, more than three thousand such epics ("exploitation films of any sort, really," he explains: "biker movies, rock 'n' roll movies, musclemen movies, 3-D movies, '60s beach movies, Mexican movies with subtitles—you get the idea"), from *Abbott and Costello Go to Mars* to *Zontar, The Thing from Venus* and *Zotz!* ("Plastic *Zotz* coins were given to the first theater patrons.") Most of these titles aren't listed in standard guides like Leonard Maltin's frequently updated *TV Movies* (NAL, $4.95). Maltin's book is still the better value, covering four times the number of films at a third the price, but Weldon's makes a nice companion volume.

Capsule descriptions are okay when you're looking up cast members during a commercial, but for really thorough coverage of the genre classics, I recommend Bill Warren's *Keep Watching the Skies!, Volume 1* (McFarland & Co., Box 611, Jefferson, NC 28640), a highly opinionated in-depth guide to SF films from 1950 to '57. The price is an outrageous $39.95 (maybe someone will have the good sense to bring it out in paperback), but for this you—or your rich friend—will get more critical insights, more entertaining personal observations, and more sheer information than you'll find anywhere else on movies such as *Them!* ("In the original prints, the titles . . . were printed in a vivid red and blue, the only instance of color titles in a black-and-white film that I have ever encountered"), *The Neanderthal Man* (whose facial makeup keeps changing, "as if different artists worked each day"), and *Voodoo Woman.* Though he dismisses this little gem as "one of the worst movies ever made," he's generous in quoting from its script. ("They mocked me, Chaka. They call me crazy. I could not tamper with nature, my colleagues said," etc.)* An appendix lists, by title, dozens of films announced but never made, some of which sound as if they'd be surefire Gold Turkey nominees (*Around the Earth in 90 Minutes, The Girl from Two Million A.D., I Buried the Devil, Snuffy Smith's Rocket Ship*).

Warren devotes nearly four pages to that strange Lovecraftian frog-man movie *The Maze* ("Either you find the story interesting if incredible, or you find it boring and ludicrous"), quotes extensively from the script (I'm told John Landis had a hand in supplying Warren with archive material), provides a rare photograph of the film's pathetic-looking frog creature, delivers commonsensical judgments on the often illogical script, and concludes on just the right affectionate note: "For those with an exotic sense of sympathy, the ending of this rather grotesque little film can be surprisingly moving." So is this book; I eagerly await Volume 2.

Speaking of Lovecraft, his hardcover publisher, Arkham House of Sauk City, Wisconsin, is busily preparing corrected editions of the master's fiction under the direction of Lovecraft scholar S. T. Joshi (*TZ* July/August '83), who—as Joyce scholars have done with *Ulysses*—has gone back to HPL's original manuscripts and discovered hundreds of errors in the standard printed text. Meanwhile, Arkham House collectors can take inventory with Sheldon Jaffery's *Horrors and Unpleasantries* (Bowling Green University, $7.95 paper, $14.95 cloth), subtitled "A Bibliographical History & Collector's Price Guide to Arkham House." The prices are rather shocking; it appears that books I bought for three dollars at Dana's dusty little bookshop on Weybosset Street in Providence are now fetching $125.

Needless to say, Jaffery is himself an Arkham House collector and understands "the suspicion that someone, somewhere, has a copy for sale for just a few dollars less than you paid." The one thing

---

*Notwithstanding the corniness of the dialogue, the cheapness of the sets, and the schlockiness of the monster suit created and worn by Paul Blaisdell, when I saw *Voodoo Woman* at age nine, on a double bill with *The Undead*, it was the scariest movie I'd ever seen.

his bibliography lacks, mysteriously, is a contents list for each book; we get pages of publishing history, but never learn what stories are included. The book does have, like Warren's, an appendix listing projects that never materialized, including an untitled collection of Robert Heinlein's fiction and an illustrated edition of William Hope Hodgson's *The House on the Borderland*. Sigh!

The Glamour
by Christopher Priest

Any editor of a genre magazine knows that stories tend to fall into familiar types. As the editor, until recently, of a magazine specializing in supernatural fantasy, I found that one of our most frequent submissions was of a type I called the Poor Misunderstood Paranormal. Most commonly the work of teenaged girls, it had as its heroine a lonely, sensitive social outcast who, unbeknownst to her family and schoolmates, secretly possessed some sort of wonderful supernatural power which set her apart from the rest of humanity.

The heroine of *The Glamour,* Susan Kewley, is a variation on this type. She's a young Londoner with the unsettling ability to turn herself invisible at will. Well, not exactly invisible: She's there just like the rest of us, casting a shadow, reflected in mirrors. You simply tend not to *notice* her—or her shadow, her reflection, or even her voice. If she stood next to you and poked you in the stomach, you'd probably wince and take some Pepto-Bismol, wondering what you'd had for lunch. If she were occupying the only remaining seat at the theater, you'd probably decide you didn't want to sit there, without quite knowing why.

As such, Susan's strange gift may remind readers less of Scottish folk tradition (a "glamour" was originally a magic spell or enchantment) than of The Shadow, who had the power "to cloud men's

---

Washington Post Book World (July 7, 1985).

minds." Indeed, when *The Glamour*'s heroine wishes to sink into invisibility, she does so by "thickening the cloud" that surrounds her.

Being "an invisible" has plenty of rewards. There's no need to pay for beer or cigarettes or the choicest merchandise from Selfridges. You can ride the London underground for free or travel the world, wherever you please; dine at the fanciest restaurants (simply pick the food right off the tray—no one will recall where it's disappeared); help yourself to money from banks; yawn in boring people's faces; stroll into strange houses and see the inhabitants naked. You never even have to flush the toilet. Best of all, you belong to an elite fraternity of fellow invisibles, a roving, lawless breed who, like gypsies, wander rowdily through London (and, presumably, other cities as well), camp in various department stores, and hang out at "a particular pub" (alas, unnamed) where "glams" congregate, invisible to everyone but themselves.

It's an intriguing notion, and in other hands it might have been good fun. Fun, however, seems the last thing a serious-minded writer like Christopher Priest has in mind. Priest is a fiercely intense young Englishman once identified with science fiction's experimental New Wave, and it's as if, like a certain film director once described by critic Andrew Sarris, he "considers himself too intellectual to tell a story." For some reason Priest has chosen to write *The Glamour* in a style as flat and colorless as a courtroom affidavit, where a sanitarium has "good food" and "attractive stands of deciduous trees," a psychiatrist's office is "a comfortable place with big leather chairs and a bookcase," a French hotel room has "a large window" and "a pleasant view," mosquitoes whine "unpleasantly," a key character is described as "a pleasant-looking middle-aged woman," and an entire metropolis is summed up this way: "Dijon was a crowded, busy city, with some kind of business convention going on." In the space of just two pages we are told that a male character, encountering Susan, "found her attractive" and "found her company very attractive," and that "she had an attractive body." There may be a logical reason why Priest's hard-to-see heroine should be referred to simply as "a young woman of medium height and build" who "lacked distinctive features," but it's deadly when everything else is described in the same bland tone— including the novel's hero, appropriately named Richard Grey.

Ostensibly a "normal" or, in the invisibles' parlance, a "flesher," Richard is in fact a pretty fleshless character. He's supposed to be suffering from amnesia after having been caught in an IRA bomb blast, but the "feeling of blankness" that troubles him seems nothing but a literary device. Though we're told of a lengthy series of operations he's supposed to have undergone, his pain never becomes real; when we meet him, he's just a melancholy, self-absorbed soul sitting picturesquely in a wheelchair. We're informed that he's been an internationally renowned news cameraman and that Susan is a freelance illustrator, yet these occupations seem little more than means of explaining how the two pay their rent; Richard's entire career is hurried through in several thin anecdotes, Susan's in a few lines. It's suggested that Richard himself may be a latent invisible ("He's only incipiently glamorous," says one observer), but Priest prefers to leave the truth ambiguous.

Until its final pages, in fact, this novel's only references to the real and the specific are limited, mysteriously, to a travelogue-like list of French cities and the names of various French restaurants, whose specialties are somewhat preciously recorded in italics, right down to a "plate of salted *bretzels*," along with the price of a dinner in New Francs and Old. Perhaps the author is simply commemorating the high points of his last vacation.

Equally mystifying is why Priest has elected to narrate the events of the novel from a variety of logically conflicting points of view: Richard's, Susan's, and finally that of Niall, Susan's former lover, a rather nasty would-be writer whose glamour is so highly developed that he can make himself invisible even to Susan herself. Their respective accounts contradict one another—Richard describes how he met Susan while traveling through France, only to have Susan tell us that she's never been abroad—so that the reader has the dubious pleasure of learning, after one 60-page section, that everything he's just read is merely the product of a character's imagination and that another lengthy episode may be no more than "a half-remembered dream."

Priest would have us believe that this deliberate confusion merely illustrates "the muddle of reality," and in his final pages, perhaps aware of how his games may have tried the reader's patience, he justifies them with some last-minute philosophizing. ("We are all fictions," Niall solemnly declares, "—you, Susan, to a lesser extent myself.") But latter-day *Rashomon*s are no longer a novelty, Marienbad has already been explored, and I suspect that most of us have had our fill of characters in a novel who discover that they're actually characters in a novel. When, at the end, Niall's long-hinted-at manuscript turns out to be the opening pages of *The Glamour,* the only surprise is that a writer of Priest's ability would stoop to so old and familiar a dodge.

Collected Stories
by Ruth Rendell

In one of her tales, "A Needle for the Devil," Ruth Rendell introduces a minor character who makes his living writing detective novels. He's forever stumbling upon ingenious—and undetectable—methods of dispatching his fictional victims, such as by means of a type of rat poison that, he explains, "inhibits the clotting of the blood. . . . If I were going to use that method in a book, I'd have the murderer give his victim warfarin plus a strong sedative. Then a small cut, say to the wrist . . ." Later he muses over a botany book: "It says here that the skunk cabbage, whatever that may be, contains irritant crystals of calcium oxalate. If you eat the stuff the inside of your mouth swells up and you die because you can't breathe."

Clearly Ruth Rendell is poking fun at herself as well as at her mystery-writing peers, for in another story—one involving her favorite sleuth, Chief Inspector Wexford—the solution to a murder hinges upon the toxic properties of two similar-looking mushrooms, *Amanita phalloides* and *Coprinus comatus;* we're even given a detailed extract on the latter (whether real or fictitious I don't know) from *British Fungi, Edible and Poisonous*. What's more, in "A Needle for the Devil," a friend of the detective novelist is so taken with his recommended method of execution that she uses it to murder her husband.

Washington Post Book World (May 15, 1988).

The murder of a spouse, often by some similarly contrived means, is something of a staple in these thirty-eight stories, reprinted from Rendell's previous four collections. And if it isn't a wife or husband who gets killed, it's a fiancée, or an ex-lover, or a secret rival. Indeed, the book is pervaded by an air of unrelieved doom, a sense that, given any pair of human beings, murder is inevitable.

Perhaps that's only as it should be in a collection such as this, but it makes for a certain numbing sameness. No sooner does a vacationing couple go for a drive in the African veldt in "The Fever Tree" than we learn, without surprise, that he's toying with the idea of killing her. No sooner do the squabbling couple in "The Fall of a Coin" check into their hotel than there's a hint of foul play in the air. ("I'll never divorce you. You've got me till death parts us. Till death, James.") Even in the bosom of a supposedly happy marriage lie thoughts of murder. In "Front Seat," a seemingly fond husband falls prey to homicidal fantasies: "Hugh thought about men who had murdered their wives, and how much easier it must have been when you could get wasp killer made out of cyanide and weed killer made of arsenic." In "Hare's House," all it takes is the periodic crash of a faulty bathroom window to drive one "apparently happy couple" to murder and another to assault.

It's not an especially encouraging vision of matrimony; nor is it an especially persuasive one. These people are, by and large, stock figures, Dagwood and Blondie gone homicidal, like the couple in "A Needle for the Devil," who fall to blows because he doesn't like the sound of her knitting. At best, it's a worldview one associates with pulp detective magazines and with TV shows like *Alfred Hitchcock Presents:* a world of gimmicky murders, populated by an all-too-familiar cast of characters—resentful spinsters, spurned wives, tyrannical bosses, mousy accountants, and heartless Don Juans.

Of all her characters, the one that appears with the most monotonous regularity is that of the shrew. In fact, one of the most striking features of these tales is their misogyny. When a husband cheats, it's because his wife is loveless and frigid; when a wife cheats, it's because she's a tramp.

And when Rendell's females are bad, they are bad beyond the point of caricature. The murderously jealous spinster in "The Venus Fly Trap," the faithless young wife in "A Case of Coincidence," the vindictive, backbiting wife in "The Fall of a Coin," the cold adulterous mother in "The Vinegar Mother," the nagging suffocating mother in "The Fallen Curtain," the neurotic would-be suicide in "The Clinging Woman," the scheming would-be heiress in "Thornapple" who has a fancy for poisons, the gluttonous date in "Bribery and Corruption" who actually passes out and drools—all these women are cartoons etched in acid; they never open their mouths except to damn themselves. One knows they're not to be trusted because they snarl when they're crossed, speak of men as "those brutes," and call other women "my dear."

In fact, one knows too much about these stories from the very first page. They all have "surprise" endings; I put that in quotes because, after reading enough of them, one learns what sort of surprise to expect, and sometimes even the details. Rendell also has a fondness for poetic irony of the most facile sort (her characters have a way of being done in by exactly the means they hoped to do in someone else), and she seems to have taken too much to heart the old theatrical axiom about never showing a gun in the first act that won't be used in the last; story after story drops a clue in the beginning—a dangerous gas meter, a lost blazer button, the fact that a character has bad eyesight or that another has a luxuriant head of hair—that one knows is going to figure in the end.

Sometimes, in fact, the axiom is taken literally. In "The Orchard Walls," set in rabbit-hunting country, we hear "the occasional sound of a shot" on the second page, and from that point on we know that someone's got to die. Once again our expectation proves correct—but not for ten long pages.

I'd have been grateful for some personal note at the start of this book, an introductory word or two about the stories' backgrounds, Rendell's intentions, or her feelings about rereading her own early work. But *Collected Stories* lacks an introduction, almost as if the author didn't care to sit down after all these years and read the stories through. Having done so myself, I think I can understand why.

The Terrors of Ice and Darkness
by Christoph Ransmayr

Whether or not truth is stranger than fiction, it's certainly stranger than Christoph Ransmayr's fiction. In *The Terrors of Ice and Darkness,* this Austrian writer has attempted to combine the two, cobbling together the documentary account of an actual nineteenth-century Arctic journey, the Austro-Hungarian North Pole Expedition, and the story of an imaginary twentieth-century traveler who sets out to follow in its frozen footsteps.

The resulting hybrid is billed as "a novel," but it's really two separate works, a novel and a history book, uneasily coexisting in alternate chapters between the same covers. The true-life chapters, complete with illustrations, photographs, and lengthy quotations from the actual explorers' diaries, letters, and memoirs, are moving, frequently horrifying in the manner of all good tales of exploration, and capable of causing a perceptible chill, even with the temperature 102 degrees outside, while the modern-day fictional chapters are tedious and unconvincing—overwhelmed by the power of the factual.

The real-life expedition, consisting of twenty-four men, mostly Italians and Austrians, set sail from Norway in July of 1872, under the command of two brave and brainy Austrian officers, Julius von

---

Washington Post Book World (August 11, 1991). This time the *Post*'s title was perfect: "The Snows of Yesteryear."

Payer and Karl Weyprecht (whom the book mysteriously insists on calling "Carl"), in the hope of finding a Northeast Passage through the Arctic Ocean to the Orient.

In this quest the voyagers failed, as had centuries of voyagers before them; but they successfully realized their second stated goal, "to explore the seas or lands to the northeast of Novaya Zemlya," two immense snow-covered islands off the northern coast of Russia visited only (and only in the summer) by whalers and seal hunters.

Their mode of exploration was a peculiarly passive one, for by the winter of 1872 their ship had become frozen fast in the middle of a titanic ice floe, leaving the crewmen prey to cold, madness, and scurvy on a sort of vast, sunless prison drifting slowly through the Arctic waters. In the spring of 1874, after more than a year of futile attempts to extricate it, the ship was finally abandoned, the half-starved men and sled dogs hauling its four massive lifeboats over miles of floating ice—but not before the wandering floe, coming to rest against a rocky coastline, had allowed them to make an important discovery: the northernmost body of land in the Eastern Hemisphere, Franz Josef Land.

Despite the grandness of its name (and Weyprecht's initial expectations), it was merely a small, ice-bound archipelago of some seventy barren little islands at around 82 degrees north latitude. But to the men of the expedition, so long adrift, the place was the fulfillment of a dream: "Wild and impetuous with excitement," wrote Payer, "we scrambled and leapt across the towering waves of ice . . . toward land, and when we surmounted its icy pedestal and actually set foot upon it, we did not see that only snow, rocks, and frozen debris surrounded us and that there could be no more dreary land on earth than the island upon which we stood. For us it was a paradise."

The book is at its best when, drawing upon the actual diaries of Weyprecht, Payer, and several members of the crew, it makes clear why so bleak a landscape might nonetheless seem welcome. We read of frozen limbs, of pervasive melancholy, and of gums so rotten with scurvy that they had to be cut off with scissors; of endless ice in all directions, clear to the horizon, and of polar air "so filled with snow that a man can breathe only with his back turned."

The expedition leaders' old-fashioned prose can sometimes turn quite purple (though it seems a forgivable fault when one is describing the aurora borealis), and the book's flow is occasionally broken by interludes of potted polar history that read as if they'd come straight from an encyclopedia; but the day-to-day account of the journey itself is a compelling one, vividly confirming the great Norwegian explorer Roald Amundsen's observation, quoted in the book, that "voyages of discovery are often no more than a race against time in the hope of escaping starvation."

By contrast, the chapters chronicling the travels of Ransmayr's modern-day hero, Josef Mazzini, seem artificial and contrived; one turns to them with a sinking heart, for the character never becomes more than a literary construct, an annoying stand-in, one assumes, for the author himself. Mazzini is a short-story writer, we're told, and a great-great-nephew of one of the Italians on the 1872 expedition. He becomes obsessed with that historic voyage because, in an effort to make the outlandish events in his own tales seem less improbable, he's "pushed the characters in his fantasies ever northward, to arrive at last in a place where not even Eskimos lived—the pack ice of the pole."

Discovering a volume on the expedition in an antiquarian bookshop, he's struck by how closely its story matches his own work: "He believed he had found in Payer's account a 'proof' for one of his own invented adventures."

This flimsy device gives Ransmayr the chance to fly his hero up into the Arctic, where he sails on a modern-day icebreaker, meets a lot of garrulous Norwegians no doubt based on people the author himself has met, learns to drive a dog sled, and eventually, like a bad idea, vanishes forever into the frozen wastes.

Bring Me Children
by David Martin

Thanks to a certain similarity in their villains, David Martin's *Bring Me Children* will inevitably be compared to *The Silence of the Lambs*. But while any comparison to the Thomas Harris bestseller should work to *Children*'s commercial advantage, I suspect that few readers are going to be pressing this book upon friends or eagerly awaiting a sequel. It's a fast read and generates, at first, some genuine suspense; but unlike Harris's *Lambs* and *Red Dragon,* which have characters of endearing humanity and moments of sublime horror, *Children* is, at bottom, a nasty piece of work.

Martin's villain is named Mason Quinndell, and if he's not exactly a Hannibal Lecter, one suspects it's not for want of trying. Like Lecter, he's a man of medicine—a wealthy West Virginia physician. He's suave and refined; he's also a serial killer, a sadistic butcher who enjoys dismembering his screaming victims as they lie strapped to an examining table. (Another peccadillo of his: leaving unwanted babies in a cave to die.) Quinndell, unlike Lecter, has been blind for several years; along with cutting limbs off, he likes to scoop his victims' eyes out with a spoon, more or less in an attempt to even the score. But he's every inch the Lecter wannabe in his aristocratic manner, his cruel wit, his keenly developed olfactory sense (especially where women are concerned), and his penchant

---

Washington Post (August 11, 1992).

for sneering at intellectual inferiors. "How wonderfully minimalist," he purrs, on discovering that the tombstone of an enemy bears only a name and the dates of birth and death.

That's the way he talks—like a cross between Anthony Hopkins and William Buckley, with "a honeyed voice . . . almost theatrical in its resonance, and cultured in the fashion of a courtly Southern gentleman." When, late one Saturday night, he rings upstairs for a hapless hireling named Mary Aurora and she makes the mistake of cursing at him in annoyance, the language in which he rebukes her is so mannered that one almost pictures Buckley's haughty grin and fluttering eyelids:

"Pray tell, to whom were you addressing that statement . . . hmm?"

When she protests that she was "half-asleep" and didn't know what she was saying, he replies that this "wounds me all the more deeply. . . . Your low opinion of me is apparently so ingrained that even when you're not fully conscious, you immediately brand me with that coarse and most common epithet—is my assessment correct?"

Later, forcing himself on Mary from behind, Quinndell lays a victim's eyeball on the small of her back and jokes, "Henry will be keeping his eye on you."

It's clear that, in sheer satanic villainy, the doctor is a bit over the top. But so are most of the other grotesques that populate this Southern Gothic tale, including a reclusive, bulb-headed backwoods dwarf who, while plainly retarded, has nonetheless amassed and read a library of do-it-yourself books; a coal-black heroine who, at twenty-six, is a professor of folklore at NYU, practices voodoo, and shows up naked in a coffin at the hero's cabin in order to make a memorable first impression ("I had to find a way to *insert* myself in your life," she explains); and a moronic, vicious 435-pound sheriff's deputy who sweats, drools, and actually goes *"har har"* when he laughs.

In contrast to these improbable but generally colorful characters, the style of the narrative itself is dishwater-thin, for the book is written in the flat, unadorned present tense of a movie script, with only the sketchiest attempt at scene-setting and no trace of atmosphere. Here's the hero, an out-of-work TV newsman, wandering around his wilderness cabin:

> He steps into the kitchen, searches through the crate for documents or messages (finding none), and tries to get a drink of water at the kitchen tap but of course the electricity is still off. The taste in Lyon's mouth is so horrible that he keeps fighting the urge to swallow.
>
> He returns to the bedroom and stands by the bed looking down at the young woman who appears now just as she did in the crate, peacefully asleep. He takes her pulse again and has just put his hand to the side of her face to check for a fever when he is startled by the overhead light coming on.

There's nothing here to quicken *our* pulse. The writing is all surface, merely chronicling the action.

Or try this for bare-bones scene-setting: "They drive off the mountain and to a state highway, which they travel for half an hour before turning onto a blacktopped road, then a dusty, rutted lane." Or this: "They are parked in the driveway of a simple one-story house in need of paint. No other houses in sight. The yard is overgrown." That's all the description we get; one half expects to come upon "DISSOLVE TO . . ."

In a sense, though, Martin's telegraphic approach may be a virtue: *Bring Me Children* may not work very well as a novel, but a screenwriter should have little trouble adapting it for the movies. And one suspects that this was the author's intention from the start.

A Curate's Egg

DERMOT CHESSON SPENCE. *Little Red Shoes and Other Tales of the Odd and Unseen*. London: Ghost Story Press, 1995. 252 pp.

To describe something as resembling "the curate's egg" is to use an English expression not generally known in America (nor even in England these days, I suspect, except among the hopelessly bookish). Its origin is a *Punch* cartoon of a century ago in which a timid clergyman, dining at a bishop's and asked if he is enjoying his egg, nervously assures his host that "parts of it are excellent."

The point of the joke, of course, is that the egg is a bad one, and that the clergyman's words are faint praise indeed. As the phrase is actually used, however—when, for example, a reviewer refers to some book, play, or exhibition as "a bit of a curate's egg"—what is meant is simply "good in parts"; and it is that more complimentary sense that best applies to *Little Red Shoes,* an English ghost-story collection first published in 1937. Parts of it—in fact, parts of nearly every one of the book's nineteen stories—are excellent, for Spence is an extremely clever writer; but there is no story that entirely succeeds in moving us, or even (a less exalted goal) in scaring us.

Maybe Spence's heart just wasn't in it; that, at least, is the impression left by the introduction that Keith Spence, the author's son, has contributed to the present edition. (It is, incidentally, the model of what an affectionate personal introduction should be:

Necrofile: The Review of Horror Fiction (Spring 1997).

filled with telling biographical detail, psychologically insightful without sounding academic, sympathetic yet not blind to the author's failings. I found it considerably more interesting than the stories themselves.)

Raised by wealthy adoptive parents in the Lake District in what his son calls "a doggy, hunting-shooting-and-fishing environment," educated at Winchester and Oxford, Dermot Chesson Spence (1904–1966) appears to have been something of a gentlemanly dilettante who preferred light verse to horror. Clearly he had his dark side, and, judging from a few of these tales, perhaps darker than most, but he emerges in his son's reminiscence as an affable, witty, pipe-smoking type who enjoyed gardening, crossword puzzles, and daily walks to the pub—in short, clubbable (in the manner of the Garrick Club, not of baby seals). A photo at the front of the book shows a prosperous-looking middle-aged man in glasses, tie, and tweedy jacket. Aside from wartime military service (most of it safely in England), he spent his career in various areas of the British publishing industry, with several years as the partner of literary agent Christine Campbell Thomson, who first brought Spence's work to public attention when she included "Little Red Shoes" in *Nightmares by Daylight* (1936), one of the volumes in her popular *Not at Night* series. The present collection, brought out a year later when Spence was thirty-three, was his first published book and remains his only book of prose (though its stories are sandwiched between two poems, both of them describing haunted houses). It was followed by five books of poetry, the last appearing in 1943; then the books stopped.

"My father might be described as a disappointed man, who never realised his early brilliant potential," writes Keith Spence. "Christine Campbell Thomson felt that his approach was rather too frivolous: 'He had a great number of interests and I don't think he ever applied himself with sufficient energy to the business of writing.' I would rather say that he was born in the wrong century; he should have lived at a time when the ability to turn out light verse at the drop of a hat was highly prized."

Little Red Shoes is dedicated "to my predecessors and superiors, Fryn Tennyson Jesse [Spence's aunt, author of the crime novel *A*

Pin to See the Peep Show], Montague Rhodes James, and William Hope Hodgson in humble emulation." I don't see much of Hodgson in these tales; while their central concern—the traditional one of a person or place haunted by some vengeful malevolent spirit—may owe something to Hodgson's Carnacki stories, Spence's writing is far more supple and sophisticated, with little of Hodgson's crude power.

The M. R. James influence seems clearer, especially in stories such as "The Dean's Bargain," about a still-potent curse found inscribed in an old Bible. Ancient maledictions figure in other tales as well, along with sinister ancestors and cryptic warnings written in Latin. As in James, characters witness monstrous things and are never again quite right in the head.

Lovingly described country houses provide the tales' most frequent settings, complete with portrait galleries, antique furniture, leaded windows, secret sliding wall-panels, and dusty libraries where searchers may discover, as James put it, "papers shut up in old books."

In James' work, however, the wry, reflective "I" who introduces most of the tales is a retiring fellow, presumably the author himself, who stands well apart from the action; he serves, with few exceptions, as a mere storyteller. Spence's narrators—more active and virile than James' stuffy antiquarians—tend to participate fully in the plots, sometimes as heroes, sometimes as horrified observers. Occasionally one may sound stilted and old-fashioned ("I was not too keen to resume my close acquaintance with the bare face of terror," says one, in the title story, "and I went early to bed to rake in my arrears of sleep"), but more frequently they adopt a breezy modern tone that is at odds with the traditional subject matter. The aristocratic narrator of "Wymondley" delights in what he calls "the tales of lechery and treachery" handed down from previous generations, and describes one particularly disreputable sixteenth-century ancestor as "a bad man, but we were proud of him in our way—he was such a great discredit to the family." Another, in "The Master of Lostwick Hall," demands of his hostess, "Look, Mrs. Brownlow. This is all too hysterical and out of Edgar Allan Poe. Is the woman a witch, or what?"

And here is another departure from James: for women, in fact, take center stage in many of these stories, most of which contain at least a hint of sex. When the young bachelor narrator of "Little Red Shoes" inherits a country estate, his eye is immediately drawn to the "buxom good looks" of the serving girls—not the sort of thing one of James' heroes would be likely to have noticed. The narrator of "Does She Want Help?" is strolling down a moonlit street when a girl steps out of a distant doorway and waves to him in distress; chivalrously he goes to her aid. "Besides," he admits, "despite her chalk-white face, I could see that she was a dashed pretty girl."

"Little Annabell" tells of a fourteen-year-old orphan who, after years of sadistic mistreatment by her "scientist" uncle ("There was one apparatus of blackened leather into which she used to be strapped and swung"), has burnt him up in his laboratory. Overreaching, she attempts to get further revenge by conjuring up his entombed corpse using a magic spell that involves standing inside a pentagram "naked as she was born." The spell goes awry, and the story ends with the reanimated corpse, armed with inch-long fingernails, giggling as it climbs through her window and attacks the screaming girl. The fact that Spence describes her, without explanation, as "a rather detestable child" does nothing to mitigate the prurience of this self-justifying child-abuse fantasy.

Several of Spence's stories deal with bitter rivalries between males in love with the same woman. In "Even the Dead Are Lucky Sometimes," two well-heeled suitors engage in a dangerous cross-country auto race over a woman "beautiful in the entirely expected yet breathtaking way of an Alpine sunrise over snow." In "James and John," a tale of wedding-night rape and revenge, the rivals are twin brothers, one "a fine figure of a fellow," the other cursed with "as twisted and misshapen a trunk as you could find anywhere." Both rivalries end in grisly deaths. (Another, though nonsexual, rivalry—between two feuding village bumpkins—is the focus of "The Last." It involves a prank using a scarecrow, and ends with one of the men going mad.)

Sometimes the male rivalry is an adulterous one, with similarly unpleasant consequences. In "The Making of the Melpomene Press," whose heroes are a pair of struggling young publishers desperate for a big sale, the firm's leading author—a flamboyant actor-manager who has dallied with the wrong titled lady—winds up in a packing-case thrown into the sea; the naked body of his mistress, "with a piece of whipcord sunk so deep in the wax of the throat that it was lost to view," winds up in another.

But nothing bad befalls the narrator of "The Master of Lostwick Hall," though he admits to being in love with his old friend's wife; in fact, he gets to claim her at the end, thanks to a curse from beyond the grave that conveniently kills off the old friend. The narrator of "The House on the Rynek," who lusts after *his* friend's wife ("I shall never forget how lovely she looked"), emerges similarly unscathed; not so the wife, who falls victim to a peculiarly horrifying family curse. I don't want to give away what was for me this collection's only genuine *frisson*, except to say that when the narrator throws his arms around her in the darkness and attempts to "snatch a kiss," he is under the impression—mistaken, it turns out—that she is naked beneath a fur coat.

Set in Cracow (which Spence had once visited) and involving the vengeful ghost of "an old and dirty Jewish furrier who had died in a three-century-old pogrom," "Rynek" is unusual for this collection in that its most memorable moment comes, as a horror tale's should, in the final pages. It is the prior events that seem contrived, clumsily designed to put the wife in harm's way while preventing the narrator and his friend from saving her. (The one is, conveniently, too heavy to climb over a railing to her rescue; the other has, conveniently, a "game leg"; all three are pawns.)

More often it is the other way around: A story begins appealingly, with a generous helping of traditional ghost-story atmosphere—a fireside whisky and soda; a chance encounter at a railroad-station bar; a group of companions swapping supernatural tales; or, as in "Even the Dead Are Lucky Sometimes," a conversation begun in the first-class compartment of a train winding its way through the countryside, and continued, that evening, in the lounge of a cozy hotel—only to bog down in an increasingly convoluted plot. Intriguing premises lead nowhere, or at least nowhere surprising.

"Knucklebones," for example, is narrated by an old seaman who, in his youth, served as cabin boy on a slave ship some time after the trade had been outlawed, and who witnessed the deliberate drowning of an entire cargo of slaves—men, women, and children brutally forced overboard because the crew feared discovery by a passing frigate. The seaman's voice is convincingly blunt ("The rights and the wrongs of it never troubled me at all. Niggers were just niggers to me and natural born slaves"), and his description of the title character is a vivid one:

> There was one nigger below that seemed to be a kind of boss among them. I should have said that his main qualification was ugliness. He was an oldish man, and his gummed wool ring was quite grey. His face was shrivelled and horrible, looking sort of tight over the cheek bones, and his few remaining teeth were filed into sharp points. He wore a double necklet of knucklebones round his neck and precious little else. Cramped though they were for space, he had a piece of clear deck to himself, rather as if he was infectiously holy and they didn't want to catch it. When he saw my mug at the combing he used to snap his bony fingers at me and jabber like anything. When he did that, all the other niggers would stop their chatter and look up too. There were no smiles then. That used to make me feel rather frightened, and I'd run forward into the fo'c'sle for human company.

It is this figure that voices the curse around which the story revolves, just before his fellow slaves are herded into the sea—a grim and powerful scene, told with great economy and skill. Each of the crew members is cursed, we are told; there will be no escape. . . .

And suddenly, like sails that have gone limp, the tale runs out of wind. Spence wraps the whole thing up in four swift pages. We learn that, over the years, one by one the men have died, though we are never told exactly how. A somewhat stagy epilogue reveals that the old seaman, now dead as well, is once more cabin boy on a ghostly version of the original slave ship, doomed to wander the earth like the *Flying Dutchman*. It is rather mild stuff, considering what preceded it.

Another strong tale that deserves a stronger ending is "Honourable Dog," whose grotesque characters—a traveling English circus troupe that is actually a gang of rogues, thieves, and murderers; an undercover detective who disguises himself as a clown; a hungry puma that paces its cave snarling "T-o-o-b-a-d-r-r-h"—would have felt right at home in a silent movie, one of those dark and cruel melodramas starring Lon Chaney and directed by Tod Browning. Unfortunately, the expected climax—a fight to the death between the puma and the detective, the latter wearing a pair of "clawed gloves" used by the Leopard Men of Africa "for their ritual killings"—proves a bit of a joke, leaving the reader feeling surprised but also slightly cheated.

The premise of "Wymondley" would also be perfect for a film: this time, however, a romantic comedy. The narrator, an impoverished young gentleman "bushwhacking" in Australia, learns that his older brother has died, leaving him the ancestral estate. With "no money and no prospect of any," he writes, "I was forced to sell—and by cable too." After the sale, conducted long-distance, the narrator discovers that his deceased brother must have secreted "a tidy little fortune" somewhere in the house. The realization "made me want to kick myself. Without any shadow of doubt my brother had hidden away somewhere bearer bonds and bank-notes enough to have saved the old place twice over, and I'd thrown in the cache with the sale. Can you wonder that I was wild enough to do a crazy thing?" He returns to England and, armed with a phony name and phony references, lands himself a job in his old home as "secretary-valet . . . and general factotum" to the new owner, a jolly American millionaire keen on horses and hounds. It is, as the narrator says, "a pleasantly farcical situation," one straight out of P. G. Wodehouse. Each night, by flashlight, he tiptoes through the mansion searching for the hidden treasure, convinced that it by rights belongs to him. When the American's daughter shows up, romance enters the picture:

> You hear and read a lot about falling in love at first sight and dismiss it probably as a fine thing for the holiday fiction market. You may. I used to. But when I saw this gorgeous creature being handed out of her Cadillac, I knew what I had been missing all my life, and made up my mind then and there to lay my hands on this missing fortune and be damned. £100,000 isn't a million, but it's a decent lot of money anywhere. I shouldn't be in the lowest class of fortune hunter with this behind me.

So far, so cute. But what are these light-hearted escapades doing in a ghost-story collection? Well, there is also an ancestral curse, which kills by a crushing blow to the throat, as if by a mailed fist: "The house does things like that every now and again to those it regards as strangers," the narrator flippantly explains.

What is remarkable is not the uneasy integration of romantic comedy with the macabre—on the screen, at least, one sees this often—but that the witty aristo-in-disguise plot is simply tossed aside, abandoned, midway through. One night the daughter catches the hero poking around: "We had a show down. I told her the whole truth, starting with the fact that I loved her." She is sympathetic; in fact, she joins him in his search. A day or two later, the narrator decides to reveal the deception to her father: "I told him the lot. . . . Old Royst was silent for a moment and then the humour of the situation burst upon him and he laughed out loud. How that man laughed."

So much for the comedy—it ends here—and so much for the elaborate mechanism that brought the hero to the house. It is eventually replaced by a mechanism of another sort (and far more unlikely), a sixteenth-century booby trap that swings out and catches the American and his daughter across their throats as they ascend a stairway, turning a Wodehousian farce into a gruesome tragedy.

Sci-Fi Entertainment

Willis O'Brien, Special Effects Genius by Steve Archer (McFarland, 239 pp, $28.50).

When most people hear the name Willis O'Brien, they think of *King Kong*. As the man who animated the ape for producers/directors Merian C. Cooper and Ernest B. Schoedsack, he bore, perhaps more than any other individual, responsibility for the film's enormous success. Cooper later called him "a bloody genius" and, more bluntly, "the best trick man in the business."

Known to people in the industry as "Obie," O'Brien also handled effects for the great silent film *The Lost World* and created the titular creatures of *The Son of Kong* and *Mighty Joe Young*. The former was such a disappointment that, as O'Brien's widow recollects in this book, he asked to have his name removed from the credits; the latter, however, was actually a greater technical achievement than *Kong,* even if the story wasn't as compelling. (It also marked the feature film debut of another great animator of the old school,

---

In the summer of 1994, after editing the first issue of *Sci-Fi Entertainment,* the magazine of TV's Sci-Fi Channel, I realized I was a bad fit and switched to writing its monthly "Bookshelf" column—on SF-related nonfiction—for editors Bob Martin and later Scott Edelman. Over the next ten years, under the name "Lawrence Tucker," I covered hundreds of reference books, art books, science books, trivia books, quiz books, movie guides, and show-biz bios. Here's a sampling.

Ray Harryhausen, who worked as O'Brien's assistant.)

In some ways, as this book makes clear, it was all downhill for O'Brien after *King Kong*. A painstaking craftsman but a poor self-promoter, he spent most of his career dreaming up visionary projects such as *War Eagles,* an epic adventure too expensive to produce, and working on low-budget productions such as *The Beast of Hollow Mountain, The Black Scorpion,* and that delightful film with the oddly redundant title, *The Giant Behemoth*. He died in 1962 at age seventy-six, during the making of *It's a Mad, Mad, Mad, Mad World*.

Judging from this volume, and from the beautiful preproduction sketches that it reproduces, the *War Eagles* project might have become one of the most stirring fantasies ever filmed. Involving a *Kong*-like expedition to the Arctic, predatory dinosaurs, and a lost race of eagle-borne Vikings, and climaxing with, in Archer's words, "an elaborate aerial battle over New York and the Statue of Liberty . . . it promised to make *King Kong* look like small meat." Merian Cooper described the story as "a super western of the air in which, instead of riders of the plains on horseback, we will have wild riders of the air on giant prehistoric eagles." He predicted that it would have "greater box-office appeal than *King Kong,* and will make more money." Alas, we'll never know.

Written by a man who is himself a special-effects expert, this tribute to O'Brien is strictly business; it's long on plot descriptions but rather skimpy, even mysterious, on the facts of its subject's life. It comes as a shock to read, in passing, that O'Brien's first wife went crazy in 1933 and murdered their two sons before fatally shooting herself. The details of this bizarre tragedy, and its consequences, are never revealed.

The book's strong points are the technical details, the colorful reminiscences of O'Brien by those who worked with him (as well as by his second wife), and the wealth of illustrations—sketches, paintings, snapshots, production stills, and photos of the pint-sized but lovingly detailed models which were the essence of O'Brien's art.

August 1994

A quartet of books on *Star Trek*'s creator depict him as a saint . . . and as a monster.

Gene Roddenberry will be dead just three years this October 23, and already there are at least four full-length books about him, including a worshipful guide to the Roddenberry Philosophy, published by a major university press, that hails him as an "American genius"; an all-out, no-holds-barred attack on the Roddenberry "myth" that bubbles over with venom and bile; and a painstakingly detailed "authorized biography" more than 600 pages long. Not bad for a TV writer whose single claim to fame, *Star Trek*, was dismissed by *Variety* the first week it aired as "an incredible and dreary mess of confusion and complexities."

Confusion and complexities abound when one attempts to form an image of the man based on the often conflicting testimonies of these four books. As reviewers will doubtless point out (the comparison is irresistible), what we have here is a *Rashomon* for the TV generation.

To James Van Hise, whose *The Man Who Created Star Trek: Gene Roddenberry* (Pioneer, 156 pp, $14.95) was the first out of the chute after Roddenberry's death, he was "a dreamer, a visionary" who "fought to bring quality and intelligent drama to television." Aimed squarely at the fans, Van Hise's book is a classic cut-and-paste job that relies heavily on quotes from previously published Roddenberry interviews and speeches but fails to reveal the sources of these quotes, though it appends, at the end, a three-page bibliography.

Its focus is, to say the least, unbalanced; it rushes through the first forty-five years of Roddenberry's life—the dangers he faced piloting a B-17 over the Pacific in World War II, the years as a pilot for Pan Am (including a near-fatal crash in the Syrian desert), his career on the Los Angeles police force, his years of struggle as a TV writer—in a mere dozen pages, yet later devotes eight pages to a heavy-breathing Tarzan movie project that understandably failed to find a backer.

Van Hise's stance is a generally uncritical one—he tends to take Roddenberry at his word—and he sometimes gets his facts wrong; he has Roddenberry serving as "a fighter pilot at the helm of a B-17" (the B, of course, is for bomber), carrying on as "one of eight survivors" of the Syrian air crash (there were twenty-two), and dying of a heart attack "in his West Los Angeles home." (He died while visiting his doctor.)

Still, the quotes Van Hise has assembled are well chosen—Roddenberry in his prime had provocative and irreverent opinions on almost any subject—and though it lacks an index, the book finds room for plenty of amusing anecdotes: on the problems Roddenberry had with network censors (in one of his early crime scripts, a character couldn't employ a tire iron as a weapon because it implied "the failure of an advertised product—tires");* the difficulty in photographing a green-skinned alien woman for the original *Star Trek* pilot ("No matter how dark they made the green, their model always looked perfectly normal. Eventually they discovered that someone at the photo lab . . . was color-correcting what he thought was a flaw in the photography"); NBC's request, to please advertisers, that the crew of the *Enterprise* include a few smokers ("I said, 'Listen, in that time they're not going to smoke.' And they said, 'Oh, you can use some square science-fiction cigarettes'"); Leonard Nimoy's obscurity (he was identified in a 1966 Hollywood Christmas parade as "Leonard Nimsy"); and Patrick Stewart's prickly personality ("A former staffer reported that Stewart walks off the set in a snit at least once a week. His co-workers have unflatteringly nicknamed him 'Baldilocks'").

If Van Hise's approach is fannish—"The trials of the past behind him, he steered his *Trek* universe to new glories. . . . He beat the odds again, achieving the allegedly impossible. He proved you can't keep a good man down"—that of Yvonne Fern in *Gene Roddenberry: The Last Conversation* (University of California Press, 228 pp, $20) is reverent to the point of hagiography. A former nun turned devout Trekkie, she encountered the wheelchair-bound Roddenberry during the final months of his life and immediately

---

*In a "campfire horror tale" for an outdoor magazine, I once had to eliminate a reference to snow that had gotten into a character's hiking boots, because boots were advertised elsewhere in the issue.

decided that the two of them had some sort of mystical bond. ("We met before we met, in the manner of children—curious, apprehensive, and eager.... Someone introduced us, or didn't.... The sun was shining—or wasn't. We looked at each other for a long time.") During a series of mind-numbingly pretentious interviews, she'd solemnly feed him questions like "What is the difference between truth and integrity?" "What is the relationship between power and creativity?" and "Tell me what the difference is between people and humanity."

It says something about Roddenberry's loneliness, his vanity, his fear of death, or his weakness for younger women, that he patiently tried to answer her. The fact that his answers are as boring and windy as her questions ("I think that humans are incredible. They are the most fascinating things in the universe") comes as no surprise.

While the aging Roddenberry drones on ("Good can be evil, and evil can be good, depending on circumstances"), Fern remains star-struck: "He reminds me of Jupiter/Zeus," she reports, "sitting so still, always in the act of creation, always in the process of generation. Physically large, mentally vast, and cosmically quiet, he has a paradoxical presence, imperious and self-effacing, as though he were winking in and out of existence, in and out of time."

It's not as if she didn't warn us; the danger signs are there on her first page, where she claims to understand "the very heart of the spiraled and unending quest of Gene Roddenberry: 'What does it mean *to be*? In this time, in this space, who are we?' His struggle to answer these questions is a tale of time slippage and alternate space, a delicate and determined unraveling of current quantum theory—physics to metaphysics and back again."

That a respected university press (which I *assume* California is) saw fit to publish this drivel is as great a mystery as any of the cosmic questions mulled over in the book.

There is another warning, a final one, embedded in the text. "I wish I could write much more of what Gene told me," Fern declares at one point. "So much is beautiful, so much is brilliant, so much is revolutionary. But I cannot"—because, she says, she has promised him "20 years' grace." She threatens, however, that in

2011, "if I feel that the time is right," the world can look forward to a second book from her. Talk about scary prospects!

To the former nun, Roddenberry was "honorable, honest, and true." To Joel Engel, author of *Gene Roddenberry: The Myth and the Man Behind "Star Trek"* (Hyperion, 283 pp, $22.95), Roddenberry was a liar, lecher, credit-chiseler, cheat, alcoholic, drug addict, and literary mediocrity.

To speak charitably of this extraordinarily uncharitable book, Engel's biography may be viewed as a useful corrective to the loony adulation of Roddenberry's fans, "the almost godlike awe," as one observer put it, "in which he was held by the Trekkies as the fount of all knowledge." And indeed, although the book re-creates private conversations and details of facial expressions that are all too plainly fictionalized, in general Engel seems to have done his homework; unlike the others reviewed here, his book has ample footnotes.

But it's a thoroughly nasty piece of work, a book-length sneer so spiteful and one-sided in its treatment of Roddenberry and so fawning toward his enemies that it borders, at times, on the comical. Engel appears to have solicited unflattering opinions from everyone who ever had a beef against the man; we learn that he stole other writers' ideas, patronized prostitutes, bored people at parties, and padded his résumé. (He didn't really fly 89 or 109 combat missions, we learn; it was probably more like 25. He wasn't really "head writer" for *Have Gun, Will Travel*, as he claimed; he simply wrote a lot of the episodes.)

Engel's hostility even pervades the index, where, under "Roddenberry," one finds just a single page listed for "accomplishments," followed by, among other goodies, "agitation enjoyed by," "barriers built by," "confrontations," "credit assumed by" (14 pages' worth), "depression," "divorce," "drinking" (another 14 pages), "drug abuse," "mental deterioration," "money sought by," "as one-trick pony," "past rewritten," "promises broken," "revenge," "scripts leaked," "self-loathing," "self-promotion," "sex as primary focus," and "womanizing."

Film critic Andrew Sarris once remarked that a fellow writer had just come out with a harshly critical study of director Ingmar Bergman; it had taken him three years to write. "Imagine," said

Sarris, "spending three years on someone you hate!" He shook his head. "Life's too short for that." It's certainly too short to waste on books like this.

There is, however, a good, rational, balanced account of Roddenberry's life. *Star Trek Creator: The Authorized Biography of Gene Roddenberry* by David Alexander (Roc, 624 pp, $23.95) is precisely the sort of colorful, well-written, sympathetic but not uncritical portrait that even those of us who aren't *Star Trek* fans can enjoy. (My only gripe is that it's miserably copy-edited and proofread.)

The book opens dramatically, with a gripping account of Roddenberry's death, which Alexander witnessed firsthand. It then returns to Roddenberry's birth in El Paso, Texas, in 1921 (his mother was just seventeen), and to his childhood in Los Angeles, where his family moved the following year. His father—like him, a Eugene—became an LAPD cop, just as Roddenberry would eventually become. Along the way, we're given a look at the young boy's first published work, "My Greedy Rabbit," written for a school paper when he was ten:

> My little rabbit
> Has a greedy habit
> Of eating the hay
> When the others play.

(Could *you* do any better?) Alexander, who interviewed Roddenberry for the freethinking magazine *The Humanist,* is particularly sympathetic to the TV writer's lifelong atheism, a stance which, considering Roddenberry's religious Baptist upbringing, took considerable courage to arrive at.

Alexander is best of all, though, in a hair-raising section on the 1947 Pan Am crash which left seven crewmen and seven passengers dead, the wreckage of their Lockheed Constellation burning in the desert night, and Roddenberry—who'd merely been along for the ride—in charge of the survivors. At dawn, Syrian tribesmen robbed the corpses and the luggage; later local villagers stole whatever was left. Back in the States, speaking of the crash, Roddenberry admitted, "I knew, for all my skills, I could not capture that moment." But he did recount, to Alexander, a moment that may have been defining:

"Something happened to me during that crash that had a big influence on my life. As we were coming down, and death was absolutely certain, I was thinking all sorts of things—should I scratch a message to my wife on the metal side of the plane? What was I going to say?—'I love you'? She already knew that. I thought, maybe I just ought to pray. I remember thinking, 'Wait a minute.' I didn't ordinarily pray, and I wouldn't have much respect for a god that would accept prayers when I was in dire straits like this. He would be bound to judge you, if he's judging you, on what you did in ordinary times. He just wouldn't accept prayers at times like this. I remember making up my mind not to pray. I thought, 'OK, take me as I am.'"

In a sense, Roddenberry asks the same of posterity; and it's on those terms, without denying the man's failings, that Alexander's biography chooses to take him: as he was.

October 1994

Star Trek isn't just a TV show. It's also a navigational guide to life in the 1990s.

People seek wisdom in the damnedest places. Some go to ashrams, some go to Yale. Some scale the Himalayas in search of monks who talk like Yoda; some burn the midnight oil poring over Heidegger, Hegel, and other names from Philosophy 101.

But true philosophers—literally "lovers of wisdom"—know that you take your wisdom where you find it, even if it's in a *Reader's Digest* snatched from the racks while you're waiting on line at the supermarket.

So there's nothing the matter with ad man Dave Marinaccio discovering, in a sci-fi TV series, the ultimate guide through life. Though *All I Really Need to Know I Learned from Watching Star Trek* (Crown, 128 pp, $14) is one of a host of recent books that take their titles from Robert Fulghum's bestselling *All I Really Need to Know I Learned in Kindergarten,* it's part of a publishing tradition that dates back to Benjamin Hoff's *Tao of Pooh* and the granddaddy of them all, Robert Short's 1964 *The Gospel According to "Peanuts."*

Marinaccio, a fortyish bachelor and self-confessed couch potato who (despite weekly workouts and plenty of girl-chasing) sports a potbelly, is both disarmingly self-confident—"I already know what's necessary to live a meaningful life," he reports, "and it isn't all that complicated"—and disarmingly modest. "For years," he admits, "I've related everything in life to *Star Trek*. But why not? Captain James Tiberius Kirk is the most successful person I've ever observed. He's a great leader, a good manager of people, dedicated, moral, adaptable, at the top of his profession, gets the girls, is well known and respected. There are worse role models."

In fact, Marinaccio sees his hero as an upholder of all the old virtues, a figure of resourcefulness, tolerance, and decency. Where a hundred years ago young men were inspired by Kipling ("If you can keep your head when all about you / Are losing theirs and blaming it on you / . . . you'll be a Man, my son!"), now, according to Marinaccio, they can learn the very same lesson from the captain of the *Enterprise:* "If you can keep your head in a crisis, you've got a fighting chance."

The book finds many other lessons in *Star Trek,* most of them deceptively simple, from the benefits of traveling light—"No one on the *Enterprise* has very much stuff"—to the importance of a satisfying resolution: "End every episode with a smile."

As a writer, Marinaccio is so laid-back that he can open a chapter with "I'm not sure how old Mick Jagger is, but it must be somewhere around fifty"—as if a few minutes' research was more than he could manage. (For the record, Mick turned fifty-one this summer.)

At 128 large-type pages, this breezy little book is exactly the right length; you can read it in an hour, and along the way you'll be entertained and occasionally even enlightened. You'll also get glimpses of Marinaccio's own past, including his years as a Catholic schoolboy (though the nuns tried to teach him the Golden Rule, they weren't as convincing as Captain Kirk), his work in a home for the retarded (where, in emulation of the "neutral zone" between the Federation and the Klingons, he turned one room into a "cool-down area" for problem patients), and his failed attempt to become a professional comic ("Standing onstage before an audience, even if the audience is only your classmates, is one of the few places in life where you can experience tremendous fear without being in any real physical danger").

One of Marinaccio's conclusions should be of particular interest to sci-fi fans. "Of all the things that *Star Trek* teaches us," he says, "the simplest and the most obvious is that mankind's future is in space.... The unknown is not to be avoided. It is to be examined, understood, and accepted."

Let's hope Congress reads this book the next time NASA appropriations come around.

The Wolf Man (266 pp, $19.95); *House of Dracula* (188 pp, $19.95); both edited by Philip Riley (MagicImage Filmbooks).

Were Americans ever so innocent that they were actually scared by movies like *The Wolf Man*? According to the first of these books, "business was a smash" when the film opened in 1941, and it quickly became "Universal's biggest money-maker of the season ... a $1,000,000 hit." Lon Chaney Jr. went on to play the same part in *Frankenstein Meets the Wolf Man* (1943), *House of Frankenstein* (1944), and *House of Dracula* (1945), all of them box-office successes.

Universal was Hollywood's preeminent purveyor of horror movies in the 1930s and 1940s, responsible for bringing to the screen such classic figures as Frankenstein, Dracula, the Mummy, and the Invisible Man. (A decade later it would give the world the Creature from the Black Lagoon.) As the late John Carradine notes in his introduction to the second of these books, "Disney has their cartoons, MGM had their musicals, but Universal is known for their monsters."

By today's standards, movies like *The Wolf Man* and *House of Dracula*—the second of Universal's multimonster horror-fests, teaming Chaney's Larry Talbot with Dracula (played by Carradine) and Frankenstein's Monster (played by Glenn Strange), as well as a mad scientist and his hunchbacked nurse—seem corny and naive; the pleasures they offer are primarily nostalgic.

But those pleasures are nonetheless real. Fortunately for nostalgia buffs, MagicImage Filmbooks has been publishing the original shooting scripts of the classic Universal horror films; the titles above are, respectively, volumes 12 and 16 of the series.

While the scripts themselves, in their original typewritten format, are the centerpieces of the books, they're accompanied by detailed background articles, interviews, lobby cards, studio publicity ("One Monster Would Be Terrific. . . . But Here Are FIVE to Bring You Five Times the Thrill!"), cast biographies, personal memoirs, and plenty of behind-the-scenes photos (though the Dracula volume unaccountably lacks a shot of Strange without his makeup). Thanks to this diversity of material, they resemble scrapbooks—affecttionate, informal, and filled with odd bits of trivia. Did you know, for example, that Bela Lugosi, who plays Maria Ouspenskaya's gypsy son in *The Wolf Man,* was actually five years older than she was? Or that the werewolf's face was made from Asian yak hair? Or that the dead trees of that film's cheesy, fog-shrouded forest had already done service in *All Quiet on the Western Front* and *Flash Gordon's Trip to Mars*? Or that Jane Adams, *House of Dracula*'s sexy hunchback, was (or so she claimed) found to have, at the age of four, "the second highest IQ in the state of California"?

Both movies—this is the oddest trivia of all—once bore the same working title, *Destiny,* with which, for some reason, Universal was enamored. (It was also a working title for *House of Frankenstein.*) Both benefited from the sure hand of Greek immigrant Janus Piccoulas, who—as a profile in the first book reveals—arrived in Los Angeles in 1906, shortly after the San Francisco earthquake, and, as the legendary "Jack P. Pierce," became Universal's presiding makeup genius. Both films may have benefited—though perhaps the opposite—from their timing: *The Wolf Man* opened on December 9, 1941, just two days after Pearl Harbor; *House of Dracula* opened on December 21, 1945, while our victorious servicemen were still returning home from overseas. Whether the horrors of war curtailed the taste for cinematic ones—or, conversely, whether real-life events created a need for escapist entertainment—is impossible to say.

One thing that's clear is that the 6-foot-3-inch Lon Chaney liked to drink. Scream queen Evelyn Ankers, his *Wolf Man* costar, puts it delicately in her foreword: "It appeared that Lon and his friends, Andy Devine and Broderick Crawford and a few others, were imbibing a bit too much and getting into wrestling matches, which usually destroyed the dressing room trailers." Cameraman

Phil Lathrop concurs: "I remember that Lon Chaney was usually drunk. In the evening, he and his pals ... would get loaded and trash out their dressing rooms." John Carradine also recalls him with the same pair of "drinking buddies" at "the local watering hole after hours." But ex-stuntman Paul Malvern, *House of Dracula*'s producer, puts a happier spin on it all: "When we went on location [for *North of the Klondike*] ... the three of them didn't have to worry about keeping warm. If they weren't beating the hell out of each other, they drank enough to generate enough heat to keep us all warm!" His conclusion: "There never was a nicer guy. He got along with everybody."

Jack's Life: A Biography of Jack Nicholson by Patrick McGilligan (Norton, 478 pp, $25).

Hollywood's most recent werewolf, Jack Nicholson, does not get along with everybody—which may be one key to his appeal. But it's easy to see, in reading about his career, that from his humble New Jersey beginnings (where the movie-struck boy took tickets and sold popcorn at his neighborhood theater) through his rise to international celebrity, Nicholson has been wonderfully adept at selling himself, flashing his famous lupine grin, and controlling his personal demons. McGilligan notes that most acquaintances from the early days remember Nicholson as "immensely likable." A high school teacher describes him as "engaging and polite to the core," and acting coach Jeff Corey remembers him, years later, as "a very agreeable kid." Later still, at the 1966 Cannes Film Festival, with his first hit, *Easy Rider,* still three years in the future, "He just smiled at everybody," a producer recalls. "His gimmick was to approach people like he was old friends with them."

McGilligan's warts-and-all biography shows how a sassy, articulate, extremely private person turned into one of Hollywood's hardest-working and highest-paid stars—and, along the way, became the windy, bad-tempered, and somewhat paranoid figure of recent interviews, giving vent, the author says, to "a deep, residual fury" (the sort of fury that, though it's too recent to have been included, may have led him to batter a stranger's automobile with a golf club during a minor traffic dispute).

Judging from *Jack's Life,* the changes in him have a lot to do, predictably, with power and money. "Nicholson," a columnist confides, "once told me he's made more money than he could ever want or spend." But one also has a sense that the aging actor is increasingly conscious of time and options running out—a concern that might make anyone impatient, especially a man as driven and ambitious as Nicholson.

This summer's modest hit, *Wolf,* does not appear in the book except as one of several upcoming projects; but it's clear from this biography that, even from the start, there's always been a lot of wolf in Jack.

December 1994

The End by R. Donna Chesher (McFarland, 230 pp, $29.95).

When I was around ten or eleven, two friends and I used to station ourselves on the roof of a neighbor's garage with binoculars and a notepad, carefully listing the time, direction, and airline of every plane that passed overhead.

If anyone had asked us why we were doing it, I'm not sure any of us could have told him. I'd not sure any of us knew, except that it was fun.

The same may be true of R. Donna Chesher, who, in the words of her book's subtitle, has spent several years compiling "Closing Lines of Over 3,000 Theatrically Released American Films."

"As far as I have been able to determine," the author informs us, "a compilation of this type has never before been attempted."

Well, yes—and for good reason, as we shall see. "I sincerely hope that you will enjoy using this compilation as much as I have enjoyed compiling it," she says.

That last seems highly unlikely. Compiling this book no doubt gave Ms. Chesher an excuse to watch a lot of movies, just as compiling a haphazard checklist of commercial aviation gave my friends and me a chance to peer at a lot of planes. But the value of all this labor seems virtually nil.

Nonetheless, it must have seemed like a good idea at the time. Every work of narrative art has a beginning, middle, and end, and it's long been axiomatic that the last of these is the most crucial.

Beginnings are undeniably important—a good author strives to hook the reader from the start (which is why it's so instructive to wander down the aisles of any good bookstore, checking out the opening paragraphs of novels and short stories)—but it's the ending, more than any other element, that determines the ultimate impact. A story may bore us, but assuming we read it all the way through, its final line can leave us with a lump in our throat; a movie may try our patience and our credulity, but a powerful last scene can send us staggering out of the theater with tears in our eyes.

Yet instead of conjuring up the final scenes of movies in all their emotional splendor, Ms. Chesher has done no more than her subtitle states: She offers us the closing lines of movies with absolutely no context or explanation, so that all too often the words are rendered virtually meaningless.

What's the final line of *Body Heat*, for example? "Yes."

That's it, you read it right—simply "Yes," followed in this book by the name of the speaker ("Matty Walker": Kathleen Turner). No explanation is provided, or even the name of the screenwriter or director. (Ms. Chesher does list—God knows why—the release year and the studio.)

What's the final line of *Bonnie and Clyde*? You'll never guess, not in a hundred million years.

"Hey."

That's it. In case you're wondering, it's uttered by Warren Beatty, just before he and Faye Dunaway get picturesquely riddled with bullets in a highly influential cinematic death scene. But informing us of this would be outside the book's rigid format, so it simply doesn't get mentioned.

Let's look at a sci-fi film whose ending choked me up: *The Terminator*. Not the overblown, rather hollow sequel, but the first film, the love story. Here's the final line, in all its glory: "I know."

Pretty underwhelming, isn't it? If Ms. Chesher had bothered to supply the haunting line that precedes it—the old Mexican man's prophetic words about the "big storm coming"—then this valedictory might have meant something. Without that context, it's meaningless.

So is, of course, the celebrated final line of *Some Like It Hot:*

"Well, nobody's perfect." I ask you, what's the point of printing the punch line if you don't supply the joke?

There are, however, a few stray pleasures to be found, if one is willing to search for them. Anthony Perkins's closing monologue in *Psycho,* here printed in full, still makes for a mild shudder or two (though this book, like some demented computer, insists on attributing the words to "'Mother's Voice': Virginia Gregg," without so much as a mention of Perkins); and Woody Allen's memorable foray into science fiction, *Sleeper,* has a final line whose wisdom we can all savor: "Sex and death. Two things that come once in a lifetime. But at least after death you're not nauseous."

Locked Room Murders and Other Impossible Crimes by Robert Adey (Crossover Press/DreamHaven, 450 pp, $45).

While Donna Chesher was watching (or fast-forwarding through) 3,000 movies, an equally indefatigable researcher was busily reading more than 2,000 locked-room mysteries—the sort in which a corpse is found alone in a locked library or (one of hundreds of variations) in the middle of a snow-covered field with no footsteps leading to it except the victim's own. Adey has exhaustively catalogued this peculiar subgenre, providing titles, detective names, and plot-lines for some 2,019 puzzlers, from Doyle's celebrated "Adventure of the Speckled Band" ("Death by fright in a locked bedroom") to more than a hundred novels and short stories by the field's acknowledged master, John Dickson Carr ("Disappearance of a man, leaving his complete suit of clothes behind," "Death by beheading in a guarded room," etc.).

What makes this reference book so special—and incidentally gives it a faint tinge of science fiction—is that a section at the end lists, in a sentence or two, the solutions to each of these mysteries, e.g., "The victim swallowed a letter sent to him that was impregnated with poison—believing it to be morphine, to which he was addicted." Many of the solutions are prosaic ("He made his exit disguised as a milkman"), but some are reminiscent of Rube Goldberg ("A rope was rigged up between two poles at either end of the tennis court, and the victim, whose throat was encircled in the middle of the court, was strangled by vigorous pulling at an end") or even Hugo Gernsback ("The gun was worked by an electromagnetic force"). And some are so bizarre that they cry out for Monty Python, e.g., "The limousine was actually being driven by a midget who sat beneath the figure of the dead chauffeur."

For those of us who like to get to the bottom of mysteries and have no patience for wading through the tedious minutia of highly improbable crimes, Adey's book is a wonderful time-saver.

February 1995

A book as thick as a cinder block yields a treasure trove of movie lore.

Though it boggles the mind, there are certain people out there—perfectly intelligent people, maybe even in your own family—who can sit and watch a movie, and actually enjoy it, without knowing the names of the actors. Incredible! And what's more, they don't even seem to care! They don't chuckle with recognition when Dick Miller and Jackie Joseph, from *The Little Shop of Horrors,* appear as a small-town couple in *Gremlins,* or when Kenneth Tobey, who saved mankind in *The Thing,* stalks through *Strange Invaders* as an alien spy, or when *Thing* alumnus Robert Cornthwaite, the quintessential egghead, plays a similar role in *Matinee.* They don't even smile when gaunt and gothic Peter Cushing, his Hammer Horror cobwebs brushed away, shows up in *Star Wars* sporting an Empire officer's uniform. When Malcolm McDowell comes bursting onscreen in *Star Trek: Generations* looking grizzled and maniacal, they don't whisper, "My God, how he's aged!" and think fond thoughts of *If . . ., A Clockwork Orange, O Lucky Man!, Time After Time, Cat People,* and *Blue Thunder.* They think, at most, "Hmm, he looks familiar."

But for true movie buffs, knowing an actor's history is half the fun, just as any self-respecting baseball fan makes sure he knows the players' batting averages, personal quirks, and the teams they played for in the past.

If you are, as I am, a dedicated reference freak, there are several all-but-indispensable books that should be sitting on your shelf within easy reach of the TV and VCR. There's the annual *Screen World* series and Leonard Maltin's comprehensive one-volume *Movie and*

Video Guide, which I'll save for another column, and for our favorite genre there's Bill Warren's *Keep Watching the Skies!* (McFarland), a lovingly detailed—and often hilarious—two-volume study of science fiction films from 1950 to 1962. At more than 1,300 pages, it's actually worth the whopping $85 price.

While the above three titles focus on individual movies, *The Film Encyclopedia* (HarperCollins, $25 pb) focuses on people—thousands of them: actors, directors, and the more important writers and producers, from straight-man Bud Abbott to director Edward Zwick (*Glory*), all of them profiled in highly readable mini-bios ranging from a few lines to full-scale essays, complete with extensive filmographies. A mammoth 1,500-pager as thick and heavy as a Manhattan phone book, it's also crammed with information—perhaps too much—on optics, special effects, and other technical matters, along with articles on the film industry in such exotic climes as Egypt, Iran, and Venezuela.

While the technical material is dull, the biographical entries are first-rate: perceptive, judicious, and always eminently browsable, making this encyclopedia the perfect desert-island gift. Its author, Ephraim Katz, brought out the first edition in 1979; he died in 1992 while preparing this updated and expanded version, and the work was completed by a dozen or more researchers.

Katz had a talent for summing up careers in just a few words: Sterling Holloway "played hillbillies, country bumpkins, delivery boys, and soda jerks in some 100 films"; Murray Hamilton was "often cast as an ambitious or conniving figure"; Dennis Hopper "is considered by some the most freaked-out personality in films." He was especially apt at differentiating among heavies: Vincent Price was "at his best as a treacherous or effete villain," Dan Duryea was "typecast as a cynical, sneering villain whom women found strangely fascinating," Claude Rains was "a suave character actor of superbly controlled sardonic manner [who] was charming even when playing villains," and Donald Pleasence is "at his most convincing as an evil villain with a fixed gaze in his unblinking blue eyes."

Katz also had a gratifying fondness for odd bits of trivia. We learn that Christopher Lee's autobiography is entitled *Tall, Dark and Gruesome,* and that Bette Midler is the author of *A View from a*

Broad. Charles Bronson was "born Charles Bunchinsky, later Buchinski, then Buchinsky." Of Nicolas Cage we are told, "Intense in his approach to roles, he is said to have slashed his arm in preparation for his part in *Racing with the Moon,* had two teeth pulled for *Birdy,* and swallowed a live cockroach for *Vampire's Kiss.*"

The *Encyclopedia* is particularly thorough on marriages and deaths. Just last night, reading an interview with British director Val Guest in one of my favorite magazines, *Scarlet Street,* my curiosity was piqued by Guest's reminiscences of Janet Munro, star of his film *The Day the Earth Caught Fire.* "She had just finished her contract with Disney.... In the Disney movies, they used to make her tie her boobs down, to make it look like she had none. We got those out, to start with! *(laughs)* She had a very tragic end."

Astonishingly, at that point the subject was simply dropped. But my trusty *Film Encyclopedia* came to the rescue: Munro's career, it notes, "was hampered by an alcohol problem.... She died freakishly at 38 as a result of choking while she was drinking tea."

For all its massive size, however, Katz's book isn't *always* so trusty; you'll find no mention, for example, of some of the names cited at the start of this column, including Kenneth Tobey. (Tobey does show up as an "American character actor of dependable types" in a rival reference work, Halliwell's *Filmgoer's and Video Viewer's Companion,* along with other players too minor for Katz.)

But Katz, at least, offers substantial entries on Peter Cushing, Malcolm McDowell, and Christopher Lee, along with such worthies as John Landis, George Romero, and Sam Raimi. None of these appear in David Thomson's *A Biographical Dictionary of Film* (Knopf, 845 pp, $25 pb), which includes just over a thousand entries—and quirky ones at that. Good lookers Madeleine Stowe, Theresa Russell, and Rebecca De Mornay receive a full column each; Jeff Goldblum isn't even listed. Nor are the Plummers (Katz includes both Christopher and Amanda) or the Carradines (Katz includes all four). Yet good old Johnny Carson, who's never even been in a movie, is given more than two pages, simply because Thomson feels like spouting off about him. ("Now, this may sound as if I don't really or entirely like Johnny. Not so. I can never resist a magnificent, triumphant performer whose appearance and aplomb are drawn tight to conceal loneliness, dismay, anger, and disgust.") A long entry on George C. Scott discusses trivia such as *Movie Movie* and *Oklahoma Crude,* yet omits any mention of *Dr. Strangelove.*

Clearly this is a most peculiar reference work. Only in passing does it provide factual information; its real aim is to air David Thomson's opinions.

As opinions go, they're literate, provocative, and sometimes fun to read. Thomson is a passionate and prolific writer of books on Hollywood, and his views are certainly informed. More important, he has what every critic needs most, confidence in his own taste—and in your *interest* in his taste.

On this last count, though, his confidence may be misplaced. After one has cheered the opinions one happens to agree with (e.g., that "Brian Cox's Lecter in *Manhunter* is arguably more intriguing and more frightening" than Anthony Hopkins's version in *The Silence of the Lambs*) and scowled at those one happens to disagree with (e.g., Thomson's praise for *The Witches of Eastwick*), one may well be left with the uncharitable thought, "Who *cares* what this guy thinks?"

April 1995

Horror director Dario Argento: Is he a master of shock, or merely of schlock?

While cultists revere Dario Argento as a sort of "Italian Hitchcock," others regard the director as, at best, a flamboyant schlockmeister. Ephraim Katz, in his *Film Encyclopedia,* dismisses Argento as one who "over the years has established a reputation as Italy's stylish master of cheap blood and gore." I'd say that's about right.

You can decide for yourself after reading *Broken Mirrors/Broken Minds: The Dark Dreams of Dario Argento* by Maitland McDonagh (Carol Publishing, 298 pp, $18.95 pb). Argento is a visually inventive director whose films, sloppily plotted and indifferently acted, tend to revolve around novel and sadistic ways of killing people, usually young women. In order to facilitate these killings, it's necessary that characters behave foolishly and implausibly, neglecting to confide in those who might help them, venturing where they shouldn't, wandering off alone when they should be on their guard, and in general—in the time-honored way of horror victims everywhere—putting themselves at risk.

It's also necessary, in these films, that the killers possess superhuman—indeed, virtually supernatural—reserves of cunning, speed, and luck; Argento's killers pop up at exactly the right moment to polish off lone and vulnerable victims with their slashing blades, then slip miraculously away without being caught. The killers themselves tend to be Jekyll-and-Hyde types, outwardly upright and trustworthy, who somehow manage to fool everybody (including the audience) until, at the end of the movie, they're revealed as secret psychotics with some convenient trumped-up grudge against the world.

Finally, in order to keep the audience guessing as to the killer's identity, Argento is forced to withhold crucial information, so we typically get lots of killer's-eye-view shots, extreme close-ups of eyeballs (and even, in one film, of a ludicrously pulsating brain), gloved hands wielding daggers (gloved so that we don't know whether the hand is that of a man or a woman), sinister whispers (which, again, disguise the killer's sex), and other means both skillful and annoying, designed to keep us in the dark.

It seems clear from his films that Argento is an impatient man: impatient with rational explanations and the need to create a convincing story, impatient to get on to the next killing. His films are scary, atmospheric, and ultimately rather mechanical.

In recent years, what's more, they have failed to find an American distributor. His best film is arguably his first, 1970's *The Bird with the Crystal Plumage,* thanks largely to an ingenious plot twist borrowed without acknowledgment from mystery writer Fredric Brown. His latest film is arguably his worst.

Given his limitations and the downward trend of his career, one has to ask whether the director really warrants as scholarly and intelligent a book as this one. Based on McDonagh's master's thesis, it acknowledges early on that "the thriller is still a low-rent genre" and generally avoids making extravagant claims for Argento's work, which it examines, film by film, with wit, insight, and affection.

Round in Circles: Poltergeists, Pranksters, and the Secret History of the Cropwatchers by Jim Schnabel (Prometheus, 302 pp, $24.95 hc). *The Bermuda Triangle Mystery—Solved* by Larry Kusche (Prometheus, 316 pp, $16.95 pb).

It's been a long time coming, but UFOs are finally official. The tiny island nation known as the Maldives has recently issued a series of full-color postage stamps, entitled "Mysteries of the Universe," commemorating flying saucers, the Loch Ness Monster, the Abominable Snowman, long-lost Atlantis, the Bermuda Triangle, and crop circles. So all of these things must be real—otherwise how can they put them on stamps?

Two titles from the hardheaded folks at Prometheus suggest otherwise. The firm publishes books on a wide range of subjects, but it specializes in debunking everything from health-food fads to creationism, with particular attention to the sort of "unexplained phenomena" featured on those stamps.

Round in Circles (wonderful title) tackles the crop circle craze, "one of the strangest popular mysteries of our time," which began in England in August 1980 when a tourist wandering the Wiltshire hills, several miles south of Stonehenge, noticed three huge circular depressions in the wheat and oat fields below him. "At first sight they appear to be spots where helicopters have landed" reported the *Wiltshire Times,* "but the circles seem too well-defined and regular to be caused that way. They are all in the middle of fields, with no tracks leading from them."

Three more circles were discovered the following summer, on a hilltop in Hampshire called Cheesefoot Head (you have to love the English), and from there the phenomenon spread. Soon such circles were cropping up by the hundreds, all over the world, in increasingly complex and beautiful designs, and local people were reporting "sulphur smells," strange "humming" and "trilling" noises, and "energy beams" of pure white light emanating from the fields. British circle sites, not surprisingly, became a mecca for New Agers, poltergeist hunters, channelers, UFO buffs seeking real-life Close Encounters of the Third Kind, meteorologists chasing whirlwinds, quasi-scientific investigators known as "cerealogists," and, of course, the media.

Some of the wind was taken out of the movement when, in

September 1991, two amiable English drinking buddies, Dave Chorley and Doug Bower, demonstrated to the press how they'd been creating these circles in local farmers' fields, using an iron bar and, later, wooden planks, since the mid-1970s; indeed, those first circles in Wiltshire and Hampshire had been their handiwork. Other circles were revealed to have been made by copycat pranksters, such as the group known as the Wessex Skeptics.

Yet while some cerealogists initially admitted they'd been gullible—"We have all been conned," said one—the rest went on believing, even when circles pronounced "genuine in every way" turned out to be fakes. "I just wish the hoaxers would come to their senses and realize it is a waste of time," wrote one true believer, after having been bamboozled.

And it *is* a waste of time. No matter how many flying saucers, faith healers, and self-proclaimed psychics are exposed as frauds, there will always be people who'll declare, as the crop circle diehards continue to do, "Surely they can't *all* be fakes."

Round in Circles is populated with a collection of pranksters, misfits, and crockpots; Jim Schnabel, a very funny writer, treats them all with amused tolerance. "Those who dismiss the subject as so much human folly," he says, "miss the point that such folly is, to a great extent, what makes us human."

Folly is also what makes bestsellers out of books that celebrate the irrational; the debunkers are never as popular. Books that touted Uri Geller's "miraculous psychokinetic powers" outsold James Randi's exposé of Geller as just another clever stage magician. Books proclaiming the perils of the so-called Bermuda Triangle, such as the meretricious 1974 bestseller by Charles Berlitz, made their authors a fortune; *The Bermuda Triangle Mystery—Solved,* by Larry Kusche, has remained relatively unknown.

Kusche was a reference librarian at Arizona State University who discovered, in the course of researching the Triangle, that this "sinister no-man's-land" bordering on Bermuda, Puerto Rico, and the tip of Florida was statistically no more dangerous—and no more mysterious—than any similar stretch of ocean. His book originally appeared in 1986; Prometheus has just reprinted it, complete with a new introduction.

Modern legend has it that the Triangle is a graveyard of lost ships and aircraft, a kind of black hole into which men and machines are continually vanishing. Some have speculated that the region contains the doorway to another dimension, that it's a "reverse gravity field" where magnets and electricity go haywire, or—again à la *Close Encounters*—that it's a happy hunting ground for UFOs.

Yet over and over, in case after case, Kusche sifts the lies from the truth and discovers that, disappointing as it may seem to the occultists among us, there's a perfectly sane, boring, natural explanation for everything.

Patiently he demonstrates that the missing ships and planes described in the press and paperbacks as having "disappeared into the Triangle in calm weather" were actually sailing into hurricanes, were in demonstrably unstable condition, or were nowhere near the Triangle when they went down. (One such plane exploded off the coast of Ireland; a ship claimed as a victim of the Triangle in fact sank in the Pacific.) Pilots described as "experienced" were in fact mere students.

In one case, terrified radio communications between a pilot and his air base—"Everything is wrong . . . strange. . . . We can't be sure of any direction. Even the ocean doesn't look as it should!"—was simply invented.

"It is no more logical to try to find a common cause for all the disappearances in the Triangle," concludes Kusche, "than, for example, to try to find one cause for all the automobile accidents in Arizona. . . . The Legend of the Bermuda Triangle is a manufactured mystery."

These two books, like others from Prometheus, document what the great Baltimore sage H. L. Mencken called "the irresistible reasonableness of the nonsensical." But I prefer the way my ex-shrink once put it: "Reality," he said, "is never enough for some people."

August 1995

From "Make my day" to "Make him an offer he can't refuse," here's a listing of the best-loved lines from a thousand films.

Speaking only half in jest, Dr. Johnson defined *lexicographer*—a breed to which he himself belonged—as "a harmless drudge." And, in fact, the image most of us have of someone who compiles a reference book is a solemn, pasty-faced fellow who spends most of his life in tedious labor, whether scribbling in the library or squinting at his computer screen. As jobs go, it sounds pretty joyless.

But Melinda Corey and George Ochoa must have had a ball putting together *The Dictionary of Film Quotations* (Crown, 448 pp, $24 pb), because they got to watch a thousand of their favorite movies, transcribing the more famous lines of dialogue—the obligatory ones such as "Rosebud," "Hasta la vista, baby," "Go ahead, make my day," "May the Force be with you," "I'm gonna make him an offer he can't refuse," and "Frankly, my dear, I don't give a damn"—but also, it's clear, choosing the lines they liked best.

The result is a reference book that's ideal for browsing, offering the same nostalgic pleasure as those compilations of "classic moments from great Hollywood films" that they show on Oscar night. Corey and Ochoa are careful to include the lines we all remember best—Geena Davis's "Be afraid. Be very afraid," so memorably spooky that it appeared on *The Fly*'s poster; Margaret Hamilton's "Oh, what a world! What a world!" as she melts in *The Wizard of Oz*; and the final, frightened monologue of *2001*'s Hal 9000 computer. But they also have a gratifying knack for picking some of the very lines I myself most cherish from films such as *Jurassic Park* ("Clever girl!"—park ranger Bob Peck's astonished tribute to the velociraptor that's about to eat him), *The Lady Eve* (Barbara Stanwyck's vengeful "I need him like the axe needs the turkey"), *Honeymoon in Vegas* (Nicolas Cage's "Did you get a job here?"—believe me, the funniest line in the movie, but you had to be there), and *Lawrence of Arabia* (nineteen separate entries, and every one a beaut).

Nostalgia aside, the book serves as a reminder that a good screenwriter really earns his money. Even in execrable films like *Total Recall*, there are lines of loony inspiration (Ronny Cox's taunt to Schwarzenegger, "In thirty seconds you'll be dead, and I'll blow this place up and be home in time for cornflakes"—assuming they eat cornflakes on Mars). You'll find knee-slappers even in so-so films like *Leap of Faith* ("A town this deep in the crapper's got nowhere to turn but God"), *The Lost Boys* ("One thing about living in Santa Carla I never could stomach was all the damn vampires"), and *I*

Was a Teenage Frankenstein ("I know you have a civil tongue in your head—I sewed it there myself").

Teenage Frankenstein isn't the only camp classic included: There's *Mommie Dearest* ("Don't f— with me, fellas. This ain't my first time at the rodeo"); *Gold Diggers of 1933* ("Can you imagine me getting sentimental, the most hard-boiled dame on the Dirty White Way?"); and the endlessly and irresistibly quotable *Plan 9 from Outer Space:* "My friends," intones Criswell in the epilogue, "you have seen this incident based on sworn testimony. Can you prove that it didn't happen? Perhaps, on your way home, someone will tap you in the dark, and you will never know it, for they will be from outer space!"

A more mercenary use for this reference book, of course, is as a bet-settler. A friend, near tears, quotes the final heartfelt line of the 1939 *Hunchback of Notre Dame,* uttered among the gargoyles by Charles Laughton: "Oh, if only I were made of stone!" You go scuttling off to your library and discover that the actual wording was "Why was I not made of stone like thee?" Another friend recites the famous line from *Casablanca,* "Play it again, Sam." You open *The Dictionary of Film Quotations* and correct him; the actual line was simply "Play it, Sam." If you have any friends left after this, you can correct them as well.

Though it sounds like a hefty amount, six thousand quotes from a thousand movies aren't all that many if you're a confirmed film buff. I wish the editors had included the haunting last lines of *The Terminator* and, for *The Shining,* something more than "He-e-e-re's Johnnie!" (They've found room for the beloved road sign in *Oz*— "I'D TURN BACK IF I WERE YOU"—and several other "quotes" are taken from letters or print; why, then, couldn't they have included *The Shining*'s unforgettable "All work and no play makes Jack a dull boy"?) I wish they had mentioned *The Go-Between,* whose haunting opening from the L. P. Hartley novel ("The past is foreign country. They do things differently there") is deservedly famous.

And though we're given a dozen hilarious examples from *A Funny Thing Happened on the Way to the Forum,* I missed my favorite exchange, probably the wisest moment of dialogue in the entire history of movies. Earlier, the Roman slave played by Zero Mostel had boasted that he was "impervious to pain." Now another slave, played by Jack Gilford, sneaks up behind him and jabs a needle into Mostel's rear. Mostel lets out a bellow of rage.

"I thought you said you were impervious to pain," sneers Gilford.

Replies the incredulous Mostel: "Not my *own!*"

Miscellaneous Writings by H. P. Lovecraft, edited by S. T. Joshi (Arkham House, 582 pp, $29.95).

Lovecraft is one of those writers who's probably best discovered before one is old enough to vote. Or at least his fiction is; by the time one hits one's twenties, it becomes increasingly difficult to summon up *frissons* over the menace to humanity posed by tentacled Cthulhu, slithering shoggoths, and various New England wizards who can come back from the dead. (I speak, incidentally, as a lifelong fan—but one aware, from painful experience, that it's hard to make converts of fellow adults.)

What *grows* in fascination, however, is Lovecraft the man: his short eccentric, somewhat solitary life in Providence, Rhode Island; his fondness for antiquarian jaunts up and down the East Coast; his astoundingly wide-ranging erudition, whether literary, historical, or scientific (augmented by a preternaturally keen memory); his deep-dyed conservatism and hostility to the modern world; his bleak (but persuasive) nihilistic philosophy, with its cynicism about human pretensions, including his own; and his thoroughly endearing love of old New England—farms, fishing villages, cobblestone streets, Colonial architecture, and vistas of towns seen at twilight.

Lovecraft's opinions—sometimes pompous, often quirky, occasionally outrageous, always passionately held—fill his letters and postcards, which he dashed off to friends the way other people talk. (Some have estimated he wrote as many as 100,000 letters.) They also fill the essays and reviews he contributed to various magazines in the world of Amateur Journalism, a queer, long-vanished movement that linked scholars, writers, and would-be poets from across the nation the way 'zines and the Internet do today.

Miscellaneous Writings presents the best of Lovecraft the essayist, as well as a generous sampling of juvenile stories, political polemics, letters to editors, literary criticism (much of it devoted to the aesthetics of verse), travel accounts (some written in a jocular mock-18th-century style), and plot ideas for horror tales—more than eighty selections in all. It's essential for Lovecraft devotees and, for newcomers too jaded for the fiction, an excellent introduction to Lovecraft's thought.

The Steampunk Trilogy by Paul Di Filippo (Four Walls Eight Windows, 352 pp, $20).

Normally this column leaves fiction to *Science Fiction Age* and *Realms of Fantasy*. But this debut book from prolific short-story writer and essayist Paul Di Filippo is unusual and ambitious enough to be worth mentioning, combining hard historical fact with the wildest of fancy and the broadest of slapstick humor. It comprises three novellas, the first set in teeming nineteenth-century London, the others in the more cerebral world of nineteenth-century Boston and its environs.

In "Victoria," which introduces us to the wealthy inventor Cosmo Cowperthwait, as well as to a silver-nosed sharpshooting villain named Lord Chuting-Payne and a passel of whores, thugs, and street people, Britain's innocent young queen has mysteriously disappeared. While the search goes on, lest the public be alarmed, Viscount Melbourne, the prime minister, secretly replaces her with one of Cowperthwait's creations, a bizarre creature, half-human, half-salamander, which answers to the name Victoria and, from a distance, might almost pass for the queen. The creature does not speak, but it very much enjoys sex; in fact, before assuming the throne, it had been the most popular choice at London's leading brothel.

Eros and erudition also meet in "Hottentots," in which the real-life Harvard biologist Louis Agassiz encounters everyone from Ralph Waldo Emerson and "Hank" Thoreau to the ace harpooner Queequeg in his search for a magical body part removed from an African woman's corpse. Before his quest is over, he even comes face to face with some classic Lovecraftian monsters lurking in the waters off Marblehead.

The final tale, a quieter excursion called "Walt and Emily," sets up a rather believable romantic encounter between the poets Emily Dickinson and Walt Whitman, who, together with other luminaries of the time, voyage into a weird green timeless dreamland worthy of fantasists George Macdonald and David Lindsay.

The result—when all three stories, with their various links to one another, are inhabiting the same book—is a sort of 19th-century *Ragtime* as enacted by Monty Python, a dizzying whirlpool of historical figures, creatures out of legend, characters out of literature, and the creations of Di Filippo's own remarkable imagination.

December 1995

The Nitpicker's Guide for Next Generation Trekkers, Volume II by Phil Farrand (Dell, 368 pp, $12.95 pb).

Fans of the first *Nitpicker's Guide*—and surely there must be a few among *Sci-Fi Entertainment* readers—now have more mind-boggling trivia to ponder and to stump their friends with: trivia such as the "number of times we see Picard buck naked" (one) and the "vintage of the champagne that christens the *Enterprise*" (Star Date 2265). Farrand, clearly an obsessive, provides insanely tough questions ("How far is it from Earth to Malcor III?") for each episode of the series, as well as maddeningly picky plot bloopers. ("When La Forge falls in the pit, his visor clearly lands off to his right. However, a few moments later he picks it up by reaching to his left.")

For hard-core Trekkers, a book like this ought to be sheer catnip. Others, however, may be reminded of what William Shatner said to a roomful of worshipful fans in that long-ago *Saturday Night Live* sketch: "Get a life!"

April 1996

Celebrating a master of horror whose classic films relied on shadows, not special effects.

Val Lewton's movies are today more revered than watched. As the producer of such 1940s horror classic as *Cat People, I Walked with a Zombie, The Seventh Victim, Isle of the Dead,* and other low-budget fare, Lewton's name has come to represent a particular style of horror—restrained, literate, and relatively subtle—that relies more on mood than on monsters, more on shadows than on special effects, and more on suggestion than on explicit violence.

It's a style highly praised by film historians, horror aficionados, and critics, but less popular with a public raised on *The Exorcist, Alien, Friday the 13th, A Nightmare on Elm Street,* and *Night of the Living Dead*. When Paul Schrader's remake of *Cat People* came out in 1982, I recall, many critics denounced its dependence on nudity, special effects, and gore; they preferred—or claimed they did—Lewton's 1942 black-and-white original. But if most video-store habitués were polled as to which version they wanted to rent again and again, the one in which Simone Simon's visit to a pet shop leaves the animals screeching in terror (a nice scene, to be sure) or the one in which Ed Begley Jr. gets his arm ripped off by a panther and Nastassia Kinski prowls naked through the grass, I suspect they'd opt for the latter.

Yet in its day, as Edmund G. Bansak demonstrates in *Fearing the Dark: The Val Lewton Career* (McFarland, 579 pp, $45), the original *Cat People* was a genuine hit, "a national phenomenon" that played to "sellout crowds" and rescued its tight-fisted studio, RKO, from financial ruin; costing less than $135,000 to make, it went on to gross more than $4 million. Bansak, whose book is clearly a labor of love—an exhaustive, richly detailed film-by-film biography that makes the case for Lewton as one of B-moviedom's most influential figures—quotes a 1946 *Life* interview in which Lewton summed up his credo: "I'll tell you a secret: If you make the screen dark enough, the mind's eye will read anything into it.... We're great ones for dark patches.... The horror addicts will populate the darkness with more horrors than all the horror writers in Hollywood could think of."

Like other "B" producers, Lewton had to contend with similarly limited budges on all his films; and Bansak reveals that in most cases, he was also forced to work with the lurid titles that the studio's front office had already cooked up. *Cat People, The Curse of the Cat People, I Walked with a Zombie, The Leopard Man, The Seventh Victim*—all these titles were decreed by RKO before any stories were concocted (or adapted) to go with them. As Bansak observes, it was, for Lewton, "a task tantamount to coordinating an entire suit of clothes to fit the choice of tie clip."

In the case of *The Curse of the Cat People,* the fit between title and subject was a particularly loose one—to the movie's misfortune. Because RKO had had a hit with *Cat People,* it demanded a sequel, or at least something it could market as one. Lewton, as the book makes clear, accommodated the studio chiefs, but only so far, penning an original treatment that had virtually nothing to do with the earlier film (though it resurrected several of its characters) and populating the new one with various feline images—ornaments, taxidermy, and so forth—that are completely extraneous to the plot. In truth, in case you haven't seen it, *Curse* is a delicate, dreamy, somewhat Disneyesque fantasy about a young girl with an imaginary (or supernatural) playmate who, in a moment of danger, becomes her protector. It's a lovely film, exquisitely shot, but it is so far removed from its title that, on first viewing, you're apt to be disappointed or even infuriated.

"When *The Curse of the Cat People* was released," says Bansak, "its title was declared ill-chosen by every film reviewer in the nation; and yet the film itself was heralded by scores of movie critics and caught the attention of universities, psychological circles, and parent groups." There's one thing we can be thankful for, at least. Bad as the title is, it's a lot better than the one Lewton himself wanted: *Amy and Her Friend.*

Sympathetic to Lewton without being blind to his weaknesses, Bansak is a painstakingly thorough historian who even gives us critiques of Lewton's early fiction (he wrote nearly a dozen quickie novels before heading for Hollywood), including a short story, "The Bagheeta," that appeared in a 1930 *Weird Tales.* Set in Lewton's native Ukraine and inspired in part by his lifelong fear of cats, the tale is a hint of themes to come, for it involves a woman who shape-shifts into a savage leopard.

So thorough is Bansak, in fact, that *Fearing the Dark* has been taken to task—by my favorite genre critic, *Filmfax*'s David J. Hogan, no less—for giving us more than we want: specifically, by providing too many unnecessary chapters on Lewton's filmmaking contemporaries and disciples, including dozens of pages on, of all people,

Orson Welles. Hogan is probably right; there's a lot of padding here. Still, when it comes to books about film, particularly when they're written as well as this one, I tend to subscribe to the theory that more is better.

Lewton died in 1951, not yet forty-seven years old. Today most of his work may seem rather dated, but the man's unusual vision lives on in intelligent, atmospheric horror films such as *Curse of the Demon* and *The Haunting,* the one directed by Jacques Tourneur, the other by Robert Wise. Both directors had worked under Val Lewton.

Human Monsters: The Bizarre Psychology of Movie Villains by George E. Turner and Michael H. Price (Kitchen Sink Press, 208 pp, $16.95 pb).

The subtitle of this book is deceptive; it is neither a study of psychology nor an examination of evil. Rather, it's an illustrated guide to sixty-five colorful B-movies of the 1930s and '40s (including *The Leopard Man* and *The Seventh Victim*), complete with production histories, casts, plot synopses, and affectionate, knowledgeable commentaries. Each movie receives three or four pages, making the book something of a sequel to Turner and Price's earlier collaboration, *Forgotten Horrors: Early Talkie Chillers from Poverty Row,* a useful reference work that belongs on every genre buff's bookshelf. If you want to know the story of *A Shriek in the Night* (1933) or *A Face in the Fog* (1936), find yourself a copy of *Forgotten Horrors.* If you want the lowdown on *Murders in the Zoo* (1933), in which Lionel Atwill feeds his wife to the crocodiles, or *The Ape* (1940), in which Boris Karloff dons a gorilla suit to commit a string of murders, check out *Human Monsters.*

Budding filmmakers reading this book, and who also read the Val Lewton biography noted above, will find themselves confronted by a sort of Ten Commandments of Horror, a set of ten axioms—by two hardheaded Hollywood veterans—that both complement and clash with one another. The Bansak book quotes Universal producer George Waggner, best known for the Lon Chaney Jr. vehicles *The Wolf Man, The Ghost of Frankenstein,* and *Frankenstein Meets the Wolf Man,* on his "seven-ingredient recipe for horror films: (1) They must be once-upon-a-time tales. (2) They must be believable in characterization. (3) They must have unusual special effects. (4) Besides the major monster, there must be a secondary character of weird appearance, such as Igor. (5) They must confess right off that the show is a horror film. (6) They must include a pish-tush character to express the normal skepticism of the audience. (7) They must be based on some pseudo-scientific premise."

Contrast this with the "three fundamental theories" of horror films that Val Lewton espouses in an RKO press release, quoted in the Turner-Price book: "First is that the audience will people any patch of darkness with more horror, suspense, and frightfulness than the most imaginative writer could ever dream up. Second, and most important, is the fact that extraordinary things can happen to very ordinary people. And third is to use the beauty of setting and camerawork to ward off audience laughter at situations which, when less beautifully photographed, might seem ludicrous."

That last piece of advice seems applicable not only to horror films but to horror fiction as well. Style counts; it counts in horror more, perhaps, than in any other genre. While science fiction, in print or on screen, may often get by on a particularly novel idea, and while mystery relies largely on an intricate plot, the style of a horror tale or film is crucial; it must be insidiously persuasive, skillfully orchestrating suspense, building up atmosphere by subtle accretion, one dab at a time. The author is trying, above all, to create a mood—and, in the process, to convince the viewer or reader of something he knows just isn't so. The major obstacle, as a fantasy critic once lamented, is that "in a fundamental way, this stuff is ridiculous." The joy of good movies is that they make us forget that fact.

June 1996

A behind-the-scenes look at a sci-fi classic—including a nuts-and-bolts tour of "Ridleyville."

Arguably one of the most important science fiction films ever made, *Blade Runner* has changed the way we think of the future. It may not be—indeed, probably *won't* be—a gleaming, sterile place like Alphaville or the glossy, high-tech world conjured up by *2001*. It won't look like an industrial park or an airport—or, à la *Star Trek*, like the hotel lobby of the Marriott. It'll be crowded, grungy, inefficient, and reeking of humanity: a Babel, a Baghdad, a Calcutta.

And it won't be all of a piece. Modern innovations will exist side by side with remnants of the past—just as they do today. Future hipsters will wear 1940s fashions; religious cults will flourish; kinky sex will still be for sale. Despite the presence of scientific miracles—space colonies, synthetic humanoids, gravity-defying automobiles—it will remain a world of chaos, crime, pollution, and decay.

This was the vision of urban America circa 2019—a distinctly dystopian vision—served up by director Ridley Scott and his talented crew of designers. It wasn't new to longtime SF readers who'd grown up on Robert A. Heinlein, John Brunner (whose *Stand on Zanzibar* explores a similarly crowded future), or Philip K. Dick, on whose novel *Do Androids Dream of Electric Sheep?* the film was based. But it was new to moviegoers, some of whom hailed *Blade Runner* as a revelation, "a masterpiece."

Yet as Paul M. Sammon reminds us in *Future Noir: The Making of 'Blade Runner'* (HarperPrism, 459 pp, $14), when the film was released in 1982, it was anything but a hit. The critics were not charmed—one that Sammon quotes described the plot as "absolutely hopeless," another dismissed it as "boring"—and as for how the movie fared at the box office, one of Sammon's chapter titles, "An Indifferent Public," says it all. Even today, the usually reliable Leonard Maltin gives *Blade Runner* a mere one-and-a-half stars.

Most moviegoers, fans and foes alike, agree that the film's strong point is its set design, its "look." The problems lie in its not-very-likable characters and its sometimes illogical plot. As Sammon concedes, "Too many narrative links were dropped and forgotten during the rewriting process."

Sammon himself, who first covered the production for a special issue of *Cinefantastique* back in 1982 and has been amassing material about it ever since, is an unabashed admirer of the film, but no apologist for it; he writes about *Blade Runner* and its creators with insight, affection, and a breathtaking grasp of the technicalities of filmmaking, yet he maintains sufficient critical distance to acknowledge personal conflicts on the set between the thorny, occasionally arrogant director and his resentful crew, as well as between the film's stars. ("Harrison hated Sean," a production executive confides about a scene between the two. "That was not a love scene, that was a hate scene. . . . He hated her, hated her.") The book is wise, well paced, abounding in fascinating trivia, and impossible to put down; it kept me reading through the night (and ruined for the next day). And while it's sure to give you a new appreciation of *Blade Runner*'s brilliance, it's thorough—and honest—enough to include a highly detailed chapter on "*Blade Runner* Blunders."

One of the things that makes it particularly entertaining is that Sammon has talked to almost all the major players in the cast and crew (including, in the appendix, a 19-page interview with Scott), and he's gotten some terrific quotes from them. The marvelous, larger-than-life actor Brion James, for example, who plays the lethal android Leon, addresses the very first question that has always bedeviled me: "Some people have asked, 'Why did Holden [the security agent] have to run a Voigt-Kampff test on me [testing whether someone is a genuine human or an android imposter] if the police already had tapes of Leon and knew what he looked like?' The answer to that one was that those tapes didn't get to the police until after I shot Holden. During my V-K test the cops didn't have that much information on us. Holden was just on a fishing expedition."

While this explanation of an apparent plot inconsistency may not convince you any more than it convinced me, it's not entirely unreasonable.

Among the book's other revelations:
- David *(Unforgiven)* Peoples' initial rewrite of the Hampton Fancher script opened with a thrilling scene set in an "'Offworld Termination Dump,' a small planetoid used for the cremation of androids whose four-year life spans have run out. Two 'Dumpers' (goggle- and fire-ensuited workmen) are introduced, routinely shoveling dead androids from a huge pile of cadavers, when one of the 'corpses' suddenly stirs. It is a very-much-alive Roy Batty, masquerading as a dead android. Batty then surreptitiously pulls Mary and Leon from the heap of bodies, and before the trio attack the defenseless Dumpers, they pause to stare up at the glittering heavens—and the beckoning planet Earth."

- From the title of Philip K. Dick's original novel (whose final question mark this book unaccountably leaves off), the film went through several title changes—from *Android* to *Mechanismo* to *Dangerous Days*—before Fancher, raiding his home library, came across "a slim, little-known book by celebrated 'beat' author William Burroughs" called *Blade Runner: (a movie)*, the title of which was duly purchased.
- Fancher's first choice to play detective Rick Deckard was Robert Mitchum. Other suggestions: Tommy Lee Jones and Christopher Walken. The first actor who actually expressed an interest in the part—thereby requiring some changes in the script—was, of all people, Dustin Hoffman.
- Contrary to popular belief, Harrison Ford's controversial voice-over narration was not forced upon the director in a last-minute effort to save the film. Explains Fancher: "Ridley was the one who initially pushed the voice-over idea. That's why it's on so many of my drafts. Scott was after the feel of a '40s detective thriller, so he liked the idea of using this *film noir* device."
- The movie's gritty urban setting was, at various times, conceived of as a future New York, a linked megalopolis of New York/Chicago, and a similar merging of San Francisco and Los Angeles dubbed "San Angeles," before the on-screen presence of L.A.'s famous Bradbury Building necessitated listing that city as the locale. (The set itself, to which Sammon proves an authoritative tour guide, was popularly known as Ridleyville. "It even *smelled* like a sleazy metropolis," Sammon reports. "Ridleyville was permeated by the aromas of burned coffee, wet trash, and boiling noodles.")
- The snake that the exotic dancer, played by Joanna Cassidy, is wearing in one photo—without much else—was in fact the actress's own pet, "a Burmese python named 'Darling.'"
- Some of Rutger Hauer's haunting final scene was invented by the actor himself. (Hauer, incidentally, comes across as witty, eccentric, and formidably intelligent.)

- As has long been rumored, the shots of the wilderness through which Deckard and Rachael travel at the end are in fact outtakes from the opening of *The Shining*.

In recent years there've been a spate of "making of" books, some of them sloppy, most of them written too fast. *Future Noir* is different; it's a true labor of love and one of those rare things, a "making of" book actually worthy of its subject.

The House on the Borderland by William Hope Hodgson (Carroll & Graf, 186 pp, $4.95 pb).

Critic E. F. Bleiler calls this novel, first published in 1908, "one of the classics of supernatural fiction." H. P. Lovecraft noted that, were it not for "a few touches of commonplace sentimentality," it would be "a classic of the first water."

The fact is, supernatural horror is a genre better suited to short stories than novels; it's hard to sustain dread over the long haul. *Borderland* is one of the genre's few near-successes; it's easily one of the weirdest, most powerful, and most spellbinding books ever written, though it's also, at times, tedious, confusing, and far too ambitious for its own good. Purporting to be a diary discovered in the ruins of an isolated house in the wastelands of western Ireland, it tells of swine-like creatures that tunnel up from the earth behind the house, and of cosmic forces from above that pull the narrator across vast stretches of space and time. It is, above all, a vision of a loneliness so profound it's almost unimaginable.

This new paperback edition—one of a number of horror classics that Carroll & Graf have been bringing out—is therefore most welcome. Unfortunately, though, it's clear that some corners were cut in its printing, which seems unusually shoddy: Ink, in places, seems to run into the cheap paper, blurring the letters; other sections are as faint as a poor Xerox. More important, this edition plunges right into the narrative, omitting the original framing device, the "Author's Introduction to the Manuscript," in which Hodgson describes the newly discovered diary's "long-damp pages . . . filled with a quaint but legible hand-writing, and writ very close. I have the queer, faint, pit-water smell of it in my nostrils now as I write." This edition also lacks the novel's full, old-fashioned title ("From the Manuscript, discovered in 1877 by Messrs. Tonnison and Berreggnog, in the Ruins that lie to the South of the Village of Kraighten, in the West of Ireland," etc.), as well as the opening dedicatory poem to Hodgson's father. Imagine, short-changing a classic just to save a sheet or two of paper!

October 1996

The science fiction of the starship *Enterprise* could become science fact, say two noted physicists.

Back in the '50s, the TV show *Disneyland* once spent an hour examining the wackily surreal physics of cartoons: Goofy strolling blithely off a cliff, unaware he isn't on solid ground, and not falling until he chances to look down; Donald Duck in an elevator, stretching as the car descends and compressing as it comes to a stop; some other character folding up like an accordion when a safe drops on his head. The episode was entitled "The Plausible Impossible"—and the same phrase came to mind as I read *The Physics of 'Star Trek'* by Lawrence M. Krauss (HarperCollins, 202 pp, $20). For just as in the world of animation, things happen in the *Star Trek* universe that defy all the known laws of physics, but it's the task of the writers to make us accept them as perfectly reasonable.

Yet in some ways, surprisingly, that's Krauss's task as well, because his book is anything but a debunking study of faster-than-light drive, antigravity, and all the other phenomena associated with SF movies and TV. In fact, Krauss is at pains through the book to point out not merely where *Star Trek* goes wrong (and he details a number of places, which I'll get to in a moment), but to demonstrate how some of the mind-stretchingly improbable things we're shown may actually be—in theory, at least—within the realm of possibility.

He reveals, for example, that "the planet Vulcan, home to Spock, actually has a venerable history in 20th-century physics." In the early 1900s, it seems astronomers were puzzled by slight deviations in Mercury's orbit, contrary to what Newtonian physics would have predicted, and they theorized that these might be caused by an as-yet-undiscovered heavenly body. "It was suggested that a new planet existed inside Mercury's orbit," says Krauss. "The name given to the hypothetical planet was Vulcan." The real reason for the orbital deviation, he explains, was not Vulcan but Einsteinian curved space—a concept that, once allowed in like some cosmic Trojan horse, allows with it a host of wild possibilities. "Along with curved space," Krauss assures us, "come black holes, wormholes, and perhaps even warp speeds and time travel."

Time travel? Can the man be serious? Well, if you don't care to take Krauss's word for it, how about that of the world's most famous living physicist? That's right; Krauss's book sports an astonishingly optimistic foreword by none other than *Star Trek* fan (and sometime actor) Stephen Hawking, who gives the show his seal of approval: "We may not yet be able to boldly go where no man (or woman) has gone before," he writes, "but at least we can do it in the mind."

Hawking acknowledges that faster-than-light travel "is absolutely essential to *Star Trek*'s story line" and that the idea is fraught with problems: An astronaut hurtling toward a distant star, for example, even if he's traveling well below the speed of light, may experience as a decade or two what, to observers on earth, would seem a voyage of thousands of years. "Fortunately," writes Hawking, "Einstein's general theory of relativity allows the possibility for a way around this difficulty: One might be able to warp space-time and create a shortcut between the places one wanted to visit. Although there are problems of negative energy, it seems that such warping might be within our capabilities in the future. . . . One of the consequences of rapid interstellar travel would be that one could also travel back in time."

I hope he's working on those little "problems of negative energy" he so offhandedly alludes to, because I have a hankering to visit the 1939 World's Fair, and maybe the Globe Theater.

Krauss himself is a professor of physics and astronomy at Case Western Reserve University. He may not be as famous as Hawking, but *The Physics of 'Star Trek'* is certainly an easier read than Hawking's *A Brief History of Time*. Interestingly, Krauss is also the author of an earlier book, *Fear of Physics: A Guide for the Perplexed*. This new one might almost deserve the same title, for it proves a quick, clever, breezy, once-over-lightly introductory course in physics, using the TV show as its jumping-off point.

Krauss defends *Star Trek*'s cast of aliens from a dismissive remark made by Nobel laureate Sheldon Glashow ("They all look like people with elephantiasis!"), noting, as a true fan should, that the show does offer, "in the sixth season of *The Next Generation,* a rationale" for this familial resemblance: It turns out that "some very ancient civilization" seeded hundreds of planets throughout the universe with the same genetic material, from which all of us, humans and aliens alike, are descended.

"There are approximately 100 billion galaxies in the observable universe, each containing more or less that many stars!" he writes elsewhere. "There are roughly 400 billion stars in our galaxy. It would seem truly remarkable if our Sun were the only one around which intelligent life developed."

But if Krauss finds things to praise for their scientific accuracy—such as the depiction of an outer-space gunfight in which all the little drops of blood flying around the ship are spherical, just as they would be in zero gravity—he also points out *Star Trek*'s many lapses, from the vast ones (he pooh-poohs the notion of "parallel universes" existing in other dimensions) to the small: He notes that in the rock-climbing scene at the start of *Star Trek V: The Final Frontier,* when Spock breaks Captain Kirk's fall just inches from the ground, the sudden stop would kill Kirk just as quickly as actually hitting the ground.

Similarly, he observes that in real life, acceleration to light-speed would reduce the *Enterprise*'s crew to what *The Star Trek Encyclopedia* describes as "chunky salsa," and he remains skeptical of what the show's writers dreamed up as a way of getting around that small problem: a passing reference, left unexplained, to "inertial dampers." Clearly writers can get away with things that scientists cannot.

Finally, there's what he calls "the infamous *Ghost* error," in which a noncorporeal spirit can pass its hand through objects or walk unimpeded through walls, yet it can also seat itself in a chair or stroll across the floor. Krauss asks, in a section title, "Which is more sensitive, your hands or your butt?" and concludes, "Matter is matter, and chairs and floors are no different from walls, and as far as I know, feet and butts are no more or less solid than hands." His parting advice strikes me as extremely wise: "Any sensible trekkerphysicist recognizes that *Star Trek* must be taken with a rather large grain of salt."

December 1996

Get acquainted with some sci-fi films that make Ed Wood's look like masterworks.

Tom Weaver is generally acknowledged to be a consummate pro in a field of doofuses. If you read many genre-movie magazines, you've no doubt discovered that most of the interviews they run are, to say the least, amateurish, especially those dealing with actors and filmmakers of the past. All too often the interviewer's questions are ignorant or overfamiliar, and the quondam celebrity—whether a half-forgotten B-movie director, a retired screenwriter, or an aging scream queen—comes off as either obnoxiously boastful or pathetically over the hill.

Weaver, however, is always a class act. Depend on him to ask the smartest questions and (no mean trick sometimes) to make his subjects sound both thoughtful and articulate.

Since 1988, Weaver has been collecting the interviews he's done for various film magazines, often expanding and updating them, into a series of books for McFarland, each containing around two dozen pieces illustrated with black-and-white photos. The books (and the selection of photos) are uniformly excellent; in fact, the only way to distinguish them is by their progressively more eccentric titles, ranging from the staid *Interviews with B Science Fiction and Horror Movie Makers* (421 pp, $38.50), the first in the series, to the fifth and most recent, *It Came from Weaver Five* (386 pp, $38.50). (The prices, you'll notice, are high; McFarland's main market is libraries, and the books all come bound in sturdy cloth library bindings.)

In the first book, Weaver makes plain his uncondescending affection for the genre—an affection that shines through the entire series. "Fans of Hollywood gloss," he writes, with just a touch of defiance, "be warned. This may not be the sort of interview book you're used to. There are no tales of multimillion-dollar productions or of pampered glitterati, no elegant Tinseltown soirées, big premieres, or jet-set ostentation. Most of the films discussed in this book are medium- to low-budget productions, some of them made by people who are at best footnotes in the big book of Hollywood history. Perhaps it *does* require something of an open and tolerant mind to see the good in pictures about Styrofoam crab monsters, Martian Jell-O, hubcaps, sparklers, and bathospheres from outer space, thirtyish teenagers and bald midgets armed with vacuum cleaners. But this is not meant as any sort of apology. It takes far more talent and imagination to make a good film on a low budget than to make one with all the materials and means of a major studio at one's disposal."

One such talent—more than a footnote, but certainly a name few would recognize—is Gene Fowler, Jr., who directed two of the 1950s' most celebrated B-movies, famous (even among those who've never seen them) for their lurid titles: *I Was a Teenage Werewolf* and *I Married a Monster from Outer Space*. Interviewed in the second book in the series, *Science Fiction Stars and Horror Heroes* (458 pp, $38.50), Fowler displays the humility and good humor that saw him through these and other low-budget productions— and that typifies the men and women Weaver interviews. Like most of them, instead of griping, he did his best with the hand (or title) he was dealt: "I did not try to make just an exploitation picture," he says. "I was trying to do something with a little substance to it." That included making the first film's mad-scientist villain somewhat sympathetic: "I always figured that a villain, in his own eyes, was a very good, very nice fellow. . . . He was actually trying to do good for the world."

Fowler expresses one opinion that, for a Hollywood director, is decidedly unconventional: "Directors," he says, "shouldn't be allowed to edit their own movies"; indeed, he's convinced that many a "director's cut" can be an exercise in sheer self-indulgence. "I think you should allow the editor to put the picture together without any kind of supervision whatsoever," he says, "because he sometimes can find things that you don't even know you shot." I'm not sure whether to attribute this view to Fowler's modesty (and maybe plain good sense) or to the fact that he himself is a former film editor.

One of the highlights, for me, of Weaver's third book, *Attack of the Monster Movie Makers* (393 pp, $35), is his interview with Kenneth Tobey, star of the classic 1951 version of *The Thing*. Talk about modesty and good humor! Tobey is extremely self-deprecating, quick to criticize his own work ("I don't think I was very *good* in it," he says of his portrayal of what he terms "the head cricket"—the alien leader—in *Strange Invaders*, "but the director seemed to like it"), candid about the ups and downs of his rocky career, and grateful for those, such as director Joe Dante and fellow actor James Arness, who've kept him working. And for the record, he confirms that, despite Christian Nyby's name in the credits, it was producer Howard Hawks who really directed *The Thing*—"all except one scene. Chris Nyby directed us coming through a door, and it's the worst scene in the picture."

My favorite is the fourth book in the series, *They Fought in the Creature Features* (326 pp, $38.50), in part because of its frontispiece, a posed photo, hilarious yet somehow touching, of the gorgeous Julie Adams shaking hands with the Creature from the Black Lagoon—or rather, with her costar in the 1954 movie, the underwater performer Ricou Browning, dressed in what appears to be an early stage of his Gill Man costume, a body suit with fish-faced creature mask but no scales yet attached. Adams is beaming affectionately and flashing a 600-watt smile; the Creature, staring pop-eyed at her as it stiffly grips her hand, seems as amazed at her beauty as we are.

"The Creature scared people," says Adams, in the book's first interview, "but there was also a sort of sweetness about it. In the real classics, there always is that feeling of compassion for the monster. I think maybe it touches something in ourselves, maybe the darker parts of ourselves, that long to be loved and think they really *can't* ever be loved."

Browning, interviewed later in the book, talks about the beloved film and TV series *Flipper*, which he created, and recalls some of the difficulties of playing the Creature. "It was kind of like swimming in your overcoat.... The eyes of the Creature mask were a couple of inches beyond my eyes, so it was kind of like looking through a keyhole." A photo shows him in full Creature costume with the headpiece removed; he looks like a rugged movie star, smiling and handsome.

This volume in the series also contains interviews with three cast members of the 1956 sci-fi film *Forbidden Planet:* Richard Anderson (the Id Creature's first victim), George Wallace (best remembered as the flying Commando Cody in the 1952 serial *Radar Men from the Moon*), and Anne Francis, who says that playing the movie's naïve young heroine required "no great preparation on my part; I wasn't that worldly-wise at that point myself."

Francis voices a sentiment common to many of the performers interviewed in these books: astonishment—and gratitude—that the movie in question has proved so popular. "At the time, I don't think that any of us really were aware of the fact that it was going to turn into a longtime cult film. . . . *Forbidden Planet* just had a life of its own, something that none of us was aware was going to happen." Ricou Browning expresses the same feeling: "As far as I see it, *Creature from the Black Lagoon* was just another movie, just another job. I've done many things since then that I am much more proud of. But I've gotten more reaction out of the Creature thing than anything else." And so does Robert Cornthwaite, still best known for playing the foolishly idealistic scientist in *The Thing:* "When I saw it, I thought, 'Ah, it's a good movie. Thank *God* it's a good movie!' Because, I confess, I really didn't know *what* to expect!"

And here, in fact, is a great truth worth keeping in mind as one sits in the darkness watching a movie unfold and, at times, wondering whatever possessed the actors, director, and producer to have wasted their time on it: the fact that, while one is working on a film, one has *no idea* whether it's any good until it's shot, assembled, scored, and offered to the world. And even then, there's no telling what the public will make of it. Or as Kim Hunter says in the second book in the series, quoting the makeup man on *Planet of the Apes:* "We're either gonna be real or it's gonna be Mickey Mouse. And we won't know until it gets on the screen."

Finally, there is one theme that emerges rather movingly in nearly every interview, a kind of nostalgic refrain: Our budgets were tiny, we had to work quickly (and often under miserable conditions), the pay was lousy, but we were young, we liked each other, and, dammit, we had fun.

April 1997

You'll have to rely on your imagination, because these 50 intriguing movies never made it to the screen.

Remember that great scene in *Starfleet Academy*—you know, the sixth *Star Trek* movie—in which the young cadet Spock, the school's first alien, endures racist taunts from his classmates, only to be defended by fellow student James Kirk? And remember that deeply affecting scene where the two meet again on the maiden voyage of the *Enterprise*?

You don't? Well, maybe that's because *Starfleet Academy* was never actually filmed. As Chris Gore tells it in *The 50 Greatest Movies Never Made* (St. Martin's, 249 pp, $13.95 pb), a combination of "studio meddling, actors' egos, and petty Hollywood power plays . . . deprived us of what could have been the greatest *Star Trek* tale of all."

It's a neat idea for a book—a celebration of movies that might have been—and Lord knows there's no end of material, since what Gore calls "the alternate universe of unfinished cinema" is many times vaster than the mass of completed films. In fact, the figures he cites are pretty scary: Approximately 42,000 screenplays are registered each year with the Writers Guild, he says, but only 3,000 of them get optioned or bought. And of these, "fewer than fifty actually get made." (What's even scarier is how few of the ones that get made are any good.)

Another potential gem that never got made is *Timegate*, a sci-fi dinosaur adventure dreamed up by special-effects designer Jim Danforth. The story dealt with future vacationers who are transported back to the age of reptiles on a time-tripping dinosaur hunt. Things predictably go wrong, the timegate gets damaged, and in order to return to the future, the group must journey through this primitive world to a distant place of rescue, battling various prehistoric monsters along the way.

From Gore's description, the special effects would probably have been fun: lots of painstakingly detailed miniature models and even a life-size "walking machine." (This was in the late 1970s, before computer animation made dinosaurs' movements smoother and more realistic, but also robbed them of a certain wonder.) According to Danforth, "We created a warehouse full of esoteric props and future vehicles. We shot thousands of feet of second-unit background plates and high-speed miniatures." Alas, what was intended to be a low-budget production grew more and more costly; eventually the studio, AIP, pulled the plug. "The props," Gore reports, "were thrown out for the taking."

Some of the projects Gore focuses on barely made it out of the idea stage, such as a Marx Brothers comedy involving the mob, the United Nations, and a scheme to steal four suitcases full of diamonds from Tiffany's. (Judging from Gore's summary of the plot, based on a 40-page treatment written for director Billy Wilder, the film wouldn't have been very funny anyway.) Others actually made it onto celluloid, such as the famous 1936–37 production of *I, Claudius*, with Charles Laughton in the title role. Set in ancient Rome, the film was never completed, largely because its leading lady, Merle Oberon, was injured in a car accident; but Gore quotes someone who, after viewing the existing footage, hailed Laughton's acting as "one of the greatest performances in the history of the cinema."

Of course, virtually *any* unfinished film, like virtually any unproduced screenplay, might contain seeds of greatness. "Heard melodies are sweet," Keats reminds us, "but those unheard are sweeter," since they exist only in our imagination. Similarly, imagination can turn a list of aborted motion picture projects into a pantheon of potential masterpieces. As Gore himself explains, "Since they weren't made, they will always be great—no one will muck them up."

Nonetheless, he admits to being uneasy with the very word "greatest." "If I had my way," he confides, "I'd rather title this book something like *The 50 Best, Coolest, Weirdest, Strangest, Wildest, Most Amazing, Most Fantastic, Most Stupendous, Most Remarkable, Most Incredible, Most Bizarre, and Potentially Greatest Movies That Never Happened.*"

One of the wildest movies in his list—if not necessarily the greatest—would have been *Alien vs. Predator*, based on the comic-book series that pitted these outer-space horror icons against one another. The result? "Cool big-screen fighting between alien races," says Gore, smacking his lips. "That's what this kind of movie is all about." It seems only fitting that when the project was scrapped, its screenwriter, Peter Briggs, was hired to write another monster/monster death-match, *Freddy vs. Jason,* merging the worlds of *Friday the 13th* and *Nightmare on Elm Street.*

Several other sci-fi projects make Gore's list, including *The Disappearance*—based on a Philip Wylie novel in which all the men on earth find themselves trapped in one dimension, all the women in another—and *Statical Planets,* the brainchild of *Mystery Science Theater 3000* creator Joel Hodgson. *Statical* was to be a witty parody of the sort of films Hodgson had ridiculed on *MST3K,* complete with '50s-style black-and-white photography and a filmmaking process he dubbed "Static-A-Matic," in which audiences were encouraged to shock themselves at designated moments by generating their own static electricity—a takeoff on the notorious stunt (was it ever really used?) in which producer William Castle claimed to have wired up theater seats during showings of *The Tingler.*

Like so many stories in the book, *Statical*'s ends in frustration: "Unfortunately, financing issues prevented further production beyond the making of the trailer." Still, says Gore, the trailer alone had audiences squealing with delight.

Last year, reviewing a collection of Hollywood interviews, I noted that Alfred Hitchcock had once been hired to direct a film about the *Titanic*. Gore doesn't mention this project, but he does describe another Hitchcock nonstarter, *The Blind Man,* a thriller that the director and *North by Northwest* screenwriter Ernest Lehman cooked up somewhere between *Psycho* and *The Birds.* James Stewart was to star as a pianist, blind since birth, who is given a corneal transplant and elects to spend his initial day of sight in a rather famous locale: "The picture takes place in Disneyland," reports Gore, "as the blind man, seeing for the first time in his life, discovers he has been given the eyes of a murdered man. He attempts to track down the killer, who in turn is trying to kill him." What doomed this project was a combination of creative indecision—Lehman appears to have lost confidence in the script—and a veto by Walt Disney himself, who, understandably, wasn't too keen on the notion of a killer stalking Disneyland.

There's no reference to *The Blind Man* in *The Alfred Hitchcock Triviography & Quiz Book* by Kathleen Kaska (Renaissance, 223 pp,

$12.95 pb), but all of his completed movies—and a number of his TV show's episodes—are included among the book's thousand or so trivia questions. (There's also a biographical chronology and a section listing the casts and credits of his films.)

Are the questions hard? Well, not if you've seen that particular movie within the past few minutes. Otherwise, they're hard indeed—hard and more than somewhat dry. In *Marnie,* for example, "What is the name of the horse Marnie rides at the stable? . . . What is the cost of the engagement ring that Mark buys Marnie?" (The answers, if you care, are "Forio" and "$42,000.") In *Psycho,* what record can be found on Norman Bates's turntable? A. "Vienna Blood"; B. "Funeral March of a Marionette"; C. "Eroica"; or D. "Un Bel Di." Does it strike you as interesting that the correct answer is C? If so, then maybe you'll enjoy this book. (I myself was disappointed that answer B—obviously thrown in because it's the music from Hitchcock's TV series—was not identified as such in the answers.)

The author has also provided several lists of "Trivia Facts." Some really *are* trivial—"Hitchcock loved American food and would often eat, in one sitting, several hot dogs covered with sauerkraut"—but some are genuinely provocative, e.g., that Hitch's own daughter refused to let her kids watch *Frenzy* (quite wisely, I'd say), and that "Hitchcock claimed that he had an ankle fetish, which explained why there were so many shots of women's ankles in his films." No doubt we have the subject here of a future grad-school dissertation.

Speaking of trivia, you'll find fascinating examples of it in *Resist or Serve: The Official Guide to 'The X-Files,' Volume 4,* by Andy Meisler (HarperEntertainment, 288 pp, $16 pb), a stylish, highly detailed, and profusely illustrated episode-by-episode guide to the TV show's fifth season, complete with representative dialogue—so much dialogue, in fact, that you'll feel you're reading a short-story collection rather than a series of plot synopses. What's more, Meisler provides a behind-the-scenes account of every episode: where filming took place, problems on the set, last-minute changes in the story line, and candid comments by the cast and crew.

You may know, for example, that the season's tenth episode, "Chinga," featuring a malign enchanted doll, was cowritten by Stephen King and series creator Chris Carter. You probably didn't know that the two of them have yet to meet face to face (Carter adapted King's original script to better fit the series), and that what led King to *The X-Files* was his appearance on *Celebrity Jeopardy,* where he encountered—and beat—David Duchovny.

The episode's gruesome images were created by visual effects supervisor Laurie Kallsen-George, who then tested them out on her two sons, ages nine and eleven. "I gauge a lot of the shows by whether my kids can stand them or not," Kallsen-George told Meisler, laughing. "If they can't, I figure it succeeded—and 'Chinga' bothered them a lot."

Trying to shock two impressionable kids? One doubts that Hitchcock's daughter would have approved.

October 1999

With the exception of a few old dependables—John Grisham, Stephen King, Bill Shakespeare—authors' names don't sell movies. *Bram Stoker's Dracula* would probably have done better business if it had invoked director Francis Ford Coppola's name instead of Stoker's. Robert Bloch may have been the author of *Psycho,* but it was Hitchcock's name that drew the crowds.

But Edgar Allan Poe has always had a special cachet. Sticking his name in front of a movie title has proven so commercial that it's been used for films that have almost nothing to do with him.

Take three horror films, for example, starring the late Vincent Price—all of them described in *The Poe Cinema: A Critical Filmography* by Don G. Smith (McFarland, 312 pp, $55). In *The Conqueror Worm,* Price plays the real-life 17th-century "witch-finder" Matthew Hopkins; the film's only connection to Poe is that, in voice-over, Price recites some stanzas from Poe's poem of the same title. In *The City Under the Sea* (a.k.a. *War Gods of the Deep*), Price recites another Poe poem. (The movie itself owes less to Poe than to *Creature from the Black Lagoon.*) And *The Haunted Palace*—frequently billed as *Edgar Allan Poe's Haunted Palace*—is really an adaptation, by Richard Matheson, of H. P. Lovecraft's *The Case of Charles Dexter Ward*.

"I fought against calling it a Poe film," claims producer/director Roger Corman, "but AIP had made so much money with Poe films that they just stuck his name on it for box-office appeal."

Incidentally, of the eight films in Corman's Poe series, Smith prefers *The Masque of the Red Death*, finding in it "a welcome philosophical depth," and least likes *The Premature Burial* (the only one not starring Price), though he still considers it "a well-sustained horror film."

These are among the 81 titles from 13 countries that Smith's book examines, dating all the way back to an obscure 1908 silent called *Sherlock Holmes in the Great Murder Mystery*. In view of the box-office magic that Poe's name on a movie would later provide, it's ironic that this "Holmes" film was actually Poe's classic detective tale "The Murders in the Rue Morgue" in disguise.

But as early as 1912, another silent—*The Bells,* from the Edison studios—was invoking Poe's name to sell tickets. Some of its title cards quoted lines from Poe's poem "The Bells," adding a touch of literary distinction to what was really just another corny melodrama about a poor girl forced by her father to marry a miser.

This well-researched book, scholarly but never dry, reflects the author's lifelong enthusiasm for Poe and, it's clear, for movies in general. The one thing missing, I think, is some sort of broad critical overview—assuming one is possible—of Poe's influence on the cinema. Instead, the only introduction we're offered is a brief Poe biography, whereupon Smith plunges into the film-by-film appraisals that make up the book.

Still, the films themselves are so colorful and so varied, ranging from the gory and sadistic to the ethereal, that one forgives the author his impatience.

The career of one of the screen's longest-lived character actors was similarly wide-ranging and colorful; as Tom Weaver acknowledges at the start of *John Carradine: The Films* (McFarland, 405 pp, $65), throughout six decades the actor appeared in "some of the worst movies in the history of Hollywood," as well as "some of the best."

The latter would certainly include *The Grapes of Wrath*, which gave him his most celebrated role, that of the ex-preacher turned labor organizer Jim Casy. It would also include *Captains Courageous* (his personal favorite) and the classic Western *Stagecoach*.

As for the lousy films—well, consider some of the titles: *Superchick. Horror of the Blood Monsters. Billy the Kid versus Dracula*. (Actually, Weaver speaks kindly of this one: "It's every bit as silly as its title implies, but it isn't unwatchable.")

The twin lures of art and exploitation in a single career—the Carradine who founded his own acting troupe and could quote Shakespeare for hours, and the Carradine who'd appear in any film, no matter how benighted, so long as he was paid—form the central theme of this book. Here is a man who played the title roles in *Hamlet* and *Richard III*—as well as in *The Cosmic Man* and *The Wizard of Mars*. Here is an actor capable of turning out Oscar-worthy performances, but whose "bad side," in the words of Gregory William Mank, comprised "scores of 'B' and 'C' horror-exploitation films, heavy hamming, perennial rumors of drinking and eccentricities, garish marital woes, arrest for alimony contempt, drunk driving and traffic violations, a prostitution scandal, bankruptcy. . . . It was a pathetic indictment against the movie industry that this 'classic man,' who could recite entire Shakespearean plays by heart, who was a living link with some of the greatest films in Hollywood's history, survived primarily as a marquee name in truly horrid, abominably produced splatter films."

The bulk of this book is Weaver's, but Mank (whose *Hollywood Cauldron* I've already written about here) contributes a fascinating 43-page biography that traces his subject's life from 1906—when he was born Richmond Reed Carradine to a cultured, well-to-do family in New York City—through his four rocky marriages, to his mysterious death in Italy in 1988. The book also sports two guest introductions, by directors Joe Dante (who cast Carradine in *The Howling*) and Fred Olen Ray (who says, "I truly believe that Carradine was convinced that if he ever stopped working, he would die").

According to Mank, Carradine was invited to audition for the monster in *Frankenstein,* but turned it down because the role offered no dialogue, merely grunts. That aside, there's little the actor didn't play, from geniuses to imbeciles, gentlemen to low-lives. His specialty, however, was heavies: Westerners (the treacherous Bob Ford in *Jesse James*), vampires (the infamous Count in *House of Frankenstein* and *House of Dracula*), Nazis (the title role in *Hitler's Madman*), and just plain madmen (the serial strangler in *Bluebeard*). "I made my reputation as an evildoer," he boasted, "and I can't spoil it by going straight!"

Bluebeard's director, Edgar Ulmer, offers a judicious assessment of Carradine's style: "When directing John, one must be mindful of the fact that one is handling dynamite. John, without half trying, can overpower a scene. . . . One must remind him to put the brakes on, lest he chew up the sprocket holes on the film." As Carradine himself once told a reporter, "I am a *ham!* And the ham in an actor is what makes him interesting."

Carradine's formidable ego would have been extremely gratified by this book, particularly by the wealth of material it contains. In what represents a really monumental feat of film scholarship, Weaver surveys, by my count, some 210 films Carradine appeared in, and he does so in depth. (Carradine's TV work—such as the *Twilight Zone* episode "The Howling Man"—is mentioned only in passing.) Weaver's plot summaries, always lucid, are admirably succinct (no mean feat), and he is one of those rare writers who's consistently entertaining even when commenting on a film you haven't seen and never expect to.

On *Voodoo Man*: "Carradine baby-talks, prances around (his loose limbs bouncing every which way), and does such a good job of convincing us he's a moron that it isn't possible to picture him belting out Shakespeare during take-fives, even though that's probably what happened."

He excerpts irresistible passages of dialogue, like this from *The Unearthly,* in which Carradine plays a mad scientist and wrestler Tor Johnson *(Plan 9 from Outer Space)* his servant: "My servant Lobo came here a puny, broken man. Now he possesses the strength of a Hercules." "And the brain of a chicken," notes the film's hero. "Unfortunate!" Carradine admits.

And he has an eye for bloopers, such as this one in *Legacy of Blood:* "During the playing of Carradine's tape-recorded will, his voice is heard during a brief shot of the tape machine *not* in operation."

When it comes to movie gaffes, *Film Flubs: Memorable Movie Mistakes* by Bill Givens (Citadel, 187 pp, $12 pb) manages to find them not in the lowly B-movies that were Carradine's bread and butter, but in big-time blockbusters.

Titanic, for example, contains anachronisms such as a reference to the "United States Postal Service," the Santa Monica Pier, Wisconsin's Lake Wissota (a man-made lake constructed later), and a gospel verse bewailing the perils of air travel. Similarly, in *Indiana Jones and the Last Crusade,* "Indy and his father ride in the German zeppelin *Hindenberg*" in 1938; the famous aircraft blew up in 1937.

Givens notes that the first Indiana Jones film confused the biblical Mount Ararat with Mount Sinai and called a Mexican character Sapito onscreen, Saripo in the credits, and Satipo in the novelization. In one scene, he adds, you can see the glass separating Harrison Ford from a deadly cobra. (Which reminds me, I could swear I've noticed wires attached to the crablike creature's legs in an early scene in *Alien.*)

Twister is dubbed 1996's "Flubbed-Up Movie of the Year" for featuring a shirt that is both buttoned and unbuttoned, depending on the shot, "a one-lane dirt road" that turns into "a four-lane highway," a truck odometer that runs backward, a smashed windshield that mysteriously repairs itself, and binoculars on the dashboard that never budge, even as the vehicle gets tossed around.

Many flubs, of course, derive from sloppy continuity: An actress who starts a scene in black high heels and ends it in white (*Vertigo*), a tie that appears tied and untied (*Mars Attacks*), graveside flowers that turn from purple to yellow (*Pet Sematary*), or a neck wound that moves from one side to the other (*Bram Stoker's Dracula*). Other films (*Excalibur, Silver Streak, Scream,* and *The Fly*) afford glimpses of a cameraman or his reflection.

This little stocking-stuffer has at least one gaffe of its own: Though the index lists *Raiders of the Lost Ark* on page 31, you'll find nary a mention of it there.

June 2000

In a world he helped shape and a year he made famous, two new books honor science fiction's grandest old man.

Each time you feel a little tingle of wonder and excitement at writing "2001" on your letters and checks—and if you don't, you're probably reading the wrong magazine—you have Arthur C. Clarke to thank. What a blessing that Clarke (born 1917) was around to welcome in this momentous year, even if Stanley Kubrick (born 1928) was not.

As a prophet who's bridged the worlds of science and sci-fi, Clarke has had the pleasure of seeing many a prediction come true; he was a leading proponent of space flight as early as the 1940s and famously proposed, in a 1945 magazine article, the concept of "geosynchronous satellites" in fixed positions above the earth to facilitate global communications. At the time of Apollo 11's triumphant lunar landing, the novel and film of *2001: A Space Odyssey* had already been out for a year, and Clark found himself one of the world's most widely quoted authorities on interplanetary exploration. "The Apollo astronauts had already seen the film when they left for the Moon," Clarke recalls. "The crew of Apollo 8, who at Christmas 1968 became the first men ever to set eyes upon the lunar far side, told me that they had been tempted to radio back the discovery of a large black monolith. Alas," he adds, "discretion prevailed."

Clarke's reminiscences of that era, as well as his groundbreaking article on communications satellites, are reprinted in *Greetings, Carbon-Based Bipeds!: Collected Essays, 1934–1998* (St. Martin's, 572 pp, $16.95 pb), along with more than a hundred other pieces on subjects ranging from giant squids to SETI—the Search for Extra-Terrestrial Intelligence, a project celebrated in the book's title essay. There are also speeches (including a 1988 address to the first graduating class of International Space University), reviews (nuclear physicist Freeman Dyson's *Imagined Worlds,* and the 1951 disaster film *When Worlds Collide*), affectionate memoirs of fellow writers such as Isaac Asimov and Robert Bloch, as well as travel pieces about his adopted home, Sri Lanka, and the seas around it. Though I could do without the latter—aside from encounters with sharks, I don't find much of interest in Clarke's descriptions of beaches, spearfishing, and island living—there's not an essay in the book that isn't cogent, wise, and thought-provoking.

For all his braininess, however (or perhaps because of it), Clarke has never been the most eloquent or stylish of writers. He's hardheaded, straightforward, and not given to heights of shimmering prose—so it's both surprising and rather touching to discover that the earliest essay in the book is a tribute to one of the most lyrical and ethereal of fantasists, Lord Dunsany: "Under the magic of his art," writes the young Clarke, "the commonest things become enchanted, and when his imagination soars away from earth, we enter realms of fantasy indeed."

That essay, we're told, was written in 1942 and published two years later. Notice anything wrong? Yes—the title of the book promises work as far back as 1934, but there's nothing from the '30s at all. And the title is misleading in an even more important respect: These are not "collected" essays; far from it. Clarke's preface informs us that throughout his career he's written "at least a thousand pieces of nonfiction," but this book includes merely a fraction of them. When it comes to single-author books, "collected" generally means *all*; what this book presents are *selected* essays.

I'm disappointed, because there's a long-ago Clarke article that I really hoped would be included, and it isn't. What brought it to mind after many years was something Clarke writes early in this book. He recalls, with amusement, the very first 1930 issue of *Astounding,* whose cover "neatly combines all the clichés of pulp fiction. In the foreground, an aviator who has crashed near the South Pole is battling with an unusual species of beetle; an entomologist would be more amazed to discover that it has a fine set of needle-sharp teeth, rather than the minor detail that it is man-sized. And you will not be surprised that there is a damsel in a very skimpy fur coat, especially for the Antarctic."

That wry reference to the man-sized beetle reminded me of a brilliant piece that Clarke—at least I *think* it was Clarke, and not Asimov—wrote some forty years ago for *Playboy,* a magazine I regularly stole from my father's dresser drawer. The article made as lasting an impression on me as the girls. Noting that, as animals grow in size, their surface areas increase by squares but their mass increases cubically, it explained why the giant insects one sees in sci-fi movies are scientifically impossible; they'd need legs as thick as an elephant's. It also explained why cockroaches have such fast reflexes and why ants seem so preternaturally strong. I would have liked to reread that article without having to worry about getting caught by my father; a shame it isn't in the book.

A shame, too, that, despite an eons-spanning vision and a truly celestial perspective, Clarke himself seems awfully prone—how shall I put it?—to ordinary human vanity. Now in his ninth decade, he's beloved around the world, yet at every opportunity he reminds us of his awards, titles, honors, and famous friends. Nearly every photo in the 16-page photo section shows him with a celebrity; tributes to deceased comrades such as Carl Sagan and Gene Roddenberry become the occasions for Clarke to quote the flattering things they wrote about him; an "About the Author" note at the end goes on for more than a page listing his achievements, not omitting such trivia as his honorary vice presidency of the H. G. Wells Society, honorary chairmanship of the Society of Satellite Professionals, and NASA Distinguished Public Service Medal. (This is followed, almost comically, by a similar half-page biography of the book's editor, Ian T. Macauley, who's at pains to inform us that he's a member of the Space Explorers Network and is listed in *Who's Who in Science and Engineering*. Aside from writing a sentence or two in italics at the start of each selection, he is quite invisible throughout the book, and it's a shock when, on the final page, he insists on stepping forward and reciting his credentials.)

Now, there's nothing actually *wrong* with an author who starts off a memoir of the 1990s, say, by pointing out that he was among the first to warn about the Y2K bug, and who alludes to his being feted on *This Is Your Life* (with Buzz Aldrin and a cosmonaut putting in an appearance) and being honored with a Sri Lankan postage stamp. There's nothing wrong with his writing, one paragraph later, "The next year I made my first visit to China to receive the von Karman award," or with his delight in having been knighted in 1998 for "services to literature." But there's a tad too much of this throughout the book; it's like one of those Christmas cards in which distant friends enclose a Xeroxed sheet or two of "family news" that reads like a press release. Maybe I was just put off by the fact that he signs both the preface and acknowledgments "Sir Arthur C. Clarke, CBE." Referring to oneself as "Sir" reminds me of those college professors with Ph.D.'s in musicology or education who insist on being addressed as "Dr." It's unseemly.

And yet, dammit, Clarke has earned the right to boast. Winston Churchill once acknowledged that his political rival Clement Attlee was "a modest man," but added disdainfully, "He has a lot to be modest about." The reverse can be said of Clarke. Does the old boy seem a bit conceited? Well, he's got a lot to be conceited about.

One area in *Greetings* where Clarke hits exactly the right note is flying saucers. Technically he's an agnostic—as what thoughtful person is not?—but he's pretty persuasive, and in admirably few words, as to their improbability. "In the first place," he writes, "they have been observed to travel at accelerations that no material body could stand." Secondly, "despite the enormous speeds reported, no sounds are ever heard from any UFOs," though such objects would normally cause "concussions that would have blasted hundreds of square miles." Finally, no truly convincing photographs have ever been taken of them.

But while Clarke is a thoroughgoing rationalist—he excoriates both fundamentalists and New Agers, and regards astrology, reincarnation, psychic claims, and creationism as "mind-rotting rubbish"—he's open-minded (he half believes there's *something* in Loch Ness) and, more important, famous. So it's not surprising that, twenty years ago, he was invited to host a TV series syndicated in Britain, Europe, and the U.S. The result, *Arthur C. Clarke's Mysterious World,* was so successful that it led to another, his *World of Strange Powers;* together they spawned three TV-based British books. Now portions of the three have been combined into *Arthur C. Clarke's Mysteries* by series creators John Fairley and Simon Welfare (Prometheus, 256 pp, $24).

Some of the unexplained phenomena the authors examine are familiar—Bigfoot, the stigmata, rains of frogs—and some less so, including "the strangest objects ever discovered by archaeologists," the Giant Balls of Costa Rica. As filmmakers offering once-over-lightly profiles of these topics, they're surprisingly conscientious, and (perhaps this is Clarke's influence) their approach is commendably skeptical and cautious. Writing about one of the famous giant figures stretching over the British landscape, they remark, "It is odd, if the Giant is ancient, that he is not mentioned in any document written before 1751." And when it comes to old Nessie, they're virtual debunkers.

After each chapter, Clarke himself contributes a brief addendum, thus enjoying the last word. He is, as always, a model of good sense; after a discussion of prehistoric stone circles, he observes, "One thing can be stated with certainty about such structures as Stonehenge: The people who built them were much more intelligent than many who have written books about them."

June 2001

Yet another book about movies never made . . .

Welcome to the dark side of Hollywood, a place of frustration, futility, and failure, where hopes are dashed, dreams are blighted, and every hour spent laboring on a screenplay is an hour wasted. *The Greatest Sci-Fi Movies Never Made* by David Hughes (London: Titan, 255 pp, £18.99) is a scary corrective to all those "making of" books in which filmmakers tell how they overcame adversity, shot the picture they wanted, and brought it successfully to the screen. This one's a history of abandoned projects and aborted deals—hot properties that ended up in limbo, discarded scripts that ended up in someone's bottom drawer.

Take, for example, Arthur C. Clarke's classic sci-fi novel *Childhood's End,* which has inspired thoughts of film adaptation ever since it came out in 1954. The late Stanley Kubrick was among those interested. Eager to make a movie "of mythic grandeur," as he put it, about extraterrestrial intelligence, he instead collaborated with Clarke on what became *2001*. Later, Universal planned to turn the book into a six-hour miniseries for CBS; later still, it was going to be a two- or three-hour TV movie for ABC. Today, all that's still just a dream. "It fills you with a sense of wonder and enlightenment," says a producer who admires the novel, but he goes on to list the problems that have kept it from the screen: *"Childhood's End* doesn't have a clearly etched battle between good and evil, a group of people running around shooting at each other, a great deal of jeopardy, or a life-and-death situation as far as the characters are concerned." In other words, it ain't *Star Wars*.

The late Douglas Adams encountered that same mind-set in his quest to turn his *Hitchhiker's Guide to the Galaxy*—a hit on British radio and TV—into a feature film. One supposedly interested producer, he discovered, simply wanted "*Star Wars* with jokes." In the end, Adams ruefully concluded that getting a movie made was as hard as "trying to grill a steak by having a succession of people coming into the room and breathing on it."

When you consider all the clashing egos involved, as well as the cost—and sheer chaos—of movie production, it's a wonder that anything of any worth makes it to the screen. Hughes chronicles the incredibly complicated history of the *Alien* series, littered with rejected treatments for an *Aliens vs. Predator* film and unused scripts by, among others, Eric Red and novelist William Gibson. Typically, *Alien*^{3} was rushed into production without a completed screenplay. "We started shooting with only forty pages," recalls director David Fincher, "and the script changed so much and so fast that we were receiving stuff off the fax and shooting it the next day. It was just insane."

Hughes also gives us detailed—and depressing—accounts of early, failed attempts to bring *Dune* to the screen (before David Lynch's feature and the Science Fiction Channel's miniseries), and of dead ends in the history of the *Star Trek* franchise; for every story that was filmed, it seems as if a dozen were discarded. We learn, too, how Steven Spielberg, in the midst of filming *Raiders of the Lost Ark*, had an epiphany: "I was sitting there in the middle of Tunisia, scratching my head and saying, 'I've got to get back to the tranquility, or at least the spirituality, of *Close Encounters*.'" The result was *E.T.*; dropped was a project called *Night Skies*, in which a farm family is attacked by what screenwriter John Sayles describes as a "group of killer aliens."

Call Hughes' book a eulogy for those killer aliens that never reached the screen. It's also a warning for anyone contemplating a career in the movies: Think twice.

Destiny can be awfully cruel to writers and artists. They have a way of dying without ever getting to taste the fruits of their greatest success. One victim of this all-too-familiar cosmic irony was Philip K. Dick, who succumbed to a series of strokes in March of 1982, just a few months before the release of *Blade Runner,* based on his novel *Do Androids Dream of Electric Sheep?* He was only fifty-three years old.

But while Dick never got to see the finished movie, he did see a 20-minute compilation of scenes from it. "The opening is simply the most stupendous thing I have ever seen in the way of a film," he enthused. Harrison Ford in the lead role was "fabulous . . . absolutely incredible. . . . He looks exactly [what] I imagined the character Rick Deckard will look like."

Dick told all this to journalist Gwen Lee, who taped a series of freewheeling interviews with him that January, less than two months before his death. Now, nearly twenty years later, these interviews have been published as *What If Our World Is Their Heaven? The Final Conversations of Philip K. Dick* (Overlook, 204 pp., $26.95). Along with Lee, listed as the book's coeditor is a longtime friend and onetime lover of PKD's, Doris Elaine Sauter. (Dick was married at least five times. Women, like his writing, were something of an obsession.)

On Lee's tape, Dick is clearly ecstatic over the prospect of being connected with a Hollywood blockbuster—"We're going to have sleepwear, we're going to have coloring books, we're going to have comic books. We're going to have everything!"—but his excitement was not confined to marketing; he could see, even from his brief glimpse, that the film's greatest strength was the crowded, dirty, real-life big-city look of its futuristic setting. "They're creating an actual world," he noted excitedly. "It's a world that people actually live in. Uh, there'll be dents on the cars, there'll be scraped paint here and there on the cars."

That "uh," incidentally, hints at what, for some, will be this book's greatest weakness, though for others, perhaps, a welcome proof of authenticity: Despite the "edited by" before Lee and Sauter's names, there doesn't seem to have *been* any editing. What you get are the raw unedited transcripts, complete with fragments, stammerings, and repetitions, right down to responses such as "I, I, uh—" and, at one point, when he leaves the room, a shout of "I can't hear ya!"

This all-inclusiveness makes for difficult reading. Still, that Dick's every stray utterance should be so lovingly, faithfully recorded is in some respects only fitting, for he was—and is, in death, even more so today—a true cult figure. To his fans, he's more than just another genre writer capable of turning out a finished sci-fi novel in eight to ten days of near-sleepless work; they revere him as a mystic, a visionary, a prophet.

That's in part because his fiction played with Big Ideas, even for a field that, more than any other, is idea-driven. It speculated about the nature of reality, the mystery of identity, and, in James's phrase, the varieties of religious experience—"gonzo-theology," as Dick's friend, the science fiction writer Tim Powers, calls it in his foreword to Lee and Sauter's book. Powers goes on to dismiss, albeit gently, the Philip K. Dick of fan legends, "the image of the crazed, mystical hermit-genius"—but in fact that's an image that the book does little to dispel.

Indeed, "crazed" (or "mystical") is exactly what comes to mind when Dick describes a vision he had in 1974—complete with a blinding "flash of light" and a pink glow—that enabled him to pinpoint an "undiagnosed birth defect" which might have cost his son's life: "This presence appeared and told me about my little boy's defect," he claims. "Exactly down to anatomical details." Later in the interview, he explains that "For almost eight years I've been in touch with some kind of mind that has given every evidence of being God. . . . And I think now that it's another species of life. . . . [It] looks like a praying mantis."

Ironically, one of Dick's strengths as a writer is the very one the movies have ignored. Dick specialized in ordinary, humdrum characters, not superhero types—which is why Arnold Schwarzenegger was all wrong as the hero of *Total Recall*, based on Dick's story "We Can Remember It for You Wholesale." Remember that scene near the end in which Arnie is strapped to a chair, with a gizmo attached to his head that'll wipe out his identity? The villain, at that point, bids him adieu and conveniently leaves the room. Remember how

Arnie gets away? By flexing his oversized muscles and yanking free of his bonds!

What an absolutely pathetic failure of imagination! And what a betrayal of an author whose imagination is still delighting us two decades after his death.

In a recent men's-magazine symposium on "The Most Frightened I've Ever Been," Stephen King recalled how, as a child, he was addicted to Edgar Allan Poe movies starring Vincent Price. One day, at the supermarket, he thought he saw Price ahead of him in line. "The man turned around very tall and very handsome. He looked down at me and I looked up at him, and I knew it was Vincent Price and he knew that I knew he was Vincent Price." No words passed between them, King recalls. "He just gave me this sort of sweet smile that said, 'I understand how intimidating I am for a young fellow like you,' and that was it."

The man profiled in *Vincent Price: A Daughter's Biography* by Victoria Price (St. Martin's, 477 pp., $17.95 pb) is every inch the tall, handsome, and sweet-natured character we all suspected he was: a consistently lucky soul, born to wealth in St. Louis, educated at Yale, who moved easily to the London and Broadway stage and then to Hollywood, where he seems to have known just about everyone. Sure, he was too hammy and too refined to have been a thoroughly convincing villain; but he made a great host on *Mystery!*, and there's something to be said for an actor regarded with affection by everyone he worked with.

February 2002

Watching a man turn into a werewolf by the light of a full moon, or a gang of green gremlins trash a Manhattan department store, it's unlikely you've ever asked yourself, "Could that really happen?" You know you're watching fantasy.

But sci-fi films are more problematic and persuasive. Those that aren't actually based on science at least present their stories amid science's trappings: lab tables, Bunsen burners, hypodermic needles, and computers. Their heroes (or villains) wear white coats and speak in scientific terms. Their credits may even list a technical advisor. Asking "Could that really happen?"—or perhaps just "Is any of it possible?"—makes perfectly good sense.

Since the mid-'90s, largely inspired by Prof. Lawrence Krauss's *The Physics of 'Star Trek,'* a number of books have sought to answer those questions. Examining not only *Star Trek* but *The X-Files, Independence Day,* and other sci-fi films and TV shows, they've also attempted to spoon-feed us a few science lessons along the way.

Like Krauss, Mark C. Glassy is an academic—he teaches at the University of California in San Diego—and his book, *The Biology of Science Fiction Cinema* (McFarland, 302 pp, $39.95), has the same twofold goal: to teach us a bit of science while weighing the validity of Hollywood sci-fi thrillers and horror films, from 1932's *White Zombie* and *Doctor X* through 1998's *Blade*. Unlike Krauss (whose book he lauds but whose name he twice misspells), Glassy is also a hands-on scientist; he's a cancer researcher whose specialties are molecular immunology and human monoclonal antibodies, but he seems to know about everything from entomology ("In the fruit fly, such viable mutations as an extra eye on the end of antennae, or an extra set of wings, have been created") to geology ("Coal is the carbonaceous residue of plant matter that has been preserved and altered by heat and pressure"). He is not a terribly stylish writer, and anyone who turns to this book expecting a sort of sugarcoated biology primer, the way Krauss's served as an introduction to physics, will be disappointed; but in some ways Glassy's is more fun. It's an enthusiast's book, filled with arcane facts, quirky personal asides, provocative opinions, and painstakingly detailed descriptions of the eighty-odd films under review—along with large helpings of med-school-textbook prose that sometimes makes for heavy going.

One of the first things you notice is how widely varied Glassy's selection is: There are some big names like *Jurassic Park* and *Alien,* some classics like *Island of Lost Souls,* but also lots of cheesy little B-movies like *Ticks, Astro-Zombies, Frankenstein's Daughter,* and *The Leech Woman.* "The films presented in this book," he admits, "were chosen because they represent examples of interesting and thoughtful biological science—which unfortunately does not always mean interesting and thoughtful cinema. Quite frankly, some of the movies are dreadful."

Whether *The Killer Shrews* fits that description is a matter of taste—it's that silly but fun 1959 cheapie in which a band of people in an island compound are menaced by "giant shrews," played by dogs with phony hair and fangs—but Glassy uses it as the occasion for a lesson on the perils of being too small:

"Shrews must eat their own body weight every few hours.... The bigger the mammal, the more 'insulation' there is from the body's mass; this insulation helps to maintain the body's internal heat. Small mammals, like the shrew, have to consume a lot of food to maintain their body heat because they have very little insulation to keep the heat in."

But size has its drawbacks if you're an insect, as Glassy illustrates with a 1993 movie called *Skeeter,* whose flying pests are six to eight inches long. ("Mosquitoes of this size would have some trouble flying, particularly after gorging themselves on blood and taking on the added weight.") He next critiques a 1994 film called *Mosquito,* in which the bugs run to nearly three feet. (They "are identified as being '*Aedes aegypti*,' which is the yellow fever mosquito. What the yellow fever mosquito is doing on Midwest farmland is not explained.")

"As a child," Glassy recalls, "I intuitively knew that big bugs just could not happen; after all, if they were 'real,' then where were they? I had no problem believing in aliens and spaceships, but big bugs just did not seem possible nor reasonable. However, this did not prevent my thorough enjoyment of this subgenre of SF films. It wasn't until much later in life, when I began to seriously learn some of the simple laws of biology, that I realized that insects bigger than say, half a meter, just could not and will not happen."

The biggest problem for oversize insects is apparently respiration, since they possess no lungs, relying instead on tiny tubules called tracheae that supply the cells with oxygen through simple diffusion and ventilation. "The tracheal system," Glassy explains, "is adequate over distances measured in millimeters, but not more than a few centimeters." Whew!

For each movie he discusses, he concentrates on several key issues that are repeated in boldface throughout the book, including "What Is Right with the Biological Science Presented," "What Is Wrong with the Biological Science Presented," and "Could It Actually Happen." Often the answer to "What Is Wrong" turns out to be speed: "The biggest biological science mistakes made in this film are those of time," he says of the alien's transformations in *Species*. "Everything happens way too fast." He praises *The Incredible Shrinking Man* for the same reason: "Unlike the film *The Devil-Doll*, in which the shrinking procedures are very rapid and occur in a matter of moments, the shrinking in this film occurs over months."

On this score the 1995 movie *Outbreak*—in which Dustin Hoffman and company save a plague-ravaged town by manufacturing a cure in what appears to be mere hours—receives a well-deserved spanking. "You just do not go out and make 'liters' of an antiserum with the snap of a finger nor the bark of a commanding officer," says Glassy. "It takes several months to make an effective antiserum, so in the meantime all the people of Cedar Creek would have died, not to mention the rest of mankind exposed to airborne virus!"

I was pleased by his professorial scorn for a movie I've long regarded as preposterous. (And don't get me started on the film's equally ludicrous helicopter stunts.) Glassy is even more reassuring, at least some of the time, when he considers that final question, "Could It Actually Happen"—his answer is generally "No." Of *Island of Terror,* he writes: "Creating life forms out of silicon will not happen on Earth, so no need to worry about a silicate creature eating all your bones." He is also comforting as to *The Brain Eaters* (which, he notes, is "suspiciously similar to Robert Heinlein's famous book *The Puppet Masters*"): "You need not worry about 300-million-year-old Carboniferous parasites coming up from the ground and attaching themselves to the backs of our necks." And here's his soothing verdict on *Mimic*: "Regarding the development of large insects that mimic man—and those who develop lungs—you need not fear, since this will not happen."

No need to worry; nothing to fear. That's exactly the kind of reassurance that the little kid in us craves, and Glassy is just the sort of brainy, lab-coated uncle that we turn to first in search of answers.

Glassy, needless to say, discusses *Them!*—that wonderful 1954 movie about SUV-sized desert-dwelling ants—in terms of formic acid, exoskeletons, and taxonomic names. (The film's "myrmecologist," or ant specialist, identifies them as *Camponotus ficitus,* carpenter ants—which, as Glassy points out, don't actually live in the desert.)

But to Charles P. Mitchell, author of *A Guide to Apocalyptic Cinema* (Greenwood, 323 pp, $85), *Them!* is "a pivotal film, one of the first to link nuclear radiation with giant mutants, an idea that became a major theme in the realm of science fiction." Out of the fifty films he analyzes, he gives it a full five stars, along with *The Man Who Could Work Miracles* (1936), a droll English fantasy written by H. G. Wells; *On the Beach* (1959), Nevil Shute's somber tale of the last humans waiting to die in Australia from the fallout of a nuclear war (Mitchell calls it "the first and foremost example of mainstream apocalyptic cinema"); *The Day the Earth Caught Fire* (1961), an intelligent, little-known English film in which nuclear testing jogs the earth from its axis, leaving humanity unsure whether—as two headlines being readied for a London tabloid put it—WORLD SAVED or WORLD DOOMED; *Dr. Strangelove* (1964), Stanley Kubrick's black comedy about an accidental WW3, which was "originally conceived as a serious thriller"; Peter Weir's *The Last Wave* (1977), in which Australian aboriginal legends and mystical dreams may spell doom for the modern world; and Tim Burton's *Mars Attacks!* (1996), subversively faithful to the bubble-gum cards that inspired it.

Mitchell, a thoughtful writer with impeccable taste in films, is a particularly keen judge of acting—an element too often slighted in this idea- and FX-driven genre. When he says that one actor "appears to be doing a pale imitation of Robert Shaw in *From Russia with Love*," or that Mia Farrow would have been better in *On the Beach* than Donna Anderson if only she'd "been old enough to tackle the role," you're inclined to believe him. Too bad the book is so outrageously expensive.

Aimed at young readers, Susan Goldman Rubin's *Steven Spielberg: Crazy for Movies* (Abrams, 94 pp, $19.95) suggests how the director's boyhood enthusiasms may have shaped his adult work. It's filled with charming old family photos: A chapter on the making of *Jaws* has, among production shots, a snap of Steve, his mom, and sisters at the seaside; one on *Empire of the Sun* shows young Steve clutching a Tinkertoy airplane. Though there's a picture of

Kate Capshaw, you won't find one of Amy Irving, and their divorce gets all of two sentences; but then, this is a sunny biography intended for budding Spielbergs not yet of bar mitzvah age. There's even a glossary of filmmaking terms at the back.

April 2002

The good news, for lovers of tradition, is that the days of foam latex monsters, stop-motion animation, and hand-painted miniatures are not yet over. Mechanical dinosaurs are by no means extinct—you can see them full-size in *The Lost World*, for example—and there's still work available for a guy who can climb into a creature costume and run around menacing people. According to the *Encyclopedia of Movie Special Effects* by Patricia D. Netzley (Checkmark, 302 pp, $18.95 pb), even a movie as up-to-date as *Jurassic Park* featured, in some scenes, "men in mechanized suits" playing the velociraptors; and inside *The Relic*'s bizarre South American jungle monster was, of all things, a human actor.

The bad news—at least for those of us who hate to see the passing of an art form—is that those days are numbered; at least that's the impression left by Netzley's book. As computer-generated graphics become more sophisticated and more affordable, they're steadily replacing the old hands-on special-effects techniques invented and developed by generations of Hollywood craftsmen.

Take, for instance, the four *Alien* movies. While each has employed "a man in a foam latex suit to portray the main alien," the most recent of them has turned to the new technology: "*Alien Resurrection* relied on computer work for many of its 205 special effects shots," says Netzley, "sometimes even using digital techniques to fix problems that occurred during filming. For example, an underwater scene was first created using the alien suit with a slit in the throat, through which the stuntman could place a breathing device between takes (this was very similar to the filming conditions involved in making the 1954 movie *The Creature from the Black Lagoon*). The footage, however, was disappointing, so a computer-generated alien later replaced the live-action one, except for a few close-up shots."

And then there's Tim Burton, who, she notes, originally planned to film *Mars Attacks!* using the painstaking stop-motion animation he'd used so successfully in *The Nightmare Before Christmas,* only to abandon that, under time pressure, for the speed and ease of computer animation.

As if to symbolize the transition from old FX to new, there's a scene in *The Lost World* in which a man is eaten by a Tyrannosaurus rex. "At the beginning of the shot," Netzley notes, "the person is a stuntman lifted into the air by a full-sized mechanical T-rex. By the time the dinosaur flips him into the air, however, both the man and the T-rex are computer-generated."

Of course, one advantage of going digital—aside from the creative freedom it offers filmmakers—is that stuntmen no longer risk being dropped or chewed up by those mechanical dinosaurs. Netzley cites a government survey of on-the-job accidents—around seven people get hurt during the making of each movie, more than half of them due to stunt work—and reports that "there are 2.5 deaths for every 1,000 stunt-related injuries." (Got your calculator out? Mine says there must be a stunt-related fatality for nearly one percent of movies.)

The *Encyclopedia* is filled with good, earnest information like this, covering everything from the silents (the Keystone Kops, *The Perils of Pauline,* and Harold Lloyd—who, incidentally, lost two fingers in an explosion while filming one of his slapstick comedies) to *Star Wars: The Phantom Menace,* including entries for every film to have won an Oscar for special effects, as well as for more than a hundred filmmakers.

Unfortunately, for virtually all the modern films she covers, Netzley relies, at least in part, on back issues of *Cinefex,* the premier magazine on movie special effects; indeed, the typical entry in this book reads like a dry though conscientious précis of some *Cinefex* article. There's nothing wrong with that—one has to find one's information somewhere—but at least the original pieces had good color photographs. This book tries to get by with some sixty-odd small, muddy, ill-chosen black-and-white photos (not a single one from a James Bond, giant ape, *Alien,* or *Jurassic Park* movie, yet two—two!—from *Small Soldiers*) and nary a single diagram. Try to imagine an entry explaining "Rotoscoping," "Bluescreen Process," or "Travelling Matte" without a photo or diagram and you'll appreciate that old line about what a picture is worth.

One source the *Encyclopedia* cites several times is *Cheap Tricks and Class Acts* by John Johnson (McFarland, 410 pp, $49.95). Subtitled "Special Effects, Makeup and Stunts from the Films of the Fantastic Fifties," it focuses on those more innocent days when the suspension wires making spacemen float and giant spiders leap had to be carefully painted (and repainted) flat black so that they would remain invisible to the camera, as opposed to nowadays, when they're digitally erased.

Johnson's book came out several years ago in one of those heavy, high-priced full-cloth editions presumably designed for libraries and serious collectors. Nonetheless, it's a delightful book, the sort one reads cover to cover at a single sitting, and it offers a far more generous selection of sharp, interesting black-and-white photos, many a full page in size, some of them surprising (4-foot-5-inch midget actor Billy Curtis posing beside 6-foot-5 James Arness, both made up as the title creature in the 1951 film *The Thing*—which, you'll recall, shrinks as it is electrocuted), some unnerving (before and after shots of 8-foot-6, 450-pound stuntman Max Palmer outfitted with hair and huge teeth for his title role in *Killer Ape*), and some hilarious (two actors from the low-budget *Monster from Green Hell* holding the pincers of a giant wasp around their necks and pretending they're struggling to get away).

Arranged not by film but by FX technique ("Pyrotechnic Effects," "Stop Motion Animation and Monster Models," "Ape Suits and Fur-Bearing Fiends," "Hodgepodge Horrors," even "Hand Puppets"), the book is filled with amusing behind-the-scenes anecdotes, reminiscences from actors and filmmakers (many from the fan magazines or from Tom Weaver's excellent volumes of interviews), and background information that'll make you look twice at some of these B-movie classics—such as a gaffe in *The Blob* (you can see, in one shot, that it's just "a decorated weather balloon pulled by wires"), a blooper in *The Thing* (the camera momentarily pans above the "Arctic sky" cyclorama backdrop to reveal real sky), and an uncharacteristic scientific inaccuracy in "the first great science fiction movie of the decade," *Destination Moon* (the severely cracked lunar surface couldn't have gotten that way without water).

Will anyone be able to write a book like this about the computer-concocted movies of today? I doubt it—and it's a shame.

With a joke every sentence or two, *The Horror Movie Survival Guide* by Matteo Molinari and Jim Kamm (Berkley, 350 pp, $14.95 pb) reads as if it were written by a couple of overgrown *Mad*-magazine-reading high-school cut-ups who've spent their lives in front of their TVs, obsessively watching horror films, giggling at them, yet curiously entranced. Just like the title says, the book purports to be a handbook—humorous yet genuinely informative—for surviving dozens of monsters, aliens, maniacs, serial killers, supernatural creatures, and sundry other dangers.

For each particular threat, we're given the movie or movies where it makes an appearance, along with a "funny" scientific name (the Terminator is listed as *Terminus onetrackmindum,* the plant from *Little Shop of Horrors* as *Flowerius chompschomps*), followed by a memorable movie quote (from 1998's *Godzilla:* "Running would be a good idea"), a short bio and advice on identification (*Psycho*'s Norman Bates is described as "a thin, sensitive man, with a slight stutter and an Oedipus complex as big as the whole Ramada chain"), characteristic cravings (the Scanners are into "simple stuff, like world domination"), behavior patterns, danger (the giant worms from *Tremors* can sense the vibrations of whoever's on the ground, so "Our best advice: learn how to fly"), current status (Dracula is "dead and getting tired of it"), and a body count (for the alien in *Men in Black,* it's "5 people, 2 Arguillians, 1 truck, and half a jewelry store").

Most crucial of all is the advice, with each creature, on What to Do If You Meet It ("They say you have to hit the [*Jaws*] shark in the eyes or the gills. This means being close enough to its mouth—we don't like this approach. You might have better luck showing your Greenpeace badge") and How to Kill It ("Keep in mind that the replicants [of *Blade Runner*] have a life span of only four years. Hook them on *General Hospital* or *Days of Our Lives.* Time will fly. . . ."). As for the bugs in *Starship Troopers,* "Get ready by stocking up on roach motels—supersized."

If you find such stuff risible (or, God forbid, useful), then this book is for you.

August 2002

A tabloid TV show specializing in Hollywood scandals once detailed the bizarre story of B-movie actress Susan Cabot, star of *The Wasp Woman,* beaten to death in 1986 by her son. Most of the talking heads interviewed on the show made her out to be a pathetic madwoman who all but deserved to be murdered. Only one person spoke of her kindly: a gentleman named Tom Weaver, identified onscreen as "Cult Film Expert & Friend."

Weaver is the author of *Science Fiction Confidential* (McFarland, 320 pp, $38.50) and nine other books, most of them interviews with bygone actors, actresses, and directors. As it happens, "cult film expert & friend" is not a bad description of his talents: He appears to have seen, and remembered in detail, just about every movie ever made, and he treats the subjects of his interviews with the sympathy and good humor of a friend. More important, his interviews are polished, well constructed, and uncommonly professional; as novelist Les Daniels put it, "He is one of the rare writers in the genre whose pages do not cry out for a copy editor."

This new collection looks at "23 Monster Stars and Filmmakers," and each interview offers a glimpse—usually an irreverent but affectionate one—into the world of low-budget cinema. Here's Weaver himself, for example, on the cheesy 1959 remake of *Tarzan, the Ape Man*: "The Technicolor movie is filled with stock footage from *King Solomon's Mines* (1950) and other oldies (including some in black-and-white!), afflicted with a bongo-heavy jazz score, and packs more phony rear-projection and fake animals than you could shake a spear at."

That movie's Tarzan, former UCLA sports star Denny Miller, recalls one disastrous fight scene: "They put me in there with a stuffed leopard and a rubber knife, and I rolled around and around with the silly thing! The scene was *so* bad that everybody mentions it." Says Weaver: "It's those awful close-ups of the leopard's face that ruin it. You just have to wonder—" Miller interrupts: "You have to wonder who was in charge there."

Former beauty queen Darlene Tompkins reveals that her nude swim scene in *Beyond the Time Barrier* was actually performed by a body double so uncannily similar-looking that she thought for a moment she was looking at herself; whereas Tod Griffin, star of *She Demons,* had no such luck: "When I was shooting that scene [a climactic fistfight]," he complains, "I didn't know that there would be a double . . . somebody that couldn't be further from me! He was half my size, blond hair [*laughs*]—it seems to me they could have gone to a *little* bit more trouble! Color his hair, or *some*thing!"

The book's first subject is John Alvin, who played opposite Peter Lorre in *The Beast With Five Fingers* and Christopher Reeve in *Somewhere in Time*. Weaver notes that Reeve rode a bicycle in that film, while the rest of the cast rode on horses or in horse-drawn carriages, because Reeve was allergic to horses at the time; "the ironic part of that is, if he hadn't gotten over his allergy, he wouldn't be paralyzed today."

That's the sort of trivia—here tragic, more often amusing, always delicious—that makes books like this so intriguing. Early on, Weaver mentions in passing that "we now know that it was the director's future wife inside the Abominable Snowman costume in *Man Beast* (1956); that the spaceship scenes in *The Brain Eaters* (1958) were actually shot in the star's Pomona garage; and that the butler in *The Maze* (1953) has an unusual gliding walk only because the actor had just had an operation on his buttocks."

No question about it, the man has seen every movie ever made.

"Most people find business stories dull," the editor of a financial magazine once remarked to me. "But they can be fascinating, if they're told right." *Comic Wars* (Broadway Books, 318 pp, $24.95), by CBS News correspondent Dan Raviv, is told right. Subtitled "How Two Tycoons Battled Over the Marvel Comics Empire—and Both Lost," it's a blow-by-blow account of how billionaire businessman Carl Icahn—"considered the most dangerous of the corporate raiders for the sheer joy he seemed to take in ripping prey apart"—tried to take over Marvel Entertainment from another high-powered billionaire, Revlon's Ronald Perelman, "America's richest short, bald, 46-year-old chain-cigar-chomper," a man who has his blood pressure tested at least twice a day. Raviv describes it as a fight between two sharks, motivated as much by sheer personal competitiveness as by greed.

With its talk of junk bonds, leveraged buyouts, and bankruptcy hearings, this is a book that readers of newspapers' business pages will relish. But readers of *Spider-Man* may find it harder going, and will have to make sure they don't confuse Ron Perelman with Ike Perlmutter, an Israeli-born toy manufacturer specializing in Marvel action figures, who is the closest thing the book has to a hero. (He offered the prescient advice that to survive, the company needed to "take advantage of the Marvel characters! . . . Make movies!") The villain is probably the icily intimidating Icahn, who, Raviv suggests, talks like the heavy in a James Bond film: "Nothing personal, Ike, but if you don't do it my way, I'll crush your company. Just like I did at TWA, at Texaco, and at U.S. Steel."

A crucial element in this battle of the titans, one that's never sufficiently explained, is the decline of the entire comic-book industry—including a decline in the value of Marvel shares that nearly enabled Icahn to seize control of the company. We read that in 1995 "the collecting bubble burst" and that sales, in consequence, "suffered a sudden tumble." But though Raviv shows how Marvel "shot itself in the foot" when its high-pressure "*Godfather*-like" distribution arrangements antagonized struggling neighborhood comic-book stores, and how changes in the characters and art staff alienated longtime Marvel fans, there are sociological aspects of the story that remain a bit mysterious.

October 2002

You've probably seen ads for really scary horror novels that warn, "Don't read this alone at night." Well, here's a book—a reference book—that ought to bear a label warning, "Don't read this in the bathroom!" If you do, you run the risk of staying in there for an hour or two.

VideoHound's Cult Flicks & Trash Pics (Visible Ink, 862 pp, $24.95 pb) also poses another danger to bathroom-bound readers:

It's as thick as a phone book and weighs several pounds, so you run the definite risk of leaving a dent in your thighs.

Essentially it's a Maltin guide on steroids: lively fact-filled entries, many of them sizable, on more than 1,300 films from *Abbott & Costello Go to Mars* to *Zu: Warriors from the Magic Mountain,* "quite possibly the ultimate Hong Kong fantasy flick." Practically every page has either a movie photo—with a straight caption, thank God, not a silly one—or a memorable quote, such as "Something's terribly wrong in Pleasantville" (ad line for *I Was a Zombie for the FBI*) or "Don't grieve, Admiral. It is logical" (Spock's dying words in *Star Trek 2*).

Lest your attention wander for even a moment, there are also dozens of sidebars, running a page or two, on cult-movie icons from Stanley Kubrick to Godzilla. The final 300 pages are devoted to indexes of actors, directors, and the like. You could easily skip them—in this age of *IMDb.com* they're pretty useless—except that they too are spiced up with classic quotes. I never realized that in *Island of Lost Souls* Charles Laughton actually says, "The natives . . . they are restless tonight."

Movie critic Roger Ebert can be a bit pompous on TV, and to my mind he gives his famous thumbs-up far too freely. But in *The Great Movies* (New York: Broadway Books, 532 pp, $27.50), a hundred essays on the films he likes best, he comes across as appealingly humble in the face of work he respects.

Around a fifth of his selections have some sci-fi or fantasy content, including *E.T.* and *Star Wars* (yes, they're there), and the book leads off with an insightful appraisal of *2001*. Ebert is especially perceptive about how the classical music enhances this film—and how, in turn, the music is itself enhanced through its association with the film's cosmic images.

He also offers a useful reminder about how unsuited films like *Lawrence of Arabia* are to television, and a welcome salute to the peculiar bittersweet humor of *Mr. Hulot's Holiday,* an endearing French comedy with remarkably few laughs: "It is about the hope that underlies all vacations and the sadness that ends them."

While he's appreciative enough of directors, Ebert occasionally scants the writers. You'd never know that part of the brilliance of Robert Altman's *Nashville* comes from Joan Tewkesbury's script; or that the characters in Spielberg's *E.T.* speak lines written by Melissa Mathison; or that Hitchcock's *Psycho* owes a thing or two to novelist Robert Bloch and screenwriter Joseph Stefano; or that *2001* had something to do with a man named Arthur C. Clarke.

December 2002

What would you do if, as a writer, you discovered that some comic-book publisher in a distant state was using your story ideas without credit or compensation? Ray Bradbury was faced with that problem just as his career was beginning to take off in the early 1950s. EC Comics, based in New York, had already taken two of his published short stories and had retitled and reworked them for their horror-comic line. When they appropriated two more in a 1952 issue of *Weird Fantasy*, the California-based Bradbury wrote them a letter.

But it wasn't an angry letter; in fact, it was disarmingly nice. "Dear Sir," he wrote, "Just a note to remind you of an oversight. You have not as yet sent on the check for $50.00 to cover the use of secondary rights on my two stories *The Rocket Man* and *Kaleidoscope*. . . . I feel this was probably overlooked in the general confusion of office work, and look forward to your payment in the near future. My very best wishes to you." And he went on to suggest, in a postscript, that EC consider putting out an all-Bradbury issue based on one of his story collections.

Bradbury's gentle approach paid off. EC immediately mailed him a check—"Although we do not agree with your conclusions, we are completely disinclined to quibble with one who writes as charming a letter as yours"—and thereby began a fruitful and extremely cordial collaboration. In fact, Bradbury became EC's best-known writer.

The saga of that relationship, in which the author displayed the good nature and canny diplomatic skill that's characterized his entire career, is told in considerable detail in *Bradbury: An Illustrated Life* by Jerry Weist (HarperCollins, 221 pp, $34.95).

Not many other episodes in Bradbury's life are recounted at such length, however, for despite its title, the book is not really a biography, nor is it a study of the man's work; rather, it's a gorgeous, gloriously lavish guided tour through the collection of Donn Albright, the world's preeminent Bradbury collector, conducted not by Albright himself—though he contributes a short, modest foreword—but by Jerry Weist, a collectibles expert at Sotheby's and a lifelong Bradbury fan. Weist is a graceful writer and manages throughout the book to express tremendous admiration bordering on reverence for Bradbury's work without ever sounding gushy, but his text is relatively spare and definitely takes second place to the hundreds of pictures, including full-color reproductions of book covers, magazine illustrations, posters, comic strips, original paintings, movie stills, personal photographs, and sketches by Bradbury himself. (The latter, incidentally, are quite clever, reminiscent of children's book illustrator Maurice Sendak and *New Yorker* cartoonist William Steig.) Not all the visual material comes from Albright's collection—some artwork was loaned by other sources, including Bradbury and his wife—but Albright's vast archives form, as Weist acknowledges, "the backbone of this book."

Those unaware of the full extent of Bradbury's connection with Hollywood will be interested in the material from two 1953 films, the 3-D *It Came from Outer Space,* which he wrote, and *The Beast from 20,000 Fathoms,* "suggested by" a Bradbury story. The author went on to share screenplay credit for John Huston's magnificent 1956 *Moby Dick,* which brought him an Oscar nomination. The book also includes photos of the life-size tattooed torso used as a makeup guide in 1968's *The Illustrated Man,* and selections—in fact, too many—from the journal François Truffaut kept while shooting his 1966 adaptation of *Fahrenheit 451.*

What fascinated me the most were not the rarities but the chapter that reproduces, side by side, the jackets adorning successive editions of Bradbury's various books. You can compare, for example, what two dozen different artists and designers, here and abroad, have done with *The Martian Chronicles*—known in Britain as *The Silver Locusts*—or what three dozen of them have made of *Fahrenheit 451,* from the abstract designs on some European editions to the images on others reproduced directly from the movie. Richly atmospheric books such as *Dandelion Wine, The October Country,* and *Something Wicked This Way Comes* have inspired particularly memorable cover art. Inevitably you find yourself trying to decide which cover is the most beautiful, the scariest, the most startling, or the most appropriate for Bradbury's text.

On this latter score, there's no doubt that Bradbury himself would choose the work of artist Joseph Mugnaini, whose work Bradbury first saw in the window of a Venice, California, gallery and immediately fell in love with. Bradbury, throughout his career, has always been extremely lucky in his illustrators—the book includes work by Virgil Finlay, Hannes Bok, Ben Shahn, Lee Brown Coye, Stanley Meltzoff, Frank Frazetta, Kelly Freas, Jack Davis, Wallace Wood, Charles Addams, Gahan Wilson, Ian Miller, Jim Burns, Michael Whelan, and other celebrated names in the worlds of art, comics, and cartoons—but just as Lewis Carroll will always be most closely associated with the illustrations of John Tenniel, Baum with John R. Neill, and Milne and Grahame with Ernest Shepard, Bradbury's favorite illustrator—one might almost say his designated illustrator—was Mugnaini, who produced the wonderfully gnarled-looking artwork that graces *The October Country,* as well as the portrait of Bradbury on the cover of this present book, but whose best-known work is undoubtedly the striking cover image he created for the original hardcover edition of *Fahrenheit 451*: a stark figure, dressed from head to toe in a suit of burning newsprint, wiping his weary brow. It's interesting, incidentally, to see three rough sketches of Mugnaini's, probably made before Bradbury had come up with the novel's precise title; they all identify the future classic as "Fahrenheit 204."

I'm Working on That: A Trek from Science Fiction to Science Fact by William Shatner and Chip Walter (Pocket Books, 398 pp, $25).

It is said that the great Joe DiMaggio not only did not *write* the 1946 autobiography attributed to him, but in fact did not even bother to *read* it. Forgive my shameful suspicion—I know it sounds horribly ungracious—but that thought did cross my mind for a moment when I saw William Shatner's name in large letters on this book's cover, dwarfing that of his co-author.

Well, whoever wrote it, he's done a bang-up job at presenting a vast amount of scientific information. The book offers a breezy, once-over-lightly tour of current research and recent technological advances that echo the gadgetry seen in sci-fi TV shows. (Sometimes, admittedly, the breeziness, the jokes, and the desperate desire to be entertaining get on one's nerves, like a standup comic who's trying a little too hard to hold our wandering attention.) The impulse behind the book, we're told, was "a kind of déjà vu. . . . Every day the world was becoming more and more like *Star Trek!*" It isn't just that cell phones and PDAs look a lot like the *Enterprise* crew's communicators; virtual reality, artificial intelligence, superhuman longevity, even time travel—this optimistic survey suggests that we're inching steadily toward them all.

And some of the neat stuff, like wearable computers and robot nurses for the elderly, is already here. One scientist, for example— and we meet dozens in the course of the book, all of them described in awestruck prose befitting an Einstein or a Gandalf—has invented "electronic paper" that can display any given text or image like a normal piece of typing paper, but then can instantly change it to a new one. Imagine, a sheet of paper folded in your pocket will be able to contain, in itself, an entire novel or, someday, an entire library.

It was the celebrated British physicist Stephen Hawking who gave the book its title. Paralyzed and wheelchair-bound, he was visiting the set of *Star Trek: The Next Generation* when he was shown a mockup of the warp drive engine, the miraculous invention that enables the *Enterprise* to travel faster than the speed of light—at least on TV. To Hawking, the concept was a familiar one; he smiled and said in his synthesized voice, "I'm working on that."

February 2003

After a lifetime of watching *King Kong* on TV and video, middle-aged movie enthusiast Mark F. Berry was finally getting the chance to see this epic adventure in a neighborhood theater. "The audience that night spanned the generations," he recalls, "and only after the film started did I realize that some of the younger ones were there not to experience a film classic, but to watch what they surely perceived as a hokey, old-timey movie far too naive for their modern sensibilities."

By the end of the film's initial sea voyage, however, with its destination a mysterious island not found on any chart, "the condescension from the younger audience members began to dwindle.... As the *Venture* emerged from the fog and Skull Mountain loomed, slouching bodies straightened up and leaned forward, whispered commentary gave way to breath holding, and giggles turned into *oohs* and *ahhs*. Even those street-wise 1990s kids, accustomed to knockout computer-generated visuals in everything from movies to fungicide commercials, fell under Kong's spell."

As *The Dinosaur Filmography* (McFarland, 491 pp, $65) makes engagingly clear, those *oohs* and *ahhs* are central to the appeal not only of the giant ape but of the giant reptiles that Kong spends his time pummeling. Berry quotes a worldly bit of wisdom voiced early in the second *Jurassic Park* by Jeff Goldblum, when the newcomers he's guiding are stunned by the sight of a magnificent herd of stegosaurs: "Yeah, 'ooh, ahh'—that's how it always starts," says Goldblum. "But then later there's running and screaming."

Observes Berry: "That line sums up the two basic elements of a dinosaur film: 'ooh, ahh' and 'running and screaming.'"

An illustrated encyclopedia of the genre (and, I suppose, the only one of its kind), Berry's book examines in detail nearly 150 movies, and one of its appendices lists two dozen more that don't quite make the grade but feature "Dinosaurian Themes, Plot Elements, or Isolated Dinosaur Scenes"—in short, as he puts it, "dinocameos." But Gojira fans be warned: All the Godzilla movies are relegated to still another appendix, just four pages long, entitled "It Came from Japan," for Berry, it seems, has decided that Godzilla's "paleontological connections" are just too tenuous and that the creature is not technically a dinosaur. (He does acknowledge that one film in the series describes the monster as "a cross between a Tyrannosaurus and a Stegosaurus," but such a notion only increases his scorn. He's particularly down on the "dreadful" 1998 American *Godzilla*, which he dismisses as "a ham-handed self-parody.")

His favorites come as no surprise. "It's difficult to imagine," he writes, "that any dinosaur film will ever equal the pure, wide-eyed delight of that first viewing of the original *Jurassic Park*"—and who can disagree? But that film receives, in his book, only three and a half stars. There's just one that gets the full four: "*King Kong* represents one of those rare moments in any creative arena when the planets aligned and the deities smiled and everything fell into place." I've never heard it said better.

Berry also champions, and analyzes at great length, three key sci-fi films from the middle of the last century that pretty much set the pattern for dino-in-the-city movies: *The Beast from 20,000 Fathoms* (1953), *The Giant Behemoth* (1959), and *Gorgo* (1961). He calls *Behemoth*—a taut, well-acted, atmospheric film shot in near-documentary style—"perhaps the most underrated dinosaur film of all." Its one great flaw, he admits, is the cost-cutting that resulted in "the infamous 'car crush' shot": The identical image of a car being crushed on a London street by a giant claw is used three times in the film.

Bet you didn't know—unless you're a trivia whiz—that this trio of dinosaur films were all directed by the same man, Eugène Lourié, who drew on his background as a production designer to make the most of his limited budgets. "If *Beast* looks like it costs more than its measly $200,000—which it does," says Berry, "a huge chunk of the credit is due to Lourié." Credit is also due to the famed stop-motion animator Ray Harryhausen, who designed the film's fictional monster, described as a "Rhedosaurus." (Harryhausen always denied that the first two letters of the creature's name were based on his initials.)

How much credit goes to Ray Bradbury is a thornier question. Bradbury's short story of the same title (later changed to "The Fog Horn"), about a giant sea creature that mistakes a lighthouse's foghorn for a mating call, may have been an inspiration for *Beast*, though only a single scene uses Bradbury's plot. This book does a fine job sorting out the several conflicting explanations.

As you might expect, Berry is also a fan of Walt Disney's *Fantasia*, which he calls "a watershed in animation history." He's great on the aesthetics of the famous dinosaur sequence; but for a more scientific slant, you'll have to turn to *Starring T. Rex! Dinosaur Mythology and Popular Culture* (Indiana University Press, 166 pp, $17.95 pb) by José Luis Sanz, a distinguished Spanish paleontologist and self-proclaimed "lover of all things dinosaurian."

Sanz reveals that Disney's dinosaurs were intended to be scientifically accurate—but not at the expense of a good dustup: "The climax of the story is a dramatic fight between a stegosaur (Upper Jurassic) and a tyrannosaur (Upper Cretaceous) with blood-red eyes. The two animals are separated in time by about 80 million years."

According to Sanz, the 1940 film also ran afoul of church authorities, who correctly perceived that it promoted the theory of evolution. "Disney's original idea," he says, "was to continue to tell the story of life up to the origin of humanity, but this was made an impossible task as a result of the threats from some religious fundamentalists."

Sanz's book, which examines everything from archeological expeditions to the lore of dragons, nicely complements the Berry volume. Though technical at times regarding saurian taxonomy, it's so readable—thanks to a graceful translation by Philip Mason—that you almost forget it was published by an academic press.

As the *Star Wars* films have grown more technically sophisticated and more grandiose in scale, filling the screen with ever more breathtaking settings, outlandish creatures, and massive battle scenes, their stories and characters have grown less satisfying. Whether Episode II is an improvement on Episode I or represents a further decline in the series is like trying to decide which breakfast cereal commercial is the most fun.

That's not to deny that an extraordinary amount of artistic creativity, talent, brains, and scientific expertise has gone into these films. You can see it on display in *The Art of Star Wars: Episode II: "Attack of the Clones"* by Mark Cotta Vaz (Ballantine, 224 pp, $19.95 pb), which presents page after page of graphic artwork—costume designs; landscape paintings; sketches of spacecraft and war machines; conceptions of various aliens, robots, and beasts—which guided the filmmakers during production. It reminds you that some amazingly gifted illustrators—and sculptors, too—have found employment in this series.

Amid all the graceful-looking costumes for senators, nobles, and Jedi knights, as well as the drawings of gleaming, streamlined space vehicles, it's a relief to see several artists' conceptions of the nasty little *kouhuns*, the poisonous centipede-like creatures sent to assassinate the sleeping Padmé, along with preliminary sketches and a Sculpey sculpture of Dexter Jettster, the slobbish, unshaven, four-armed cook at Dexter's Diner.

By way of appendix, the book also includes the complete Episode II screenplay by George Lucas and Jonathan Hales. Considering how lame, ill-conceived, and confusing that screenplay is, it's perhaps a dubious bonus, though no doubt nice to have for the record.

A few of the same designs appear in the companion volume, *Star Wars Mythmaking: Behind the Scenes of 'Attack of the Clones'* by Jody Duncan (Ballantine, 224 pp, $19.95 pb), but this book is illustrated almost entirely with revealing color photographs detailing the creation of the film. After an introduction by producer Rick McCallum, who notes that "the production . . . began less than a week after the release of Episode I," and a further chapter on the film's genesis, Duncan wisely chooses not to tell the story of its production chronologically—there's nothing duller than a "making of" diary—but instead follows the movie scene by scene, briefly sketching the plot and then filling in the background.

She seems to have had plenty of access to cast and crew, so the book is filled with recollections—overwhelmingly positive, as you might expect from this authorized account by everyone from seventy-eight-year-old Christopher Lee (who, in the climactic swordfight scene, had his face patched digitally over his stunt double's) to Lucas himself. The latter is appealingly modest; of one of the film's central themes, the forbidden romance between Padmé and Anakin, he says, "The challenge was that I wanted to tell the love story in a style that was extremely old-fashioned, and, frankly, I didn't know if I was going to be able to pull it off. In many ways, this was much more like a movie from the 1930s than any of the others had been, with a slightly over-the-top, poetic style—and they just don't do that in movies anymore. I was very happy with the way it turned out in the script and in the performances, but I knew a lot of people might not buy it. . . . I didn't know if people would laugh at it and throw things at the screen."

While I neither laughed nor threw things, I'm one who didn't buy it; yet these two books make me wish I had. When a director does a magnificent job promoting his latest film on talk shows and in press interviews but the film itself isn't very good, industry types like to joke, "Forget the movie—distribute the director!" You might almost say the same about these books; the film they conjure up with their gorgeous artwork and dazzling images of rockets, armor, weaponry, monsters, towering cities, royal pageantry, and epic battles is a lot more thrilling than the one actually released last spring.

April 2003

"When in doubt," a veteran magazine publisher used to say, "give 'em a list." Readers love lists, and a magazine should always mention one on the cover: 7 investing mistakes to avoid; 15 celebrity beauty tips; television's 50 most memorable characters. (A friend of mine sold that idea to *TV Guide*.) So there's something irresistible about *10 Sure Signs a Movie Character Is Doomed & Other Surprising Movie Lists* (Hyperion, 300 pp, $14.00 pb) by Richard Roeper, Roger Ebert's partner on their thumbs-up-or-thumbs-down TV show.

One problem, unfortunately, is that the book's title notwithstanding, there's nothing very "surprising" about a list of doomed characters. In fact, back in the 1950s, a *Mad* magazine clone called *Humbug* ran a series exactly like this, titled "You Know Who Gets Killed." A typical scene showed an old man standing guard at the site where, earlier that night, a mysterious flying saucer has crashed. A scientist, heading home for the night, warns him, "If anything strange happens, call me at once!" "What could happen?" shrugs the old man.

Another scene featured a soldier in a foxhole boasting to his buddies, "Tomorrow my enlistment is up and I'm going home!" In his hand are snapshots of his wife and kids.

Guess who's in the third spot on Roeper's list: Yes, that same doomed soldier from *Humbug*, this time gazing lovingly at a photo of his pregnant girlfriend. The poor guy also appears—in the "Death" category—on the hilarious website *moviecliches.com*, which Roeper credits at the end of this book.

Still, there's much that's new here, and much that's amusing. You'll find Actresses Who Have Yet to Do a Nude Scene (including—and this *is* a surprise—Raquel Welch), as well as Actors and

Actresses Who Took Their Clothes Off When They Should Have Kept Them On (including a pre-*Sopranos* Aida Turturro). There's a list of seventeen movie characters' "555-" phone numbers, eleven Movies That Employed James Brown's "I Feel Good" to Indicate That a Character Feels Good, the 25 Best Sports Movies of All Time, and the 25 Worst. You'll find the Best Movies About the Newspaper Business, the Best Easter Movies, and the Best Porn Titles Based on Legit Movies—including *Position: Impossible* and *Buffy the Vampire Layer*.

And best of all, often courtesy the web, there are loads of movie clichés, from the car that crashes through the guardrails and over a cliff, immediately bursting into flame, to the guy that slouches up to a bar and orders "beer" without the bartender ever asking, "What *kind* do you want?"

Just in case anyone might mistake this pleasant ten-minute read for a serious work of film scholarship, Roeper sets him straight at the outset: "If you're looking for a book of movie lists that tells you the real names of Cary Grant and John Wayne, this isn't it. But if you'd like to see the definitive list of movies in which Ben Affleck cries like a big fat baby, proceed directly to the register." He begins the book, in fact, by approvingly quoting Michael Keaton's remark to a pompous critic who went on too long about *Batman Returns:* "You know what? It's just a f— movie."

But that's not the way sci-fi writer David Gerrold feels about *The Matrix.* In his introduction to *Taking the Red Pill: Science, Philosophy and Religion in 'The Matrix'* (BenBella, 280 pp, $17.95 pb), edited by Glen Yeffeth (who supplies some useful mini-introductions), Gerrold manages to find in this 1999 film the "the permeating flavors of George Orwell, Harlan Ellison, Philip K. Dick, and William Gibson," along with echoes of *Beowulf,* St. George and the Dragon, samurai tales, the Prometheus and Orpheus myths, and of course, as the film's central archetype, Christ. Here he pauses and asks, as if with a grin: "And you thought *The Matrix* was just a movie, right?"

Gerrold is the only one in this earnest collection who displays a sense of humor, and even he seems to feel that it's a mistake to see a film of such richness and depth only once: "A single exposure," he maintains, "is not enough." At least he's aware of what attracted the crowds: the film's "breathless pace, astonishing eye-candy, a sense of mythic adventure, and an acid-tinged sensibility. Like *Star Wars,* it opened up a new continent of imagination."

The first installment of *The Matrix* was certainly a treat to watch: the cool leather trench coats and shades, the gymnastic battles, the sense that you, the viewer, were privy to a vision denied the rest of mankind. But only one of the fourteen essayists in this book seems embarrassed by how ludicrously pretentious the movie is (perhaps because they're pretty pretentious themselves) or bothered by its meretricious message: that it's okay to murder policemen as if they were mere videogame figures because, after all, they're just minions of the machine.

Instead, the movie is grist for some provocative, impressively erudite, but often tedious analyses. It's described as a parable of the Messiah or of Buddha; an examination of the nature of reality; a meditation on Artificial Intelligence; an heir to many well-established science fiction traditions, and to Heinlein in particular (this in an essay by James Gunn); a "paradigm of postmodernism"; a warning about technological slavery; and the product of "cross-cultural looting" by a pair of brothers weaned on comics and sci-fi movies.

This last take comes from Andrew Gordon, who argues that "the primary pleasures of *The Matrix* are not intellectual but visceral, in the innovative visual tricks and stunts and the almost nonstop action." One of the media critics he quotes goes further, dismissing the film as "a muddily pretentious mixture of postmodern literary theory, slam-bang special effects, and Superman heroics" that ultimately degenerate into "a frightening form of nihilism . . . as the well-armed hero sets out to save humanity by killing as many humans as possible."

Think you need a work as highfalutin as *The Matrix* to wax philosophical over? Not at all. In *'Buffy the Vampire Slayer' and Philosophy: Fear and Trembling in Sunnydale* (Open Court, 329 pp, $24.95 hc, $17.95 pb), edited by James B. South, what the book describes as twenty-five "up-and-coming young philosophers" turn to the popular TV series and ask, among other probing questions, "What would Buffy do?"

As the subtitle, with its wink at Kierkegaard, suggests, these academics take themselves a lot less seriously than the *Matrix* crew, yet they still find plenty of elements in the Buffy universe (or "Buffyverse") that bear examination through the teachings of Plato, Aristotle, Kant, and Nietzsche. One essay suggests that Buffy and her gang are proto-fascists ("Do they not kill on sight, wisecracking as they go, with no obvious guilt about their incremental genocide?"); another finds "Marxist tendencies" in the show's "persistent association of capitalist values . . . with literal inhumanity."

Many of the writers, and not just the women, are thrilled with *Buffy*'s feminist subtext, and all of them are obviously fans. The ideal reader for this book would be a fan as well, one who's also a prospective philosophy major.

When a book is called *Joss Whedon: The Genius Behind Buffy* (BenBella, 176 pp, $15.95), you may wonder if the title is meant ironically—the way, five years ago, *The Encyclopedia Shatnerica* turned out to be a book that, for 300 pages, made hilarious wicked fun of William Shatner. But no, this one is as unashamedly adulatory as its title, from its introduction—which asks the question "Who is Joss Whedon? What makes him tick? And, most importantly, how does he manage to create such magic?"—to the final chapter, which reminds us that "with all his accomplishments, it's sometimes difficult to remember that Joss is still a young man, that his best work is probably still ahead of him," and predicts that he'll "blossom into one of the great filmmakers of his generation."

But though the book is clearly a piece of p.r. puffery, so liberally relying on quoted reminiscences, reflections, and opinions from Whedon himself that he should almost be listed as co-author, *Genius* offers much information that may be of interest to *Buffy* fans. Granted, author Candace Havens's sheer breathless desire to flatter him sometimes grows monotonous—"A brilliant writer, he is equally adept at drama, comedy, horror, and action. A producer with a self-proclaimed feminist agenda, Joss makes a point of defying convention and Hollywood norms. A shy, reclusive child, Joss has overcome his inherent introversion to achieve great success in a variety of leadership roles. . . . Genuinely kind and easygoing, Joss is also a perfectionist. . . . A longtime Anglophile, Joss was thrilled at the prospect of living in England. . . . A keen observer, Joss studied his classmates"—and so on, sentence after sentence. Still, we do get an impression of Whedon himself as a fairly nice fellow, funny and (but for his involvement in this book) engagingly modest.

He had the good sense to be born into a show-biz family—both his father and grandfather were TV writers—and to have enjoyed a privileged prep-school-to-Wesleyan education. He also had the good sense, upon moving to Los Angeles, to change his name from Joe to Joss. In short order he turned out the spec script for what would become the feature film *Buffy the Vampire Slayer*. "The idea for the film," says Whedon, "came from seeing too many blondes [in horror movies] walking into dark alleyways and being killed. I wanted, just once, for her to fight back when the monster attacked, and kick his ass."

The film itself proved something of a disaster. Though Paul Reubens was a pleasure to work with, Donald Sutherland was rude, contemptuous, and uncooperative—"Whedon said several times that working with Sutherland was one of the worst experiences of his life"—and Rutger Hauer, as a vampire, tried to push his own "bizarre" ideas, which included playing one scene in the nude. The result was, as Havens says, "a very mediocre film." Not surprisingly, she takes Whedon's side—"His hip, scary script had been turned into a silly, campy film"—and typically gives him the last word: "The director ruined it."

History repeated itself, the book suggests, with Whedon's screenplay for *Alien Resurrection:* "The harshest criticism of the movie came from Whedon himself, who felt the director had ruined an excellent script." But that film had one positive result: "The next person who ruins one of my scripts," Whedon vowed, "is going to be me."

Havens's book describes the happy consequence of that vow, the *Buffy* TV series, which for some reason, at least in my experience, seems to have an enormous appeal for a lot of intelligent women. The author traces the show's plotline and what Whedon calls his "genre-busting mission" through seven seasons, while interviewing, along the way, various members of the Whedon-worshiping cast and crew ("His brain just doesn't work like the rest of us mortals," says an executive producer; "You just have to trust in that genius," agrees Sarah Michelle Gellar) as well as critics ("Joss is a master of everything," gushes a Pittsburgh newspaperman). Visiting the *Buffy* set—and she proves a fine tour guide—Havens is in heaven: "Time got away from me while I explored the world that had come straight from Joss's vivid imagination."

We mustn't sneer; books like this have a long and honorable history. Don't forget that Hawthorne wrote an adulatory campaign biography of Franklin Pierce—though Pierce, at least, was a college friend.

June 2003

Dreamer of Dune by Brian Herbert (Tor, 560 pp, $27.95).

Frank Herbert's *Dune*—the fat 1965 book that started it all, begetting sequels, a movie, and (so far) two miniseries—is generally regarded as a classic example of "ecological science fiction." With breathtaking imagination, but also with painstaking logic and a fair amount of science, it demonstrates how society might evolve on a desert planet where water is as precious as the rarest wine.

Yet for me, at least, what's even more memorable than the stillsuits and sandworms is the sensibility that animates the book, its peculiar vision of human relationships. The story itself is a paranoid nightmare of rivalries and vendettas, deceptions and betrayals, plots and counterplots, power struggles both interpersonal and interplanetary. Feelings of mistrust and suspicion lurk beneath every human encounter; aside from battle scenes and spice harvests, the book is a series of intrigues, assassinations, conspiracies, and coups d'état. It's a worldview that I, for one, found deeply disturbing and unpleasant.

Now, thanks to a superb 560-page warts-and-all biography written by Herbert's son, we have a chance to meet the creator of that world. And it probably shouldn't surprise anyone that, while highly intelligent, capable, and forceful, he emerges as a rather unpleasant man—at least if you happened to have him as a father.

Brian Herbert doesn't mince words. Right up front—literally

the second sentence of the book, in fact—he writes, "Frank Herbert was not always a heroic figure to me, for I did not get along well with him in my childhood, and only grew close to him when we were both adults."

Today, Brian is successfully carrying on his father's work, having cowritten half a dozen books in the *Dune* series. As a boy, however, his feelings and opinions didn't matter. "My status in the household," he says, "was not dissimilar to that of a dog or a human subspecies. If I didn't please the master, I was dispatched from his sight."

In *Dune,* haunted as it is by deadly political conspiracies, characters are forever weighing one another's language for "nuances of meaning." Brian and his younger brother's speech faced similar scrutiny in the Herbert household: "He picked our sentences apart. 'What do you mean you'll *try* to do it?' he would say to me, in a voice reaching crescendo. 'Don't ever use the word *try* on me! That word signifies failure, the likelihood of defeat. You'll do it, god damn it, Brian, you won't *try* to do it!' Another intolerable word to him was 'can't.' We didn't dare use that word or 'try,' because they triggered something in the man and he would fly into blind rages."

Part of the problem was simply Frank Herbert's difficult choice of profession, which, until the success of *Dune,* kept him under terrible financial pressure. It's not easy being a freelance writer trying to support a family—nor is it easy on the family. Brian observes that his father's "impatience with children was perhaps his worst fault, the one that troubled me most. Children were noisy and boisterous, his *bête noire*. They clattered through the house and yard, driving him crazy when he tried to write, when he tried to think."

When Brian came home from school, he would have to tiptoe around the house so as not to arouse the elder Herbert's wrath. "I was a rather hyperactive child," he recalls, "and my father, when home, often lost patience with me. He was trying to write, or to do extensive research. He needed quiet, contemplative time to consider important matters. I remember him yelling at me constantly, and if I didn't do exactly as instructed, he was quick to administer corporal punishment."

The picture he paints of Herbert is a scary one, "a burly, barrel-chested man" with lots of blond hair on arms and chest. "Later, when he grew a full beard, he would look even larger to me, and quite wild. . . . He'd been a tough kid, and was even tougher now. No one pushed him around. He knew judo. . . . He could open any jar in an instant, and had what Mom called 'asbestos skin,' enabling him to touch hot pans and casserole dishes without burning himself. His presence was overpowering, with more than a hint of police militarism, stemming from his highway patrolman father. When Dad questioned me, it was *with intensity,* the way the police did it."

The questioning sometimes resembled police interrogation in another way: Along with various weapons and firearms, Herbert kept in his home a genuine naval-surplus lie detector, which he used on his sons, presaging the menacing lethal device with which *Dune* opens. "The machine," Brian recalls, "was kept in his study, and he only brought it out when I was in trouble. . . . After each question, he studied the machine intently and invariably pronounced me guilty of something."

"He could not handle children," Brian writes elsewhere—then adds, as if in exoneration, "Perhaps this was because he had never really been a child himself."

It's true that, as the book recounts in colorful detail, Frank Herbert—born in 1920 in the state of Washington—had a rough-and-tumble Depression-era childhood and left home early; both his parents were "on-again, off-again alcoholics." His father, Frank senior, in addition to working as a motorcycle cop, was also at times a farmer, deputy sheriff, and failed businessman. Both father and son were macho types—avid outdoorsmen, hikers, campers, fishermen, and hunters.

Frank junior, though, was also bookish. He was reading the newspaper by age five, by twelve had "read the complete works of Shakespeare," and later claimed that school tests measured his IQ at 190. He made his first magazine sale, to a Western pulp, at age seventeen while still in high school, though it was eight years before he made another sale.

Aside from the man's failings as a parent, Brian's portrait of his father is, by and large, an admiring one. We read of Herbert's wartime stint in the navy; his first brief youthful marriage (which ended with a Dear John letter); his varied West Coast newspaper work as a reporter, editor, and photographer; his speechwriting for several Republican politicians; his first encounter with his next wife at a college creative-writing class; his travels, with his family, in Mexico; the sale of his first novel, followed by more years of rejection, poverty, and struggle. The family never remained long at an address. "One symbol of our frequent moves," writes Brian, "was a waxed cardboard stencil, 'F. HERBERT,' with black paint smeared on it. Each time we moved, Dad used it and painted his name on our mailbox . . . in order to make absolutely certain that the mailman did not miss our stop. Letters from agents and publishers as well as checks arrived in the mail. The mail became, to a large extent, the lifeline of our family."

And then came the serialization, in *Analog,* of what was at the time called *Dune World,* followed by its publication in book form by a company best known for auto-repair manuals. And with it, everything changed: A Nebula and a Hugo came Herbert's way; money and more money; worldwide fame as an environmental guru; a midlife mellowing, a "truce," a "new relationship," and eventually literary collaboration with his now-grown son. The final chapters of the book are poignant, marked by Brian's description of his mother's death in 1984, at fifty-seven, and his father's just two years later, at sixty-five. By this time we have come to understand how he can now describe his father as "this phenomenal man" and sincerely mourn him: "He was a great and loving man, and his flaws were infinitesimal."

Matrix Warrior: Being the One by Jake Horsley (London: Gollancz, 240 pp, £6.99)

This sometimes earnest, sometimes tongue-in-cheek response to *The Matrix* takes as its starting point "the possibility that everything in the movie might be absolutely and totally true"—in short, that the world *is* an illusion, we *are* all slaves, and "humanity is a food source." Offering itself as "a field manual" (or as the subtitle suggests, "The Unofficial Handbook"), it promises to help us unplug ourselves, free ourselves of illusion, and at last know the truth.

It's a cute idea. Alas, the book does little more than filibuster upon it, chapter after chapter, in the sort of empty, b.s.-ridden, turgid prose with which generations of bright, glib, but lazy students have answered essay questions on exams. Nor is the tedium relieved by an assortment of scientific-looking diagrams scattered here and there in the text: circles within circles, circles overlapping circles, circles in various molecular patterns, all bearing portentous labels such as "Humaton," "Ruthlessness and detachment," "Money (Shopping)," "Gatekeepers," "Fame (Sex) Loneliness," and "Real World."

Beneath the book's philosophizing there's an air of condescension, one that has something of the Eastern guru in it but is closer to the attitude generally associated with self-pitying, alienated adolescent misfits. "Humatons," we're told, "do not think for themselves. Their so-called 'minds' are actually intricate recordings fixed on a loop of endless repetition." The true matrix warrior must be "indifferent to and contemptuous of the trinkets and baubles of matrix life that humatons so ceaselessly chase after." And what are these "petty baubles"? "Love, food, money, fame, and above all social acceptance."

There's a particular contempt, not surprisingly, for "the institutions of government, congress, elections, and so forth," and for politics: "Nothing is quite so amusing from a Lucid point of view as the institution of politics. Like religion, only even more insidious, politics provides humatons with the illusion of somehow having their destiny in hand and being on a path that will eventually lead somewhere; if not to utopia, then at least democracy!" It's a pity, but I suspect this book is not going to be endorsed by the League of Women Voters.

Japanese Movie Posters by Tetsuda Masuda and Kairakutei Black (Tokyo: DH Publishing, 96 pp, $30 pb).

Offering full-color reproductions of eighty movie posters, this handsomely produced oversized paperback may be a bit pricey for most of us, but where else are fans of samurai movies going to find a copy of the poster for *Zatoichi, the Fugitive* (the fourth in a twenty-six-film series that, we're told, "gained even more notoriety ... when an actor using a real sword killed an extra on set during a fight scene")? And where else will sci-fi fans find the posters for

Rodan, Mothra, Mothra 2, and *Gamera vs. Giant Sea Monster Jigura* and horror fans the poster for *Ship of Blood-Sucking Skulls*? ("Unfortunately," a caption says, "the poster is better made than the film.")

Happily, the book includes a striking poster from *Spirited Away,* the powerful *Alice in Wonderland*–like animated film, now distributed by Disney, that's become "the biggest hit in the history of Japanese cinema." I'm not so sure *Spirited* is really for kids—it's pretty damned disturbing—and this book is not for kids either: The section titled "Pink" contains a generous helping of Japanese starlets, some depicted in bondage, some in schoolgirl outfits, most seminude, and all unashamedly lurid.

So Crazy Japanese Toys! by Jimbo Matison and Michael Garlington (Chronicle, 132 pp, $18.95 pb).

Subtitled *Live-Action TV Show Toys from the 1950s to Now,* this oversized paperback—gorgeously designed, like all Chronicle products—is a gallery of 153 colorful plastic Japanese toys: figures of men, women, animals, aliens, and monsters, some of them vaguely winsome, most of them futuristic and extremely bizarre. All are photographed in high style against suitably contrasting backgrounds, turning them into little works of art. Except for five amusing chapter introductions ("Men in Rubber," "Rockin' Chicks," "Cute 'n' Cuddly," "Motor Heroes," and "Freaky Foes"), the book has virtually no text; even the information normally found in captions is relegated to the back of the book, in the interest of sheer coolness.

August 2003

The Twilight Zone Scripts of Earl Hamner by Earl Hamner and Tony Albarella (Cumberland House, 312 pp, $16.95 pb).

Fans of *The Twilight Zone* are probably aware that Rod Serling, its creator and host, wrote most of the original series' 156 episodes. In fact, of the first season's 36 episodes, Serling wrote an astounding 28—and for the entire series, 92. After him, in the number of their contributions, are two names long identified with the fantasy genre: Charles Beaumont (18 episodes) and Richard Matheson (14).

The fourth most prolific contributor, however, with eight

shows to his credit, is less well known—at least as a writer of the *Twilight Zone* school. That's because Earl Hamner made his name in a very different area of TV. As Tony Albarella explains in his introduction to this handsomely designed eight-script collection, "Mr. Hamner's work is overshadowed by his success as creator, writer, producer, and narrator of *The Waltons,* arguably the best-loved family series in television history." He later created another popular series, *Falcon Crest.*

In writing *The Waltons,* as well as novels such as *Spencer's Mountain* and *The Homecoming,* Hamner drew on his boyhood in rural Virginia, where he was born in 1923. He used the same Blue Ridge background for his first *Twilight Zone* contribution, "The Hunt," a folksy tale about a coonhunter's devotion to his dog. Although as a dead-but-doesn't-know-it yarn it makes use of one of the most familiar of supernatural plot devices, it ends with a rustic vision of the afterlife, in a scene I challenge anyone—or at least any animal-lover—to read without getting a little choked up.

Another Hamner script, "Jess-Belle," employs the same hillbilly milieu, complete with barn dances, shotguns, lantern light, even a backwoods witch-woman. (It also employed the same actress, Jeanette Nolan, as well as young stars Anne Francis and James Best, who'd already appeared together in *Forbidden Planet.*) Like "The Hunt," in which characters spied omens in the natural world—"Three nights ago I saw blood on the moon. And two days ago, a bird flew in the house and lit on your side of the bed"—"Jess-Belle" serves up even more portentous birds: "I saw [a female whippoorwill] on the trail tonight," reports the title character. "Wingin' up against the sky, then a nighthawk swooped up out of the pines and tore her breast open." Replies the hero, named Billy-Ben: "It was a bad omen."

Albarella—who, after each script, contributes a thoughtful discussion of its genesis, themes, and on-air presentation—calls this one "arguably Hamner's finest contribution to the series," but maybe it plays better than it reads. (I confess it's been years since I've seen it.) On the page, "Jess-Belle" comes off like *Cat People* set amid the world of *Li'l Abner,* swollen here and there by some purplish dialogue: "Remember when we clung together in the sweet night grass on Rockfish Mountain and the moonlight made a sea of silver mist on the fog below?" What's remarkable is that the script, created for the season of hour-long *Twilight Zone*s, was written from scratch and ready to shoot in a single week.

Hamner clearly had a knack for conjuring up stories with a classic Serling flavor. His "You Drive" and "A Piano in the House" feature machines with magical powers: a car that brings a hit-and-run driver to justice and a player piano whose songs inspire people to reveal their true selves. (Serling, you'll recall, had—as the title of one of his own scripts puts it—"A Thing about Machines.") "Stopover in a Quiet Town"—like so many of the Serling episodes, including the very first, "Where Is Everybody?"—plays on our fear of isolation and loneliness; as Albarella points out, it also has a touch of Serling's distaste for slick, sophisticated urban types, a theme carried further in Hamner's final script, "The Bewitchin' Pool," which also became the final show of the series. Here, as in so many *Twilight Zone* stories, characters—in this case a suburban brother and sister oppressed by squabbling, selfish parents—escape to an old-fashioned rural world, Huck Finn by way of Norman Rockwell, where kindly old ladies stitch quilts and boys in straw hats fish for minnows. Call it watered-down *Waltons,* if you like, but it sure is seductive.

Picturing Extraterrestrials: Alien Images in Modern Mass Culture by John F. Moffitt (Prometheus, 595 pp, $30).

As someone who lives just down the road from the cabin where horror writer Whitley Strieber claims to have been abducted by aliens, I'm a sucker for books on UFOs. This one—by John Moffitt, a retired art-history professor living in New Mexico "not all that far from Roswell"—examines the cultural and commercial forces that have spawned what Moffitt calls "the 'classic' alien . . . small in stature, hairless, usually pale gray in color, [with] a proportionately oversized, triangular-shaped and somewhat bulbous head, and large, dark, and reflective, wrap-around eyes"—a type he also dubs "the bug-eyed space waif."

This ubiquitous figure owes something to Spielberg and something to the cover of Strieber's *Communion,* a book Moffitt treats with undisguised contempt. Dismissing Strieber's account of mind and anal probes as "pornography of the masochistic sort," he traces elements in it that may well have been inspired by earlier abduction tales. Indeed, a smirking contempt sets the tone for much of this book, for Moffitt seems at pains lest we think even for a moment that he himself believes in such tommyrot. While it's hard not to share, and even applaud, his skepticism, his unceasing derision soon grows wearisome; in quoting the testimony of self-proclaimed abductees, he constantly injects his own sarcastic observations instead of letting his subjects hang themselves.

Still, there are genuine riches here, if one hunts for them; Moffitt seems to have read and digested entire libraries, not only of UFO lore but of psychology, history, and the arts, from ancient icons to modern film and TV, from Karl Marx to Virginia Woolf. His wide-ranging knowledge undoes him, however, for the text is maddeningly rambling and digressive, as if the author saw in it a chance to express opinions on whatever struck his fancy, no matter how marginally related to his ostensible topic. While his style is blessedly free of academic jargon, at times it resembles a garrulous monologue, by turns pretentious or colloquial, filled with fussy little parenthetical asides, some of them donnishly playful, some oddly self-conscious.

And like many a monologist, Moffitt sometimes repeats himself. On page 36, we read: "Twenty years ago a Gallup poll found that only 30 percent of American college graduates believed the flying saucers visited earth in some form; today, 42 percent of college graduates accept the credulous premise—further proof that the quality of higher education in the United States has surely diminished by (at least) half." This entire passage reappears virtually word for word on page 129, except that "higher" has been stuck inside sneer quotes and "42 percent" has mysteriously grown to "nearly 60 percent." Such carelessness does not inspire confidence.

One wishes that *Picturing Extraterrestrials* included more pictures; there are just 16 pages of black-and-white illustrations, compared with nearly 600 pages of text. How irresistible this book would have been if that ratio had been reversed.

The Prisoner: The Official Companion to the Classic TV Series by Robert Fairclough (ibooks, 144 pp, $24.95 pb).

Though it's a cult favorite with fans around the world, *The Prisoner* was a commercial disappointment. Filmed in the real-life Welsh hamlet of Portmeirion and debuting in the fall of 1967, this surreal British series—about an unnamed secret agent known only as "Number 6" who, upon attempting to resign, is imprisoned by his former employers in a charming but isolated theme-park-looking place known only as "the village"—lasted just seventeen episodes.

There are three things you should know about this excellent book: It provides a detailed show-by-show guide to the series, complete with behind-the-scenes production notes; it has tons of color photos; and it offers, as a bonus, a DVD of the first episode and an alternate version of the second.

According to author Robert Fairclough, one reason for the series' early demise—aside from its odd, Kafkaesque premise—was friction between its creators: writer George Markstein (seen each week as the administrator to whom the agent submitted his resignation) and star Patrick McGoohan (who, we're told, had been offered, and turned down, the chance to play James Bond). Though Fairclough repeatedly praises the Irish actor for his uncompromising integrity, it's easy to see that McGoohan took himself very seriously indeed and that his ego may have made him no picnic to work with. He rejected one script because it had Number 6 attempting to orient himself by studying bird migration—"heroes don't birdwatch," he declared—and another because it had him perspiring; "heroes," he said, "don't sweat."

October 2003

The Art of X2: The Making of the Blockbuster Movie, designed and edited by Timothy Shaner (Newmarket, 160 pp, $19.95 pb).

"There's nothing like a successful movie to breed a bigger sequel," says Avi Arad, head of Marvel Studio—and *X-Men* was an extremely successful movie, generating what Oscar Richards, in this book's introduction, says was "the second-biggest opening of any film in Twentieth Century Fox history." The sequel, *X2,* is indeed bigger, with more elaborate sets, additional characters, and, according to

Richards, "800 on-screen F/X sequences versus 500 in *X-Men*."

Special effects are a raison d'être of books like this. As popular movies—and sci-fi movies in particular—become increasingly dependent on dazzling the audience with futuristic vehicles, marvelous costumes, spectacular sets (sometimes encompassing entire cities), and characters with superhuman powers, we're going to see more and more films entitled *The Making of* and books entitled *The Art of*. This one contains very little text and consists largely of pictures—costume sketches, set designs (including, sitting weirdly in the middle of a Vancouver soundstage, a mockup of the Oval Office), production stills, storyboards (resembling the comics on which the film was based), behind-the-scenes shots of the performers, and preliminary "concept" art—making it a perfect souvenir book for fans. Alas, though we're offered a test shot of Nightcrawler's blue makeup being applied, we don't get to see exactly how Mystique's skintight blue costume—or was it merely body paint?—was put on Rebecca Romijn-Stamos. That would be worth a book in itself.

Ironically, amid all the stunning art and lavish color, my favorite picture is the book's only black-and-white photo, depicting director Bryan Singer and twelve cast members seated at a long table during a Vancouver press conference. As they wait patiently for questions, each facing a microphone and a bottle of water, they look just like guests of honor at a sci-fi convention.

Fangoria's 101 Best Horror Movies You've Never Seen by Adam Lukeman (Three Rivers, 273 pp, $13 pb).

The premise is hard to resist. Here's a book that celebrates the terrific little horror movies you missed . . . or never even heard of. As *Fangoria* editor Anthony Timpone says in his introduction, these 101 "treasures" are "the unheralded gems you might not know or might have forgotten, as well as films that deserve reevaluation," including commercial flops and "straight-to-video sleepers."

Immediately I was won over when I spied, among the titles covered, three favorites of mine from the early '70s: *Let's Scare Jessica to Death*, a moody, quiet film set in the New England countryside and featuring some excellent method actors from New York (it doesn't make a great deal of sense, but it's atmospheric as hell); *The Asphyx*, a supernatural obscurity set in Victorian England with fine Hammer-like production values (no treasure, perhaps, but heartening to see it unearthed); and *The Other,* a superb, gorgeously photographed adaptation of Thomas Tryon's novel. Score three for *Fango.*

Even though you've likely never heard of many of these films and will disagree about some that are included (*Swamp Thing?*), chances are you'll find a few of your own faves as well, for the book casts a very wide net, from art films (*Paperhouse*) to gorefests (*Two Thousand Maniacs!*), from lighthearted romps (*Night of the Comet; Lair of the White Worm*) to films that'll plunge you into week-long depressions (*Henry: Portrait of a Serial Killer; The Vanishing*).

Each film receives a two-page write-up that's long on plot and way too short on commentary, and the cast lists are annoyingly incomplete. What's best are the two or three items of "Terror Trivia" included for each title. Some samples: Before he cast porn star Marilyn Chambers as the lead in *Rabid,* David Cronenberg contemplated giving the role to a pre-*Carrie* Sissy Spacek; a pre-*Kojak* Telly Savalas sucks his trademark lollipop in *Horror Express.* Among those considered to play Hannibal Lecter in *Manhunter* were Brian Dennehy, John Lithgow, and Mandy Patinkin. Don Siegel, director of the 1956 *Invasion of the Body Snatchers,* played a cab driver in the 1978 remake; in a lovers'-lane murder scene in *Maniac,* makeup artist Tom Savini "played both killer and victim"; and ex-surgeon general C. Everett Koop shows up in a restaurant scene in *The Exorcist III.*

The Universe: 365 Days edited by Robert J. Nemiroff and Jerry T. Bonnell (Abrams, 744 pp, $29.95).

There are plenty of books containing photos of the planets, stars, and galaxies, and all such photos tend to be glorious; but there's probably never been a book at once so single-minded and yet so voluminous as this. As thick as a phonebook and so heavy you might use it for your morning exercises, *The Universe: 365 Days* consists of 365 full-page full-color photos of celestial phenomena with, on each facing page, a few succinct sentences of technical explanation. The explanations are useful and often entertaining—one starts off by informing us, tongue in cheek, that "using the new camera on the recently refitted Hubble Space Telescope, astronomers have been able to confirm that the Moon is in fact made of green cheese"—but even without the text, the beauty of the photos is excuse enough for preserving them between covers. Here's an "hourglass nebula," startlingly reminiscent of Sauron's sinister unwinking eye in the *Lord of the Rings* films; turn the page and there's a close-up of the Crab Nebula, a swirling pattern resembling the marbled covers of old books; turn one more page and you'll find an eruption on one of Jupiter's moons, fiery lava frothing up into what looks like the Sahara. It's the hardcover equivalent of an outer-space slide show—or, more up to date, of an elaborate and colorful PowerPoint presentation.

As the engagingly modest foreword explains, the editors selected these images from six years' worth—mostly NASA photos from various interplanetary probes and Apollo missions, as well as from observatories around the world—that appeared on *Astronomy Picture of the Day,* a website the pair established in 1995. The selection is endlessly varied, from a U.S. Navy photo of an F/A-18 Hornet breaking the sound barrier to a fly-by view of Neptune sent back by Voyager 2, to the blurred image of "dark matter" provided by a group of microwave telescopes in Spain, depicting "some of the oldest objects ever seen." My only criticism of the selection is that it's formless—utterly random, in fact. Each of the photos is designated by a single day of the year, but there's no link between image and date: April 27th depicts Enceladus, a moon of Saturn; the 28th and 29th depict the red giants Betelgeuse and Mira; the 30th, a computer-generated 3-D picture of a teapot, the sort of thing you squint at until the image appears. The "365" may work as a marketing tool, but the book could just as easily have contained 300 pictures—or twice that many.

The Zombie Survival Guide: Complete Protection from the Living Dead by Max Brooks (Three Rivers, 257 pp, $12.95 pb).

Now that *28 Days Later* has brought zombies back to the screen (although this time they're overrunning London and Manchester instead of Pittsburgh or Rome), it's high time we innocent humans were provided with some practical advice on combating this threat. Two years ago *The Horror Movie Survival Guide* took on the task, offering tips on how to deal with everything from space aliens to killer sharks, but it did so for laughs (and tried a bit too hard).

What's odd about *The Zombie Survival Guide* is that it plays it straight, like a real survival manual. We're told, in earnest detail, about zombies' physical attributes ("Despite legends and ancient folklore, undead physiology has been proven to possess no powers of regeneration.... Unlike a living body, adrenal glands have not been known to function in the dead, denying zombies the temporary burst of power we humans enjoy"); hand-to-hand combat ("When using a blunt weapon, the goal is to crush the brain.... This is not as easy as it sounds"); the use of fire as a defense ("Flesh—human, undead, or otherwise—takes a long time to burn. In the minutes or hours before a blazing zombie succumbs, it will become a walking—or to be perfectly accurate, a *shambling*—torch"); the wisdom of retreating to an offshore oil rig ("When choosing a fortress purely for its safety, nothing on earth holds a candle to these artificial islands"); and the usefulness of a good scuba outfit ("Because the undead can exist, operate, even kill in a liquid environment, hunting them may require occasional underwater warfare"). A long section at the back recounts, with scholarly exactitude, dozens of "recorded attacks" from all over the world.

What's even odder is that the author of this straight-faced spoof is the son of Mel Brooks and Anne Bancroft and has written for *Saturday Night Live*. You'd think the guy would be funny, but the book he's produced is, if anything, somewhat tedious, like those stage appearances in which the late Andy Kaufman would read aloud from *The Great Gatsby;* the joke was that there *was* no joke. If *The Horror Movie Survival Guide*'s humor failed because it was too broad, the humor in *Zombie* fails because it is, like its subject, preternaturally dry.*

Double Feature Creature Attack by Tom Weaver (McFarland, 721 pp, $30 pb).

"Much that once was is lost, for none now live who remember."

---

*Maybe I just didn't get the joke, because the book became a bestseller; and ten years later Brooks's next zombie history, *World War Z,* became, of course, the blockbuster Brad Pitt film.

Something akin to those haunting words—from the opening of *The Fellowship of the Ring*—must have echoed in Tom Weaver's head as he set out to meet the B-movie actors and filmmakers who turned 1940s and '50s Hollywood into a golden age—or okay, bronze age—of horror and sci-fi. The films themselves were shown at drive-ins, Saturday matinees, and later on TV shows like *Chiller Theater;* the people who made them are now elderly or dead, though a fortunate few are still working. Weaver, a genre-film historian, has made a career out of interviewing the survivors, gathering their recollections—which are invariably amusing, colorful, and ultimately quite touching—first for periodicals, then for a series of books, most of which I've reviewed for this magazine.

Two of them, *Attack of the Monster Movie Makers* and *They Fought in the Creature Features,* published in 1994 and '95, have now been packaged into this eminently rereadable 700-page double volume, containing forty-three interviews with the likes of Herman Cohen, producer of *I Was a Teenage Werewolf;* Ben Chapman and Ricou Browning, who together (on land and water, respectively) played the titular Gill Man in *The Creature from the Black Lagoon;* Kenneth Tobey, stalwart star of *The Thing;* Jeff Morrow, chief alien in *This Island Earth;* Turhan Bey, villain in *The Mummy's Tomb;* Candace Hilligoss, star of *Carnival of Souls;* John Agar, star of *Tarantula;* and Anne Francis, star of *Forbidden Planet* and later two *Twilight Zones*.

"When I started on this kick," explains Weaver, "I wanted to be the *first* person to talk to the Richard E. Cunhas [*She Demons*] and the Susan Cabots [*The Wasp Woman*] and the Reginald LeBorgs [*The Black Sleep*]—not the five-hundred-and-first guy to elicit the same old, dog-tired reminiscences out of, say, Roger Corman or Christopher Lee." In fact, the only really familiar figure interviewed here is Vincent Price; and typically, it's the best Price interview I've ever seen.

December 2003

Profoundly Disturbing by Joe Bob Briggs (Rizzoli/Universe, 256 pp, $24.95 pb).

To many genre fans, the pseudonymous Joe Bob Briggs will always be known as the redneck reviewer who evaluates exploitation movies, B-pictures, and drive-in fare using a grisly but gleeful cinematic body count: this number of severed heads, that number of hacked-off limbs; this many bare breasts, that many corpses.

But welcome to a new Joe Bob Briggs, who, if he isn't exactly more refined, is certainly more scholarly and intellectual than the lip-smacking Texas gorehound who hailed *The Killer Shrews* for, among other things, its excellent "character-actor eating." The latter-day Briggs is perfectly comfortable making allusions to German Expressionism, to Stendhal, to Picasso, Braque, and Duchamp, and to the film historian Siegfried Kracauer.

The movies he focuses on in this new book—*Blood Feast; The Texas Chain Saw Massacre; Ilsa, She-Wolf of the SS;* and a dozen more—are mostly the same sort of lurid productions he's celebrated in the past, only here he discusses them like a professor rather than a frat boy. The subtitle describes these films as "Shocking Movies That Changed History!" and in his intro he argues that "all the films I've chosen for this book have been banned, censored, condemned, or despised because in one way or another they expanded what the camera sees into some area that was previously verboten. These films . . . ultimately rearrange our whole view of what constitutes reality."

That's a pretty heavy claim; and even after reading his insightful examination of, say, *Creature from the Black Lagoon*, I can't quite see that film as especially groundbreaking or precedent-shattering. True, *Creature* carries an unspoken sexual subtext for a large part of its intended audience—"It doesn't take a master psychologist to see how a pubescent boy, struggling with feelings of being ugly, unloved, and half-formed, would not only identify with the creature (who has acne-like protuberances on his face) but imagine a girl just like Julia Adams, who would finally come to rescue him from the lonely black lagoon called his room"—but that's nothing new; virtually every film has a sexual subtext. Still, whether or not the book's fifteen selections all qualify as genuine pioneers, they're the occasion for some fascinating analysis that manages to single out these productions for what makes them special while placing each in its historical tradition; and writing that good needs no excuse.

The one silent film included, *The Cabinet of Dr. Caligari,* gives

Briggs room to discourse on post–World War I Europe's political and social turmoil, but also to point out that this innovative horror film was "designed to be seen with a full orchestra playing modernist music—Debussy, Schoenberg, Stravinsky"—and is consequently ruined when accompanied, as it usually is, by a conventional silent-movie organ or piano score. His piece on a, for me, unheard-of 1947 cheapie called *Mom and Dad*—an hour and a half of pious family-values fluff, with some clinical footage about childbirth and syphilis spliced in at the end—allows him to discuss the economics of the exploitation film, along with a social history of small-town American taboos. He treats a 1957 Hammer title, *The Curse of Frankenstein*, as the first splatter film—"This was the first film to show preserved eyeballs, brains in glass jars," the first to show "graphic gore"—and mentions in passing that Hammer's earliest production was a 1935 parody of *The Private Life of Henry the Eighth* called *The Public Life of Henry the Ninth*.

Bet you didn't know that Hammer went back that far. Or that *Creature from the Black Lagoon* was originally shot in 3-D (which "explains otherwise strange moments in the film, such as when the Gill Man seems to be walking toward the camera or waving his arms in a menacing manner for no apparent reason"). Or that before he wrote *The Exorcist*, William Peter Blatty was considered "a master of light comedy." Or that before *Reservoir Dogs* (whose genesis, incidentally, along with its similarities to the 1987 Hong Kong thriller *City on Fire*, is expertly recounted here), Quentin Tarantino had made one TV appearance—"a walk-on part as an Elvis impersonator on the sitcom *The Golden Girls*." Or that a reader's report on J. G. Ballard's novel *Crash* warned, "This author is beyond psychiatric help. Do Not Publish!" You can see, in this outraged reaction, proof that the novel was Profoundly Disturbing—as was David Cronenberg's eventual film of it; and as are, in their own individual ways, all the movies in this terrific book.

H. G. Wells on Film: The Utopian Nightmare by Don G. Smith (McFarland, 203 pp, $39.95).

The French have Jules Verne, with his Tom Swiftian submarines and flying machines, but the British have Herbert George

Wells—in versatility, literary ability, intellect, and sheer imagination the true progenitor of modern science fiction. It's astonishing how many classic films his works have spawned—sometimes followed by multiple remakes. Smith's book covers nearly all of them in scholarly detail, methodically contrasting them with the original stories or novels.

Still, with ideas as provocative as Wells's, it is impossible to stay up to date; though the book discusses ten films inspired by *The Invisible Man*, for example, including three French silents, a Mexican production, and even *Abbott and Costello Meet the Invisible Man*, it doesn't include 2003's *The League of Extraordinary Gentlemen*, in which a character one step removed from the Wells original plays a key role. (Nor will you find the nasty 2000 Paul Verhoeven film *Hollow Man*, which has no connection to Wells—at least none that is credited.)

The Island of Doctor Moreau has inspired at least five movies, three of them major Hollywood productions, all of them wonderfully erotic and creepy and touching, with mad-scientist leads played by Charles Laughton (1933), Burt Lancaster (1977), and Marlon Brando (1996)—the latter in an underrated version that I'm glad to see Smith defending: "The best thing about this film is that it presents an occasion for people to think. But in America, most people don't go to movies to think. They go to buy popcorn and be entertained." All three versions gain immense power from the presence of a seductively slinky panther-woman character who, Smith reminds us, never appeared in the original novel. Both other *Moreau*-inspired films are Filipino: *Terror Is a Man* ("the best horror/science fiction film made in the Philippines") and *The Twilight People* ("what a mess!").

Especially welcome, to me, was a chapter on *The Man Who Could Work Miracles*, a charming 1936 English fantasy that Wells himself adapted from one of his stories. You'll also find excellent discussions of *The Time Machine*, *The War of the Worlds*, and the visionary saga *Things to Come*, another film for which Wells himself wrote the script, featuring futuristic cityscapes resembling the covers of 1930s *Amazing Stories*.

Hitchhiker: A Biography of Douglas Adams by M. J. Simpson (Boston: Justin Charles, 426 pp, $27.95).

Douglas Adams, the six-foot-five Cambridge-born, Cambridge-educated author of *The Hitchhiker's Guide to the Galaxy*, died in 2001 of a heart attack while working out in a Santa Barbara health club. He was only forty-nine, and had been embroiled in a frustrating struggle to bring *Guide* to the screen. In this affectionate but not-uncritical biography—divided into forty-two chapters because that number is, according to the *Guide*, "the Answer to the Great Question of Life, the Universe and Everything"—M. J. Simpson introduces us to a flawed genius with a penchant for monologuing (he would talk nonstop for over an hour if something was on his mind) and a formidable talent for missing deadlines ("Douglas certainly raised procrastination to an art form," says a colleague). His greatest influences were Monty Python and the Beatles; he revered Kurt Vonnegut and Robert Sheckley but was no sci-fi fan—"in fact," remembers an acquaintance, "he was quite dismissive of it."

Guide began as a hit BBC radio series that had the good luck to air in 1978 just a few weeks after *Star Wars* opened in Britain. Only later did Adams turn his quirky comedy into a novel. "A publisher came and asked me to write a book," he recalled, "which is a very good way of breaking into publishing." Sequels followed, and computer games, and a heartfelt celebration of endangered species, *Last Chance to See*. Still, one comes away with the impression that Adams never lived up to his early success and spent too much time collecting fine wines, expensive cars, and "what was confidently believed to be the largest collection of left-handed guitars in the world."

Hitchhiker is one of two Adams biographies to be published this fall; the other, *Don't Panic*, by *Sandman* creator Neil Gaiman, is a fast, delightful read but not as thorough as Simpson's. Curiously, Simpson has contributed four chapters to Gaiman's book and Gaiman has contributed a foreword to this one—probably the only time two seemingly competing authors have collaborated on each other's books, and surely the sort of generous cooperation that the genial Adams would have approved of.

Future Perfect: Vintage Futuristic Graphics edited by Jim Heimann (Cologne, Germany: Taschen, 192 pp, $9.99 pb).

The German publisher Taschen produces some of the handsomest and most intriguing art books available today; and whether they're $10 (like this one) or $60 (like the full-color facsimile of the 1493 *Nuremberg Chronicle,* the original of which sells for $98,500), all are bargain-priced.

Future Perfect is a sort of pocket-sized coffee-table book, a collection of color illustrations from magazines of the 1920s, '30s, '40s, and '50s depicting what daily life was going to be like—or at least what daily life *ought* to be like if people got their act together—in the America of the future. "That roughly four-decade period was, in hindsight, a golden age of galloping optimism," writes artist Bruce McCall in a preface entitled, alas, "Futures That Never Arrived."

Aside from the preface, the book has no text; but the images—from ads, sci-fi pulps, and the covers of magazines like *Popular Science* and *Modern Mechanix and Inventions*—paint something that needs no explanation, the picture of a sleek, clean, efficient, comfortable future: impossibly streamlined automobiles cruising down impossibly trafficless highways; space vehicles that Tom Corbett, Space Cadet, might have used; hovercars, monorails, and robot gardeners; gleaming futuristic cities, their skies filled with helicopters, dirigibles, and flying wings; a five-story seaplane as big as an ocean liner; a plane that looks like a giant microphone; a railroad train running on what appears to be, improbably, an enormous ball bearing; a mailman bouncing across suburban lawns using some sort of antigravity backpack; and a happy housewife purchasing a wardrobe via telephone and TV screen. Well, at least there's one prediction that's come true.

February 2004

Lost in Space: The Fall of NASA and the Dream of a New Space Age by Greg Klerkx (Pantheon, 416 pp, $27.95).

Early in this hard-hitting book, the author quotes Graham Greene: "There is always one moment in childhood when the door opens and lets the future in." For Greg Klerkx, who dreamed of growing up to be an astronaut, that moment was when the men of

Apollo 11 first set foot on the moon. As it happens, Klerkx became a senior manager at the SETI Institute, devoted to the Search for Extra-Terrestrial Intelligence, but he still identifies with individuals who long to clamber aboard a spaceship and visit the moon or Mars, and he defends "what is derisively dubbed space tourism." As he argues near the end, "The average man or woman's desire to travel into space is no less noble than that of any NASA astronaut"—and he holds the space agency responsible for discouraging that dream.

In fact, Klerkx's passionate and rather anguished account might just as easily be titled "The Case Against NASA." Over and over, Klerkx hammers home his criticisms: that NASA has become "a fractious bureaucracy roiling with politics and infighting, thick with red tape and feral self-interest" and "a desperate bureaucracy concerned, above all else, with its own survival." He sees NASA's current preoccupation with the space shuttle and the International Space Station—projects he terms a "two-headed albatross"—as driven by financial and political concerns: "NASA and its chief contractors, Boeing and Lockheed Martin, have what amounts to a state-sponsored market monopoly—with the market in this case being near-Earth human spaceflight."

The shuttle program, he argues, has had the unintended effect of tying humanity "more tightly to Earth," and he dismisses the rocket itself—perhaps a little too flippantly—as "the spacefaring equivalent of a Ford Pinto: It keeps chugging along not because it is a fundamentally good vehicle, but because it is serviced relentlessly by a swarm of technicians and has virtually every component replaced, repaired, or refurbished after every trip." And what, he asks, is the point of all this labor? "After its first few flights, beginning with the launch of *Columbia* in 1981, it began to dawn on the public (and on Congress) that the shuttle didn't seem to have any particular purpose."

As for the space station, he sees it as equally pointless. "When the space station was announced in 1984, it was promoted loudly as the staging post for missions to Mars and, critically, the first outpost of an orbital commerce revolution that would create a busy hub of human enterprise around the planet. Those promises, too, were quickly unmasked as little more than hype: The space station was built, first and foremost, to give the space shuttle something obvious to do." Elsewhere he calls the station "a money-gobbling albatross"—he's obviously fond of that image—"whose original intent and design have become so subverted by politics, spin, and greed that not even NASA can give a straight answer anymore as to what, in fact, it's for."

With taxpayer dollars being funneled into these two projects, "leaving space in the hands of the experts, with the public cheering from the sidelines and dutifully footing the bill," Klerkx is not surprised that the cheering has begun to subside, along with the public's willingness to pay. After all, Americans' initial interest in space—and the race to the moon—was fueled in part by fear and the spirit of competition: We didn't want the Russians to get there first. Today, though the president now talks of a return to the moon, the race is perceived as over. "The Apollo generations will give way, soon," Klerkx predicts, "to generations for whom human spaceflight is at best mildly entertaining and at worst a burden."

The best hope of rekindling an interest in space travel, he suggests, is to privatize it, just as earth-bound aviation—aside from its military uses—is in the hands of commercial airlines and private individuals. It's a view that's been espoused by science fiction writers such as Robert A. Heinlein (check out his "The Man Who Sold the Moon" and "Requiem"), and in fact Klerkx offers a keen political analysis of Heinlein's work, one of whose abiding themes was rugged American individualism. However, "the idea of space as an individual frontier was anathema to NASA's way of doing business," Klerkx says, and—in addition to describing NASA as a "truncheon-swinging government bully"—he compares the agency's group-think mentality to that of the *Star Trek* race the Borg.

Lost in Space is provocative and probably important, though for my taste it spends a few too many chapters profiling various entrepreneurs and visionaries, one of whom has "proposed turning the [space] station into a purely commercial enterprise and getting NASA out of the picture altogether." Another, the multimillionaire philanthropist Dennis Tito, in April 2001 became "the first person in history to pay his own way into space." Writes Klerkx: "As the date of Tito's flight grew closer, the tone of NASA's rhetoric became increasingly shrill and uncomfortably personal." He alludes to "Tito's cheerfulness and NASA's loutishness"—just in case you've forgotten, even for a moment, which side he's on.

The Art of John Berkey by Jane Frank (London: Paper Tiger, 128 pp, £20.00/$29.95).

There are science fiction artists who specialize in extraterrestrial landscapes—the great Chesley Bonestell comes to mind—and there are some who specialize, like Wayne Barlowe, in extraterrestrials themselves. But no one does *vehicles*—vast starships, complex space stations, battle cruisers bristling with guns—as convincingly as John Berkey. He imparts to them, among other things, a certain *blur*—Jane Frank refers to his "unique Impressionistic style, which makes things 'realer than real'"—so that, for all their detail, they seem too gigantic and moving at too great a speed for the eye to fully encompass. And what's astonishing is that these illustrations of his look almost effortless.

They're not. In fact, judging from what one reads about him in this collection of more than a hundred of his paintings, he's been, all his life, a diligent and conscientious worker. Now in his early seventies, he emerges not only as talented and hardworking but becomingly modest, a family man who spends his Sundays fishing. "This is a man," writes Frank, "who, according to his own telling, 'just happens' to have painted spaceships for the past forty years. . . . He is a man so courteous and gentlemanly in his demeanour that it would be a physical impossibility for him to slam the phone down on any telemarketer."

Born in North Dakota, raised in Montana and Minnesota, he went to art school in Minneapolis and learned his craft turning out calendar illustrations. "My first job was a painting of cows walking along a fence-line towards a town in the snow," he recalls. "I was paid $300. My most recent piece was a book cover for the Science Fiction Book Club. I was paid $3,000." Though most of the pictures in this collection are solidly sci-fi (including covers for *Science Fiction Age*), illustrations for *National Geographic, Sports Afield,* and *Popular Mechanics* are also represented, along with a number of personal works: glowing country landscapes and a few nudes. Vehicles may be his specialty, from 15th-century sailing ships to futuristic spaceships, but he even breathes life into a study of pebbles and rocks.

The Complete Tolkien Companion by J. E. A. Tyler (St. Martin's, 720 pp, $27.95).

Do we really need help reading Tolkien? Sure we do. Granted, *The Lord of the Rings* and *The Hobbit* are not as demanding as, say, *Ulysses* or, God forbid, *Finnegans Wake*. You can't fully appreciate Joyce without a guidebook (or an unusually knowledgeable professor), but you can read and love and understand Tolkien's fantasy epics right off the bookshelf, without benefit of exegesis. And millions have done so.

Still, anyone who's ever gotten confused between Sauron, Saruman, Sméagol, and Smaug may discover that there's some truth in the old adage that you can't tell the players without a program; and Tyler's book fills that need splendidly. It's a fat, handsomely designed, immensely detailed guide to Middle-earth, part Who's Who, part gazetteer. With the possible exception of Tom Shippey's erudite and insightful *J.R.R. Tolkien: Author of the Century*, it's the single most indispensable book to have in your backpack when you're setting out on a journey to Mirkwood or Mordor. (Stay-at-homes will want to keep it on their night table.)

What makes it a particular joy to read, though perhaps less user-friendly, is that the *Companion* is written in a heightened, elegant prose that sometimes seems to echo *The Silmarillion*. Typical is this description of Elrond's abode: "The House of Rivendell was not a fortress, nor a camp of war. It was a place of learning, merriment, and quiet, beside a running stream, deep in a forest-clad northern valley." Or savor, for example, the biblical language Tyler uses to describe Sauron's final great attack: "This occurred in 3019 Third Age, when a mighty host came down from the mountains and captured West Osgiliath, pouring across the Great River in many boats." Only rarely is there a hint of humor: "The labours they [the Rangers] undertook in their worthy purpose were long, hard, and yet not without result. Of course the Northlands were still threatened by groups of pillaging Orcs from the Misty Mountains, and the occasional cave-troll in business on his own account; but the hoped-for result was, by and large, attained, and the folk of Eriador were safely guarded, although they knew it not."

Couched in such a style and adorned with medieval-looking woodcuts that introduce each new letter of the alphabet, the book has the flavor of something written on parchment with a quill pen.

Adventures of a Suburban Boy by John Boorman (London: Faber & Faber/New York: Farrar, Straus & Giroux, 320 pp, $27).

Even for a movie director, a justly envied breed, John Boorman seems to have led a particularly enviable life. Though not all his films have been box-office hits, he's had the privilege of selecting—and writing—his own projects; he's shot pictures in exotic corners of the world (such as the Amazon jungle for *The Emerald Forest,* with his own son as star); and in *Hope and Glory* he was lucky enough to re-create, with lovingly remembered detail, his own London childhood during the Blitz.

He's also had the opportunity to work with some memorable characters, all of whom come to life in this droll, charming, and often very funny autobiography. Boorman was especially fond of the late Lee Marvin, a difficult and clearly troubled man, who became a close friend while starring in *Point Blank* and *Hell in the Pacific:* "He leapt from metaphor to metaphor, and when he was drinking, the leaps got wider. I would follow him as far as I could, and there was always wisdom there . . . but beyond a certain level of vodka, he sailed out on his own into deeper waters where no mortal could follow."

Another drinker (though only on weekends), Richard Burton, starred in *The Heretic,* the *Exorcist* sequel, which proved to be an unqualified disaster: "He acted from the neck up, face and voice. His body was rigid, completely inexpressive. When alcoholics are on the wagon there is a hollowness about them. . . . I persuaded myself that this emptiness could work for the film. He said, 'This is my sixtieth film. I've never seen any of them except the first two. I was shocked. I was looking at my father's face. Unbearable.'"

Filming *Deliverance*—by far, I think, his greatest achievement—on Georgia's Chattooga River, Boorman worked with Burt Reynolds, Jon Voight (who comes across as sensitive and thoroughly decent), and still another alcoholic, the poet James Dickey, author of the gripping novel on which the film was based. Dickey proved to be an imperious drunk who intimidated the actors, and Boorman had to throw him off the set (though he later cast him as the sheriff). Dickey took in the assembled cast with an angry glare. "'It *appears*,' he italicised, 'that my *presence* would be most *efficacious* by its *absence*.' He let that sink in for a long moment, turned on his heel, and left. Burt looked perplexed. 'Does that mean he's going or staying?' You could never be sure with Burt whether he was being dumb or acting dumb."

In contrast, Marcello Mastroianni, star of *Leo the Last,* was the soul of tranquility, an affable fellow who found acting as natural as making love: "I had a scene where he was asleep in bed. While we were lighting and lining up, he simply fell asleep in the bed. I had to wake him up, so that he could act being asleep." Boorman was equally fond of Sean Connery, star of his sci-fi fable *Zardoz:* "He lived in my house for several weeks. He was a model guest: entertaining, thoughtful—he moved around the house turning off lights, a frugal Scot." Boorman discovered that the mercurial Nicol Williamson, whom he cast as Merlin in *Excalibur,* was "a notorious hypochondriac. He had two fatal diseases during the course of the picture."

In the early '70s, with J.R.R. Tolkien's blessing, Boorman labored on an adaptation of *The Lord of the Rings* but couldn't find the financing. Despite this disappointment, he has nothing but praise for Peter Jackson's version, which he compares to a Gothic cathedral. "My concept shrivels by comparison," he says modestly. "For instance, to solve the half-size Hobbit problem I was intending to cast ten-year-old boys, give them facial hair, and dub them with adult voices!"

Boorman recalls that as a boy he dreamed of being a writer, a career that, in desperation, "I hoped would transport me to another life away from the suburbs. I nurtured dreams of greatness." He may be revered today as a filmmaker, not a writer, but in this memoir he proves that he had at least one great book in him.

April 2004

Strange Universe: The Weird and Wild Science of Everyday Life—on Earth and Beyond by Bob Berman (Times Books/Holt, 219 pp, $25).

Popular-science books are, well . . . popular. And among the most popular is the type that seeks to demonstrate the laws of nature and the cosmos in the events of daily life. (James Trefill, for one, has made a career out of such writing.) Now astronomer Bob Berman has come up with a worthy example of the breed, finding lessons not only in the night sky but in such mundane objects as lightbulbs, tea kettles, and snowflakes.

However, *Strange Universe* tries to cover too much ground. It jumps about from subject to subject as if afraid we might be bored—and ironically, we *are,* because we're coaxed along so fast that we're never engaged. Ultimately, the book's frenetic once-over-lightly pace grows wearisome.

Berman devotes a mere six sentences, for example, to the fact that a shower curtain's tendency to draw inward toward the rushing water illustrates Bernoulli's principle, the same one that "makes tornadoes lift roofs and lets airplanes fly." A page later, he's explaining, in just five sentences, that the change in the pitch of a speeding police car's siren is an example of "the wonderful Doppler shift." In the very next paragraph, he's off talking about the color spectrum. *Hey,* we want to cry, *slow down!*

I remember reading, as a boy, how with each breath we take, we inhale atoms once breathed by—among others—Leonardo da Vinci. I remember being thrilled by the idea. Here the same mind-boggling concept is hurried by in just three sentences.

But maybe I shouldn't complain, because Berman has, after all, a wealth of things to teach us: that meteors, by the time they reach the earth, are barely warm; that four-fifths of the air we breathe is nitrogen; that women pay lower auto insurance but have 15 percent more accidents; that a third of all ultraviolet waves strike us sideways; that the moon is "one of the few totally gray objects in the known universe," and that its gravity causes foot-high deformations in the very ground we walk on; that the center of every rainbow you see is "the shadow of your head"; that the animal whose menstrual cycle is most similar to humans' is the opossum; and that Jupiter and its moons stink of methane, sulfur, and ammonia, making their vicinity "arguably the foulest-smelling place in the known universe outside of certain locker rooms."

June 2004

I Am Alive and You Are Dead: A Journey into the Mind of Philip K. Dick by Emmanuel Carrère (Holt, 328 pp, $26).

Despite this biography's provocative title, Philip K. Dick is indeed dead (and you, dear reader, are alive). But so persuasive is the book's ability to put us inside the skull of this visionary science fiction writer—a man who spent his life and literary career questioning our most fundamental assumptions about memory, human identity, and the ultimate nature of reality—that we're half inclined to wonder if the title may not have a bit of truth to it.

But no, as is well known, Dick died of a series of strokes in 1982, just a few months before the release of *Blade Runner,* based on his short novel *Do Androids Dream of Electric Sheep?* He was only fifty-three—and judging from this biography, it's not hard to see why he died so young. The picture Carrère paints is of an anxious, unstable, emotionally needy man, prey to paranoia, whose life was ruled by three compulsions: writing, womanizing, and drugs.

The drugs, which fueled the writing, were presumably his undoing. Supercharged on amphetamines, Carrère says, Dick could churn out a novel in a couple of sleepless weeks—"in two years he published a dozen—but he paid for the boost they gave him with terrible bouts of depression." (It's no surprise to learn that, before his death, he'd made at least two suicide attempts.) Later we read that, unsettled by marital tensions and the birth of a daughter, "Phil went through his medicine cabinet and took pills by the handful, hoping to calm his nerves. He also took them to strengthen his resolve, to lift his spirits, and to cope with other people; he took them to fall asleep and to wake up, to work and to relax from his labors. . . . He needed half a dozen or so doctors to keep his medicine cabinet stocked. . . . And like any prescription junkie, he spread his purchases among as many pharmacies as possible. . . . Eventually he was forced to buy drugs on the street." In 1969 "an overdose of amphetamines sent Phil to the hospital. . . . The moment he got out, however, he was back on speed again."

The womanizing is, if anything, even less attractive. Dick was married five times and had numerous affairs. Throughout the book he's forever encountering some sympathetic and impressionable young woman—and they seem to get younger as he grows older, till at last he marries an eighteen-year-old—ditching his current partner and moving in with the new one; though in fact, just as often, it's the women who leave him. "He couldn't stop himself from hitting on any woman who came through the door," writes Carrère. "Every woman he met he fell in love with. . . . Most of these women were the wives or girlfriends of his friends." (I know one veteran sci-fi writer who, with his fiancée, had to flee California because Dick had fixated on her and was bombarding her with phone calls and letters.) It's true that one young actress he befriended at the end of his life recalls "his kindness, his warmth, his loyalty"; but the main impression we get is of a man who preferred his women to be essentially homebound chattels and went to pieces the moment they showed a trace of independence.

Fortunately, however, we have the writing. (No reader should miss Dick's quietly haunting, Hugo-winning 1962 alternate-world novel, *The Man in the High Castle*, about an America conquered, and divided down the center, by the Axis powers.) Carrère—who, curiously, scants the final year of the author's life, not even mentioning *Blade Runner* by name—quotes liberally from the books, always to good effect, turning them into the steps of an intellectual and religious journey that ends, ironically, with a Zenlike renunciation of all the wild theories, drug-induced visions, cosmic speculations, and paranoid fantasies on which the books were based.

"There's nothing more pathetic than the mistrust of immediate reality by people who never stop splitting hairs over Ultimate Reality," he has the mature Dick thinking. "In life, what you need to know, Dick now insisted, is how to repair your car. Not some hypothetical car, not cars in general—because nothing exists *in general;* only particular things exist, and those that we happen to encounter along our path should suffice us. Those who want something else, something more, are looking for trouble: They start off noticing impossible repetitions and making ludicrous connections between unrelated events, and before they know it they're believing that everything that happens is the result of a secret master plan that it is their job to get to the bottom of; in short, they become paranoid. *Be careful kids*, Dick seems to be saying, . . . *it's all too easy to get caught up in this sort of thing. And I should know."*

August 2004

The Unseen Force: The Films of Sam Raimi by John Kenneth Muir (Applause, 349 pp, $18.95 pb).

Director Sam Raimi may be too old today to qualify as a wunderkind, the way he did as a twenty-two-year-old back in 1982 when his first movie, *The Evil Dead,* was released and was hailed by Stephen King as "the most ferociously original horror film of the year." But Raimi's work is still marked by that same youthful energy and inventiveness, from the pyrotechnics and nonstop action of *Darkman* to the glorious skyscraper-swinging of *Spider-Man* and *Spider-Man 2*.

A classic summer blockbuster, *Spider-Man* broke box-office records—a far cry from *The Evil Dead*, which cost just $110,000 to shoot (the money, says a crew member, came from "lawyers, doctors, and friends and family") and around twice that for post-production and promotion, grossed barely over $1 million in theaters, but was saved by the providential advent of the VCR. Originally titled *Book of the Dead*, it's a gripping and grisly movie, half Lovecraft, half George Romero, filled with breathtaking special effects despite its shoestring budget. Its sequel, *Evil Dead 2: Dead by Dawn*, rehashed the same haunted-cabin plot but turned it into slapstick comedy, complete with a closely observed flying eyeball that lands in someone's mouth; Raimi, as this book makes clear, is a lifelong Three Stooges fan.

And author John Muir is a staunch Raimi fan, waxing enthusiastic about each of Raimi's films—they're given a chapter apiece—from the comic-bookish *Darkman* ("a resounding success . . . a high point in the superhero genre") to the heart-poundingly suspenseful cautionary tale *A Simple Plan* ("a cinematic perfect storm, an ideal marriage of a literate, involving, and human story with the visuals of a confident director who knows exactly how to present it"), as well as *Spider-Man* ("nothing short of spectacular") and the quirky gunfight saga *The Quick and the Dead* ("the most accessible of modern Westerns, and also the most fun").

Raimi made his name as a horror director, but nothing in this book is as chilling as the experiences recounted by *Quick*'s original screenwriter, the Englishman Simon Moore: "Sharon Stone [one of the stars] just treated me as though I was the guy who brought her latte or something," he recalls. "The first meeting I had with her, she sat down and told me who this character was and what this character would do. She never once asked a single question." As for his idol, Gene Hackman, "We had a read-through . . . and he just stopped every five minutes or so and said, 'That's a terrible line,' 'God, that line stinks,' or 'We've got to change that.'. . . All the stars felt their parts were underwritten and wanted more dialogue, and more scenes where they talked about their pain." Thoroughly disillusioned, Moore realized that in Hollywood the writer is "an entirely marginal figure who is quite literally asked to stand outside the door when the meetings are going on."

Muir has put this book together without any input from Raimi himself, but—despite an off-puttingly crude cover—it's more than a cut-and-paste job; he's interviewed assorted cast and crew and makes excellent use of their recollections. And he writes splendidly. An insightful chapter, for example, on the Raimi film I most admire, *A Simple Plan,* demonstrates how much it owes to the Cain and Abel story, *Macbeth, Of Mice and Men,* and (John Huston being Raimi's favorite director) *The Treasure of the Sierra Madre.* Chapter by chapter, the book builds a case for Raimi as one of our most accomplished filmmakers—and certainly the perfect genre-film maker; he got the nod to direct *Spider-Man,* a studio executive explained, because he was "everything we were looking for. He was incredibly stylish, he had tons of heart, and he's a total *Spider-Man* geek."

Cool Tools edited by Kevin Kelly (www.cool-tools.org, 140 pp, $20 pb).

Forget sex, sports, or mountain scenery. The height of bliss, as anyone with any sense knows, is to sit in your kitchen eating a little something while leafing through a catalogue—ideally one like this, successor to the groundbreaking, consciousness-transforming *Whole Earth Catalog*s of the '60s and '70s, which promoted, as this one does, the virtues of eco-friendliness, self-sufficiency, and boundless curiosity about our planet. In fact, Kevin Kelly, *Tools*' editor, principal writer, and all-round Renaissance man, edited later incarnations of *Whole Earth,* and that legendary catalogue's founder, Stewart Brand, contributes many of the articles in this one.

The "Tools" of the title are, as Kelly explains, "anything useful": maps, websites, software, camping gear, videos, DIY kits, optical and electronic equipment, medical supplies, and just plain neat stuff, from a "weed wrench" for your garden to a site where you can buy Silly Putty by the pound—all described by intelligent, enthusiastic users. A large portion of the items are books—travel books, science books, handbooks, field guides, reference works—and since we're offered brief samples of their contents, *Tools* packs more than its share of wisdom. Kelly publishes the catalogue himself; you can find much of the same material for free on his *cool-tools.org* website, though you won't have the pleasure of reading it at your kitchen table.

As Timeless as Infinity: The Complete Twilight Zone Scripts of Rod Serling, Volume One, edited by Tony Albarella (Gauntlet, 485 pp, $60).

Here's an ambitious project—the first volume of a planned series that will reproduce Rod Serling's actual *Twilight Zone* shooting scripts from his personal collection, all ninety-two of them, complete with camera directions and the occasional scribbled annotation, as well as relevant background material for each episode.

This inaugural volume opens with "The Time Element," an hour-long Serling script for *Westinghouse Desilu Playhouse* that aired in the fall of 1958. Starring William Bendix as a man who, in his dreams, goes back in time to the Honolulu of December 6, 1941, it's a somewhat predictable exercise in frustration. Unable to convince anyone that the Japanese are about to attack Pearl Harbor, he's dismissed by one and all as a drunk or a madman. This tale—which, in its televised form, was slightly different from the version in this book (obtuse military men were changed to obtuse newspapermen)—is regarded as the unofficial pilot of *The Twilight Zone.*

The series' actual pilot, "Where Is Everybody?," aired a year later. That script is also included here, as well as scripts for "Third from the Sun," "The Purple Testament," "The Big Tall Wish," "Eye of the Beholder," "A Most Unusual Camera" (two complete drafts), "The Mind and the Matter," and "The Dummy"—an assortment that, for reasons best known to the editor, covers several seasons, rather than presenting the scripts in the order they were aired. Chronological or not, these scripts are an education in TV dramaturgy, and reading them conveys the immediacy and excitement of watching these shows for the first time.

Gunpowder: Alchemy, Bombards, and Pyrotechnics by Jack Kelly (Basic Books, 270 pp, $25).

In *2001: A Space Odyssey,* no sooner does a primitive man stumble upon the first technology—in the form of a bone—than he uses it as a weapon to kill his fellow men and beasts. And according to *Gunpowder,* once inquisitive Chinese alchemists discovered, in the 900s, that the right mixture of charcoal, sulfur, and saltpeter, touched by flame, blew up in thunderous blasts, it wasn't long before their rulers began using this miraculous "fire drug" in war.

Horrifying in content (for it is, after all, a history of wholesale slaughter) but curiously literary, even poetic, in style, Kelly's book lives up to the promise of its sub-subtitle, "The History of the Explosive That Changed the World." Gunpowder in early cannons known as "bombards" brought down castle walls, ending the feudal era; in naval artillery and soldiers' arms such as "arquebuses," it fueled Europe's conquest of Asia, Africa, and America; the British search for Concord's reputed seven tons of contraband powder in April 1775 helped spark the American Revolution.

Gunpowder has been dubbed "the devil's distillate," and it seems fittingly symbolic that saltpeter, the scarcest of its three ingredients, originally came from, among other places, putrefying manure, ordure, dung heaps, and (in the American Civil War) citizens' chamber pots. Even more appropriate, some was produced from the corpses of hastily buried soldiers killed in battle—which made for, as Kelly observes, "a macabre kind of recycling."

October 2004

Ray Bradbury: The Life of Fiction by Jonathan R. Eller and William F. Touponce (Kent State, 589 pp, $34).

In his "unauthorized autobiography," *Once Around the Bloch,* the late Robert Bloch—always a quipster as much as a horror writer—recalls attending the first Pacificon, a sci-fi convention held in Los Angeles in 1946, where, Bloch says, he met the "youthful and exuberant fan-turned-pro Ray Bradbury. I often wonder what became of him."

What became of Bradbury, of course, is that he's become one of the world's most popular—and most frequently reprinted and adapted—short-story writers, has had his work collected in more than eighty books, has been touted on his paperbacks as "The World's Greatest Living Science Fiction Writer," and has recently been the subject of a lavish pictorial biography, *Bradbury: An Illustrated Life*. And now we have further proof of his importance in *Ray Bradbury: The Life of Fiction*, a massive and exhaustive study of his work, conducted in high academic style by two professors from Indiana University. The book comes complete with all the usual scholarly apparatus, including two appendices that are alone worth the price of admission for serious Bradbury devotees—a 65-page year-by-year bibliography and a 10-page list of Bradbury's unpublished fiction (enough to fill an entire bookshelf)—as well as, to start you off in a properly reverential mood, a full page of epigraphs by sources ranging from Harlan Ellison to Nietzsche and Yeats.

Even without these trappings, you'd know from the outset that you're in the arid world of academia, because the authors treat us to "textual" six times, "texts," "intertextual," and "textuality" twice each, and for good measure "intertextuality"—all in the first two paragraphs.

If you can get past a prose style that, in places, would probably put Bradbury himself to sleep (to say nothing of his fans), there's much of interest in the book, which focuses not on Bradbury's life but on a thematic analysis of his fiction and on the nuts and bolts of his publishing career: specifically, on Bradbury's relations with his agents and publishers; on comparisons of successive drafts of stories and of the contents, and proposed contents, of various collections (a complicated business with this author, since his stories—and sometimes different versions of his stories—have been recycled many times); on Bradbury's obsessive concern, over the years, with the cover art for his books; and on his efforts, even as a fledgling author, to promote and shape his popular image. On this last point, for example, we learn that Bradbury was so anxious to suppress all references to the *Weird Tales* origin of the stories in his first collection, *Dark Carnival* (1947), for fear the mere mention of that magazine would mark him as a pulp-fiction hack, that he was willing to risk losing the copyrights on the tales.

The carnival is, of course, one of the recurring images in Bradbury's fiction, right on through his celebrated novel *Something Wicked This Way Comes* (1962)—indeed, the authors have turned it into a metaphor for Bradbury's approach to various literary genres, speaking throughout the book of what they call a "'carnivalization'... at the heart of Bradbury's authorship"—and I was interested, if not entirely surprised, to read that relations were somewhat strained between Bradbury and another fantasy writer associated with carnivals, Charles Finney, who, it seems, grumbled that *Something Wicked* bore too close a resemblance to his own novel *The Circus of Dr. Lao*. Taking their subject's side, Eller and Touponce attribute Finney's pique to jealousy, argue that "the two works have little in common," and point out that Bradbury avoided Finney's novel while working on his own—nor was he much impressed with it once he got around to reading it.

The two professors come to Bradbury's defense once more when they take apart Thomas Disch's notorious attack on Bradbury in the *New York Times Book Review*, wherein he dismissed Bradbury's work as not art but kitsch. Laboriously trotting out their chosen metaphor, the two accuse Disch of having written "a hasty piece of carnival abuse" and scold him for failing to appreciate how "a carnival entertainer" like Bradbury has produced work that can "carnivalize genres." Though their prose may be somewhat leaden at times, clearly they like cotton candy more than Disch does.

The Great Beyond: Higher Dimensions, Parallel Universes, and the Extraordinary Search for a Theory of Everything by Paul Halpern (Wiley, 336 pp, $27.95).

For physicists, it amounts to something like the holy grail—a unified field theory, or "theory of everything," that would encompass and explain in a single equation the universe's four fundamental forces: gravity, electromagnetism, and two subatomic forces, the strong and weak interactions. Einstein devoted the last three decades of his life to its pursuit—without success, in part because, according to Paul Halpern's *The Great Beyond,* he resisted hypotheses predicated upon higher dimensions. (Today's "dimension hunters," as Halpern calls them, are up to eleven.)

Such concepts are impossible for us non-mathematicians to imagine, but Halpern does his best, in this engaging history, to explain them by means of everyday analogies; there are no numbers in the book, no formulae, but plenty of guitar strings, orange slices, and inside-out gloves. The most useful analogy contrasts the Newtonian view of gravity as a force acting between two bodies at a distance—"one tugboat pulling another along with a rope"—with Einstein's, in which one boat disturbs the water, "causing the other to rock in its wake."

Even with these examples, however, you won't come away from *The Great Beyond* with much understanding of modern cosmology, for most of the book focuses not on the theories but on the men who concocted them; science takes second place to social history, brief biographies of the various theorists (brainy, of course, often eccentric, sometimes quite lovable), and just plain gossip. Though Halpern spends only a single unhelpful paragraph explaining the Michelson-Morley experiment that tested the existence of an all-pervasive "aether," he devotes two pages to describing the quaint old German university town of Göttingen, home of several groundbreaking mathematicians; another two pages on European art movements such as Cubism and Futurism; and six pages on the unlikely friendship of Einstein and Charlie Chaplin.

How to Clone the Perfect Blonde: Using Science to Make Your Wildest Dreams Come True by Sue Nelson and Richard Hollingham (Quirk, 272 pp, $16.95 pb).

The title is irresistible—and it's only the first chapter. Later chapters hold equally enticing promises: "How to Turn Back Time," "How to Live Forever," and one that, for me, is almost more intriguing and elusive than boring old immortality: "How to Lose Your Love Handles."

Authors Nelson and Hollingham have come up with a cleverly original way of explaining current scientific thought: using as a hook not *Star Trek* or the latest sci-fi blockbuster (the way so many popular-science books have), but instead examining how modern science might potentially grant a handful of our fondest wishes. The title chapter uses the quest for the perfect blonde as a way of discussing cloning, from salamanders and frogs to Dolly the sheep to—someday, probably—humans. A chapter on "How to Build a Robotic Servant" provides a short course on artificial intelligence. "How to Shorten Your Commute" segues from teleportation to quantum theory. The "Love Handles" chapter offers a once-over-lightly look at genetic engineering.

The operant word is *lightly;* you can't begin to do justice to all these topics (plus black holes, string theory, and neurochemistry) in one brief and breezy book. Worse, as if the authors were afraid they'd lose us, the style is as incessantly jokey as a barroom bore, with lame japes every few sentences and punning subsection titles that are, at best, hit or miss: "Hello, Dolly," "The Science of the Lambs," and "These Are a Few of My Favorite Strings."

The Philosopher at the End of the Universe: Philosophy Explained through Science Fiction Films by Mark Rowlands (St. Martin's, 286 pp, $23.95).

It isn't the first time sci-fi has been used as a philosophical teaching tool—we've already seen *The Ethics of Star Trek, The Metaphysics of Star Trek,* and *Buffy the Vampire Slayer and Philosophy*—but Rowlands is a tad more ambitious: he uses well over a dozen different films, from *Frankenstein* to the *Matrix* series, as his jumping-off points for explorations of philosophical issues (he calls the genre *sci-phi*). *Minority Report* illustrates free will vs. determinism; the *Terminator* films, the mind-body problem; *Hollow Man,* morality and the social contract.

Rowlands's tone is casual and colloquial, sometimes approaching the sort of voice you'd hear at a college-dorm bull session. In a chapter on *Total Recall* that discusses how personal identity is founded upon memory, he talks familiarly of "Arnie," calls a villain "the guy from the agency" and the hero "the guy whose memories were erased," and assures us that certain movie critics "wouldn't recognize a philosophical argument if it sat on their face and wiggled." This studied unpretentiousness is a bit much; still, the book is a lot more fun—and sometimes more memorable—than Philo 101.

December 2004

A Swedish Podcast

HM: Do you remember when you first got interested in horror and weird fiction?

TK: Well, I guess my introduction was pretty typical. As a schoolboy in the late 1950s, I was fascinated by lurid horror comics, monster magazines, and various old horror movies that would show up on TV. Or rather, I should say, I was fascinated by these things during the daylight hours; I couldn't get enough of them. But at bedtime, like a remorseful addict, I'd regret it, and I would terrify myself with fantasies—your standard childhood fantasies—of monsters slipping into my room, so that every sound, every shadow, became a source of fear. At which point, I would yell for my father or mother to come in and comfort me. Looking back, it doesn't take a psychoanalyst to see a pattern there, one with a fairly obvious payoff: stuff my head with images of monsters by day, scare myself at night, and thereby elicit parental reassurance.

HM: What was your initial reaction to the work of Lovecraft and Clark Ashton Smith, and what first struck you about these two authors?

Email interview conducted in August 2017 by Henrik Möller for his podcast *Udda Ting*—"odd thing"—presented partly in Swedish, partly in English. (You've got to love those Europeans.) An actor friend of Möller's stood in for me, reading aloud my replies. The effect was, appropriately, somewhat odd.

TK: I didn't discover Smith till later, and I've never quite warmed to his ornate style. But Lovecraft, when I first came across him in anthologies at my neighborhood library, conveyed something new to me; call it, as he did, cosmic terror. And his stories held a particular power, because to a youthful reader they seemed almost real, thanks to his detailed, convincing sense of place—I mean, he alluded to actual towns, actual streets, even actual houses—and thanks to the equally convincing way he'd quote from forbidden volumes that, for all I knew, might be real books.

HM: At what point did you start writing your own fiction?

TK: I remember elementary-school attempts at science fiction. One story I wrote—intended, I should add, to be humorous—was about a nightmarishly overpopulated future society where people are crowded together like New Year's Eve revelers in Times Square. At the end of the story, the hero manages to purchase the home of his dreams—which, we discover, once served as an outhouse.

HM: When did you begin writing horror stories?

TK: I don't think I wrote anything that could be described as horror till after I'd been reading that genre for years; and when I did, I was basically just trying to imitate writers I admired, Lovecraft among them. Till that time, my stories were, as I say, attempts at science fiction—in part, I think, because science fiction just seemed easier and more fun. I recall writing at least one "mainstream" story, but it was harder; and I'd probably find that just as true today.

HM: Do know how your ideas materialize? Do you have the seed of a story when you start writing, or do you just sit down with a blank mind and start to write?

TK: I keep a lot of notes—I mean, voluminous notebooks of ideas, images, phrases, quotes, all of which might be capable of providing inspiration. But as for where the ideas come from . . . well, they simply emerge. Isn't that what our brains are for?

HM: Your stories are so brilliantly constructed, with such precision. Do you have a technique, a way of mapping out the story?

TK: That's kind of you; thanks. I do worry a lot about trying to make events seem at least somewhat logical, ordering them in some effective dramatic fashion, and in general trying to disguise the fact that almost everything I'm describing, when you come right down to it, is pretty preposterous.

HM: Do you do a lot of rewrites?

TK: Lots and lots. And even today, when I get my hands on something I wrote long ago, I can't resist trying to improve it. I recently revised, albeit slightly, two of the novelettes from *Dark Gods*—"Black Man with a Horn" and "Children of the Kingdom"—and made substantial corrections to *The Ceremonies,* which badly needed them.

HM: Along with "The Events at Poroth Farm," "Black Man" and "Children" are my favorite stories of yours. Can you tell me how they came to be?

TK: Very briefly, "Poroth" was inspired—this is probably obvious—by an actual summer I spent on a farm in rural New Jersey; it belonged to friends from the city who, in some respects, were the inspiration for the farm couple in the story. "Black Man" and "Children" were attempts to set supernatural horror within my own Manhattan neighborhood; it's one way of making the world a bit more interesting.

HM: Did Frank Belknap Long ever read "Black Man," and if so, do you know what he thought of it?

TK: No, Frank never did read it. I knew him—a somewhat sad, frail little man, soft old-man's voice, slightly crazy wheelchair-bound wife, squalid apartment—and I doubt he'd have seen very much of himself in the story's narrator. In truth, there's not much resemblance. But I wouldn't have wanted to risk possibly hurting his feelings.

HM: Do you remember how you first met him?

TK: Kirby McCauley—who was later to represent Stephen King, Peter Straub, and George R. R. Martin, among others, but who was then a struggling young agent specializing in horror fiction while working out of a basement apartment in St. Paul, Minnesota—visited New York with an eye to moving here. Kirby had been Frank's agent for several years and, through the mail, had recently offered to represent me as well; in those days he had, as clients, a number of elderly writers from *Weird Tales* and other legendary pulps. Needless to say, since at that time only one story of mine had actually appeared in print—the first version of "Poroth," as it happens, in a lowly fanzine—I was thrilled. I joined Kirby and Frank for lunch at a Spanish restaurant, El Quijote, near Frank's apartment. I remember being a tad disappointed in Frank; he was already, I guess you'd say, in his dotage.

HM: I know that, for good reasons, you don't like Dario Argento's *Trauma*. It's his first bad film and the start of his downfall after a long line of great films. Did you know of his work prior to the collaboration? Can you tell me how you got involved in the project? Did you get to contribute something story-wise to the script?

TK: Oy! So I have the honor to have written Argento's first bad film? Well, I can't argue with that.

You asked me earlier about the construction of my stories, and that's somewhat relevant. I was brought in—through Kirby, bless him—to write a script based on, if memory serves, a 12-page, or maybe 16-page, untitled treatment by Argento and one or two associates. It seemed to me excessively, at times even ludicrously, violent and somewhat incoherent. Like, for no particular reason, a young boy character ended up hanged. I saw my task, in part, as trying to make the story a bit more logical and believable, but also to add, if I could, some notions here and there that struck me as unnerving. I had seen three or four of Argento's films and had been quite riveted by them, especially by *Suspiria*.

His English, I found when I met him, was somewhat limited—

that was another reason I'd been hired, as this was to be his first full-length American feature—but he was an eccentric, colorful character, and I felt fortunate to be working with him. We spent a couple of days in Pittsburgh together, looking over possible locations; it's an area, of course, where George Romero had shot his zombie films and where Jonathan Demme had shot *The Silence of the Lambs*. (I remember, while there, being somewhat uneasy, as I was also, at the time, editing a monthly crime magazine and had concealed from the staff where I was going.) Later, I gather, Argento considered filming in New Orleans. Alas, the movie ended up being shot in Minneapolis, one of the least atmospheric cities in America, for a depressingly tiny budget, and an elaborate opening scene I'd dreamed up, involving a bizarre fatal accident at a construction site, was simply never filmed. I'd thought it was rather neat, but it was obviously way too expensive.

HM: Can you describe that discarded opening scene?

TK: Well, let me try to recall it. As best I can remember, Dario's original treatment involved a mysterious killer who's running around lopping off heads. And the origin of the killer's lunacy—as we learn at the end—lies in some traumatic incident years before in which . . . was it a baby's head that was cut off in a botched obstetric procedure? That seems to ring a bell. At any rate, Dario's treatment never addressed the question of why the psychopath at the heart of the mystery would suddenly begin murdering people after years of living a peaceful, law-abiding life.

So I had this idea for opening the movie with a bizarre fatal accident at a construction site, a sort of Rube Goldberg affair, in which some object balanced on one of the topmost girders—a heavy bucket, a block of concrete, whatever—tips over and falls, snapping an attached cable whose end gets yanked through a pulley and goes whipping through the air at great speed, slicing off some luckless worker's head. (I'd once heard about something similar happening on an aircraft carrier.) And I imagined the head bouncing down a series of platforms, level after level, like a ball bearing in a pinball game, until it drops onto the sidewalk below and comes rolling up to the feet of what seems an ordinary passing pedestrian—who will turn out, in the end, to be the murderer. But we don't entirely see this passerby; we just see a close-up of the person's shoes, I think, coming to a stop beside the head, and we hear some sort of scream—a scream of horror but also, perhaps, of . . . well, not recognition, exactly, but of remembering. Obviously this would be the incident—a jarring flashback, more or less, to the original incident in the hospital—that would awaken long-buried memories and set the murderer off. I may even have suggested that the severed head—like guillotined heads have been reputed to do—might look up and mouth some sort of silent message.

I guess I should have realized that the scene would be too complicated to film, but I thought Dario might find the idea amusing and give it a try. It seemed like the sort of thing that might appeal to him. And so far as I know, he actually considered doing it, until he found himself working with a much smaller budget than he'd expected.

HM: What was it like to work with him?

TK: In general, once I'd begun writing, a typical face-to-face encounter with him consisted of me bringing him a scene I'd written, pleased with my own cleverness, and him reading it, nodding, and then running his finger down the page to indicate the length of the dialogue and saying, deflatingly, "Ah, yes. You cut, yes?" In the end, a lot of material did get cut—maybe not enough! But there was some connecting tissue, some necessary exposition, that also got cut, leaving a few plot points unexplained and confusing.

Finally—and forgive me for trying to shift some of the blame—Argento was prey to sudden enthusiasms and had a habit of latching onto ideas from whatever he'd just seen or read and urging me to incorporate them into the story, occasionally at the expense of logic. For example, at some point—I forget when—I found myself having to introduce a side plot about anorexia, because Dario had seen some sort of documentary about it and felt sorry for the girls, or perhaps just attracted to them. I remember that while we were swapping ideas for the script, he saw *Shadows and Fog*—a very strange Woody Allen film—and immediately wanted to work some elements from it into ours. And then one day he saw Hitchcock's *Shadow of a Doubt* and was influenced by that as well. At one point, he wanted to add a talking lizard (maybe there *is* one in the film now; I forget), and he did an amusing imitation of it in a high, piping voice. In the end, my friend Andy Sands, one of the production crew, summed up the film's problems by saying, "Too much plot, too little time." I've never watched the damned thing all the way through. One small, pleasant memory: getting to take Argento's then-seventeen-year-old daughter, Asia, who would star in the film, out to lunch when she came to New York.

HM: Do you have a horror/weird film that you like?

TK: When I was at film school—I actually have a fairly useless master's degree from Columbia—I went around asking my fellow students what movie had scared them the most. Not surprisingly, I suppose, most people would name some movie they'd seen when they were nine or ten years old. (One guy said nothing had ever scared him except his mother's vacuum cleaner.) A couple of films that haunted me in my own childhood were *Creature from the Black Lagoon* and *Monster on the Campus*. Oddly enough, it's only now, recalling them, that it occurs to me they were both directed by Jack Arnold.

Later, in 1979, when I saw the first *Alien,* I wondered why, as I strolled out of the theater, my right arm was aching. Then I realized it was because I'd been holding my right hand up over my eyes through most of the movie.

HM: Do you have any contemporary literary favorites?

TK: To be honest, I read very little fiction nowadays; mostly I read big fat history books. But I'll always turn, with interest, to anything by George Orwell, John Updike, or Arthur Machen—three extremely disparate names with extremely disparate styles.

www.ingramcontent.com/pod-product-compliance
Lightning Source LLC
Chambersburg PA
CBHW060310230426
43663CB00009B/1648